# ISSUES IN INTERNET LAW

## Society, Technology, and the Law

# ISSUES IN INTERNET LAW

## Society, Technology, and the Law

Seventh edition

by Dr. Keith B. Darrell

*Amber Book Company LLC*

Issues In Internet Law:
Society, Technology, and the Law
by Dr. Keith B. Darrell
Amber Book Company LLC
www.amberbookcompany.com
U.S.A.

Cover Photograph by Marc S. Sillman

Cover Concept & Design by Keith B. Darrell

Library of Congress Catalog Card Number: 2012902182
Issues In Internet Law / Keith B. Darrell

Inquiries regarding foreign rights and translation rights should be addressed
to: *info@AmberBookCompany.com*.

First edition published 2005. Second edition 2006. Third edition 2007. Fourth edition 2008. Fifth edition 2009. Sixth Edition 2011. Seventh Edition 2012. Printed and bound in the United States of America.

11 10 09 08 07 06    5 4 3 2 1

Library of Congress Cataloging-in-Publication Data
Darrell, Keith.
   Emerging issues in Internet law and the effects on, and responses from, society / Keith B. Darrell
   xxii, 488 p. : ill. ; 25 cm.
   Includes indices
   ISBN (softcover): 978-1-935971-08-5
   1. Internet 2.Law and legislation

ISBN (softcover): 978-1-935971-08-5

Seventh Edition • May 2012

This book is printed on acid-free paper.

*Dedicated to my grandmother, Muriel S. Patiteaux,
on her 101st birthday, January 17, 2012.*

*"I don't really understand what a Web site is. I haven't quite grasped the concepts."*

—Judge Peter Openshaw, Woolwich Crown Court in London, May 16, 2007, during the trial of three men accused of inciting terrorism via the Internet.

# TABLE OF CONTENTS

## PART ONE: INTRODUCTION TO LAW

### CHAPTER 1: INTRODUCTION TO LAW    1

## PART TWO: INTELLECTUAL PROPERTY

### CHAPTER 2: COPYRIGHT BASICS    17

## PART FOUR: PRIVACY

### CHAPTER 7: PRIVACY BASICS      135

### CHAPTER 8: DATA PRIVACY      157

## PART SIX: BUSINESS AND THE INTERNET

### CHAPTER 19 BUSINESS AND THE INTERNET     361

### CHAPTER 20: WEB CONTRACTS     385

# PART SEVEN: BEYOND THE HORIZON

## PREFACE TO THE CURRENT EDITION

In the BBC TV series "*Black Adder*", Samuel Johnson presents his new book "the dictionary" to the prince regent, explaining it has been his life's work for the past 40 years to write a book containing every word in the English language.[1] "How frabjupulous!" Rowan Atkinson, in the title role, snidely remarks. Johnson's face betrays an involuntary grimace as he realizes the word frabjupulous (made up on the spot by Black Adder) is not in his book. Black Adder continues to pepper his conversation with more imaginary words, until the frustrated Johnson rips the pages from his book and tosses them into the fireplace, resigned to return to the drawing board. Like Johnson, I begin each new edition filled with pride borne of accomplishment, but as work begins on the subsequent edition, I too, feel the urge to rip out pages of the earlier edition and consign them to the fire pits of some nether region.

Two factors set *Issues in Internet Law: Society, Technology, and the Law* apart from other books on the topic. First, as may be apparent from its title, the book is prospective in its approach. It does not seek to lay out "the law" or ask the reader to memorize pages of legal canon. Where the intertwining subjects of technology and law are concerned, both are in a continual state of evolution, as is society's reaction to the changes being inflicted on it. The book you hold in your hands is about that — change brought by technological advances and its effects on society and, in turn, how the law copes with it. The book is not designed to state what "the law" is, but rather to make the reader aware of legal issues surrounding the Internet. Laws vary by jurisdiction and change constantly, especially where an evolving technology like the Internet is concerned. In the Internet Age, in a world where changes occur daily at light speed, the only state of the law (at least as it relates to technology) is the state of flux. Where necessary, legal concepts and precedents are explained, but the text of most cases and statutes referred to throughout the book are left to hyperlinks in the endnotes. Instead, this book examines the rationale — the thought processes — of courts as they struggle to apply antiquated laws to futuristic situations. As an author, my goal is not to offer fodder for pedantic rote memorization but to challenge the reader to think — to extrapolate the paths the courts and legislatures are likely to follow as they address issues in Internet law. Which brings us to the second aspect distinguishing this book from similar tomes. *Issues in Internet Law: Society, Technology, and the Law* is written in an anecdotal style, relying on actual topical issues. While other books might rely on a series of classroom hypotheticals to explain the relevant issues, life is seldom that black or white. As you shall see, the real world is often complicated by extenuating circumstances and varying shades of gray. Answers are not always clear cut, as in textbook examples, and sometimes raise more questions than they resolve. The anecdotes serve as food for thought, and debate, and that is a good thing. One's thought process should begin, not end, once the last page has been read. The anecdotal nature of the book makes it entertaining and easier to read, but do not be fooled: there is a wealth of information contained within.

*Issues in Internet Law: Society, Technology, and the Law* is written for laymen. The reader need not be a lawyer or an IT engineer. Many readers purchase the book to gain an understanding of legal and Internet concepts because they are using the Internet in their daily personal and business lives, from shopping online, communicating through e-mail, creating Web sites, blogging, and interacting with others on social networks. Yet, the book has also been adopted as a textbook by dozens of colleges, universities, vocational schools, and online courses, throughout the United States and abroad. Teachers have discovered the book's anecdotal approach and prospective outlook enliven the material, meaning students actually read it because they find it entertaining as well as informative. Technical phrases are defined along the way and in the glossary. Just enough detail is provided so the reader can visualize a situation. Those seeking a more detailed explanation should peruse the endnotes and read the source material cited.

At the end of the book is a glossary, a list of acronyms, a case index, a statute and treaty index, and a topic index. Throughout the book, key phrases are highlighted in *italics*, defined terms are printed in **semi-bold**, and phrases that are defined in the glossary are highlighted in ***semi-bold italics***. American statutes are highlighted in **this font**. Chapter questions and quizzes are available on the Issues In Internet Law Web site at IssuesInInternetLaw.com/student/index. html. To report an error, please visit IssuesInInternetLaw.com/forms/error.html. To view reported errors in this and previous editions, visit IssuesInInternetLaw.com/text/updates.html.

*Issues in Internet Law: Society, Technology, and the Law* covers a wide selection of topics, making the book more of a survey of emerging issues and trends. Even in nearly 500 pages, it is not possible to delve into this vast array of subjects in depth. The reader is encouraged to seek out books devoted entirely to any specific topic he or she finds particularly intriguing. Likewise, since technology and the law are constantly changing, readers may wish to order a new edition of *Issues in Internet Law: Society, Technology, and the Law* each year to keep up.

**End Notes**

[1] "Ink and Incapacity", *Black Adder the Third*, BBC television, original air date September 24, 1987.

## ACKNOWLEDGMENTS

This book would not have been possible without the contributions of many individuals. Some lent moral support and encouragement, others technical prowess; some graciously allowed use of their documents, while others contributed by being active participants in the development of Internet law. The latter group, and those who chronicled their exploits before me, are acknowledged separately within the text and accompanying endnotes.

Deep within the pages of this book lurks the profound influence of many teachers who made time to help me learn to read, listen, think, and write: Russell Brines, William J. Carney, Frank Mulhall, Betty Owen, John Smolko, and Cindy J. Wilmer.

Several colleagues perused portions of the manuscript in its later stages and suggested revisions: Larry Brown, John Collins III, Ronald Dupont, Jr., Scott Greenberg, Jennifer Jackson, Jeremy Pound, and Marc Sillman. Carol Moncrief, John Parker, Denise Schmeichler, and Dan Wallach allowed me to publish their e-mails or contracts in previous editions so readers could learn from them. Thanks to Brenton Cleeland for permission to use his photograph of the billboard in Australia at the heart of the _Chang_ case discussed in Chapters 1 and 2, and to Aaron Wall and Mark W. Voigt for taking time to correspond with me about their ongoing cases discussed in this book. A special note of thanks to all the eagle-eyed readers who have caught errors in previous editions and alerted us via our Web site, **IssuesInInternetLaw.com**.

Finally, those individuals whose existence provided continual encouragement: Rino diStefano, Hero Joy Nightingale, Alison Pestcoe, and of course, Amber.

# NOTE TO TEACHERS & LIBRARIANS

Amber Book Company values your input in making each edition of this book an improvement over the previous one. Internet technology is changing at warp speed every year, resulting in new legal and social consequences. To stay current, Amber Book Company has released a new edition of *Issues in Internet Law: Society, Technology, and the Law* every year for seven of the past eight years.

**Teachers** can help by e-mailing info@AmberBookCompany.com and describing how they use the book in their classrooms, what they would like to see covered in future editions, and what, if any, errors they have found in this edition. As our way of thanking you for your assistance, Amber Book Company will send complimentary copies of future editions to selected instructors.

**Librarians** should plan to order every annual edition of *Issues in Internet Law: Society, Technology, and the Law,* as even a year-old edition will quickly be made obsolete by the rapid advances in technology and law.

Students, IT professionals, attorneys, and casual readers may wish to keep the most current edition on their bookshelves, as technological advances and recent court decisions may render information in this edition obsolete.

While you may order copies of *Issues in Internet Law: Society, Technology, and the Law* through your traditional vendors or online booksellers like Amazon.com, Amber Book Company does sell direct with volume discounts. And be sure to check out some of the other fine books offered on **AmberBookCompany.com**.

# PURCHASING COPIES OF THIS BOOK

Many schools use this book as a required textbook. It is available at the list price from college bookstores, the publisher directly, and many fine Web sites, including Amazon.com and Barnes & Noble (bn.com). Unfortunately, a few disreputable Web sites also offer it for sale at an outrageous premium over the publisher's list price. While we have no control over this, we advise you to check the list price on the publisher's site before ordering online. There is never a reason to pay over the list price; if your bookstore does not have the book, Amber Book Company always has the current edition available to ship at the list price.

We work hard to keep this book affordable and students can help by asking their professors not to photocopy portions for use as handouts or coursepacks.

# INTRODUCTION

As the Internet evolves from a nascent technology to an integral part of our daily personal and business lives, it will have a profound effect on how we interact with others, personally and professionally. Familiar "offline" legal issues will arise in an "online" context. As legislative bodies struggle to understand the new medium and draft laws to address these new issues, more often than not, it is left to courts to interpret and apply existing laws and previous court decisions to issues of Internet law. Many, including, for example, the First Amendment to the U.S. Constitution drafted more than two centuries ago, were written by men who could ill conceive of modern technologies (*e.g.,* telephones, fax machines, computers, and the Internet) to which their words would be applied. Legislatures and courts must distill the fundamental legal concepts ingrained within the framework of those early cases and statutes and apply them to issues arising from 21$^{st}$ century technologies. The Internet is an innovation that opens a Pandora's Box of legal issues. As Canadian Justice Sharlow commented:[1]

> The issue of the proper balance in matters of copyright plays out against the much larger conundrum of trying to apply national laws to a fast-evolving technology that in essence respects no national boundaries. Thus in _Citron v. Zündel,_[2] the Canadian Human Rights Tribunal wrestled with jurisdiction over an alleged hate Web site supplied with content from Toronto but posted from a host server in California. In _Reference re Earth Future Lottery_,[3] the issue was whether sales of tickets from an Internet lottery in Prince Edward Island constituted gambling "in the province" when almost all of the targeted on-line purchasers resided elsewhere. The "cyber libel" cases multiply. In _Braintech, Inc. v. Kostiuk_,[4] the British Columbia Court of Appeal refused to enforce a Texas judgment for Internet defamation against a B.C. resident where the B.C. resident's only connection with Texas was "passive posting on an electronic bulletin board."[5] There was no proof that anyone in Texas had actually looked at it. On the other hand, in _Dow Jones & Co. v. Gutnick_,[6] the High Court of Australia accepted jurisdiction over a defamation action in respect of material uploaded onto the defendant's server in New Jersey and downloaded by end users in the State of Victoria. The issue of global forum shopping for actions for Internet torts has scarcely been addressed. The availability of child pornography on the Internet is a matter of serious concern. E-commerce is growing. Internet liability is thus a vast field where the legal harvest is only beginning to ripen.

Anyone in contact with the Internet can benefit from an understanding of the legal issues related to it. Such contact may come through browsing the World Wide Web; participating in a Usenet newsgroup, electronic mailing list, chat room, online forum, or social network; blogging; making an online purchase; or by sending or receiving e-mail. The contact may involve issues of commerce and contract law, or sexual harassment in the workplace, or freedom of speech, or invasion of privacy. Was that online contract you clicked enforceable, even if you scrolled down and did not read it? Does receiving pornography in office e-mail from other employees constitute sexual harassment? Can someone get away with insulting you online? Can stalkers find your personal information online? What can you legally place on your Web site; and what is not allowed? Do you own your domain name? Can a library censor your Internet use?

Do you know who is reading your e-mail? Is it legal to gamble online? How "private" is your private information once you disclose it to a Web site? Can a student be suspended for online comments about a teacher? Is a student exercising his First Amendment rights when he creates a hate site on a public school's Internet server? Can you get in trouble for making a gripe site about a business that ripped you off? Did you know the sites you visit and the words you type into search engines are being logged? Do other countries address these issues differently from the U.S.? Which country's laws apply on the Internet? These are just some of the issues addressed in this book. To paraphrase Justice Shaw, Internet law "is thus a vast field where the legal harvest is only beginning to ripen."

Law does not exist in a vacuum. Laws are a response to societal needs, often stimulated by technological change. Thousands of years ago, societies crafted laws to deal with false and malicious statements spread orally by their members (slander). With the advent of the printing press, such lies (libel) were able to be endowed with both permanence and the ability to travel unaided by human voice or physical accompaniment; indeed, one could anonymously post a flyer filled with lies and misrepresentations about another individual for all eyes in the kingdom to view. Another thousand year leap has turned that anonymous flyer on a tree into an Internet post that reaches all eyes worldwide and instantly achieves viral permanence.

While the Internet has created a new stage on which for society to act, it is merely an extension of society itself. As one of the Internet's founding fathers, Vincent Cerf, stated, "Most of the content on the network is contributed by the users of the Internet. So what we're seeing on the Net is a reflection of the society we live in."[7] He correctly points out we do not need to fix the Internet with a slew of new laws but rather need to address those societal ills directly. "When you have a problem in the mirror you do not fix the mirror, you fix that which is reflected in the mirror."[8] Or to paraphrase Walt Kelly, "We have met the Internet and it is us."[9]

### End Notes

[1] *Society of Composers, Authors & Music Publishers of Canada v. Canadian Ass'n of Internet Providers*, 2004 SCC 45. (Included in the Cases Section on the Issues in Internet Law site, www.IssuesinInternetLaw.com).

[2] *Citron v. Zündel* (18 January 2002), T460/1596 (Can. H.R.Trib.).

[3] *Reference re Earth Future Lottery*, [2003] 1 S.C.R. 123, 2003 SCC 10.

[4] *Braintech, Inc. v. Kostiuk* (1999), 171 D.L.R. (4th) 46 (CA) [leave denied [1999] S.C.C.A. No. 236].

[5] *Ibid.*, (para. 66).

[6] *Dow Jones & Co. v. Gutnick* 194 A.L.R. 433, 2002 HCA 56 (Austl. 2002), holding "defamation is to be located at the place where the damage to reputation occurs."

[7] "Call to Regulate the Net Rejected," BBC News, August 29, 2007.

[8] *Ibid.*

[9] Walt Kelly, *Pogo* comic strip, 1970: "We have met the enemy and he is us."

# Methodology

*Issues in Internet Law: Society, Technology, and the Law* is reader-friendly. It is written in an anecdotal fashion, using real-life stories to illustrate the application of legal principles. Many textbooks take a more pedantic approach. They will list a series of statutes and black letter law, suitable for rote learning where the student is expected to memorize the material and regurgitate it on an exam paper. What is missing from this approach is any kind of cognitive thought process. Students are not being asked to think, merely to retain information in their minds until tested, when it can be safely forgotten. That may be sufficient in academia, but not in the real world. Poetry may be memorized and recited, but the key to law is those cases and statutes must be interpreted, their rationales understood, and, most importantly, applied to specific and variable fact situations.

Fact situations, and the lawsuits that arise from them, seldom present themselves in a straight-forward manner. There may be multiple legal issues involved, some obvious and some open to creative interpretation. Who would think to apply arcane or superannuated legal theories like trespass to chattels to spam or cyberbullying? Yet attorneys and judges have done so by studying the reasoning behind the court decisions and enactment of statutes and extrapolating where the law is headed. If information seems scattered throughout multiple chapters and footnotes, that is by design, to enable the reader to see how concepts pull together. Plaintiffs do not file lawsuits based on a single cause of action: a libel suit may include a count for false light and intentional infliction of emotional distress; a breach of contract claim may include charges of misrepresentation, fraud, and unjust enrichment; a copyright infringement suit may also include violation of the Copyright Act, trademark infringement, and appropriation. The student of law must understand each legal theory, how they interact, how they are applied to specific factual settings, and how variations in the facts may change the applicability and the outcome.

The anecdotal approach is beneficial because students learn better through stories that show the application of principles than from simply listing those principles. Aesop learned that a long time ago, and his parables have proven the efficacy of allegorical teaching. Because *Issues in Internet Law: Society, Technology, and the Law* deals with emerging issues, sometimes there are no answers, only yet to be resolved questions. But hopefully, the reader has been given the cognitive tools to formulate educated guesses as to where the courts might rule on these issues. Equally important, the reader will have valuable insight into discerning the nuanced fact situations that may lead to differing results.

As a survey book, *Issues in Internet Law: Society, Technology, and the Law* must be a mile wide and an inch thick. Its goal is to introduce the reader to important, relevant emerging issues in Internet law and provide enough understanding so the reader may seek out in-depth material on any particular topic he or she wishes to learn more about.

## CHANGES SINCE THE PREVIOUS EDITION

Advances in the state of technology and new laws and court decisions necessitate a new edition of *Issues in Internet Law: Society, Technology, and the Law* be published every year, in order to keep it the most up to date resource on the market. The book is written for lay people as a survey of emerging issues in Internet law, but many colleges and universities, IT programs, corporate training departments, and online courses have chosen to adopt it as a textbook, both in the United States and abroad. Cognizant many teachers use the book's table of contents as their syllabus, I have taken care to make as few modifications as possible that might affect the order of presentation of material, to minimize the transition from one edition to the next.

I do stress the importance of always using the latest edition, as even a year-old edition is woefully out-of-date in the fast-paced world of technology and law. When the first edition of *Issues In Internet Law* was published, Facebook and Twitter did not exist. A lot has happened in a short time. *Issues in Internet Law: Society, Technology, and the Law* has been on the cutting edge and has been the first to address dozens of emerging issues that are now mainstream topics. It has also correctly predicted how certain issues would ultimately be resolved by the courts. It was one of the first book of its kind; now, there are more than 100 books dealing with various aspects of Internet law. Whether you are a student, teacher, IT professional, or attorney, you should consider updating your copy each year by purchasing the latest edition for your bookshelf.

Publishing a nearly 500-page technical book every 12 months is not without its hazards. Typos and other errors occur in any publication, and every attempt is made to eliminate them from *Issues in Internet Law: Society, Technology, and the Law* prior to going to press. Unlike textbooks with five years between editions to iron out the bugs, *Issues in Internet Law: Society, Technology, and the Law* has only months before the next edition is finalized. Also, to remain the most up-to-date book on Internet law, breaking news is often added at the last minute, leaving even less time for review than typical textbooks. Nonetheless, if you notify us of any errors, they will be corrected immediately and not appear in subsequent printings of the current edition, nor in future editions.

Each year, I begin by making any necessary corrections to the text. Then, I update the material, adding new laws enacted and court decisions handed down since the previous edition. Often these court rulings settle unanswered questions or overturn cases referenced in the previous edition. I also update changes in technology and societal trends (*e.g.*, Facebook is in, MySpace is out; will Pintrest be the next Twitter?). Next, I revise sections and chapters, rewriting them to address concerns brought to my attention by readers, students, and teachers, Finally, I add new content, such as advances in technology (*e.g.*, geofiltering and facial recognition software) societal impact (*e.g.*, new chapters on journalism in the digital age, and business and the Internet), and legal changes (hundreds of new cases and statutes). Below are some of the major highlighted changes since the previous edition:

**Chapter 1:**
  Added discussion of Substantive and Procedural law
  Added discussion of Judgments and Damages
  Added discussion of Equitable Relief
**Chapter 2:**
  New VARA case: *Mass. Museum of Contemporary Art Found., Inc. v. Büchel*
  Update on *Golan v. Holder*

**Chapter 3:**
 Update on linking liability
 Added the "Hot News" tort and misappropriation
 Update on the First Sale Doctrine
**Chapter 4:**
 Added the new **America Invents Act**
**Chapter 6:**
 All the cybercrimes chapters have been merged
 Revised Computer Trespass section
 Update on cyberstalking
 Update on online gambling
**Chapter 7:**
 Revised The Right to Privacy section
 Update on Public Disclosure of Private Facts
 Revised False Light section
 New False Light case: *Jews for Jesus, Inc. v. Rapp*
 Revised Federal Laws Affecting Privacy section
 Revised Social Networks section
 Update on The Electronic Trail (facial recognition technology)
**Chapter 8:**
 New chapter on Data Privacy
 Update on Data Breaches
 Revised Types of Data Breaches
 Revised Consequences of Data Breaches
**Chapter 9:**
 Revised Expectation of Privacy in E-mail
 Update on Expectation of Privacy in One's Own Hard Drive
 New case: *United States v. Fricosu*
 New case: *In re Subpoena Duces Tecum Dated March 25, 2011*
 Update on Web cam cases
 New Section: Expectation of Privacy in Web Posts
 New Section: Government Intrusion into Individual Privacy
**Chapter 10:**
 Revised Behavioral Marketing section
 Update on Flash Cookies
**Chapter 11:**
 Update on Web Monitoring Software section
 Update on "sexting"
**Chapter 12:**
 Update on Social Networks
 New case: *Phonedog v. Kravitz*
 New case: *Maremont v. Susan Fredman Design Grp., Ltd.*
**Chapter 13:**
 Major Revision of Free Speech chapter
 New sections on Political Speech, Commercial Speech, and Expressive Conduct

New section on Unprotected Speech
New section on Regulation of the Airwaves
New case: _FCC v. Fox Television Stations_
**Chapter 14:**
Major Revision of Defamation section
Major Revision of Anonymous Free Speech section
Update on WikiLeaks
**Chapter 15:**
New Chapter on Student Speech
Update on _Layshock_ and _Blue Mountain_ cases
Update on Cyberbullying
**Chapter 16:**
New chapter: Journalism in the Digital Age
Update on Shield Laws
New case: _Too Much Media, LLC v. Hale_
New case: _Obsidian Finance Group, LLC v. Cox_
**Chapter 17:**
Revised What is Possession? section
**Chapter 18:**
Revised Online Harassment section
Update to Repression of Speech section
Update to Web Speech Under Totalitarianism section
**Chapter 19:**
New Chapter: Business and the Internet
Update on E-Discovery
Update on Corporate Securities section
Update on Crowdfunding
Update on FINRA
Update on Sales Tax
Update on Employee Bloggers section
New case: _Am. Med. Response of Conn._
New case: _Hispanics United of Buffalo, Inc. v. Ortiz_
**Chapter 20:**
Update Affirmative Defenses
Revised Terms of Use Agreements section
Revised Clickwrap Agreements section
New case: _CX Digital Media, Inc. v. Smoking Everywhere, Inc._
**Chapter 21:**
New Section: Digital Estate Planning
Update Net Neutrality section
New Section: Geolocation Filtering
**Revised Glossary**

# CHAPTER

# 1

———

# INTRODUCTION
# TO LAW

> This chapter provides an overview of the American legal system, with special attention paid to the concepts of federalism and jurisdiction. Also discussed is how to read and analyze a court's written opinion.

*"It is one of the happy incidents of the federal system that a single courageous state may, if its citizens choose, serve as a laboratory, and try novel social and economic experiments without risk to the rest of the country."* — Justice Louis Brandeis

WHEN THE U.S. CONSTITUTION was written, the drafters purposely set up a system of checks and balances to disburse power among three distinct branches of government. This separation of powers resulted in the creation of Congress (the legislative branch), the presidency (the executive branch), and the judiciary (the judicial branch). The legislative branch makes laws (called statutes), the executive branch enforces laws (through attorneys general who prosecute lawbreakers), and the judicial branch interprets those laws through judges and courts. The executive branch also promulgates executive orders and administrative rules for federal agencies. Executive orders are issued by the head of the executive branch (the president, at the federal level, or a governor or mayor at the state or local level) and have the force of law.[1] The courts' interpretation of statutes has created a body of case law, known as common law.[2] State governments also follow the three-tier separation of powers model.

## How Many Jurisdictions in the U.S.?

*Jurisdiction* is the limit or territory within which a court has the power, right, or authority to interpret and apply the law. Each state has its own jurisdiction, and both laws enacted by different state legislatures and interpretation of those laws by different state courts may vary.

You might guess there are 50 jurisdictions, since there are 50 states. But the correct answer is 51! There are indeed 50 state jurisdictions, but the federal government also exercises jurisdiction in certain matters. This is due to the concept of federalism.

Figure 1-1

## Federalism

*Federalism* is a system of government where a written constitution divides power between a centralized government and a number of regional governments. Each is supreme within its proper sphere of authority, and both the centralized and regional governments act directly on the people through their officials and laws. The federal government's powers are enumerated in the U.S. Constitution. The Tenth Amendment to the Constitution reserves to the states all powers not specifically granted to the federal government. At times, there may be overlapping areas where both state and federal governments have an interest.

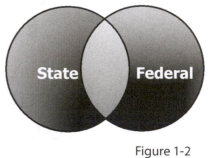

Figure 1-2

If a state law conflicts with either the U.S. Constitution or a valid federal law, then the U.S. Supreme Court can declare the state law unconstitutional.[3] The U.S. Supreme Court can also declare laws passed by Congress unconstitutional.[4]

## The American Court System

- **The United States Supreme Court** consists of nine justices and is based in Washington, DC. It can hear appeals involving issues of federal law, regardless of whether the cases arise in state or federal courts. It may choose to accept or reject cases; however, it must hear certain rare mandatory appeals and cases within its original jurisdiction (specified by Article III of the U.S. Constitution) (see Figure 1-3). If it agrees to hear a case, it grants a writ of *certiorari*.
- **The United States Court of Appeals for the Federal Circuit** (CAFC) consists of 12 judges appointed for life by the president with the advice and consent of the Senate. This court is unique in that it is the only one of the 13 federal circuit courts whose jurisdiction is based on subject matter rather than geography. It has nationwide jurisdiction in several subject areas, including international trade disputes, government contracts, patents, trademarks, nontort monetary claims under $10,000 against the federal government,[5] federal personnel, and veterans' benefits. This court hears appeals from all U.S. district courts, the U.S. Court of Federal Claims, the U.S. Court of International Trade, and the U.S. Court of Appeals for Veterans Claims. It also accepts appeals of decisions by certain administrative agencies. Appeals from this court go to the U.S. Supreme Court (see Figure 1-3).
- **The United States Court of Federal Claims** (formerly the United States Claims Court) consists of 16 judges appointed for a term of 15 years by the president with the advice and consent of the Senate. This court has limited jurisdiction in federal cases involving monetary claims founded on the U.S. Constitution, federal statutes, executive regulations, or contracts with the federal government; and pending conflicts transferred from the defunct Indian Claims Commission. A significant portion of this court's cases deal with tax refund suits and civilian and military pay questions. Appeals go to the U.S. CAFC (see Figure 1-3).
- **The United States Court of International Trade** consists of nine judges appointed for life by the president with the advice and consent of the Senate. This court specializes in — and its jurisdiction is limited to — cases that involve international trade and customs law. It has nationwide jurisdiction and is authorized to hold hearings in foreign countries. Appeals from this court go to the U.S. CAFC (see Figure 1-3).

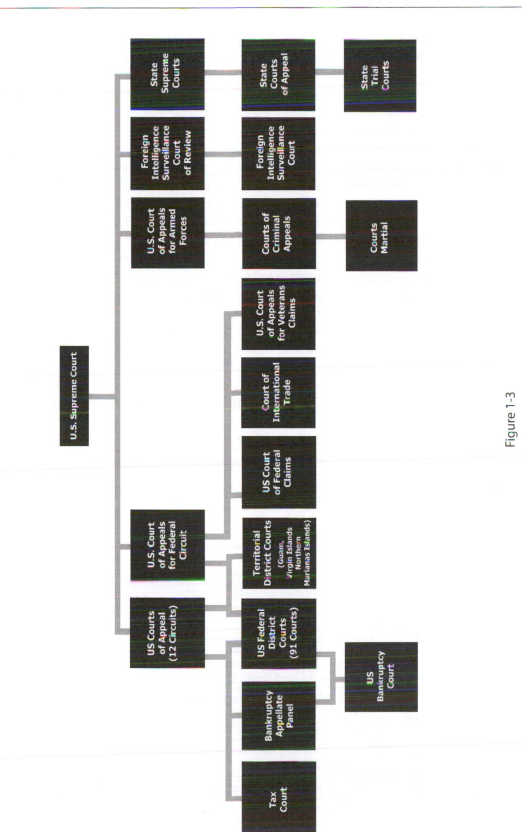

Figure 1-3

- **The United States Court of Appeals for Veterans' Claims** consists of seven judges appointed by the president with the advice and consent of the Senate to serve either 13– or 15–year terms. This court hears appeals from the Board of Veterans' Appeals, an administrative board hearing appeals from the Department of Veterans' Affairs. Appeals from this court go to the U.S. CAFC (see Figure 1-3).

- **United States Circuit Courts of Appeal** review cases from U.S. District Courts in their respective circuits, as well as appeals of federal administrative agencies decisions. Appellate courts limit their review to whether the lower court made the correct legal decision; they do not hear direct evidence, examine the facts of a case, or consider arguments based on a theory raised for the first time in the appeal. In addition to the U.S. CAFC, discussed above, there are 12 other U.S. Courts of Appeal — each state is assigned to one of 11 geographic circuits (the District of Columbia has its own circuit) served by a U.S. District Court of Appeal (see Figure 1-4). The number of judges in each circuit varies (see Figure 1-4). Except for the District of Columbia, each circuit judge must be a resident of the circuit for which he or she is appointed. Appeals go to the U.S. Supreme Court (see Figure 1-3).

- **United States District Courts** consist of 94 general trial courts that handle criminal and civil cases involving federal statutes or the U.S. Constitution, admiralty and maritime cases, and civil cases between citizens from different states where the amount at stake exceeds $75,000 (*i.e., "diversity jurisdiction"*). Three U.S. territories — Guam, the Virgin Islands, and the Northern Mariana Islands — have U.S. district courts with both federal and local jurisdiction (see Figure 1-3). U.S. district judges are appointed for life by the president

| Circuit | Judges | States | Location |
|---------|--------|--------|----------|
| 1st | 6 | Maine, Massachusetts, New Hampshire, Rhode Island, and Puerto Rico | Boston |
| 2nd | 13 | Connecticut, New York, and Vermont | New York |
| 3rd | 14 | Delaware, New Jersey, Pennsylvania, and the Virgin Islands | Philadelphia |
| 4th | 16 | Maryland, North Carolina, South Carolina, Virginia, and West Virginia | Richmond |
| 5th | 17 | Louisiana, Mississippi, and Texas | New Orleans |
| 6th | 16 | Kentucky, Michigan, Ohio, and Tennessee | Cincinnati |
| 7th | 11 | Illinois, Indiana, and Wisconsin | Chicago |
| 8th | 11 | Arkansas, Iowa, Minnesota, Missouri, Nebraska, North Dakota, and South Dakota | St. Louis |
| 9th | 28 | Alaska, Arizona, California, Guam, Hawaii, Idaho, Montana, Nevada, Northern Mariana Islands, Oregon, and Washington | San Francisco |
| 10th | 10 | Colorado, Kansas, New Mexico, Oklahoma, Utah, and Wyoming | Denver |
| 11th | 12 | Alabama, Florida, and Georgia | Atlanta |
| D.C. | 12 | District of Columbia | D.C. |

Figure 1-4

with the advice and consent of the Senate; however, the three territorial district judges are only appointed for 10-year terms. Appeals go to the U.S. Courts of Appeal (*i.e.*, the Circuit Courts).

- **The United States Tax Court** consists of 19 judges appointed by the president with the advice and consent of the Senate. This court has jurisdiction involving disputes over federal income tax assessments. While other courts may also hear tax disputes, this is the only court in which taxpayers may litigate the dispute prior to paying the disputed tax amount. It is located in Washington, D.C., but the judges travel nationwide to conduct trials. Appeals go to the U.S. Courts of Appeal (*i.e.*, the Circuit Courts, see Figure 1-3).

- **Bankruptcy Appellate Panels** are composed of bankruptcy judges from the districts in each respective circuit and appointed by a judicial council. The number of panels varies by the circuit but is typically a three-judge panel. Each panel hears U.S. Bankruptcy Court appeals from its judicial circuit. As shown in Figure 1-3, U.S. Bankruptcy Court appeals can go to either the circuit's bankruptcy appellate panel or its district court; this is because bankruptcy appellate panels were authorized by the 1978 **Bankruptcy Reform Act**[6] but not every circuit has established a panel. In those circuits without panels — the Second, Third, Fourth, Fifth, Seventh, and Eleventh Circuits — U.S. Bankruptcy Court appeals go to the U.S. district court within the respective circuit. The First, Sixth, Eighth, Ninth, and Tenth Circuits have panels. Appeals from the Bankruptcy Appellate Panels go to the U.S. Circuit Courts (see Figure 1-3).

- **The United States Bankruptcy Court** is a federal court that has subject matter jurisdiction over bankruptcy cases (state courts cannot hear bankruptcy cases). Each of the 94 federal judicial districts handles bankruptcy matters. Bankruptcy judges are appointed by the majority of judges of the respective U.S. court of appeals for a term of 14 years. Appeals can go to either the circuit's bankruptcy appellate panel or its district court (see Figure 1-3).

- **United States Court of Appeals for the Armed Forces** is composed of five civilian judges appointed for 15-year terms by the president of the United States with the advice and consent of the Senate. It has worldwide appellate jurisdiction over active duty U.S. military personnel and other persons subject to the **Uniform Code of Military Justice** (UCMJ). Appeals go to the U.S. Supreme Court (see Figure 1-3).

- **United States Courts of Criminal Appeals for Branches of the U.S. Armed Forces** review courts-martial cases (*i.e.*, judicial proceedings conducted under the **UCMJ** by the armed forces). There are four different courts — the Army Court of Criminal Appeals, the Navy-Marine Corps Court of Criminal Appeals, the Air Force Court of Criminal Appeals, and the Coast Guard Court of Criminal Appeals. Appeals from these courts — for example, death sentences affirmed by a Court of Criminal Appeals — go to the U.S. Court of Appeals for the Armed Forces (see Figure 1-3).

- **Courts Martial** are military tribunals consisting of a panel of military officers trying military offenses and are governed by the **UCMJ**. A court-martial is established under Article I of the U.S. Constitution and does not exist until its creation is ordered by a commanding officer. Courts martial have worldwide jurisdiction over active duty U.S. military personnel. Appeals go to the appropriate United States Court of Criminal Appeals for Branches of the U.S. Armed Forces (see Figure 1-3).

- **The Foreign Intelligence Surveillance Court** (FISC) consists of 11 U.S. district court judges from different circuits, appointed by the chief justice of the United States for staggered terms. This court has limited jurisdiction "to hear applications for and grant orders approving electronic surveillance anywhere within the United States under the procedures set forth in" the **Foreign Intelligence Surveillance Act of 1978**.[7] Individual judges review the government's applications for authorization of electronic surveillance (**FISA** warrants) designed to procure foreign intelligence information (see Figure 1-3) Applications for **FISA** warrants are rarely denied but should the **FISA** court turn down the government's application, that decision may be appealed to the United States Foreign Intelligence Surveillance Court of Review[8] (see Figure 1-3).

• **United States Foreign Intelligence Surveillance Court of Review** is a three-judge panel comprised of district or appellate federal judges, appointed by the chief justice of the U.S. Supreme Court for staggered seven-year terms. This court reviews denials of applications for electronic surveillance warrants (**FISA** warrants) by the United States Foreign Intelligence Surveillance Court.

• **State Supreme Courts**, called the state Supreme Court in almost all states, are the final court of appeal for all but a small number of state cases.[9] However, if a case involves a right protected by the U.S. Constitution, then the losing party may appeal to the U.S. Supreme Court (see Figure 1-3).

• **State Trial Courts** are where almost all cases involving state civil and criminal laws are initially filed (typically called Municipal, County, District, Circuit, or Superior Courts). Appeals usually go to state Courts of Appeal (see Figure 1-3).

## Jurisdiction and Venue

There are a lot of courts; in which one should a plaintiff (the individual or corporation suing) file the lawsuit? *Venue*, *i.e.*, the proper location for trial, is determined by whether the court has authority to hear the case. For example, venue in criminal cases is the judicial district or county where the crime was committed; and in civil cases, venue is usually the district or county where the defendant resides, where the contract was executed or is to be performed, or where the act occurred.[10]

Jurisdiction involves the court's authority to hear the case. On review of the complaint, if the court determines it lacks jurisdiction, it must dismiss it. By dismissal on grounds of lack of jurisdiction, the court is not addressing — let alone deciding — the merits of the case; only that it is not allowed to hear it. The court must have jurisdiction over either the parties, the subject matter, or the thing in dispute. These three types of jurisdiction are known, respectively, as personal jurisdiction, subject matter jurisdiction, and *in rem* jurisdiction (Latin for "jurisdiction over the thing itself"). Since in rem jurisdiction seldom arises, and subject matter jurisdiction is relatively straightforward, most jurisdictional questions will turn on personal jurisdiction. But where is the proper place to file cyberspace lawsuits, where the dispute arises in an intangible location with parties potentially residing anywhere in the world? Before we can answer this question, we must first review the three forms of jurisdiction.

### Personal Jurisdiction

Personal jurisdiction (also known as *in personam jurisdiction*, Latin for "jurisdiction over a person") asks: Does the court have authority over the parties? Since the plaintiff submits to jurisdiction by filing the suit, the question really is: Does the court have authority over the defendant? There are several ways it may have personal jurisdiction:

- If the defendant resides or operates a business in the state
- If there is a meaningful connection or contact between the defendant and the state where the lawsuit is filed
- "Gotcha" Jurisdiction — where the defendant sets foot into the state
- If the defendant has caused an injury within the state
- "*Minimum Contacts*" — if a business regularly solicits business in the state, derives substantial revenue from goods or services sold in the state, or engages in some other persistent course of conduct there
- By consent, through appointment of a registered agent for service of process, or by contractual agreement, including an online click-wrap agreement

## Subject Matter Jurisdiction

Subject matter jurisdiction asks: Does the court have authority to hear the case? Recall from our discussion of federalism and the Tenth Amendment, all power not granted to the federal government resides with the states. Thus, state courts have "general" jurisdiction and can hear any type of case not exclusively delegated to federal courts. However, federal courts have exclusive subject matter jurisdiction if the case arises under the U.S. Constitution or federal laws related to patent, bankruptcy, copyright, maritime, securities, [11] or aviation laws. In those cases, the lawsuit must be filed in federal court.

## In Rem Jurisdiction

Some litigants employ inventive means to allow their case to be tried in their desired forum. Famous London department store Harrods wanted to sue a former affiliate in Buenos Aires, South America. The affiliate had registered 60 variations of Harrods' name with a domain name registrar in Virginia. Unable or unwilling to get jurisdiction over the affiliate in the United Kingdom or Argentina, Harrods chose to file its trademark infringement and dilution case in Virginia, site of the Internet domain name registry. The case, *Harrods Ltd. v. Sixty Internet Domain Names*, [12] was filed in federal court in Virginia as an *in rem* action against the 60 domain names themselves. An action *in rem* means the plaintiff is proceeding against a "thing" as opposed to a "person" (*in personam*). The court found in rem jurisdiction existed because the registry was in Virginia. Thus, the court regarded the domain name as a piece of property that can be sued in its own right. (The effect of a domain name being regarded as a property right versus a contract right is discussed in Chapter 5). Harrods would probably not have been able to avail itself of this tactic in a jurisdiction outside the United States because most countries view domain names as contractual, not property rights. The case illustrates an inventive method to obtain jurisdiction in a desired forum.

## Jurisdiction in Cyberspace

Let us return to our question: Where is the proper place to file cyberspace lawsuits, where the dispute arises in an intangible location with parties potentially residing anywhere in the world? The European Union's answer is straightforward; its law looks to where the harm occurred, not to whether the defendant targeted a specific state. Australia's High Court, in a defamation suit, found since the harm occurs where the comments are read or heard, not where they are written, publication takes place where the material is downloaded and that is the appropriate venue for jurisdiction.[13] Unfortunately, the United States applies a more complex approach to finding personal jurisdiction. Rather than focusing on where the injury occurred, U.S. law looks at whether the defendant "purposefully availed" himself (or itself, if a corporation) of the forum state. U.S. courts look for some action by the defendant to establish purposeful ties with the state; simply posting an ad on a Web site viewable in that state would not be enough to find jurisdiction, since anyone, anywhere could view it. (But, were the ad targeted specifically to that state's residents, that might establish a purposeful tie). In addition to purposeful availment, the court looks to whether it was foreseeable the defendant would be haled into court in that forum. Of course, it is foreseeable merely by establishing a Web site a nonresident defendant's product or services might end up in the forum state; however, the key is whether the defendant's conduct and connection with the forum state would make it reasonable to anticipate he would be haled into court there.[14]

Next, the court will consider fairness factors; these include the burden on the defendant, the interest of the plaintiff, and the forum state's interest (see the _Scarcella_ case, below). Finally, the court will determine if there have been sufficient _minimum contacts_ with the forum state to warrant a finding of personal jurisdiction.[15] One method often employed is the concept of a "sliding scale of Internet activity."[16] At one end is the "active Web site" where the defendant has transmitted files to the forum state or contracted with its residents.[17] In the middle is the gray area of the level of "interactivity" and the commercial nature of any information exchanged.[18] At the opposite end of the spectrum lies the "passive Web site", where only information has been posted or limited communication has occurred.[19] In the latter case, most courts would conclude creating a site was not by itself an act purposefully directed toward the forum state. But if the defendant were to do something additional to serve or exploit the forum state (_e.g.,_ directly targeting or encouraging its residents to use the site) then it might find jurisdiction. Other factors the court might consider are: the location of the site's server, the location of the defendant's principal place of business, the defendant's state of residence, the defendant's sales to the forum state, and solicitation of the forum state's residents by the defendant.

### Jurisdictional Examples

Now let us examine some Internet jurisdiction cases. DontDateHimGirl.com was designed as the Internet equivalent of the bathroom wall: the Florida-based site invited disgruntled women to "tell all" about bad ex-boyfriends. A Pennsylvania attorney found himself allegedly described on the site as a herpes-ridden gay or bisexual who had passed on a sexually-transmitted disease and fathered multiple children with different women. Understandably upset, he sued the site creator for defamation in a Pennsylvania court (The merits of this case are discussed further in Chapter 14, but it is relevant here for its procedural issues).[20] The defendant raised the **Communications Decency Act** (CDA) as a defense but the court never considered her defense or the plaintiff's defamation claim; instead, it dismissed the case for lack of personal jurisdiction over the defendant.[21] The court found the plaintiff did not have sufficient minimum contacts with Pennsylvania for it to be able to exert jurisdiction. The site's server was in Florida, the defendant resided in Florida, and the site had solicited comments from all states, not specifically from Pennsylvania. Did this mean the defendant bore no liability for comments posted on her site, or that other sites could now engage in the same behavior with impunity? No, because the court never addressed the issues in the case; it simply said the Pennsylvania court was not the right venue to debate them. The plaintiff might find Florida would be a more proper venue for his lawsuit against the Florida-based defendant. The Pennsylvania court might have found jurisdiction had the plaintiff sued only the Pennsylvanian residents who posted the comments about him, instead of suing the out-of-state site owner.

A New York plaintiff, dissatisfied with an engine purchased on eBay, sued the Missouri seller. The New York court held the online auction process—a single transaction—did not rise to the level of purposeful conduct required to establish personal jurisdiction in a breach of contract action. It ruled a single sale, "without more, does not constitute sufficient purposeful availment to satisfy the minimum contacts necessary to justify summoning across state lines, to a New York court, the seller of an allegedly nonconforming good."[22]

A *long-arm statute* allows a state to exercise personal jurisdiction over a nonresident individual or company, whose actions caused damage in that state or to one of its residents, based on some action of the defendant establishing his minimum contacts with the forum state. For personal jurisdiction to be valid under a state's long-arm statute, the defendant must have been given reasonable notice of the action against him. Each state may specify what it considers sufficient contacts to establish jurisdiction.[23] An Iowa resident who created a gripe site (see Chapter 19 for a discussion of gripe sites) soliciting comments from disgruntled moving van firm customers was sued for defamation by a New York-based firm.[24] The defendant had posted comments claiming the moving company was operating without legal authorization and legally required insurance. The federal district court in New York dismissed the case for lack of personal jurisdiction, holding the plaintiff failed to demonstrate personal jurisdiction under New York's long-arm statute because the defendant had not transacted business in New York, nor had the lawsuit arisen from such transactions.[25] Posting defamatory comments on a Web site accessible in New York was not enough to meet the long-arm statute's requirements.

In another case involving New York's long-arm statute, a Manhattan attorney sued his aunt and uncle, Florida residents, for hacking his law firm's Web site and replacing his résumé with a photograph of him labeled "Pig of the Year".[26] The couple moved to dismiss the suit claiming lack of personal jurisdiction. While they did have certain minimum contacts with New York (both had New York professional licenses but did not derive business income from the state), the court held it lacked personal jurisdiction because the state long-arm statute set a stricter requirement for jurisdiction — while it does not require the defendant's physical presence to find jurisdiction, the tortious act must have been committed in New York.[27] If, as here, the tortious act (*i.e.*, defamation) was committed in Florida, even if the damage from the act occurred in New York, the court will not find personal jurisdiction over the out-of-state defendants.

A federal district court in Virginia dismissed a lawsuit by America Online (AOL) accusing Florida computer technicians of maintaining a computer network that spammed AOL, holding sending e-mails through AOL's Virginia-based computers did not grant Virginia jurisdiction. More than half of all worldwide Internet traffic passed through Virginia because it was home to AOL and 1,300 other Internet Service Providers (ISPs) and technology firms. The ruling would not prevent AOL from suing the defendants in Florida, where they resided. AOL probably chose to sue in Virginia because it had the country's toughest anti-spam law. In 2003, its anti-spam statute was used to indict two North Carolina men, the first in the U.S. charged with felonies for spamming. [28] In 2004, one defendants' sister and a Texan were also indicted under the statute. Each charge carried a sentence of one–to–five years in prison and a fine of up to $2,500. The Virginia statute targeted spammers who intentionally alter an e-mail header or other routing information and try to send either 10,000 e-mails within a 24-hour period or 100,000 in a 30-day period. [29] A spammer could also be prosecuted if a specific transmission generated more than $1,000 in revenue, or total transmissions generated $50,000. Because of this tough anti-spam statute, ISPs such as AOL would prefer to litigate spam cases in Virginia.

As discussed in greater detail in the next chapter, a photographer uploaded his photo of a 16-year-old girl at a car wash to his Flickr account. The photo was allegedly downloaded and doctored by an Australian ad agency and used in a billboard advertising campaign for an Australian mobile phone company. The Texas teen was astounded to learn her face was appearing on billboards on the opposite side of the world with what she viewed as disparaging text captions. The Texas court dismissed her case for lack of personal jurisdiction over the Australian defendant, holding the plaintiff had failed to demonstrate the defendant had minimum contacts with the forum state of Texas. [30] The defendant had argued three minimum contacts with Texas: (1) Flickr had servers in Texas; (2) the Creative Commons license effectively created a contract with a Texas resident; and (3) intrastate effects of the ad campaign's use of the photo. The court found: (1) the defendant failed to prove the downloaded photo was on the Texas server and not one of Flickr's servers in another state; (2) the Creative Commons license did not require the mobile phone firm to perform any of its obligations in Texas; and (3) though the plaintiff may have shown she was affected in Texas, she failed to prove the defendant's conduct was intentionally directed into the forum. Jurisdiction in cyberspace is often ambiguous, leaving a judge free to make a legally sound finding either way. After all, the photographer resided in Texas, as did the photo's subject, the photo was taken in Texas, and the photo resided on a server in Texas, whether or not downloaded from that particular server. While the court could make a legally rational argument for not finding jurisdiction, such a finding from a public policy perspective has a harsh result for the plaintiff, who is left with no practical recourse. The court's holding effectively suggested if the 16-year-old wanted justice, she should save her after-school job money to travel to Australia and hire an Australian law firm to sue in an Australian court. A legally correct option? Yes. A pragmatic option? No.

## Jurisdictional Balance

The Internet has changed the dynamics of legal jurisdiction. As Judge Warren Ferguson, of the Ninth Circuit, wrote: [31]

> It is increasingly clear that modern businesses no longer require an actual physical presence in a state to engage in commercial activity there. Businesses may set up shop, so to speak, without ever actually setting foot in the state where they intend to sell their wares. Our conceptions of jurisdiction must be flexible enough to respond to the realities of the modern marketplace.

Companies doing business on the Internet now face the burden of having to defend against lawsuits in multiple jurisdictions anywhere, at anytime. In deciding jurisdictional questions, courts must balance the burden faced by the defendant with the legitimate interests of the plaintiff.

To avoid the expense of litigating all over the country, companies often insert "*choice of forum*" clauses in customer agreements. AOL had such a clause in its online click-wrap agreement, but it was held unenforceable. In *Scarcella v. America Online, Inc.*, [32] the plaintiff sued AOL after an AOL technical support person told him to delete a folder, resulting in the loss of 1,500 e-mail addresses. The plaintiff sued in Manhattan's small claims court, despite the choice of forum clause's stipulation all claims be filed in Virginia. AOL moved to dismiss, arguing the New York court lacked subject matter jurisdiction because of the choice of forum clause. The court denied AOL's motion, finding the clause unenforceable on public policy grounds: "The general policy of giving effect to forum-selection clauses must yield to the scheme enacted by the legislature specifically to ensure that civil justice is meaningfully accessible to those seeking the adjudication of small claims." It found the public policy interest of providing an inexpensive and informal venue for small claims, *i.e.*, establishment of small claims courts, outweighed enforcement of the choice of forum clause. It added, "The essential features of a small claims court are extremely low costs or none at all, no formal pleadings, no lawyers, and the direct examination of parties and witnesses without formality by a trained judge who knows and applies the substantive law," noting the expense the plaintiff would have to bear in traveling to, and litigating in, Virginia. The decision has no effect on the enforceability of forum clauses in cases that fall outside of the requirements (*i.e.*, dollar amounts) of small claims court.

Conversely, under the doctrine of *forum non conveniens*, a nonresident defendant may ask a court to transfer the case to a more convenient court if the venue poses an undue hardship.

## Anatomy of a Court Decision

*"Four things belong to a judge: to hear courteously, to answer wisely, to consider soberly, and to decide impartially." — Socrates*

Courts do not make laws. Only legislatures can enact laws. Courts interpret laws enacted by a legislative body and then apply that interpretation to a specific fact pattern. A court's written opinion can be dissected into four parts. The first part is the *Fact Situation*; this is a description of the facts specific to the case at hand, *i.e.*, who the players are and what happened. The second part is the specific *Issue* of law raised by this fact situation; this is the issue the court is being asked to decide. The third part is the *Holding*; this is the court's ruling, the answer to the question raised in the issue. This is the part that causes one side to leave the courtroom smiling while the other party displays less sanguine emotions. The holding (also called the decision or ruling) becomes a binding rule of law. The fourth part is the court's *Rationale*. This is the thought process used by the court in arriving at its decision. The rationale is extremely important because it gives observers valuable insight into how the court might apply the law in a similar circumstance, albeit with a somewhat different fact situation.

As we look at various issues in Internet law, we will encounter issues not yet addressed by courts, and issues where courts in varying jurisdictions have decided the same issue in opposite ways. By studying the rationales of previous decisions, we can infer the direction a court might take on first addressing an issue or how an appellate court might resolve a split of opinion.

Once a court has issued its decision, its holding takes on the force of law. The doctrine of *stare decisis* (Latin for "let the decision stand") requires a court follow its own decisions and those of higher courts within the same jurisdiction. Courts are loath to

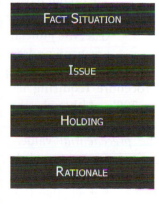

FACT SITUATION

ISSUE

HOLDING

RATIONALE

Figure 1-5

overturn rulings once made because of the instability that would ensue from a constantly changing landscape of legal decisions continually being overruled.[33] Thus, courts adhere to the concept of **binding precedence**. Reliance on precedence assures stability and uniformity to the law, allowing individuals and businesses to plan accordingly, and engendering confidence in the legal system. If there is no binding precedent in the jurisdiction, a court may look to precedents in other jurisdictions, examining the rationale of their decisions for guidance; while not binding, such **persuasive precedents** may be adopted or discarded by the court. Courts rarely overrule a previous decision, instead preferring to "**distinguish**" the fact situation of the current case from fact situation of the previous case, rationalizing a different result.

Court decisions are filed in the clerk's office of the courthouse and available for the public to read or copy. A small percentage of these decisions are published in books called "**reporters**"; these reporters are published periodically and stocked by various law libraries. In this manner, an attorney in Delaware can read about a case that occurred in California. While a case from another jurisdiction has no precedential effect, the attorney may find the rationale useful in making a similar argument to his own court. Of course, if the case is from the same jurisdiction, then it can be cited as precedent.

Decisions that are not submitted to the reporters but remain filed away at the clerk's office are called "**unpublished opinions**." Generally, unpublished opinions may not be cited as precedent; some courts do not allow unpublished opinions to be cited for any reason[34] and go so far as to sanction lawyers who cite them.[35] Published opinions differ from unpublished opinions in that they are written by judges rather than law clerks and go through many drafts and much editing and revision before being released. It makes sense a judge would spend more time crafting and dressing up an opinion that will be read by his peers and available worldwide than an opinion that will sit unnoticed in a file cabinet in the local courthouse. At least, that was the case until the technology of the Internet enabled unpublished opinions to be published in legal databases and on the World Wide Web. This caused a movement among some courts and lawyers to allow citation of unpublished opinions.[36] Even U.S. Supreme Court Chief Justice John Roberts said, "A lawyer ought to be able to tell a court what it has done."[37] The opposing view was expressed by Ninth Circuit Judge Alex Kozinski, who said because unpublished opinions are drafted by staff attorneys and law clerks instead of judges, "When the people making the sausage tell you it's not safe for human consumption, it seems strange indeed to have a committee in Washington tell people to go ahead and eat it anyway."[38] However, as Judge Richard Arnold of the Eighth Circuit succinctly put it:[39]

> We do not have time to do a decent enough job, the argument runs, when put
> in plain language, to justify treating every opinion as a precedent. If this is
> true, the judicial system is indeed in serious trouble, but the remedy is not to
> create an underground body of law good for one place and time only.

In 2006, the U.S. Supreme Court adopted Rule 32.1 of the Federal Rules of Appellate Procedure requiring federal courts allow citation of unpublished cases, effective January 1, 2007. Although the rule allows lawyers to *cite* unpublished opinions in federal circuit courts (it does not apply to state courts), it leaves to the circuit courts' discretion the *precedential* value, if any, to be assigned to unpublished opinions. So the issue of precedence in unpublished opinions remains unresolved. To quote Judge Arnold again:[40]

> The question presented here is not whether opinions ought to be published,
> but whether they ought to have precedential effect, whether published or not.
> We point out, in addition, that "unpublished" in this context has never meant

"secret." So far as we are aware, every opinion and every order of any court in this country, at least of any appellate court, is available to the public. You may have to walk into a clerk's office and pay a per-page fee, but you can get the opinion if you want it.

## Onward to Court

Jurisdiction and venue are matters of procedural law, as opposed to substantive law. *Procedural law* governs the machinery of the courts, specifically the process and procedure of enforcing substantive rights. *Substantive law* creates, defines, and regulates rights. Examples of substantive law include the law of contracts, torts, real property, and wills. Substantive law comes from *common law* (which is derived from judicial decisions and the general body of case law and statutes that governed England and the American colonies prior to the American Revolution) and *statutory law* passed by legislative bodies.

Substantive law is divided into civil law and criminal law. In matters of *civil law,* a plaintiff sues a defendant, while in *criminal law* cases, the state prosecutes an action against a defendant. Procedural law is governed by rules. All courts have procedural rules for practice in them. In civil cases in federal courts, the Federal Rules of Civil Procedure (FRCP) apply. State courts have their own rules of civil procedure. In criminal cases in federal courts, the Federal Rules of Criminal Procedure (FRCRP) apply. State courts have their own rules of criminal procedure. The Federal Rules of Appellate Procedure (FRAP) apply in all U.S. Circuit Courts of Appeal. Federal and state courts will also apply their own evidentiary rules regarding the admissibility of evidence at trial.

Trials may be before a judge (*i.e.,* a *bench trial*) or before a judge and jury (*i.e.,* a jury trial). In a jury trial, the jury acts as the trier of fact (deciding the truthfulness of the evidence that has been presented) and the judge acts as the trier of law, applying the law to the facts of the case. In a bench trial, the judge assumes both roles.

Prior to the trial, the parties in a civil suit engage in the process of *discovery* to obtain evidence from the opposing party. The purpose of discovery is to discover facts that may lead to admissible evidence at trial. This may take the form of requests for answers to interrogatories, production of documents, and admissions. Parties may be deposed (*i.e.,* have their deposition taken under oath and transcribed) and nonparties (*i.e.,* witnesses) may be subpoenaed for depositions and or court appearance. Objects may also be subpoenaed, as may an object's custodian who would receive a *subpoena duces tecum* (Latin for "bring it with you"). In the 21st century, parties now engage in *electronic discovery* (e-discovery), seeking e-mail, social network profiles and posts, and metadata. Corporations, on notice of the initiation of a lawsuit, should place a *litigation hold* on their relevant electronic data in anticipation it will be subject to e-discovery by the plaintiff's attorney and subjected to digital forensic procedures. The purpose of the litigation hold is to avoid *spoilation* (tampering with or destruction) of evidence. *Metadata* is defined as data about data. It is usually not visible in the document itself but can be extracted from it. Metadata may include the identity of the document's author and the time and date it was written. As discussed in Chapter 19, the FRCP were amended in 2006 to deal with electronic discovery.

At the conclusion of the trial, the judge or jury will render its judgment in the case. [41] A jury's judgment is called its *verdict.* A judge's judgment may be referred to as his decision, ruling, or holding. A judge may also issue a declaratory judgment, a summary judgment, or a default judgment. A *declaratory judgment* is a conclusive and legally binding declaration by the court, in a civil case, advising the parties as to their rights and responsibilities, without awarding damages or ordering them to do anything. It is usually sought by a potential party after a legal controversy has arisen but before any damages have occurred or any laws have been violated. A *summary judgment* is a decision by the judge to dismiss a civil case because it presents no genuine issue of material fact in dispute (*i.e.*, no factual questions exist for a judge or jury to decide). A *default judgment* is granted when one party fails to perform a court ordered action, such as appearing in court thereby preventing the legal issue from being presented before the court, and the judge rules in favor of the compliant party (the one who showed up, usually the plaintiff).

Plaintiffs sue for damages, equitable relief, or both. Damages may take several forms. *Actual damages* are compensation for losses suffered by the plaintiff due to harm caused by the defendant. *Compensatory damages* provide a plaintiff with the amount of money needed to replace what was lost. *Punitive damages* (also referred to as exemplary damages) may be awarded by the trier of fact in addition to actual damages to punish the defendant and serve as an example to prospective defendants not to commit the same act. *Statutory damages* are set amounts stipulated by a specific statute. Some statutes, such as the Racketeer Influenced and Corrupt Organizations (RICO) Act, provide for *treble damages* — triple the amount of actual or compensatory damages awarded the defendant. Treble damages are established under specific statutes and are meant to penalize the guilty party and discourage others from similar behavior. *Nominal damages* are trivial amounts awarded where the plaintiff's legal right has been proven to have been violated but he has suffered minimal or no harm or loss. *Liquidated damages* are damages for breach of contract, stipulated in advance, in the contract, by the parties.

Equitable relief falls under a court's powers of equity, and include issuing an *injunction* (court order requiring a party to do or refrain from doing a specific act, *e.g.*, a temporary restraining order or permanent injunction), *specific performance* (compelling a party to perform a specific act, usually pursuant to a contract), restitution (*e.g.*, disgorgement of profits to prevent unjust enrichment), declaratory relief (issuance of a declaratory judgment), recission of contracts, and reformation of contracts (rewriting a contract to make it reflect what it should have said).

Cases may be appealed from the trial court to an appellate court. Sometimes, a case will continue under a different name of one of the parties, for example, where the attorney general is a named party but a new individual has assumed that position since the initial case was filed. In this situation, the case will be retitled with the new party's name and the phrase "*sub nom.*" (abbreviation for the Latin phrase *sub nominee*, which translates to "under the name of") followed by the names of the original parties. An appellate case may be heard by a panel of the court (usually three judges) or by the full court, referred to as an *en banc* hearing. A panel decision may be appealed to the full court. The appellate court may remand (*i.e.*, send back) a case to the lower court for further action.

There are some other Latin phrases that appear in this book. *Pro se* means a defendant has chosen to act as his own attorney. *Sua sponte* means a judge has acted of his own accord, without prompting from either party in a case. This most often occurs when a judge decides he lacks jurisdiction over a case or believe a conflict of interest may exist (in which case he will recuse himself from the case). The abbreviations *i.e.*, *e.g.*, and *cf.* appear frequently throughout this book. *I.e.* is the abbreviation for the Latin term *id est*, which means "that is". *E.g.* is the abbreviation for the Latin phrase "*exempli gratia*" and means "in example of". *Cf.* is the abbreviation for the Latin word "*confer*" and means to compare or contrast the immediately preceding statement or case.

## Chapter 1 Notes

[1] While executive orders have the force of law, the executive is not technically making law, as that is a power reserved for the judicial branch. In _Youngstown Sheet & Tube Co. v. Sawyer_, 343 U.S. 579 (1952), the Supreme Court invalidated President Harry S. Truman's Executive Order 10340 that sought to place the nation's steel mills under federal control because it attempted to make law, rather than clarify or further an existing statute.

[2] Judges may adhere to a philosophy of **judicial restraint**, where they defer to the legislature and respect precedent, or **judicial activism**, where judges allow their personal views on public policy to influence their decisions. Judicial activists are often criticized as making law from the bench, rather than interpreting it.

[3] The Supremacy Clause of the Constitution (Art. VI, Cl. 2) establishes the U.S. Constitution, U.S. treaties, and federal statutes as "the supreme law of the land" mandating where a state law or state constitution conflicts with federal law (_i.e._, the U.S. Constitution, U.S. treaties, and federal statutes), the state court must follow federal law.

[4] _Marbury v. Madison_, 5 U.S. 137 (1803), which established the concept of **Judicial Review** under Article III of the U.S. Constitution, enabling courts to invalidate legislation found to conflict with the Constitution.

[5] While the **Tucker Act** grants the U.S. CAFC exclusive jurisdiction over claims in excess of $10,000, the so-called "**Little Tucker Act**", 28 U.S.C. § 1346(a)(2), allows concurrent jurisdiction between the CAFC and the federal district courts for claims of less than $10,000 against the United States.

[6] **The Bankruptcy Reform Act of 1978** (Pub. L. 95-598, 92 Stat. 2549, November 6, 1978) made it easier for both businesses and individuals to file bankruptcy and to reorganize.

[7] **The Foreign Intelligence Surveillance Act of 1978** (FISA), Pub. L. No. 95-511, 92 Stat. 1783 (codified as amended at 50 U.S.C. §§ 1801-1811, 1821-1829, 1841-1846, 1861-62).

[8] If an application is denied, the government cannot resubmit it to another Foreign Intelligence Surveillance Court (FISC) judge but must appeal to the U.S. Foreign Intelligence Surveillance Court of Review. 50 U.S.C. §§ 1803(a), (b). Although created in 1978, the U.S. Foreign Intelligence Surveillance Court of Review was the "Maytag repairman" of the judicial system, having to wait until 2002 to receive its first appeal from the FISC. In a redacted public version of the opinion, the FISA appellate court reversed the FISA court and found for the government. _In re: Sealed Case No. 02-001_, (USFISCR Nov. 2002). Interestingly, the government raised an argument on appeal it never advanced in the lower court; the appellate court allowed this, stating _supra_, at n.6, "Since proceedings before the FISA court and the Court of Review are _ex parte_ — not adversary — we can entertain an argument supporting the government's position not presented to the lower court."

[9] In the states of New York and Maryland, and in the District of Columbia, the highest court is called "Court of Appeals". Maine's highest court is the "Supreme Judicial Court". The state of Massachusetts' highest court is the "Supreme Judicial Court". Oklahoma and Texas have two separate supreme courts: one for criminal appeals (the Court of Criminal Appeals) and one for civil cases (the Supreme Court). West Virginia's highest court is the Supreme Court of Appeals.

[10] Once _venue_ and _jurisdiction_ have been addressed, the court will turn to **choice of law** to apply the case. In civil cases involving a nonresident defendant, a court will apply its own state's procedural law to determine if it has jurisdiction, but then may choose to apply the substantive law of the defendant's state or nation. (In criminal cases, the forum state's procedural and substantive law is always applied).

[11] Some securities lawsuits may be brought under state fraud statutes.

[12] _Harrods, Ltd. v. Sixty Internet Domain Names_, 302 F.3d 214, 225 (4th Cir. 2002).

[13] _Dow Jones & Co. v. Gutnick_ 194 A.L.R. 433, 2002 HCA 56 (Austl. 2002), holding "defamation is to be located at the place where the damage to reputation occurs."

[14] "The foreseeability that is critical to due process analysis is not the mere likelihood that a product will find its way into the forum state. Rather, it is that the defendant's conduct and connection with the forum state are such that he should reasonably anticipate being haled into court there." _World-Wide Volkswagen Corp. v. Woodson_, 444 U.S. 286 (1980). _See also Asahi Metal Indus. Co. v. Superior Court_, 480 U.S. 102, 112, (1987) (the "placement of a product in the stream of commerce, without more, is not an act the defendant purposefully directed toward the forum State.").

[15] *See Int'l Shoe Co. v. Washington*, 326 U.S. 310 (1945).

[16] *Zippo Mfg. Co. v. Zippo Dot Com*, 952 F. Supp. 1119 (W.D. Pa. 1997).

[17] "…contracts with residents of the forum state that involve the knowing and repeated transmission of computer files over the Internet, personal jurisdiction is proper." *Zippo, ibid. at* 1124.

[18] "The exercise of jurisdiction is determined by the level of interactivity and commercial nature of the exchange of information that occurs on the Web site." *Ibid. at* 1124 (citing *Maritz, Inc. v. Cybergold, Inc.*, 947 F. Supp. 1328 (E.D. Mo. 1996).

[19] *Zippo at* 1124.

[20] *Hollis v. Joseph*, Case No. GD06-012677 (Allegheny Ct. Com. Pl. Pa. 2007).

[21] The Communications Decency Act of 1996, 47 U.S.C. § 230(c)(1).

[22] *Sayeedi v. Walser*, 835 N.Y.S.2d 840 (N.Y.C. Civ. Ct. 2007).

[23] *See* Vedder Price, "Long-Arm Statutes: A Fifty State Survey," 2003 *available at* http://euro.ecom.cmu.edu/program/law/08-732/Jurisdiction/LongArmSurvey.pdf (accessed Mar. 23, 2012), listing the text of all 50 U.S. state long arm statutes.

[24] *Best Van Lines, Inc. v. Walker*, Civil No. 03-6585, 2004 WL 964009 (S.D.N.Y. dismissed May 4, 2004), aff'd 490 F.3d 239 (2ᵈ Cir. 2007).

[25] New York long-arm statute, New York Civil Practice Law § 302.

[26] *Davidoff v. Davidoff*, 819 N.Y.S.2d 209 (N.Y. Supr. Ct. 2006) (Unpublished).

[27] A **tort** is a civil (noncriminal) wrongful act, whether negligent or intentional.

[28] Jeremy Jaynes and his sister Jessica DeGroot were convicted on November 3, 2004; the third defendant, Richard Rutkowski, was acquitted. All three defendants were North Carolina residents.

[29] Jaynes and DeGroot allegedly used fake Internet addresses to send more than 10,000 spam e-mails to AOL subscribers on three days in July 2003 — a volume that made the crime a felony under the Virginia statute.

[30] *Chang v. Virgin Mobile USA, LLC*, 2009 WL 111570 (N.D. Tex. 2009).

[31] *Gator.com Corp. v. L.L. Bean, Inc.*, 341 F.3d 1072 (9ᵗʰ Cir. 2003), vacated 366 F.3d 789 (9ᵗʰ Cir. 2004).

[32] *Scarcella v. Am. Online, Inc.*, 4 Misc. 3d 1024A (N.Y. Civ. Ct. 2004), aff'd 11 Misc. 3d 19 (N.Y. App. Term 2005).

[33] Especially if a court is overturning one of its own prior rulings, since doing so is a public admission of a previous mistake; instead, courts often use spurious grounds to distinguish previous cases that conflict with its present ruling.

[34] Prior to January 1, 2007 when Rule 32.1 of the Federal Rules of Appellate Procedure went into effect, the U.S. Courts of Appeals for the Second (based in New York City), Seventh (based in Chicago), Ninth (based in San Francisco), and federal circuits prohibited citation of unpublished opinions, while six other circuits discouraged it. *See* Tony Mauro, "Supreme Court Votes to Allow Citation to Unpublished Opinions in Federal Courts," Legal Times, April 13, 2006.

[35] *Sorchini v. Covina*, 250 F.3d 706 (9ᵗʰ Cir. 2001), which states in part: "Counsel represents that she violated the rule (against citing unpublished opinions)…we may bear part of the responsibility by issuing unpublished dispositions…and so tempt lawyers to cite them as precedent." The court then declined to sanction the attorney and ironically, in one of its only two footnotes to the opinion, cited *Bush v. Gore*, 531 U.S. 98 (2000), the case the U.S. Supreme Court insisted was "limited to the present circumstances" and could not be cited as precedent.

[36] Molly McDonough, "Door Slowly Opens for Unpublished Opinions," ABA Journal Report, April 21, 2006.

[37] Dennis Crouch, Patently O: Patent Law Blog, April 13, 2006, *available at* www.patentlyo.com/patent/2006/04/unpublished_opi.html (accessed Mar. 23, 2012).

[38] Tony Mauro, "Supreme Court Votes to Allow Citation to Unpublished Opinions in Federal Courts," Legal Times, April 13, 2006.

[39] *Anastasoff v. United States*, 223 F.3d 898, 904 (8ᵗʰ Cir. 2000).

[40] *Anastasoff*, 223 F.3d 898 *at* 904.

[41] Please note the spelling, as the word **judgment** is frequently misspelled. The word "judgement" is a British spelling that applies to nonjudicial uses (*e.g.*, poor judgement). In America, the word is always spelled "judgment".

# CHAPTER

# 2

# COPYRIGHT BASICS

This chapter discusses what a copyright is, how to obtain one, what it does and does not protect, and the concepts of "fair use" and "public domain." It also explores the Visual Artists Rights Act and Creative Commons, an innovative alternative to traditional copyright.

*"Only one thing is impossible for God: To find any sense in any copyright law on the planet." — Mark Twain*

COPYRIGHT IS ONE OF the four forms of intellectual property, the others being trademarks, patents, and trade secrets. Certain things are not copyrightable: facts, ideas or concepts, procedures or methods of operation, U.S. government works, titles, names, short phrases and slogans, symbols, designs, and lists. However, while copyright might not apply, patent or trademark might be applicable.

## The Copyright Act

Copyright law protects original works, which the **Copyright Act of 1976**[1] defines as:

- Literary works
- Musical works, including accompanying words
- Dramatic works, including accompanying music
- Pantomimes and choreographed works
- Pictorial, graphic, and sculptural works
- Motion pictures and other audiovisual works
- Sound recordings
- Architectural works

The Act also covers compilations, meaning the selection, ordering, and presentation of otherwise unprotectable facts (*e.g.*, databases) may be protectable.[2] Other Web site components protected by copyright include written words; software programs; photographs (*e.g.*, JPG, GIF, and PNG digital formats); and music and sound recordings (*e.g.*, MP3 format).

## Exclusive Rights of the Copyright Owner

**The Copyright Act** grants the copyright holder exclusive rights of:
- Reproduction
- Derivative Works
- Distribution
- Public Performance
- Display
- Audio/Video transmission

## Filing a Copyright

An applicant for copyright registration must either mail an Form CO to the Copyright Office or register online.[3] At the time of this book's publication, Form CO could be downloaded from the Copyright Office's site (www.copyright.gov/forms) and needed to be accompanied by a $50 fee ($35 if filed online) and one copy of the unpublished work (two copies if published).[4] Filing an application is not necessary to create a copyright. Original works are automatically protected once *created and fixed in a tangible medium*. But registration establishes a public record of claim (eliminating the "**innocent infringement defense**"[5]) and is a statutory prerequisite for an infringement suit. It also establishes prima facie evidence of the copyright's validity if made within five years of publication. If registered within three months after publication or prior to infringement, the copyright holder can receive statutory damages and attorneys' fees; otherwise only actual damages and profits are recoverable.

## The © Symbol

Registration is not required to use the © symbol, since a common law copyright arises on the work's publication and, under the **1976 Copyright Act**, a statutory copyright exists once the work is created. A 1989 amendment to the 1976 Act[6] brought it in line with provisions of the Berne Convention[7] and made use of the copyright notice optional; but lack of notice may reduce possible damages in an infringement suit. If used, the copyright notice must be in valid form. A valid copyright notice consists of all of the following:
- The © symbol, or the word "copyright", or abbreviation "Copr.";
- The year of *first* publication of the work (not necessarily the current year); and
- The name of copyright owner.

"(c) 2012 My Company, Inc." is not a valid copyright notice; the letter "c" within parentheses is not legally sufficient to replace the actual © symbol.

## Length of Protection

The **Copyright Clause** is found in Article I, § 8, Clause 8 of the U. S. Constitution, ratified in 1788. It reads:[8]

> To promote the Progress of Science and useful Arts, by securing *for limited Times* to Authors and Inventors the exclusive Right to their respective Writings and Discoveries *[emphasis added]*.

What is a "limited time"? Two years later, when the first copyright statute was enacted in 1790, it provided a federal copyright term of 14 years from the publication date, renewable for an additional 14 years if the author survived and applied for an additional term.[9] In 1831, Congress expanded the federal copyright term to 42 years (28 years from publication, renewable for 14 years).[10] In 1909, Congress further expanded the term to 56 years (28 years from publication, renewable for an additional 28 years).[11] In 1976, Congress overhauled the **Copyright Act** and how copyright terms were computed.[12] For works created by identified natural persons, the 1976 Act provided copyright protection would run from the work's creation, not from publication, as in the previous Acts and mandated protection would last until 50 years after the author's death.[13] For anonymous works, pseudonymous works, and work-made-for-hire, it provided a term of 75 years from publication or 100 years from creation, whichever expired first.[14] Any works in existence prior to the Act's effective date of January 1, 1978 were granted a copyright term of 75 years from the publication date. The most recent extension was the **Sonny Bono Copyright Term Extension Act** (CTEA) in 1998, extending copyright protection by 20 years for works copyrighted after January 1, 1923.[15] Works created by identified natural persons now have a term lasting from creation until 70 years after the author's death. Work created by two or more authors now has a term of 70 years after the death of the last surviving author. For anonymous works, pseudonymous works, and work-made-for-hire, the term is 95 years from publication or 120 years from creation, whichever occurs first. For works published before 1978 with existing copyrights as of the **CTEA**'s January 1, 1978 effective date, the term was extended to 95 years from publication. (For further reference, see the exhaustive chart of copyright terms and public domain at Cornell University's Web site.[16] The **CTEA** is both a retroactive and a prospective extension, resulting in the prevention of many works, beginning with those published in 1923, from entering the public domain. Thousands of works were instead preserved under private ownership until at least 2019.

Intuitively, one might argue permitting Congress to extend existing copyrights allows it to evade the "limited times" constraint of the Copyright Clause by effectively creating perpetual copyrights through repeated extensions. Yet, the U.S. Supreme Court, in a challenge to **CTEA**, ruled 7–to–2 the Act was constitutional, rationalizing **CTEA** does not violate the "limited times" restriction because its terms, though longer than the 1976 Act's, are nonetheless limited, not perpetual.[17]

Copyright law can be complex. A recent case extended copyright protection for 130 years to works created before 1917.[18] How this anomaly occurred is as fascinating as it is convoluted. Between 1913 and 1917, Pierre-Auguste Renoir (1841-1919) and his assistant, Richard Guino, collaborated in the creation of 11 sculptures made in France on or before 1917 (yes, copyright law protects sculptures). The U.S. Copyright Office and many commentators (including this author) argued because publication occurred before 1923, the works are now in the public domain in the United States. But…

Guino acquired the exclusive right to produce and reproduce sculptures from the original plaster casts. In 1984, years after he had died, his successor, a trust, registered copyright in the sculptures with the U.S. Copyright Office. In 2003, Renoir's great-grandson sold some of the sculptures and castings and the trust sued him for copyright infringement.

How can copyright protection be afforded to works in the public domain? In _Twin Books Corp. v. Walt Disney Co.,_ the Ninth Circuit held if a foreign work did not secure U.S. copyright protection, then it did not enter the public domain in the United States.[19] Instead, the logic went, the work was effectively unpublished for purposes of U.S. copyright law. In other words, a work only published abroad has not really been published in the eyes of American copyright law. Therefore, the **Copyright Act of 1976** would extend protection to works created before January 1, 1978 but had previously neither fallen into the public domain nor been copyrighted.[20] The statutory protection lasts for 70 years after the death of the last surviving author. Since Guino died in 1973, the copyright will last until 2043.

The district court granted summary judgment to the trust, even though it criticized _Twin Books_.[21] The lower court was forced to follow the opinion of its appellate court. The same thing happened in _Vernor v. Autodesk, Inc._ (discussed in Chapter 3), where a district court was bound by **stare decisis** to follow the earlier of two conflicting Ninth Circuit panel decisions because, absent an intervening Supreme Court precedent on point or a contrary **en banc** decision, a three-judge panel may not overrule the Ninth circuit's binding precedent — only the full court can do that.[22] The Ninth Circuit upheld the lower court's finding of infringement.[23] So we are left with the odd result a work created in 1913 is deemed protected by U.S. copyright law for 130 years, until 2043.

## Work-made-for-hire

In a _"work-made-for-hire"_, one who commissions a work is deemed its author and owner of all rights, including copyright, worldwide, for the duration of the term. Under this doctrine, the work's creator has no rights to the creation unless specified in the contract. A work product may be considered work-made-for-hire where the creator is an **employee** or an independent contractor. If prepared by an employee within the **scope of employment**, then the employer owns the copyright. "Within the scope of employment" means creation of the work was part of the job duties; creating a work later acquired by one's employer does not make it work-made-for-hire.

If the work was **specially ordered or commissioned** (_i.e._, prepared by an independent contractor) as part of a collective work and the parties agree in writing it is work-made-for-hire, then it is considered work-made-for-hire. This writing requirement poses a dilemma. Suppose an independent contractor (not an employee) is hired to write a book or a song, or design a Web site, or create any other work. Further suppose based on the initial conversation, the independent contractor begins the project before a written contract is given to her. The contract arrives either midway through the project or after she has finished and she signs it. Is it "work-made-for-hire"? Circuit courts are split and the U.S. Supreme Court has yet to hear a case to resolve the conflict. The Second Circuit held the **Copyright Act** requires parties agree _before_ the work's creation it will be a work-made-for-hire, **but** the _actual writing memorializing_ the agreement need not be executed before creation of the work.[24] However, the Seventh Circuit disagrees, requiring a writing prior to the work's creation.[25]

While there is no writing requirement for copyright, absent a written agreement, patent rights belong to the employee (rather than the employer) who develops an invention within the scope of employment.

## Elements of a Civil Copyright Infringement Claim

In a civil copyright infringement lawsuit, the plaintiff must prove three elements: (1) **ownership of a valid copyright**, (2) **actual copying**, and (3) **misappropriation**. The first element is established by authorship (either by the plaintiff or the assignor, where the rights were assigned to the plaintiff) of an _original work fixed in a tangible medium_. Registration of the copyright is a jurisdictional prerequisite to filing a lawsuit. The second element is established by direct evidence (*e.g.*, an admission or witness testimony) or indirect evidence to show a "*striking similarity*" between the protected work and the alleged copy and *access* (with *use of that access*) to the protected work. The third element is established by a showing the portion of the protected work alleged to be copied was in fact *protectable* (*e.g.*, not in the public domain) and the *intended audience would recognize substantial similarities* between the protected work and the alleged copy.

## Defenses to a Civil Copyright Infringement Claim

Certain defenses to a civil copyright infringement claim are obvious, such as *permission from the copyright holder* to use the protected work, or where the *copyright has expired*. Another defense is *lack of jurisdiction*, *i.e.*, if the copyright was not properly registered, the court may lack jurisdiction to hear the case. Likewise, if the work is in the public domain, arose from an independent creation, was de minimis, or met the Fair Use test, then infringement would not be found.

### Public Domain

Public domain refers to created materials that are ineligible for copyright protection (*e.g.*, government-created documents, like statutes and published judicial opinions) or whose protection under the law has lapsed. Since materials in public domain lack copyright protection, permission to use them is not required. Whether materials are in public has no bearing on whether they fall into public domain. One should not erroneously assume everything on the Internet is in "public" and therefore in public domain and freely usable without permission. Material is only in public domain if the copyright has expired or it was not copyrightable in the first place.

It had long been considered a "bedrock principle" once in the public domain, works remain in the public domain. However, a 2010 case upended that notion when the Tenth Circuit ruled constitutional a trade treaty restoring copyright protection to foreign works previously in the public domain.[26] In 1989, the United States joined the Berne Convention. Article 18 provides when a country joins, it must grant copyright protection to preexisting foreign works even if those works were in the public domain in that country; however, the U.S. legislation implementing the treaty did not extend copyrights to foreign works already in U.S. public domain. But in 1994, the United States signed trade agreements in the Uruguay Round General Agreement on Tariffs and Trade, including one that extended copyright protection to all works of foreign origin whose term of protection had not expired.[27] To comply with these international treaties, Congress enacted the **Uruguay Round Agreements Act** (URAA).[28] Section 514 of the **URAA** implements Article 18 of the Berne Convention by granting copyright protection to works that lost protection for failing to comply with various formalities, as well as works that never obtained U.S. copyrights. By removing works from the U.S. public domain, the **URAA** arguably interferes with free expression, undermining First Amendment values the public domain is designed to protect. In the 2010 case, the plaintiffs were "orchestra conductors, educators, performers, publishers, film archivists, and motion picture distributors who have relied on artistic works in the public domain for their livelihoods. They perform, distribute, and sell public domain works."[29] Granting a motion for summary judgment, the

Tenth Circuit reversed the district court, holding Congress acted within its authority under the Copyright Clause in enacting § 514. In a 6–to–2 vote, the U.S. Supreme Court affirmed the Tenth Circuit, ruling Congress had the right to change the status of these works to make them consistent with an international agreement.[30] As a result, millions of works were taken out of the public domain and their use will now require payment of licensing fees.

## Independent Creation

There is an old saying, "great minds think alike." Sometimes two individuals create a similar work by coincidence. If the alleged infringer can show his work was created independently of the protected work and he lacked access to the protected work, then he may successfully rebut an allegation of infringement.

## De Minimis Copying

The notion the use of the protected work is too trivial may be a valid defense. Judges obviously do not want their courts clogged with trivial lawsuits; thus, the legal doctrine of *de minimis non curat lex* (Latin for "the law does not care about trifles") has developed to weed out cases considered trivial. However, this defense will usually only apply if the work is used briefly and not recognizably, such as when a copyrighted poster is seen in a movie for a few seconds, or from a distance, or is filmed out of focus. Courts have reached opposing results on similar fact situations. Where several copyrighted photographs appeared in a film, one court found no infringement because the photos "appear fleetingly and are obscured, severely out of focus, and virtually unidentifiable."[31] But where a copyrighted poster was shown for 27 seconds in the background of the TV show "*Roc*", another court rejected the de minimis defense.[32]

## "Fair Use" Doctrine

The "*Fair Use*" doctrine is an affirmative defense to a copyright infringement claim. It allows limited use of a copyrighted work for criticism, comment, news reporting, research, scholarship, or teaching. The Fair Use doctrine is not a simple test, but a delicate balancing of interests; only a court can determine if a particular use qualifies as a fair use. To make that determination, the court looks at four factors:

- **What is the purpose and character of the use?** Is it educational (tipping the scales toward a finding of fair use) or commercial (less likely fair use)? The court will apply a transformative test to determine if the original work has been transformed by the addition of new expression or meaning.

- **What is the nature of the work?** Is it factual (more likely fair use) or creative (less likely)? Creative works receive more protection than fact-based works. Quoting from unpublished materials creates greater risk than quoting from published materials.

- **How does the amount and substantiality of the portion of the work used relate to the entire work?** Generally, the less of the original material copied, the more likely a finding of fair use. For example, in <u>*Kelly v. Arriba Soft Corp.*</u>,[33] the court held an image search engine site could use low resolution thumbnails of copyrighted photographs but not full-size images.

- **What is the effect of the use on the potential market for, or value of, the work?** A finding the use would decrease the potential market for, or value of, the copyrighted work would militate against fair use.

These factors are not always easy to ascertain, even for courts. In _Perfect 10 v. Google, Inc.,_[34] a California federal court issued a preliminary injunction against Google for infringing on a pornographic site's copyright by indexing and displaying thumbnails of its images in search results. The court distinguished this case from _Arriba_ on two grounds. First, applying the "use" test, it found Google's use of the photographs was commercial. In _Arriba_, clicking on the thumbnail took a user to the copyright holder's site, but here users were taken to sites infringing on Perfect 10's copyright by displaying its photos without permission and where Google would receive revenue if the infringing site was also a Google AdSense partner. In those instances, the court wrote, "Google's thumbnails lead users to sites that directly benefit Google's bottom line."[35] Second, applying the "effect of the use on the potential market for and value of the copyrighted work" test, the court found Google's use likely did harm Perfect 10's efforts to sell small thumbnail-sized images to mobile phone users. But the Ninth Circuit reversed, reasoning Google's use of the thumbnails was "highly transformative" and the public benefit of its search engine outweighed any potential commercial use.[36] This case is a perfect example of courts attempting to balance the free flow of information online with the protection of copyright holders.

Close paraphrasing, if extensive, may constitute copyright infringement. Lack of attribution or credit, or improper credit, weighs against a finding of fair use. However, acknowledging the copyrighted material's source does not substitute for permission. Placing a copyrighted image on a Web site and adding the copyright holder's copyright information below the image does not protect one from an infringement suit. Nor will disclaimers necessarily provide protection; in fact, they may establish evidence of the defendant's awareness of the law and therefore willfulness (a key element in criminal copyright infringement, discussed below). The court will weigh all the above factors in determining whether fair use can be used as an affirmative defense.

Many college professors provide students with "coursepacks"—photocopied compilations of reading materials from assorted books and articles. The question arises whether such coursepacks fall under fair use or if permission should be sought from, and licensing fees paid to, the publishers. Kinko's, a commercial photocopy store, was found to be infringing book publishers' copyrights by offering photocopied book chapters as part of coursepacks sold to students.[37] Using the balancing test discussed above, the court noted the purpose of the use was commercial, not educational (Kinko's was profiting from the sale); the amount of the work used (from 5-to-25 percent of the original work) was excessive; and the use had a direct effect on the market for the original books since students who bought the coursepacks would forego buying the original books.

Fast forward to the Internet Age, where professors scan copyrighted materials into digital files and post them on college Web sites as electronic coursepacks, estimated to account for up to half of all syllabus reading at American colleges and universities.[38] Is this fair use or copyright infringement? The answer may hinge, in part, on whether the court finds the use to be noncommercial as well as the direct effect on the textbook market. Several textbook publishers have joined in a lawsuit against Georgia State University for providing electronic coursepacks without permission from the publishers or payment of licensing fees.[39] Unlike the Kinko's case, where the coursepacks were sold by a commercial entity, here the coursepacks are being freely distributed to students by the university on its site.

## Parody

Parody may be a defense to a copyright infringement claim. A parody is a humorous spoof of the underlying copyrighted work and therefore derivative of it. Normally derivative works are an exclusive right of the copyright holder, but an exception is made for works that qualify as parody. Important elements of a parody are:

- A derivative work
- based on a famous copyrighted work
- taking only so much of the original work as necessary to invoke the original
- that involves the conveyance of two *simultaneous* but contradictory messages — it must target the copyrighted work but be apparent it is not the original, and
- the copyrighted work itself must be the subject of the parody

Parody is often linked with fair use, but it is not included in the statutory fair use limitation on a copyright holder's rights. [40] It is difficult to apply the four-pronged fair use balancing test to parody because (1) contrasting commercial versus nonprofit educational use is meaningless when considering "nearly all of the illustrative uses listed in the preamble paragraph of § 107 [of the **Copyright Act**], including news reporting, comment, criticism, teaching, scholarship, and research … are generally conducted for profit in this country," [41] (2) how much of the original incorporated into a parody becomes "too much" is an amorphous standard that varies depending on the particular work, [42] and (3) the effect on the market for the original is negligible because parodies seldom substitute for it, as they serve different market functions. [43]

As discussed, the copyrighted work itself must be the subject of the parody. Parody alludes to, and comments on, the work itself, instead of using the work to make a general statement. For example, when a defendant published a book about the O.J. Simpson trial written in the stylized rhyming manner of *The Cat in The Hat* books by Dr. Seuss, it did not qualify as a parody because it did not satirize or comment on the original work ("*The Cat in the Hat*"), but rather on an unrelated event (the trial). [44]

As parody is also a form of expression, including political expression (*e.g.,* George Orwell's "*Animal Farm*"), there is often a free speech element associated with it; however, the property interest of the copyright holder have usually prevailed over the First Amendment in such cases.

## Transformative Use

The U.S. Supreme Court has held a commercial parody can be a fair use. When rap music group 2 Live Crew released a parody of Roy Orbison's song "*Oh, Pretty Woman*", after the licensor had refused their request for permission to do so, the Co urt held its commercial parody was a fair use within the meaning of the **Copyright Act**'s language, with the deciding factor being the degree to which the parody was a transformative work. [45]

In contrast, the Second Circuit found any transformative use of the derivative work was "slight to nonexistent" where a publisher released a trivia book based on events in the fictional television comedy "*Seinfeld*." [46] The defendant published *SAT: The Seinfeld Aptitude Test*, a 132-page book of 643 trivia questions and answers about events and characters from the show. The copyright holder won a summary judgment for infringement, [47] sustained on appeal. The appellate court reasoned (1) the amount of material copied was not de minimis, (2) facts about fictional works — *i.e.*, "fictional facts"[48] — are not comparable to facts that would make the nature of the work educational (recall fair use is more likely to be found in factual than fictional works), and (3) there was no significant transformative use, since the book's purpose was to entertain the *Seinfeld* fans with a work about *Seinfeld*, much the same purpose as the TV show. While the book was not claimed to be a parody, this case and the preceding one are illustrative in clarifying the concept of a transformative use as differentiated from a derivative work, and in showing how a true parody may be a permissible transformative use.

Sound like a bunch of legal hocus-pocus? Consider the case where the publisher and author of the Harry Potter series of children's books about a boy wizard sued a fan who had maintained a site devoted to the books and movies when he announced plans to publish a reference guide to the franchise. The proposed "lexicon" would alphabetically list characters, places, spells, creatures, and objects from the Harry Potter universe. The plaintiffs (author J. K. Rowling and publisher Warner Bros. Entertainment, Inc.) argued the proposed book "compiles and repackages Ms. Rowling's fictional facts derived wholesale from the Harry Potter works without adding any new creativity, commentary, insight, or criticism."[49] The defendants (RDR Books and the lexicon's author) argued the book was a printed and bound version of his site, which had existed for years, unchallenged by the plaintiffs (in fact, the plaintiff-author was quoted as using the site as a reference tool and gave it a "Fan Site Award" in 2004, and Warner Bros. had invited the defendant to the filming of one of the Harry Potter movies, explaining they used his site daily as a guide).[50] The defendants also pointed out nearly 200 books on the Harry Potter universe had been published by others,[51] raising the question why this particular work was singled out. Rowling had publicly stated her intent to publish a Harry Potter encyclopedia at some unspecified point in the future.

The case raised several salient issues and the court directly addressed some of them:

- Is the lexicon a transformative use or merely a derivative work?
- Should Rowling's intent (or, conversely, lack of intent) to publish a lexicon have any bearing on the questions of infringement or fair use?
- How might the outcome affect the legality of third-party publications of popular culture compendia, "companion" books, and "fan fiction"?[52]
- When the publisher of a $15 billion franchise and a major entertainment conglomerate sue a small press publisher, do legal principles yield to financial realities?[53]

The defendants did not deny the lexicon infringed on the plaintiffs' copyright, but argued, as a reference book, it was a fair use.[54] The court found the book was not entitled to the fair use defense because it relied on "the verbatim copying of language", contained "a troubling amount of direct quotation or close paraphrasing of Rowling's original language", and did not add any new creativity, commentary, insight, or criticism (as distinguished from the Web site, noting the latter contained "fan art, commentary, essays, timelines, forums, and interactive data").[55] The court permanently enjoined publication of the lexicon.

As a district court decision, it lacks precedential value beyond its jurisdiction, but may gain authoritative weight as a persuasive precedent if cited heavily in future cases. Since the defendants withdrew their appeal, the decision will not be subject to review. The defendants announced plans to publish a different version of the guide that would adhere to the specifications for such a book laid out in the ruling (*i.e.,* more analysis and commentary; no plot spoilers).[56]

*Was the lexicon a transformative use or merely a derivative work?*

The plaintiffs alleged the lexicon violated their right to control the production of derivative works. But the court noted "a work is not derivative, however, simply because it is 'based upon' the pre-existing works" because, in the Second Circuit, "if the secondary work sufficiently transforms the expression of the original work such that the two works cease to be substantially similar, then the secondary work is not a derivative work and ... does not infringe the copyright of the original work." [57] The court found the plaintiffs failed to show the lexicon was a derivative work and gave the copyrighted material another purpose, providing readers with "a ready understanding of individual elements in the elaborate world of Harry Potter". [58]

*Should Rowling's intent (or, conversely, lack of intent) to publish a lexicon have any bearing on the questions of infringement or fair use?*

In examining the fourth fair use factor, market harm, the court first noted "notwithstanding Rowling's public statements of her intention to publish her own encyclopedia, the market for reference guides to the Harry Potter works is not exclusively hers to exploit or license, no matter the commercial success attributable to the popularity of the original works" but then back-pedalled. [59] While finding the lexicon would not potentially compete directly with, and impair sales of, any similar lexicon Rowling might write one day, the court found it could impair sales of two of her companion books that were copied almost verbatim, as well as the future marketability of songs and poems also copied verbatim. [60]

*How might the outcome affect the legality of third-party publications of popular culture compendia, "companion" books, and "fan fiction"?*

The court noted, "the Lexicon fits in the narrow genre of non-fiction reference guides to fictional works". [61] Therefore, the holding and analysis should be applicable to similar "companion" books, and "fan fiction".

*Does current U.S. copyright law, as applied in this case, undermine the underlying public policy of the copyright law by protecting too much of the original work?*

The **Copyright Act** establishes a de facto monopoly for creators of original works as an incentive to create original works, while at the same time allowing and encouraging others to build on such works. The common law fair use doctrine was incorporated into the **Copyright Act** and has been interpreted by courts to allow secondary works that add value to the original work resulting in a transformative purpose for the work. The court found a transformative purpose in the lexicon's use of the Harry Potter series, *i.e.*, as a reference guide to the fictional series. However, it ruled against the defendants, holding "a finding of verbatim copying in excess of what is reasonably necessary diminishes a finding of a transformative use." [62]

It could be argued U.S. copyright law, as applied in this case, undermines the Act's underlying public policy by protecting too much of the original work. The constitutional justification for the copyright law is to "promote ... the useful arts." [63] The defendants gave the public a useful work and it exists in the present. The plaintiff proposes to give the public a useful work "one day, maybe." Should the plaintiff never write her own lexicon, the public will have been deprived of an existing useful work, contrary to the public policy justification of the **Copyright Act** (*i.e.*, promoting the useful arts).

## Criminal Infringement

Copyright infringers may face both *civil* and *criminal* liability. Historically, criminal copyright infringement had been a misdemeanor, but in 1982 the **Copyright Act** was amended to make certain types of first-time infringement felonies, depending on the number of copies made or sold within a 180-day period. The 1909 Act requirement the criminal infringement be "for profit" was changed by the **1976 Copyright Act** to infringement conducted "willfully and for purposes of commercial advantage or private financial gain." The ease of infringement through the Internet led Congress to reevaluate and ultimately change the profit motive requirement. Internet infringers were posting copyrighted software, music, and movies online not for profit but to share freely with fellow Internet users. Also, in many cases the infringers were juveniles and thus sympathetic defendants. In 1997, Congress passed the **No Electronic Theft Act**, [64] eliminating the felony copyright infringement requirement to show a profit motive — only distribution need be shown. Two years later, the first felony conviction was obtained under the Act against a defendant who illegally posted software programs, music, and movies on his Web site for public downloading. [65]

The elements of felony copyright infringement are: (1) existence of a copyright; (2) infringement by the defendant (*i.e.*, reproduction or distribution of the copyrighted work); (3) the defendant acted "willfully"; and (4) the defendant infringed at least 10 copies of one or more copyrighted works with a total retail value of more than $2,500 within a 180-day period. [66]

## Damages

The **Copyright Act** provides remedies for infringement: injunctive relief (a court order to cease the infringing activity), impoundment (court-ordered confiscation of the infringing products), destruction of infringing products, damages, and court costs. [67] If the plaintiff has filed a *timely registered* copyright claim with the copyright office, then he may seek statutory damages and attorneys' fees. Timely registration is determined differently for published and unpublished works. If published, then registration is considered timely if made within three months from first publication and the infringement occurred after first publication. [68] If unpublished, registration is deemed timely if made prior to the infringement. [69] A copyright owner who has timely registered his claim may, before judgment, elect statutory damages in place of actual damages and profits, but may not receive both. [70] Statutory damages may be greater, for example, in cases where multiple copyrights have been infringed. Courts retain discretion to award statutory damages in addition to actual damages and disgorgement of profits. [71]

Statutory damages for copyright infringement are described in § 504 of the **Copyright Act**. A copyright owner may recover actual damages resulting from the infringement and disgorgement of any profits attributable to the infringement (if not already accounted for in computing actual damages). [72] For example, if the infringing work is not the entire work but part of a larger work (as in a chapter of a book), the court will consider what portion of the total net profits are attributable to the use of the infringing material and what portion are attributable to other factors and then apportion the profits. [73] But if the copyrighted portions are too entwined with the non-infringing work, then the defendant's entire profits will be awarded to the plaintiff.

The **Copyright Act** does not define the term "actual damages" but they are typically calculated to reflect "the extent of which the market value of the copyright has been injured or destroyed by an infringement." [74] This is obviously an uncertain and speculative damage model. Courts will look at how sales of the infringing product have displaced sales the copyright owner otherwise might have made. Such lost sales can be a measure of *actual damages*. In determining *lost profits*, the copyright owner must prove not just the dollar amount of lost sales, but also his profit margin. After the plaintiff has established the infringer's gross revenue and the relationship between the revenue and the infringement, the burden of proof shifts to the defendant to prove any deductible expenses and elements of profit attributable to factors besides the copyrighted work. Deductible expenses include those directly related to the infringing use, such as production, marketing, and distribution costs, but with the caveat "a plagiarist may not charge for his labor in exploiting what he has taken."[75]

## Alternative Creator Rights Protection

The **Visual Artists Rights Act** and Creative Commons are two alternatives to the **Copyright Act** for creators to preserve and protect their rights.

### The Visual Artists Rights Act

In 1990, Congress passed the **Visual Artists Rights Act** (VARA), which protects the moral rights of artists who produce a "work of visual art."[76] Moral rights ensure authors the ability to control the eventual fate of their works. The concept of moral rights is not about ownership of the work, but rather about ensuring its integrity by preventing revision, alteration, or distortion, regardless of who the ultimate owner may be.

**VARA** only protects an artist's moral rights in paintings, drawings, prints, sculptures, and photographs, existing in a single copy or a limited edition of 200 signed and numbered copies or fewer.[77] Additionally, the photographs must have been taken for exhibition purposes only. The Act does not apply to posters, maps, globes, charts, technical drawings, diagrams, models, applied art, motion pictures or other audiovisual work, books, magazines, newspapers, periodicals, databases, electronic information services, electronic publications, merchandising items or advertising, or any promotional, descriptive, covering, or packaging material or container.[78] **VARA** also does not apply to work-made-for-hire.[79]

Moral rights under **VARA** are exercisable only by the artist and are not transferable. They end with the artist's life (or last surviving artist, if co-creators), but the artist may waive them, usually by contract at the time of commission or purchase. **VARA** grants the artist the rights of attribution and integrity. The *right of attribution* entitles the artist to be properly credited for her work; or conversely, to demand her name be removed from work distorted, mutilated, or modified; or to demand her name be removed from work she did not create.[80] The *right of integrity* precludes others from distorting, mutilating, or modifying her work; it also prevents the destruction of works of "recognized stature."[81] Both rights are recognized under the Berne Convention.

Legal remedies for **VARA** violations are damages, disgorgement of profits made by the infringer, injunctions, and/or impoundment or destruction of the work. Statutory damages range from \$750-to-\$30,000;[82] however, if the infringement was committed willfully, the court in its discretion may increase the statutory damages up to \$150,000.[83] The court also has discretion to reduce damages to \$200 if the infringer was unaware and had no reason to believe her acts constituted copyright infringement.[84] **VARA** does not preclude state law claims, such as right of publicity, misappropriation, trademark infringement, and defamation.

The First Circuit has held **VARA**'s protection of an artist's moral rights extends to unfinished creations that are "works of art" within the meaning of the **Copyright Act**. [85] In that case, a museum sought a declaration it was entitled to present an uncompleted project to the public. The artist counterclaimed, seeking an injunction preventing the display of his unfinished work, and damages for violations of his rights under **VARA** and the **Copyright Act**. The district court had ruled the museum had a right to exhibit the unfinished work against the artist's wishes but must not refer to the artist in signage and include a disclaimer the work was an unfinished project that did not carry out the creator's intent. However, the First Circuit reversed, becoming the first federal circuit court to issue a decision under **VARA**. The appellate court reasoned although **VARA** does not specify when an artistic work becomes subject to it, it is part of the **Copyright Act**, which states a work is created when "fixed" in a tangible medium of expression and "where a work is prepared over a period of time, the portion of it that has been fixed at any particular time constitutes the work as of that time." It also held a plaintiff can seek only an injunction, not damages, for violation of the right of attribution.

### Creative Commons

Creative Commons, a methodology developed by Stanford law professor Lawrence Lessig, is a new approach to copyright gaining prominence on the Web. His view is the "all or none" copyright approach, where a creator either allows or prohibits use of his work, stifles artistic growth in the digital age. Lessig proffers what he terms "a more flexible approach," described on his Creative Commons site [86] as having "built upon the 'all rights reserved' of traditional copyright to create a voluntary 'some rights reserved' copyright." Under Creative Commons, a creator offers a portion of rights but subject to certain conditions. There are four conditions, used in various combinations to form six distinct *Creative Commons licenses*: "Attribution" (permission to publish if properly credited), "Noncommercial" use (permission to publish for noncommercial purposes), "No Derivative Works" (permission to publish the original but no works derived from it), and "Share Alike" (permission to distribute derivative works only under a license identical to the license that governs the creator's work).

Creative Commons licenses are based on copyright concepts, and therefore only apply to works that would be copyrightable. Traditional copyright is restrictive, in that it vests the sole rights of reproduction and distribution in the copyright holder — the focus is on ownership of a single bundle of rights. Creative Commons is a less restrictive licensing scheme, where the focus is on use, through a smorgasbord of licensable rights. Under traditional copyright law, a copyright holder can license his work, with the duration and revocability subject to the licensing agreement terms. However, Creative Commons licenses are nonrevocable. [87] As this may be equivalent to giving away commercial rights to one's creative work, the least restrictive Creative Commons licenses may be most beneficial for unknown creators seeking exposure rather than wealth. However, the more restrictive Creative Commons license may ultimately be embraced by traditional media companies, who view the Internet as the greatest threat to their rights. The motion picture and music industries are decrying the downloading of films and music, much as they did the invention of the video tape recorder, and much as record companies feared radio. "At every turn in history we see this new model of distribution that people say is going to destroy art itself," author Cory Doctorow said, noting such fears have historically been disproven.[88] Traditional media companies might be wise to embrace technologies such as file-sharing and digital copying and co-opt them, and Creative Commons may offer them one means to do so.

A work protected by a Creative Commons license may identify itself as such by use of a Creative Commons ⓒⓒ symbol (similar to the copyright © symbol but with a double 'C') or be listed in the CreativeCommons.org searchable archives.[89] Also, both the Yahoo! search engine and the Firefox Web browser allow users to search the Web for works of art licensed by Creative Commons.

Justin Wong used a Creative Commons Attribution 2.0 license on photos posted to his Yahoo! Flickr photo-sharing account. The particular license allowed any use, even commercial, as long as he was credited. Wong, a church youth counselor, photographed 15-year-old Alison Chang at a church-sponsored car wash in Dallas, Texas and posted the photo to his Flickr account.[90] Apparently, an Australian ad agency decided rather than hire a model for its new ad campaign, it would simply search Flickr's collection of photos to find one it liked. They must have liked Alison's photo a lot, because her image was cropped out of the photo, flipped, and blown up to appear on a billboard in Adelaide, Australia as part of mobile phone company Virgin Mobile's ad campaign. The billboard touted the double-entendre "virgin–to–virgin" text services beneath Alison's photo and above her photo, in large letters read: "Dump Your Pen Friend."[91] Chang sued Virgin's American subsidiary, Virgin Mobile, USA and Australian-based Virgin Mobile Pty., Ltd., reportedly seeking damages under the right of publicity (see Chapter 12).[92] Wong, co-plaintiff in the suit, alleged Virgin did not honor all the Creative Commons license terms.[93] The case would have been one of the first to deal with Creative Commons; however, Virgin Mobile, USA claimed it had nothing to do with its Australian counterpart, and the Texas court dismissed the case for lack of personal jurisdiction over the Australian defendant.

The Chang lawsuit is not the only case of personal photographs appropriated by businesses. In 2012, Jubeerich Consultancy, an Indian company offering "overseas study opportunities and placement services," used University of North Carolina Student Body President Eve Carson's photograph on a billboard to promote its business. Four years earlier, Carson had been abducted, robbed, and murdered. The picture was apparently taken off the Internet and used without permission from the deceased student's family or the copyright holder, UNC.[94] The photograph was her official student body president portrait, taken by a university photographer.[95] In an ironic and even more distasteful move, the NewsObserver, Web site of the North Carolina based *News & Observer* that reported the story, reprinted the billboard with Carson's photo and placed a "Buy Photo" link beneath it, allowing readers to purchase a print of the photo (matted and framed) or have it placed on a coffee mug, mouse pad, deck of playing cards, or drink coasters.[96]

One woman reported a photograph of her pug in a Santa Claus outfit was used without permission as a Christmas icon in the corner of an NFL football game broadcast on Fox television. She eloquently and succinctly summed up the copyright issue: "It's a picture of a stupid dog. But it's my dog and it's *my* photo!" (emphasis added), noting with irony that during the same game Fox repeatedly admonished against infringing its own copyright.[97] A man who complained of software copyright audits at work by Microsoft was similarly shocked by such corporate hypocrisy when he found one of his own photographs on a Microsoft-owned blog.[98]

Another man discovered a photograph of his young daughter had been lifted from Flickr and misappropriated onto an online parenting site featuring a story about the dangers of lead paint. The photograph showed his daughter playing in front of a paint-peeling wall, creating an inference he was a negligent father — highlighting the risk of a potential false light claim, in addition to an infringement claim, against the site.[99] And iStockphoto, a division of Getty Images that licenses photos and frequently issues takedown notices to sites it finds infringing its copyright, ironically offered photos owned by an Icelandic professional photographer, taken from her Flickr account.[100]

These examples underscore the point copyright is vested in the work's creator and just because a photograph is publicly posted on the Internet does not mean it is in the public domain. If a photo is subject to a Creative Commons license, both the photographer uploading it and the individual downloading it must be aware of, and comprehend, the terms of the license.

## Chapter 2 Notes

[1] The Copyright Act of 1976, as amended, 17 U.S.C. § 101, *et seq.*

[2] Databases are generally protected by copyright law as compilations, 17. U.S.C. § 101, but the database must contain a minimum level of creativity to be protectable, and be original in its selection, coordination, and arrangement. *Feist Publ's, Inc. v. Rural Telephone Serv. Co.* However, copyright protection in a compilation extends only to the compilation itself, and not to the underlying materials or data. 17 U.S.C. § 103(b). So while a database of facts or ideas may be protected, the facts or ideas themselves are not.

[3] Copyright information is available online at Library of Congress, U.S. Copyright Office, *at* www.copyright.gov (accessed Mar. 23, 2012).

[4] For current fees, visit the Copyright Office site, *available at* www.copyright.gov/docs/fees.html.

[5] **Innocent Infringement** is not a defense against a finding of infringement. The infringer remains liable but a court may reduce or remit damages. Innocent Infringement may be claimed where (1) a defendant's work is copied subconsciously and in good faith, having forgotten the plaintiffs' work was the source; (2) the infringing work is based on an infringing work supplied by a third party, or (3) the infringer had a good faith belief his actions were not infringing.

[6] The Berne Convention Implementation Act of 1988, Pub. L. No. 100-568, 102 Stat. 2853.

[7] The Berne Convention for the Protection of Literary and Artistic Works.

[8] The Copyright and Patent Clause, U.S. Const., Art. I, § 8, cl. 8.

[9] The Copyright Act of 1790, ch. 15, § 1, 1 Stat. 124 (1790 Act).

[10] The Copyright Act of 1831, ch. 16, §§ 1, 16, 4 Stat. 436, 439 (1831 Act).

[11] The Copyright Act of 1909, ch. 320, §§ 23–24, 35 Stat. 1080–1081 (1909 Act).

[12] The Copyright Act of 1976, 17 U.S.C. §§ 302–304.

[13] 17 U.S.C. § 302(a).

[14] 17 U.S.C. § 302(c).

[15] 17 U.S.C. § 302(a).

[16] *Available at* http://copyright.cornell.edu/resources/publicdomain.cfm (accessed Mar. 23, 2012).

[17] *Eldred v. Ashcroft*, 537 U.S. 186, 221 (2003).

[18] *Societe Civile Succession Richard Guino v. Renoir*, No. 07-15582 (9th Cir. Dec. 10, 2008).

[19] *Twin Books Corp. v. Walt Disney Co.*, 83 F.3d 1162 (9th Cir. 1996).

[20] 17 U.S.C. 303(a).

[21] *Societe Civile Succession Richard Guino v. Beseder, Inc.*, 414 F. Supp. 2d 944, 952 (D. Ariz. 2006).

[22] *Vernor v. Autodesk, Inc.*, 555 F. Supp. 2d 1164 (W.D. Wash. 2008), rev'd 621 F.3d 1102 (9th Cir. 2010).

[23] *Renoir*, No. 07-15582.

[24] *Playboy Enter., Inc. v. Dumas*, 53 F.3d 549 (2ᵈ Cir. 1995) cert. denied, 516 U.S. 1010 (1995).

[25] *Schiller & Schmidt, Inc. v. Nordisco Corp.*, 969 F.2d 410 (7ᵗʰ Cir. 1992).

[26] *Golan v. Holder*, Case No. 09-1234 (10ᵗʰ Cir. 2010).

[27] The Agreement on Trade Related Aspects of Intellectual Property Rights.

[28] 17 U.S.C. § 104(A).

[29] *Golan*, fn. 26, *supra*.

[30] *Golan v. Holder*, 565 U. S. ___ (2012), aff'ing *Golan v. Holder*, Case No. 09-1234 (10ᵗʰ Cir. 2010).

[31] *Sandoval v. New Line Cinema Corp.*, 147 F.3d 215 (2ᵈ Cir. 1998). *See also Gottlieb Dev., LLC v. Paramount Pictures Corp.*, 590 F. Supp. 2d 625 (S.D.N.Y. 2008) holding fuzzy views of copyrighted designs on a pinball machine in the background of a scene in the movie *"What Women Want"* were de minimis.

[32] *Ringgold v. Black Entm't Television, Inc.*, 126 F.3d 70 (2ᵈ Cir. 1997).

[33] *Kelly v. Arriba Soft Corp.*, 280 F.3d 934 (9ᵗʰ Cir. 2002) withdrawn, 311 F.3d 811 (9ᵗʰ Cir. 2003). (Included in the Cases Section on the Issues in Internet Law site, www.IssuesinInternetLaw.com).

[34] *Perfect 10, Inc. v. Google, Inc.*, 416 F. Supp. 2d 828 (C.D. Cal. 2006), aff'd in part, rev'd in part, remanded, *sub nom. Perfect 10, Inc. v. Amazon.com*, 487 F.3d 701 (9ᵗʰ Cir. 2007).

[35] *Ibid.*

[36] *Ibid.*

[37] *Basic Books, Inc. v. Kinko's Graphics Corp.*, 758 F. Supp. 1522 (S.D.N.Y. 1991).

[38] Katie Hafner, "Publishers Sue Georgia State on Digital Reading Matter," The New York Times, April 16, 2008.

[39] Complaint, *Cambridge Univ. Press v. Patton*, Case No. 1:2008-cv-01425 (N.D. Ga. filed Apr. 15, 2008).

[40] 17 U.S.C. § 107. Limitations on Exclusive Rights: Fair Use:

> Notwithstanding the provisions of sections 106 and 106A, the fair use of a copyrighted work, including such use by reproduction in copies or phonorecords or by any other means specified by that section, for purposes such as criticism, comment, news reporting, teaching (including multiple copies for classroom use), scholarship, or research, is not an infringement of copyright. In determining whether the use made of a work in any particular case is a fair use the factors to be considered shall include —
> (1) the purpose and character of the use, including whether such use is of a commercial nature or is for nonprofit educational purposes;
> (2) the nature of the copyrighted work;
> (3) the amount and substantiality of the portion used in relation to the copyrighted work as a whole; and
> (4) the effect of the use upon the potential market for or value of the copyrighted work.
> The fact that a work is unpublished shall not itself bar a finding of fair use if such finding is made upon consideration of all the above factors.

[41] *Campbell v. Acuff-Rose Music*, 510 U.S. 569, 584 (1994).

[42] Even the U.S. Supreme Court standard enunciated in *Campbell supra,* at 586-87: "[T]he extent of … copying" must be consistent with or no more than necessary to further "the purpose and character of the use" — is a vague and subjective standard.

[43] *Campbell*, 510 U.S. 569.

[44] *Dr. Seuss Enter., L.P., v. Penguin Books USA, Inc.*, 109 F.3d 1394 (9ᵗʰ Cir.), cert. denied, 521 U.S. 1146 (1997). The book, titled *"The Cat is Not in the Hat"* by "Dr. Juice" featured a narrator wearing a red and white stove-pipe hat (like Dr. Seuss' Cat in the Hat) spouting lines like: "I do not like pre-trial exams. Green-fisted witnesses, surely shams" (recalling Dr. Seuss' *"Green Eggs and Ham"*). Another stanza recalls Dr. Seuss' *"One Fish, Two Fish, Red Fish, Blue Fish"*: "One Knife? Two Knife? Red Knife. Dead Wife."

[45] *Campbell*, 510 U.S. 569.

[46] *Castle Rock Entm't v. Carol Publ'g Grp., Inc.*, 150 F.3d 132 (2ᵈ Cir. 1998).

[47] *Castle Rock Entm't v. Carol Publ'g Grp., Inc.*, 955 F. Supp. 260, 274 (S.D.N.Y. 1997).

[48] Fictional facts relate to the characters, settings, and events described within a fictional work. That Sherlock Holmes was a detective, smoked a pipe, and lived at 221B Baker Street, London England are all accurate "fictional" facts; however, they are not "true" facts because Sherlock Holmes is a fictional character who did not exist and never lived at that address.

[49] Complaint, *Warner Bros. Entm't Inc. v. RDR Books*, Case No. 1:2007-cv-09667 (S.D.N.Y. filed Oct. 31, 2007).

[50] Mark Hamblett, "Harry Potter Author Fights Creator of Lexicon, Calling It 'Wholesale Theft,'" New York Law Journal, April 15, 2008. Harry Potter author J.K. Rowling wrote: "This is such a great site that I have been known to sneak into an Internet café while out writing and check a fact rather than go into a bookshop and buy a copy of Harry Potter (which is embarrassing)," "J.K. Rowling vs. Vander Ark: the Whole Story," eitb.com, April 14, 2008, *was available at* www.eitb24.com/new/en/B24_94534/entertainment/HARRY-POTTER-LEXICON-J.K.-Rowling-Vs.-Vander-Ark-whole-story (accessed Jul. 1, 2009) but no longer available.

[51] David Glovin, "Rowling Warns of Potter Plagiarism in Trial Testimony," Bloomberg.com, April 14, 2008.

[52] Fan fiction refers to fiction written by fans of fictional characters or settings (*e.g.*, Sherlock Holmes, Oz, Star Trek) created by another. Such derivative stories, usually unauthorized by the original creator, often take the format of sequels or prequels to the original material and are circulated among other fans either through "fanzines" or fan Web sites, free or at minimal cost.

[53] Hamblett, fn. 50 *supra. See also* Joe Nocera, "A Tight Grip Can Choke Creativity," The New York Times, February 9, 2008, for an excellent analysis of the case.

[54] The plaintiffs were awarded $6,750 in statutory damages.

[55] *Warner Bros. Entm't Inc. v. RDR Books*, 575 F. Supp. 2d 513 (S.D.N.Y. 2008).

[56] James Prichard, "New Version of 'Harry Potter' Guide to be Released," Associated Press wire service report, December 5, 2008.

[57] Quoting *Well-Made Toy Mfg. Corp. v. Goffa Int'l Corp.*, 354 F.3d 112, 117 (2ᵈ Cir. 2003) (in turn, quoting *Castle Rock*, 150 F.3d at 143 n. 9).

[58] *RDR Books*, 575 F. Supp. 2d 513.

[59] *Ibid.*

[60] "Fantastic Beasts & Where to Find Them" and "Quidditch through the Ages".

[61] *RDR Books*, 575 F. Supp. 2d 513.

[62] *Ibid.*

[63] The Copyright and Patent Clause, U.S. Const., Art. I, § 8, cl. 8.

[64] The No Electronic Theft Act of 1997, 17 U.S.C. § 101.

[65] "First Criminal Copyright Conviction under the "No Electronic Theft" (NET) Act for Unlawful Distribution of Software on the Internet," Press Release, U.S. Attorney's Office, District of Oregon, August 20, 1999. Jeffery Gerard Levy, a 22-year-old University of Oregon student, pleaded guilty and faced maximum penalties under the NET Act but received only two years probation.

[66] 17 U.S.C. § 506(a)(2); 18 U.S.C. § 2319(a), (c)(1).

[67] 17 U.S.C. § 502-505.

[68] 17 U.S.C. § 412(2).

[69] 17 U.S.C. § 412(1).

[70] 17 U.S.C. § 504(c)(1). *See Twin Peaks Prods., Inc. v. Publ'ns Int'l, Ltd.*, 996 F.2d. 1366 (2ᵈ Cir. 1993).

[71] However, most relevant case law is based on the 1909 Copyright Act, not the 1976 Copyright Act. *See Robert Stigwood Grp., Ltd. v. O'Reilly*, 530 F.2d 1096 (2ᵈ Cir. 1976), cert. denied, 429 U.S. 848 (1976); *F. W. Woolworth Co. v. Contemporary Arts, Inc.*, 344 U.S. 228 (1952); *L.A. Westermann Co. v. Dispatch Printing Co.*, 249 U.S. 100 (1919).

[72] 17 U.S.C. § 504(b).

[73] *Sheldon v. Metro-Goldwyn Pictures Corp.*, 309 U.S. 390 (1940).

[74] *Frank Music Corp. v. Metro-Goldwyn-Mayer, Inc.*, 772 F.2d 505, 512 (9ᵗʰ Cir. 1985).

[75] *Sheldon v. Metro-Goldwyn Pictures Corp.*, 106 F.2d 45, 51 (2ᵈ Cir. 1939).

[76] The Visual Artists Rights Act of 1990 (VARA), 17 U.S.C. § 106(A).

[77] The Copyright Act of 1976, 17 U.S.C. § 101.

[78] *Ibid.*

[79] *Ibid.*

[80] 17 U.S.C. § 106A(a)(1) and (2).

[81] 17 U.S.C. § 106A(a)(3).

[82] 17 U.S.C. § 504(c)(1).

[83] 17 U.S.C. § 504(c)(2).

[84] *Ibid.*

[85] *Mass. Museum of Contemporary Art Found., Inc. v. Büchel*, 565 F. Supp. 2d 245, (D. Mass. 2008), aff'd in part and vacated in part, 593 F.3d 38 (1ˢᵗ Cir. 2010).

[86] Creative Commons, *available at* http://creativecommons.org (accessed Mar. 23, 2012).

[87] *Ibid.*

[88] Ariana Eunjung Cha, "Creative Commons is Rewriting Rules of Copyright," The Washington Post, March 15, 2005, p. E01.

[89] Creative Commons site, fn. 86, *supra.*

[90] Noam Cohen, "Use My Photo? Not without Permission," The New York Times, October 1, 2007.

[91] A photograph of the billboard advertisement, taken on a public street, Churchill Road, in Adelaide, Australia, by photographer Brenton Cleeland, is *available at* www.flickr.com/photos/sesh00/515961023 (accessed Mar. 23, 2012). The original photograph taken by Wong is *available at* http://lh4.ggpht.com/fisherwy/RvPKV4pBF7I/AAAAAAAAIyM/kL463iozl_Q/alison+chang+flickr+picture%5B8%5D.jpg (accessed Mar. 23, 2012).

[92] *Chang v. Virgin Mobile USA, LLC*, 2009 WL 111570 (N.D. Tex. 2009).

[93] This assertion, which forms the crux of the complaint, appears in doubt, however. The photo was originally posted on Wong's Flickr account (and can be viewed as used on the billboard on Brenton Cleeland's Flickr account at www.flickr.com/photos/sesh00/515961023, last accessed Mar. 23, 2012) under a Creative Commons Attribution license, which allows free use as long as the copyright holder is credited. The license states: "You must attribute the work in the manner specified by the author or licensor (but not in any way that suggests that they endorse you or your use of the work)." Both the photo posted on the Flickr site and a contemporaneous comment below it alerting the rights holder to its use by Virgin showed the ad did have a line with a hyperlink to Wong's Flickr account, meaning Virgin appears to have complied with the license terms. (Creative Commons does also offer the option to add a no commercial use restriction to the attribution license; it is unclear whether Wong had added this restriction). There are two distinct rights at issue. First, is the photographer's right to control the disposition of his creative work, which was addressed by the terms of the Creative Commons license, and second, is the right of the subject to control the use of the commercial value of her likeness (see the discussion on appropriation in Chapter 12). A photographer typically licenses photographs to others to publish, assigning to the publisher the rights granted him by the subject in the model release. Here, Chang did not sign a release assenting to the use of her likeness for commercial purposes, so while the photographer may have granted a license of his rights in the photograph, he was unable to convey any rights of behalf of the subject, absent an executed model release assigned to him. Chang may have a valid right of publicity case against Virgin, as the license terms also state "Rights other persons may have either in the work itself or in how the work is used, such as publicity or privacy rights" are in no way affected by the license. It is telling Chang's initial reaction on learning of her image having been appropriated for use on the billboard was, "hey that's me! no joke. i think i'm being insulted... can you tell me where this was taken." (Comment she posted below Cleeland's snapshot of the billboard, at www.flickr.com/photos/sesh00/515961023).

[94] Jane Stancill and Bruce Siceloff, "Image of Slain UNC Student Body President on Advertising in India," Newsobserver.com, March 21, 2012. *See also* Eric Pfeiffer, Image of Murdered Former UNC Student-Body President Being Used in India Advertising," Yahoo! News, March 22, 2012.

[95] For comparison purposes, Eve Carson's UNC photo is *available at* http://media.zenfs.com/en/blogs/thesideshow/EveCarson.jpg (last accessed Mar. 22, 2012). The billboard photo is *available at* www.newsobserver.com/2012/03/21/1947979/image-of-slain-unc-student-body.html (last accessed Mar. 22, 2012).

[96] NewsObserver's order form for prints of the photo is *available at* http://photostore.newsobserver.com/mycapture/enlarge_remote.asp?source=&remoteimageid=4251774 (last accessed Mar. 22, 2012).

[97] Monica Hesse, "Hey, isn't That... People are Doing Double-Takes, and Taking Action, as Web Snapshots are Nabbed for Commercial Uses," The Washington Post, p. C01, January 9, 2008.

[98] *Ibid.*

[99] *Ibid.*

[100] Stephen Shankland, "Photographer Finds Flickr Pics Sold on iStockphoto," CNET News.com, February 7, 2008.

# CHAPTER

# 3

———

# COPYRIGHT
# INFRINGEMENT

> This chapter examines direct, contributory, and vicarious infringement of copyrighted content online, with a focus on hypertext linking, inline linking, deep-linking, framing, file-sharing, the Digital Millennium Copyright Act, and the First Sale doctrine.

*"Shame may restrain what law does not prohibit."* — *Seneca*

## Copyright Infringement

COPYRIGHT INFRINGEMENT OCCURS WHEN the infringer publishes or distributes copyrighted material without permission from copyright holder. The plaintiff must show ownership of the copyright and that the defendant violated his exclusive rights under the **Copyright Act**. There is no copyright infringement if:

- **The material is not published or distributed.** "Published or distributed" includes posting to a Web site, social network, blog, or Usenet group, or e-mailing or sending as an attachment in chat or IM (Instant Messaging). However, one court has determined making music files available for download on a hard drive on a peer-2-peer (P2P) network is not infringement absent evidence of actual distribution. [1]
- **The material is not copyrighted.** If in the public domain (*e.g.*, the copyright period has expired or the material was produced by the government)
- **The copyright holder has given permission** (*e.g.*, stated in the material, in a separate letter authorizing its use, or pursuant to a license, contract, or Creative Commons license). Permission may be limited to specific uses, formats, or media.

In addition to direct infringement, courts have fashioned three distinct types of secondary liability for copyright infringement: contributory infringement, vicarious infringement, and inducement. A ***direct infringer*** commits the copyright infringement directly by engaging in a volitional act;[2] most instances of direct infringement involve either placing copyrighted material on one's Web site or publishing a site to which one does not hold the copyright. A ***contributory infringer*** helps others commit copyright infringement. A ***vicarious infringer*** has the right and ability to control an infringer's activity and receives direct financial benefit from the infringement. An *inducer* distributes a device with the object of promoting its use to infringe copyright.

## Direct Infringement

### Web Site Content

When collating content to place on a site, it is essential to bear in mind under U.S. copyright law[3] it is illegal to copy and publish on a Web site someone's text, artwork, music, or photographs without their permission. A site owner must either own the copyright to materials placed on the site or have the copyright owner's permission to use such them.

Take the case of _Playboy v. Sanfilippo_.[4] One can imagine the defendant sitting in his room staring at stacks of his lifetime collection of _Playboy_ magazine and a beat-up copy of a "Create Your Own Web Site" book when the epiphany hit him — why not set up an adult site where visitors could pay to see his collection of 7,500 photographs of naked women — all scanned from copies of _Playboy_ magazine? Playboy, however, was not happy about this and promptly sued for copyright infringement. Playboy prevailed because it showed the necessary elements of an infringement claim: (1) **ownership of a valid copyright**, (2) **actual copying**, and (3) **misappropriation**. Intent, knowledge, injury, or damage are not required elements of a copyright infringement action. At the time of the lawsuit, statutory damages ranged from $500–to–$100,000 per infringement (_i.e._, per photo) — Playboy asked for damages of $285,420,000! However, the court awarded a more reasonable $3,737,500. Still, think how elated you would be to win $3.7 million in the lottery; now picture how a defendant would feel having to write a check for that amount. So remember, it is illegal to copy someone's photos and put them on your site.

An interesting case arose when conservative group USA Next published a Web advertisement criticizing the American Association of Retired Persons (AARP).[5] It contained a photograph of a soldier with a red "X" over him and two men kissing, captioned "The REAL AARP Agenda." The gay couple in the photograph sued the ad's producer for $25 million for libel and invasion of privacy, contending they "did not consent to serve as models for a homophobic and mean-spirited campaign for a political group with whose views they strongly disagree."[6] USA Next said the ad was meant to show the AARP is out of touch with "mainstream America", while the plaintiffs argued it portrayed them in a false light[7] as unpatriotic during wartime. Ironically, the defendants countered they did not need permission from the men pictured, since the photo was taken (to accompany a story on the issuance of marriage licenses to same-sex couples) by a Portland newspaper and they had posed for it. However, the defendants admitted USA Next's consultant had taken the photograph from the _Portland Tribune_'s Web site without the newspaper's permission. It would appear the paper might have a valid cause of action for copyright infringement against USA Next, regardless of this lawsuit's outcome.

Suppose the local newspaper publishes a favorable story about, or review of, your business, or a complimentary article detailing your years of community service, and you wish to republish it on your site. After all, the article is about you, or your business. However, since it was created by someone else and already published in a tangible medium, it is a copyrighted work and you would be infringing on the copyright holder's exclusive rights of reproduction and distribution if you reproduced it on your site.

What if you want to place your company brochure on your site? While you may hold the copyright to a brochure you created, suppose it has a copyrighted photograph you paid the photo's copyright holder to license for use in your brochure. Can you post the brochure, with the licensed photo, on your site? The answer is probably no, unless it is a broad license that includes republication in other media like the Internet. This is an example of permission being limited to specific uses, formats, or media. When negotiating licenses, the licensee should negotiate as broad a license as possible to accommodate future uses, while the licensor should be mindful of potential loss of future revenue by agreeing to a broad license.

### The Web Site Itself

The copyrightable elements of a Web site include its overall "look and feel", software applications, scripts, graphics (photographs and artwork), and text. Many sites are designed by professional Web designers for clients, who use them for personal or business use. Who owns the copyright to a site created for a client by a Web designer? Recall from the previous chapter, a work's creator is the copyright holder; by default, the Web designer becomes the copyright owner, unless the Web site development agreement (*i.e.*, contract between the designer and her client) states otherwise. The contract may define "developer content" and "company content" and assign rights to each. It may grant the client a license to use a copyrighted work, while the designer holds the actual copyright. A license to use a copyrighted work does not grant a right to create a derivative work (recall from the previous chapter, derivative works are an exclusive right of the copyright owner). So, if the designer retains the copyright and grants the client only a license, should the client later publish an updated version of the site, it may be a derivative work and thus an infringement of the designer's copyright.

In a case illustrating copyright ownership of a Web site absent a written agreement,[8] a designer hired by a magazine began work based on an oral agreement, creating files, code, graphics, and the site design. While the contract was being drafted, a dispute arose. It had not been signed, but the parties had both performed according to their prior understandings under the contract. The designer claimed ownership of the files, code, programming, and graphics for the site, and threatened to shut it down unless additional fees were paid. The issue raised was who owned the copyright to the site, as there was no written agreement regarding copyright ownership or license rights.[9] The court held, absent a signed contract, the designer had granted an implied nonexclusive license to the client to use copyrighted software and files on the site by virtue of the parties' course of dealings and industry custom, and for which the designer had been paid. Therefore, the client did not violate the designer's copyright, since its use was under a lawful license. However, the court added the implied license was revocable absent proper consideration (*i.e.*, payment), but where there was proper consideration, the nonexclusive license would remain irrevocable. The nonexclusive license does not have to be in writing. The court declined to rule on whether the site was a work-made for-hire.

## Contributory Infringement

If third-parties are allowed to publish material on a Web site, the site owner may incur liability for what they post.[10] While not a direct infringer (since the owner did not post the infringing material) he might be a contributory infringer by providing the means for the infringement to occur. Third-party posts might consist of copyrighted material (infringing on the holder's valid copyright), or libelous or defamatory comments,[11] or profanity (what this author calls the "Graffiti Factor"). Some places third parties might publish (*i.e.*, upload content) on a site include discussion forums and message boards, chat rooms, guestbooks, and blogs. While the federal **Communications Decency Act** (CDA, discussed at length in Chapter 14) broadly protects ISPs, Web site owners, and other "publishers" from liability for certain content posted by others, it is not a license to infringe copyrights, defame, or violate trade secrets.

Copyright infringement is not the only risk from third-party posts, They may also contain defamation (see Chapter 14) or reveal trade secrets (see Chapter 4). One blogger was sued for both defamation and publication of trade secrets after the content in question was posted by readers in his blog's comments section. He maintained a blog on search engine optimization (*i.e.*, how to make a site rank higher in search engine results), and a search engine optimization software maker objected to negative comments posted by blog readers about its software and marketing practices. [12] The case was dismissed for lack of personal jurisdiction by the Nevada federal court.

The safest way to avoid liability would be to not allow third-party posts. However, that may not be feasible, given the site's nature or purpose. If a site hosts discussion forums, message boards, or blogs, it should have a moderator responsible for policing and cleaning up posts. Chat room software often comes with filters to block certain words and phrases, including profanity. Instead of using a guestbook that automatically posts comments, the guestbook form can use a "mailto: form" to send comments directly to the site owner for review before posting to the site.

To find copyright infringement, a court does not need to find the site owner intended to infringe, or even knew the third-party had posted the material. Still, lack of intent to infringe or knowledge of infringement may reduce statutory damages.

## Linking

The World Wide Web is so-named because every Web page contains hyperlinks to other Web pages, analogous to navigating through a spider's web. There are three types of links to other Web pages: simple hypertext links, inline links, and deep-links.

A *hypertext link or hyperlink* is a word or phrase (usually underlined) which, when clicked, will take the user to a new Web page. For example, a Web site could contain a sentence that reads "My bicycle is a <u>Schwinn</u>", where Schwinn is a hyperlink which, when clicked, takes the user to the Schwinn site. But what if Schwinn does not want to be associated with the referring site? Does a Web site need permission from another site to link to it?

Accounting firm KPGM apparently believed so when it e-mailed a young man in Great Britain, advising him to remove his link to its site from his Web page, stating: "Please be aware such links require that a formal agreement exist between our two parties, as mandated by our organization's Web Link Policy." [13] KPGM's e-mail prompts two issues: (1) legally, is a site entitled to enforce provisions or restriction in its online policy statements on others unilaterally, and (2) practically, how could it follow through on such enforcement? The situation is reminiscent of President Andrew Jackson's response to a U.S. Supreme Court ruling he did not like: "The court has made its decision; now let them enforce it," [14] a quip referring to the judicial branch's lack of enforcement power. None of this was lost on the savvy 22-year-old Web consultant, who e-mailed back, "my own organization's Web Link Policy requires no such formal agreement." [15] He summed up the obvious fallacy of KPMG's policy: "If every hyperlink used on the Web required parties at both sides of the link to enter into a formal agreement, I sincerely doubt that the Web would be in existence today."

As no American court has ruled on this issue, it would be advisable to obtain permission before linking to another site. While links from a referring site tend to improve a site's search engine ranking, it might not wish to be associated with the referring page. For example, a hate group might link to the target of its hatred. A neo-Nazi site might have an article on "Jewish Control of the Media" and link to a Jewish celebrity's site. Then, search engine queries for that celebrity would yield the neo-Nazi Web site among the results. The Jewish celebrity might object to being linked to the neo-Nazi site.

Can a government entity stop someone from linking to its site? A Wisconsin woman maintained a personal Web site devoted to local government affairs and a business site, where she hyperlinked to the local police department. The city attorney sent her a cease-and-desist notice to remove the link as "maintenance of this link could be construed as having been authorized or endorsed by the City and/or its Police Department."[16] After she complied with the notice, police told her they were conducting "an official police investigation relative to the linking."[17] The next month, the city notified her it had decided not to pursue legal action and the mayor publicly apologized. Unsatisfied, she sued the city, mayor, police chief, and city clerk for violating her First Amendment rights, claiming the cease-and-desist notice and subsequent criminal investigation had been in retaliation for her support of an unsuccessful mayoral recall attempt.[18]

From a copyright standpoint, hyperlinking is equivalent to telling one where to find the source of the information. A text-only hyperlink would likely not be considered an infringement.[19] Yet, there may be circumstances where hyperlinking might be considered a form of contributory infringement.

In the previous chapter, we discussed *Perfect 10 v. Google, Inc.*,[20] where Google was sued by a pornographic Web site for displaying thumbnail photos from that site in its search engine results. While the court ruled the public benefit of Google's transformative use of the photos outweighed protecting the copyrighted material, it added a surprising comment that could reshape American law on linking. In addition to displaying thumbnail photos in its search results, Google also displays a hyperlink to the full size image and a hyperlink to the referring page. Some of these referring pages were not the Perfect 10 site but other pornographic sites illegally posting Perfect 10's copyrighted photos. The court stated these hyperlinks could make Google a contributory infringer, since it was providing access to the infringing sites:[21]

> There is no dispute that Google substantially assists Web sites to distribute their infringing copies to a worldwide market and assists a worldwide audience of users to access infringing materials. * * * Google could be held contributorily liable if it had knowledge that infringing Perfect 10 images were available using its search engine, could take simple measures to prevent further damage to Perfect 10's copyrighted works, and failed to take such steps.

The case was remanded to the lower court to determine if, based on the facts, Google had failed to take steps to prevent harm to Perfect 10's copyrighted material. Unfortunately, the court did not elaborate on what "simple measures" would be appropriate, so more litigation in this area may be expected.

Google lost two similar cases in Germany in 2008, as the courts arrived at an opposite ruling to the American *Perfect 10* case. The German Regional Court of Hamburg ruled Google violated German copyright law by displaying thumbnail previews of copyrighted images because "no new work is created" by the display. German photographer Michael Bernhard's photos and cartoonist Thomas Horn's artwork had appeared as thumbnails in Google search results. [22] However, in a similar 2008 German case, an appellate court agreed there was no exemption under the German Copyright Act for creation and display of thumbnail copyrighted images by search engines, yet dismissed the case under the rationale the plaintiff had engaged in search engine optimization, therefore deliberately attracting spiders and robots, and was estopped from raising claims against search engines. [23] None of the German courts addressed the fact the plaintiffs could have prevented indexing of the images simply by using a robots.txt file in their site's root directory.

In Australia, where copyright infringement is a crime punishable by fine and/or imprisonment, courts have applied the contributory infringement concept to include Web site owners who hyperlink to infringing sites. [24] An 18-year-old was prosecuted for linking to a site that may have offered infringing downloads. [25] This case is notable because the man (a minor when he placed the link) had no relation to the infringing site and subsequently faced criminal, not civil penalties. In another Australian case, the court found both the Web site operator and ISP guilty of contributory infringement. [26] A retired policeman set up a site, mp3s4free.net, that linked to music files on sites he did not own; the copyright owners (several large music companies) sued for infringement. In ruling illegal linking without permission to copyrighted music posted elsewhere, a three-judge panel of the Federal Court of Australia relied on the Australian Copyright Act, which lists the following three factors as relevant to determining whether a person has authorized infringement of copyrighted sound recording:

- The extent (if any) of the person's power to prevent the infringement
- The nature of any relationship between the person and the infringer, and
- Whether the person took other reasonable steps to prevent or avoid the infringement, including compliance with relevant codes of practice

From _Perfect 10 v. Google, Inc._, it appears U.S. courts may be headed toward a similar analysis (although the Australian court based its analysis on a test contained in its own statute). [27] However, the Australian court held both the site linking to the infringing site and its ISP liable as contributory infringers, even though neither offered or hosted the copyrighted MP3 files. This is much further than any American or European court has stretched the definition of contributory infringement. In the United States, the **CDA** § 230 might preclude ISP liability on the basis the ISPs lack control over content hosted on their systems by their customers. [28]

In a case pending before the Seventh Circuit, a site owner is appealing a verdict of contributory infringement for allowing users to embed videos hosted on third-party sites. [29]

In 2011, the U.S. Department of Homeland Security claimed linking to copyrighted material is a crime. Acting in concert with Immigration and Customs Enforcement, it seized a New York man's domain, replacing its content with a government warning: [30]

> This domain has been seized by ICE — Homeland Security Investigations, Special Agent in Charge, New York Office.
> It is unlawful to reproduce copyrighted material, such as movies, music, software or games, without authorization… First-time offenders convicted of a criminal felony copyright law will face up to five years in federal prison, restitution, forfeiture and fine.

The site owner claimed he never reproduced copyrighted material, only linked to other sites. [31]

The Motion Picture Association of America (MPAA) in 2008 sued a content aggregator (a site that syndicates or links to, but does not host, third-party content, which may include infringing content) on the novel theory it was "profiting" from providing hyperlinks because it had related advertising (such as online movie rental company Netflix video ads) on the same Web page.[32] This pending case, filed in California federal court, raises interesting issues, including the prospect of contributory liability for RSS feeds that link to infringing content.

Many sites use *RSS* feeds to aggregate content, usually in the form of a headline and/ or brief description of a news article, followed by a link to that article. This presents the issue of whether news aggregators can be liable for copyright infringement for copying the opening paragraphs (ledes) of news articles from other sites or whether such practice qualifies as fair use. Even if considered fair use, there is another issue: Are news aggregators liable under state laws that retain the doctrine of "hot news" misappropriation?[33]

The U.S. Supreme Court created the *"hot news" tort* in 1918, a legal doctrine granting news organizations a short-term monopoly on their reporting, whether or not copied verbatim.[34] That case, however, is no longer precedential law because it relied on the concept of federal common law, which the Supreme Court ruled 20 years later, federal courts lacked the power to create.[35] Yet state courts have relied on the case's reasoning to create "hot news" torts under their states' unfair competition laws. The 1976 **Copyright Act** provides federal copyright law preempts any state law claim involving "exclusive rights within the general scope of copyright" such as reproduction, distribution, performance, or display of the work.[36] However, the Act's legislative history specifically mentions the "hot news" tort as a state law claim that potentially survives preemption. Thus, under the "hot news" tort, states may offer a remedy for "misappropriation" of another's property interest.

In 2008, GateHouse Media, publisher of more than 100 small Massachusetts newspapers, sued the New York Times Company over its aggregation of news headlines on its Boston.com site. Filed in Massachusetts federal court, the suit alleged the Times had infringed Gatehouse's copyright by allowing its Boston Globe site to copy verbatim headlines and ledes from articles published on GateHouse-owned sites. As in the case of framing (discussed below), the plaintiff argued by linking directly to the articles, the defendant had caused visitors to bypass the site's home page and miss its ads, resulting in lost advertising. The case was settled when GateHouse agreed to erect technical barriers preventing Boston.com's automated "scraping" of its content and the Times agreed to honor those barriers.[37] As with the German cases discussed above, there are often technical solutions aggrieved site owners can implement before turning to costly lawsuits. Here, the plaintiff could easily block Boston.com's computer program from aggregating articles for conversion to links. The settlement affected only GateHouse and had no effect on the Times' content aggregation from other sources. So, the issue of whether aggregation through RSS feeds is copyright infringement remains unresolved.

Blues Destiny Records (BDR) sued German host Rapidshare for allegedly hosting infringing music files. It also sued Google and Microsoft (owner of the Bing search engine) for linking in search engine results to Rapidshare and other download sites allegedly hosting its copyrighted content.[38] On notification from BDR, Google and Microsoft removed or disabled links to pages alleged to allow downloading of copyrighted material, complying with **DMCA** takedown provisions. BDR asked a Florida court to dismiss the case without prejudice (meaning BDR could refile its claim).[39] Google then sought a declaratory judgment from a California court it had not contributed to the infringement of BDR's copyrights and was entitled to the protection of **DMCA** safe harbor clauses.[40] While it appeared Google, having followed the **DMCA** takedown provisions, would be entitled to safe harbor, the more interesting issue was whether the court might rule merely linking to an infringer (especially through search results) constituted contributory infringement. Google voluntarily dismissed the case after Rapidshare reportedly agreed not to file claims for past actions on Google's part.

When dealing with hyperlinks, the safest course for a site owner would be to get *express consent* from the other site or *implied consent*, as through use of reciprocal links. Generally, hyperlinks to other pages should not be problematic unless the pages contain infringing copyrighted material. However, before using graphic links comprised of trademarks from the linked site, express consent should be obtained to avoid a trademark infringement claim. It is also advisable to use a linking disclaimer, such as: "Our Web site does not guarantee, approve, or endorse the information or products available at these Web sites, nor does a link indicate any association with or endorsement by the linked Web site." Conversely, what if one wishes to link *from* a third-party's site? In *LiveUniverse, Inc. v. MySpace, Inc.*, a federal district court addressed whether a social network can prevent users from posting certain links.[41] MySpace had deactivated links from competitor Vidilife.com (owned by LiveUniverse). MySpace claimed it does not prevent anyone from visiting its competitors' sites, but had "no responsibility to build a moving walkway to a competitor's store."[42] The court agreed, dismissing the case.

Web pages are coded in Hyper Text Markup Language (HTML). The code not only tells the browser where to place graphics on the page but where to find them. The graphics will reside either on the site's server or on someone else's. **Inline linking**, or "inlining", is the process of displaying a graphic file on one site that originates at another (and therefore is hosted on a different server). It is also known as **hotlinking** by those who do it and as **bandwidth theft** by those victimized by it. Forum and message board software often allow use of graphic avatars in posts. Frequently, users hotlink to an image (often copyrighted) found on the Web, so each time they post, the forum server downloads the graphic from the original site's server, increasing bandwidth usage and cost for the original site owner. Each instance of someone loading the forum page containing the graphic counts toward the original site's bandwidth usage allocation.

A *Dilbert* comic strip fan inlined a link to the strip on his site. He did not copy the graphic to his server. It remained on the copyright holder's server, but the strip appeared on his page because of an inline link to the image file on the copyright holder's server. The copyright holder's attorney sent the fan a cease and desist e-mail explaining the strip was copyrighted material and insisting he remove the link.[43] The fan replied he had created the site so as to avoid copyright problems in that he "*pulled images from the copyright owner's server*" but did not store any copyrighted images on his server. (One might argue, before even examining the technical details, "pulling images from the copyright owner's server" has the sound of taking something that does not belong to you). The attorney replied, since the **Copyright Act**[44] prohibits unauthorized *display* of a copyrighted work, inlining the comic strip was a violation. This mooted the issue of whether the images had been "copied or reproduced" onto his server, because the Act also protects the copyright holder's exclusive right of display.[45] He pointed out the Act's statutory damages for infringements after notice to an infringer could be up to $100,000 per infringement. Since the fan's site was coded to link to each day's comic strip, that would be $100,000 per day! The inline link was quickly removed. The attorney also explained his client was in the business of selling intellectual property rights — its only product was selling to others the right to copy and display those rights (the comic strip characters). If others were allowed to use them without paying, his client would lose its ability to make money. Were inline linking allowed, the copyright holder would also lose control over the context in which the property is displayed. He cited as an example inlining the *Dilbert* comic strip to the Ku Klux Klan's Web page, which could "erode the value of the property in a way that will be very difficult to measure." Ironically, the exchange ended with the fan granted the right to display a single *Dilbert* comic strip on his site, albeit in reduced form.

The legal status of inline linking has not been completely resolved. Proponents argue in inline linking no copy is made by the alleged infringer; instead, the object inlined is pulled directly from the host server. However, as seen above, this does not address the fact the work is still *displayed*, even if not copied. Opponents argue the copyrighted work effectively appears as part of a Web page belonging to someone other than the copyright holder. Inlining is likelier than hypertext linking to violate copyright as it creates a potential for creating a derivative work and could cause confusion as to the association, if any, between the two sites.

*Deep-linking* refers to a hypertext link that bypasses a site's home page and takes the user directly to an internal page. There are no U.S. laws prohibiting deep-linking but recent U.S. court decisions have called into question the practice's legality. Controversy exists over whether the practice constitutes copyright infringement. Opponents argue the **Copyright Act** protects the creative process, which includes the decision of how much of a work to display and in what order to display it. Control over these factors is important because deep-linking can cause sites to lose income, as their revenues are often tied to the number of viewers who pass through their home page; if visitors bypass home page ads by entering through a deep-link, then the ads are never seen. Also, it may erroneously create an impression the linked Web sites are associated or endorse each other.

Proponents argue the World Wide Web was created to promote fast and easy dissemination of information. Direct links to a site's interior pages enhance usability since, unlike generic links, they specifically relate to users' goals. An e-commerce usability study showed more than a quarter of purchase failures were due to difficulty getting from the home page to the correct product page;[46] preventing deep-linking would eliminate a quarter of potential sales from visitors from search engines. In *Ticketmaster Corp. v. Microsoft Corp.*,[47] Microsoft's "Sidewalk" events Web guide offered users a deep-link to Ticketmaster's ticket purchase page. Although Microsoft was promoting Ticketmaster sales and sending it thousands of customers, Ticketmaster was upset despite the increased traffic because the link took users directly to the event page, bypassing advertisers on its home page. (The case was settled in early 1999, with Microsoft agreeing not to deep-link but instead point visitors to Ticketmaster's home page).

With the rise in popularity of video sharing sites such as YouTube, the practice of deep-linking to podcasts or videos with infringing content on such sites has buttressed the contributory infringement argument.

Sometimes deep-linking may present a case for direct, rather than contributory infringement. In Texas, a federal district court held providing an unauthorized deep link to a live audio Webcast infringed on the holder's copyright.[48] SFX Motor Sports produced "Supercross" motorcycle racing events and streamed live audio of the events on its site, where sponsors had paid for ads. By deep-linking to the Webcasts, the defendant enabled visitors to bypass the SFX site — and its advertisers — causing economic harm to SFX. In this case, since the linked content was on the copyright holder's site, the defendant was not contributing to an existing infringement; he was committing it, making him not a contributory infringer but rather a direct infringer.

## Framing Issues

*Framing* is the process of allowing a user to view the contents of a second Web site (or page) while framed by information from the first site. Framing takes deep-linking one step further. The problem is it could cause confusion about, or be used intentionally to misrepresent, an affiliation or endorsement by the framer of the framed site.[49] The framed site lacks control over the content surrounding it. Many arguments for and against deep-linking also apply to framing, but the combination of display of copyrighted material and juxtaposition of the material with the framer's own material in a manner that could cause confusion or be misleading would likely be a strong factor toward a finding of infringement.

A Web site may expressly prohibit inline linking or framing of its site in its published *Terms of Use agreement*. But as discussed above (and later in Chapter 20), enforceability of a unilateral Terms of Use "agreement" is questionable. In *Ticketmaster v. Tickets. com*,[50] the court held a contract is not created simply by use of a Web site; there must be affirmative assent, such as clicking on a click-wrap agreement. The concept is unilateral agreement on terms of Web site usage cannot be imposed — there must be mutually expressed agreement. There is an inherent Catch-22[51] in conditioning a visitor's use of a site on terms in a page he may not see until he has completed his use or perusal of the site, as visitors often can view an entire site before stumbling onto the Terms of Use page, if at all.

## The Digital Millennium Copyright Act

*"The idea of copyright did not exist in ancient times, when authors frequently copied other authors at length in works of nonfiction. This practice was useful, and is the only way many authors' works have survived even in part." — Richard Stallman*

The **Digital Millennium Copyright Act** (DMCA)[52] is a 1998 amendment to the U.S. **Copyright Act of 1976**. Title I provides up to 10 years imprisonment for circumventing technical measures that protect copyrighted works. It was first applied in the case of an individual who developed software to override manufacturers' copyguard so copyrighted DVDs could be freely copied. Title II, the **Online Copyright Infringement Liability Limitation Act** (OCILLA), establishes protection (*safe harbor*) for Online Service Providers (OSPs) whose customers commit online copyright infringement.[53] An OSP might be an Internet Service Provider (ISP) who provides Internet access (*e.g.*, AOL or a broadband ISP) or a Web site providing a service (*e.g.*, a search engine; a bulletin board system [BBS] operator; a video site like YouTube or auction site like eBay).[54] Under the **DMCA**, an OSP need not monitor its service for infringements; the burden rests on the copyright holder. To qualify for the safe harbor provision, an OSP must:

- Implement, and notify users of, a policy to terminate infringers;[55]
- Designate a "copyright agent" to receive infringement complaints;
- Provide means for notice to the OSP to delete the infringement (or hotlink);
- Been unaware of the infringement (*i.e.*, no "blind eye" to customers' infringements);
- Not gain financial benefit attributable to the infringing material; and
- On notification of claimed infringement, "respond expeditiously to remove, or disable access to, the material."

The safe harbor provision protects from liability for illegal user posted copyrighted content if the OSP removes such content "expeditiously" on notification of the infringement. (No court has yet defined what amount of time qualifies as "expeditiously"). Notice of alleged infringement is referred to as a "takedown notice." In 2010, a federal court reaffirmed the principle in a case where Viacom (owner of MTV, Comedy Central, and Nickelodeon) sent YouTube takedown notices for 100,000 videos and sued Google (YouTube's owner), alleging YouTube had promoted unlicensed use of videos from its TV channels. The court held, by removing almost all 100,000 videos in 24 hours, YouTube fell within the **DMCA's** safe harbor. [56]

The safe harbor is unavailable if an OSP was aware of the infringement and failed to remove it. It is not required to determine if content is copyrighted and posted without permission; in fact, any delay to determine so could subject it to liability, as counter to the statute's "expeditiously" language. Most will immediately remove material without investigating if it is infringing. That happened in 2007, when Viacom sent YouTube a takedown notice, alleging a parody of its Comedy Central TV show "*The Colbert Report*" had infringed its copyright. [57] As seen in Chapter 2, it is permissible to reference a copyrighted work for purpose of parody. If the material in question were a true legal parody, then it would not have been an infringement and should not have been removed.

Under the **DMCA**, the right of redress for wrongfully removed content is not against the OSP who removed it, but rather the takedown notice sender. The alleged infringer may file a *counter notification* with the OSP, who then has 10 business days to provide the filer with a copy of the counter notification and replace the material within 10–to–14 business days following receipt of the counter notification, unless the filer notifies the OSP it has filed a restraining order against the subscriber to prohibit the infringement.

There is a tendency for some copyright holders to engage in "takedown fever". When an independent filmmaker promoted his school board candidacy with a homemade video clip uploaded to YouTube, *Web Junk 2.0* (a Viacom TV show) broadcast his entire clip (without obtaining his permission) in a segment on Web videos (note: broadcasting one's entire work without permission is copyright infringement!). He then posted a clip of the Viacom show spotlighting his own clip on YouTube. Ironically, Viacom claimed he was infringing on its content and sent YouTube a takedown notice. YouTube warned if he repeated such copyright infringement, his YouTube account would be canceled. [58]

But takedown fever may be slowed in the wake of the actions of a Pennsylvania mother. Stephanie Lenz uploaded a 29-second video to YouTube of her 13-month-old boy dancing to a Prince song; many viewers thought it was cute, but not Universal Music Group (UMG), the song's copyright holder. UMG fired off a takedown notice to YouTube, which immediately removed it. But Lenz dusted off her copy of the **DMCA** — specifically, the §512(g) counter-notification provision — and demanded her video be reposted. [59] Six weeks later, Lenz's baby was back dancing on YouTube. But she was not ready to put her copy of the **DMCA** away. She turned to §512(f), a provision imposing liability on anyone who files **DMCA** notices without a good faith belief the material infringes on the copyright holder's rights. [60] UMG moved to dismiss, claiming it did not need to consider fair use when sending a **DMCA** notice. The court disagreed: [61]

> In order for a copyright owner to proceed under the **DMCA** with 'a good-faith
> belief that use of the material in the manner complained of is not authorized
> by the copyright owner, its agent, or the law,' the owner must evaluate whether
> the material makes fair use of the copyright.

Thus, the court held copyright holders must consider fair use before sending **DMCA** takedown notices. UMG argued it would be too difficult to evaluate if a particular use were fair use. A valid point, since fair use is a subjective standard, a finding of which may vary based on the individual judge hearing the case. Nonetheless, the court disagreed, perhaps thinking the requirement to stop and examine each video subjectively might stem the tide of takedown fever and discourage copyright holders from misusing the **DMCA**. Lenz still needed to prove UMG acted in bad faith for her to prevail at trial.

### The Effect of the DMCA — Before and After

Prior to passage of the **DMCA**, the U.S. Supreme Court was faced with one of the most far-reaching copyright decisions of the 20th century. Sony Electronics had begun commercially marketing a videotape recorder that allowed users to copy TV programs onto a videotape cassette. The motion picture industry sued Sony as a contributory infringer, since its videotape recorder enabled others to commit copyright infringement. However, in 1984 in *Sony Corp. of America v. Universal City Studios,*[62] the U.S. Supreme Court found while the Sony Betamax videotape recorder could be used to copy movies and TV shows it also had *"commercially significant non-infringing uses"* (*e.g.,* "time-shifting" — recording TV shows for later viewing and for viewing home movies). Thus, the Supreme Court created the *Betamax Test*: Is the technology capable of commercially significant non-infringing uses?

Two years after the **DMCA**'s passage, in 2000, the motion picture industry again tried to block a new technology that would allow users to copy movies, this time from DVDs. The defendant offered for download on his Web site, software to copy DVDs protected by the Content Scramble System. A federal court ruled this a copyright infringement that violated the **DMCA**.[63] Had the **DMCA** existed 20 years earlier, the home video recording industry might never have gotten off the ground.

### Peer–2–Peer Networking

Peer–2–Peer (P2P) networking enables direct communication or sharing of information between individual users through their computers. In a traditional computer network, traffic travels to the server and back to each node in a highly centralized system where all activity centers around the server. A true P2P network is a decentralized model of computer networking where traffic travels between two users' computers and not through a central server.

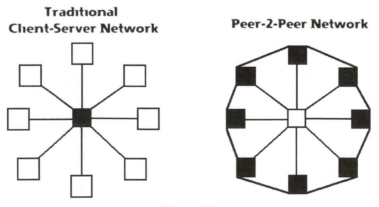

**Traditional Client-Server Network**      **Peer-2-Peer Network**

Figure 4-1

P2P networking became a (if not *the*) major issue in online copyright infringement with the launch of Napster and its progeny in 1999. Devised by college student Shawn Fanning, Napster was a software program that let millions link computers and share songs in a common pool of downloadable files. Users interested in specific music tracks perused the online catalogs and downloaded the music file directly from other members' computers. Napster was a *centralized* file-sharing P2P service. Users connected to the central server and told it what files they had; Napster's central server indexed the available files of all users and cross-referenced this with incoming requests for specific files. When it found a match, the two users connected to transfer the file. Thus, Napster was a *modified P2P network* with its server performing an indexing function, while the actual music files remained on the users' computers.

## Contributory Infringement

Recall from the discussion of linking, a direct infringer is one who makes and shares copies, and a contributory infringer is one who knows or has reason to know of the infringement and induces, causes, or materially contributes to infringing conduct of another. Napster was not a direct infringer because it did not make or distribute the copyrighted works. But in 2001, the Ninth Circuit held Napster was a contributory infringer.[64] The court applied a two-part test: The contributory infringer must (1) "know or have reason to know" of a direct infringement, and (2) materially contribute to the infringing activity. Since Napster was a centralized file-sharing P2P service, it was materially contributing to the infringement.

Likewise, in *In re Aimster*,[65] the court ruled P2P network Aimster was a contributory infringer because it (1) offered no evidence its P2P software had any non-infringing use, and (2) had clear knowledge of infringement. The court focused on the fact Aimster's software tutorial's lone example of file-sharing was the sharing of copyrighted music, which showed knowledge of the infringing activity and a material contribution to it. Aimster failed to use the Betamax Defense; *i.e.*, showing the technology is capable of commercially significant non-infringing uses.

## A Defeat For the Recording Industry

In 2003, a federal district court in California ruled against several movie and recording studios in a copyright infringement suit against P2P firms Grokster and StreamCast (the Morpheus P2P software maker).[66] This was the first victory by P2P developers over the powerful recording industry. The court found the P2P firms not guilty of contributory infringement because of the Betamax Defense, citing non-infringing uses such as the circulation of e-books, promotional videos, and demo games on their networks. Significantly, the court distinguished between centralized and decentralized file-sharing services. The P2P firms escaped liability because they were *decentralized* — they did not actively facilitate and could not stop their users' infringing activity.

The Ninth Circuit upheld the decision, ruling P2P networks legal and makers of decentralized P2P software not responsible for their users' actions.[67] In a major defeat for the film industry, it reaffirmed the Betamax rationale: while sometimes used to download copyrighted material, P2P software is also used in non-infringing ways. (P2P software has been used by computer programmers to exchange code, by scholars to share treatises, and by political organizations to exchange ideas, as in the 2004 election campaign, when political group MoveOn.org distributed political ads and political site OutragedModerates.org disseminated government documents via P2P networks.). The court rebuked the film industry, saying it is unwise to alter copyright law in a way that could stifle innovation just to suit well-established players in a market, as technology often changes the market for the better in the long run. The case was appealed to the U.S. Supreme Court and that decision is discussed below, but first we must examine the concepts of vicarious infringement and inducement, and review the situational context of file-sharing at the time the courts were deciding these issues.

## Vicarious Infringement

*Vicarious infringement* is liability for the infringing acts of another. The theory of vicarious infringement is if one controls the infringer and profits from his infringements, she can be held liable in his place. Vicarious infringement occurs when a party has the right and ability to control an infringer's activity and receives direct financial benefit from the infringement. [68]

A California federal court ruled credit card companies cannot be liable for copyright infringements committed by their customers. Perfect 10, a site offering subscribers photographs of naked women, sued Visa and MasterCard under the theory of vicarious infringement. [69] It claimed by completing transactions at sites selling stolen Perfect 10 images, the companies were vicarious infringers. The court disagreed: [70]

> The ability to process credit cards does not directly assist the allegedly infring-
> ing Web sites in copying plaintiff's works. * * * Defendants do not provide the
> means for distributing those works to others, nor do they provide bandwidth
> or storage space with which to transfer or store the works.

The Ninth Circuit upheld the decision [71] and the U.S. Supreme Court refused Perfect 10's appeal in a related case against another credit card processor. [72] In a similar case, after a media conglomerate bought Napster, record companies sought to hold *investors* liable for vicarious infringement of copyrighted songs, by suing shareholders on the theory by financing Napster while infringement was occurring, they were enabling it. [73]

## Illegal Music File-sharing

In 2003, the Recording Industry Association of America (RIAA) announced plans to sue individual music file-sharers and by 2007 it had sued 30,000 people. [74] While the tactic scared many from file-sharing and resulted in quick settlements, it engendered negative publicity and embarrassment from the nature of some of the named defendants. One was a 12-year-old New York honor student who settled with the multimillion dollar music industry by paying $2,000 (statutory damages for copyright infringements range between $750–to–$150,000 per song). [75] The RIAA was less successful in seeking up to $150,000 per song from a 66-year-old Boston woman it alleged illegally shared 2,000 songs through the Kazaa P2P network: the fact she owned a Macintosh computer (Kazaa ran only on Windows) led the RIAA to drop the suit although it reserved "the right to refile the complaint if and when circumstances warrant." [76] Or, as one blogger sarcastically put it, "just in case she buys a PC, installs Kazaa, acquires a taste for hip-hop, and decides to start sharing files." [77] Other defendants included a woman who did not own a computer, [78] a grandmother accused of downloading music by a band called "Incubus" [79] and a dead woman. The RIAA claimed the deceased 83-year-old had uploaded more than 700 pop, rock, and rap songs under the screen name "smittenedkitten." Her daughter claimed her mother hated computers and would not allow one in her house, and the RIAA later admitted it was unlikely the deceased was actually "smittenedkitten."[80] Cases like these highlight the problems and inaccuracies replete in RIAA's lawsuits.[81]

To date, only two RIAA file-sharing cases have gone to jury trial, as most defendants settle to avoid an expensive, prolonged legal battle.[82] In 2007, the RIAA convinced a jury Jammie Thomas had used Kazaa to download music. She was ordered to pay $9,250 per song for 24 songs, totaling $220,000. But the judge granted her motion for a new trial based on what he determined had been an error in his jury instructions. Instruction No. 14 stated the mere act of downloading constituted infringement, and Instruction No. 15 stated making songs available for distribution on a P2P network constituted infringement, regardless of whether actual distribution was shown. Thomas may have downloaded the songs to a folder on her computer accessible to other Kazaa users, but there was no evidence Kazaa users actually accessed her computer. Is there infringement absent distribution? Is downloading alone, without distribution, merely theft and not infringement? The issue is whether the RIAA has to prove anyone besides their agents downloaded the copyrighted songs, or if it is sufficient the defendant made copyrighted music available on a hard drive for copying via a P2P network. In *Atlantic Recording Corp. v. Howell*, the court denied a motion for summary judgment, ruling merely making an unauthorized copy of a copyrighted work available to the public is not an infringement, absent distribution.[83] The so-called "***making available***" argument had been the basis for most RIAA file-sharing suits.

Not all courts agree with *Howell*'s logic. Most rulings have come on motions before the court, not in final opinions on the cases. A federal judge in Connecticut denied an RIAA's motion for default judgment, based on her belief the absent defendant might have a valid defense, as there was no actual distribution of the files.[84] A federal court in New York denied a defendant's motion to dismiss for failure to state a claim, reasoning the copyright holder's distribution right is analogous to its publication right under the **Copyright Act** and may be infringed by an offer to distribute the copyrighted material, while in the same breath rejecting the "making available" theory.[85] It made a semantic distinction between "offering to distribute copies" — which it held infringement — and "making available." At the same time, a federal court in Massachusetts granted a motion to quash a subpoena to disclose a John Doe defendant's identity in a file-sharing case, reasoning distribution is not analogous to publication, and ruling making copyrighted files available on a hard drive via a P2P network is not infringement.[86] The "making available" theory is a hotly contested issue among the federal courts.

The *Thomas* case judge granted a new trial because he became convinced merely making files available for distribution was not an infringement, as he had instructed the jury. He also voiced concern the fine was disproportionate to the RIAA's actual damages, noting the music allegedly downloaded would fill only three CDs, but the damages awarded totaled 4,000 times the cost of three CDs.[87] In his earlier order granting the new trial, Judge Michael Davis, Chief Justice of the Minnesota District Court, wrote:[88]

> While the Court does not discount Plaintiffs' claim that, cumulatively, illegal downloading has far-reaching effects on their businesses, the damages awarded in this case are wholly disproportionate to the damages suffered by Plaintiffs. Thomas allegedly infringed on the copyrights of 24 songs — the equivalent of approximately three CDs, costing less than $54, and yet the total damages

awarded is $222,000 — more than five hundred times the cost of buying 24 separate CDs and more than four thousand times the cost of three CDs. While the **Copyright Act** was intended to permit statutory damages that are larger than the simple cost of the infringed works in order to make infringing a far less attractive alternative than legitimately purchasing the songs, surely damages that are more than one hundred times the cost of the works would serve as a sufficient deterrent…

The Court would be remiss if it did not take this opportunity to implore Congress to amend the **Copyright Act** to address liability and damages in peer-to-peer network cases such as the one currently before this Court. The Court begins its analysis by recognizing the unique nature of this case. The defendant is an individual, a consumer. She is not a business. She sought no profit from her acts… The Court does not condone Thomas's actions, but it would be a farce to say that a single mother's acts of using Kazaa are the equivalent, for example, to the acts of global financial firms illegally infringing on copyrights in order to profit…

In the 2009 retrial, a new jury found Thomas guilty of copyright infringement and set damages at an astounding $1.92 million, or $80,000 for each of the 24 songs allegedly shared.[89] The huge disparity between the actual harm and the damages awarded prompted some to question whether the award might be unconstitutional. The judge reduced the award to $54,000 ($2,250 per song) calling the jury's verdict "monstrous and shocking."[90]

The disparity between actual and statutory damages in file-sharing cases provided the basis of one defendant's attack against an RIAA suit. The RIAA alleged Joel Tenenbaum illegally downloaded and shared seven songs on a P2P network.[91] Seven songs could fit on a single $10 CD; yet Tenenbaum faced liability of up to $1 million in damages if he lost. His counterclaim alleged the statutory damages increased by the 1999 **Digital Theft Deterrence and Copyright Damages Improvement Act** amendment to the **Copyright Act** were unconstitutional, as was use of what he termed a criminal statute in a civil case.[92] However, the **Copyright Act** is not a criminal statute; it is a federal law containing both civil and criminal provisions. Tenenbaum argued the excessively disproportionate statutory damages were punitive damages that, if assessed, would deprive him, or any noncommercial defendant, of due process:[93]

If 17 U.S.C. 504(c) applies, it violates due process because the damages threatening the defendant are "wholly disproportionate to his alleged offense" and "so severe and oppressive" that they are "obviously unreasonable," {citation omitted}. The injury to plaintiffs by Tenenbaum's alleged conduct, a noncommercial person, is "at most de minimis" and yet he is threatened with "the maximum punitive damages recoverable from a willful commercial infringer" — $1,050,000 in damages.

Tenenbaum admitted in court he downloaded and distributed 30 songs, leaving only the damages issue for the jury to decide. It ordered him to pay $675,000, but a federal district court reduced the damages to $67,500, agreeing the jury award was "unconstitutionally excessive".[94]

Defendants often find themselves "bullied into accepting a carefully chosen sum that is substantially smaller than the legal fees required to fight the accusations."[95] But that may change after _Capitol Records, Inc. v. Foster,_[96] where a defendant turned the tables on the record company that sued her and recovered $70,000 in attorney's fees. The RIAA sued Deborah Foster in 2004, claiming it had evidence an IP address associated with her ISP account engaged in illegal file-sharing. She denied it and the following year the RIAA added her adult daughter (against whom it later won a default judgment) to its complaint. The RIAA claimed Foster — if not a direct infringer — was nonetheless a vicarious infringer, as she provided the account her daughter allegedly used to commit the infringement. However, the RIAA abandoned its claim, as the court explained: [97]

> The plaintiffs assert that had the case continued, they would have proved their secondary liability claims. Specifically, they contend they would have been able to show that the defendant knew or "should have known" that her Internet account was being used by a member of her household to infringe the plaintiffs' copyrights. That may be so. The plaintiffs, however, chose not to pursue the claim. The Court finds disingenuous the plaintiffs' assertion that "had they been given an opportunity, they would have been able to prove vicarious infringement." The plaintiffs were in no way deprived of an opportunity to prove their allegations. They moved, voluntarily, to dismiss their claims after the defendant had already made a substantial investment toward defending against those claims.

Foster's award of attorney's fees, the first file-sharing case in which the RIAA had to pay a defendant's legal fees, set an important precedent for wrongfully-sued defendants and might encourage others.

The RIAA seems to follow a poker strategy toward its litigation: bluff strongly, then fold if the stakes look too high. In 2005, a disabled, single mother living on Social Security received a letter from a law firm accusing her of downloading 1,300 gangsta rap songs under the name "gotenkito@kazaa.com" [98] and claiming she owed hundreds of thousands of dollars for infringement. [99] She denied the accusations and offered to let the RIAA inspect her computer. Using Google, she found "gotenkito@kazaa.com" on a MySpace page of a teen who allegedly admitted illegally downloading music. [100] She gave this information to the RIAA, who responded by suing her. Only when she moved to force them to prove she illegally downloaded music did the RIAA, hours before the motion deadline, drop its case. In another example of the RIAA folding as the stakes increased, a defendant sued for file-sharing argued he was a victim of RIAA inaccuracies like the ones described earlier. [101] He moved for summary judgment, citing mistaken identity based solely on his name, an IP address, and a list of songs flagged by file-sharing software. The RIAA moved for expedited discovery to find enough evidence to prevent dismissal, which would seem an admission the three factors it typically uses to bring cases might not withstand a motion for summary judgment, let alone prove infringement. It dropped the case amid speculation of the potential damage a loss might have to future RIAA lawsuits.

Since most file-sharers remain anonymous behind screen names, the RIAA had resorted to using IP addresses to track down file-sharing ISP accounts, a method rife with inaccuracies, as recounted above. The U.S. Court of Appeals for the District of Columbia held the RIAA could not use the **DMCA** subpoena process to obtain the name of a Verizon Internet Services customer it suspected of file-sharing. [102] As RIAA lawsuits rely on the **DMCA**'s subpoena process, rulings like this make it difficult for the RIAA to identify prospective defendants.

Some courts have provided limited protection to ISP customers. A federal district court in Pennsylvania held before complying with a subpoena demanding file-sharers' names, ISPs must first provide customers with detailed notice of their rights and information on challenging it, including a list of attorneys and jurisdictional requirements. The notice reads, in part: "To maintain a lawsuit against you in the District Court in Philadelphia, the record companies must establish jurisdiction over you in Pennsylvania. If you do not live or work in Pennsylvania, or visit the state regularly, you may be able to challenge the Pennsylvania court's jurisdiction over you." This might affect ISP customers living in neighboring states. While applicable only to the Eastern District of Pennsylvania, the decision represents another step in the evolution of the law in this area, as American courts move to protect privacy and due process rights of those accused of copyright infringement. [103] In contrast, the British High Court ruled subpoenaed ISPs must reveal names and addresses of those accused of file-sharing. [104] After obtaining the information from the ISP, the British Phonographic Industry and the International Federation of the Phonographic Industry would notify file-sharers of the charges and offer to settle.

After suing more than 35,000 live individuals and one corpse, the RIAA, perhaps, recognized its litigation policy had been a massive public relations disaster on the scale of what the Hindenburg did for air travel promotion. [105] In December 2008, it unveiled a new strategy of working with ISPs, who would admonish subscribers engaged in illegal file-sharing, rather than reliance on lawsuits. [106] Only if subscribers ignored the warnings, would the RIAA sue, it stated. Disturbingly, it is unclear from the RIAA's statements how ISPs would determine if subscribers were file-sharing, or if the shared files were copyrighted and shared in violation of the copyright holder's rights, without violating their subscribers' privacy rights by examining the content of the files being transferred. In the first example of this new cooperation between record companies and ISPs, U.K. ISP Virgin Media announced it would temporarily disconnect customers or interrupt service if they were "persistent file-sharers". [107] This raises troubling issues:

(1) Since file-sharing is legal and only sharing of copyrighted works is an infringement, why should all file-sharers be targeted?

(2) How would an ISP know whether the shared content is copyrighted or not unless it is snooping on its subscribers by looking at the content itself?

(3) Virgin said it will determine which customers are "persistent file-sharers" not from its own logs but from information supplied by UMG; does this effectively turn the ISP into a private police force for the record companies?

The RIAA announced July 1, 2012 was the implementation date for the full rollout of its "graduated response" program, where participating ISPs like Comcast, Cablevision, Verizon, Time Warner Cable, and other bandwidth providers would first warn customers and then slow their connection speed or suspend their service. [108]

The RIAA claims music sales continue to decrease annually, as nearly one in five online users download music. [109] Yet, legal fee-based online music services have evolved and prospered, with Apple's iTunes and Roxio's revamped version of Napster finding a large market. [110] Rather than adhering to a policy of alienating and suing its current and potential customer base — a dubious business stratagem at best — it might do better to develop new business models to reflect the Internet Age. One possibility might be an advertising-based model, where free music is accompanied by paid ads. Another might be a licensing system allowing consumers to pay a fee, either to individual downloading sites or to ISPs, that would be paid to the RIAA like a royalty in exchange for unlimited file downloading.

As discussed in the previous chapter, copyright infringement is subject not only to civil but criminal prosecution. The U.S. Justice Department's Computer Crime and Intellectual Property Section has convicted two individuals for conspiracy to commit felony criminal copyright infringement, after targeting illegal distribution of copyrighted movies, software, games, and music on *private* P2P networks (rather than going after *public* P2Ps like Kazaa or e-Donkey).[111] The federal government also won its first jury verdict against a defendant who ran a private P2P network for sharing thousands of copyrighted entertainment files, with the defendant facing up to five years in prison and a $250,000 fine.[112]

States, too, have cracked down on criminal copyright infringement. Arizona prosecuted a University of Arizona student for uploading digital copies of recently released movies and music.[113] Charged with felony possession of unauthorized copies of intellectual property, he was sentenced to three months in jail, deferred with three years probation, community service, and fined $5,400. Unlike many who download copyrighted files for personal use or to trade, this student was selling the files. Yet, sometimes states can go too far. Tennessee passed a law backed by the recording industry to thwart hackers and thieves who sell login passwords to legal movie and music downloading sites that had the effect of criminalizing using a friend's login, even with permission, to hear songs or view movies from sites like Rhapsody or Netflix.[114]

However, both the states and the U.S. federal government are powerless to stop copyright infringement by foreign entities. While treaties such as the Berne Convention or the World Intellectual Property Organization (WIPO) Copyright Treaty may enable the United States to lodge a complaint with a foreign government, enforcement of alleged infringement remains with the foreign government, whose laws or definitions of infringement may differ from the United States, and not all nations are signatories to the treaties. For example, until recently, Moscow prosecutors refused to press criminal charges against AllofMP3.com, a popular Russian site that sold copyrighted American songs for pennies and entire albums for a dollar.[115]

The Inducing of Copyright Infringement Act of 2004 (the INDUCE Act) was a bill that would have eliminated the Betamax Standard used the last two decades to determine liability in infringement cases. Recall the Betamax Standard states if the technology is capable of commercially significant non-infringing uses, then it does not violate the law. Under the bill, it would have made no difference if the technology has substantial non-infringing uses; makers of devices with multiple uses, (*e.g.*, computers and copy machines), could be liable for inducing infringement. Any device that could be used to store or play illegally obtained files could be targeted in a lawsuit — the result of which could ban file-sharing networks, P2P networks, Tivo, and even VCRs. Extremely favorable to the music and motion picture industries, the proposed law was sponsored by conservative Utah Republican Sen. Orrin Hatch, who previously proposed in 2003 copyright holders be allowed to destroy remotely computers used by individuals who download copyrighted songs. Hatch, who reportedly received $158,000 in campaign contributions from TV, movie, and music industries, co-authored the **DMCA**.[116] Titled as the INDUCE Act — "Inducement Devolves into Unlawful Child Exploitation Act" — the bill was labeled as anti-child pornography but was really a back-door effort to eliminate P2P file-sharing. Although not enacted into law, it — or similar legislation — could resurface in a future session of Congress.

The recording industry won the next round in the copyright battle when the U.S. Supreme Court handed down its unanimous decision in *MGM v. Grokster* in 2005.[117] It overturned the Ninth Circuit's ruling decentralized P2P software producers should not be held responsible for their users' actions but did not go so far as to rule the technology, *i.e.*, P2P networks, illegal, as the recording industry had desired. Rather than address that issue, the court focused on how Grokster and StreamCast had marketed and promoted themselves to potential customers and whether they had encouraged illegal use of their technology. Justice David Souter wrote in the majority opinion:[118]

> We hold that one who distributes a device with the object of promoting its use
> to infringe copyright ... is liable for the resulting acts of infringement by third
> parties.

That concept has been referred to as "*inducement*", *i.e.*, actively encouraging users to engage in infringing activities. Thus, the U.S. Supreme Court effectively adopted the rationale of the Induce Act that would have punished companies that induced customers to violate copyright law.[119] The Induce Act had been proposed in response to the Ninth Circuit's earlier decision in favor of Grokster and StreamCast. Souter called Grokster and StreamCast's unlawful intent "unmistakable", stating there was "substantial evidence" Streamcast had "induced" people to use its software to share copyrighted files illegally. (However, the Supreme Court remanded the case for a trial on the issue of whether the firms *did* induce copyright infringement. In 2006, the same federal judge who, in 2003, had ruled file-sharing firms could not be liable for their software users' actions, held the Morpheus software distributor had induced file-sharing of copyrighted music, stating "evidence of StreamCast's unlawful intent is overwhelming.").[120]

The decision applied a standard of vicarious liability on manufacturers for their customers' illegal uses of their technology, *e.g.*, file-sharing companies are to blame for what users do with their software. However, makers of other technology, such as photocopiers, cameras, i-Pods, i-Phones, and even computers could also be liable under the vicarious liability standard enunciated in <u>Grokster</u>. The test is whether they actively and knowingly encourage illegal use, such as copyright infringement. The recording industry had argued the defendants had control over end-users because they could have modified the software to prevent users from sharing copyrighted files. This "control" would impute vicarious liability, they argued. Recall the Ninth Circuit had ruled P2P networks could not be liable for copyright infringement as they could be used for legitimate purposes as well (the Betamax Standard). The U.S. Supreme Court said the Betamax Standard was still valid but the Ninth Circuit had interpreted the <u>Sony</u> decision too broadly. But the court did not elaborate because it was itself split on whether Grokster and StreamCast had violated <u>Sony</u>. So the Supreme Court appears to have upheld the Betamax Standard and the apparent legality of the underlying technology, while subjecting manufacturers to vicarious liability for illegal uses of that technology if they actively promoted and marketed such illegal uses.

On the one hand, the decision may have a chilling effect on producers of digital media products, who now have to guard against lawsuits for contributing to, or inadvertently encouraging, copyright infringement. On the other hand, this case could be interpreted as a road map laid out by the court for other P2P companies to follow to avoid infringement liability. The opinion's rationale was liability will turn on whether the defendant's actions (*i.e.*, marketing and promotion) reveal an intent to contribute (indirectly or vicariously) to copyright infringement. Companies that avoid the appearance of such intent may avoid liability.

While the U.S. Supreme Court has not yet addressed the issue of whether the underlying P2P technology itself is legal, it is possible Congress could declare it illegal. At hearings in 2007, several congressmen claimed P2P networks posed a "national security threat" by virtue of enabling federal government employees unintentionally to share sensitive or classified documents from their computers.[121] One example cited was of a Department of Transportation employee whose daughter installed the P2P file-sharing program Limewire on her home computer, exposing certain government documents to the network. This begs the questions: Why did a government employee have sensitive or classified files on a home computer? Why would a government employee allow a child access to a computer containing sensitive or classified files? The solution to any perceived threat to national security is not to prohibit a technology that enables communication among its users (an action that would probably be in direct violation of First Amendment free speech rights) but rather to regulate and control those in the government who handle sensitive or classified files. The government should require written authorization for installation of P2P programs on its computers and properly train its employees on file security. Laws already exist against leaking classified documents. Any perceived "national security threat" emanates not from the technology itself, but rather from the way individuals use that technology.

## The First Sale Doctrine

The ability to download music raises interesting questions. Can a legally down-loaded song be resold? You can buy a music CD at the music store and legally sell it to your friend or on eBay. What if you legally purchased a downloaded song and burned it to a single CD and sold it to the same friend or on eBay? Is there a difference? What if you burned the song to multiple CDs and sold them all? Would it make a difference? Would it be infringement if you burned the song to multiple CDs for personal use?

In 1908, the U.S. Supreme Court established the *"First Sale" doctrine*, holding a buyer of a copyrighted work can sell or give it away without the copyright owner's permission. [122] In that case, Macy's Department Store sold a book for 89¢ even though the publisher had inserted a notice in the book that any retail sale under a dollar would be considered copyright infringement. Although the 1908 court decision (and its subsequent codification into the **1909 Copyright Act**) applied to copies that had been sold, the **Copyright Act of 1976** codified the doctrine to apply to any "owner" of a lawfully made copy, eliminating the requirement of a sale. [123]

In 2007, UMG sued a man, whose livelihood consisted of buying collectible record albums and CDs at used record stores and selling them on eBay, for copyright infringement. [124] UMG claimed the First Sale doctrine did not apply because the CDs at issue were promotional CDs given by record companies to radio stations and reviewers. (Interestingly, UMG did not appear to have sued any used record stores for selling promotional, or other, records and CDs). The federal district court in California granted the defendant's motion for summary judgment, ruling the First Sale doctrine protected his sale of the promotional CDs. [125] It dismissed UMG's contention its "For Promotional Use Only" label constituted a license rather than a transfer of ownership. Under the First Sale doctrine, once the copyright holder sells or gives away a copy of a phonograph record, CD, DVD, or book, the recipient may resell it without further permission.

The issue turns on ownership, *i.e*, whether the copyrighted material is sold and subsequently owned by the purchaser, or merely licensed with the copyright holder retaining ownership. Software publishers have contended the First Sale doctrine does not apply to computer software because it is not sold but licensed under terms of an End User License Agreement (EULA). Many software publishers have complained about online resales of their products on eBay, but until 2008 none had claimed copyright infringement. [126] Then, software maker Autodesk sent eBay **DMCA** takedown notices alleging Timothy Vernor, an eBay seller, was violating its copyright by offering its CDs for sale on the auction site. After eBay suspended Vernor's account, he sued, seeking declaratory and injunctive relief against Autodesk. [127] Vernor sought a declaration his sales were legal under the First Sale doctrine and an injunction barring Autodesk from interfering with future sales. Autodesk countered copies of its software were licensed, not sold. The district court looked at two conflicting Ninth Circuit cases. In _United States v. Wise_, which involved the sales and licenses of film prints, the court held the determinative issue was whether the transaction gave rise to a right of perpetual possession in the transferee. [128] If the transferee were entitled to keep the copy, it was a sale; whereas if the copyright holder could demand its return, it was merely a license. In _MAI Sys. Corp. v. Peak Computer_, the court held (without citing any precedent and contrary to _Wise_) by including a license with its software, MAI's customers who purchased it were licensees, not owners. [129] Relying on _Wise_, the older case, the district court held the transfer of copies of Autodesk's software were sales because the realities of the transfers implied a right of perpetual possession, and the First Sale doctrine would apply. [130] The court was bound by **stare decisis** to follow its earliest panel decision absent an intervening Supreme Court precedent on point or a contrary **en banc** decision. On appeal, a Ninth Circuit panel ruled 3–to–0 a user agreement could ban software resales, clearly delineating the distinction between a sale and a license. [131] It rejected the lower court's interpretation of _Wise_ as holding a transferee's right to indefinite possession alone established a first sale, instead looking additionally to whether the copyright owner had (1) specified the user was granted a license, (2) significantly restricted the user's ability to transfer the subject matter, and (3) imposed notable use restrictions. A sale has no restrictions, whereas a license may restrict transfer, for example, within a stated geographic area or without written consent. Because software is generally sold subject to licensing agreements, most individuals do not own their software. The same analysis could be applied to e-books, especially if a license agreement were included within the e-book. The _Vernor_ decision means copyright owners may prohibit resale of their works by inserting clauses in shrink-wrap and click-wrap licenses. [132] It does not vitiate the First Sale doctrine; it merely means the doctrine does not apply to a one who possesses a copy of the copyrighted work without owning it, such as a licensee.

The distinction between sales and licenses of music has far reaching ramifications. Under most recording contracts, artists are entitled to 50 percent of revenue from licensed uses of their music (_e.g._, movie soundtracks, TV shows, and ad jingles) but typically less than 20 percent royalties from sales. The Ninth Circuit held iTunes downloads are encumbered by enough restrictions they cannot be considered sales, ruling songs downloaded from Apple's iTunes store are not actually purchased, but instead "licensed" by the downloader. [133]

At the start of this discussion, we asked, "Can a legally downloaded song be resold?" That question may soon be answered. The issue of application of the First Sale doctrine rose again in 2011 when a firm dubbing itself "The World's First Online Marketplace for Used Digital Music" offered a service for individuals to buy and sell legally purchased music files. [134] ReDigi claimed its software analyzed the metadata of each uploaded song to ensure it had been legally acquired and not ripped from a CD. Once determined legitimate, the file was deleted from the uploader's computer. According to the company, its software could tell if a user tries to replace a file on his computer after having uploaded it for resale. The RIAA argued ReDigi could not avail itself of the First Sale doctrine as a defense because its software must first duplicate the user's copy, watermark it, store the copy on its server, and delete the original from the user's hard drive or mobile device — meaning it is the copy offered for sale, in violation of the **Copyright Act**. It contended the Act does not allow a copy of the original to be resold, even if the original is deleted as part of the process. As of this writing, the RIAA had sent

ReDigi a cease and desist letter. ReDigi announced plans to offer a similar market for e-books. Should this progress into a lawsuit, it will be interesting to see how a court addresses the issue, especially in light of the *Vernor* case.

## Chapter 3 Notes

[1] *Atlantic Recording Corp. v. Howell*, 554 F. Supp. 2d 976 (D. Ariz. 2008), denying a motion for summary judgment: "The court agrees with the great weight of authority that section 106(3) is not violated unless the defendant has actually distributed an unauthorized copy of the work to a member of the public. Merely making an unauthorized copy of a copyrighted work available to the public does not violate a copyright holder's exclusive right of distribution." *But cf. Motown Record Co. v. DePietro*, 2007 U.S. Dist. LEXIS 11626, 2007 WL 576284 (E.D. Pa. 2007) which reached an opposite result, relying on a 2002 letter from Marybeth Peters, Register of Copyrights, stating: "[M]aking [a work] available for other users of [a] peer to peer network to download … constitutes an infringement of the exclusive distribution right, as well as the production right." Also, one might argue merely displaying copyrighted files in a P2P shared folder violates the Copyright Act's prohibition against "display" of copyrighted material.

[2] *Religious Tech. Ctr. v. Netcom On-Line Commc'ns Servs., Inc.*, 907 F. Supp. 1361 (N.D. Cal. 1995).

[3] The Copyright Act of 1976, as amended, 17 U.S.C. § 101, *et seq.*

[4] *Playboy Enters., Inc. v. Sanfilippo*, 46 U.S.P.Q.2D (BNA) 1350 (S.D. Cal. 1998). (Included in the Cases Section on the Issues in Internet Law site, www.IssuesinInternetLaw.com).

[5] "Gay Couple Sues Conservative Group over Use of Their Photo in Internet Ad," Associated Press wire service report, March 11, 2005.

[6] According to the complaint filed in the case.

[7] See Chapter 12 for a discussion of the privacy tort of false light.

[8] *Holtzbrinck Publ'g Holdings, L.P. v. Vyne Commc'ns, Inc.*, Case No. 97 Civ. 1082, 2000 U.S. Dist. LEXIS 5444 (S.D.N.Y. 2000).

[9] Note, there was no question as to the oral contract's validity; the issue was not whether there was a valid contract, but whether the client or the designer held the site copyright, since there was no dispositive written memorandum of their agreement. The court noted the Statute of Frauds, which bars certain oral contracts, was inapplicable because the license is implied from the parties' conduct (this was not the first site the designer had made for the client).

[10] As discussed in Chapter 14, *infra*, there are circumstances where the site owner (or ISP) may be shielded from liability for third-party posts by § 230 of the Communications Decency Act (CDA).

[11] Defamation online is discussed at length in Chapter 14, *infra*.

[12] *Software Dev. & Inv. of Nev. d/b/a Traffic Power.com v. Aaron Wall, d/b/a SEO Book.com*, Case No. 05-A-508400-C (8th Judicial Dist., Clark Cnty., Nev. 2005); *Software Dev. & Inv. of Nev. d/b/a Traffic-Power. com v. Wall d/b/a Seobook.com*, Case No. 2:05-cv-01109-RLH-LRL (D. Nev. motion to dismiss granted Feb. 13, 2006).

[13] E-mail dated November 29, 2001, posted on Chris Raettig's site, together with his reply, *was available at* http://chris.raettig.org/email/jnl00036.html (accessed Jul. 1, 2009) but no longer available.

[14] In 1832, the Cherokee Indians lived on land guaranteed them by a treaty with the U.S. government. After gold was discovered, Georgia attempted to seize the land. The Cherokees sued and in *Worcester v. Georgia*, 31 U.S. 515 (1832) the U.S. Supreme Court ruled in their favor. Georgia refused to obey the court. President Andrew Jackson said, "[Chief Justice] John Marshall has made his decision; now let him enforce it." Jackson sent federal troops to evict the Cherokees, who were forced to travel the "Trail of Tears" to Oklahoma, with thousands dying enroute.

[15] Chris Raettig's site, fn. 13, *supra*.

[16] *Reisinger v. Perez*, Case No. 2:2008-cv-00708 (E.D. Wis. filed Aug. 20, 2008).

[17] *Ibid.*

[18] *Ibid.*

[19] *Ticketmaster Corp. v. Tickets.com, Inc.*, 54 U.S.P.Q.2D (BNA) 1344 (C.D. Cal. 2000) ("[H]yperlinking does not itself involve a [direct] violation of the Copyright Act (whatever it may do for other claims) since no copying is involved."); *Online Policy Grp. v. Diebold, Inc.*, 337 F. Supp. 2d 1195, 1202 n.12 (N.D. Cal. 2004) ("Hyperlinking per se does not constitute direct copyright infringement because there is no copying.").

[20] *Perfect 10, Inc. v. Google, Inc.*, 416 F. Supp. 2d 828 (C.D. Cal. 2006), aff'd in part, rev'd in part, remanded, *sub nom. Perfect 10, Inc. v. Amazon.com, Inc.*, 487 F.3d 701 (9th Cir. 2007).

[21] *Ibid.*

[22] Case Nos. 308 O 42/06 and 308 O 248/07 (Hamburg Regional Court, Germany 2008).

[23] Case No. 2 U 319/07 (Thuringian Higher Regional Court, Germany, 2008).

[24] Chris Jenkins, "ISP Liable in 'MP3s4free' Case," Australian IT, July 15, 2005.

[25] Simon Hayes, "Man Charged in Copyright Case," Australian IT, June 7, 2005.

[26] *Cooper v. Universal Music Australia Pty, Ltd.*, [2006] FCAFC 187 (2006).

[27] In June 2007, the High Court of Australia refused to hear an appeal, upholding the decisions of the trial judge and Full Federal Court the defendant had authorized copyright infringement.

[28] *See* further discussion on the CDA and publisher liability in Chapter 14.

[29] *Flavia Works, Inc. v. Gunter*, Case No. 10 C 6517 (N.D. Ill. Sept. 1, 2011), on appeal to Seventh Circuit.

[30] *Was available at* www.channelsurfing.net (accessed Mar. 10, 2011) but no longer available.

[31] David Edwards, "New York Man Faces Five Years in Jail for 'Linking' to Online Videos," *available at* http://www.rawstory.com/rs/2011/03/10/new-york-man-faces-five-years-in-jail-for-linking-to-online-videos/ (accessed March 23, 2012).

[32] Gina Keating, "MPAA Accuses Pullmylink.com of Aiding Movie Piracy," Reuters wire service report, April 17, 2008. *See also* Jacqui Cheng, "Oops! MPAA Lawsuit Gives Free Publicity to Torrent Site," ArsTechnica.com, April 20, 2008.

[33] See *Barclays Capital, Inc. v. Theflyonthewall.com* ("Fly I "), 700 F. Supp. 2d 310 (S.D.N.Y. 2010).

[34] *Int'l News Serv. v. Associated Press*, 248 U.S. 215 (1918).

[35] *Erie R.R. Co. v. Tompkins*, 304 U.S. 64 (1938).

[36] 17 U.S.C. §§ 106, 301.

[37] "NYT, Gatehouse Release Settlement Details," The Boston Globe, January 26, 2009.

[38] *Blues Destiny Records, LLC v. Google, Inc.*, Case No. 3:09-cv-00538-WS-EMT (N.D. Fla. filed Dec. 7, 2009; voluntarily dismissed without prejudice, Mar. 2010).

[39] Dan Nystedt, "Google Sues for Decision on Links to Copyrighted Songs," IDG News Service, May 6, 2010.

[40] *Google, Inc. v. Blues Destiny Records, LLC*, Case No. 3:2010-cv-01824 (N.D. Cal. filed Apr. 28, 2010; voluntarily dismissed without prejudice, Jun. 15, 2010).

[41] *LiveUniverse, Inc. v. MySpace, Inc.*, Case No. 2:06-cv-06994-AHM-RZx, 2007 U.S. Dist. LEXIS 43739 (C.D. Cal. 2007).

[42] Kellie Schmitt, "Judge Lets MySpace Block Links to Its Competition," The Recorder, July 25, 2007.

[43] E-mails on Dan Wallach's site, *available at* www.cs.rice.edu/~dwallach/dilbert/um_letters.html (accessed Mar. 23, 2012).

[44] The Copyright Act of 1976, as amended, 17 U.S.C. § 101, *et seq.*

[45] *See* Chapter 2, *supra.*

[46] Jakob Nielsen's Alertbox, "Deep Linking is Good," March 3, 2002, *available at* www.useit.com/alertbox/20020303.html (accessed Mar. 23, 2012).

[47] *Ticketmaster Corp. v. Microsoft Corp.*, Civil Action No. 97-3055 DDP (C.D. Cal. 1997); case settled in January 1999; Microsoft agreed not to deep-link into Ticketmaster's site.

[48] *Live Nation Motor Sports, Inc. v. Davis*, 81 U.S.P.Q.2d 1267 (N.D. Tex. 2006).

[49] In at least one case, a court has found the degree of confusion created sufficient to warrant a finding of trademark infringement under the Lanham Act where the defendant framed trademarked elements of the plaintiff's Web site around its own page to sell CDs. *See Hard Rock Cafe Int'l, Inc. v. Morton*, No. 97 Civ. 9483, 1999 WL. 717995 (S.D.N.Y. 1999) (Unpublished):

> In this case, defendants do not themselves offer goods for sale on one of their Web pages. Instead, the CDs are sold by Tunes on a Web page created by Tunes but "framed" by the Hard Rock Hotel Web page. Through the framing mechanism, the Hard Rock Hotel logo appears around the border of a computer screen otherwise filled by the Tunes Web page. * * * Through framing, the Hard Rock Hotel Mark and the Tunes site are combined together into a single visual presentation and the Hard Rock Hotel Mark is used to promote the

sale of CDs by Tunes. Because the Tunes material appears as a window within the original lining page, it is not clear to the computer user that she or he has left the Hard Rock Hotel Web site. The domain name appearing at the top of the computer screen, which indicates the location of the user in the World Wide Web, continues to indicate the domain name of Hard Rock Hotel, not that of Tunes. * * * In light of this seamless presentation of the Tunes Web page within the Hard Rock Hotel Web site, the only possible conclusion is that the Hard Rock Hotel Mark is used or exploited to advertise and sell CDs.

[50] *Ticketmaster*, 54 U.S.P.Q.2d (BNA) 1344.

[51] The phrase "Catch-22", derived from the 1961 novel of the same name by Joseph Heller about the madness of war, has evolved into common use to mean a cyclical conundrum.

[52] The Digital Millennium Copyright Act, 17 U.S.C. § 512.

[53] There are actually four safe harbor provisions under the OCILLA: (1) transitory digital network communications (17 U.S.C. § 512(a)); (2) system caching (17 U.S.C. § 512(b)); (3) information residing on systems or networks at the direction of users (17 U.S.C. § 512(c)); and (4) information location tools (17 U.S.C. § 512(d)). For purposes of this chapter, our discussion centers on the third safe harbor.

[54] The issue of whether P2P networks also qualify for safe harbor protection under § 512 of the Digital Millennium Copyright Act was left unsettled by the court in *A & M Records*, fn. 13 *infra*, when it chose not to extend the safe harbor provisions to the Napster software program and service.

[55] When AOL changed its e-mail address for notification of copyright infringements from "copyright@aol.com" to "aolcopyright@aol.com" but failed to configure the old e-mail address to either forward or bounce messages — allowing "notices of potential copyright infringement to fall into a vacuum and to go unheeded" — it suggested AOL did not have an effective notification procedure and therefore might not qualify for the safe harbor. *Ellison v. Robertson*, 357 F.3d 1072 (9th Cir. 2004).

[56] *Viacom Int'l, Inc. v. YouTube, Inc. & Google, Inc.*, Case No. 1:2007-cv-02103 (S.D.N.Y. 2010), granting Google's motion for summary judgment. In April 2012, the Second Circuit vacated the ruling, stating "a reasonable jury could conclude that YouTube had knowledge or awareness" of infringement "at least with respect to a handful of specific clips" and remanded the case for the lower court to decide whether YouTube had turned a blind eye to its users uploading copyrighted videos. The decision raised concern whether adherence to the DMCA's takedown notice requirements provides a safe harbor, although the statute has always denied safe harbor for those turning a blind eye. *See* Brian Stelter, "Appeals Court Revives Viacom Suit Against YouTube," The New York Times, April 5, 2012.

[57] It was one of more than 100,000 takedown notices sent by Viacom to YouTube. *See* Nate Anderson, "DMCA Takedown Backlash: EFF Sues Viacom over Colbert Parody Clip," Arstechnica.com, March 22, 2007. In the Viacom case, the Electronic Frontier Foundation and Stanford Law School's Center for Internet and Society sued Viacom; the suit was dropped a month later after Viacom agreed to establish a Web site and e-mail "hotline", and promised to review any complaint within one business day and reinstate content erroneously taken down.

[58] Christopher Knight, "Viacom Hits Me with Copyright Infringement for Posting on YouTube a Video That Viacom Made by Infringing on My Own Copyright!" The Knight Shift blog, August 29, 2007, *available at* http://theknightshift.blogspot.com/2007/08/viacom-hits-me-with-copyright.html (accessed Mar. 23, 2012).

[59] The Digital Millennium Copyright Act, 17 U.S.C. § 512(g).

[60] The Digital Millennium Copyright Act, 17 U.S.C. § 512(f).

[61] *Lenz v. Universal Music Corp.*, 572 F. Supp. 2d 1150 (N.D. Cal. 2008) (copyright owner must consider any fair use doctrine defenses prior to issuing DMCA notice). The Northern District of California held a plaintiff suing over a wrongful DMCA takedown notice can only recover damages proximately caused by the notice. *Lenz v. Universal Music Corp.*, Case No. 5:07-cv-03783-JF (N.D. Cal. Feb. 25, 2010). This ruling effectively limits a plaintiff's recovery to attorney's fees and might discourage other plaintiffs from suing under § 512(f).

[62] *Sony Corp. of Am. v. Universal City Studios, Inc.*, 464 U.S. 417 (1984).

[63] *Universal City Studios, Inc. v. Reimerdes*, 111 F. Supp. 2d 294 (S.D.N.Y. 2000). (Included in the Cases Section on the Issues in Internet Law site, www.IssuesinInternetLaw.com).

[64] *A & M Records, Inc. v. Napster, Inc.*, 239 F.3d 1004 (9th Cir. 2001). (Included in the Cases Section on the Issues in Internet Law site, (www.IssuesinInternetLaw.com).

[65] *In re Aimster*, 334 F.3d 643 (7th Cir. 2003).

[66] *MGM Studios, Inc. v. Grokster, Ltd.*, 259 F. Supp. 2d 1029 (C.D. Cal. 2003).

[67] *MGM Studios, Inc. v. Grokster, Ltd.*, 380 F.3d 1154 (9th Cir. 2004).

[68] *Fonovisa, Inc. v. Cherry Auction, Inc.*, 76 F.3d 259, 262 (9th Cir. 1996).

[69] *Perfect 10, Inc. v. Visa Int'l Servs. Ass'n*, 71 U.S.P.Q.2D (BNA) 1914 (N.D. Cal. 2004).

[70] *Ibid.*

[71] *Perfect 10, Inc. v. Visa Int'l Servs. Ass'n*, 494 F.3d 788 (9th Cir. 2007).

[72] *Perfect 10, Inc. v. CCBill, LLC*, 488 F.3d 1102 (9th Cir. 2007), cert. denied, 522 U.S. 1062 (2007).

[73] *UMG Recordings, Inc. v. Bertelsmann AG*, 222 F.R.D. 408 (N.D. Cal. 2004), although the court sidestepped that issue in deciding the case.

[74] Jeff Leeds, "Labels Win Suit against Song Sharer," The New York Times, October 5, 2007.

[75] Jefferson Graham, "RIAA Lawsuits Bring Consternation, Chaos," USA Today, September 10, 2003.

[76] Chris Gaither, "Recording Industry Withdraws Suit," The Boston Globe, September 24, 2003.

[77] Eric Bangeman, "Et Cetera: Bullet for Bullet," ArsTechnica.com, September 24, 2003.

[78] Dan Tuohy, "Music Industry Ends Legal Battle with NH Woman," Union Leader, June 20, 2009.

[79] Graham, fn. 75, *supra.*

[80] Nate Mook, "RIAA Sues Deceased Grandmother," BetaNews, February 4, 2005, *available at* www.betanews.com/article/RIAA_Sues_Deceased_Grandmother/1107532260 (accessed Mar. 23, 2012).

[81] Bruce Gain, "RIAA Takes Shotgun to Traders," Wired News, October 4, 2005.

[82] *Capitol Records, Inc. v. Thomas* (formerly *Virgin Records Am., Inc. v. Thomas*), 579 F. Supp. 2d 1210 (D. Minn. 2008). In May 2008, U.S. District Judge Michael J. Davis announced he had come across an earlier Eighth Circuit decision that said infringement requires "an actual dissemination" in contradiction to his jury instructions making sound recordings available without permission was an infringement "regardless of whether actual distribution has been shown", raising the prospect of a new trial.

[83] *Atlantic Recording Corp. v. Howell*, 554 F. Supp. 2d 976 (D. Ariz. 2008).

[84] *Atlantic Recording Corp. v. Brennan*, 534 F. Supp. 2d 278 (D. Conn. 2008). When a defendant fails to appear in court to defend against the plaintiff's complaint, the plaintiff may ask the clerk of the court to issue a default, and then file a motion with the judge for entry of a *default judgment*. Such motions are usually granted, though the defendant may subsequently file a motion pursuant to Fed.R.Civ.P. 55(c) and 60(b) to set aside the entry of default and of the default judgment. In exercising its discretion to set aside a default judgment, a court must consider three factors: (1) whether the plaintiff will be prejudiced; (2) whether the defendant has a meritorious defense; and (3) whether the default was the result of the defendant's culpable conduct. *Gross v. Stereo Component Sys., Inc.*, 700 F.2d 120 *at* 122 (3d Cir. 1983); *Feliciano v. Reliant Tooling Co.*, 691 F.2d 653, *at* 656 (3d Cir. 1982); *Farnese v. Bagnasco*, 687 F.2d 761, *at* 764 (3d Cir. 1982). A meritous defense is one that, if established at trial, would constitute a complete defense. Here, there was no default judgment to be set aside, as the judge denied the motion for default judgment, appearing to have acted *sua sponte* in raising the issue of a possible meritous defense, *i.e.*, there needs to be an actual distribution to violate the Copyright Act.

[85] *Elektra Entm't Grp., Inc. v. Barker*, 551 F. Supp. 2d 234 (S.D.N.Y. 2008).

[86] *London-Sire Records, Inc. v. Does*, 542 F. Supp. 2d 153 (D. Mass. 2008).

[87] *Thomas*, 579 F. Supp. 2d 1210, fn. 82 *supra.*

[88] Order of Judge Michael Davis, Chief Justice of the Minnesota District Court, granting new trial in *Capitol Records, Inc. v. Thomas*, 579 F. Supp. 2d 1210 (D. Minn. 2008).

[89] Greg Sandoval, "Court Orders Jammie Thomas to Pay RIAA $1.92 Million," CNET News.com, June 18, 2009.

[90] Patrick Condon, "Judge Cuts $2 Million Penalty in Song-sharing Case," Associated Press wire service report, January 22, 2010. The defendant rejected a $25,000 settlement offer with a condition to ask the judge to "vacate" his decision, *i.e.*, remove it from the record. The RIAA said it would challenge the ruling reducing her damages while the defendant said she would challenge the damage award as unconstitutional. *See* Greg Sandoval, "Jammie Thomas Rejects RIAA's $25,000 Settlement Offer," CNET News.com, January 27, 2010.

[91] *Sony BMG Music Entm't v. Tenenbaum*, Civ. Act. No. 07-cv-11446-NG (D. Mass. Jul. 9, 2010).

[92] The Digital Theft Deterrence and Copyright Damages Improvement Act of 1999 (Pub. L. No. 106-160).

[93] *Tenenbaum*, fn. 91, *supra*, Memorandum in Support of Defendant Joel Tenenbaum's Motion to Dismiss (filed Mar. 9, 2009).

[94] Jonathan Saltzman, "Judge Slashes Downloading Penalty," The Boston Globe, July 10, 2010. *See also* Denise Lavoie, "Jury Awards $675K in Boston Music Downloading Case," Associated Press wire service report, August 3, 2009. However, the First Circuit reinstated the $675,000 jury verdict in 2011. *See* Phillip Caulfield, "Court Orders Student Joel Tenenbaum to Pay $675G for Illegally Downloading Music—Again," New York Daily News, September 20, 2011.

[95] Eliot Van Buskirk, "Scoop: Label Must Pay P2P Defendant's Legal Fees," Wired Listening Post, February 7, 2007.

[96] *Capitol Records, Inc. v. Foster*, 86 U.S.P.Q.2D (BNA) 1203 (W. D. Okla. 2007).

[97] *Ibid.*

[98] Florin Tibu, "Atlantic Records Sues 7-Year-Old Girl," Softpedia, March 27, 2007, *available at* http://news.softpedia.com/news/Atlantic-Records-Sues-7-yo-Girl-50342.shtml (accessed Mar. 23, 2012).

[99] Complaint, *Andersen v. Atlantic Recording Corp.*, Case No. 3:2007-cv-00934, 2008 U.S. Dist. LEXIS 13207 (D. Ore. filed Jun. 22, 2007), *was available at* www.ilrweb.com/viewILRPDF.asp?filename=andersen_riaa_070816AmendedComplaint (accessed Jul. 23, 2010) but no longer available.

[100] Ashbel S. Green, "Woman: I'm No Music Pirate," The Oregonian, June 27, 2007.

[101] *Elektra Entm't Grp., Inc. v. Wilke*, Case No. 06-cv-2717 (N.D. Ill. dismissed, Oct. 13, 2006).

[102] *Recording Indus. Ass'n of Am., Inc. v. Verizon Internet Servs., Inc.*, 351 F.3d 1229 (D.C. Cir. 2003).

[103] Katie Dean, "File Sharers Win More Protection," Wired News, October 28, 2004.

[104] Matthew Caron, "Good to Be an American," Copyfutures blog, October 16, 2004, *available at* http://lsolum.typepad.com/copyfutures/2004/10/good_to_be_an_a.html (accessed Mar. 23, 2012).

[105] To be fair, the RIAA is not the only organization going to extreme lengths in an effort to adjust to the new realities of the digital world. The American Society of Composers, Authors and Publishers (ASCAP) argued digital downloads were also public performances for which copyright owners must be compensated, an argument rejected by a federal district court and the Second Circuit. The U.S. Supreme Court denied the appeal. *See Am. Soc'y of Composers, Authors & Publishers (ASCAP) v. United States*, 627 F.3d 64 (2d Cir. 2010), cert. denied, (No. 10-1337) 565 U.S. __ (Oct. 3, 2011).

[106] Alex Dobuzinskis, "Music Industry Ends Mass Piracy Lawsuits," Reuters wire service report, December 19, 2008.

[107] David Meyer, "Virgin-Universal Deal May Hit 'Persistent' File Sharers," CNET News.com, June 15, 2009.

[108] Greg Sandoval, "RIAA Chief: ISPs to Start Policing Copyright by July 1," CNET News.com, March 14, 2012.

[109] Sarah McBride and Ethan Smith, "Music Industry to Abandon Mass Suits," The Wall Street Journal, December 19, 2008.

[110] Charles Duhig, "Digital Music Sales Soar; Industry Hopes Downloads Eventually Offset CDs' Decline," The Los Angeles Times, October 4, 2005.

[111] *See* Joris Evers, IDG News Service, "Feds Bust File-Sharing Sites," PCWorld.com, August 25, 2004 *and* Grant Gross, IDG News Service, "P-to-P Operators Plead Guilty," PCWorld.com, January 19, 2005.

[112] Alexandre Carst, "Online Piracy May Not Be the Way to Go," enews20.com, May 25, 2008.

[113] Associated Press wire service report, March 8, 2005.

[114] Shelia Burke and Lucas L. Johnson II, "Tenn. Passes Web Entertainment Theft Bill," Associated Press wire service report, June 1, 2011.

[115] John Borland, "Legal Reprieve for Russian MP3 Site?" CNET News.com, March 7, 2005. In 2005, the Moscow prosecutor ruled Russian copyright laws do not cover online distribution of creative works, but reversed its position in 2006 and began a criminal probe against AllofMP3.com. In October 2006, Visa stopped processing transactions for AllofMP3.com and the Bush administration warned allowing the site to continue could jeopardize Russia's entry into the World Trade Organization (WTO). *See* Greg Sandoval, "Visa Halts Its Service for allofmp3.com," CNET News.com, October 18, 2006. In June 2007, the site was shut down, but its owner set up an identical site, mp3Sparks.com. A Russian court acquitted the owner of copyright infringement after he argued he had paid royalties to the Russian Multimedia and Internet Society (which many Western firms refuse to recognize or accept payments from). The site said it would resume business, but as part of Russia's entry into the WTO, the United States and Russia agreed in principle "on the objective of shutting down Web sites that permit illegal distribution of music and other copyright works", and listed AllofMP3.com as an example. *See* "Russia Throws out Net Piracy Case," BBC News, August 15, 2007.

[116] "INDUCE Act Will Ban P2P Networks and Apple iPod, Critics Say," Legal News Watch, June 22, 2004; *see also* Joanna Glasner, "File-Trading Bill Stokes Fury," Wired News, June 24, 2004.

[117] *MGM Studios, Inc. v. Grokster, Ltd.*, 545 U.S. 913 (2005).

[118] *Ibid*. Several weeks after the *Grokster* decision, Bush White House spokesman Scott McClellan, stated, "The president believes that the manufacturer of a legal product should not be held liable for the criminal misuse of that product by others. We look at it from a standpoint of stopping lawsuit abuse." Ironically, he was referring to proposed legislation to protect gun manufacturers and dealers from lawsuits over gun crimes, not to P2P software.

[119] Lawrence Lessig has written an interesting op-ed article contending the U.S. Supreme Court in *Grokster* usurped Congress' copyright-making policy, noting historically it had deferred to Congress to define the scope of copyright, as in *Sony*, 464 U.S. 417. He argues the *Grokster* court expanded the Copyright Act "to cover a form of liability it had never before recognized in the context of copyright — the wrong of providing technology that induces copyright infringement." Lawrence Lessig, "Make Way for Copyright Chaos," The New York Times, March 18, 2007.

[120] Associated Press wire service report, September 27, 2006. Kazaa and Grokster settled out-of-court.

[121] Anne Broache, "Congress: P2P Networks Harm National Security," CNET News.com, July 24, 2007.

[122] *Bobbs-Merrill Co. v. Straus*, 210 U.S. 339 (1908).

[123] The Copyright Act of 1976, 17 U.S.C. § 109.

[124] *Universal Recordings, Inc. v. Augusto*, 558 F. Supp. 2d 1055 (C.D. Cal. 2008).

[125] *Ibid*.

[126] *See* Elaine Hughes, "Online Resales Worry Retailers," USA Today, August 1, 2007.

[127] *Vernor v. Autodesk, Inc.*, Complaint No. 2:07-cv-01189-JLR (W.D. Wash. filed Aug. 1, 2007).

[128] *United States v. Wise*, 550 F.2d 1180 (9th Cir. 1977).

[129] *MAI Sys. Corp. v. Peak Computer, Inc.*, 991 F.2d 511 (9th Cir. 1993).

[130] *Vernor v. Autodesk, Inc.*, 555 F. Supp. 2d 1164 (W.D. Wash. 2008).

[131] *Vernor v. Autodesk, Inc.*, 621 F.3d 1102 (9th Cir. 2010).

[132] *See* the discussion of shrink-wrap and click-wrap agreements in Chapter 20, *infra*.

[133] *F.B.T. Prods. v. Aftermath Records*, 621 F.3d 958 (9th Cir. 2010).

[134] Ben Sisario, "Site to Resell Music Files Has Critics," The New York Times, November 14, 2011.

# CHAPTER

# 4

# TRADEMARK, PATENTS, AND TRADE SECRETS

This chapter discusses trademarks, patents, and trade secrets, focusing on the Lanham Act, international trademarks, the Madrid System, the Anti-Dilution Act, the concepts of direct and contributory infringement, dilution, blurring, tarnishment, parody, the Paris Convention of 1883, the Patent Cooperation Treaty of 1970, and the Convention on the Grant of European Patents of 1973.

*"He goes by the brand, yet imagines he goes by the flavor." — Mark Twain*

## The Lanham Act

TRADEMARKS ARE THE SECOND of the four forms of intellectual property we will examine in this section. U.S. trademark law falls under the purview of the **Lanham Act** of 1945. The Act expanded the concept of infringement, permitted registration of service marks, provided incontestability status for marks in continuous use for five years, and decreed federal trademark registration would constitute "***constructive notice*** of the registrant's claim of ownership thereof." *Trademarks* identify goods, while *service marks* identify services. It defines a trademark as:[1]

> Any word, name, symbol, or device, or any combination thereof used by a person ... to identify and distinguish his or her goods, including a unique product, from those manufactured and sold by others and to indicate the source of the goods, even if the source is unknown.

## Filing A Trademark

In America, *trademarks arise from use*, so registration is unnecessary; however, as with copyright, there are compelling reasons to register. Registration with the U.S. Patent and Trademark Office (USPTO) establishes a public record of claim (*i.e.*, "***constructive notice***"), evidence of ownership, and the right to invoke federal jurisdiction in a dispute.[2] U.S. registration can also serve as the basis for securing registration in foreign countries. Once filed with U.S. Customs, registration can help a trademark owner stop imports of infringing foreign goods from entering the country.

## Trademark Search

The trademark registration process begins with a search by the applicant (or patent attorney) to determine if anyone has applied for the same trademark. Searches can be conducted online using TESS (the Trademark Electronic Search System) at http://tess2.uspto.gov. The first place to look is in the USPTO Trademark Database, which contains only federal trademarks. It is not current, not all-inclusive, limited to text marks, and does not include alternate spellings, state trademarks, common law trademarks, foreign trademarks, or domain names. The next resource to search, especially if contemplating use of a trademark as part of a domain name, is WHO IS,[3] a database maintained by domain name registrars, and AllWhoIs,[4] a mega search engine that searches WHO IS databases at multiple domain name registries. Finally, trademarks can be searched internationally through the International Archives from the Madrid Protocol countries.

## Trademark Registration

To register a U.S. trademark, an application must contain:
- The applicant's name
- Name and address for correspondence
- A clear drawing of the trademark
- A list of the goods or services
- Five specimens showing the trademark as actually used
- The required filing fee for at least one class of goods or services

Applications may be filed online using TEAS (Trademark Electronic Application System) at www.uspto.gov/teas or mailed to Commissioner for Trademarks, Box-New App-Fee, 2900 Crystal Drive, Arlington, VA 22202-3513. Registration is not immediate; it may take more than a year from filing, if approved. The USPTO compares the trademark and the goods and services described in the application against those already registered. If the proposed trademark passes the examination, it is published in the *Official Gazette of the Patent and Trademark Office*, affording an opportunity for objections by anyone who feels potentially harmed by registration of the trademark.

The USPTO may issue an "*office action*", *i.e.*, a nonfinal rejection, because of the existence of "identical or similar marks" or if it believes a mark is "generic or descriptive." Once obtained, protection can last indefinitely, but must be renewed (with an affidavit of use) every 10 years and the trademark must be maintained or will be deemed lost. Failure to use the trademark in commerce (or file a § 8 Declaration of Continued Use between the fifth and sixth years after registration) results in **abandonment.** An abandoned trademark falls into the public domain but may be re-registered by a party that re-establishes exclusive and active use and is associated with the original trademark owner. A trademark will also fall into public domain if it becomes a part of the common usage (*i.e., genericized*), so it is important trademark owners educate businesses and consumers on appropriate trademark use by visibly and actively promoting use of their trademarks as adjectives and not as nouns or verbs. For example, Google would insist on the phrase "conduct a search using Google" instead of "Google the term".

*Genericization* or *trademark erosion* can lead to loss of trademark protection. These phrases began as trademarks for specific products but were gradually genericized through common usage, falling into public domain: Allen Wrench, Aspirin, Cellophane, Celluloid, Corn Flakes,

Dry Ice, Escalator, Gramophone, Granola, Heroin, Jungle Gym, Kerosine, Lanolin, Linoleum, Mimeograph, Nylon, Photostat, Plasterboard, Pogo Stick, Raisin Bran, Shredded Wheat, Spandex, Teleprompter, Thermos, Trampoline, Webster's Dictionary, Yo-Yo, Zeppelin, and Zipper.

Trademark owners have mounted aggressive educational campaigns to raise public awareness and preserve their marks, sometimes adding the word "brand" after the trademark. The following trademarked names are still valid but often misused to refer to a generic product: *Adrenaline* (epinephrine), *Astroturf* (artificial grass), *Baggies* (food bags), *BAND-AID* (self-adhesive bandage), *Bic* (ball point pen), *Breathalyzer* (breath alcohol analyzer), *Bubble Wrap* (air-filled plastic packing material), *Chap Stick* (lip balm), *Crock-Pot* (slow cooker), *Dictaphone* (dictation recorder), *Dixie cups* (disposable bathroom cups), *Dumpster* (large trash can), *Fiberglass* (glass fiber), *Frisbee* (flying disc), *Formica* (laminated plastic surface), *Go-Kart* (mini racing cars), *Google* (Web search engine), *Hoover* (vacuum cleaner), *Hula Hoop* (dancing ring), *Jacuzzi* (whirlpool bath), *Jeep* (army vehicle), *Jell-O* (gelatin dessert), *Kitty Litter* (cat litter), *Kleenex* (tissue), *Krazy Glue* (glue), *Laundromat* (self-service laundry), *Magic Marker* (felt-tip marker), *Muzak* (background music), *Pablum* (baby cereal), *Photoshop* (a software program), *Ping-Pong* (table tennis), *Playbill* (theater program), *Plexiglas* (clear plastic sheets), *Post-It* (self-adhering notepaper), *Polaroid* (instant photograph), *Popsicle* (frozen confection), *Q-tip* (cotton swab), *Realtor* (real estate agent), *Rolodex* (rotary card file), *Rollerblade* (inline skates), *Saran wrap* (transparent plastic wrap), *Scotch tape* (transparent adhesive tape), *Sharpie* (marker), *Sheetrock* (gypsum panels), *Spackle* (wall filling compound), *SPAM* (packaged meat product), *Speedo* (tight-fitting swimsuit), *Stetson* (cowboy hat), *Styrofoam* (polystyrene filler), *Tabasco* (hot spicy sauce), *Taser* (electric shock weapon), *Teflon* (nonstick surface), *TiVo* (digital video recorder), *Tupperware* (food storage ware), *Valium* (tranquilizer), *Vaseline* (petroleum jelly), *Velcro* (re-usable fastening tape), *Windex* (glass cleaner), and *Xerox* (photocopy).

## International Trademarks

The Internet has opened new avenues to international commerce. A lone individual can create a Web site and begin marketing and distributing goods and services around the world. Today, it is more important than ever to protect a trademark worldwide, especially in any country where revenue is derived. Nike learned this the hard way during the 1990 Olympics in Barcelona, Spain, when it had to make its sponsored athletes cover the Nike name because a Spanish firm had been granted a Spanish trademark for sportswear under the Nike trademark. There are three ways to protect a trademark in the European Community:

- Apply for separate national trademark registrations in each European nation
- Community Trade Mark registration (CTM)
- International registration (Madrid Protocol)

### European Registration

In 1992, 12 European nations formed the European Common Market. Shortly thereafter, the European Community Trademark Registry was created, allowing a single trademark application to be valid in all member nations, rather than having to file separately in each country. A trademark owner files a single application with the Office for Harmonization in the Internal Market (OHIM), based in Alicante, Spain, in one of the designated language

(English, French, German, Italian, or Spanish), granting the trademark owner, on registration, rights in all EU countries. Any individual or company can file a Community Trade Mark (CTM) application; the CTM is available to European and non-European companies, lasts 10 years, and is renewable every 10 years. However, to remain valid, the mark must be used within at least one EU nation within five years of registration, lest it be open to cancellation on the ground of non-use. Registration protection only applies to member nations; applicants must still file separately in nonmember countries. The registration process averages 18–to–24 months. Registration of a trademark in the registry prevents others from using it within the E.C. and enables the holder to bring a cause of action concerning its use within the member states through the E.C. trademark law and courts. Infringement suits are brought in member states in special courts designated to hear CTM cases; these courts apply EU law instead of local law. The E.C. Trademark Registry includes all 27 member states. Trademarks registered with the E.C. Trademark Registry are permitted to use the ® symbol in all member states.

## The Madrid System

*The Madrid System* is an international clearinghouse for trademark registration in multiple jurisdictions, administered by the International Bureau of the World Intellectual Property Organization (WIPO) in Geneva, Switzerland. Two treaties drafted nearly a century apart — the Madrid Agreement Concerning the International Registration of Marks (1891) and the Madrid Protocol (1989) — comprise the Madrid System. The Madrid Agreement and the Madrid Protocol are collateral but independent of each other. The Madrid System enables trademark protection in multiple countries by filing one application directly with one's own national or regional trademark office. It is a convenient and cost-effective way of filing and maintaining trademark rights in foreign countries. After a trademark owner has applied for or registered a trademark in his home country (and paid the domestic filing fee), he need only file a single additional application in one language (English, French, or Spanish) and pay a fee in the local currency, rather than file multiple applications with each member country. The Madrid System provides a process of international registration, not a single international trademark — applicants get a bundle of national rights, not a single international right. Two major differences between the Madrid System and the CTM are:
- Madrid applicants must have a business in, or be domiciled in or a national of, one of the member states.
- Madrid registrants must be able to show use of the mark in *each* of the designated countries on expiration of the initial 5-year dependency period or the mark will be open to revocation in any jurisdiction where not in use.

*The Madrid Protocol,* an international trademark registration treaty adopted in Madrid, Spain, on June 27, 1989, took effect in America in November 2003.[5] It applies only to treaty signatories; Canada and Mexico are not signatories but the United States is (however, the United States is not a signatory to the Madrid Agreement). The treaty provides a single application is valid for 10 years and renewable for further 10-year terms. The Madrid Protocol signatories are: Albania, Antigua and Barbuda, Armenia, Australia, Austria, Belarus, Benelux (Belgium, Netherlands, and Luxembourg), Bhutan, Bulgaria, China, Croatia, Cuba, Cyprus, the Czech Republic, Denmark, Estonia, Finland, France, Georgia, Germany, Greece, Hungary, Iceland, Iran, Ireland, Italy, Japan, Kenya, North Korea, South Korea, Kyrgyzstan, Latvia, Lesotho,

Liechtenstein, Lithuania, Macedonia, Moldova, Monaco, Mongolia, Morocco, Mozambique, Namibia, Norway, Poland, Portugal, Romania, the Russian Federation, Serbia and Montenegro, Sierra Leone, Singapore, the Slovak Republic, Slovenia, Spain, Swaziland, Sweden, Switzerland, Turkey, Turkmenistan, Ukraine, the United Kingdom, the United States, and Zambia.

## The ® Symbol

The ® registered trademark symbol identifies a trademark as registered with the USPTO. A valid registration notice consists of the ® symbol, and/or "Registered in the U.S. Patent and Trademark Office" or the abbreviation "Reg. U.S. Pat. and Tm. Off." Failure to use the notice does not affect the trademark's validity. However, if used, the trademark owner need not prove the defendant had actual notice of registration to recover damages and profits, since registration serves as *constructive notice*. The ® symbol should not be used if the trademark is not registered with the USPTO. Instead, the ™ symbol should be used to designate trademarks not protected by federal registration (*i.e.*, state or common law marks). In the case of a service mark, the $^{SM}$ symbol is used.

## Trademark Infringement and Dilution

Trademarks are protected by law from both infringement and dilution. In determining *infringement*, a court looks at whether the similarity between trademarks is "likely to cause confusion" in the minds of consumers,[6] because the law's stated objective is consumer protection.

Congress passed the **Anti-Dilution Act of 1996** as an amendment to the **Lanham Act**. Previously, trademark owners had to rely on state anti-dilution laws as remedies, as no federal anti-dilution laws existed. The Act is sometimes more useful to the trademark owner than an infringement claim because it does not require a showing of a "likelihood of confusion." Instead, the test is a "commercial use in commerce" of a "famous mark" if the use "causes dilution of the distinctive quality of the famous mark." The Act only applies to "famous" trademarks. While Congress did not define "famous" within the Act, it did list eight factors for determining if a trademark is "famous."[7] Courts make this determination on a case-by-case basis. The test for dilution is: Would the strong association the public has between the famous trademark and the plaintiff be diluted?

Under the **Lanham Act**, to prove trademark dilution, the plaintiff must show:[8]
- Ownership of a trademark qualifying as a "distinctive and famous" trademark as measured by the totality of the eight factors listed in the **Lanham Act** § 43(c)(1), and
- The defendant is making commercial use,
- In interstate commerce,
- Of a trademark or trade name, and
- The defendant's use began after the plaintiff's trademark became famous, and
- The defendant's use causes dilution by lessening the capacity of the plaintiff's trademark to identify and distinguish goods or services.

To be considered as "distinctive and famous", the Lanham Act provides the following factors may be weighed:
- The degree of inherent or acquired distinctiveness of the trademark,
- The duration and extent of use of the trademark in connection with the goods or services with which the trademark is used,

- The duration and extent of advertising and publicity of the trademark,
- The geographical extent of the trading area in which the trademark is used,
- The channels of trade for the goods or services with which the trademark is used,
- The degree of recognition of the mark in the trading areas and channels of trade used by the mark's owner and the person against whom the injunction is sought,
- The nature and extent of use of the same or similar trademarks by third-parties, and
- Whether the trademark was registered under the Act of March 3, 1881, or the Act of February 20, 1905, or on the principal register.

The court weighs several factors to determine if a mark has been infringed, including its strength, the similarity of parties' service, evidence of actual confusion, the degree of care likely to be exercised by consumer; and, in domain name disputes, the similarity of the trademark to the domain name and the domain name registrant's intent in choosing the name. Under the Act, dilution can occur even when a famous mark is used by another on noncompeting goods, *e.g.*, "Maytag cameras" or "Smith & Wesson washing machines." This would be an example of "*blurring*", where consumers see the trademark used by another to identify a noncompeting good, thereby diluting the unique and distinctive significance of the mark.

A second type of dilution is *tarnishment*, when the other party's use of the mark tarnishes, degrades, or brings ridicule to the distinctive quality of the mark. For example, when a site with the domain name AdultsRUs.com was launched, Toys "R" Us sued under the **Anti-Dilution Act** with little difficulty persuading the court of the dilution of its famous trademark by tarnishment.[9] By contrast, Hormel, maker of Spam (the meat product, not the junk e-mail) tried unsuccessfully to convince the Second Circuit Court of Appeals a forthcoming Muppets movie character had tarnished its trademark.[10] The film "*Muppet Treasure Island*" introduced a new Muppet character, Spa'am, the high priest of a tribe of wild boars that worships Miss Piggy as its queen. Hormel feared tarnishment of its trademark, as the court explained:[11]

> Hormel also expresses concern that even comic association with an unclean "grotesque" boar will call into question the purity and high quality of its meat product. But the district court found no evidence that Spa'am was unhygienic. At worst, he might be described as "untidy." * * * Moreover, by now Hormel should be inured to any such ridicule. Although SPAM is in fact made from pork shoulder and ham meat, and the name itself supposedly is a portmanteau word for spiced ham, countless jokes have played off the public's unfounded suspicion that SPAM is a product of less than savory ingredients. For example, in one episode of the television cartoon "*Duckman*", Duckman is shown discovering "the secret ingredient to SPAM" as he looks on at "Murray's Incontinent Camel Farm." In a recent newspaper column it was noted that "In one little can, Spam contains the five major food groups: Snouts. Ears. Feet. Tails. Brains." * * * In view of the more or less humorous takeoffs such as these, one might think Hormel would welcome the association with a genuine source of pork. Nevertheless, on July 25, 1995, Hormel filed this suit alleging both trademark infringement and dilution.

The court noted while a trademark may be tarnished when its likeness is placed in the context of sexual activity, obscenity, or illegal activity, here there was no negative association through its use:[12]

> The *sine qua non* of tarnishment is a finding that plaintiff's mark will suffer negative associations through defendant's use. Hormel claims that linking its

luncheon meat with a wild boar will adversely color consumers' impressions of SPAM. However, the district court found that Spa'am, a likeable, positive character, will not generate any negative associations. Moreover, contrary to Hormel's contentions, the district court also found no evidence that Spa'am is unhygienic or that his character places Hormel's mark in an unsavory context. Indeed, many of Henson's own plans involve placing the Spa'am likeness on food products. In addition, the court also noted that a simple humorous reference to the fact that SPAM is made from pork is unlikely to tarnish Hormel's mark. Absent any showing that Henson's use will create negative associations with the SPAM mark, there was little likelihood of dilution.

The **Anti-Dilution Act** has been used to force cybersquatters to relinquish domain names to trademark owners. The theory is dilution occurs when Web visitors give up searching for the trademark holder's goods in frustration after countless encounters with the cybersquatters' sites instead of the true mark holder's site. However, the Act is only applicable where a "famous" trademark is at issue. Holders of nonfamous trademarks must seek recourse through the **Anti-cybersquatting Consumer Protection Act.** Domain name disputes and cybersquatting are discussed at length in the next chapter.

### Trademark Infringement or Parody?

It is permissible to reference a copyrighted work or trademark for the purpose of *parody*. Courts have accepted the dictionary definition of parody as "literary or artistic work that imitates the characteristic style of an author or work for comic effect or ridicule."[13] A legal parody involves the conveyance of two *simultaneous* but contradictory messages — it must target the work but be apparent it is not the original.

PETA, People for the Ethical Treatment of Animals, filed a trademark infringement suit against a defendant who had registered the domain name PETA.org and set up a site at that URL titled "People Eating Tasty Animals."[14] The site linked to meat, fur, hunting, leather, and animal research, all of course, opposed by PETA. The court held it was not a legal parody because the domain name alone did not convey the second message (*i.e.*, parody). The defendant argued the second message was in the content of the site itself, but court rejected that view, stating it was not conveyed *simultaneously*.

Search engine firm Google accused Booble.com, which marketed itself as an adult search engine, of trademark infringement, alleging Booble copied its distinctive look with similar logo design and page layout. Google sent Booble a standard cease and desist letter, evoking a detailed and well-written response from Bobble's attorneys raising the defense the Booble site was a parody of Google. The letter stated, in part, "Our client's Web site is in fact a successful parody, which simultaneously brings to mind the original, while also conveying that it is not the original."[15] The letter attempted to show Booble had not met the necessary element of confusion in the minds of consumers for a finding of trademark infringement, by stating the domain names were entirely different; Booble only searched the Web for adult content; and the Booble mark differed from Google's in that it "features a woman's chest…uses the phrase, 'The Adult Search Engine'…posts a warning that the Web site contains explicit content…and…disclaims any association with Google.com."[16] The letter ended by tweaking the Google lawyers, noting the sole case referenced in their cease and desist letter was a copyright, not trademark case, and "although some analytic similarities exist between copyright and trademark parody cases, Google neither claims copyright infringement in its letter, nor is any relevant portion of its Web site copyrightable."[17] Ouch! The site owners reached an agreement and Booble modified its page design.[18] Ironically, on revamping the design and abandoning any attempt at parody, Booble's owner reported the site started as a joke had begun generating significant traffic as a serious adult search engine.[19]

## Direct and Contributory Infringement

The concepts of direct and contributory infringement, discussed as applied to copyright in the previous chapters, also apply to trademarks. Upscale jeweler Tiffany & Co. sued eBay for trademark infringement, claiming nearly three-quarters of items labeled as "Tiffany & Co." on the auction site were fakes.[20] Tiffany alleged while eBay did not directly sell counterfeits — and thus was not a *direct infringer* — it was a *contributory infringer* by facilitating and promoting the sale of thousands of pieces of counterfeit Tiffany & Co. jewelry. The issue of whether eBay was a contributory infringer turned on whether the auctioneer or the trademark owner should bear the burden of policing goods sold on auction sites for counterfeits. eBay argued it had anti-fraud mechanisms in place to reduce the sale of counterfeit goods — such as its "feedback" system where buyers rate sellers publicly, the fact it allowed firms like Tiffany to shut down sellers they claimed violated their intellectual property rights,[21] and its willingness to remove any auction listings in "obvious violation" of intellectual property laws.

A federal district court in New York ruled companies like Tiffany are responsible for policing their trademarks online, not auction sites like eBay.[22] Tiffany had also argued eBay was a contributory infringer because the amount of fake goods sold on eBay was so substantial it profited significantly from the trade and promoted it. (Unlike the business model of a newspaper publishing classified ads, eBay collects part of the sale price, effectively sharing in each transaction's profits.) However, while a contributory infringement claim might arise by allowing counterfeits to be sold on its site,[23] to be deemed a contributory infringer eBay must have "knowingly facilitated" the counterfeiting. The court held "companies like eBay cannot be held liable for trademark infringement based solely on their generalized knowledge that trademark infringement might be occurring on their Web sites."[24]

Tiffany also claimed direct infringement, because eBay bought advertising links on Yahoo! and Google. A search for "Tiffany" or "Tiffany's" with these search engines results in eBay's links appearing atop the page. Tiffany argued these links led to sellers who offered counterfeit goods on eBay's site and by advertising them eBay was infringing on its trademark. But the court held this was "*nominative use*", *i.e.*, there is no infringement liability merely for using a trademarked phrase to describe the actual trademarked product one is speaking or writing about.[23] It wrote:[25]

> Indeed, were eBay precluded from using the term "Tiffany" to describe Tiffany jewelry, eBay would be forced into absurd circumlocutions. To identify Tiffany jewelry without using the term Tiffany — perhaps by describing it as "silver jewelry from a prestigious New York company where Audrey Hepburn once liked to breakfast," or "jewelry bearing the same name as a 1980s pop star" — would be both impractical and ineffectual in identifying the type of silver jewelry available on eBay.

In the first U.S. appellate decision to address contributory trademark infringement in e-commerce, the Second Circuit upheld the lower court in eBay's favor.[26]

## Patents

*"Everything that can be invented has been invented."*
— (attributed) Charles H. Duell, Commissioner, U.S. patent office, 1899

Patents are the third of the four forms of intellectual property we will examine in this section. Internet companies have availed themselves of patents to procure monopoly rights in certain inventions. The concept of being awarded a monopoly for a new invention is not an idea borne of the Internet Age, but rather dates back to the Founding Fathers, who included that right within the U.S. Constitution. [27] As trademarks fall under the purview of the **Lanham Act**, patents are governed by the **Patent Act**. [28] A patent is a *government-issued grant* conferring on an inventor the right to *exclude* others from making, using, offering for sale, or selling the invention for a period of 20 years, [29] measured from the filing date [30] of the patent application. "Any new and useful process, machine, manufacture, or composition of matter, or any new and useful improvement thereof" may be patented. [31] The term "process" is defined as "process, art or method" and includes a new use of a known process, machine, manufacture, composition of matter, or material.

Abstract ideas, laws of nature, and physical phenomena are not patentable. Patents are similar to copyrights in that one cannot copyright or patent an idea. Copyright law prevents the copying of the expression of ideas, but does not protect the ideas themselves; likewise, patent law protects inventions, but not ideas. In both cases, there must be some identifiable embodiment of the idea before there can be intellectual property protection. Patents are, in one respect, the opposite of trade secrets, another form of intellectual property discussed later in this chapter: The inventor must make a full disclosure of the invention (*i.e.,* not hold back any secrets) to obtain a patent; in exchange for patent rights, the patent (*i.e.,* how the invention works) becomes public information. Thus, a patent is the opposite of a trade secret, (*e.g.,* the formula for Coca-Cola), which by its very nature is secret, whereas a patent is open and public.

Patent rights are *exclusionary*; the holder does not necessarily have the right to use the invention, but has the right to *exclude* others from making, using, selling, or offering to sell the invention. He can *stop* others from using it; or *license* his patent in exchange for royalties. A patent's true value comes from licensing revenue or preventing a competitor's use. A license can be one of three types:

- *Exclusive license* to a single licensee
- *Nonexclusive license* to multiple licensees, or
- *License within a limited field* of use

There are three types of patents. The most common is the *utility patent*, which applies to inventions that have a use and protects functionality. *Design patents* protect an object's appearance. *Plant patents* protect the appearance and color of plants. Most patents expire after 20 years (except design patents, which expire after 14 years). U.S. patents are enforceable only in the United States and its territories; separate patent systems exist in most countries.

To obtain a patent, the invention must be:

- **Novel**. Not known or used by others, or patented, or described in a printed publication, or in public use, or on sale more than one year prior to the patent application. [32] Telling friends and family about the invention may toll the one-year grace period. An inventor must file for patent protection within that grace period or lose all rights to patent protection. While the United States has a one-year grace period, most countries do not, so it is advisable for inventors to file before any public disclosure. Otherwise, such public disclosure might preclude the filing of international applications.

- **Non-obvious.** Not obvious to a person having ordinary skill in the pertinent art as it existed when the invention was made. The patent examiner will compare the invention with *prior art* (*i.e.,* everything publicly known before the invention as shown in earlier patents and other published material) and judge whether differences between the prior art and the invention would have been "obvious to a person having ordinary skill in the pertinent art as it existed when the invention was made". A change in size or substitution of one material for another would probably be considered obvious and hence not patentable.

- **Useful.** It must have current, significant, and beneficial use as a process, machine, manufacture, composition of matter, or improvements to one of these. ("Composition of matter" relates to chemical compositions and may include mixtures of ingredients as well as new chemical compounds). If a machine, it must also perform its intended purpose to be patentable, otherwise it is not considered useful. For example, a perpetual motion machine would not be patentable because it would not work (the concept violates the laws of physics).

### Filing the Application

Before filing a patent application, a search for *prior art* (*i.e.,* what already exists anywhere in the world) must be made. Prior art is important because the most common ground to invalidate a patent is the invention is not novel or is obvious in light of prior art. Once the prior art search has been completed, a patent application must be filed with the U.S. Patent and Trademark Office (USPTO). [33] Filing *is* necessary — *patents do not arise from use,* as do copyrights and trademarks. As this is a specialized area of law, one should always use a *patent attorney* with knowledge and experience in patent law who has passed a special exam and is registered to practice before the USPTO. Nonlawyers who act as "*patent agents*" and can prepare patent applications but not practice law (*e.g.,* litigate patent matters or write contracts related to patents) are also registered with the USPTO. Once filed, the application is reviewed by a patent examiner, which may take nine–to–18 months. The review is similar to the trademark application process, as the examiner issues an "office action" citing his findings, often resulting in a denial. The patent attorney then responds either by arguing the points raised or amending the application. Obtaining a patent can be *expensive* and *time-consuming.* There are both filing and issue fees (if the patent is granted) and in some cases periodic maintenance fees. The USPTO only processes patent applications; it does not enforce patents or deal with infringement claims; those are handled by the federal courts.

### The Patent Application

The patent application has several parts:
- The *petition* — the formal request for a patent
- The *abstract* — a short technical summary of the invention including a statement of its use
- The *specification* — a detailed description of the invention's features, including how to make and use it
- The *claims* section — a brief statement in precise legal language of what is being patented, written primarily to show the examiner how the invention differs from prior art (the claims section is the most important part of the application)

- The *drawings* section — a graphical representation of the invention (or in the case of software or chemicals, a flowchart)

As stated earlier, the grace period is strict. Failure to file a timely patent application can result in effective donation of patent rights to the public domain. The patent application *must* be filed within *one year* of occurrence of any one of the following:

- Description of the invention in a publication
- Public use of the invention
- Patenting of the invention by another
- An offer to sell the invention

## Who Is the Patent Holder?

Prior to 2011, the United States had a "first to invent" patent system as opposed to most other countries that have a "first to file" system. Under the "first to invent" system, if two inventors attempted to patent the same invention, an "interference proceeding" would be held and the one who could prove he conceived the invention first would get the patent. In 2011, President Barack Obama signed into law the **America Invents Act**, which established a "first to file" standard for patent approval (eliminating the interference proceeding) and created a post-grant review system to weed out bad patents.[34] The law, the most significant change to the U.S. patent system since 1952, affects applications filed on or after March 16, 2013.

If two inventors worked jointly on an invention, then they should file as joint inventors. But one who is merely a financial backer may not file as a joint inventor. If the inventor is deceased, then his or her legal representatives may apply. Likewise, if the inventor has been declared legally insane, then her guardian may file the application. U.S. patents are filed in the *inventor's* name, unlike the rest of the world, which allows companies to file for patent ownership. Companies would be wise to require a written contract obligating the employee or independent contractor to transfer patent ownership to the company. In fact, most firms routinely include a patent rights assignment clause in employment contracts. (Under the new Act, assignees may apply for the patent). There are three scenarios where an employer might have patent rights:

- **Employment Agreement.** Prior to creating the invention, the inventor signed an employment contract requiring assignment of all patent rights to the employer. A few states restrict the scope of these assignment clauses.[35]
- **Hired to Invent.** The employee was specifically hired for the purpose of inventing the item or solving a stated problem.
- **Shop Right.** A common law right granting a nonexclusive and nontransferable license to the employer allowing use of an invention created during the course of employment by its employee.[36] The nonexclusive nature of this right means the employee could simultaneously license the invention to his employer's competitor. The shop right normally arises only where the employee has used the employer's resources (*e.g.*, time, money, supplies, labor) to create the invention.

## Patents and the Internet

On the Internet, patents protect software (also protected by copyright) and business methodology. One example of a *software patent* is the GIF patent, the source of a patent infringement case that could have affected many of the images on the Web. In 1987,

CompuServe, a major ISP at the time, created GIF, an efficient image file format, using the LZW file compression scheme. Seven years later, Unisys announced it had filed for, and received in 1985, a patent on the LZW algorithm. (This was a "submarine" patent, *i.e.*, submerged unseen until it surfaces to fire at its target). While Unisys had owned the patent since 1985, it had only pursued hardware, not software licenses. Unisys sued CompuServe for infringement. The case was settled and the developers had to pay Unisys royalties. Meanwhile, other developers, concerned they could no longer use GIFs on the Internet without paying royalties, created PNG as a royalty-free graphic format alternative to GIF.[37]

Some examples of ***business methodology patents*** granted to Internet firms are the Priceline. com "Reverse Auction" and the Amazon.com "One-Click." Priceline's Reverse Auction business methodology is a service where consumers name the price they are willing to pay and Priceline finds sellers to meet the buyers' stated needs and price. Amazon's One-Click patent, issued in 1998, is described in its application as "a business methodology for placing an order whereby in response to a single act (a mouse click) an item may be ordered from an e-commerce Web site." Through the use of cookies, additional information needed to complete the order will have been previously obtained and stored on Amazon's database, so the order can be processed with only one mouse click. Many critics object to the notion of patenting business methodologies, on the basis methodologies like Priceline's and Amazon's are neither novel nor non-obvious. Amazon demonstrated its use of its exclusionary rights as a patent holder in December 1999, before the busy online holiday shopping season, by obtaining an injunction against competitor Barnes and Noble (www.bn.com), forcing it to replace its own one-click ordering system with a more complicated one.[38]

There have now been many *Web-related patent filings*, including one-click online shopping, online shopping carts, the hyperlink, video streaming, internationalizing domain names, pop-up windows, targeted banner ads, paying with a credit card online, framed browsing, and affiliate linking. Some patents involve innovative uses of existing technology. Digital Envoy was granted a patent for its IP Intelligence technology, which pinpoints a Web user's physical location down to the city level, based on the user's Internet Protocol (IP) address.[39] Google then licensed Digital Envoy's patent to deliver geo-targeted ads on its site. Google later applied the technology to deliver geo-targeted ads to its Google AdSense partners on their sites, prompting Digital Envoy to sue Google for allegedly exceeding the patent license by allowing the technology's use on third-party sites.[40]

### Patent Infringement

As discussed, the patent application "claims" section contains a set of claims defining what the inventor seeks to protect with his patent. Infringement is determined by comparing the claims language with the actual product. For the patent to be infringed upon, the product must match the definition given in at least one claim. To infringe, each and every element of that claim must be present in the infringing product; if an element is missing, then the product does not infringe. Since a patent examiner has examined it, a patent is presumed by the court to be valid and the burden of proof is on the accused infringer to prove it is invalid and should not have been granted, due to any one of the following:

- Prior art not previously considered
- Insufficient disclosure of the invention
- Fraud

Because the federal government grants patents, federal courts have jurisdiction in patent infringement cases. If a court finds infringement, the patent holder may seek an injunction to prevent further infringement, or monetary damages. As shown in Chapter 1, all appeals in patent cases go to the U.S. Court of Appeals for the Federal Circuit (CAFC), in Washington, DC (established in 1982), with further appeal possible to the U.S. Supreme Court.

### International Patents

U.S. patent protection extends *only* throughout the United States and its territories and possessions. It does not give an inventor the right to exclude those in foreign countries from making or using the invention. Patent protection usually *must be sought in each individual country* in which it is desired. Many countries require the patented product be manufactured in that country within a specified time frame (often three years). Failure to meet this "*working requirement*" will void the patent in some countries, but others grant compulsory licenses to any applicant.

The *Paris Convention of 1883* protects industrial property (*i.e.*, patents, utility models, industrial designs, trademarks, service marks, and trade names).[41] It is one of the most important treaties in intellectual property law, assuring signatory nations will grant the same patent and trademark rights to citizens of other signatories as they have to their own citizens. It provides if an inventor subsequently files patent applications for the same invention in other member countries within one year after filing the first one, later applications receive a fictional filing date equal to the first one's filing date. This is known as "convention priority." The Paris Convention is supervised by the World Intellectual Property Organization (WIPO).

The *Patent Cooperation Treaty of 1970* lets an inventor seek patent protection simultaneously in many countries through a single application.[42] There are 137 signatories to the treaty, including the United States, most of the European Community, and Japan. The process begins with filing of an international patent application in one country's "receiving office." An international patent search is conducted for prior art, and an opinion regarding patentability is issued, along with an "International Search Report." Eventually, both the report and the application are published.

The *Convention on the Grant of European Patents of 1973* (European Patent Convention or EPC), set up the European Patent Organization and a legal framework for the granting of European patents.[43] The contracting nations are: Austria, Belgium, Bulgaria, Croatia, Cyprus, the Czech Republic, Denmark, Estonia, Finland, France, Germany Greece, Hungary, Iceland, Ireland, Italy, Latvia, Liechtenstein, Lithuania, Luxembourg, Malta, Monaco, the Netherlands, Norway, Poland, Portugal, Romania, Slovakia, Slovenia, Spain, Sweden, Switzerland, Turkey, and the United Kingdom. Once granted, a European patent has the same force and effect as a national patent in each of the contracting nations.

## Trade Secrets

*"Three may keep a secret, if two of them are dead." — Benjamin Franklin*

*Trade secrets* are confidential practices, methods, processes, designs, or other information used by a company to compete with other businesses. The elements of a trade secret are:

- Information not generally publicly known
- Information conferring on its holder an economic benefit derived from its secrecy
- Information that is the subject of reasonable efforts to maintain that secrecy

Trade secrets, like copyrights, trademarks, and patents, are a form of intellectual property. In one respect, a trade secret is the opposite of a patent. Recall from earlier in this chapter, in exchange for patent rights, the patent (*i.e.*, how the invention works) becomes public information. Thus, a trade secret is by its nature secret, whereas a patent is open and public.

With one exception, noted below, trade secrets are subject to state, not federal law, so the law on trade secrets will vary by jurisdiction. However, about 45 states have adopted a model statute known as the **Uniform Trade Secrets Act** (UTSA).[44] The **UTSA** defines trade secrets as "information, including a formula, pattern, compilation, program, device, method, technique, or process that derives independent economic value from not being generally known and not being readily ascertainable and is subject to reasonable efforts to maintain secrecy."[45]

Inventions, formulas, recipes, designs, software designs, manufacturing processes, instructional methods, document tracking processes, and customer or supplier lists can comprise trade secrets.[46] Even Google's search code has been deemed a trade secret.[47] One does not file a trade secret, as is the case with other intellectual property; trade secret protection is automatic when information of value to the owner is kept secret by the owner. Simply locking the information in a file cabinet marked "Confidential" is sufficient. But trade secret protection may be lost if the owner fails to take reasonable measures to protect it. Unlike copyrights and patents, trade secrets do not expire within a set period.

## Misappropriation of Trade Secrets

Trade secrets are subject to misappropriation, usually by either corporate espionage or breach of a confidentiality agreement. But discovery of protected information by independent research or reverse engineering is not misappropriation. So, if a soft beverage scientist stumbles across the exact formula for Coca Cola in his laboratory, he has not misappropriated a trade secret. Remedies for misappropriation include monetary damages, recovered profits, reasonable royalties, and injunctive relief.

**The Economic Espionage Act of 1996** makes misappropriation or theft of trade secrets a federal offense.[48] The Act's first part deals with theft of trade secrets to benefit foreign governments, but the second part focuses on theft or misappropriation in the corporate environment. Section 1832, titled "Theft of Trade Secrets", applies to products produced for, or placed in, interstate or foreign commerce. Penalties include fines (up to $5 million) and imprisonment (up to 10 years). It applies not only to one who steals the trade secrets but also to whomever "receives, buys, or possesses such information, knowing the same to have been stolen or appropriated, obtained, or converted without authorization."[49]

In a one case, Apple Computer sued a student for disclosing trade secrets on his site. As a 13-year-old boy, Nicholas Ciarelli built a site in 1998 and under the alias "Nick dePlume" began publishing insider news and rumors about Apple.[50] After breaking the news Apple would launch a G4 version of the PowerBook laptop, his site quickly became a leading source for Apple insider news among Apple fans, with millions of monthly page views. Despite Apple's warnings to cease publishing proprietary information, he continued, and in 2004, after another revelation by his site, Apple sued him for illegally misappropriating trade secrets.[51]

Although Ciarelli did not have a direct relationship with the company, Apple's lawsuit alleged his site induced tipsters to break nondisclosure agreements. The site had a phone number for tips and an e-mail form link labeled *"Got Dirt?"* stating he "appreciates your news tips and insider information." Third parties are prohibited by the **UTSA** from exposing information knowingly obtained from sources bound by confidentiality agreements. Ciarelli, a 19-year-old Harvard student at the time of the lawsuit, claimed he was a "journalist" protected by the First Amendment. [52] (See the discussion of news blogs in Chapter 16). But critics argued his site also had a commercial component, [53] as it featured paid ads from technology companies. He countered his site benefited Apple by creating valuable "buzz" about forthcoming products. The lawsuit had the potential to backfire on Apple, antagonizing many Apple fans who saw one of their own attacked by the computer giant. [54] One blogger commented Apple should hire Ciarelli, not sue him. In 2007, a settlement was reached, resulting in the site being shut down. [55]

**Chapter 4 Notes**

[1] The Lanham Act, 15 U.S.C. § 1125.

[2] U.S. Patent and Trademark Office, *available at* www.uspto.gov (accessed Mar. 23, 2012).

[3] WhoIs Web site, *available at* www.whois.com (accessed Mar. 23, 2012).

[4] AllWhoIs, *available at* www.allwhois.com (accessed Mar. 23, 2012).

[5] Madrid Protocol, *available at* www.wipo.int/madrid/en (accessed Mar. 23, 2012).

[6] *See Hormel Foods Corp. v. Jim Henson Prods., Inc.*, 73 F.3d. 497 (2[d] Cir. 1996), where the court found an "unclean grotesque boar" porcine Muppet named "Spa'am" would not cause confusion in the minds of consumers with plaintiff's pork product, "Spam." (Included in the Cases Section on the Issues in Internet Law site, www.IssuesinInternetLaw.com).

[7] The 1996 Anti-Dilution Act, The Lanham Act § 43(c)(1).

[8] The Lanham Act, fn. 1, *supra*. The Anti-Dilution Act, § 43(c)(1) of the Lanham Act, was amended in 2006 to eliminate the requirement of a showing of actual economic harm to the famous mark's economic value, in response to the U.S. Supreme Court decision in *Moseley v. V Secret Catalogue, Inc.*, 537 U.S. 418 (2003), as well as the split decisions among the federal circuits. Under the new standard, a party is entitled to an injunction against the user of a trademark "likely to cause dilution." *See* The Trademark Dilution Revision Act of 2006, 15 U.S.C. § 1125(c)(1).

[9] *Toys 'R' Us, Inc. v. Akkaoui*, 40 U.S.P.Q.2D (BNA) 1836, 1836-39 (N.D. Cal. 1996).

[10] *Hormel Foods Corp.*, 73 F.3d. 497. The case was filed under New York's anti-dilution statute, N.Y. Gen. Bus. Law § 368(d) (McKinney 1984), not under the federal Anti-Dilution Act which was not signed into law until 1996.

[11] *Ibid.*

[12] *Ibid.*

[13] *Campbell v. Acuff-Rose Music, Inc.*, 510 U.S. 569, 582 (1994).

[14] *PETA, Inc. v. Doughney*, 113 F. Supp. 2d 915 (E.D. Va. 2000). (Included in the Cases Section on the Issues in Internet Law site, www.IssuesinInternetLaw.com).

[15] Garrett French, "Booble Responds to Google: Read Letter," WebProNews, *available at* www.Webpronews.com/ebusiness/seo/wpn-4-20040129BoobleRespondsToGoogleReadLetter.html (accessed Mar. 23, 2012).

[16] *Ibid.*

[17] *Ibid.*

[18] Gretchen Gallen, "Booble Tests Mainstream Ad Blitz," XBiz News, November 12, 2004.

[19] *Ibid.*

[20] *Tiffany (NJ), Inc. v. eBay, Inc.*, 576 F. Supp. 2d 463 (S.D.N.Y. 2008).

[21] eBay's VeRO (Verified Rights Owner) program allows participants (mostly software, media or fashion trademark owners) to notify eBay of fakes, request removal of infringing eBay listings, and request personal information about alleged infringers.

[22] *Tiffany (NJ), Inc.*, fn. 20, *supra*.

[23] eBay did not "allow" counterfeit goods to be sold; on notification, eBay would terminate the listing.

[24] *Ibid.*

[25] This is the same principle raised in a Ninth Circuit case where a defendant used the trademark "Volkswagen" in advertising to describe he specialized in repairing Volkswagens. In *Volkswagenwerk Aktiengesellschaft v. Church*, 411 F.2d 350, 352 (9th Cir. 1969), the court held the defendant was able to advertise he repaired Volkswagens as long as he did not do so in a manner "likely to suggest to his prospective customers that he is part of Volkswagen's organization of franchised dealers and repairmen."

[26] *Tiffany (NJ), Inc. v. eBay, Inc.*, 600 F.3d 93 (2d Cir. 2010).

[27] U.S. Const., Art. I, § 8: "Congress shall have power … to promote the progress of science and useful arts, by securing for limited times to authors and inventors the exclusive right to their respective writings and discoveries."

[28] The Patent Act, 35 U.S.C. § 101. "Inventions patentable: Whoever invents or discovers any new and useful process, machine, manufacture, or composition of matter, or any new and useful improvement thereof, may obtain a patent therefor, subject to the conditions and requirements of this title."

[29] Most patents expire after 20 years (an exception is design patents, which expire after 14 years).

[30] However, patents are not enforceable until the day of issuance.

[31] The Patent Act, fn. 28, *supra*.

[32] The America Invents Act of 2011 (H.R. 1249), effective for applications filed on or after March 16, 2013, eliminates geographic and English-language distinctions among types of prior art.

[33] U.S. Patent and Trademark Office, *available at* www.uspto.gov (accessed Mar. 23, 2012).

[34] The America Invents Act of 2011 (H.R. 1249), fn. 6, *supra*.

[35] California, Delaware, Illinois, Kansas, Minnesota, North Carolina, Utah, and Washington all have statutes imposing limited restrictions on the scope of assignment clauses in employer contracts.

[36] *See Gill v. United States*, 160 U.S. 426 (1896), establishing an estoppel principle, if an employee acquiesces and participates in the use of the invention in the employer's business, he is estopped from preventing the employer's use of the invention or requiring the employer to pay royalties.

[37] In June 2003, Unisys' U.S. patent on LZW expired, but the patent remained valid in Europe and Japan until June 2004, and in Canada until July 2004. A patent IBM had filed on the same algorithm expired in August 2006.

[38] *Amazon.com, Inc. v. BarnesandNoble.com, Inc.*, 73 F. Supp. 2d 500 (W.D. Wash. 1999) vacated and remanded 239 F.3d 1343 (Fed. Cir. 2001). In 2007, a three-judge USPTO panel reversed an earlier decision approving Amazon.com's One-Click online purchasing system patent because of evidence another patent predated it. *See* Elinor Mills, "Amazon 1-Click Patent Rejected," CNET News.com, October 17, 2007. Amazon's One-Click patent was held non-infringing by the U.S. Court of Appeals for the Federal Circuit in 2011. *Cordance Corp. v. Amazon.com, Inc.*, Docket Number 2010-1502 (2011).

[39] Digital Envoy press release, June 29, 2004, *available at* www.digitalenvoy.net/news/press_releases/2004/pr_062904.html (accessed Mar. 23, 2012).

[40] Jonathan Skillings and Stefanie Olsen, "Google Hit with 'Geo-location' Lawsuit," CNET News.com, March 30, 2004. Digital Envoy lost the case.

[41] Paris Convention of 1883, *available at* www.wipo.int/treaties/en/ip/paris/trtdocs_wo020.html (accessed Mar. 23, 2012).

[42] Patent Cooperation Treaty of 1970, *available at* www.wipo.int/pct/en/texts/articles/atoc.htm (accessed Mar. 23, 2012).

[43] Convention on the Grant of European Patents of 1973, *available at* www.wipo.int/clea/docs_new/pdf/en/ep/ep001en.pdf (accessed Mar. 23, 2012).

[44] The text of the Uniform Trade Secrets Act is included in the Cases Section on the Issues in Internet Law site (www.IssuesinInternetLaw.com).

[45] *Ibid.*

[46] Adding walnut dust to a recipe for baking chocolate chip cookies constituted a trade secret. *Peggy Lawton Kitchens, Inc. v. Hogan*, 466 N.E.2d 138 (Mass. App. Ct. 1984).

[47] A federal court held Google did not have to give Viacom its search code, ruling it a trade secret that could not be disclosed without risking the loss of business. *See* Steven Musil, "YouTube Privacy at Risk in Google-Viacom Ruling," CNET News.com, July 2, 2008.

[48] The Economic Espionage Act of 1996, 18 U.S.C. § 1831, *et seq.* The Act defines a trade secret as "all forms and types of financial, business, scientific, technical, economic, or engineering information, including patterns, plans, compilations, program devices, formulas, designs, prototypes, methods, techniques, processes, procedures, programs, or codes, whether tangible or intangible, and whether or how stored, compiled, or memorialized physically, electronically, graphically, photographically, or in writing if:

(A) the owner thereof has taken reasonable measures to keep such information secret; and

(B) the information derives independent economic value, actual or potential, from not being generally known to, and not being readily ascertainable through proper means by, the public..." 18 U.S.C. § 1839(3).

[49] *Ibid.*, § 1832(a)(3).

[50] A "nom de plume" is a French phrase meaning "pen name" or pseudonym.

[51] *Apple Computer, Inc. v. DePlume*, Case No. 05-cv-33341 (Cal. Super. Ct., Santa Clara Cnty. filed Jan. 4, 2005); *see also* Jonathan Finer, "Teen Web Editor Drives Apple to Court Action," The Washington Post, p. A01, January 14, 2005.

[52] While this raises the interesting issue of 'What is a journalist?' or more precisely, 'Who may be considered a journalist?' the First Amendment was not written merely to protect journalists; the First Amendment is a broad restriction on government prohibiting it from restricting speech by its citizens.

[53] The U.S. Supreme Court has ruled the First Amendment protects commercial speech, but to a lesser degree than noncommercial speech. However, even newspapers, which solicit and contain paid advertising, do not forfeit their First Amendment protection by doing so.

[54] See the discussion on company lawsuits against cybergripers and the risk of negative publicity, in Chapter 18.

[55] Duncan Martell, "Popular Apple Rumor Web Site to Shut Down," Reuters wire service report, December 20, 2007.

# CHAPTER

# 5

———

# TRADEMARK AND
# THE INTERNET

This chapter explores trademarks and domain names, the Truth in Domain Names Act, cybersquatting, the Anti-cybersquatting Consumer Protection Act, the Uniform Domain Name Dispute Resolution Policy, meta tags, and keyword advertising.

*"What's in a name? That which we call a rose*
*By any other name would smell as sweet."*
— *William Shakespeare, "Romeo and Juliet" Act 2, Scene 2*

THERE ARE THREE MAIN areas in which trademarks become a concern online. The first is *cybersquatting*, where individuals buy domain names of trademarked brands and attempt to resell them to the trademark holder for a profit. The second is *cybergriping*, where disgruntled consumers use a trademarked name or phrase as part of their domain name for a site used to gripe about the trademark holder's firm or product. The last area is *keyword advertising*, where trademark holders attempt to stop their brands from being purchased as keywords in Internet search advertising. As seen later in this chapter, American courts have trended toward allowing companies to buy the trademarked brand names of rivals as keywords, but European jurisdictions, most notably France, take the opposite view.

## Are Domain Names Property?

There are contrasting views regarding the legal status of domain names. One sees domain names as *intellectual property rights*, while the other holds they are licenses, thus *contractual rights*. The distinction is important because property rights offer more protections than contract rights. Also, a property right lasts indefinitely until conveyed, whereas a contract right is limited to an express (*i.e.*, defined) term on which it will expire. Another way of looking at the domain name issue is, do you *lease* it or do you *own* it?

The Ninth Circuit has accepted the view a domain name is "property." Sometimes the "property" can be very valuable. Stephen Cohen stole Gary Kremen's domain name, sex.com, simply by submitting a fake transfer letter with a forged signature to the domain registrar.[1] Cohen made at least $40 million from the site. Kremen subsequently won a $65 million judgment against Cohen, who promptly transferred his assets overseas and fled to Tijuana, Mexico.[2] The court found the registrar liable for giving the name to someone without properly informing its rightful owner,[3] under the theory Kremen had a property right in the domain name and the registrar committed the tort of conversion by giving it to Cohen (reversing that portion of the lower court's decision).[4] In finding a property right, the court compared registering a domain name to staking a claim to a plot of land at the title office. An apt analogy, as the rush for domain names is reminiscent of the 19th century Gold Rush, when prospectors descended on claims offices to file land claims for what they perceived as valuable property. While not every claim turned into a small fortune, some did. The same is true today with Web real estate. Purchase and sale of domain names is a multi-billion dollar industry, with a projected $5.3 billion market value by 2011.[5] Domain names are registered at a rate of 90,000 per day![6] In 2006, sex.com sold for $14 million[7] and three years later insure.com sold for $16 million.[8]

Although bankruptcy courts treat domains as property, and the IRS treats them as a form of intellectual property (allowing amortization similar to a trademark), there are federal cases ruling a domain name is *not* tangible property.[9] One state supreme court even held domain names should be considered services rather than property. (The lower court holding in Kremen, subsequently reversed, also had considered a domain name not as property but as a service, likening it to a phone number. A better analogy might be to view the numeric IP address underlying the domain name as akin to a phone number, whereas the domain name itself is more like a trademark.). The counterview to the domain name as property right is it is merely a contract between the owner and registrar. Network Solutions describes a domain name as a contractual license between itself and the registrant. Lawyers from most countries outside of the United States agree a domain name is a contract right from a domain registry.

If considered a property right, then the *scope* of a property interest in a domain name may vary widely in the United States, *since states create and define property interests, not federal courts.* Property rights are established through either a state's supreme court decisions under common law or through statutes enacted by state legislators. So if domain names are property interests, the state will define the scope of such property rights.

Fraudulent domain name transfers as in Kremen continue. In 2004, a 19-year-old German faced computer sabotage charges after hijacking the German eBay domain eBay.de, redirecting visitors to a different domain name server (DNS). The teen said he had requested DNS transfers for several sites, including Google.de, Web.de, Amazon.de and eBay.de "just for fun", after discovering how to do a DNS transfer online.[10] The other requests were denied, but the eBay transfer went through, with no explanation for how it could have been transferred without the owner's consent. (In 2007, Google.de, the German Google domain, was hijacked the same way).[11] Four months later, a New York ISP discovered its domain had been hijacked.[12] Officials at Panix.com, which provides Internet access and e-mail services to New York City, Long Island, Westchester, Rockland County, and New Jersey, discovered its domain's ownership had been moved during the night to a company in Australia, the DNS records moved to the United Kingdom, and the company's e-mail redirected to a Canadian company! Improbable as it may seem, fraudulent domain transfers without the owner's consent continue, affecting even major companies. In 2009, a New Jersey man was charged with felony theft by unlawful taking or deception, identity theft, and computer theft for allegedly stealing a domain name and reselling it for $111,000. He allegedly hacked into the domain name owner's account, transferred ownership to himself, and resold it on eBay to a professional basketball player.[13] Revised 2004 rules governing domain name ownership transfer only exacerbated the problem. The amended ICANN rules automatically approve inter-registry transfer requests after five days unless countermanded by the domain owner; previously domain ownership and name servers were unchanged until the owner had replied affirmatively to the transfer request.

# Domain Name Tricks

## Domain Misspellings

*Typosquatting* is a form of cybersquatting (discussed later in this chapter) where the typosquatter registers a misspelled version of a prominent trademarked domain name in the hope visitors will reach the site by accidentally mistyping the trademarked URL. The aim is to drive traffic to his site, where visitors click on advertising links that generate revenue for the typosquatter (often the landing page is a domain parking site with no real content other than hyperlinks based on keywords similar to the misspelled word in the domain name). Courts will find trademark infringement where the trademark owner's name has been intentionally misspelled in a bad faith attempt to divert visitors from the targeted site to the violator's site. One district court has ruled registering domain names that are intentional misspellings of distinctive or famous trademarks violates the **ACPA**. [14]

When a new domain name is registered, the registrant often lacks a site prepared to place at the domain. Registrars offer to "park" the domain on their servers, providing a placeholder Web page filled with keyword ads tied to the domain name. Many typosquatters have purchased domain names that are commonly misspelled variations of famous trademarks, also filling the empty page with keyword ads tied to the domain name. Their intent is to profit from click-through ad revenue from visitors landing on the page by mistyping a domain name. [15] Purposely creating consumer confusion over trademarked brand names to profit from the misdirection is the essence of what U.S. trademark laws are meant to prevent. In 2007, computer manufacturer Dell sued three registrars for typosquatting on and counterfeiting its trademark (perhaps the first time a counterfeiting claim has been used in a domain registration case). [16]

In addition to landing on pay-per-click sites, visitors are frequently rerouted to a competitor's site or to a pornographic site — and in at least one case, both! In Calgary, Canada, a defendant was fined $15,000 after buying a domain name similar to his former employer's and redirecting visitors to a gay porn site. The defendant, who had worked for a bicycle shop with the domain name InformCycle.ca, bought the domain name InformCycle.com. Banking on the prospect of Web users accidentally typing ".com" instead of ".ca", he initially forwarded visitors to his current employer's site (a competing bike shop) but later redirected traffic to the porn site. The court found his motive was to "embarrass and harm" his former employer. [17] Often on being redirected to a pornographic site, visitors find themselves "mousetrapped."

## Mousetrapping

*Mousetrapping* is when a visitor cannot leave a site without clicking on a succession of pop-up windows. Typically, the visitor's Web browser's back button is disabled. Each pop-up contains another ad for a pornographic site, and the owner is usually paid between 10¢ and 25¢ per click by advertisers. One defendant admitted earning between $800,000-to-$1 million per year through mousetrapping. [18] Mousetrapping may be considered a "deceptive practice" under the **Federal Trade Commission Act**.

## Pagejacking

*Pagejacking* occurs where an offender steals a site's contents by copying pages, putting them on a site that appears to be the real one, and luring people to it through deceptive means. By moving enough of a site's content and page description metadata, pagejackers can submit the fake site to search engines to be indexed. Search engine users then receive results from both the real and fake sites and may be easily misled into clicking on the wrong one, being redirected to a pornographic or other undesired site. As an additional annoyance, visitors subjected to pagejacking may also be mousetrapped. Pagejacking is prohibited as a "deceptive practice" under the **Federal Trade Commission Act**. Pagejacking is also used in phishing schemes, where the fake page is set up to procure account numbers and passwords or other personal data from visitors. Phishing is discussed in greater detail in the cybercrimes section (Chapter 6) of this book.

## Truth in Domain Names

### The Truth in Domain Names Act

Enacted by Congress in 2003 as part of the **PROTECT Act**,[19] the **Truth in Domain Names Act**[20] criminalizes use of a "misleading domain name" with intent to deceive a person into viewing obscenity or to deceive a minor into viewing "material that is harmful to minors." The Act may be vulnerable to a First Amendment challenge because the terms "misleading", "obscenity", and "harmful to minors" are inherently vague. It was used to arrest an infamous cybersquatter[21] who for years had made millions of dollars linking pornographic sites to domain names similar to popular trademarks.[22] Taking advantage of children who typed domain names incorrectly, he had registered 3,000 names, including "Teltubbies.com", "Bobthebiulder.com", "Dinseyland.com", and 41 variations on celebrity Britney Spears' name that directed visitors to a pornographic site.

### The Fraudulent Online Identity Sanctions Act

The **Fraudulent Online Identity Sanctions Act** amended the **Lanham** and **Copyright Acts** to provide trademark or copyright infringement will be considered "willful" if the infringer knowingly provided misleading or false contact information in making, maintaining, or renewing a domain name's registration.[23] It also mandated judges double or increase by seven years the sentence for a felony involving use of a falsely registered domain name.

## Cybersquatting

A "*cybersquatter*" is one who deliberately and in bad faith registers domain names in violation of a trademark owner's rights. Cybersquatters' motives include extorting payment from trademark owners, hoarding names to resell to the highest bidder, diverting visitors to pornographic sites, diverting consumers to a competitor's site, and defrauding consumers.

### Anti-cybersquatting Consumer Protection Act

To win an infringement suit, trademark law required a "*use in commerce*" of the infringing trademark. Cybersquatters got around this by refusing to sell the domain name (*i.e.*, no offer of sale, thus no commerce) or by registering a name but not creating a site at the URL, since if there was no Web page, there could be no "use in commerce." Not creating a Web page also effectively eliminated any claim of *consumer confusion.*" If they did have a Web page on the domain name URL, the cybersquatters could reduce "consumer confusion" by posting a disclaimer to the effect the site was unrelated to the trademark holder's mark.

The **Anti-cybersquatting Consumer Protection Act** (ACPA)[24] closed these loopholes in existing trademark laws. It does not require actual "use" in commerce. The test is "registers, traffics in, or uses a domain name", which means mere registration will suffice.[25] However, the plaintiff must show both the domain name registrant had a *"bad faith intent to profit from"* a trademark and he registered, trafficked in, or used a domain name identically or confusingly similar to the trademark.[26] The **ACPA** does not mention any provision for contributory liability, yet several courts have allowed claims of contributory cybersquatting, so long as its "bad faith intent" requirement is met.[27]

A federal appeals court ruled, in 2004, an anti-abortion activist violated trademark law by registering multiple domains (including drinkcoke.org, mycoca-cola.com, mymcdonalds.com, mypepsi.org, and my-washingtonpost.com) and using them to point visitors to his anti-abortion sites with pictures of aborted and dismembered fetuses.[28] By registering "WPNI.org", which is similar to WPNI.com, the domain name for Post-Newsweek employees' e-mail addresses, the anti-abortion activist was able to intercept e-mails to reporters. The Eighth Circuit held the names he had registered were "confusingly similar" to the trademarked ones and thus violated the **ACPA**. It upheld a preliminary injunction ordering him to relinquish the names. The defendant contended he was exercising his First Amendment right to criticize companies he claimed promoted abortion and not using the domain names for commercial profit, thus lacking the required "bad faith intent to profit". But since he had included some commercial messages on his sites, the court did not have to decide if the outcome would be the same on a "noncommercial" site. It ruled, while the defendant had a right to express his message online, the First Amendment would not allow trademark misappropriation to do so, citing confusion that would be created in consumers' minds.

## Cyberpoachers

*Cyberpoachers* grab domain names when a name a company had previously registered becomes available for any of a number of reasons; *e.g.,* if it let the registration expire by mistake, or through domain name registrar error or fraud. A company may not even realize it has lost its domain name. In one case, a large private game reserve's name lapsed before it was due to publish a full-page ad in *The New York Times,* leading them to discover their domain name had been cyberpoached and now led to an animal porn site.[29] Where the cyberpoacher has purchased the domain name with intent to resell it to the original owner, the court may deem that a "bad faith" violation of the **ACPA**.[30]

## Personal Names as Domain Names

Can using another person's name as your domain name be misleading?[31] Likewise, do you have a property interest in your own name? A father registered the domain name "Veronica.org" and filled the site with photographs of his two-year-old daughter Veronica. He was shocked when Archie Comics fired off a letter from its attorney accusing him of trademark infringement and demanding he turn over the domain name to the comic book publisher, known for publishing stories about a group of teenagers named Archie, Jughead,

Reggie, Betty and *Veronica*. The father replied he had purchased the domain name for his daughter Veronica, it was a noncommercial ".org" domain, and it made no reference to Archie Comics, its trademarks or products. He assured Archie Comics it would be several years before his two-year-old would have the necessary skills to design a logo that could be confused with Archie's. [32] The following news excerpt shows the risk of negative publicity and ridicule corporations take when attempting to pursue such specious claims: [33]

> Archie Comic Publications has been forced to slink away with its tail between
> its legs after the public relations debacle that followed its threats against two-
> year-old Veronica Sams of Los Angeles. Lawyers for Archie Comics apparently
> were worried that the public might confuse pictures of little Veronica sitting
> in her bathtub with the teenage cartoon character named Veronica that graces
> the pages of Archie Comics.

In a similar situation, computer manufacturer Dell (named after company founder Michael Dell) took umbrage with the URL of Spanish Web designer Paul Dell (no relation to Michael), www.dellwebsites.com. Dell's trademark infringement claim cited a "risk of confusion" between the Web designer's site and its own and demanded Paul Dell sign over the domain to the PC manufacturer at his own expense. [34] One news report sarcastically noted the amount of confusion allegedly caused by Paul Dell's Web design site had not seemed to have had a noticeable effect on Dell Computer's revenue, which during that period had increased by 20 percent to $23 billion. [35]

Penguin Books published "Katie.com" — a book by Katie Tarbox, a teenage victim of an online predator. Tarbox expanded the book into a TV show and a school curriculum to teach children online safety. But there was a slight problem — the domain Katie.com was owned by a completely different "Katie" — Katie Jones, who had purchased it four years earlier. Jones complained of massive undesired e-mail and heavy site traffic resulting from the book's publication, claiming she felt uncomfortable keeping her child's photos on a site marketed as part of a book about pedophiles. Jones revamped it into a public protest against Penguin, whom she alleged had co-opted her domain name, aware she owned Katie.com when it titled the book. (Tarbox, the author, had her own site at Katiet.com). Penguin continued to promote Katie.com, pausing only to print this small addition to the copyright notice in the 2001 paperback edition: "the publishers wish to make clear the author of Katie.com and events described in Katie.com have no connection whatsoever with the Web site found at domain name address www.katie.com, or with e-mail address katie@katie.com." Jones compared it to publishing a book with her home phone number or address as the title. Ironically, the book is about Internet abuse disrupting an innocent girl's life. Penguin relented and renamed Katie.com *"A Girl's Life Online."* Katie.com later became a hosted Web page filled with pay-per-click ads and then a porn site; as of 2012, it was a fashion site for adolescent girls. [36]

Uzi Nissan, an Israeli, came to America in 1976 and started several businesses with his family name — "Nissan Foreign Car Mobile Repair Service" in 1980, "Nissan International, Ltd.", an import-export firm, in 1987, and "Nissan Computer Corp." in 1991. As he explains on his site, Nissan is proud of the long heritage of his family name, which is also the biblical word for the seventh month in the Hebrew calendar. [37] In 1994, he registered the domain name Nissan.com to promote his computer business. The next year, he registered a service mark for Nissan and his logo with North Carolina. Five years later, [38] Nissan Motors Ltd., a Japanese automobile manufacturer, [39] sued Uzi Nissan to enjoin him from using his family name for business purposes on the Internet and $10 million in damages. [40] The district court stated: [41]

> Although there is no absolute right to use one's name as a trademark, the Ninth
> Circuit has recognized a "judicial reluctance to enjoin use of a personal name."
> _E. & J. Gallo Winery v. Gallo Cattle Co._, 967 F.2d 1280, 1288 (9ᵗʰ Cir. 1992)
> * * * An injunction limiting the use of an infringing personal name should
> be 'carefully tailored to balance the interest in using one's name against the
> interest in avoiding public confusion.' _E. & J. Gallo Winery_, 967 F.2d at 1288.

The district court found automobile-related advertising on Uzi Nissan's site infringed on the plaintiff's trademark, but the non-automobile advertising did not. It enjoined the defendant to post a disclaimer he was unaffiliated with Nissan Motor Co. with a link to the plaintiff's site, and not to display automobile-related information, ads, promotions, or hyperlinks on his site.[42] On appeal, the court held the lower court's injunction prohibiting displaying links to disparaging comments about Nissan Motor Co. an unconstitutional content-based restriction in violation of the First Amendment. The appellate court upheld the finding the automobile-related advertising infringed on the plaintiff's trademark, but the non-automobile advertising did not, and remanded the case to determine the issue of trademark dilution.[43]

The previous cases involved individuals and/or corporations each claiming a right to a name in which each had some legitimate interest. Archie Comics had a character named Veronica and David Sams had a daughter with that name. Michael Dell and Paul Dell were both born with the Dell surname and each had a legitimate interest in using his surname to describe his business. Likewise, both Katie Tarbox and Katie Jones were born with the name "Katie." And Uzi Nissan was also born with his surname and had a legitimate interest in using it in his business. But what about the situation where an individual usurps another's name?

While the focus of the **ACPA** is on preventing trademark-based cybersquatting, it does protect trademarked names. Generally, for a personal name to be registrable as a trademark it must (1) be with the consent of the person, and (2) serve to distinguish the registrant's goods from the goods of another.[44] The first requirement would prohibit someone from trademarking an individual's personal name without that individual's permission. The second requirement means the personal name must have attained a secondary meaning associating it with particular goods or services, _e.g.,_ Mary Kay cosmetics, Calvin Klein clothing, Martha Stewart housewares. Not all trademarks are registered; it is possible a personal name may have attained a common law trademark status.

The **ACPA** not only protects a trademarked personal name, but a separate section also protects personal names of individuals.[45] However, one federal court chose to ignore that provision, when a Democratic candidate's paid consultant launched a disparaging site using his Republican opponent's name as the domain name. Applying a specious First Amendment rationale, the court denied a temporary injunction, ruling the site owner's free speech rights outweighed the **ACPA**'s protections.[46] Astoundingly, the court found "no irreparable harm" to the plaintiff Robin Ficker by the launch of an attack site in his own name, RobinFicker.com, days before the election. The court attempted to rationalize its decision, stating, "by entering public arena he invited comments and critiques." Since the election ended days later, appealing the case was moot. But had it been appealed, a more rational court might have overturned this decision. The court's finding potential damage to the defendant's First Amendment free speech rights outweighed any actual damage to the plaintiff ignores the fact the defendant's freedom of expression could have been accomplished with a different domain name not misleading as was the one he had chosen. While the First Amendment supersedes any statute, the U.S. Supreme Court has ruled on many occasions free speech rights are not absolute and are subject to reasonable restrictions on time, place, and manner. Here, the plaintiff was not asking for a prohibition or a prior restraint on the content of the speech, but merely the disparaging content not be misleadingly placed on a domain with his own name. It would have been well within the court's power to find the manner of speech improper and enjoin the defendant from stating the content using his opponent's name as the domain name, while allowing the same content stated in a different manner, *i.e.*, on a site with a different domain name. The court said it found "the likelihood of harm to the Defendants is significant. The Court is particularly concerned with the threat to Defendants' right to free speech under the First Amendment" yet gave no explanation as to what significant harm was posed by requiring the defendant to change the domain name (not the speech itself).[47] Also, the court stated there was no irreparable harm, despite the obvious harm given the site's intent to sully a candidate's reputation days before an election; voters would come to RobinFicker.com, read the disparaging articles posted by his opponent's political consultant and presumably vote for the opponent. Though not a defamation case, the court borrowed the "public figure" standard from defamation law, (*i.e.*, public figures, because they choose to thrust themselves into the public limelight to influence the resolution of issues in a particular public controversy[48] must meet a higher burden of proof to show libel)[49] stating: "by entering the public arena as a candidate for political office, he has invited comments and critique."[50] This analogy is not only misplaced but ignores the fact public figures retain rights, including, no matter how diminished, privacy and publicity rights. The court did not consider the plaintiff's right of publicity (*i.e.*, an individual's right to control and profit from commercial use of his name, likeness, and persona).[51] Obviously, the plaintiff had no control over this unauthorized appropriation of his identity, although arguably the context of a political campaign might not be a commercial use.

Another political domain name dispute occurred in the 2008 presidential election campaign when the Barack Obama campaign sought to take over a site created by an ardent supporter. Joe Anthony began a MySpace fan page — myspace.com/barackobama — for Sen. Obama after listening to his 2004 Democratic convention keynote address. After Obama became a presidential candidate, Anthony's page gained 160,000 "friends."[52] Anthony collaborated informally with the campaign on the site, but as it grew in popularity, he asked the campaign for compensation, citing the time involved in maintaining it. The campaign balked at the $39,000 he wanted and raised concerns over someone not on their staff — indeed someone they had never met — controlling what had become a valuable campaign asset. It asked MySpace to transfer the URL, claiming the candidate should have the right to control his own MySpace subdomain name. MySpace resolved the conflict with a brilliant solution: it gave the name to the Obama campaign transferred the 160,000 "friends" to Anthony's replacement site.[53] MySpace executive Jeff Berman explained the company's reasoning:[54]

> We felt under the circumstances that Sen. Obama had the right to the URL containing his name and to the official campaign content that was provided, but that the user should retain the basic elements of the profile, including the friends who had been accumulated.

An individual's personal name may be protected under the **ACPA** even if not trademarked. A separate section of the Act protects personal names of individuals. **ACPA** § 1129 "Cyberpiracy Protections for Individuals", provides civil liability for:[55]

> Any person who registers a domain name that consists of the name of another living person, or a name substantially and confusingly similar thereto, without that person's consent, with the specific intent to profit from such name by

selling the domain name for financial gain to that person or any third party,
shall be liable in a civil action by such person.

While § 1129 does not require the personal name be trademarked to be protected, it does require specific intent to profit from sale of the name; a situation where a cybersquatter purchases a candidate's name and attempts to resell it to the campaign would be covered by § 1129, but a situation like *Ficker* would not fall under this section, as there was no resale attempt. [56]

Some factors to consider in determining if a personal name has been improperly registered as a domain name include:

- Does the registrant have a legitimate reason for using the name (*i.e.*, no "bad faith"?)

- How specifically does the domain name identify the person? Many women named Hillary might in good faith register Hillary.com; even hundreds named Hillary Clinton could in good faith register their domain as HillaryClinton.com. But a domain registration for HillaryRodhamClinton.com by anyone other than the former First Lady might raise legitimate "bad faith" questions

- Is the name a registered trademark?

- Has the name attained a common law trademark status?

- If it has not been trademarked, does the registrant lack the requisite intent to resell the name, precluding § 1129 from applying?

- Is the right of publicity recognized in the state?

### Shared Domain Name

It is possible for two trademark owners to coexist amicably using the same trademark with different products/services, or regions. One method used by some companies is to register the common trademark as a domain name and, on the home page at the URL, provide a split screen for each trademark. Playtex.com states "Although we may have a name in common … we are two completely separate companies" followed by images and links to Playtex Products on the left side of the screen and images and links to Playtex Apparel (the famous bras) on the right. [57] Pez Candy once split its page in half — clicking on the left side took visitors to the Pez subsidiary for North and South America, while clicking on the right half took visitors to the Pez subsidiary for Europe, Asia, Oceania, and Africa. [58] Likewise, scrabble.com uses a split screen to let visitors choose between Hasbro Inc.'s North American site and a Mattel subsidiary's site for the rest of the world. [59]

### Uniform Domain Name Dispute Resolution Policy

The Internet Corporation for Assigned Names and Numbers (ICANN) [60] is responsible for domain name registration oversight and has set up an administrative (*i.e.*, nonjudicial) process to resolve disputes. The Uniform Domain Name Dispute Resolution Policy (UDRP) is a quick, cost-effective alternative to a lawsuit, as arbitration is usually settled within months from filing. [61] There is no appeal, but parties can still go to court if they wish. Unlike the U.S. court system, there is no reliance on precedent, so results can be uncertain. The UDRP applies to *all* Global Top Level Domains (.com, .net, .org, .aero, .biz, .coop, .info, .museum, .name, .pro); and *some* Country Top Level Domains (.nu, .tv, .ws); but not to

.gov, .mil, or .int domains. Most registrars inform anyone registering a new domain name the registration is subject to the UDRP.

A complaint will fail unless all three UDRP threshold requirements for transfer or cancellation of the domain name registration are proved:

- Identical or confusingly similar domain names; and
- Registrant lacking legitimate interest in the name; and
- The domain name registered and used in bad faith

The complainant begins by suing the domain name holder or filing a complaint with an approved dispute resolution service provider, such as the Asian Domain Name Dispute Resolution Centre, CPR Institute for Dispute Resolution, the National Arbitration Forum (NAF), and the World Intellectual Property Organization (WIPO).[62] The latter two deal with the majority of domain name dispute arbitration cases.[63]

A recent NAF case illustrates how the process works and may reach surprising results.[64] In 2009, President Bill Clinton filed a complaint (making him the *complainant* in the proceeding) against an alleged cybersquatter doing business as "Web of Deception" (the *respondent*). The respondent had registered three domains: williamclinton.com, williamjclinton.com and presidentbillclinton.com. The complainant claimed a common law trademark in his name and the registered domains were identical to or confusingly similar to it. To support his common law trademark, he noted he: (1) had been elected and served as the 42nd president of the United States; (2) had been governor of Arkansas for two terms; (3) had written a series of best-selling books; (4) was *Time* magazine's Man of the Year in 1992; (5) was selected as the 17th Most Admired Person of the 20th Century in a Gallop poll; and (6) had founded philanthropic foundations bearing his name, several of which held registered federal trademarks. He alleged the respondent was a cybersquatter who (1) had no rights or legitimate interest in the domain names and had not made any demonstrable preparation to use them in any "bona fide offering of goods or services", and (2) acted in bad faith by choosing a domain name identical to his common law trademark and by linking his site to forward visitors to a Republican National Committee site.

The *arbitration panelist* concluded the complainant had established a common law mark in his name.[65] A trademark registration is unnecessary if a complainant can prove common law rights by establishing its mark has acquired secondary meaning. The panelist then reached his decision by determining whether all three UDRP threshold requirements for transfer or cancellation of the domain name registration had been met. *Were the domain names identical or confusingly similar to the common law trademark?* The panelist agreed with the complainant they were. *Did the registrant have a legitimate interest in the name?* The panelist found the respondent had no rights in the name. *Was the domain name "registered and used in bad faith"?* The panelist said no. The elements of bad faith under UDRP 4(b) are: a showing the names were registered or acquired for the purpose of (1) selling or transferring the name to the mark holder; (2) preventing the mark holder from registering the domain; (3) disrupting a competitor's business; or (4) attracting Internet users by confusing them. While the first element was not met because the respondent had not attempted to sell the names, the second element appears questionable. Was the complainant not prevented from registering the names by the respondent's act of registration? The third element would not appear to have been met, but the fourth is extremely questionable — attracting Internet users by confusing them. However, the panelist explained his reasoning:[66]

The Panelist simply cannot find bad faith in this case. None of the elements of bad faith are met within the UDRP definition of bad faith. * * * the Panelist cannot find that Respondent's registration and subsequent use of the disputed domain names to resolve to a website in direct competition with Complainant constitutes a disruption of Complainant's business and qualifies as bad faith registration and use. * * * Respondent is allegedly using the disputed domain names in order to intentionally attract Internet users to an opposing website by creating confusion among Internet users who are seeking Complainant's WILLIAM CLINTON mark. Allegedly, the disputed domain names resolve to the official Republican party website in direct competition with Complainant, giving the impression Complainant is affiliated with its political competitor. The Panelist declines to find that this is a violation of Policy and is not bad faith registration and use.

As a result of not finding bad faith, the third UDRP requirement, the complaint failed and the panelist found in favor of the respondent.

As apparent from the _Clinton_ case, the outcome of domain name arbitration can be unpredictable. One dispute resolution service resolved a case in favor of News Corporation's MySpace.com against Total Web Solutions of Stockport (TWSS), even though TWSS had registered the domain myspace.co.uk six years before MySpace launched its social network. [67] At first, TWSS had used the domain to offer e-mail services, but as MySpace's popularity grew, it relaunched as a parked page filled with pay-per-click ads for social networks like MySpace. The arbitrator concluded TWSS was unfairly profiting from association with MySpace and this represented evidence of abusive registration. The presumption a party has the right to a domain name registered first in time and prior to the existence of an opposing party's trademark can be rebutted by a showing of future unfair profiting from association with the trademark. It is a fairly wide-reaching ruling (with no precedential value) because shows a party with an established domain name can lose it years later to a newcomer who happens to have subsequently trademarked the name. The arbitrator based his decision on the rationale TWSS was responsible for the content (and thereby the associations) on its site. But this may not have been the case, as ads appearing on the page were not selected by TWSS but rather determined by algorithms linked to search terms by search engine users.

## Social Network Subdomains

While domain names are purchased from registrars, subdomains are obtained directly from the domain owner. A personalized URL on a social network, like www.MySpace.com/YourName, must be obtained directly from MySpace. The social networks are owned by private companies that make their own rules on if and how personalized names are allocated and what measures, if any, are available for disputes and trademark infringement claims. As discussed in this chapter, the domain name process is relatively straightforward. Names are first-come, first-served. They can be bought and sold by the owners. Disputes can be settled in arbitration or the courts. But the subdomain process differs markedly. Social media names are assigned arbitrarily, if at all. They cannot be resold (and in fact, are not purchased initially, either). Subdomains can be reclaimed at any time by the social network. Name disputes, imposters using a celebrity's name, and trademark disputes are all subject to the whims and policies of each organization.

## Search Terms and Infringement

### Meta Tags

Meta tags are relevant keywords used by search engines to index pages, allowing Web users to find tagged pages in searches. Since meta tags are placed in the HTML document, they are entirely within the Web designer's control. So, if a site owner places someone's trademark in his meta tags, has he committed infringement? It depends on why he placed the trademarked terms in his meta tags. If his purpose was to divert traffic from the trademark owner's site to his own, then he may have infringed on the owner's trademark rights. But using the terms to describe his content in a factual manner would be considered "*nominative fair use.*" The test for nominative fair use is whether:[68]

> (1) The product or service cannot be readily identified without using the trademark
>
> (2) The user only uses so much of the mark as is reasonably necessary to identify the product or service
>
> (3) The user does nothing to suggest sponsorship or endorsement by the trademark holder.

Where the defendant used the plaintiff's trademark "Pycnogenol" in meta tags on its site to sell competing products, the court ruled such use was not nominative fair use.[69] In *Niton Corporation v. Radiation Monitoring Devices, Inc.,*[70] a rival x-ray manufacturing firm copied Niton's meta tags onto its site, including phrases like "The Home Page of Niton Corporation, makers of the finest lead, radon, and multi-element detectors."[71] This blatant and willful meta tag infringement was sufficient for the court to grant a preliminary injunction against the defendant's use of the meta tags.

However, in *Playboy v. Welles,*[72] former Playboy "Playmate of the Year" Terri Wells used the trademarked phrases "Playboy" and "Playmate" in her site's meta tags. The court held use of the trademarks a fair use because it accurately described and identified her.[73] Her site made no effort to trick or confuse consumers into believing it was related to Playboy; in fact, it included a disclaimer. (Of course, search engine robots and spiders could index the disclaimer, causing searchers for those terms to end up on her site). However, the court did find Welles' repeated use of "PMOY '81" in her site's wallpaper not nominative fair use, since it was unnecessary to describe her. Similarly, when Devco, a seller of replacement parts for the Bijur lubrication system, placed the trademarked name "Bijur" in its meta tags, the court held its use of Bijur's trademark did not constitute infringement or dilution because it was nominative fair use.[74]

### Keyword Advertising

*Keyword advertising* is a form of *contextual marketing* where search engines respond to a query for one company's products with paid ads of another's alongside the requested results. Google lets advertisers bid for placement in "sponsored" areas of search-result listings, pairing ads with listings generated by relevant keywords. Since Web searches are the primary way people find products and services online, keyword advertising is highly effective for marketers — enabling them to reach searchers but pay only when their links are clicked — and a big money maker for search engines like Google. About 98 percent of its revenues come from keyword advertising.[76] But many of these ads are linked to branded or trademarked names of products and services. The question arises if, for example, on entering the phrase "Adidas sneakers" into a search engine, a banner ad for competitor Nike appears, does this violate Adidas' trademark? In other words, when does use of keyword ads become abuse?

Courts consider three factors in finding trademark infringement:

    (1) If there has been a "*use*" of the plaintiff's trademark,
    (2) If the use creates a "*likelihood of confusion*", and
    (3) If the use qualifies as a *nominative fair use*.

Some are obvious **nominative fair uses** — how do you say you repair Volkswagens without using the trademarked term "Volkswagen"?[76] But some marketers bid for rivals' keywords to divert their traffic. U.S. federal trademark laws protect a trademark against a "use in commerce", but courts are split over whether using a competitor's trademark as a keyword to trigger ads in search results is a "use in commerce" under the statute. Many district courts have found the sale of trademarked keywords to be a use under the **Lanham Act**[77] but others have not.[78] A federal court dismissed a case against Google by a computer repair firm over its practice of letting businesses purchase keyword ads to be displayed when users typed in a competitor's name, holding selling keyword advertising is not a trademark use in commerce.[79] Playboy lost a lawsuit to prevent Web portals Netscape and Excite from displaying hardcore sex ads in search results for its trademarked terms "Playboy" and "Playmate," but the Ninth Circuit reversed, ruling its trademarked terms should be protected even in searches that prompt pop-up ads.[80] The Second Circuit, however, took the opposite view, rejecting a trademark infringement claim based on pop-up ads.[81]

Utah enacted the **Trademark Protection Act**, which let firms register trademarks as "electronic registration marks" and prohibited use of trademarks registered under the Act to trigger online ads.[82] While questionable whether the Utah law could withstand a constitutional challenge, the act was subsequently amended to eliminate electronic registration, punitive damages, and state enforcement against advertisers using their competitors' marks (but it still allows civil suits).

Google has had limited success in this area domestically, and until 2010, had not fared well overseas. A French court ruled in 2004 Google's French subsidiary could not link competitors' ads to the trademarks of a European resort.[83] Google's subsidiary also failed in the Court of Appeals in Versailles to overturn a decision barring display of keyword ads next to search results for a French travel agent's trademarks.[84] However, after losing a similar keyword ad case against Louis Vuitton SA in France, Google prevailed on appeal to the European Court of Justice in Luxembourg, with a ruling it had respected trademark law by allowing advertisers to bid for keywords relating to third-party trademarks.[85] As a result, Google announced it would change its European search policy to allow advertisers to buy and use as keywords trademarked by others.

In April 2012, the Fourth Circuit overturned portions of a lower court's ruling, reinstating claims Google committed direct trademark infringement and diluted Rosetta Stone's brand by selling other companies' trademarks as sponsored links.[86] The three-judge panel wrote "A reasonable trier of fact could find that Google intended to cause confusion in that it acted with the knowledge that confusion was very likely to result from its use of the marks." The case was remanded with instructions the lower court reconsider when Google first appeared to dilute the trademark and whether it was "famous" at the time.[87]

A Florida district court required a defendant to use an infringing term as a negative keyword in any future keyword advertising it purchased.[88] ("*Negative keyword*" means instructing the search engine never to display the phrase in search results.) Orion Bancorp sued Orion Residential Finance (ORF) for infringement by using its trademarked word "Orion" as a keyword for financial services and products. Both firms offered housing finance services. The court ordered ORF to use "negative keywords" to avoid association with the plaintiff's trademark. The injunction prohibited ORF from:[89]

> [P]urchasing or using any form of advertising including keywords or 'adwords' in Internet advertising containing any mark incorporating Plaintiff's mark, or any confusingly similar mark, and shall, when purchasing Internet advertising using keywords, adwords or the like, require the activation of the term 'Orion' as negative keywords or negative adwords in any Internet advertising purchased or used.

U.S. law is unclear about the responsibility, if any, of search engines to police trademarks in paid searches. Google claims advertisers are responsible for keywords and ad text they use, but on request will perform a limited investigation. The law is also unclear about the responsibility, if any, of search engines to give trademark holders visibility in search results based on keywords related to their trademarked terms (*i.e.*, the term may appear as a buried link in a long list of results). Trademark owners seek to assert their rights to trademarked keyword ads because, as discussed in the previous chapter, by law they risk losing their trademarks if the terms become a part of the common usage and they cannot show they have tried to contest it. That happened to Sony in Austria, where it lost the right to its "Walkman" trademark in 1994. Sony had sued Austrian company Time Tron Corporation for describing its range of portable cassette players as Walkmans in a sales catalog, effectively using the trademarked term generically to mean any portable cassette player. The court found Sony had not taken sufficient steps to prevent the generic use of its trademark after failing to seek a retraction when it appeared listed as a noun in a 1994 German dictionary.[90] Of course, sometimes keyword advertising can backfire. An Associated Press wire story titled "Fatal Fire Caused by Candle, Official Says" describing how a Philadelphia firefighter was killed in a fire caused by "an unattended fragrance candle" automatically pulled up next to the article ads for fire department uniforms, and immediately below it an ad from a fragrance candle manufacturer, complete with a picture of one of its products, a lit candle. And when a TV station's site ran the headline "Man Gets 6 Months For Putting Urine In Co-Workers' Coffee" accompanying it was a generated keyword ad that read "Tempt Your Taste Buds With Our Recipes."

## Chapter 5 Notes

[1] Gary Kremen is also the founder of Match.com, the Internet's largest dating site.

[2] Cohen was captured by Mexican police in 2005 after six years as a fugitive and returned to America.

[3] *Kremen v. Cohen*, 337 F.3d 1024 (9th Cir. 2003). (Included in the Cases Section on the Issues in Internet Law site, www.IssuesinInternetLaw.com).

[4] *Kremen v. Cohen*, 99 F. Supp. 2d 1168 (N.D. Cal. 2000).

[5] *See* "MAP Research Releases Global Domain Registration Industry Report," Domainnews.com, January 21, 2009.

[6] Adam Goldman, "Internet Domains Snagging Huge Amounts of Money," Associated Press wire service report, July 16, 2007.

[7] The domain name sex.com sold in 2006 to Escom, LLC for an estimated $14 million. "Sex.com Sold," CNET News.com, January 19, 2006.

[8] Chris Irvine, "Top 10 Most Expensive Domain Names," The (U.K.) Telegraph, March 10, 2010. *See* "Domain Name Sold for Record Nearly $10 Million," DNJournal.com, March 12, 2008. In 2007, Porn.com sold for more than $9 million, and Beer.com, Business.com, and Diamond.com, all sold in excess of $7 million. *See also* Joseph Menn, "No Real Estate Slump Online," The Los Angeles Times, January 24, 2008.

[9] Adam Strong "First Ever Criminal Prosecution for Domain Name Theft Underway," DomainNameNews. com, *available at* www.domainnamenews.com/featured/criminal-prosecution-domain-theft-underway/5675 (accessed Mar. 23, 2012).

[10] Martin Fiutak, "Teenager Admits eBay Domain Hijack," CNET News.com, September 8, 2004. Many teens commit computer crimes, but their motivation is mostly "curiosity and a hunger for excitement rather than wanting to cause trouble," according to psychologist Shirley McGuire of the University of San Francisco, who surveyed 4,800 San Diego high school students. She reported only 10 percent said they committed computer crimes "to cause trouble or make money." *See* Marilyn Elias, "Most Teen Hackers More Curious Than Criminal," USA Today, August 19, 2007.

[11] John Blau, "Google.de Domain Gets Kidnapped," IDG News Service, January 23, 2007.

[12] Steven Musil, "ISP Suffers Apparent Domain Hijacking," CNET News.com, January 16, 2005.

[13] *See* Strong, fn. 9, *supra. See also*, "NJ Man Charged with Web Name Theft, Sale on eBay," Associated Press wire service report, August 3, 2009.

[14] *Shields v. Zuccarini*, 254 F.3d 476 (3d Cir. 2001).

[15] Leslie Walker and Brian Krebs, "The Web's Million-Dollar Typos," The Washington Post, p. F01 April 30, 2006.

[16] Brian Krebs, "Dell Takes Cybersquatters to Court," The Washington Post, November 28, 2007.

[17] Richard Cuthbertson, "Porn Re-router Fined $15,000," The Calgary Herald, June 24, 2008.

[18] John Zuccarini, discussed at fn. 21, *infra*. Associated Press wire service report, May 24, 2002.

[19] The PROTECT Act of 2003 (Pub. L. No. 108-21).

[20] The Truth in Domain Names Act, 18 U.S.C. § 2252(B).

[21] John Zuccarini, *see FTC v. Zuccarini*, Civil Action No. 01-cv-4854, (E.D. Pa. 2002).

[22] "Man Sentenced for Registering Misleading Web Site Names," USA Today, February 27, 2004.

[23] The Fraudulent Online Identity Sanctions Act (Title II of the Intellectual Property Protection and Courts Amendments Act of 2004), Pub. L. No. 108-482.

[24] The Anti-cybersquatting Consumer Protection Act, 15 U.S.C. § 1125(d).

[25] *Jack In The Box, Inc. v. Jackinthebox.org*, 143 F. Supp. 2d 590 (E.D. Va. 2001) holding the act of registering a domain name is sufficient to trigger the protection of the ACPA.

[26] *Taubman Co. v. Webfeats*, Case No. 01-72987 (E.D. Mich. 2001) (granting preliminary injunction), rev'd 319 F.3d 770 (6th Cir. 2003), holding, in part, merely discussing the sale of a domain name did not constitute bad faith under the ACPA where the discussions were initiated by the buying party.

[27] *Microsoft Corp. v. Shah*, Case No. C10-0653 (W.D. Wash. 2011) denying defendants' motion to dismiss claims for contributory cybersquatting and contributory dilution as unrecognized by law. If upheld, the decision may broaden the ACPA's scope to allow claims against those that facilitate cybersquatting or induce others to violate the Act.

[28] *Coca-Cola Co. v. Purdy*, 2002 U.S. Dist. LEXIS 13443 (D. Minn. 2002) (motion for preliminary injunction), aff'd 382 F.3d 774 (8th Cir. 2004).

[29] Catherine Rampell, "Firms Fight Back in Site Name Game; Web Domains, or Variations thereof, Can Define a Company or Product," The Washington Post, December 1, 2007, p. D01.

[30] *BroadBridge Media, LLC v. Hypercd.com*, 106 F. Supp. 2d 505 (S.D.N.Y. 2000).

[31] If the person's name is trademarked, then any attempt to mislead or confuse consumers would trigger the Anti-cybersquatting Consumer Protection Act, 15 U.S.C. § 1125(D)(1)(A). The Act protects "the owner of a mark, including a personal name which is protected as a mark." *Ibid.*

[32] Beth Lipton Krigel, "Archie Comics Fights Parent for Domain," CNET News.com, January 15, 1999.

[33] David Loundy and Blake Bell, "E-Law Updates: Domain Name Disputes (Big Company vs. Little Baby)," March 1999.

[34] Kieren McCarthy, "Dell Joins Domain Name Hall of Shame (Again)," The Register, January 26, 2005.

[35] *Ibid.*

[36] Katie Jones site, *was available at* www.katie.com (accessed Sept. 25, 2007); but the URL had become a parked page filled with pay-per-click ads when accessed on Aug. 5, 2008, a porn site when accessed on Jul. 1, 2009, and an adolescent girl's fashion site when accessed on Mar. 23, 2012.

[37] Uzi Nissan site, "The Story", *available at* www.ncchelp.org/The_Story/the_story.htm (accessed Mar. 23, 2012).

[38] Nissan attorney Leland Dutcher claimed in 1994 "there wasn't an understanding of the power of the Internet as a marketing tool" but five years later the company "became concerned that a very large number of [customers] were going looking for us at a Web site at nissan.com that we didn't have," Stephen Cass, Spectrum Careers site, "Nissan v. Nissan", *was available at* www.spectrum.ieee.org/careers/careerstemplate. jsp?ArticleId=i100302 (accessed Aug. 5, 2008) but no longer available. This raises the interesting question of whether a corporation not sharp enough to register its own name as a URL deserves the right to usurp the name from a more prescient registrant bearing the same name. Taken at face value, Dutcher's comments would appear to suggest Nissan Motor Co.'s admitted shortsightedness and lack of vision justify a court ordering the transfer of the domain name to it.

[39] Nissan Motor Co. first registered its trademark in the U.S. in 1959. *Nissan Motor Co., Ltd. v. Nissan Computer Corp.*, 89 F. Supp. 2d 1154 (C.D. Cal. 2000), aff'd 246 F.3d 675 (9th Cir. 2000); 204 F.R.D. 460 (C.D. Cal. 2001) (defendant's motion for leave to add counterclaims denied); 2002 U.S. Dist. LEXIS 6365 (C.D. Cal. 2002) (plaintiff's motion for partial summary judgment granted); 61 U.S.P.Q.2d 183 (C.D. Cal. 2002) (defendant's motion for partial summary judgment granted); 231 F. Supp. 2d 977 (C.D. Cal. 2002) (plaintiff's motion for permanent injunction granted), aff'd in part, rev'd in part 378 F.3d 1002 (9th Cir. 2004). Although the Nissan trademark was not used in the United States until 1983; before that, Nissan Motor Co. marketed its cars under the Datsun brand name. (Uzi Nissan's name was first registered on his birth certificate in 1951), Uzi Nissan site, fn. 37, *supra.*

[40] *Nissan Motor Co.*, fn. 39, *supra.* The district court in California admitted the defendant was not located in, and did not sell any products or services in, California but nonetheless found jurisdiction based on the fact the defendant placed advertising on his site through contracts with five California-based companies — Asimba, Inc., Ask Jeeves, Inc., CNET, Inc., GoTo.com, Inc., and RemarQ Communities, Inc.

[41] *Ibid.*

[42] *Ibid.*

[43] *Nissan Motor Co., Ltd. v. Nissan Computer Corp.*, 378 F.3d 1002 (9th Cir. 2004).

[44] The Lanham Act, 15 U.S.C. § 1052(c).

[45] The Anti-cybersquatting Consumer Protection Act, 15 U.S.C. § 1125(D)(1)(A) protects "the owner of a mark, including a personal name which is protected as a mark." However a separate section of the Act also protects personal names of individuals. ACPA § 1129 "Cyberpiracy Protections for Individuals" provides civil liability for:

> Any person who registers a domain name that consists of the name of another living person, or a name substantially and confusingly similar thereto, without that person's consent, with the specific intent to profit from such name by selling the domain name for financial gain to that person or any third party, shall be liable in a civil action by such person.

Section 1129 does not require the personal name be trademarked to be protected; however it does require a specific intent to profit from the name's sale. *See Schmidheiny v. Weber*, 319 F.3d 581 (3d Cir. 2003), where a cybersquatter purchased Schmidheiny.com and attempted to resell the name to Stephan Schmidheiny, named by *Forbes Magazine* as one of the world's wealthiest individuals with a net worth of $3.1 billion. The court ruled the ACPA could be applied retroactively, even though the domain name was registered prior to enactment of the statute.

[46] *Ficker v. Tuohy*, 305 F. Supp. 2d 569 (D. Md. 2004). (Included in the Cases Section on the Issues in Internet Law site, www.IssuesinInternetLaw.com). *See also* "Forrest Claypool Launches JoeBerrios.com, Slams Opponent's Record in Assessor's Race," The Huffington Post, August 17, 2010, detailing how the independent candidate for assessor launched JoeBerrios.com, a Web site with the name of his Democratic opponent, displaying as cloud tags "clout, corruption, pay-to-play, and FBI investigation".

[47] *Ibid.*

[48] *Time, Inc. v. Firestone*, 424 U.S. 448 (1976).

[49] *New York Times Co. v. Sullivan*, 376 U.S. 254 (1964).

[50] *Ficker*, 305 F. Supp. 2d 569.

[51] The **right of publicity** is a common law right, the applicability of which varies from state to state. See the discussion in Chapter 12.

[52] MySpace is a social network and a "friend" is one who joins the user's social network.

[53] Micah L. Sifry, "The Battle to Control Obama's MySpace," TechPresident.com, May 1, 2007. Contrast the Obama situation with the way CNN gained control of the URL Twitter.com/CNNBrk from a CNN fan who had managed to get 1.5 million followers on his Twitter account: rather than accept Twitter's offer simply to take the name from the fan, CNN hired the fan as a consultant to train its staff in the use of Twitter. That way, CNN achieved its aim without the negative publicity attached with tearing away the account from a diehard fan. *See* Julia Angwin, "Who Owns Your Name on Twitter?" The Wall Street Journal, May 19, 2009.

[54] *Ibid.*

[55] The Anti-cybersquatting Consumer Protection Act, 15 U.S.C. § 1129.

[56] *Ficker*, 305 F. Supp. 2d 569.

[57] Playtex site, *available at* www.playtex.com (accessed Mar. 23, 2012).

[58] Pez site, *available at* www.pez.com (accessed July 23, 2010) but no longer a split site as of Feb. 3, 2012.

[59] Scrabble site, *available at* www.scrabble.com (accessed Mar. 23, 2012).

[60] Internet Corporation For Assigned Names and Numbers, *available at* www.icann.org (accessed Mar. 23, 2012).

[61] Sheri Qualters, "Arbitration is Weapon of Choice in Growing Number of Domain Name Disputes," National Law Journal, October 9, 2006.

[62] *Available at* www.icann.org/udrp/approved-providers.htm (accessed Mar. 23, 2012).

[63] Qualters, fn. 61, *supra.*

[64] *William J. Clinton & The William J. Clinton Presidential Found. v. Web of Deception*, Claim No. FA0904001256123 (Jun. 2009).

[65] *Ibid.* "Reluctantly, the Panelist concludes that President Clinton has established a common law mark in his name. President Clinton's best-selling books are probably enough to qualify his personal name as a common law mark. A finding that a common law mark exists that the first element of the UDRP has been established."

[66] *Web of Deception*, fn. 64, *supra.*

[67] Mark Sweney, "MySpace Wins Domain Name Fight," The Guardian, January 31, 2008.

[68] *New Kids on the Block, Inc. v. News Am., Inc., d/b/a USA Today, Inc.*, 971 F.2d 302, 306 (9th Cir. 1992).

[69] *Horphag v. Pellegrini*, 337 F.3d 1036 (9th Cir. 2003).

[70] *Niton Corp. v. Radiation Monitoring Devices, Inc.*, 27 F. Supp. 2d 102, 105 (D. Mass. 1998).

[71] *Niton Corp.* at 104.

[72] *Playboy Enters., Inc. v. Welles*, 7 F. Supp. 2d 1098 (S.D. Cal. 1998)(preliminary injunction), aff'd 162 F.3d 1169 (9th Cir. 1998); 78 F. Supp. 2d 1066 (S.D. Cal. 1999) (summary judgment), aff'd in part, rev'd in part 279 F.3d 796 (9th Cir. 2002), aff'd 30 Fed. Appx. 734 (9th Cir. 2002).

[73] In a similar case, Half Price Books sued BarnesandNoble.com in November 2002, claiming it infringed and diluted its trademark by advertising sale books in a subtitle "Half-Price Books & Special Values" on a menu tab. Following the rationale of Welles, this might be considered a permissible truthful description by a competitor of the price of their books, or the use of a generic term. However, on a motion for summary judgment, the court ruled against BarnesandNoble.com, allowing the case to go forward, concluding because the defendant's display of the phrase "was sufficiently prominent to suggest . . . an affiliation between [the parties]," there was sufficient evidence from which a reasonable jury could find in favor of plaintiff. *Half Price Books, Records, Magazines, Inc. v. BarnesandNoble.com, LLC*, 2004 U.S. Dist. LEXIS 223691 (N.D. Tex. Nov. 22, 2004).

[74] *Bijur Lubricating Corp. v. Devco Corp.*, 332 F. Supp. 2d 722 (D.N.J. 2004).

[75] Stefanie Olsen, "Google Loses Trademark Dispute in France," CNET News.com, January 20, 2005.

[76] In *Volkswagenwerk Aktiengesellschaft v. Church*, 411 F.2d 350, 352 (9th Cir. 1969), the Ninth Circuit held the defendant could advertise he repaired Volkswagen vehicles as long as he did not do so in a manner "likely to suggest to his prospective customers that he is part of Volkswagen's organization of franchised

dealers and repairmen." Likewise, in *Bijur Lubricating Corp.* 332 F. Supp. 2d 722, the court held replacement parts seller Devco's placement of Bijur's trademarked name in its meta tags did not constitute infringement or dilution in violation of the **Lanham Act** but was nominative fair use because it could not identify the replacement part without using the mark. *See also Toyota Motor Sales v. Tabari*, No. 07-55344 (9th Cir. Jul. 8, 2010) holding an automobile brokerage firm's use of the string "lexus" in domain names "buy-a-lexus.com" and "buyorleaselexus.com" under which he operated was **nominative fair use**.

[77] *Buying for the Home, LLC v. Humble Abode, LLC*, 459 F. Supp. 2d 310 (D.N.J. 2006), where a New Jersey court denied a motion for summary judgment holding search engine keyword-triggered advertising had satisfied the "use" requirement of the **Lanham Act**. *See also Gov't Emples. Ins. Co. v. Google, Inc.*, 330 F. Supp. 2d 700 (E.D. Va. 2004); *800-JR Cigar, Inc. v. Goto.com, Inc.*, 437 F. Supp. 2d 273 (D. N.J. 2006); *Edina Realty, Inc. v. TheMLSonline.com*, 80 U.S.P.Q.2D (BNA) 1039 (D. Minn. 2006); *Google, Inc. v. Am. Blind & Wallpaper Factory, Inc.*, 2005 WL 832398 (N.D. Cal. 2005).

[78] *Rescuecom Corp. v. Google, Inc.*, 456 F. Supp. 2d 393 (N.D.N.Y. 2006); *Merck & Co. v. Mediplan Health Consulting, Inc.*, 431 F. Supp. 2d 425 (S.D.N.Y. 2006). As district court holdings, they do not set binding precedents, but other courts may be persuaded by the reasoning and agree search engines do not infringing on trademarks by selling keyword advertising. Ironically, Rescuecom dropped its appeal of the decision dismissing its suit over Google's keyword-based ad practice, as it was simultaneously engaged in a similar lawsuit, this time as a defendant, accused by Best Buy of using its trademarked phrase "geek squad" in keyword ads. In its defense, Rescuecom argued inconsistently such use was "an appropriate use of another company's trademarks in comparative advertising." *See* Tom Krazit, "Rescuecom Drops Trademark Suit against Google," CNET News.com, March 5, 2010.

[79] *Rescuecom Corp.*, 456 F. Supp. 2d 393

[80] *Playboy Enters., Inc. v. Netscape Commc'ns Inc.*, 55 F. Supp. 2d 1070 (C.D. Cal. 1999) (plaintiff's motion for preliminary injunction), aff'd 202 F.3d 278 (9th Cir. 1999), 2000 U.S. Dist. LEXIS 13418 (C.D. Cal. 2000) (defendants' motions for summary judgment), rev'd 354 F.3d 1020 (9th Cir. 2004). The Second Circuit, however, took the opposite view, rejecting a trademark infringement claim based on pop-up ads.

[81] *1-800 Contacts, Inc. v. WhenU.Com, Inc.*, 414 F.3d 400, 408-09 (2d Cir. 2005), cert. denied, 546 U.S. 1033 (2005).

[82] The (Utah) Trademark Protection Act (SB 236, Chapter Law 365) (2007).

[83] "Google Loses French AdWords Case," Outlaw.com, January 24, 2005. Google stated it would appeal.

[84] Peter Sayer, IDG News Service, "Google France Loses Appeal in AdWords Trademark Dispute," PCWorld.com, March 18, 2005.

[85] *See* Eric Pfanner, "E.U. Court Curbs Sales by Google of Brand Names as Keywords," The New York Times, March 23, 2010, *and* Matthew Saltmarsh, "Google Will Sell Brand Names as Keywords in Europe," The New York Times, August 4, 2010. The case was appealed from *SARL Google, Sté Google Inc. c/ SA Louis Vuitton Malletier*, No. 05/06968 (Cour D'Appel de Paris Jun. 28, 2006).

[86] *Rosetta Stone Ltd. v. Google Inc.*, Case No. 10-2007 (4th Cir. 2011).

[87] Terry Baynes, "Court Revives Rosetta Stone Suit vs Google," Reuters wire service report, April 9, 2012.

[88] *Orion Bancorp, Inc. v. Orion Residential Fin., LLC*, 2008 WL 816794, 2008 U.S. Dist. LEXIS 32483 (M.D. Fla. Mar. 25, 2008).

[89] *Ibid.*

[90] *Sony Europe v. Time Tron Corp.* (Austrian Supreme Court 1994).

# CHAPTER

# 6

———

# Cybercrimes

> This chapter discusses cybercimes, focusing on spam, anti-spam laws including the CAN-SPAM Act, identity theft through social engineering, e-mail spoofing, phishing, pharming, cookie poisoning, spyware, drive-by downloads, malware, wardriving, piggybacking, telecommunications theft, scams, and cyberstalking.

*"Crooks are early adopters."* — *Craig Newmark*

## Spam

*"In view of the more or less humorous takeoffs such as these, one might think Hormel would welcome the association with a genuine source of pork."*
— *Judge Ellsworth Van Graafeiland, Hormel Foods Corp. v. Jim Henson Prods., Inc.*

SPAM, NOT TO BE confused with the Hormel product, is *unsolicited e-mail*, usually fraudulent business schemes, chain letters, political, or offensive sexual messages. Most Internet users consider spam a major annoyance. It clogs e-mail boxes forcing them to waste time sorting legitimate from junk e-mail: in 2011, spam accounted for 19 percent of corporate e-mail received.[1] Spammers risk a potential *negative backlash* from consumers subjected to their mass e-mail campaigns, as the act of spamming might alienate a prospective customer. Why, then, do spammers spam? Simply, because it works. Spam is a cheap, highly effective marketing method. Marketing is a numbers game and spam allows a spammer to reach huge numbers at minimal cost. If a fraction respond favorably, the spammer will have made back the mass mailing's cost many times over his initial investment. In 2011, every dollar invested in e-mail marketing returned an estimated $44.25.[2] Twenty percent of U.S. residents say they buy products from spammers, according to a 'Yahoo! Mail' survey.[3] As some consumers welcomes spam, it is proliferating, congesting blogs, mobile phones, and instant messages. Spam is estimated to account for 80-to-90 percent of all U.S. e-mail[4] and 71 percent of e-mail worldwide.[5]

## Where Does Spam Come From?

It seems you have more e-mail from spammers than friends filling your mailbox each day, but how did they learn your e-mail address? They may *buy* it — 1.5 million e-mail addresses cost less than $15. Or they may get it using "*harvesters*" — software programs that pluck e-mail addresses from Web sites and newsgroups. Not only do spammers clog e-mail accounts with unsolicited mass mailings, they have also turned to instant messages, pop-up ads, blogs, site guestbooks, and social networks. But there are some steps you can take to limit your exposure.

## Streetwise Tips to Avoid Spam

- *"NOBODY'S HOME!"* **Never Reply to Spam!**

They promise to remove your name from their list if you reply to their e-mail, but they are lying! What spammers want is to confirm they have a valid e-mail address. By replying, you are telling them that; you will have made your e-mail address more valuable to the spammer, who will sell it to other spammers, leading you to be inundated with more spam. Replying to spam is the technological equivalent of the hobo mark of old. [6]

- *"NO SHOUT-OUTS!"* **Never Post Your E-mail Address on Your Web site!**

By posting your e-mail address on your home page, you are rolling out the welcome mat to spammers eager to use software to "harvest" e-mail addresses from Web sites. This software crawls through the Internet looking for text strings resembling "you@yoursite.com." Once found, your address joins thousands harvested in the spammer's database. An alternative to posting your e-mail address on your site is to use a query form instead of an e-mail link — visitors can message you without your e-mail address being displayed. This approach will only work on your own site, so you still need to use discretion when posting your e-mail on a third-party's site, such as on a guest book or blog. Also, check to see who else may be posting your e-mail address online (*e.g.*, do a Google search for you own e-mail address). Check the organizations to which you belong; opt-out of member directories that place e-mail addresses on their site.

- *"'ANONY MOUSE' IS IN THE HOUSE"* **Use an Alias E-mail Address in Newsgroups!**

Newsgroups are an e-mail address gold mine for spammers, since most display the poster's e-mail address on each message as well as in the message header. If you post to a newsgroup, you are going to get spam. Most newsgroup-related spam is sent to the address in the message header, even if other e-mail addresses are included in the post's text. You can participate in newsgroup discussions without being subjected to a flood of spam by using a different e-mail address from the one normally used for friends or business. Create a "public" address for newsgroups and a "private" one for friends or business (similar to having an unlisted phone number). You can set up a free Hotmail or Gmail e-mail address just for use on newsgroups.

- *"WHAT YOU TALKIN' 'BOUT, WILLIS?"* **Never Give Your E-mail Address Unless You Know How It Will Be Used!**

If a site requests your e-mail address, then it obviously wants to use it for some purpose; find out why. Read the site's "Terms of Use" and "privacy statement" before supplying your e-mail address. Ask if they plan to share or sell it.

- *"TALK TO THE HAND!"* **Use a Spam Filter!**

While there is no such thing as a perfect spam filter, e-mail filtering software can keep spam at a manageable level and reduce risk of exposure to e-mail viruses. Spam filters are available both from ISPs and commercial software companies.

- *"DO NOT FEED THE BEARS"* **Never Buy Anything Advertised in Spam!**

There is a reason parks have signs reading "Do Not Feed the Bears!" If you feed them once, they will keep coming back. Do not encourage spammers. The reason marketers spam is because they make money convincing people to buy a product. If no one buys products advertised in spam, then there will be no benefit for companies to spam. In short, do not reward spammers.

## The CAN-SPAM Act

The **CAN-SPAM Act of 2003** (Controlling Assault of Non-Solicited Pornography and Marketing Act) preempted more than 30 state laws and brought uniformity to the legal effort to fight spam.[7] But the Act is less restrictive than some state laws and, because of First Amendment free speech concerns, *does not ban sending spam*. It does not preempt state laws that prohibit "falsity and deception" in commercial e-mails, and states may retain certain portions of existing anti-spam laws, or enact new laws.

The **CAN-SPAM Act**:
- Requires accurate headers in e-mails — a valid return address must be used to deter "spoofing"
- Prohibits misleading subject headings in e-mails
- Requires a functioning return e-mail address that remains active for at least 30 days
- Requires opt-out procedures for recipients to unsubscribe from future e-mails
- Requires clear notice of the opt-out provision
- Requires the spammer comply with any opt-out request received after 10 days
- Requires clear labeling of commercial e-mail as an advertisement or solicitation
- Requires listing the sender's valid physical postal address within the e-mail
- Prohibits e-mail address harvesting
- Requires warning labels on commercial electronic mail containing sexually oriented material

The Act is enforced by the FTC, state attorneys general, and ISPs — it does not create a private right of action for individuals to sue spammers for violations. In 2004, the U.S. Department of Justice charged four Illinois men under the Act, and Massachusetts used it to charge a Florida man suspected of spamming thousands of consumers.[8] In 2005, a timeshare spammer was sentenced to a year in prison under the Act.[9] The first trial conviction under the Act came in 2007, when a California man was convicted of misrepresenting himself as the AOL billing department in e-mails to thousands of AOL subscribers and requesting their credit card information.[10] (This kind of "phishing" attempt is discussed in detail later in this chapter). A New York teenager gained the dubious distinction of the first conviction under the **CAN-SPAM Act** for sending spam through instant messaging (known as *"spim"*). Not only did the teen spam the MySpace IM system with 1.5 million messages, but he allegedly attempted a not-so-brilliant extortion scheme, threatening the social network with further spim attacks unless it hired him as a consultant; he was arrested by police and U.S. Secret Service officials while enroute to his arranged meeting with MySpace executives.[11]

Social Networks have aggressively pursued spammers. MySpace won $234 million against a defendant under the **CAN-SPAM Act**, whom it claimed sent 735,925 messages to its members.[12] It also received an arbitration award against Media Breakaway for $4.8 million in damages and $1.2 million in legal fees.[13] Facebook won the largest judgment to date under the **CAN-SPAM Act**: $873 million in 2008 against Adam Guerbuez, of Montreal, and his company, Atlantis Blue Capital for luring members to phishing sites to steal their logins and passwords, which he then used to send four million fake messages from members' profiles.[14] Spammers target social networks because members are more likely to look at the spam if they believe it is a message from a friend. Although Facebook won the largest judgment yet under the Act, the largest penalty paid for violating the **CAN-SPAM Act** was a $900,000 civil penalty pursuant to a consent decree entered into between the FTC and Internet marketer Jumpstart Technologies, LLC.[15]

One federal court ruled while the **CAN-SPAM Act** does not impose strict liability for violations by agents of an entity, it does impose vicarious liability if the entity had knowledge of the violation and control over its agents.[16] An online pornographic firm hired affiliates to promote its site. The affiliates spammed in violation of the **CAN-SPAM Act** and the FTC sought to hold the company strictly liable for the affiliates' actions. The court ruled the Act did not impose a strict liability standard, but if it were found the company knew its affiliates were violating the Act and had failed to exercise sufficient control over them, then it could be vicariously liable.[17]

The Act does not outlaw spamming and one spammer actually argued compliance with it should prevent an organization from blocking its spam. White Buffalo Ventures set up a dating site, LonghornSingles.com, and targeted University of Texas students by obtaining their e-mail addresses through a Freedom of Information request. The school responded by blocking the site's IP address. White Buffalo Ventures sued, charging the university was violating its First Amendment rights and the **CAN-SPAM Act** precluded the blocking.[18] A Texas federal court disagreed and a Fifth Circuit three-judge panel upheld that decision, adding the **CAN-SPAM Act** was not intended to prevent ISPs from filtering out spam. The U.S. Supreme Court declined an appeal.[19]

The latest trend for spammers is to send image-based spam in an attempt to slip past the spam filters. Most image spam is used in "pump and dump" stock-scam e-mails touting a stock to raise its value, so the spammer can then quickly sell it at a profit.[20] While the **CAN-SPAM Act** appears to have had limited effect against the onslaught of spam, and there have been no other federal anti-spam laws passed yet, various state anti-spam laws do exist.

## State Spam Laws

Since e-mails travel across state lines, in drafting anti-spam laws the question invariably arises: Is the spammer subject to the laws of the state from which the spam was sent, or to the laws of every state in which it was received? Presumably, states would choose the second view, since each drafts its laws with the intent of protecting its own citizens. But to accept the latter view would mean for every e-mail address in his possession, a spammer would need to know the geographic location of each recipient. Alternatively, the spammer would need to determine if his e-mail campaign violated *any* state's laws, *i.e.*, a least common denominator approach, targeting his campaign to the most restrictive states' laws. Such confusion has led some courts to hold laws based on that view unenforceable.

Many states require a label at the beginning of the subject line of certain types of unsolicited commercial e-mail messages.[21] Alaska, Arkansas, Arizona, Colorado, Connecticut, Illinois, Indiana, Kansas, Louisiana, Maine, Michigan, Missouri, Nevada, New Mexico, Oklahoma,

Oregon, South Dakota, Tennessee, Texas, and Wisconsin require that the unsolicited e-mails contain a label ("ADV:") in the subject line and an opt-out mechanism in the body. California and Delaware have an *opt-in rule* for e-mail advertising, where the recipient must have agreed in advance to receive the e-mail, *e.g.*, by signing up for an e-mail list. States that require unsolicited bulk commercial e-mails include an e-mail address for opt-out requests and senders honor such requests: Arizona, Arkansas, Colorado, Connecticut, Idaho, Illinois, Indiana, Iowa, Kansas, Louisiana, Maine, Michigan, Missouri, Nevada, New Mexico, North Dakota, Ohio, Oklahoma, Pennsylvania, Rhode Island, Tennessee, and Texas.

States making it illegal to send unsolicited bulk e-mail containing falsified routing information are: Arkansas, Arizona, Colorado, Connecticut, Delaware, Florida, Georgia, Idaho, Illinois, Indiana, Iowa, Kansas, Louisiana, Maine, Maryland, Michigan, Nevada, North Carolina, Ohio, Oklahoma, Oregon, Pennsylvania, Rhode Island, South Dakota, Tennessee, Texas, Virginia, Washington, West Virginia, and Wyoming.

Three states (through their state bar associations) have regulated unsolicited e-mails from attorneys. A Florida Bar rule requires attorneys who advertise via unsolicited e-mail place "legal advertisement" in the subject line. [22] Kentucky requires attorneys who advertise via written, recorded, or electronic communication targeted at potential clients to include in upper case "THIS IS AN ADVERTISEMENT" prominently in each communication. [23] Louisiana requires attorneys who advertise via unsolicited e-mail targeted at potential clients to use a subject line that states "This is an advertisement for legal services." [24]

Alabama, Hawaii, Kentucky, Massachusetts, Mississippi, Montana, Nebraska, New Hampshire, New Jersey, New York, South Carolina, and Vermont have not enacted anti-spam laws. Minnesota and North Dakota's spam laws expired when the **CAN-SPAM Act** passed. Utah repealed its law.

Virginia had the toughest anti-spam law in the country. In 2003, the statute was used to indict two North Carolina men, the first individuals in the U.S. charged with felonies for spamming. [25] One was sentenced to nine years imprisonment. Five months later, his sister was indicted for violating Virginia's anti-spam laws, as was a Texan in 2004. Each charge carried a prison sentence of one–to–five years and a fine of up to $2,500. The Virginia statute targeted spammers who intentionally alter an e-mail header or other routing information and try to send either 10,000 e-mails within a 24-hour period or 100,000 in a 30-day period. [26] A spammer could also be prosecuted under the statute if a specific transmission generated more than $1,000 in revenue or total transmissions generated $50,000. [27] However, in 2008, the Virginia Supreme Court declared the state's anti-spam statute unconstitutional because it applied to all anonymous transmission of unsolicited bulk e-mail, without exceptions for political, religious, or other noncommercial speech protected by the First Amendment. [28] The state court decision invalidating Virginia's **Computer Crimes Act** [29] had no effect on the federal **CAN-SPAM Act**, which still regulates transmission of spam in Virginia and other states.

## Foreign Spam Laws

Some countries have *"opt-in" laws* forbidding unsolicited e-mail unless the recipients have previously indicated a willingness to receive it. Of course, the question remains, 'How would a foreign country *enforce* that law against an American spammer?'

## Using Existing U.S. Laws to Fight Spam

As discussed at the beginning of this chapter, spammers risk negative feedback from unhappy recipients of their unsolicited e-mails. They may be willing to send a million e-mails at once, but they do not want to receive a million complaints in their e-mail in-box the next morning. Therefore, most spammers use false headers to avoid negative feedback following a large scale unsolicited e-mailing. *Trademark and unfair competition laws* have been used against spammers who identify their messages as coming from someone else. The FTC has promulgated stringent truth in advertising laws that apply to e-mail marketing, so spam containing misleading or false statements can subject the spammer to purview of the FTC.

Most states have existing laws that can be adapted to fight spam. For example, a federal court in Iowa awarded an ISP more than a billion dollars against a spammer, using the Iowa **Ongoing Criminal Conduct Act** in combination with the federal **Racketeer Influenced and Corrupt Organizations Act** (RICO) that allows for treble damages.[30]

Sometimes, there may be both criminal and civil remedies to spam. A defendant accused by Earthlink, a major ISP, of using 343 e-mail accounts to send 825 million spam messages for products like herbal sexual stimulants was sentenced to three years in prison.[31] In a separate civil case, Earthlink won a $16 million judgment against the same spammer.[32] ISPs fight spam by expressly prohibiting users from spamming in their *Terms of Use* agreements and by offering free spam-blocking tools. Commercial spam-blocking tools are also available from software retailers. Lawsuits are one unique anti-spam weapon. In at least two cases, spam recipients have sued a product's manufacturer for failing to live up to its advertised claims. A New Jersey man sued a Florida company for false advertising, alleging its herbal penis enlargement pills did not work.[33] In response to an unsolicited e-mail, a California man paid Leading Edge Marketing $160 for its "VigRx Oil." When the penis enlargement herbal supplements failed to work, he sued the British Colombian company for fraud, theft, and money-laundering.[34]

## The Computer Fraud and Abuse Act

The **Computer Fraud and Abuse Act** criminalizes knowingly accessing a computer without authorization or in excess of authorization.[35] It has been used to fight spammers who access a plaintiff's computer system without authorization to obtain e-mail addresses for spamming.[36]

## Murking

A *Murkogram* is spam that includes a *disclaimer* stating the message cannot be considered spam because it is in compliance with Bill S.1618 Title III, known as the Inbox Privacy Act.[37] That alone should be a tip-off, as the astute reader knows, only statutes, *i.e.*, laws enacted by the legislature, have the force of law; *bills* are merely proposed laws that only become law when passed by the legislature (state legislature or Congress) and signed into law by the chief executive (governor or president). In 1999, U.S. Sen. Frank Murkowski, for whom the Murkogram is dubiously named, proposed a law requiring spam include the sender's correct name, physical address, IP address, phone number, and an option for recipients to remove themselves from the sender's list (an opt-out option). The proposal was not enacted because of ISP's objections the requirements would be too burdensome. But many spammers cite the proposed law as a way of legitimizing their spam. A typical boilerplate statement in the spam suggests (1) though not requested, it is in conformity with the (nonexistent) law since it identified the sender, and (2) the recipient had no grounds for legal action against the sender. Such spammers are said to be "Murking."

## Mail Bombs

Every e-mail account is allocated a certain amount of disk space on an ISP's server. Disk space is a finite, limited resource that must be shared among all accounts on a server. A huge amount of mail could fill recipient's allocated space or overwhelm the server, causing it to stop functioning. A *mail bomb* is a massive amount of e-mail sent to a specific person or computer network with the intention of disrupting service to all mail server customers. Mail bombs are a form of denial of service attack. Internet users who have been spammed or flamed (*i.e.*, publicly attacked) in a newsgroup often retaliate with mail bombs, although the practice is illegal.

## Permission-based Marketing

Not all bulk e-mail is spam. Only *unsolicited* bulk e-mail is considered spam. Some is permission-based, meaning a recipient has asked to receive it. This occurs when a Web site visitor agrees to receive a newsletter or other e-mail, known as "opt-in e-mail."

# Social Engineering And Identity Theft

*"I don't need to worry about identity theft because no one wants to be me." — Jay London*

Savvy cybercrooks have developed both high-tech and low-tech social engineering techniques to capture passwords and personally identifiable information about users that can be used to steal their identities. Identity theft is one of the major crimes of the Information Age.

## E-mail Spoofing

*E-mail spoofing* is forgery of an e-mail header so the message looks like it came from someone other than the sender. Spammers spoof with the hope the recipient will open the e-mail and possibly respond, while hiding their own e-mail address to avoid a negative backlash. An unscrupulous spammer could send a spoofed e-mail that appears to be from someone else with a message that person did not write. E-mail spoofing is illegal under the **CAN-SPAM Act**. Spammers spoof to:
- Avoid identification and subsequent liability under anti-spam laws
- Hide their true identity because the e-mail content violates state or federal law (*e.g.,* obscenity, child pornography, offers of prostitution or illegal drugs, threats, or harassment)
- Trick the recipient into opening an e-mail appearing to come from a known sender to infect the recipient's computer with a virus or Trojan horse [38]
- Initiate a phishing attempt
- Initiate a "*social engineering*" attack to trick the recipient into divulging confidential information (*e.g.,* a spoofed e-mail claiming to be from one in a position of authority, seeking passwords, credit card numbers, or other personal information — any of which can then be used for a variety of criminal purposes.

## Phishing

*Phishing* (pronounced "fishing") is an online scam in which unsuspecting users receive official-looking e-mails to trick them into revealing passwords, user names, and personal information. A victim is tricked into clicking a link that leads to a "spoofed" (*i.e.*, fake) version of the real organization's site. She is then tricked into revealing account numbers, credit card numbers, Social Security numbers, and passwords. (Such pagejacking,[39] where the fake page is set up to procure a victim's personal information, is also discussed in Chapter 5). One form of pagejacking modifies a victim's browser by replacing the address bar with a Java applet allowing the scammer to divert the victim to any site but still show the true organization's URL in the browser address line, so when the user clicks the phishing e-mail link, he is taken to a phony site that looks authentic.[40] Phishing (an allusion to fishing for information) is a form of *social engineering* to trick the recipient into revealing confidential information. The unfortunate effect is it undermines consumer confidence in Web-based transactions. Even if a familiar site (*e.g.*, one's bank or credit card company) e-mails the recipient claiming he needs to verify or update account information, he should go directly to their site and then verify it, not click the e-mailed link. Reputable financial institutions will not ask customers to update confidential information through e-mail. If the e-mail has a phone number, he should contact the institution first to ensure the listed phone number is legitimate and not a direct line to an identity thief. The latest browser versions of Internet Explorer, Firefox, Google Chrome, and Opera all have anti-phishing software offering some protection by alerting users to suspicious sites that might be spoofed phishing sites.

According to one e-mail security firm, the number of "phishing" e-mails increased from 279 to 215,643 over a six-month period in 2004.[41] By 2007, it was estimated there were 6.1 billion daily phishing attacks.[42] Phishing cost Americans $3.2 billion in 2007.[43] Phishing e-mails often claim to be from trusted sources, such as eBay, PayPal, banks, and even the IRS. Can you tell the difference between a legitimate e-mail and a phishing scam? Take an online phishing quiz at: www.sonicwall.com/phishing.

*Personalized phishing* is a targeted variation where the victim gets an e-mail personalized with accurate account information previously obtained by the phisher from misappropriated consumer data. Addressing the victim by name, the phisher asks for more personal information, which he plans to sell to other identity thieves at a premium.

*Spear-phishing*, a more targeted variation, occurs when the phisher poses as a high-level executive in the targeted corporation and demands confidential information from an employee. With the obtained passwords, he can install Trojan horses or other malware to access company data. Spear-phishers are normally not random hackers but sophisticated criminals seeking financial gain, or military or trade secrets.[44] In one spear phishing attack, executives received e-mails purportedly from a federal district court, each with his name, company and phone number, commanding him to appear before a grand jury, with a link to a "subpoena". Clicking it installed a keystroke logger on the victim's computer.[45] When spear-phishers go after big fish like top executives they refer to it as "*whaling*."[46] Other spear-phishing e-mails claim to come from the FBI or the IRS, insisting the victim click a link to view a complaint filed against his company, Spear-phishing has been particularly effective in military settings, where soldiers are trained to follow orders without questions. Consider the U.S. Military Academy at West Point, N.Y., where 500 cadets received an e-mail from

Col. Robert Melville informing them of a grading error and ordering them to click a link to correct their grades. More than 80 percent clicked the link, as ordered. But there was no such officer as Col. Robert Melville; he was an invention of an National Security Agency computer security analyst offering the cadets a real-life training exercise in spear-phishing. [47]

In a more recent and egregious whaling incident, Thomas Ryan, co-founder and managing partner of cyber operations and threat intelligence for Provide Security, devised a social engineering experiment in 2010, targeting the military industrial complex. [48] He set up a fake profile on Facebook, Twitter, and LinkedIn for "Robin Sage" a woman in her twenties, who supposedly worked for the Naval Network Warfare Command. In the course of the 28-day experiment, "Robin" amassed 300 LinkedIn connections, 110 Facebook friends, and 141 Twitter followers. Her "friends" included individuals in the Joint Chiefs of Staff, the CIO of the National Security Agency, a U.S. Marines intelligence director, a U.S. House of Representatives chief of staff, and several Pentagon and Defense Department employees. An Army Ranger uploaded photos from the field in Afghanistan with Geo-IP data from his camera in them, inadvertently revealing his classified location to "Robin". Robin's profile and sexy photo caught the eye of several defense contractors as well, reportedly Lockheed Martin, Northrop Grumman, and Booz Allen Hamilton. Lockheed was cited as one of several firms that offered "Robin" a job; others invited her to dinner to discuss employment prospects. The social engineer chose the name "Robin Sage" as an inside joke because Robin Sage is the last phase of U.S. Army Special Forces training before becoming a Green Beret. Apparently, no one in military intelligence got the joke.

Another phishing trend is use of instant messaging instead of e-mail. The victim receives an IM (Instant Message), either from a friend's IM signature or from *spim* (spam sent through an IM). It links to a page where the victim must first enter a user name and password. Of course, the page has hidden code that e-mails the victim's information to the phisher. With a victim's Yahoo! user name and password, a phisher could easily read the victim's e-mail, access his Yahoo! wallet account, view his stock portfolio on his Yahoo! home page, impersonate him on Yahoo! Chat, and trade or sell any of this information. Since the phisher now has access to the victim's buddy list, he can IM the same phishing lure to the victim's entire list, making it appear they are receiving a message from a friend as well. The moral is be cautious before clicking links in IMs or e-mails.

Similar to phishing, *pharming* diverts an unsuspecting Web user from a legitimate commercial site to a fake one. Pharming is a malicious Web redirect — a blend of domain spoofing and DNS hijacking or DNS poisoning — that exploits the Domain Name System (DNS) used to translate a site's domain name into a numerical code for Internet routing. One method of pharming uses a virus or *Trojan horse* to attack the host file on the victim's computer. (The host file converts URLs into numeric strings a computer understands). Another pharming method is *DNS poisoning*, which attacks the equivalent of a host file on the domain name server, with the potential to misdirect large numbers of users to the spoofed site. (Recall the two pharming attacks from Chapter 5, where someone fraudulently changed the DNS address for a New York ISP's domain and a German youth hijacked the eBay.de domain). Pharming attacks can be hard to detect, since the fake site will look identical to the real one and appear to have the proper URL shown in the address bar. However, pharming spoofs can be avoided if the user only accesses an institution's site by HTTPS (Hypertext Transfer Protocol over Secure Socket Layer, or HTTP over SSL, *i.e.*, a secured URL) and not by ordinary HTTP Hypertext Transfer Protocol, *i.e.*, with no SSL protection), or if the user follows browser warnings about sites with invalid server certificates (*i.e.*, when a dialogue box asks the user if he wishes to trust the certificate because the name on it does not match the site he is trying to reach).

Most phishing scams rely on the victim being duped into revealing personal information to the phisher. However, one variant known as *keystroke phishing* attempts to retrieve personal information without the victim's knowledge. Instead of directing the victim to a fake site asking for personal information, the e-mail installs a Trojan horse onto the computer. The Trojan is a *keystroke logger* that records keystrokes typed on the keyboard and writes the information (such as the victim's login user ID and passwords for online bank accounts) to a text log file, which is then sent to the phisher.

## Identity Theft

*Identity theft* is a federal crime under the **Identify Theft and Assumption Deterrence Act.** [49] Under the Act, identity theft occurs when someone "knowingly transfers, possesses, or uses, without lawful authority, a means of identification of another person with the intent to commit, or to aid or abet, or in connection with, any unlawful activity that constitutes a violation of federal law or that constitutes a felony under any applicable state or local law." Federal identity theft cases are investigated by federal law enforcement agencies and prosecuted by the U.S. Department of Justice.

The crime of identity theft begins when an impostor obtains key pieces of personal information to impersonate the victim to get credit, merchandise, or services in her name or to provide the thief with false credentials. The thief might run up debt in victim's name, or give the false identity to the police, creating a criminal record or outstanding arrest warrants for the unsuspecting victim. The thief can obtain information by *phishing, database cracking, or social engineering (e.g.,* survey). *Database cracking* occurs when a hacker breaks into a database. *Social engineering* is a collection of techniques to trick or manipulate people into revealing confidential information (*e.g.,* passwords). One technique is *pretexting* — using a false scenario to procure information (*e.g.,* a phone call pretending to be from the victim's bank). Another is *survey,* where using an innocent survey with innocuous questions about the victim's mother's maiden name, the names of his children and pets, or his birth date can yield a surprising number of passwords and user names, which taken together with other known information about the victim can be used to access accounts and obtain even more personal data.

Social engineering techniques range from simple to innovative and tricky. On the simple side, a social engineering susceptibility survey of 576 office workers polled outside a London rail station showed 21 percent willing to reveal account passwords in exchange for a candy bar. [50] More than four times as many women than men surveyed admitted they would share passwords with "attractive, well dressed market researchers". Fifty-eight percent of respondents would give their passwords over the phone to anyone claiming to be from the information technology department. Nearly a third used one password for everything and 61 percent gave out their birth dates (essential data for identity thieves).

On the tricky side, CyberLover was a program that mimicked online flirting and extracted personal information from unsuspecting chatters in Russian dating chat rooms. The software emulated a real conversation so the chatter believed he or she was chatting with a real person and revealed personal information. CyberLover established up to 10 relationships in 30 minutes, with profiles from "romantic lover" to "sexual predator," reporting back with each chatter's name, contact information, and photos. [51]

Once a phisher has a victim's credit card number, what does he do with it? A Russian phisher accumulated hundreds of credit card numbers and distributed them among his American "*cashers*" — young men who would encode the numbers onto plastic cards and use them to withdraw money from ATMs. The cashers would then wire the funds — less their percentage — back to the Russian phisher.[52] Such cashers can make hundreds of thousands of dollars, according to postal inspectors.[53]

Identity thieves have created sites to exchange stolen information internationally. In 2004, 28 individuals were arrested for running sites designed to steal, sell, and forge credit cards and identification documents. Hosting sites on non-U.S. servers in countries like Belarus, Canada, Sweden, and Ukraine, the suspects bought, sold, and traded stolen credit cards, driver's licenses, birth certificates, and passports. About 1.7 million stolen credit card numbers were involved in the operation.[54] Scammers can buy someone's identity — birth date, Social Security number, bank account number, passwords, and mother's maiden name — for $14-to-$18 on underground online forums.[55] A credit card number alone costs as little as a dollar.[56] About 5,000 credit cards were traded or sold on the online black market in the second half of 2006.[57]

Identity theft may be spreading to the Internet, but it is not new. According to the FTC, in 2001 only 3 percent of reported identity fraud cited misuse of Internet accounts; 97 percent of identity theft came from offline causes![58] Despite risks inherent online, discussed further in this chapter, it is still safer to give out a credit card number on a secured Web page than to hand a card to an unknown waiter or salesperson.

## Social Security Numbers

The Social Security Administration reported misuse of Social Security numbers (SSN) jumped from 11,000 instances in 1998 to 65,000 in 2001.[59] The identity theft crisis can be traced to the fact the SSN has become Americans' de facto national identifier. From mobile phone companies to public utilities, businesses routinely ask American consumers for their SSNs, when there is no need for them to have it. One poll found almost 90 percent of Americans were asked for their SSNs by businesses.[60] The SSN was never meant to be a national identity number. So how did it reach this point?

The **Social Security Act of 1935**[61] did not mention SSNs. It merely authorized creation of a record-keeping scheme to track employee contributions to Social Security. SSNs were created in 1936 for tracking workers' Social Security earnings records.[62] Unlike many European countries, America neither had nor desired a national identity card.[63] By executive order, President Franklin Roosevelt required all federal agencies to use the SSN "exclusively" to identify individuals.[64] In 1961, the Civil Service Commission adopted the SSN as an official federal employee identifier and that same year the Internal Revenue Code was amended to require taxpayers to use it on tax returns.[65] In 1964, the Treasury Department required savings bond purchasers to disclose their SSNs before purchasing bonds. With the creation of Medicare in 1965, individuals over age 65 were required to obtain a SSN, which serves as their Medicare number.[66] The next year, the Veterans Administration began using the SSN as the hospital admissions number and for patient record keeping. In 1967, during the Vietnam War, the Defense Department substituted the SSN in place of the military service number for Armed Forces personnel. Then, in 1970, the **Bank Records and Foreign Transactions Act** required all banks, savings and loan associations, credit unions, and securities brokers/dealers obtain their customers' SSNs. [67] In 1972, the **Social Security Act** was amended to mandate the Social Security Administration issue SSNs to all legally admitted aliens (including foreign workers with visas) and anyone applying for or receiving benefits paid from federal funds. [68] It also authorized the Social Security Administration to issue SSNs to school children. The **Tax Reform Act of 1976** let states use SSNs in the administration of taxes, general public assistance, and driver's license or motor vehicle registration so individuals were then required to provide their SSNs to the states for these purposes. [69] (However, the **Intelligence Reform and Terrorism Prevention Act of 2004** prohibits states from displaying SSNs on drivers' licenses, state ID cards, or motor-vehicle registrations). [70] The **Food Stamp Act of 1977** [71] mandated disclosure of SSNs of all household members as a condition of eligibility for the food stamp program and in 1981 such disclosure became necessary for participation in the school lunch program. [72] That same year, potential inductees were required to disclosure their SSNs to the Selective Service System on draft registration. [74] The following year, all federal loan applicants had to disclose their SSNs to the lender. [74] In 1988, disclosure of an applicant's SSN was made a condition of eligibility for HUD housing. [75] And in 1994, Congress authorized use of SSNs for jury selection. [76]

As Congress continually expanded the use of the SSN over the years, it steadfastly proclaimed (through various studies and committee reports) the SSN should not be used as a national identifier; but in fact, that was what it was becoming. Since its introduction, the SSN has been used by many institutions, including hospitals, banks, and brokerage firms, as a means of customer identification. The problem is when multiple databases and record systems are indexed to the same identifier, it is difficult to permit access to only some of the information about a person while restricting other topics. That is why the SSN is so valuable to identity thieves; it truly is the key to one's identity.

Except as noted above, no federal law governs — or even limits — use or disclosure of SSNs among *private* entities. There is no legal requirement for anyone to provide one's SSN to a private business. Conversely, private companies are free to deny credit, services, or membership to anyone refusing to divulge his SSN. But there are laws limiting public and publicly funded entities. The **Privacy Act of 1974** requires all government agencies (federal, state, and local) requesting SSNs provide a disclosure statement on the request form explaining if the disclosure is mandatory or optional, how the SSN will be used, and under what statutory authority it is requested. [77] The Act prohibits denial of government benefits or services for refusal to disclose the SSN, unless disclosure is required by federal law or is to an agency using SSNs prior to January 1975 (**FERPA**'s effective date).

The *Buckley Amendment*, also known as the **Family Educational Rights and Privacy Act** *(FERPA)*, permits the federal government to cut funding to public schools that violate the privacy of student records. It applies to state colleges, universities, and technical schools receiving federal funds. [78] Its purpose is to protect students' privacy and give them access to their records to assure accuracy. School officials may not disclose students' personally identifiable information (including SSNs) or permit inspection of their records without the student's written permission, except where permitted by the Act. But while the Act creates a federal restriction on the institutions' actions, *it does not create a right of private suit*. In <u>Gonzaga University v. Doe</u>, a recent college graduate sued his school, claiming a university employee had revealed personal information without his consent, damaging his chance to get a job. [79] The U.S. Supreme Court held the graduate could not bring a private cause of action under § 1983 of the **Civil Rights Act** (a federal statute often used to sue to enforce one's rights in federal court) to enforce his rights under **FERPA**. [80] It held **FERPA** does not grant individuals the right to sue in their own right; instead, the individual must file a complaint with the institution or with the Secretary of Education, the latter then being required to investigate, review, order compliance and, if necessary, terminate federal funding if the school does not comply.

Even with protections like the Buckley Amendment, SSNs can be found both online (even on government sites) and offline in many government records, such as civil and criminal court filings, traffic tickets, creditors' filings, land deeds, and death certificates. In 2001, federal courts prohibited SSNs from appearing on public documents, but that does not affect federal court records prior to 2001 or state court records. [81]

### Safeguard Your ID Information

An identity thief can get an individual's personal identification information by:
- *Pretexting* — posing as a bank, credit card issuer, phone or electric company, or other service provider allegedly to confirm or update the victim's information
- "**Dumpster Diving**" — pilfering through garbage or mailboxes for credit card offers, account statements, and bill payments
- **Insecure Web Form** — from the victim entering information on an insecure site
- **Retail Theft** — from stores in which the victim shops (*i.e.,* dishonest clerks)

To safeguard personal identification information and prevent identity theft:
- Cross-shred (not just tear) documents with personal identification information
- Periodically obtain and review credit reports (you are entitled to one free copy annually). The three credit bureau sites are: equifax.com, experian.com, and transunion.com
- Opt-out of pre-approved credit card offers by mail, either online at optoutprescreen.com or by calling the Credit Card Industry's Opt-out Hotline at (888) 567-8688 [*888*-5OptOut]. The toll-free number was enacted as a requirement of a 1996 amendment to the **Fair Credit Reporting Act**
- Protect mail from theft by (1) noticing when bills have not arrived on time and contacting the sender, and (2) if planning an extended trip, calling the U.S. Postal Service at (800) 275-8777 [*800*-ASK-USPS] to request a "vacation hold" on mail delivery service. A vacation hold can be requested online at the U.S. Postal Service site, usps.com
- Do not reveal your SSN unless absolutely necessary! Remember, when you give someone your SSN, you are giving away the key to your personal identification.
- Do not carry seldom-used credit cards or any unnecessary identification (*e.g.,* voter registration card, insurance card with SSN)
- Identity thieves are not always strangers; they may be people from work, casual acquaintances, close friends, ex-lovers, or even relatives
- Do not give out personal information by phone, mail, or online
- Overwrite data on, and reformat, old hard drives

One often overlooked source of personal information for identity thieves is discarded hard drives. When a computer is disposed of, if the hard drive is not wiped clean then the data still remain on the drive and may be easily retrieved. Even files placed in the Windows Recycle Bin and deleted may be recovered through file recovery software. [82] The Windows command to delete files does not actually delete data from the hard drive; it merely deletes the computer's own record of the fact the disk space the data reside on is unavailable. The only method of irretrievably destroying data (other than physically destroying the drive), is to use software that wipes or overwrites data on the disk through multiple passes. The U.S. Department of Defense uses DOD 5220.22-M, a standard that generates and records random characters across the entire hard drive surface, destroying all the data and resetting file sizes to zero.

Computers at schools, businesses, and doctor's offices hold highly personal information from financial data to medical histories, which often remain on the drives when the computers are donated or sold. In one study, confidential or personal data was found on 113 of 200 drives purchased on eBay.[83] An audit discovered Montana state agencies had neglected to remove private information before donating old computers to schools: eight still contained 386 SSNs, financial records for 182 people, 84 business files, and job applicant information.[84] New Jersey almost made a similar blunder, but a review of computers the state was preparing to auction to the public found 46 out of 58 hard drives (79 percent) had confidential data, including SSNs, tax returns, passwords, employee evaluations, files on abused children, and names, addresses, birth dates and other information on hundreds of foster and abused children; one laptop, used by a judge, contained confidential memos about possible misconduct by attorneys, as well as the judge's own tax returns.[85] One man who bought a computer on eBay for £77 discovered it contained information on several million bank customers, including account details, customers' signatures, mobile phone numbers and mothers' maiden names.[86] Computers belonging to individuals (as opposed to governments and businesses) may hold everything from passwords and bank account numbers to e-mailed love letters and personal diaries.

The problem is not limited to computers *owned* by individuals or businesses, as many businesses also *lease* computers. What happens when the leased computer is returned? Unless it has been "wiped" as described above, the data will remain on the drive, available to anyone at the leasing organization or to subsequent lessees.

Not only hard drives in desktop and laptop computers are at risk — multimedia players, smart phones, and photocopiers have drives that may also hold private data. Merely handing someone your driver's license to make a photocopy may put you at risk of identity theft — and not necessarily from the person making the copy. Many doctor's offices and labs routinely photocopy patients' IDs and insurance cards (Medicare cards show the patient's SSN). Merchants often photocopy driver's licenses and personal checks. But what most people do not realize is almost every digital copier built since 2002 has a hard drive, like a computer, that stores an image of each document copied, scanned, or e-mailed. Such documents may include SSNs, driver's licenses, bank and tax records, and medical records. In 2010, a CBS news investigation purchased three used photocopiers.[87] One still had documents from a police sex crimes division on the copier glass. In 12 hours, using software available free online, they removed the hard drives and downloaded tens of thousands of documents. These included detailed domestic violence complaints; targets in a major drug raid; pay stubs with names, addresses and SSNs; and 300 pages of individual medical records. Hundreds of used copiers are stored in warehouses waiting to be sold. The threat to privacy is compounded by the fact many businesses lease copiers, only to return them — their hard drives intact — to the leasing company, where they are released to others with the sensitive information still on the drives. Many used copiers are also shipped to buyers overseas. Software is available to wipe the hard drives before they are resold or returned to lessors, but according to the CBS News investigation, few companies purchase or use the software.[88] At present, there are no American laws requiring copier hard drives be replaced or wiped clean. While some nations have laws (such as the U.K. Data Protection Act) mandating organizations delete personal data before disposing of hard drives, many do not comply with the law, making discarded drives a treasure trove for identity thieves.[89]

### The Identity Theft Penalty Enhancement Act

**The Identity Theft Penalty Enhancement Act of 2004**, provides mandatory prison time for possession of another's identity-related information with the intent to commit a crime. [90] It updates existing penalties, adding two years for those who "knowingly transfer, possess, or use another's identity to commit a felony" and five years for "terror-related crimes." The Act has been characterized as a knee-jerk reaction to the growing identity theft problem, as it is unlikely the minimum two-year sentence will deter one intent on committing a crime that already carries a 15-year prison term. Of course, the real problem is not a lack of existing laws, but that the government must first identify and capture the lawbreaker. A more practical solution might be to pass laws holding information handlers more accountable for the security of the data they collect and store. Still, the Act is a step toward centralizing enforcement at the federal level to resolve the problem of inadequate state enforcement.

Many states have statutes:

- specifically creating a separate crime for identity theft
- requiring credit agencies block inaccurate information resulting from identity theft
- requiring government agencies aid victims with repairing their credit reports
- allowing individuals to place a credit freeze or fraud alert on credit reports until the identity theft is resolved.

Many cybercrimes target a user's computer or Internet connection. Cookies may be modified and malware may be surreptitiously downloaded to a user's computer. Cybercrooks might even hijack an innocent user's Internet connection to commit a crime.

## Cookie Poisoning

*Cookies* are data placed on a user's computer by a site to enable it to personalize the user's visit (*e.g.*, on e-commerce sites this might mean pulling up a previously completed customer profile), speed up transactions, and monitor the user's behavior (see the discussion of behavioral marketing in Chapter 10). *Cookie poisoning* is the modification of a cookie by an attacker to gain unauthorized information about the user for purposes such as identity theft. Cookies are "poisoned" when any of the stored values (*e.g.*, user IDs, passwords, account numbers and session keys) are altered. The cookie then follows the user from one part of the site to another. If hackers get on a site and steal a user's cookie, then they have access to that user's session. Web sites should protect cookies (*e.g.*, through encryption of the stored values) before they are sent to the user's computer to prevent cookie poisoning.

## Malware

*Malware* is any form of malicious computer software that infiltrates a users' computer. The phrase is short for "malicious software" and refers to any software program or file developed for the purpose of doing harm. It can take the form of adware, spyware, or ransomware. Malware is often loaded surreptitiously onto users' computers when they download wallpaper, screen savers, and ringtones. One study found users have an 18 percent chance of downloading malware when they search for news and photos of celebrities. [91] Malware includes computer viruses, worms, and Trojan horses. A *worm* is a self-replicating virus that does not alter files but resides in the computer's active memory and duplicates itself. A *Trojan horse* is a program in which malicious or harmful code is hidden inside an apparently harmless program or data to later gain control and cause damage. The phrase comes from Homer's *Iliad* — during the Trojan War, the Greeks presented the citizens of Troy with a large wooden horse in which they had secretly hidden their warriors; at night, the warriors emerged from the wooden horse and overran and conquered Troy.

## Adware vs. Spyware

*Adware* is software that displays ads as the program runs. Software developers justify placing ads in their products to recover programming development costs, thereby lowering the overall user cost. Adware is legal, though often an alternative "full cost" version of the software without ads is available. *Spyware* is software that accesses and uses an Internet connection in the background without the user's knowledge or explicit permission. It often includes programming code that tracks a user's personal information and forwards it to third-parties, again without the user's knowledge or authorization. Spyware can infiltrate a computer when a user installs new software (either by download or CD). Spyware and adware both may contain data collecting programs, but the difference is in spyware the data collecting program is installed for malevolent purposes without the user's knowledge or consent, whereas in adware, it is installed for commercial purposes with the user's knowledge and consent, (although such disclosure may have been buried in a long click-wrap agreement and consent may only have been given when the user clicked on it while downloading other programs). [92]

Some online advertisers and P2P networks place programs on users' computers to monitor their activity or to use their computers' processors. Many users are unaware they are being monitored. Spyware can crash computers or slow performance and be difficult to find and remove; however, software programs like Spybot, Spy Sweeper, and Ad-Aware can remove it.

Undisclosed spyware may violate communications and computer trespass laws. In one case, both a spyware firm marketing to suspicious spouses, and its customers, were charged with violating federal computer privacy laws. The "Loverspy" program, disguised as an e-mailed greeting card with flowers and puppies, hid spyware to record out-going e-mails and sites visited. A thousand copies of Loverspy were sold, but only four purchasers were indicted and charged with "illegal computer hacking" and "illegally intercepting the electronic communications of their victims," each facing up to five years in prison and a maximum fine of $250,000. [93] The spyware creator was indicted on 35 counts of manufacturing, sending, and advertising a surreptitious interception device, unlawfully intercepting electronic communications, disclosing unlawfully intercepted electronic communications, and obtaining unauthorized access to protected computers for financial gain. An arrest warrant was issued for the fugitive, who faced up to 175 years in prison if caught and convicted. [94]

During the 2007 holiday season, users of the Sears Holdings Community Web site were surprised to discover a program installed on their computer had allegedly recorded and transmitted their actions — such as logging into bank accounts, sites they visited, e-mails sent and received (headers, not the message content), and items purchased — back to Sears, without providing notice to the user it was running in the background. On being accused of placing spyware on computers, Sears provided customers with information about the software's function, added start menu shortcuts to indicate the application's presence, and provided uninstallation instructions. [95]

Spyware can be used to rob people. U.S. investors have 10 million online brokerage accounts and approximately one-quarter of all retail U.S. stock transactions are made online. [96] Thieves place spyware on a computer and, using keystroke loggers, capture an investor's account user name and password to access the account and either sell off the account's portfolio and keep the proceeds or use the account for *"pump and dump" schemes* [97] to manipulate stock prices for profit. While spyware can easily be uploaded to a personal computer through an e-mail attachment or by a drive-by download, computers in publics places, such as brokerage office lobbies, libraries, hotel rooms, and Internet cafés, are the preferred targets since they get a high volume of multiple users. The best protection against falling victim to spyware includes frequently changing passwords and avoiding public computers for transactions requiring entry of an account number or password. If you must do so, then empty the browser cache so subsequent users of the computer will not have access to your user name and password.

### Ransomware

*Ransomware* is a type of malware that encrypts a user's hard drive or selected files (*e.g.,* music, photos, or documents) and demands payment to decrypt it. The FTC filed its first spyware case against three software companies, accused of infecting computers with malware when users downloaded screensavers and P2P software and then trying to sell them software to remove it. [98] The infected computers displayed pop-up ads offering to remove the malware for $30. One individual owned all three companies and the FTC settlement reached in 2006 imposed a $1.86 million fine. [99]

In one scam, a virus causes pop-up windows to appear on the user's screen, allegedly from "the ICPP Copyright Foundation". The pop-ups inform the user a computer scan has detected illegal content on the hard drive and offer a "pretrial settlement" fine of $400 payable by credit card as an alternative to expensive litigation or prison. The ransomware also changes the desktop's wallpaper to read "Warning! Piracy detected!" Of course, the malware has not actually found anything, or even scanned the drive, and "the ICPP Copyright Foundation" does not exist. But many victims pay the "fine" online with their credit card. In this scam, the scammers do not take the money but instead sell the credit card information to crooks and identity thieves. [100] A Japanese virus variation of ransomware, called Kenzero, infects hard drives of file-sharing site users, takes screenshots of their browsing history, and publishes them with identifying information on a Web site. The ransomware then e-mails the victim demanding a credit card payment to "settle your violation of copyright law" and remove the Web page. [101]

### Drive-by Download

A *drive-by download* is a program automatically downloaded to a user's computer, often without the user's knowledge or consent. Unlike a pop-up download, which asks for consent (although usually in a way calculated to lead the user to respond affirmatively), a drive-by download occurs invisibly. It can be initiated by simply visiting a site or viewing an HTML e-mail message where code in the HTML uses ActiveX controls (a plug-in for

Microsoft's Internet Explorer Web browser) to install the software in the background. The code is often hidden in parts of the site not designed or controlled by its owner, *e.g.*, banner ads and *widgets* (third-party programs embedded into an HTML page). Trojan horses have been discovered in banner ads placed on popular sites like MySpace and Photobucket.[102] Often, a drive-by download is installed invisibly along with another application. Drive-by downloads are used to infect a computer or steal sensitive data. Some change bookmarks, install unwanted toolbars or substitute a new browser home page, while others install Trojan keystroke loggers. An in-depth Google study of 4.5 million Web pages revealed 10 percent contained malicious code that could infect a user's computer through drive-by downloads.[103] The best defense against drive-by downloads is for users to set browser settings to the highest security level and to use up-to-date security software. Drive-by downloads are illegal and fall under the crime of *computer trespass*.

## Computer Trespass

*Trespass to chattels* is a superannuated common law doctrine created to protect physical property. It is defined as "intentionally dispossessing another of the chattel or using or intermeddling with a chattel in the possession of another."[104] If the disposition is total, rather than partial, the common law tort of *conversion* would apply instead of trespass to chattels. A requisite element of trespass to chattels is substantial interference with the chattel, such as removal, damage, or impairment of its physical condition.

In 1996, a California appellate court took the novel approach of pulling the trespass to chattels tort out of the mothballs and applying it to modern technology.[105] Some teenage boys used computer technology to crack a telephone carrier's access and authorization codes and make long distance phone calls without paying for them. They ran a computer program for nearly seven hours, generating more than 1,300 calls. The small phone carrier' system, having relatively few telephone lines, was so overtaxed by the automated calling some subscribers were denied access to phones lines. The trial court found the defendants guilty of fraud and conversion, but the appellate court ruled there cannot be conversion of an intangible object unless there is a corresponding tangible object. The court then decided, *sua sponte*, the trial court had "mislabel[ed] the cause of action" and "It has long been recognized that this court has the power to modify the conclusion of the court below, where the record supports it" and held the defendants had committed a trespass to chattels. Thus, the court found electronic signals were sufficiently physical and tangible to constitute trespass to chattels.

Other courts followed California's lead, allowing trespass to chattel actions where there was no physical contact but electronic intrusion instead, applying the tort to the Internet, holding spamming was actionable as a trespass to chattels.[106] Courts also applied the doctrine to spiders (automated software that scan Web pages for search engines, also called crawlers, robots, and bots) crawling Internet-accessible databases, ruling they were trespassing on the database servers, beginning with a case where eBay successfully asserted a trespass to chattels claim against an online auction aggregator.[107] The court ruled the crawling constituted unauthorized interference with eBay's possession of its personal property and equated the consumption of eBay's bandwidth with actual harm. But in 2003, a California court refused to apply the doctrine to an alleged spammer, finding the requisite element of harm had not been met.[108]

Some states have specific computer trespass statutes. State statutes address the concept of computer trespass in varying ways, so one must look to the specific wording of the applicable statute. Generally, computer trespass occurs when an individual gains unauthorized access to a computer system or exceeds his authorized access. This access may with be with an intent to examine personal data and records (Computer Invasion of Privacy); an intent to defraud (Fraudulent Trespass); an intent to destroy data or damage the network (Destructive Trespass); or without destructive intent but nonetheless resulting in harm (Reckless Trespass). Penalties may range from misdemeanor to felony. For example, computer intrusion was one of seven felonies a California man pleaded guilty to after breaking into 3,200 e-mail accounts of women in 17 states. He used the social engineering technique of perusing Facebook accounts for answers to the security questions used by Web-based e-mail services like Yahoo! Mail and Gmail. Once he had accessed the account, he would change the password (locking out his victim) and search for explicit photographs, which he would post to her Facebook profile or send to her entire e-mail address book. The thief also accessed some Facebook accounts by clicking the "Forgot Your Password?" link and requesting a new password be sent to the victim's e-mail account, which he now controlled. He blackmailed one victim into sending him more explicit photographs by threatening to post the ones he had. Investigators found 172 nude or semi-nude photos of the women, including a film actress, on his hard drive. [109]

Computer trespass statutes have been extended beyond their original hacker targets. A husband who suspected his wife of infidelity used a password list she kept next to the family's computer to log into her Gmail account and confirm his suspicions. [110] Michigan prosecutors charged him with felony computer misuse under an anti-hacking statute, which carries a five-year prison term. [111] In December 2011, a Michigan Court of Appeals panel ruled the case should proceed to trial, noting the state's computer hacking law has "no spousal exception," and as written was applicable to the case. [112]

The federal **Computer Fraud and Abuse Act** criminalizes knowingly accessing a computer without authorization or in excess of authorization. [113] It has been used against spammers who access a plaintiff's computer system without authorization to obtain e-mail addresses for spamming, and against computer hackers. Federal prosecutors expanded its use when they charged a woman with violation of the **CFAA** for breaching the MySpace's Terms of Use agreement. The novel approach alleged by creating a MySpace account with a fictitious name, in violation of the Terms of Use agreement, she lacked authority to access its server, which in turn was a violation of the Act. [114] However, in April 2012, the Ninth Circuit in a 9-to-2 ruling, sought to limit the reach of the **CFAA**, holding prosecutors could not use the statute to punish employees who access workplace computers in violation of corporate policy. [115] In that case, the defendant was charged with inducing Korn/Ferry employees into stealing confidential client information so he could set up a competing firm.

Ohio prosecutors also made innovative use of their state computer trespass statute to convict a defendant who used his work computer to upload his nude photos to an adult site and view other photos on porn sites, by charging him with felony hacking under the statute. [116] The jury found by accessing the porn sites he had exceeded his authorization to use the computer.

## Wardriving, Piggybacking, and Telecommunications Theft

"*Wardriving*" is the practice of driving with a Wi-Fi enabled laptop, mapping houses and businesses that have wireless access points. "*Piggybacking*" is use of a wireless

Internet connection without permission. Theft of Internet access or bandwidth is the crime of **telecommunications theft**. Those who use wireless Internet access at home or business are often unaware their wireless signals can be transmitted 500 feet or further. If a user has not encrypted them, these signals can be intercepted, allowing the interceptor to "piggyback" on them and log onto the Internet on a Wi-Fi equipped laptop.

A Florida man wardriving with a laptop in his car was charged with unauthorized access to a computer network, a third degree felony, [117] while across the pond in the United Kingdom, in a case of first impression, a man caught with a laptop in front of a residential building, piggybacking on a homeowner's wireless network, was fined £500 and sentenced to 12 months probation. [118] An infamous 2003 wardriving case occurred when Toronto, Canada police noticed a man driving the wrong way on a one-way street. Pulling the car over, they discovered he was naked from the waist down, with his laptop downloading child pornography from the Wi-Fi connection of a nearby home. [119] Situations like this raise the specter of other potential problems. As Jeff Beard wrote in his *LawTechGuru* blog: "Now imagine that it was your Wi-Fi connection he hijacked, except that the authorities didn't catch the wardriver, but instead tracked the downloads back to your network from your ISP's logs. Talk about some explaining to do." [120] It is possible Wi-Fi owners who negligently fail to secure their networks might be liable for acts of wardrivers and other unauthorized users of their networks. Unauthorized access to a wireless network can not only involve downloading but uploading, too; spam, viruses, and Trojans could all be uploaded, potentially harming third-parties.

Wardriving — driving with a Wi-Fi enabled laptop computer, mapping houses and businesses that have wireless access points — is not by itself a crime. It is the unauthorized use of a wireless Internet connection — the telecommunications theft — that makes the act illegal. If a business offers patrons the use of its Wi-Fi signals (as many do), then the users are not making unauthorized use of a wireless Internet connection. However, that scenario does raise the issue of what liability, if any, the business might have for any illegal acts committed by authorized users of its wireless Internet connection. Suppose a patron at a popular coffeehouse avails himself of its free Wi-Fi and downloads child pornography as he sips his Java. Or perhaps he uploads a Trojan to steal data from a business rival. Does the coffeehouse, as the Wi-Fi access provider, bear any liability? Or might a court label the coffee house an Online Service Provider protected by the **CDA**? [121] What if the patron e-mails spam with an unauthorized copyrighted image; would the coffeehouse be considered a contributory infringer, since it enabled the copyright infringement by making the technology available? These are issues yet to reach the courts. However, in 2009, a U.K. pub owner was fined £8,000 in a civil case, after a patron illegally downloaded copyrighted material over the pub's open Wi-Fi hotspot. [122] No similar cases have yet been reported in America.

The FBI has documented several cybercrime incidents involving unauthorized use of open Wi-Fi access points, including an attempt to steal credit card transaction data from a Michigan department store, an attempt to extort $17 million from a patent company through use of unsecured wireless access points, and a phishing scheme in Georgia that used open wireless access points to send e-mail to trick recipients into revealing credit card and banking information. [123] In the Michigan case, dubbed by the press as the first criminal conviction for wardriving, the defendant pleaded guilty to a federal misdemeanor of unauthorized access to a protected computer. [124] A man and his roommate wardriving came across an unsecured network at Lowe's store. He used the private corporate network to check his e-mail and, six months later, his roommate returned with a friend, a young man on probation for a juvenile computer crime conviction. In the parking lot, they accessed the network again, connecting to Lowe's branches in Kansas, North Carolina, Kentucky, South Dakota, Florida, and California. They altered the store's proprietary software to enable them to retrieve customer credit card numbers. Both pleaded guilty to computer intrusion, damage, and fraud. [125] The 21-year-old was sentenced to nine years in prison, the longest sentence yet for computer hacking. [126] His companion received a 26-month sentence. [127]

## Pod Slurping

Apparently, not even the seemingly innocuous iPod is without its dark side — it is not just for music. High school students, hiding iPods and other digital media players beneath their clothes, have been caught playing back voice-recorded test answers during school exams (mobile phone texting of test answers being "so '90s."). Schools in Idaho, Washington, Ontario, and even Australia have banned digital media players once the non-tech generation of teachers and administrators got wise to the dual use of such devices. [128]

There have been reported instances of "*pod slurping*", *i.e.*, data thieves hooking iPods or other portable media players into corporate computers and networks to use as portable hard drives to siphon information. [129] Relatively inexpensive, easily concealable, prosaic in appearance, and with hard drives holding up to 320 gigabytes of memory, portable media players are understandably a data thief's best friend. [130] A keyboard is not necessary; the data thief merely plugs the device into an open USB port and begins downloading. To casual observers, he would appear to be listening to music on his iPod. Besides music files, portable media players can store other files, such as documents, photographs, and spreadsheets. A typical word-processing file averages 25k–to–30k in size, meaning an average 120-gigabyte portable media player is capable of storing more than 4.5 million documents!

Of course, data transfer works both ways. A corporate spy or disgruntled employee could use a portable data device deliberately to inject viruses and spyware into the corporate network (pod burping?). [131] Data thieves can also simply walk away with data already stored on disks or USB flash drives. According to computer security firm Symantec, 54 percent of all identity theft-related data breaches were attributable to lost or stolen data storage media. [132]

## Electromagnetic Keyboard Sniffing

Cybercriminals soon may not need to touch a computer to steal data from it. Swiss researchers have discovered by analyzing electromagnetic signals produced by every key pressed on a computer keyboard they can determine what was typed from 65 feet away. [133] Since 2000, it has been rumored the U.S. government has a classified program called "TEMPEST" aimed at electromagnetic computer monitoring technology. [134]

*"Crime and the fear of crime have permeated the fabric of American life."*

— *Chief Justice Warren E. Burger*

## The Mule Scam

Cybercriminals in search of a way to launder illegal gains often turn to mules. In criminal parlance, a "mule" is an innocent-appearing individual chosen by drug dealers to smuggle drugs across borders. In cyber parlance, a mule is one used (usually unknowingly) to launder funds stolen online. The prospective mule receives an e-mail offer of a work-at-home job completing sales for an overseas firm, whose site appears legitimate, bearing names, trademarks and page content of real companies copied from their sites. The mule is asked to add an e-mail address to his PayPal account, to transfer money on the company's behalf. Soon, funds are deposited into the account, with instructions to transfer them to the mule's checking account, and withdraw and wire all but a 10 percent commission to an overseas address provided by the company. The catch? The mule can expect to be contacted by a defrauded victim, for example, an eBay bidder inquiring why he has not received an item paid for via PayPal to the mule's e-mail address. When this scenario has occurred, eBay has held the mule responsible for repaying the full amount to the innocent auction winner. [135]

## Cyberstalking

*Cyberstalking* is crime in which an attacker harasses the victim using electronic communication, such as e-mail, instant messaging, or messages posted to a Web site, blog, chat room, or a discussion group. Cyberstalkers may also incite others against their victims by impersonation, *e.g.*, sending offensive e-mails to employers, posting inflammatory messages on message boards (*i.e.*, "flaming"), or simultaneously offending dozens of chat room participants disguised as the victim. The victim is then banned from message boards, accused of improper conduct, and flooded with threats. Cyberstalkers rely on the Internet's *anonymity* to stalk victims undetected. Cyberstalking may develop from real world stalking and continue online, as in the Amy Boyer incident discussed in Chapter 12, or begin online followed by stalking in the physical world.

A 2009 study reported 45 percent of cyberstalkers were male and 35 percent female (gender was unreported in 20 percent of responses); victims were 21 percent male and 78 percent female (1 percent unreported). [136] A third of the victims were between 18 and 30; 30 percent between 31 and 40; and 32 percent over 41. [137] Twenty-seven percent were unmarried, and 69.5 percent were Caucasian. Sixty-one percent had a prior relationship with the cyberstalker and, of those, 22 percent had met online, 43 percent were from former intimate relationships, 14 percent were family, 7.5 percent were friends, 8 percent were co-workers, and 4 percent were from school. Thirty-four percent of incidents stemmed from e-mail, 13 percent from IMs, 8.5 percent from message boards, 6 percent from chat rooms, 7 percent from Web sites, and 11 percent from Facebook and MySpace. [138] Threats of offline physical violence were reported by 16.5 percent of respondents.

*Corporate cyberstalking* usually involves an organization stalking an individual. Often initiated by a high-ranking executive with a grudge, any employee may conduct corporate cyberstalking (*e.g.*, targeting a former customer or employee who has sued the corporation. Less frequently, it may involve an individual stalking a corporation.

Despite the multijurisdictional nature of cyberstalking, no federal law exists to protect victims or define OSP responsibilities and liabilities. However, federal law does impose a

$1,000 fine or five years imprisonment for anyone transmitting in interstate commerce any threat to kidnap or injure someone. State laws differ on definitions, protections, and penalties. Forty-one states expressly prohibit harassing conduct online or through other electronic means. (Online harassment is discussed in detail in Chapter 18). When does harassment rise to the level of stalking? State cyberstalking laws vary widely. Some consider a threat against the victim's family as cyberstalking, while others say the threat must be directed against the individual. Some require a showing of the stalker's intent to cause "imminent fear", whereas others look to the victim, requiring knowledge the stalker is causing fear. Some statutes require direct communication with the victim, while others would find cyberstalking if the stalker sent a message the victim was likely to receive, even if not actually received. For some states, threat of injury to the victim's reputation meets the definition of cyberstalking, while others require threat of physical injury. Certain states have low thresholds: Arizona requires the victim be "seriously alarmed" or "annoyed." Four (Idaho, Nebraska, New Jersey, and Utah) and the District of Columbia lack cyberstalking statutes.

A cyberstalking prank led to a civil lawsuit when an online advertising campaign backfired. [139] A woman sued Toyota and its ad agency, Saatchi & Saatchi, in 2009 after she was cyberstalked as part of its intrusive "Your Other You" sales campaign. For five days, she received e-mails from a stranger who had her home address, in which he said he was running from the law and needed to hide out at her house with his pit bull. He sent her a link to a MySpace profile describing him as a 25-year-old Englishman who "enjoyed drinking alcohol to excess" and said he would arrive at her home in a few days. He later e-mailed he had had some "trouble" at a motel and she received an e-mailed bill from the "motel manager" claiming she was financially responsible for the man's damage to the motel room. The panicked woman eventually received an e-mail linked to a video explaining her stalker was a fictional character and the prank was part of an online ad campaign for Toyota's Matrix automobile. Toyota claimed someone had signed her up for the campaign at its Web site and she had clicked on its Terms of Service agreement authorizing it to send her the e-mails and containing an arbitration clause. But a California appeals court voided the Terms of Service agreement based on fraud in the inception of the contract, finding the defendants "misrepresented and concealed (whether intentionally or not) the true nature of the conduct to which [plaintiff] was to be subjected," clearing the way for the case to be tried. While the agreement said she would receive e-mails from Toyota, the stalker never identified himself as representing Toyota and the agreement led her to believe she was agreeing to take a personality exam, with no mention of the prank or its stalking aspect. The woman sought $10 million in damages for intentional infliction of emotional distress; unfair, unlawful, and deceptive trade practices; and negligent misrepresentation.

## Federal Statutes Used to Fight Cybercrime

### The Securities Act of 1933 and the Securities Exchange Act of 1934

Securities fraud is another offline crime that has entered the Internet Age. Defrauders use online stock market message boards and chat rooms to hype various stocks, making wrongful posts attempting to manipulate securities prices with false "facts", "rumors", and alleged "inside information." Defrauders mass e-mail bullish announcements to "pump up" highly volatile share prices in small companies and then sell their own shares in those companies into the false demand they created. These *"pump and dump" schemes* violate both state and federal securities laws. Often promoters create a *"sock puppet"*, i.e., a false online identity to deceive others or promote a product or company. [140] The chat rooms and e-mails of the Internet Age have replaced the boiler rooms and cold calls of the penny stock boom, as faster and cheaper alternatives for stock promoters. [141] The SEC estimated 100 million stock spam messages are e-mailed weekly, spiking share prices and trading volume, and contributing to investor losses. [142]

Sales of securities are subject, on the state level, to state securities laws and state common law fraud statutes, and on the federal level, to the **Securities Act of 1933** [143] and the **Securities Exchange Act of 1934**. [144] Both the federal government and the states have watchdog agencies to administer the laws and guard against securities fraud, i.e., respectively, the SEC and state securities administrators and divisions. SEC regulations on corporate communications restrict what publicly-held companies are allowed to say, especially immediately following a new securities offering. A careless blog post or tweet on Twitter by a company official may subject the company to liability under federal securities laws.

## The USA PATRIOT Act

Congress enacted the **USA PATRIOT Act** ("Uniting and Strengthening America by Providing Appropriate Tools Required to Intercept and Obstruct Terrorism Act of 2001") on October 26, 2001 in response to the September 11th terrorist attacks. [145] It is a comprehensive piece of legislation and beyond the scope of this book to do more than give a brief overview of the Act and how it applies to the Internet. Introduced on the heels on the September 11th attacks, the bill was rushed through Congress and passed into law with exceptional speed. Normally a bill would be debated in Congress; the House and Senate would draft different versions; the two versions would then be meshed into a unified bill by a committee; and a legislative history of commentary from that committee and other legal commentators would be created and serve as a resource for courts to infer the intent of the bill's drafters. In this case, the 342-page bill amending multiple federal statutes was enacted into law in a mere five weeks, due to the prevailing public anxiety over the terrorist attacks. America had been attacked on its own soil, the first attack on the continental United States since the War of 1812; more than 3,000 civilians had been killed in attacks on the two most prominent cities in the country, New York City and Washington, D.C. The Pentagon itself had been attacked and letters containing deadly anthrax were circulating through the U.S. postal system. The country's mood was one of intense fear, and Americans turned to their government demanding protection and security. Congress and the president responded with the **USA PATRIOT Act**. In times of such intense public fear, civil liberties are often not a consideration, and simplistic knee-jerk responses that would never be seriously contemplated suddenly become established reality. If a democracy like America were to be attacked by a foreign country or culture, one simplistic and knee-jerk response might be to round up everyone in the United States from that foreign country or culture (even if now U.S. citizens) and put them in concentration camps (with no hearings, no judicial process, and no habeas corpus rights). [146] It would be effective, of course, but so offensive to the notions of civil liberties, freedom, and democracy on which America is based, it would never happen. Except it did. With the stroke of a pen, President Franklin

Roosevelt signed Executive Order 9066, and more than 110,000 people of Japanese ancestry on the Pacific Coast of the United States were physically removed from their homes and placed behind barbed wire in "War Relocation Centers." [147] This is not to say the **USA PATRIOT Act** was unnecessary. But it was rushed into law so quickly and under such extreme public anxiety it lacked the necessary protection of civil liberties inherent in other legislation.

**The USA PATRIOT Act** amended many federal statutes, including:

- **The Bank Secrecy Act of 1970** (BSA) [148]
- **The Computer Fraud and Abuse Act of 1986** (CFAA) [149]
- **The Electronic Communications Privacy Act** (ECPA) [150]
- **The Fair Credit Reporting Act** (FCRA) [151]
- **The Family Educational Rights and Privacy Act** (FERPA) [152]
- **The Foreign Intelligence Surveillance Act** (FISA) [153]
- **The Immigration and Nationality Act** (INA) [154]
- **The Anti-Money Laundering Act** (AMLA) [155]
- **The Money Laundering Control Act** (MLCA) [156]
- **The Pen Register and Trap and Trace Statute** (PRTTS) [157]
- **The Right to Financial Privacy Act** (RFPA) [158]
- **The Federal Wiretap Act** (Title I of the ECPA) [159]

Among its provisions, the Act lessened the standard by which the federal government may intercept electronic messages. It is now allowed to intercept all messages "relevant to an ongoing criminal investigation" — previously it required a crime have been committed before interception. Additionally, the Act's guidelines apply to all surveillance cases, not just suspected terrorists. It also lowered the legal bar by which the government can obtain Internet routing information, creating a civil liberties concern — since content and routing information are usually combined, the government could exceed its stated purpose and intrude deeper into an individual's privacy. [160] For example, a data packet containing an e-mail header also holds the rest of the e-mail; would it not be naive to think government investigators, after obtaining the header, would not read the content? With Internet browsing, the Web site routing automatically reveals what sites the individual has visited and what he did on those sites. Some methods used to obtain routing information also include information on other ISP customers, so not only are the investigation's target's privacy rights compromised, but those of unrelated individuals.

The Act amended the law to allow the government to subpoena customer credit card and bank account numbers from ISPs, in addition to the information it was already allowed to subpoena (*i.e.*, customer's name, address, length of service, and method of payment). [161] It also allowed ISPs to disclose voluntarily customer records and content of electronic transmissions to the government "if the provider reasonably believes that an emergency involving immediate danger of death or serious physical injury to any person justifies disclosure of the information." [162] This makes sense in a situation where the ISP has reason to believe a customer intends to harm himself (*e.g.*, posting a suicide note online) or others (*e.g.*, see the Amy Boyer cyberstalking case in Chapter 12); however, in a broad reading it can be construed to apply to harm from any potential "terrorist" — terrorism by its nature implies a constant state of emergency involving immediate danger of death or serious physical injury. So in effect, by labeling a suspect a terror suspect, the government could conceivably request ISP customer records and e-mails without a subpoena (of course, the ISPs could refuse the request). [163]

The **USA PATRIOT Act** also introduced the "sneak and peek" search warrant, where the government executes a warrant without notice or with delayed notice. The Fourth Amendment to the U.S. Constitution guarantees citizens protection from unreasonable searches and seizures. The U.S. Supreme Court has ruled law enforcement officials must obtain a search warrant and provide notice to any party whose property is to be searched before the search is conducted. Section 213 of the Act eliminated this notice requirement in situations where "the investigation will be jeopardized" by giving notice. Again, a broad reading of the phrase "jeopardized" would make this an expansive search power.

Section 215 of the Act modified § 505 of **FISA** to allow the FBI, the U.S. Department of Defense, and other government agencies, secretly to demand information from ISPs without a court order by issuing secret *"National Security Letters"* (NSLs). These NSLs demand information about subscribers, such as home addresses, phone calls placed, e-mail subject lines, and logs of sites visited. The **ECPA** had restricted the FBI from sending NSLs to telecommunications firms except in relation to an investigation of "an agent of a foreign power."[164] Prior to the **USA PATRIOT Act**, NSLs could only be used in investigations of suspected terrorists and spies, but now the FBI need only say an NSL may be "relevant" to a terrorist-related investigation and no court approval is required. The FBI issues more than 30,000 NSLs annually,[165] and not just to ISPs.[166] Librarians have been served with NSLs demanding they turn over "all subscriber information, billing information and access logs" of patrons who used library computers.[167] Unlike subpoenas, NSLs do not require approval by a judge, grand jury, or prosecutor, but are instead issued by FBI field supervisors.

A federal court declared provisions of the **USA PATRIOT Act** unconstitutional in 2004, holding NSLs violated both the First and Fourth Amendments. The Act forbids an NSL recipient from ever disclosing its existence "to any person." The court held the mandatory gag order amounted to an "unconstitutional prior restraint of speech in violation of the First Amendment." (**Prior restraint** is discussed in detail in Chapter 18). Ironically, the American Civil Liberties Union, which brought the suit, was unable to disclose information about the case, so as to avoid penalties for violating the Act's gag provision. In <u>Doe v. Ashcroft</u>,[168] the ACLU sued on an ISP's behalf that received an NSL, challenging the constitutionality of one statute amended by the Act,[169] requiring ISPs to comply with FBI requests for subscriber information (specifically name, address and subscriber's length of service) and forbidding disclosure of the order to anyone (*i.e.*, a "gag order"). The court wrote:[170]

> Because neither the statute, nor an NSL, nor the FBI agents dealing with the recipient say as much, all but the most mettlesome and undaunted NSL recipients would consider themselves effectively barred from consulting an attorney or anyone else who might advise them otherwise, as well as bound to absolute silence about the very existence of the NSL.

The court then addressed the overbreadth of the statute:[171]

> The evidence * * * demonstrates that the information available through a § 2709 NSL served upon an ISP could easily be used to disclose vast amounts of anonymous speech and associational activity. For instance, § 2709 imposes a duty to provide "electronic communication transactional records," a phrase which, though undefined in the statute, certainly encompasses a log of email addresses with whom a subscriber has corresponded and the Web pages that a subscriber visits. Those transactional records can reveal, among other

things, the anonymous message boards to which a person logs on or posts, the electronic newsletters to which he subscribes, and the advocacy Web sites he visits. Moreover, § 2709 imposes a duty on ISPs to provide the names and addresses of subscribers, thus enabling the Government to specifically identify someone who has written anonymously on the internet.

A federal court in Connecticut subsequently enjoined the government from enforcing a gag order under the same statute where an NSL had been served on a library.[172] Both cases were combined in _Doe I v. Gonzales_.[173] While the appeals were pending, and despite civil libertarians' objections over the sweeping powers the **USA PATRIOT Act** granted the federal government, Congress renewed it with minor changes in 2006.[174] In light of those changes, the Second Circuit remanded the first case to the lower court and dismissed the second case as moot. In 2007, the lower court held, despite the revisions, the NSL's gag order provision violated First Amendment free speech rights, as both a prior restraint on speech and a content-based ban. But FBI agents can still use other means to obtain information from ISPs, including a subpoena, warrant, or court order.

Until 2005, the federal government had intercepted e-mail through its Carnivore program, an FBI Internet surveillance system to monitor electronic transmissions of criminal suspects. Carnivore could capture all e-mail to and from a user's account and all network traffic to and from a user or IP address. It could also capture all e-mail headers (including e-mail addresses) to and from an e-mail account, but not the actual contents or subject line. Carnivore could list the servers the user accessed, track everyone who accessed a specific Web page or FTP (_i.e.,_ uploaded or downloaded) file and track all Web pages or FTP files a user accessed. Critics claimed Carnivore did not include proper safeguards to prevent misuse and might have violated individual constitutional rights. In January 2005, the FBI announced it was replacing Carnivore with commercial software to eavesdrop on computer traffic, reported to be more effective and less expensive[175] than Carnivore's estimated $6–to–$15 million price tag.[176]

## The Wire Wager Act and Online Gambling

Online gambling revenues, estimated at $12 billion in 2006, were projected to have reached $25 billion by 2010, with half from U.S. gamblers.[177] Online gambling's legality has been questionable. States prohibit or regulate most or all forms of gambling. However, the Internet, with its ability to reach across state lines, again raises the issue of how states can enforce their regulations and prohibitions on this nascent technology. Although gambling sites may be based in countries where taking bets is legal, it is not necessarily legal for U.S. citizens to place bets through them. Eight states prohibit Internet gambling: Illinois, Indiana, Louisiana, Nevada, Oregon, South Dakota, Michigan, and Washington. Federal prosecutors have contended it is illegal for sites to solicit or accept bets from U.S. citizens, even if their operations are outside the United States.[178] In two separate instances in 2006, British online gambling executives were arrested when they touched U.S. soil.[179]

The main concern about online gambling is the accessibility for _minors_ and _pathological gamblers_. A U.K. study found 30 U.K. gambling sites had registered children as young as 11.[180] Gambling sites use credit and debit cards for age verification, but in the U.K. children over age 11 can obtain debit cards. Some hold banks responsible "because issuing these cards to minors gives them access to all types of adult services, including porn sites."[181]

Others argue banks should not be viewed as gatekeepers to the realm of moral turpitude and responsibility lies with the online gambling industry to devise better age verification.

There are two types of online gambling. ***Casino-style gambling*** consists of a variety of interactive games (*e.g.*, blackjack, poker, roulette, slot machines) with software-generated colorful graphics and background music. The main concern about from the gambler's view is whether the games are fair or rigged. In contrast, ***sports gambling*** sites typically are not interactive or software-intensive and thus cheaper to run. Gamblers have no concern over results tampering, since sports events outcomes are public knowledge.

Gambling sites are usually offshore, in island nations and Australia, Austria, Belgium, Germany, and South Africa. U.S. attempts to ban online gambling have been unsuccessful. In 2000, the Internet Gambling Prohibition Act failed in Congress by 25 votes. U.S. efforts to ban Americans gambling online led Antigua and Barbuda to complain to the World Trade Organization (WTO). In 2004, a WTO panel sided with them, ruling the ban violated global trade rules. The ruling was upheld twice by the WTO's appellate body and in 2007 it declared America out of compliance. [182] To comply, the United States would have to allow citizens to gamble online or ban all forms of online gambling (including buying lottery tickets online). The WTO faced a Hobson's choice, as backing down would undermine its credibility, while sanctioning the United States risked a political backlash from its most powerful backer.

Lacking an existing federal law to ban online gambling, prosecutors, as with most Internet issues, have tried to tailor existing laws to deal with emerging legal issues. They have focused on the **Wire Wager Act**, a 1961 law prohibiting use of "wire communication facilities for transmission in interstate or foreign commerce of bets or wagers or information assisting in placing of bets or wagers on any *sporting event or contest.*" [183] In 2000, the first defendant in an Internet offshore sports betting case—the co-owner of an Antigua gambling site—was convicted under the Act, fined $5,000 and sentenced to 21 months in prison. Until a law specifically outlawing Internet gambling is passed, offshore betting site prosecutions will be limited to the **Wire Wager Act**. Under it, the government must prove the defendant:

- Was engaged in the business of betting or wagering, (*i.e.*, deriving all or much income from the business of gambling; the law is mainly enforced against bookmakers, not casual bettors), and
- Transmitted, in interstate or foreign commerce: (a) bets or wagers, (b) information assisting in placement of bets or wagers, or (c) communication that entitled the recipient to receive money or credit as a result of a bet or wager, and
- Used a "wire communication facility" to transmit these materials, and
- Acted "knowingly", *i.e.*, not by accident or mistake

Congress next focused on going after the money instead of the players. It passed the **Unlawful Internet Gambling Enforcement Act**, [184] criminalizing payment processing by banks, credit card companies, and online payment systems to online gambling firms (with the exception of "fantasy" sports, lotteries, horse racing, and harness racing). Its passage caught the online gambling industry by surprise, as it was attached to the **Safe Port Act** bill shortly before Congress recessed. Since U.S. citizens account for more than half of industrywide revenue, its impact was immediately felt, with the likelihood online gambling firms would have to concentrate on growing their non-American markets or go out of business. There remained the possibility U.S. citizens might be able to place online bets through non-U.S. payment processors, effectively emaciating the law.

In 2011, a Justice Department legal opinion reversed the federal government's long opposition to Internet gambling, suggesting the **Wire Wager Act** applies only to betting on "sporting events or contests," leading some cash-strapped states to consider legalizing, licensing and taxing other forms of online gambling. [185] Most are looking at online poker, rationalizing it involves more skill and less chance than other casino-style gambling, or the sale of lottery tickets. Online poker players have been gambling on illegal sites, risking the sites would not cheat or refuse to pay out winnings. Legal, regulated sites might attract more players. However, an Iowa study has raised the concern legalized Internet gambling might pose the risk of gambling addiction and related problems for residents. [186]

## Virtual Crime

Can one be charged with stealing something that does not exist? If so, are murder charges for killing imaginary people next? What sound like absurd questions might in fact be the next frontier of Internet law. Many now play games online in *massively multiplayer online* (MMO) environments consisting of computer-generated virtual worlds in which large numbers of players interact using avatars.

For example, Habbo is a popular social network for children, with 80 million registered users in 31 countries and an estimated $77 million in annual revenue. Kids log on and create their own characters using avatars. They play games and chat with other members in the Hotel, a chat room animated to appear like a virtual hotel. Members decorate their hotel rooms with virtual furniture to suit their personalities, but the furniture must be purchased with real money from Habbo, whose revenue is derived in large part from selling virtual items like furniture and clothes to members.

In some MMOs, like the extremely popular "Second Life", members earn their real-life livings by creating items for players in the virtual world, such as avatar clothing and accessories for other players' avatars and environments. Some have online virtual stores within the MMO where they sell virtual goods for real money. South Korea has begun taxing virtual property transactions within MMOs. [187]

Of course, with virtual goods comes virtual theft. But do virtual goods, which have been paid for with real money, have legal status as goods? Can you call the police if someone online steals your virtual goods? One American man did just that! However, police in Blaine, Minnesota refused to arrest the alleged virtual thief accused of stealing $4,000 worth of virtual goods, saying it was not a "crime" because virtual items "are devoid of monetary value," and therefore no crime had actually been committed. [188]

Dutch police took a different view when they arrested a teenager for virtual theft of £2,800 worth of virtual furniture from rooms in the Habbo Hotel. He was part of a teen gang that allegedly used social engineering techniques and phishing to trick members into revealing login details and passwords, which they then used to move the stolen furniture to their own online hotel rooms. [189] In a 2008 Dutch case, an Amsterdam court found two teens guilty of theft for stealing virtual items in the computer game "RuneScape". The victim, a 13-year-old, was physically assaulted in his room and threatened with a knife if he did not log on and transfer a virtual amulet and a virtual mask from the online game to his attackers' game accounts. The assailants, ages 14 and 15, were sentenced to community service. The Leeuwarden District Court treated the virtual goods as material goods, stating "these virtual goods are goods (under Dutch law), so this is theft." [190]

Sound surreal? Having trouble picturing people suing over virtual theft in "Second Life?" Think they need to worry about getting a first life? Think again; there is real money at stake. Commerce within "Second Life" tops $1 million dollars every day![191] And under the "Second Life" Terms of Use agreement, players retain all intellectual property rights in the digital content they own, create, or otherwise place within the virtual world. Intellectual property rights can translate into big money. Six "Second Life" vendor-players sued a man in 2007 in New York federal court, alleging he violated both the **Lanham Act** and the **Copyright Act** by stealing specific computer code to copy virtual goods they had created to sell to other players. The goods included virtual clothes and virtual sex toys. The parties entered into a consent judgment.[192] A Florida "Second Life" vendor-player also sued a man for violating the **Lanham** and **Copyright Acts**, alleging theft of his virtual product — the "SexGen bed" that allowed players to place their avatars in various sexual positions and had sold for $45 each to more than 1,000 players that year.[193]

### Chapter 6 Notes

[1] "Internet 2011 in Numbers," Pingdom.com, *available at* http://royal.pingdom.com/2012/01/17/internet-2011-in-numbers (accessed Mar. 23, 2012).

[2] *Ibid.*

[3] Jon Swartz, "Poll Shows Some Look Forward to Reading Spam," USA Today, July 27, 2004.

[4] Bob Sullivan, "Now, Two-thirds of All E-mail is Spam, and in the U.S., Spam Tops 80 Percent Mark," MSNBC.com, May 22, 2004, *available at* www.msnbc.msn.com/id/5032714 (accessed Mar. 23, 2012); *see also* Sharon Gaudin, "90% of E-mail Will Be Spam by Year's End," InformationWeek, February 22, 2007.

[5] "Internet 2011 in Numbers," fn. 1, *supra.*

[6] During the Great Depression, hobos would leave a mark on the door of a home where they had received a handout as a sign to other hobos the home was a "soft touch."

[7] The CAN-SPAM Act of 2003, 15 U.S.C. § 7701-7713. The Act initially mandated a feasibility study of a "do not e-mail" registry, similar to the popular "do not call" registry, but the Federal Trade Commission (FTC) concluded the proposed registry would not be feasible.

[8] The defendants — Daniel J. Lin, James J. Lin, Mark M. Sadek and Christopher Chung, and a company (Phoenix Avatar) — were charged with sending hundreds of thousands of spam e-mails for fake diet and hormone products.

[9] "EarthLink Helps Put 'Timeshare Spammer' in the Slammer," Atlanta Business Chronicle, November 17, 2005.

[10] *United States v. Goodin*, Case No. 06-110 (C.D. Cal. 2007).

[11] *United States v. Greco* (C.D. Cal. 2005). *See also* John Leyden, "NY Teen Charged over IM Spam Attack," The Register, February 22, 2005.

[12] Steven Musil, "MySpace Wins $234 Million Antispam Judgment," CNET News.com, May 13, 2008.

[13] Greg Sandoval, "Accused Spammer Must Pay MySpace $6 Million," CNET News.com, June 16, 2008.

[14] Deborah Gage, "Facebook Wins $873 Million Case against Spammer," The San Francisco Chronicle, p. D1, November 25, 2008.

[15] FTC Press Release, "FTC Slams Spammer in Pocketbook," March 23, 2006.

[16] *United States v. Cyberheat, Inc.*, 2007 WL 686678 (D. Ariz. 2007).

[17] **Strict liability**, in criminal law, is liability for which defendants will be convicted even if ignorant of one or more factors that made their acts or omissions criminal. **Vicarious liability** is liability imputed to one for the actions of another. Agency law is based on the doctrine of **respondeat superior**, whereby a principal (*e.g.*, an employer) is liable for the actions of his agent (*e.g.*, an employee).

[18] *White Buffalo Ventures, LLC v. Univ. of Tex.*, 420 F.3d 366 (5th Cir. 2005) cert. denied, 546 U.S. 1091 (2006).

[19] Anne Broache, "Supreme Court Won't Hear Spam Appeal," CNET News.com, January 9, 2006.

[20] Eric B. Parizo, "Image Spam Paints a Troubling Picture," SearchSecurity.com, July 26, 2006.

[21] Alaska, Arkansas, Illinois, Indiana, Kansas, Louisiana, Maine, Minnesota, North Dakota, Oklahoma, Pennsylvania, South Dakota, Tennessee, Texas, Utah, and Wisconsin had required a label ("ADV: ADLT") at the beginning of the subject line of any sexually explicit unsolicited commercial e-mail message, if the sender knew the recipient was a resident of that state; however, the FTC's 2004 labeling requirement all sexually-oriented spam to be labeled "SEXUALLY EXPLICIT" in the subject line has now superseded the states' requirements.

[22] Fla. R.P.C. 4-7.6(c)(3).

[23] Kentucky Supreme Court Rules, SCR 3.130-7.09(3), Kentucky Bar Association Attorneys' Advertising Commission, AAC Regulation No. 3: Communications That Require The Disclaimer "THIS IS AN ADVERTISEMENT" (Effective January 1, 2006).

[24] Louisiana State Bar Rules of Professional Conduct, Rule 7.6(c)(3) (Effective December 1, 2008).

[25] *Jaynes v. Commonwealth*, 48 Va. App. 673 (2006). Jeremy Jaynes and his sister Jessica DeGroot were convicted on November 3, 2004. Jaynes was sentenced to nine years imprisonment (overturned on appeal when the statute was declared unconstitutional); DeGroot did not receive a prison sentence and the third defendant, Richard Rutkowski, was acquitted. All were North Carolina residents. *See* Larry O'dell, "Va. Court Upholds Spammer's Conviction," Associated Press wire service report, February 29, 2008.

[26] Jaynes and DeGroot allegedly used fake Internet addresses to send more than 10 million spam e-mails a day to AOL subscribers on three days in July 2003 — a volume that made the crime a felony under the Virginia statute; Associated Press wire service report, "Trial Shows How Spammers Operate," USA Today, November 14, 2004.

[27] *Ibid.* Jaynes' alleged spamming yielded him as much as $750,000 per month, though he only averaged one response for every 30,000 e-mails, at $40 per response.

[28] *Virginia v. Jaynes*, 666 S.E.2d 303 (Va. 2008).

[29] The Virginia Computer Crimes Act, Va. Code §§ 18.2-152.1 – 18.2-152.14.

[30] Associated Press wire service report, December 18, 2004. The Iowa law allowed plaintiffs damages of $10 per spam e-mail and RICO tripled that amount. The defendants failed to appear in court and the plaintiffs were granted a default judgment, although unlikely to be collected, as the defendants' whereabouts are unknown. The ISP's inbound mail servers had received up to 10 million spam e-mails a day in 2000.

[31] Howard Carmack of Buffalo, New York, also known as the "Buffalo Spammer." *See* Julia Angwin, "How Ruthless Youngblood Cracked an Elusive Spammer," The Wall Street Journal, May 13, 2003.

[32] Paul Roberts, "Buffalo Spammer Gets 3.5 to 7 Years," IDG News Service, May 27, 2004.

[33] Lester Haines, "Man Sues Bigger Penis Pill Company," The Register, February 16, 2005.

[34] John Leyden, "Californian Sues Penis Pill Spammers For Fraud," The Register, February 9, 2004.

[35] The Computer Fraud and Abuse Act, 18 U.S.C. § 1030.

[36] *See Am. Online, Inc. v. Christian Bros.*, Case No. 98 Civ. 8959 (S.D.N.Y. 1999); *Am. Online, Inc. v. LCGM, Inc.*, 46 F. Supp. 2d 444 (E.D. Va. 1998); and *Am. Online, Inc. v. Nat'l. Health Care Disc., Inc.*, 174 F. Supp. 2d 890 (N.D. Va. 2001).

[37] The Inbox Privacy Act of 1999, *available at* www.spamlaws.com/federal/106s759.shtml (accessed Mar. 23, 2012).

[38] A **Trojan horse** program is a malicious software program uploaded to the victim's computer without his knowledge, usually installed while the victim is downloading a different file. The name is derived from the Trojan horse from Homer's *Iliad*; during the Trojan War, the Greeks presented the citizens of Troy with a large wooden horse in which they had secretly hidden their warriors. At night, the warriors emerged from the wooden horse and overran and conquered Troy.

[39] **Pagejacking** is theft of a site's contents by copying its pages, placing them on another site that appears to be the legitimate site, and then inviting people to the illegal site through deceptive means.

[40] "Phishing Con Hijacks Browser Bar," BBC News, April 8, 2004, *available at* http://news.bbc.co.uk/1/hi/technology/3608943.stm (accessed Mar. 23, 2012).

[41] E-mail security firm MessageLabs, *available at* www.messagelabs.com/default.aspx (accessed Mar. 23, 2012).

[42] Dan Grabham, "10 Years of Phishing Attacks," tech.co.uk, March 26, 2007, *available at* www.tech.co.uk/computing/internet-and-broadband/news/10-years-of-phishing-attacks?articleid=1864041047 (accessed Mar. 23, 2012).

[43] Brian Krebs, "Cyber Crime 2.0," The Washington Post, December 20, 2007.

[44] Timothy L. O'Brien, "Gone Spear-Phishin'," The New York Times, December 4, 2005.

[45] John Markoff, "Larger Prey are Targets of Phishing," The New York Times, April 16, 2008.

[46] *Ibid. See also* Cara Garretson, "Whaling: Latest E-Mail Scam Targets Executives: Social Engineering Fuels New Form of Phishing," Network World, November 14, 2007.

[47] David Bank, "'Spear Phishing' Tests Educate People about Online Scams," The Wall Street Journal, August 17, 2005.

[48] Kelly Jackson Higgins, "'Robin Sage' Profile Duped Military Intelligence, IT Security Pros," DarkReading, July 6, 2010, *available at* www.darkreading.com/insiderthreat/security/privacy/showArticle. jhtml?articleID=225702468 (accessed Mar. 23, 2012).

[49] The Identify Theft and Assumption Deterrence Act, 18 U.S.C. §1028.

[50] Mark Adams, "Your Password for a Candy Bar?" Information Security, April 21, 2008, *available at* www.spamstopshere.com/blog/2008/04/21/your-password-for-a-candy-bar (accessed Mar. 23, 2012).

[51] Ina Fried, "Warning Sounded over 'Flirting Robots,'" CNET News.com, December 7, 2007.

[52] Kim Zetter, "Confessions of a Cybermule," Wired News, July 28, 2006.

[53] *Ibid.*

[54] From a U.S. Department of Justice press release, "Shadowcrew Organization Called 'One-Stop Online Marketplace for Identity Theft,'" October 28, 2004, *available at* www.cybercrime.gov/mantovaniIndict.htm (accessed Mar. 23, 2012):

> [I]ndividuals from across the United States and in several foreign countries conspired with others to operate "Shadowcrew", a Web site with approximately 4,000 members that was dedicated to facilitating malicious computer hacking and the dissemination of stolen credit card, debit card and bank account numbers and counterfeit identification documents, such as drivers' licenses, passports and Social Security cards. The indictment alleges a conspiracy to commit activity often referred to as "carding" — the use of account numbers and counterfeit identity documents to complete identity theft and defraud banks and retailers.

[55] Symantec Press Release, March 19, 2007, *available at* www.symantec.com/about/news/release/article. jsp?prid=20070319_01 (accessed Mar. 23, 2012). *See also* "Online Crooks Getting More Professional," Associated Press wire service report, September 17, 2007. A Symantec report for the first half of 2007 stated America hosted 64 percent of "underground economy" servers; Germany was second and Sweden ranked third. China had one-third of the world's computers taken over by *bots* (Web robots that, in this case, are used to spam without a computer owner's knowledge or consent).

[56] *Ibid.*

[57] *Ibid.*

[58] Declan McCullagh, "Season over for 'Phishing'?" CNET News.com, July 15, 2004.

[59] Statement by Sen. Strom Thurmond before the U.S. Senate Judiciary Subcommittee on Technology, Terrorism, and Government Information regarding identity theft, July 9, 2002.

[60] According to a Consumers Union telephone poll. *See* Emily Brandon, "Who's Got Your Number," U.S. News & World Report, May 29, 2008.

[61] The Social Security Act of 1935 (Pub. L. No. 74-271).

[62] Pursuant to Treasury Decision 4704.

[63] However, in the post-9/11 world, Congress has shown an inclination toward creation of a national identity card, most recently with the passage of the Real I.D. Act of 2005 (Pub. L. No. 109-13).

[64] Exec. Order No. 9397 (3 CFR (1943-1948 Comp.) 283-284).

[65] Internal Revenue Code Amendments (Pub. L. No. 87-397).

[66] Internal Revenue Code Amendments (Pub. L. No. 89-384).

[67] The Bank Records and Foreign Transactions Act (Pub. L. No. 91-508).

[68] Social Security Amendments of 1972 (Pub. L. No. 92-603).

[69] The Tax Reform Act of 1976 (Pub. L. No. 94-455).

[70] The law, effective on December 17, 2005, applies to all licenses, registrations, and identification cards issued after that date, but is not retroactive. Ironically, the federal government still uses an individual's SSN as a Medicare identifier. *See* Cathie Gandal, "Medicare Card Security under Scrutiny," AARP Bulletin, p. 4, September 2008.

[71] The Food Stamp Act of 1977 (Pub. L. No. 96-58).

[72] The Omnibus Budget Reconciliation Act of 1981 (Pub. L. No. 97-35).

[73] The Department of Defense Authorization Act (Pub. L. No. 97-86).

[74] The Debt Collection Act (Pub. L. No. 97-365).

[75] The Housing and Community Development Act of 1987 (Pub. L. No. 100-242).

[76] The Social Security Independence and Program Improvements Act of 1994 (Pub. L. No. 103-296).

[77] The Privacy Act of 1974, 5 U.S.C. § 552(a): "It shall be unlawful for any Federal, State or local government agency to deny to any individual any right, benefit, or privilege provided by law because of such individual's refusal to disclose his Social Security account number."

[78] The Buckley Amendment, 20 U.S.C. § 1232(g).

[79] *Gonzaga Univ. v. Doe*, 536 U.S. 273 (2002). This case is included in the Cases Section on the Issues in Internet Law site (www.IssuesinInternetLaw.com).

[80] 42 U.S.C. § 1983. Civil Action for Deprivation of Rights:

Every person who, under color of any statute, ordinance, regulation, custom, or usage, of any State or Territory or the District of Columbia, subjects, or causes to be subjected, any citizen of the United States or other person within the jurisdiction thereof to the deprivation of any rights, privileges, or immunities secured by the Constitution and laws, shall be liable to the party injured in an action at law, suit in equity, or other proper proceeding for redress, except that in any action brought against a judicial officer for an act or omission taken in such officer's judicial capacity, injunctive relief shall not be granted unless a declaratory decree was violated or declaratory relief was unavailable.

[81] Bill Brubaker, "Online Records May Aid ID Theft; Government Sites Post Personal Data," The Washington Post, p. A01, January 2, 2008.

[82] There is even a National Association for Information Destruction, *available at* www.naidonline.org/index.html (accessed Mar. 23, 2012).

[83] Joris Evers, "Dumped Hard Drives Tell All," CNET News.com, May 31, 2005.

[84] "Agencies Left Private Information on Discarded Computers, Audit Shows," Associated Press wire service report, May 25, 2005.

[85] Richard Pérez-Peña, "New Jersey nearly Sold Secret Data," The New York Times, March 10, 2011, p. A24.

[86] "Bank Customer Data Sold on eBay," BBC News, August 26, 2008.

[87] Armen Keteyian, "Digital Photocopiers Loaded with Secrets," cbsnews.com, April 15, 2010.

[88] For example, the New Jersey state comptroller stated only one agency had a device to magnetically erase hard drives, but "employees did not like to use it because it was noisy." Pérez-Peña, fn. 48, *supra*.

[89] Lucy Sherriff, "Investigators Uncover Dismal Data Disposal," The Register, February 17, 2005.

[90] The Identity Theft Penalty Enhancement Act (Pub. L. No. 108-275).

[91] Christian Wiessner, "Cybercriminals Use Celebrity Names to Lure Victims," Reuters wire service, September 16, 2008.

[92] Click-wrap agreements are discussed further in Chapter 20, *infra*.

[93] "Creator and Four Users of Loverspy Spyware Program Indicted," U.S. Department of Justice press release, August 26, 2005.

[94] "Jealous Lovers: No Web Snooping," Associated Press wire service report, August 27, 2005.

[95] *See* Robert Vamosi, "Spyware Found in Sears Online Community Installation," CNET News.com, January 3, 2008 *and* Maxim Weinstein, "My SHC Community Report Released," January 8, 2008, *available at* http://blogs.stopbadware.org/articles/2008/01/08/my-shc-community-report-released (accessed Mar. 23, 2012).

[96] "Online Brokerage Account Scams Worry SEC," Reuters wire service report, October 13, 2006.

[97] Discussed *infra* in this chapter.

[98] *FTC v. Seismic Entm't Prods., Inc.*, Civ. No. 04-377-JD (D. N.H. 2004); Stipulated Final Order for Permanent Injunction (2006).

[99] Roy Mark, "Spyware Operators Settles with FTC," InternetNewsBureau.com, November 22, 2006, *was available at* www.internetnews.com/bus-news/article.php/3645466 (accessed Jul. 23, 2010) but no longer available.

[100] "Porn Virus Publishes Web History of Victims on the Net," BBC News, April 15, 2010.

[101] *Ibid.*

[102] Brian Krebs, "Banner Ad Trojan Served on MySpace, Photobucket," The Washington Post, September 9, 2007.

[103] "Google Searches Web's Dark Side," BBC News, May 11, 2007.

[104] Restatement (Second) of Torts § 217 (1965).

[105] *Thrifty-Tel, Inc. v. Bezenek*, 46 Cal. App. 4th 1559 (1996).

[106] *CompuServe, Inc. v. Cyber Promotions, Inc.*, 962 F. Supp. 1015 (S.D. Ohio 1997).

[107] *eBay, Inc. v. Bidder's Edge, Inc.*, 100 F. Supp. 2d 1058 (N.D. Cal. 2000).

[108] *Intel Corp. v. Hamidi*, 30 Cal. 4th 1342 (Cal. 2003).

[109] *See* Robert McMillan, "Man Stole Nude Photos from Women's E-mail Accounts," IDG News, January 13, 2011; and "Attorney General Kamala D. Harris Warns about Identity Theft as Predator Pleads Guilty to Hacking Hundreds of E-Mail Accounts," Press Release, January 13, 2011, *available at* http://oag.ca.gov/news/press_release?id=2026 (accessed Mar. 23, 2012).

[110] Brennon Slattery, "Husband's E-mail Snooping May Lead to Five Years in Prison," PCWorld, December 28, 2010.

[111] Mich. Comp. Laws § 752.795, which reads, in relevant part:
> A person shall not intentionally and without authorization or by exceeding valid authorization do any of the following: Access or cause access to be made to a computer program, computer, computer system or computer network to acquire, alter, damage delete or destroy property or otherwise use the service of a computer program, computer, computer system or computer network.

[112] *Michigan v. Walker*, Dkt. Nos. 304593 and 304702 (Oakland Cir. Ct. entered September 6, 2011 and June 22, 2011, respectively) (Unpublished) *available at* http://coa.courts.mi.gov/documents/opinions/final/coa/20111227_c304593_54_304593.opn.pdf (accessed Mar. 23, 2012).

[113] The Computer Fraud and Abuse Act, 18 U.S.C. § 1030.

[114] See the discussion in Chapter 18 of the *Drew* case, in which federal prosecutors charged a woman with violation of the **Computer Fraud and Abuse Act** (CFAA), a federal anti-hacking statute, for violating the MySpace's Terms of Use agreement.

[115] *United States v. Nosal*, Case No. 10-10038 (9th Cir. 2011), reversing 642 F.3d 781 (9th Cir. 2011).

[116] *State v. Wolf*, Case No. 08 CA 16 (Ohio 5th App. Dist. 2009).

[117] "Florida Man Charged with Stealing Wi-Fi Signal," Associated Press wire service report, July 18, 2005.

[118] Dan Ilett, "Wireless Network Hijacker Found Guilty," Silicon.com, July 22, 2005.

[119] Richard Shim, "Wi-Fi Arrest Highlights Security Dangers," CNET News.com, November 28, 2003.

[120] Jeff Beard, "Wi-Fi Hacker Arrest Raises Security & Liability Concerns," Law Tech Guru Blog, *available at* www.lawtechguru.com./archives/2003/12/02_wifi_hacker_arrest_raises_security_liability_concerns.html (accessed Mar. 23, 2012).

[121] See the discussion of the **Communications Decency Act** (CDA) in Chapter 14, *infra*.

[122] David Meyer, "Pub Fined $13k for Wi-Fi Copyright Infringement," CNET News.com, November 28, 2009.

[123] Twenty-one year old Brian Salcedo was sentenced to nine years in prison for hacking into the computer system of Lowe's Department Store, the longest prison sentence to date for computer hacking. U.S. Department of Justice Press Release, *available at* www.usdoj.gov/criminal/cybercrime/salcedoSent.htm (accessed Mar. 23, 2012).

[124] Kevin Poulsen, "Wardriving Guilty Plea in Lowe's Wi-Fi Case," SecurityFocus.com, August 5, 2004, *available at* www.securityfocus.com/news/9281 (accessed Mar. 23, 2012).

[125] *Ibid.*

[126] *See* Beard, fn. 120, *supra*.

[127] Kevin Poulsen, "Crazy-Long Hacker Sentence Upheld," Wired.com, July 11, 2006.

[128] "Some Schools Banning iPods to Stop Cheating," Associated Press wire service report, April 27, 2007.

[129] Even Apple Computer discovered its employees had used their iPods to smuggle corporate secrets out of the building. Hiawatha Bray, "iPod Can Be Music to a Data Thief's Ear," The Boston Globe, June 6, 2005.

[130] For example, the Archos 7 Wi-Fi portable media player has a 320 GB drive.

[131] The author hereby humbly coins the phrase "pod burping" to refer to use of a portable media device to inject viruses or malicious code into a corporate network.

[132] Symantec Press Release, March 19, 2007, *available at* www.symantec.com/about/news/release/article.jsp?prid=20070319_01 (accessed Mar. 23, 2012).

[133] "Keyboard Sniffers to Steal Data," BBC News, October 21, 2008.

[134] Will Knight, "A Year Ago: Cypherpunks Publish Proof of Tempest," ZDNet UK, October 26, 2000. Reports vary on what TEMPEST is. Some say TEMPEST stands for "Transient Electromagnetic Pulse Surveillance Technology" and is a U.S. government program to use electromagnetic emanations from keyboards for surveillance. *See* FAS Intelligence Resource Program at www.fas.org/irp/program/security/

tempest.htm (accessed Mar. 23, 2012). Others claim the acronym stands for "Telecommunications Electronics Material Protected from Emanating Spurious Transmissions" and is a U.S. government program designed to find ways to shield computers from electromagnetic eavesdropping—a defensive application rather than a spying tool, but nonetheless confirming the existence of the technology. *See* Arik Hesseldahl, "The Tempest Surrounding Tempest," Forbes, October 2008. Still other sources claim TEMPEST is a U.S. government standard for measuring electromagnetic emanations. However, a Forbes report, *supra*, lumped TEMPEST in with Echelon (the global telecommunications surveillance network run by the National Security Agency) and Carnivore (an Internet eavesdropping tool used by the FBI, discussed in this chapter).

[135] Brian Krebs, "'Money Mules' Help Haul Cyber Criminals' Loot," The Washington Post, January 25, 2008.

[136] Working to Halt Online Abuse site, *available at* www.haltabuse.org/resources/stats (accessed Mar. 23, 2012).

[137] *Ibid.*

[138] *Ibid.*

[139] *Duick v. Toyota Motor Sales USA, Inc.*, Case No. B224839 (Cal. Ct. App. Aug. 31, 2011).

[140] Sock puppets have also been used by individuals to alter Wikipedia entries (either in self-promotion in their own entries or to detract from others in their entries) and to praise (their own) books on Amazon.com. Whole Foods Market's C.E.O. used a sock puppet on Yahoo! message boards from 1999 to 2006 to promote his company's stock (including making stock price predictions) and attack its competitor Wild Oats Markets; although the SEC announced it was examining the blog posts to determine if they violated securities laws, in May 2008 it recommended no action be taken. *See* David Kesmodel and Jonathan Eig, "A Grocer's Brash Style Takes Unhealthy Turn," The Wall Street Journal, July 20, 2007. *See also* Brad Stone and Matt Richtel, "The Hand That Controls the Sock Puppet Could Get Slapped," The New York Times, July 16, 2007.

[141] Kit R. Roane, "Taking Penny Stocks out of the Boiler Room," U.S. News & World Report, June 4, 2007, pp. 55-56.

[142] Karey Wutkowski, "SEC Cracks down on Spam-driven Stocks," Reuters wire service report, March 8, 2007.

[143] The Securities Act of 1933, 15 U.S.C. § 77(a), *et seq.*

[144] The Securities Exchange Act of 1934, 15 U.S.C. § 78, *et seq.*

[145] The USA PATRIOT Act, (Pub. L. No. 107-56).

[146] **Habeas corpus** (Latin for "you have the body") is a writ directed to one holding an individual in custody or detention commanding the detained individual be brought before a court to determine the legality of his detention. Its purpose is to ensure individuals are not unlawfully detained. The writ of habeas corpus dates back to 13th century England and was adopted by the United States.

[147] The Supreme Court upheld the constitutionality of Executive Order 9066 in *Korematsu v. United States*, 323 U.S. 214 (1944).

[148] The Bank Secrecy Act of 1970, 31 U.S.C. §§ 5311-5355.

[149] The Computer Fraud and Abuse Act of 1986 (CFAA), 18 U.S.C. § 1030.

[150] The Electronic Communications Privacy Act (ECPA), 18 U.S.C. § 2510, *et seq.*

[151] The Fair Credit Reporting Act (FCRA), 15 U.S.C. § 1681.

[152] The Family Educational Rights and Privacy Act (FERPA), 20 U.S.C. § 1232(g).

[153] The Foreign Intelligence Surveillance Act (FISA), 50 U.S.C. § 1801, *et seq.*

[154] The Immigration and Nationality Act (INA), 12 U.S.C. § 1101.

[155] The Anti-Money Laundering Act (AMLA), 31 U.S.C. § 5318(h).

[156] The Money Laundering Control Act (MLCA), 18 U.S.C. §§ 1956-57.

[157] The Pen Register and Trap and Trace Statute (PRTTS), 18 U.S.C. §§ 3121-27.

[158] The Right to Financial Privacy Act (RFPA), 12 U.S.C. § 3401, *et seq.*

[159] The Federal Wiretap Act, 18 U.S.C. §§ 2510-22 (Title I of the ECPA).

[160] The USA PATRIOT Act § 216.

[161] The USA PATRIOT Act § 210.

[162] The USA PATRIOT Act § 212 (The "Cyber Security Enhancement Act").

[163] Google even refused to comply with a government subpoena requesting user search information. *See* Andrew Orlowski, "US Gov Demands Google Search Records," The Register, January 19, 2006.

[164] The Electronic Communications Privacy Act, fn. 143, *supra.*

[165] NSLs can also be issued by the U.S. Department of Defense and other agencies.

[166] Barton Gellman, "The FBI's Secret Scrutiny: In Hunt for Terrorists Bureau Examines Records of Ordinary Americans," The Washington Post, p. A01, November 6, 2005.

[167] *Ibid.*

[168] *Doe v. Ashcroft*, 334 F. Supp. 2d 471 (S.D.N.Y. 2004).

[169] 18 U.S.C. § 2709. Counterintelligence Access to Telephone Toll and Transactional Record.

[170] *Ashcroft*, 334 F. Supp. 2d 471.

[171] *Ibid.*

[172] *Doe v. Gonzales*, 386 F. Supp. 2d 66, 82 (D. Conn. 2005).

[173] *Doe I v. Gonzales*, 449 F.3d 415 (2ᵈ Cir. 2006).

[174] One change was redefining the phrase "wire or electronic communication service provider" to exclude libraries. *See* The USA PATRIOT Improvement and Reauthorization Act of 2005, Pub. L. No. 109-177, 120 Stat. 192 (March 9, 2006).

[175] "FBI Tosses Carnivore to the Dogs," Associated Press wire service report, January 18, 2005.

[176] *Ibid.*

[177] Michael A. Hiltzik, "Latest Arrest Chips Away at Online Betting," The Los Angeles Time, September 8, 2006).

[178] *Ibid.*

[179] *Ibid.* Peter Dicks, London-based Sportingbet, PLC chairman, was arrested on a layover at a New York airport on a Louisiana criminal warrant for violating a Louisiana law against computer gambling with a maximum five-year prison sentence and $25,000 fine. He was released after New York's governor declined to extradite him to Louisiana. David Carruthers, C.E.O. of BetOnSports.com, arrested on a layover at the Dallas-Ft. Worth Airport, was charged with violating federal racketeering and mail fraud laws. "N.Y. Judge Declines to Hold Former British Online Gambling Exec," Associated Press wire service report, September 29, 2006. Three BetOnSports executives pleaded guilty to federal racketeering charges in St. Louis, Missouri. BetOnSports handled $1.8 billion annually in bets. *See* Jim Salter, "Three Plead Guilty in BetOnSports Online Gambling Case," Associated Press wire service report, June 23, 2009.

[180] Melissa Kite, "Government to Crack down on Online Gambling by Children," telegraph.co.uk (daily online U.K. newspaper), August 1, 2004, *available at* www.telegraph.co.uk/news/uknews/1468358/Government-to-crack-down-on-online-gambling-by-children.html (accessed Mar. 23, 2012).

[181] David Hood, spokesman for bookmaker William Hill, *see* Sarah Womack, "Gambling Web Sites Let Punters as Young as 11 Set up Accounts," telegraph.co.uk, July 27, 2004, *available at www.telegraph.co.uk/news/uknews/1467932/Gambling-websites-let-punters-as-young-as-11-set-up-accounts.html* (accessed Mar. 23, 2012); "Children Able to Gamble on Net," BBC News, July 27, 2004, *available at* http://news.bbc.co.uk/1/hi/uk/3927645.stm (accessed Mar. 23, 2012).

[182] Gary Rivlin, "Gambling Dispute with a Tiny Country Puts U.S. in a Bind," The New York Times, August 23, 2007.

[183] The Wire Wager Act, 18 U.S.C. § 1084.

[184] The Unlawful Internet Gambling Enforcement Act of 2006, 31 U.S.C. §§ 5361-5367.

[185] "Whether Proposals by Illinois and New York to Use the Internet and Out-Of-State Transaction Processors to Sell Lottery Tickets to In-State Adults Violate the Wire Act," Department of Justice Memorandum, September 20, 2011 *available at* www.justice.gov/olc/2011/state-lotteries-opinion.pdf (accessed Mar. 23, 2012).

[186] Michael Cooper, "As States Weigh Online Gambling, Profit May Be Small, "The New York Times, January 17, 2012.

[187] "RMT Taxation Starts in Korea from 1 July 2007," IM69.COM-Da Kick Arse Vampire's Blog, June 27, 2007, *was available at* http://im69.com/entry/ENG-RMT-Taxation-starts-in-Korea-from-1-July-2007?TSSESSIONim69com=51fb98e06b8d366677d49d693253a101 (accessed July 1, 2009) but no longer available.

[188] Earnest Cavalli, "Police Refuse to Aid in Virtual Theft Case," Wired, February 4, 2008.

[189] Bruno Waterfield, "World's First Arrests for 'Virtual Theft'," The Telegraph (U.K.) November 14, 2007.

[190] *See* "Dutch Court Convicts 2 of Stealing Virtual Items," October 21, 2008; *and* Ben Kuchera, "Dutch Court Imposes Real-world Punishment for Virtual Theft," ArsTechica, October 23, 2008.

[191] ABA Section of Intellectual Property Law, Div. VII — Information Technology, Final Report, August 5, 2008.

[192] *Eros, LLC v. Simon*, Case No. 07-cv-4447 (E.D.N.Y. 2007). The case was settled in December 2007, for $525 and an agreement by the defendant to cease and desist.

[193] *Eros, LLC v. Leatherwood*, Dkt. No. 8:07-cv-0115-SCB-TGW (M.D. Fla. filed Jul. 3, 2007; settled Mar. 2008).

# CHAPTER

# 7

—

# PRIVACY BASICS

> This chapter discusses the right to privacy (appropriation, intrusion, false light, and public disclosure of private facts), the right of publicity, public records, and voluntary disclosure of private information, with emphasis on the First and Fourth Amendments.

*"The right to be let alone is indeed the beginning of all freedoms."* — *Justice William O. Douglas*

## The Right to Privacy

THE RIGHT TO PRIVACY is not explicitly stated anywhere within the U.S. Constitution. In fact, in the earliest case to address the concept, the New York Supreme Court ruled it did not exist.[1] A flour company used a picture of Abby Roberson, without her consent, on flyers posted around town to advertise its product. The girl's family claimed this caused her severe embarrassment and humiliation, but the court ruled 4–to–3 she had no cause of action to sue. The public outcry was so fierce, the state legislature enacted a statute making it a tort punishable as a misdemeanor to use the name, portrait, or picture of any person for "advertising purposes or for the purposes of trade" without written consent. Three years later, the Georgia Supreme Court, in what would become the leading case, resolved the issue with the opposite result of the New York court, recognizing a distinct right to privacy, when an insurance company used a man's picture, without consent, to sell insurance.[2]

The *right to privacy* is a derived right, *i.e.*, a right logically drawn from those expressly enumerated, in this case inferred from the Fourth Amendment guarantees against unreasonable search and seizures. The first legal article suggesting the existence of a right to privacy was written by Samuel Warren and Louis Brandeis in the *Harvard Law Review* in 1890.[3] This famous article discusses the "right to be let alone". The right to privacy is a common law right developed by courts (not legislatures), and varies by state. As Warren and Brandeis put it:[4]

> Thoughts, emotions, and sensations demanded legal recognition, and the beautiful capacity for growth which characterizes the common law enabled the judges to afford the requisite protection, without the interposition of the legislature.

Unlike defamation, which addresses injury to reputation,[5] American privacy law targets injury to an individual's feelings (European privacy law is more concerned with an individual's dignity).[6] The right to privacy is considered a personal right, thus there is no privacy right for corporations. However, corporations have rights analogous to an individual's right to privacy, *i.e.*, intellectual property rights. For example, they may protect their business plans, prototypes, and other confidential business matters under trade secrets laws (see Chapter 4). Privacy has been defined by the U.S. Supreme Court as the right of an individual to control dissemination of information about oneself. The right to privacy stems from a:

- Class of persons, *e.g.*, children or patients
- Specific type of information, *e.g.*, medical history or tax returns
- Set of circumstances, *e.g.*, intrusion into one's private affairs

There are four distinct categories of the tort of invasion of privacy, each based on different elements:[7]

- Appropriation of name or likeness
- Intrusion on solitude or seclusion
- Public disclosure of private facts
- False light in the public eye

## Appropriation (The Right of Publicity)

*Appropriation* involves use of an individual's name, likeness, or identity for trade or advertising purposes without consent. It is the oldest form of invasion of privacy, dating back to the <u>Roberson</u> case. The tort of appropriation is also inversely referred to as the *"right of publicity"*, *i.e.*, a right to prevent use of one's identifiable name or likeness by a third-party for commercial purposes without consent.

The right of publicity is recognized in 28 states (there is no federal right of publicity) through either statute or case law, and its scope varies by state. It has been evolving since public outcry from the <u>Roberson</u> case established the dual concept individuals should be able to control how their personas are used, or whether they are used at all. The latter proposition is a privacy right, *i.e.*, a personal interest in anonymity, the right to be left alone — a person should be able to prevent another from using his likeness without permission and be compensated for emotional distress resulting from such unauthorized use of his identity. The former proposition has been cast as a property right, as the commercial component implies an intrinsic value in one's name or likeness; and any compensation is not for emotional distress but for restitution of that intrinsic commercial value. Recently, some have deemed the right of publicity an intellectual property right, similar to copyright or trademark rights.

The notion of the right of publicity as a property right began with the 1953 case of <u>Haelan Laboratories v. Topps Chewing Gum</u>, the first case to coin the phrase "right of publicity."[8] Haelan, a chewing gum company, had signed exclusive contracts with Major League Baseball players to appear on trading cards. Rival Topps signed the same players to appear on its baseball cards. Haelan sued Topps for inducing the players to breach the exclusivity contracts. Topps' rather weak defense was the exclusivity contract was merely a release to protect Haelan from any subsequent invasion of privacy suit from the players. Instead, the Second Circuit ruled a contract did exist, Topps had tortiously interfered with Haelan's business relationship with the players, and "in addition to and independent of [the appropriation] right of privacy, * * * a man has a right in the publicity value of his photograph * * * This right might be called a 'right of publicity.'" [9] *Haelan* illustrates the difficulties celebrities and other public figures had winning appropriation cases — it was hard to claim invasion of privacy when one was actively thrusting oneself into the limelight to achieve celebrity.

As mentioned, the scope of the right varies by state. In some, it is transferable and in certain states it may survive the individual's death. Actor Bela Lugosi became famous for his movie role as the vampire Dracula from the Bram Stoker novel of the same name. After Lugosi's death, his widow and son sued Universal Pictures, alleging the movie studio was using Lugosi's likeness in its promotion of Dracula-related merchandise. The plaintiffs claimed a property interest in Lugosi's right of publicity, but the California Supreme Court held "the right to exploit one's name and likeness is personal to the artist and must be exercised, if at all, by him during his lifetime." [10] Subsequently, in 1986, the state legislature passed the California **Celebrities Rights Act**, which created an inheritable right to a person's name or likeness for 70 years after death (extended retroactively in 2007 to all individuals who had died since January 1, 1938). [11]

Appropriation, or inversely, the right of publicity, refers not merely to an individual's name but to one's identity or persona. Many people may share the same name, but identity is unique. A VCR manufacturer ran a TV ad showing a blonde robot flipping over cards on a game show; Vanna White, the blonde star of the game show "*Wheel of Fortune*", claimed it was her likeness and won her appropriation suit, as flipping over cards on a game show **was** her identity! [12] Similarly, iconic talk show host Johnny Carson, who was introduced each night by announcer Ed McMahon intoning a stylized, drawn out "Heeeeeeeeere's Johnny!" successfully sued Here's Johnny Portable Toilets, Inc. for violating his right of publicity. [13] Even though the portable toilet firm did not use Carson's name or likeness, the Sixth Circuit held it nonetheless had appropriated his persona. However, the right of publicity only protects the identity or persona of humans; it does not protect the identity or persona of a corporation, partnership, institution, or other business entity. [14]

State courts have applied different tests to determine if there has been appropriation. Some, like Missouri, consider whether the use is predominantly commercial or expressive, whereas California focuses on whether the defendant's use is transformative. The California Second District Court of Appeal held three video game companies could market a character based on a well-known former lead singer of a 1990s funk band because the company's use was transformative by adding "new expression." [15] The court said: [16]

> All that is necessary is that [Sega's] work add 'something new, with a further purpose or different character, altering the first with new expression, meaning, or message.' * * * A work is transformative if it adds 'new expression.' That expression alone is sufficient it need not convey any 'meaning or message.'

It found the First Amendment a complete defense to the singer's misappropriation claim because the game maker had added its own creative characteristics (a different hairstyle). From a more traditional analysis, it may also have been significant while the right of publicity protects one's "identity", the singer testified she had "no singular identity", and her appearance and visual style were "continually moving" because she was "not the type of artist that wants to do the same thing every time." [17] Under the transformative test, the California Supreme Court found DC Comics had substantially transformed two half-worm, half-human creatures with green tentacles sprouting from their chests (named the "Autumn brothers") from the likenesses of musicians Johnny and Edgar Winters (the "Winters brothers") in its *Jonah Hex: Riders of the Worm* comic book.[18] "Although the fictional characters * * * are less-than-subtle evocations of Johnny and Edgar Winter, the books do not depict plaintiffs literally. They are distorted for purposes of lampoon, parody, or caricature."[19] In contrast, the Missouri Supreme Court, applying the "commercial or expressive" test, found creation of a comic book villain using the name and likeness of former St. Louis Blues hockey player Tony Twist in Todd McFarlane's *Spawn* comic book commercially exploitative, awarding Twist $5 million.[20] It found the "predominant purpose" of using the hockey player's name and likeness was to sell comic books.

Defenses to appropriation are consent; failing to identify the individual; and newsworthiness (but not for advertising purposes). However, newsworthiness is not an absolute defense; the U.S. Supreme Court ruled a plaintiff whose entire 15-second circus act as a "human cannonball" was broadcast by a television station had a right to publicity value of his performance."[21]

The California **Celebrities Rights Act** was invoked by defendants in a class action against Facebook after they discovered by clicking on the "like" button for a particular page, product, or company on its site, Facebook generated paid advertisements displaying the their name, photo, and a caption asserting they liked a certain advertiser, to their friends on the social network.[22] The defendants argued using their identities (*i.e.*, names and images) for profit to promote or endorse products or businesses without their knowledge or consent, and without compensation, violated the statute. Facebook moved to dismiss the suit, countering use of its member's names and photographs fell under the Act's "newsworthy" exception, for which consent is not required, because the "plaintiffs are 'public figures' to their friends," and " 'expressions of consumer opinion' are generally newsworthy."

The determination of whether one is a "public figure" is important in defamation cases because public figures bear a higher burden of proof (*i.e.*, **actual malice**) than "private figures" (*i.e.*, negligence).[23] Social media may blur the distinction; one might ask, if a private figure creates a public Facebook profile and voluntarily posts personal details, has he "voluntarily thrust" himself into the public eye? Would the answer depend on how many people actually view the profile, or merely on the fact it could be viewed by an unlimited audience? If the latter, then would listing one's name in the phone book, which can be viewed by anyone, make one a public figure? Would the answer change based on whether his profile's privacy settings (indicating his intent, or lack thereof, to limit the audience for his posted content) made it viewable to the world at large or only to selected friends? In any event, to extend the public figure concept to "being known among one's friends" would be to vitiate it. More importantly, while the concept is relevant in defamation law, it has no bearing in a case where the cause of action lies in misappropriation for pecuniary gain.

The California District Court denied Facebook's request to dismiss, allowing the case to proceed to trial, noting (reminiscent of the "human cannonball" case):[24]

> While the Court agrees that Plaintiffs' assertion of their status as local "celebrities" within their own Facebook social networks likewise makes them subjects of public interest among the same audience, even newsworthy actions may be subjects of [the statute's] liability when published for commercial rather than journalistic purposes.

## Intrusion on Solitude or Seclusion

*Intrusion* involves intruding on one's solitude or seclusion, either physically (*i.e.*, entering onto property, *e.g.*, searching an employee's locker or opening an employee's mail marked "personal" or "confidential") or by electronic or mechanical means. The tort occurs at the stage of information gathering and does not require publication. The intrusion must be offensive and objectionable to a reasonable man. It would not be intrusion merely to photograph a woman walking down a public street; however, photographing the same woman walking down a public street at the precise moment a gust of wind were to blow her dress up would be considered intrusion.[25] Defenses to an intrusion claim are express or implied consent, and being on public property.

Google, in 2007, launched Street Views, an application for Google Maps, which provided panoramic camera views of city streets in selected cities (initially Denver, Houston, Las Vegas, Los Angeles, Miami, New York, Orlando, San Diego, and San Francisco). Google claimed it only filmed public property, comparing it to what people walking down a city street might see.[26] Pedestrians were visibly identifiable and the detail was so fine license plates could be read. While most street scenes captured on Google Street Views tend to be innocuous, recent examples appear to intrude on one's solitude in public places:

- A man urinating on the side of a road[27]
- A woman picking her nose
- A surfer changing into his swimsuit
- A man sitting inside his house in front of a window
- A man entering an adult bookstore
- A man entering a strip club

While Google has argued these activities occurred in public, instead of a handful of people viewing them, Google Street Views allows millions to view individuals working outside, picking their noses or adjusting their clothes as they walk along the street, or sunbathing in bikinis on the lawn of Stanford University (a scene so popular it was posted to multiple blogs that solicit popular Google Street Views photos).[28] The ubiquity of closed circuit filming in modern society by security cameras in stores and on public streets was best expressed by an ad in a San Francisco Nordstrom's department store window for fashion designer Kenneth Cole's clothing line — "You are on a video camera over 20 times a day. Are you dressed for it?"[29]

The issue of intrusion becomes of greater concern when one considers the effect of inferences drawn from extrinsic facts when viewing the filmed subjects. For example, while filming someone walking down a public street might not by itself be an intrusion into individual privacy, would that change if a clearly identifiable individual were walking into:

- A rape counseling center?
- An Alcoholics Anonymous meeting?
- An adult bookstore or strip club?
- A Gay and Lesbian Community Center?
- A police station, as an informant?

Google said it would "try to not have identifiable faces and licence plate numbers in any Street Views image in Canada" after the Canadian privacy commissioner voiced concerns over Street Views' impending arrival in Canada.[30] Is Google's Street Views an intrusion that would be offensive and objectionable to a reasonable man? Or merely the exercise of free speech to photograph public places and people in them, colliding with the privacy interests and expectations of individuals as they go about their daily routine?

A Pennsylvania couple sued Google for invasion of privacy after photographs of their home appeared on Street Views.[31] Ironically, a photograph of the home, along with the couple's name and a detailed property description was also listed on the Allegheny County Assessor's Office site. The First Amendment right to take pictures on a public street or photograph a home from one is well established. The issue of invasion of privacy comes into play where there is an intrusion offensive and objectionable to a reasonable man, *e.g.*, photographing a home from a public street using a telephoto lens to peer into a bedroom or physically entering private property. Google has stated it removes images from Street Views on request and even removed photographs of an entire city after a request from the city council.[32]

Consent is a defense to intrusion, *e.g.*, an invitation to enter one's home. But consent can be exceeded — an invitation to enter one's home for dinner does not entitle the guest to rifle through the host's bedroom drawers. Necessity may be another defense; *e.g.*, entering a sleeping neighbor's home to rescue him from a fire. A lack of expectation of privacy is a third defense to intrusion — this has been referred to as the "plain view" defense, *i.e.*, where the plaintiff was in plain view in a public place and therefore had no reasonable expectation of privacy. But, even in a public place it might be reasonable for one not to expect to be recorded by hidden surveillance cameras (*e.g.*, clothing store changing rooms or public restrooms).

An interesting privacy issue concerns publication of tidbits of public information collated on a single site and presented in a manner that might be intrusive. The site BlockShopper.com lists purchases and sales of neighborhood homes, including the buyer's and seller's names, home address and description, purchase price, a map to the property, and a photograph of the residence, all of which is public information available at the public records office (except for the photograph, presumably from the Multiple Listing Service [MLS] site).[33] So far, no problem. But BlockShopper goes one step further, and scours the Web to add other publicly available Internet information to its site, including a biography of the purchaser (*e.g.*, profession, graduation dates, degrees, spouse) and a photograph of the purchaser with his or her name captioned underneath. While all the information on the page is either from public records or freely accessible online, the tying together of such disparate information to create effectively a personal profile is highly intrusive. Disclosure of personally identifiable information poses serious risks, like identity theft and stalking (see the <u>Remsburg</u> case later in this chapter). BlockShopper focuses on professionals, mainly lawyers and doctors. By simply buying or selling a home, the life of a trial lawyer or abortion doctor might be at risk from a stalker, who now has one-stop access to the potential victim's home address (complete with a map, directions, and photo of the house), a photo of the potential victim, and the workplace name.

## Public Disclosure of Private Facts

*Public disclosure of private facts* involves publication of private and embarrassing facts unrelated to matters of public concern (*i.e.*, non-newsworthy). It is premised on the notion certain information about an individual is of such an intimate or offensive nature, and of so slight legitimate public interest and concern, it can and should be completely removed from public discourse. The facts must be private (*e.g.*, medical conditions and treatment, sexual relations, personal letters, or income taxes) and there must be a reasonable expectation they will remain private. Anything in the public record, regardless of how embarrassing or distasteful, is not actionable. Also, the disclosure must be relatively widespread; while disclosure to a small group might not be actionable, this requirement will seldom pose a problem on the World Wide Web. Defenses to a public disclosure of private facts claim are: the facts are related to matters of public concern (*i.e.*, newsworthy); the facts would not be offensive to a reasonable man; the facts are a matter of public record; and consent.

A hospital employee allegedly posted a patient's medical information on his Facebook page to make fun of the woman and her medical condition, publishing her name and adding: "Funny but this patient came in to cure her VD and get birth control."[34] Such actions would not only subject the poster to liability in a civil suit for invasion of privacy by public disclosure of private facts, but also violate the **Health Insurance Portability and Accountability Act** (HIPAA).[35]

## False Light in the Public Eye

*False light in the public eye* involves a statement that is false or misleading, and highly offensive (but not necessarily defamatory) and creates a false impression about the plaintiff in the public eye. While similar to the tort of defamation, the primary difference is defamation must adversely harm one's reputation, whereas the false light tort requires the representation merely be "highly offensive to a reasonable person." For example, suppose a newspaper article on police cracking down on prostitution is accompanied by a photograph of a man leaving a bordello. The obvious impression would be the man was a customer; however, what if he had delivered a pizza and was on his way out of the building to return to his car? Use of the photograph, especially in juxtaposition with, and given the context of, the article, would have cast him in a false light in the public eye.

Several states do not recognize the false light tort on the grounds it is too similar to defamation and the false light standard too subjective and likely to chill free speech. The false light tort has been recognized by 30 states, expressly rejected by 10, and 10 have yet to rule on the issue. The main difference between the two torts is the legal standard applied. The "highly offensive to a reasonable person," false light standard compensates for hurt feelings, whereas the defamation standard requiring a showing of reputational injury in the community compensates a plaintiff for damage to reputation. False light requires broad publication to many people, while defamation need only be made to a few. Also, false light provides liability for untrue implications (as in the example above) rather than express false statements. Truth can be a defense to defamation, but is irrelevant to false light. Florida declined to recognize false light, instead recognizing the tort of *defamation by implication* in its place.[36] In crafting the defamation by implication tort, the court adopted a new standard to go with it, substituting "a substantial and respectable minority" for the "reasonable person". The dissent argued the new standard was too vague.

## Privacy Defenses

Unlike defamation actions, truth is not a defense in invasion of privacy actions. Defenses to invasion of privacy claims usually fall under consent; privilege (*e.g.*, court records); information in the public record; matters of legitimate public concern (*i.e.*, newsworthiness); failure to prove a necessary element of the tort; or, in some cases, expiration of the applicable statute of limitations.

## Federal Laws Affecting Privacy

Although there are no *general* federal privacy laws, there are federal laws protecting certain aspects of an individual's right to privacy. The **Video Privacy Protection Act** of 1988 makes it illegal to disclose what videotapes an individual has rented, unless given informed, written consent at the time the disclosure is sought.[37] In 2007, a federal court ruled customers of online bookseller Amazon.com have a First Amendment right to keep their reading habits from the government.[38] Federal prosecutors had subpoenaed the identities of thousands of individuals who bought used books through Amazon. The initial subpoena sought records of 24,000 transactions dating back to 1999, but was later narrowed to 120 customers. In 2008, when a federal court granted a motion allowing records of every video watched by YouTube users, including their login names and IP addresses, to be turned over to Viacom, the Electronic Frontier Foundation argued the ruling violated the **Video Privacy Protection Act**.[39] Similarly, in 2010, Amazon sued North Carolina, claiming the state tax collector's demand for "full details" on 50 million purchases by residents between 2003 and 2010 violated its customers' privacy and First Amendment rights.[40] The state sought personally identifiable information that could be used to collect use taxes from residents. A federal court in Washington granted Amazon's summary judgment motion, holding it did not have to turn over the records because the state's demand violated the First Amendment.[41] The court found "no legitimate need" for specific customer information, since Amazon had given state tax collectors anonymized information about items shipped to specific ZIP codes.

Other federal laws affecting privacy include:

- **The Privacy Act of 1974**, granting individuals the right to see records maintained by the federal executive branch agencies about themselves, correct inaccuracies in such records, and sue the federal government if it allows unauthorized individuals access to such records[42]
- **The Family Educational Rights and Privacy Act (FERPA)**, requiring schools obtain written permission from the parent or student before releasing any information from a student's educational record[43]
- **The Federal Records Act**, governing the creation, preservation, and disposition of federal records by federal agencies, including government employees' e-mails[44]
- **The Right to Financial Privacy Act**, establishing a due process requirement mandating government agencies provide notice and an opportunity to object before a bank or other institution can disclose an individual's personal financial information to a government agency (with exceptions for the IRS and matters involving drug trafficking or espionage)[45]
- **The Gramm–Leach–Bliley Act of 1999**, requiring financial institutions to maintain privacy policies that govern their collection, disclosure, and protection of customers' personally identifiable information and to develop a data security plan describing how they will protect customers' personally identifiable information; the Act also applies to companies, whether or not financial institutions, which receive such information[46]
- **The Fair Credit Reporting Act of 1970**, portions of which govern creating, distributing, or using consumer reports online[47]

- **The Health Insurance Portability and Accountability Act of 1996** (HIPAA), limiting what personal information may be disclosed by health, medical, and doctor's office Web sites[48]

- **The Electronic Communications Privacy Act of 1986** (ECPA), which prevents unauthorized government access to private electronic communications (Title I, the **Wiretap Act**) and stored electronic communications, *e.g.*, e-mail on third-party servers (Title II, the **Stored Communications Act**)[49]

- **The Children's Online Privacy Protection Act** (COPPA, discussed in detail in Chapter 11)[50]

- **The Cable Communications Policy Act of 1984**, requiring cable service providers obtain prior written or electronic consent from customers before collecting or disclosing their personal information (with exceptions for business necessity and detection of cable piracy), and provide customers a written notice of privacy practices and access to collected information[51]

- **The Telephone Consumer Protection Act of 1991**, regulating telemarketing practices[52]

- **The Telephone Records and Privacy Protection Act of 2006**, criminalizing *pretexting*, making it illegal to buy, sell, or obtain personal phone records (with an exception for law enforcement or intelligence agencies) under false pretenses[53]

- **The Telecommunications Act of 1996 § 702**, protecting customer proprietary network information held by telecommunications carriers[54]

- **The Driver's Privacy Protection Act of 1994**, restricting the release of state motor vehicle records to unauthorized parties without the driver's consent. The Act also outlaws *pretexting*, making it illegal to make false representations to obtain such information[55]

Absent specific federal privacy laws, the Federal Trade Commission (FTC) has regulated online collection and use of personal information using its authority over "unfair" or "deceptive" commercial practices pursuant to § 5 of the **Federal Trade Commission Act**. The FTC defines "personal data" to include:

- First and last name
- Address
- E-mail address, instant messenger ID, or screen name that reveals e-mail address
- Phone number
- Social Security number
- Photograph with name
- A persistent identifier (*e.g.*, cookie retrieval)

Sometimes, people expressly or by implication waive a claim for appropriation, or even misuse, of their personally identifiable identification. Individuals often disclose much personal information on home pages, including their home address; photographs; names and details of themselves, their children, and even the family dog! They reveal intimate details of their lives in blogs. Many employers search for and peruse blogs of prospective employees before making a hiring decision. While free to disclose and share such information with the world, individuals must realize the risk of the wrong people gaining unrestricted access to such personal information. Individuals may waive or limit liability for misuse of personal information through a *customer waiver in a click-wrap agreement.*[56] Many firms put waiver clauses in click-wrap agreements stating the customer agrees not to sue the company in the event of a data breach if its database containing customers' personal information is hacked or stolen.

## Public Records

*Public records* take many forms—birth, adoption, marriage, and death certificates; recorded wills and deeds; census records; court documents; military records; motor vehicle records; licenses (*e.g.*, from pilot licenses to ham radio operator licenses); property tax records; criminal records; business filings; UCC filings; professional licenses; and campaign contributor lists are just some types of records available to the public. Until the advent of the Internet, much of an individual's sense of privacy came from realizing the lengths one would have to go through to retrieve personal information from public records. The cumbersome and inefficient process of digging through public records was itself, in many cases, a barrier protecting individual privacy. When Arthur Dent, the protagonist in Douglas Adams' novel *"The Hitchhiker's Guide to the Galaxy"*, complains about a bulldozer poised to knock down his house to make way for a new highway, he is informed the road construction plans have been a matter of public record "on display"—in the cellar, "in the bottom of a locked filing cabinet stuck in a disused lavatory with a sign on the door saying 'Beware of the Leopard.'"[57] Prior to the Internet, so-called "public" records were not much more accessible than the plans for the highway going through Arthur Dent's house. Sure, the records were available to the public, but "availability" entailed traveling to the physical location of the records, during proscribed hours of operations, and following precise rules and regulations to obtain and view such materials. Thus, most "public" information was public only to the most intrepid, resourceful, and perseverant researcher. An occasional reporter might snoop amongst filed court records to ferret out gossipy tidbits relating to divorce records, arrests, medical histories, and other private matters of public record, but not until recently could one conjure the image of a neighbor seated at her computer in her nightgown scrolling through such files while sipping her morning coffee.

Public records thus present a challenge for both privacy advocates and those favoring open records and state *"sunshine laws"*. If one can drive to the courthouse to view a public record, why not be able to view the same record online? On the other hand, does ease of availability increase the likelihood of identity theft? Saying public records should remain public—but not be made widely available—goes against the fundamental principle of open records laws. If "public means public" and all public records should be easily accessible, both in person and online, then perhaps the notion of what information should be classified as "public" in the first place needs to be re-examined.

One concern is access to public records should not be limited to those with the financial means to hire employees, law firms, or couriers to go to the courthouse to retrieve them. Making public records available online ensures a level playing field so anyone, from a poor individual to a wealthy corporation, can access the same information.[58] Another concern centers around court records, where an individual may be accused (but not convicted, and perhaps later vindicated) of a crime. The mere allegation could follow the individual online forever, causing permanent damage to his reputation. To avoid this, federal courts and some states use a record-by-record decision-making process to shield certain records[59] from public view.[60] However, this process is only set in motion after an individual makes an official request to the judge. In some cases, this may be a time-consuming, expensive, or complex task.

In Florida, the state that pioneered the concept of sunshine laws, court documents were available online until 2002, when Florida temporarily banned their release on the

Internet, partly in response to the clamor around NASCAR driver Dale Earnhardt's autopsy photographs. Earnhardt died in a crash at the Daytona 500 and under Florida law, his autopsy report and photographs were public records. Local newspapers sought copies and Earnhardt's widow and fans lobbied the state legislature to prevent their release.

A 2007 lawsuit against the Florida Department of Law Enforcement sought removal of a minor's name from the state's publicly accessible online database. The 13-year-old was arrested for allegedly stealing a can of soda.[61] Her attorneys claimed online publication of her name and the arrest details violated Florida law mandating minors' misdemeanor records be kept confidential.[62] The database apparently also listed an arrested individual's physical description and Social Security number.[63] The state Web site offered this information to anyone willing to pay the $23 per record charge and had received $52.7 million from such fees for criminal histories. The minor's argument was once such information is exposed online, it is irretrievable and can permanently harm the child's future.[64] For that reason, historically, juvenile court records were kept confidential to protect children, so as not to stigmatize them for the rest of their lives with a criminal record. However, as juvenile crime rates soared in the last quarter of the 20th century, more than 42 states made juvenile criminal records public to some extent; under Florida law, records of minors charged with felonies or more than two misdemeanors are public.

Federal judges in South Florida and eastern Pennsylvania began removing plea and sentencing memos from online case files in 2007 after a site, WhosARat.com, was started with the purpose of exposing informants and undercover agents in criminal cases.[65] While removing the documents from their own sites, the judges still allowed them to be obtainable directly from the courthouse. Although it would seem a motivated criminal would take the extra effort to go to the courthouse and retrieve a physical copy of the documents, these courts have effectively created two classes of "public" records based on accessibility — online records and in person records. This invites the question of whether effectively creating a new class of public record — one with more limited accessibility — is inherently unfair to those lacking the financial or physical (*i.e.*, those with physical disabilities that would preclude them from traveling to the courthouse) means to access the records.

### Information Broker Liability

There have always been private investigators, using various resources to ferret out personal information about individuals. But now there are online *information brokers* who supply personal information about individuals to the general public. Most, but not all, of these data are from public records, which prior to the Internet were difficult to access but are now easily accessed, searched, and collated. There are many legitimate uses for such information, such as tracking down an old school friend or a distant relative, or for genealogical purposes. But what liability does an information broker have if the information it supplies is misused by a *stalker*?

In *Remsburg v. Docusearch, Inc.*, online information broker Docusearch sold information about Amy Lynn Boyer to Liam Youens.[66] Youens had become obsessed with Boyer in school, stalked her for years, and chronicled his plans to murder her on his Web site. Although he already knew where she lived, Youens bought information, including her Social Security number and workplace address, from Docusearch.[67] He later drove to

Boyer's workplace, fatally shot her, and then himself. Boyer's mother sued Docusearch. The court held the threats posed by *stalking* and *identity theft* meant the *risk of criminal misconduct* was sufficiently *foreseeable* so an investigator has a *duty to exercise reasonable care* in disclosing a third person's personal information to a client. Chillingly, after ordering information on Boyer from Docusearch's site, Youens wrote in his online diary on his site devoted to his planned murder of Boyer: "It's accually [sic] obsene [sic] what you can find out about a person on the internet [sic]."[68]

### Insurer Liability

The Boyer case spawned a second lawsuit, this time raising the issue of insurer liability.[69] Insurers insure against risks, but what liability do they have *for the risks posed by dissemination of information*? Boyer's mother had sued Docusearch, who in turn requested a defense and indemnity from its insurer, Preferred National Insurance. Preferred filed a declaratory judgment action seeking a determination the policy it had issued Docusearch did not cover this situation. It argued, under the policy, it had no obligation to defend the company or pay claims resulting from assault and battery. The New Hampshire Supreme Court found for Preferred on the issue of coverage for assault and battery but remanded the case for consideration as to whether coverage applied to the invasion of privacy and state **Consumer Protection Act** claims, leaving open the issue of under what circumstances an insurer may be liable for an insured's dissemination of a third-party's personal information.[70]

## Voluntary Disclosure

Sometimes, the greatest threat to privacy may come from the individual himself. Many people maintain personal Web sites, profile pages, or blogs, where they detail their lives, including names of family and pets (a security risk, since people often use children's and pets' names as passwords), pictures of their home and children, their address, and information about their lives. All this could subject them to identity thieves, stalkers, or sexual predators. Children often maintain their own social network pages, giving out their names, ages, addresses, interests, and schools, as well as publishing their photographs and even their student photo-ID cards. On Facebook and MySpace, minors routinely post their mobile phone numbers, school names, and other personal information, as well as sexually provocative pictures of themselves (This issue is discussed further in Chapter 11).[71] Blogs are an especially delicate area, as bloggers often treat them as online diaries, forgetting they are viewable by millions. Bloggers disclose the most intimate details of their lives, which may include information about friends and family who do not know their private lives are being exposed on the Web. In deciding what to share with the world, one must balance the desire to share with the associated risks.

The Internet is forever; everything ever posted is cached on a hard drive somewhere. Deleting a site may not matter. The Internet Archive, known as "The Wayback Machine", archives 85 billion Web pages dating back to 1996.[72] A frivolous night of drunken revelry with friends might years later be summoned like a ghost from the digital graveyard, becoming an embarrassment during a job interview or political campaign. It may not even take years, as conservative candidate Alan Keyes found when, after making anti-gay remarks during his U.S. Senate race, his daughter's blog about being a lesbian made headlines.[73]

## Job Searches

The Internet has opened opportunities for job seekers, allowing them to post résumés online for prospective employers to peruse. But many do not realize their online résumé with their name, address, phone number, educational background, employment history, and other personal information could float in cyberspace for years, allowing an identity thief to slip into the victim's skin as if slipping into a warm coat. To avoid victimization, online résumés should use initials in place of names, a post office box in lieu of a home address, and a temporary e-mail address. Also, birth dates should be left off, as they are essential personal information for identity thieves.

Conversely, the Internet *is* one's online résumé; employers are as likely to "Google" an applicant's name and read her blogs and social network pages as intently, if not more so, than her résumé. A CareerBuilder.com survey of hiring managers revealed 22 percent used social networks to research job candidates and dropped a third of them after seeing what was on their profiles. Mention (or photos) of alcohol and drug use, and provocative or inappropriate photographs doomed many applicants, as did discriminatory remarks related to race, gender, or religion; an unprofessional screen name; and poor communication skills evident from the profile. But, a quarter of managers were positively influenced by good communications skills and a professional image on an applicant's profile. [74] A job applicant — or anyone concerned about online privacy — should ask: What does my YouTube, MySpace, or Facebook page tell a prospective employer about me?

## Virtual Tour Web Sites

"Virtual tours" on real estate sites let prospective home buyers "walk through" a home using 360-degree panoramic imagery software. But, as with personal sites and online résumés, there is a risk in disclosing personal information online: burglars may use virtual tours to case homes, seeking out valuables and unsecured entry points. [75]

## Social Networks

Social networks (see Chapter 12) might best be described as the "Me Generation" meets the Internet. Each network consists of members with "profile pages", *i.e.*, a Web page where they can tell the whole world about "me." One major social network is aptly named "MySpace." But often members fail to consider not only their friends, but the entire online world may be perusing the personal information they have placed on their profile.

Some personal information typically posted on profile pages include: first name, last name, city and state, home and/or mobile phone numbers, e-mail address, IM user name, birth dates, age, gender, sexual orientation, name of school or employer, student class schedules, and names of friends, family, and pets. There are also photographs and often intimate and highly personal blogs and/or vlogs, as well as a list of network interest groups the individual has joined. One social network, Twitter, is set up so users can constantly update their friends with a 140-character blurb on what they are doing that instant (*e.g.*, "I am doing homework" or "I am taking a shower"). Voluntary disclosure of such personal information creates a public forum for everyday interactions, as well as intense online ties because of the instantaneous  and continual updates. That is the essence of social networking: the unabashed disclosure of both personal data and intimate blog revelations enables strangers sharing the network to feel they know each other. Many social networkers have virtual "friends" whose lives they know all about and who know intimate details of their lives, but whom they have never met in person. Such friends are but "a mouse click away" —whether around the corner or around the globe.

Social media inherently engender a willingness to share personal information with strangers. An IT security firm study found 41 percent of Facebook users revealed personal information to "Freddi Staur" (an anagram for "ID fraudster"), a fake member it made up. The information disclosed was sufficient to target spear-phishing e-mails, guess their passwords, pretend to be them, or even stalk them.[76]

An app for geolocator social network Fourquare tapped into Foursquare and Facebook data to pinpoint the location of specific women near users. All the data had been freely volunteered by users; the app merely collated it. The "What Girls Around Me" app displayed females (and males) who had told Foursquare they had "checked in" at a specific location near the app user. It then displayed each individual Facebook photo, name, and data from her (or his) profile.[77]

Social networks can be a gold mine of personal data for stalkers, employers, insurance companies, private investigators, defense attorneys, or even judges. Trial consultants peruse them to create psychological profiles of potential jurors, raising concerns whether courts are adequately supervising the process.[78] In a Connecticut case, a recent graduate sued a high school superintendent for failing to protect her from a volunteer basketball coach's sexual advances. She filed an anonymous "Jane Doe" complaint, but the superintendent's attorney uncovered her identity by searching for MySpace profiles of the school's class. He found two for her with her true first and last names, seven photos of her, and an autobiographical account. Armed with this information, he filed a motion to reconsider her anonymous status, arguing she had waived anonymity by voluntarily publicizing her name, image, and the "circumstances of her case" on the Web. She moved for contempt and sanctions, on the grounds his motion had violated the standing "Jane Doe" order. The judge agreed, fined him $1,000, and ordered the motions revealing the student's identity sealed and replaced with redacted copies. The profiles were removed from the site.[79]

A 20-year-old student dressed as a convict at a Halloween party two weeks after causing an alcohol-related automobile accident that seriously injured a woman. The prosecutor collated photographs of him in a black-and-white striped shirt and an orange jumpsuit labeled "Jail Bird" from a Facebook page into a Power Point presentation under the title "Remorseful?" at his sentencing hearing. The judge said the slide show influenced his decision to sentence the student to two years in prison.[80] A California prosecutor said he changed his mind about recommending probation for a 22-year-old whose drunk driving accident killed her passenger after seeing her MySpace profile with post-crash photographs of the woman holding a wine glass, captioned with jokes about drinking. Result: the prosecutor argued for prison instead of probation — the woman received two years in prison.[81] Another California lawyer told his client — a recent college graduate charged with a fatal drunk driving accident — to delete her MySpace page if she had one. She had one, but did not delete it. The attorney was understandably surprised when, at her sentencing hearing, the prosecutor introduced photographs from her profile posted after the crash, showing her holding a beer bottle and wearing a shirt advertising tequila. Result: a five-year prison sentence.[82]

A Canadian woman on long-term sick leave for depression lost her benefits after her insurance agent saw her Facebook photos of her having fun at a Chippendales bar show.[83] And the Florida Board of Bar Examiners adopted a policy to investigate social network profiles of bar applicants. [84]

The rise of the Internet Generation has spawned a privacy generation gap. Members of the Internet Generation beginning college in 2007 were born in 1989. They grew up in, and cannot imagine, a world without:

- Desktop computers
- Laptop computers
- 3–Dimensional video games
- The World Wide Web
- E-mail
- Mobile phones
- Smart phones
- CDs and DVDs
- Portable media players
- UPC barcodes and scanners
- Digital cameras
- Cable television
- E-book readers

All of these recent technological innovations are prosaic to them, whereas older generations marvel at phones without cords, cameras without film, and television with more than three channels. Children of that generation went to the movies; kids in today's Internet Generation make their own movies and upload them for other kids to watch and critique. The older generation has a greater expectation of privacy and is surprised to discover the degree to which personal information is available online. The Internet Generation, having grown up in an environment of friends armed with mobile phone cameras and surrounded by closed circuit television cameras in stores and on streets, has developed a diminished expectation of privacy. The Internet Generation photograph each other at parties and post the pictures on their sites or social networks; the older generation might look askance at being photographed at a party and would probably feel their privacy had been violated on finding the photo posted on a Web site (most probably would not have a MySpace or Facebook page). The Internet Generation not only have a diminished expectation of privacy; they are self-proclaimed "attention whores", posting intimate photos, online diaries, and even attempts at poetry, having concluded privacy in the modern world an illusion. As New York Magazine's Emily Nussbaum writes, their generational icon is Paris Hilton, "blurring as she does the distinction between exposing oneself and being exposed. We live in a time in which humiliation and fame are not such easily distinguished quantities." [85]

By the time they reach college, today's grade schoolers will have become inured to an ever-diminishing expectation of privacy as they "graduate" from one social network to the next. The preteen set can network at *Club Penguin*; migrate to *Xanga* during junior high; switch to *MySpace* in high school; join the college crowd at *Facebook*; and after graduation, network with their peers at *LinkedIn*.

A parent on a social network should exercise caution in revealing information about children, such as names, photographs, and the school they attend. Social networks offer many benefits, but members must carefully consider the consequences of what they post, as often the greatest threat to privacy comes from the individual.

Burglars also read Twitter and Facebook status updates—do you really want to tell them you are miles away from home, especially after raving about the widescreen TV you just bought? A U.K. survey revealed 38 percent of social networkers post holiday plans. [86] Combined with the fact many add individuals they do not know as "friends", such voluntary disclosures pose a serious risk to the security of homes and possessions. A European survey found 13 percent of random friend requests were accepted on Facebook and 92 percent on Twitter. [87] It also found 13 percent of men and 7 percent of women listed their mobile phone number on their profiles, and 9 percent of men (4 percent of women) posted home phone numbers. Younger users were most likely to reveal their whereabouts. Burglars appreciate this type of information, as they do your travel plans and photos taken inside your homes showing the layout and your possessions, or, as one source phrased it, "Internet shopping for burglars." [88] Social networks are awash with a geolocation craze in which members report their physical location throughout the day. Facebook, Twitter, and Foursquare encourage users to broadcast when they check-in somewhere outside their home. This, of course, is valuable information for burglars, who prefer empty homes, as in the case of three New Hampshire burglars who stole $200,000 of personal property, using Facebook updates from local residents to target unguarded homes. [89] PleaseRobMe.com was a site that automatically aggregated tweeted vacation plans and Foursquare check-ins at locations, listing these updates in categories like "recent empty homes" and "new opportunities," to emphasize how over-sharing one's personal life makes it easy for burglars to take advantage of the information. [90]

Users may set their network privacy settings to control how much of their profile information is visible by strangers and which details friends may view, but social networks frequently change the way their privacy settings function and information may default to public view. Setting the network's privacy to the highest level may be complicated and even complete anonymity cannot protect one's identity. As discussed in the section on data reidentification in Chapter 8, there are ways to link a user's identity to her account. Another factor is friends within the network may share information with individuals who are strangers to the user. Social networks also share user information with third parties. Their (frequently revised) Terms of Use and privacy policies list whom they may allow access to user data. Facebook, for example, changed its Terms of Use agreement in 2010 to make members' data more accessible to other members. Employees of the network can see all of a user's information, even that deemed "private" or "hidden". It grants third parties access to user data to sell their products. And most applications ("apps") receive data about users. Do you know where that information goes and who reads it?

## The Electronic Trail

In today's society, everyone leaves an electronic trail. These digital breadcrumbs lead back to us, eviscerating our privacy. Every phone number you dial and every text message you send or receive is stored in a database. Your mobile phone's geodata chip can disclose your location, no matter where you are. Your itinerary stored in airline databases shows where you have been. Your credit card company's database, holding your entire buying history, can reconstruct where you were and what you did. It can also reveal almost everything about you: the clothes you buy, where you shop, and what you shop for. Business suits or swimsuits? Health food or ice cream sundaes? Church donation or bondage toys?

Pet food, cigarettes, diapers, or medicine — your purchases paint a portrait of who you are. Credit cards have usurped cash, and with it, our privacy. Online merchants store lists of everything you purchase... and everything you looked at but did not buy. ISPs log the sites you browse. Your medical records will soon be online, as your bank records already are. Face-to-face conversations are being replaced by texting, e-mail, instant messages, and Facebook chats — all saved to hard drives and archived on servers. Even if you delete information from your computer or account, it probably still resides on another computer or server.

The advent of controversial facial recognition technology for photographs combined with the ubiquity of social media has created new privacy concerns. Facial recognition software scans photographs, matching faces with stored photos. Goggle's Picasa and Apple's iPhoto use facial recognition technology on photo storage sites, but it becomes of greater concern when applied to a social network, where, depending on one's privacy settings, information may be shared among many users. On Facebook, when a match is found, users are prompted to "tag" or label the person in the photo. The potential exists for the technology to be used in more invasive ways. One concern is what personally identifiable information in a database (*i.e.*, Facebook or any other social network employing the technology) could be associated with photographs. For example, the software might match a random Web photo (*e.g.*, from a dating Web site or a news story) and match it with a similar photo on Facebook, pulling up the associated profile with the subject's identifying personal information. In addition to the privacy concerns, there is the risk of misidentifications occurring, as the technology is not foolproof.

Technology, like an evil djinn, once freed from the bottle cannot be recorked. Instead, as you shall see in the remainder of the Privacy portion of this book, society must devise comprehensive data privacy laws that safeguard personal information and communications regardless of where it is stored or how it is transmitted;[91] that mandate data be kept confidential when stored, protected from breach, and deleted when no longer necessary to be retained.[92] Privacy laws must shift their focus from notification (of policies and breaches) to control (over collection, use, and retention), and also address third-party access to, use and retention of personal data.[93] The borderless nature of the Internet makes international cooperation implicit in this approach to data privacy laws.

## Non-U.S. Privacy Laws

Each state may have its own privacy laws. Also, foreign laws may apply in certain circumstances. Two major areas of foreign privacy laws are the Canadian Privacy Laws and the European Union Privacy Directive.

### Canadian Privacy Laws

Canada has two federal privacy laws. The *Canadian Privacy Act of 1983* protects personal information collected by the Canadian government.[94] It allows Canadians to access such information and to challenge its accuracy. The Privacy Commissioner of Canada, authorized to investigate complaints, oversees the Act. The *Personal Information Protection and Electronic Documents Act* (PIPEDA) applies to the collection, storage, and use of personal information by nongovernmental organizations.[95] PIPEDA requires businesses to inform consumers who collects the information, why it is collected, and the purposes for which it will be used. The Privacy Commissioner also oversees this Act. All organizations in Canada must designate an individual to handle privacy matters and complaints. PIPEDA also applies to information collected, used, or disclosed by federally regulated agencies, such as telecommunications companies, ISPs, broadcasters, airlines, and banks; and to provincially-regulated private-sector organizations, such as insurance companies and retail stores, unless the province has passed "substantially similar" legislation.[96] PIPEDA requires *consent* when collecting, using, or disclosing personal information. The business or Web site requesting the information must provide the *right to access* the personal information and challenge its accuracy. Use of the collected information is *limited* to the stated purpose for which it was collected and the scope of the consent given. If the business or Web site wishes to use the information collected for another purpose, PIPEDA requires *additional consent* be obtained. PIPEDA applies retroactively to information collected prior to the Act's passage.

## The European Union Privacy Directive

The ***European Union Directive on Data Protection*** requires EU member nations to implement national legislation to protect the privacy of individuals.[97] The European Union, as of 2012, consisted of 27 member states: Austria, Belgium, Bulgaria, Cyprus, the Czech Republic, Denmark, Estonia, Finland, France, Germany, Greece, Hungary, Ireland, Italy, Latvia, Lithuania, Luxembourg, Malta, the Netherlands, Poland, Portugal, Romania, Slovakia, Slovenia, Spain, Sweden, and the United Kingdom.

The Directive broadly defines personal data as any information relating to an individual. European law allows personal information to flow outside Europe only if there is an adequate level of protection in the receiving country. It prohibits transfer of personal data to non-European Union countries that do not meet its "adequacy" standard for privacy protection. However, the European Commission has approved a "*safe harbor*" arrangement whereby companies and organizations in the United States can commit themselves to comply with a set of data protection principles and be deemed to have met the adequacy standard.

The differences between the European Union and the United States in their approaches to privacy stem from a fundamental difference in their conception of the role of government in society. In the European Union, privacy is a fundamental right *requiring* the government to pass comprehensive legislation to protect personal information; in the United States, the First Amendment *restricts* the government's ability to control the free flow of information (including personal information).

**Chapter 7 Notes**

[1] *Roberson v. Rochester Folding-Box Co.*, 171 N.Y. 538, 64 N.E. 442 (1902).

[2] *Pavesich v. New England Life Ins. Co.*, 122 Ga. 190, 50 S.E. 68 (1905).

[3] Warren and Brandeis, The Right to Privacy, 4 Harvard L.R. 193 (1890), *available at* http://groups.csail. mit.edu/mac/classes/6.805/articles/privacy/Privacy_brand_warr2.html (accessed Mar. 23, 2012).

[4] *Ibid.*

[5] Injury to feelings is nonetheless a recognized element of damages in defamation actions but not an essential element of the tort. Defamation deals only with damage to reputation and the lowering of esteem or respect for an individual within the community. *Ibid.*, *at* note 14.

[6] *See* James Q. Whitman, The Two Western Cultures of Privacy: Dignity Versus Liberty, 113 Yale L. Jnl. 1153 (2004), *available at* http://digitalcommons.law.yale.edu/fss_papers/649 (accessed Mar. 23, 2012).

[7] Prosser, Restatement (Second) of Torts, §§ 652(A)-652(I). Invasion of Privacy is a tort with civil penalties, however some jurisdictions, in response to Internet or high tech invasion of privacy, have drafted Invasion of Privacy criminal statutes (*e.g.*, criminal invasion of computer privacy or video voyeurism). Criminal invasion of computer privacy statutes usually involve unauthorized use of a computer to view confidential information about someone. For example, the Virginia Computer Crimes Act, Va. Code § 18.2-152.1, *et seq.*, provides:

> A person is guilty of the crime of computer invasion of privacy when he uses a computer or computer network and intentionally examines without authority any employment, salary, credit or any other financial or personal information relating to any other person. "Examination" under this section requires the offender to review the information relating to any other person after the time at which the offender knows or should know that he is without authority to view the information displayed.

*See e.g.*, *Plasters v. Commonwealth*, Case No. 1870-99-3, 2000 Va. App. LEXIS 473 (Va. Ct. App. 2000) (Unpublished). Note, this statute is concerned with *viewing* the private information. *Downloading* the information might fall under a state's computer theft statutes, while *republication* of the information might run afoul of copyright laws. Related video voyeurism statutes typically criminalize nonconsensual photography or video recording of an individual in a state of undress or nudity in places where one has a reasonable expectation of privacy. Photos and videos of people in department store changing rooms, locker rooms, and in one case, their own home (a video voyeurism law was passed in New York after a woman discovered her landlord had placed hidden video cameras in her apartment) have appeared on the Internet. The Video Voyeurism Prevention Act of 2004, 18 U.S.C.A. § 180, is limited to acts occurring on federal property, but most states have some sort of video voyeurism statutes. Some states criminalize invasion of privacy through forms of online harassment, *e.g.*, posting nude photos or sex tapes on the Internet for revenge or to embarrass an ex-boyfriend or girlfriend. *See* the discussion of online harassment in Chapter 21.

[8] *Haelan Labs., Inc. v. Topps Chewing Gum, Inc.*, 202 F.2d 866 (2[d] Cir. 1953), cert. denied, 346 U.S. 816 (1953).

[9] *Ibid.*

[10] *Lugosi v. Universal Pictures*, 603 P.2d 425 (Cal. 1979).

[11] The California Celebrities Rights Act, California Civil Code § 3344, *et seq.*, § 3344.1 is the Astaire Celebrity Image Protection Act, which extends the right of publicity to heirs of a deceased celebrity and establishes liability for the use of a deceased celebrity's image, without consent, on or in products, merchandise, or goods.

[12] *White v. Samsung Elecs. of Am., Inc.*, 971 F. 2d 1395 (9th Cir. 1992), cert. denied, 508 U.S. 951 (1993).

[13] *Carson v. Here's Johnny Portable Toilets, Inc.*, 698 F.2d 831 (6th Cir. 1983)

[14] *Eagle's Eye, Inc. v. Amber Fashion Shop, Inc.*, 627 F. Supp. 856, 862 (E.D. Pa. 1985).

[15] *Kirby v. Sega of Am., Inc.*, 144 Cal. App. 4th 47 (2006).

[16] *Ibid.*

[17] "Game Maker May Use Celebrity's Likeness if 'New Expression' Added — C.A.," Metropolitan News-Enterprise, September 26, 2006.

[18] *Winter v. DC Comics, Inc.*, 30 Cal. 4th 881 (2003).

[19] *Ibid.*

[20] *Doe v. TCI Cablevision*, 110 S.W.3d 363 (Mo. 2003); verdict aff'd *sub nom.*, *Doe v. McFarlane*, 207 S.W.3d 52 (E.D. Mo. App. 2006).

[21] *Zacchini v. Scripps-Howard Broad. Co.*, 433 U.S. 562 (1977).

[22] *Fraley v. Facebook, Inc.*, Case No. 11-cv-01726-LHK (N.D. Cal. Dec. 16, 2012), order granting in part and denying in part defendant's motion to dismiss.

[23] See the discussion of defamation law in Chapter 14, *infra.*

[24] *Ibid.*

[25] *Daily Times Democrat v. Graham*, 276 Ala. 380 (1964).

[26] Miguel Helft, "Google Zooms in Too Close for Some," The New York Times, June 1, 2007.

[27] *See* Guillaume Frouin and Catherine Bremer, "Frenchman Sues over Google Views Urination Photo," Reuters wire service report, March 1, 2012.

[28] LaudonTech's Google Street Views Sightings site, *available at http://www.streetviewfunny.com/street-viewfunny/index.php* (accessed Mar. 23, 2012).

[29] "Eye Spy," The Chandler Times, Phoenix, AZ, 2007. Ironically, the ad was visible on Google Street Views.

[30] Carly Weeks, "Street View Blurred by Canadian Privacy Concerns," CanWest News Service, September 24, 2007.

[31] *Boring v. Google, Inc.*, Case No. 2:2008-cv-00694 (W.D. Pa. 2009). The case was dismissed in 2009 for failure to state a claim. Aaron and Christine Boring had claimed finding their home clearly visible on Google's Street Views caused them "mental suffering" and diluted their home value.

[32] Lora Pabst, "North Oaks Tells Google Maps: Keep Out—We Mean It," Minneapolis-St.Paul Star Tribune, May 31, 2008. The roads in the city of 4,500 residents are privately owned by the residents. Along with its request to remove photographs of the town, the North Oaks City Council's letter to Google included a threat it might cite Google for violation of the city's trespassing ordinance.

[33] Lynne Marek, "Lawyers Shrink from Web Real Estate Spotlight," The National Law Journal, September 9, 2008.

[34] Susan Abram, "Hospital Employee Allegedly Makes Fun of Patient's Medical Condition on Facebook; Officials Investigating," The Los Angeles Daily News, December 29, 2011.

[35] The Health Insurance Portability and Accountability Act, 42 U.S.C. § 300(gg) and 29 U.S.C. § 1181, *et seq.*

[36] *Jews for Jesus, Inc. v. Rapp*, 997 So.2d 1098 (Fla. 2008). Defamation by implication is similar to defamation per quod. **Defamation per quod** exists where statements are not defamatory on their face but extrinsic facts or circumstances exist that imply or convey defamatory meaning. **Defamation by implication** arises where a defendant either juxtaposes a series of facts, or omits facts, so as to imply a defamatory connection between them.

[37] The Video Privacy Protection Act, 18 U.S.C. § 2710, *et seq.*; *see* Electronic Privacy Information Center, *available at* www.epic.org/privacy/vppa (accessed Mar. 23, 2012) for general overview of the Act and Cornell University Law School, *available at www.law.cornell.edu/uscode/18/2710.html* (accessed Mar. 23, 2012) for text of the Act.

[38] Ryan J. Foley, "Feds Cancel Amazon Customer ID Request," Associated Press wire service report, November 27, 2007.

[39] Steven Musil, "YouTube Privacy at Risk in Google-Viacom Ruling," CNET News.com, July 2, 2008.

[40] *See* Elinor Mills, "ACLU Fights N.C. Quest for Amazon Customer Data," CNET News.com, June 23, 2010; *and* Declan McCullagh, "Amazon Fights Demand for Customer Records," CNET News.com, April 19, 2010.

[41] *Amazon.com, LLC v. Lay*, Case No. C10-664 MJP (W.D. Wash. 2010).

[42] The Privacy Act of 1974, 37 5 U.S.C.S. § 552(a).

[43] The Family Educational Rights and Privacy Act (FERPA) 20 U.S.C. § 1232(g).

[44] The Federal Records Act, 44 U.S.C. §§ 2101-2118.

[45] The Right to Financial Privacy Act, 12 U.S.C. §§ 3401-13.

[46] The Gramm-Leach-Bliley Act, 15 U.S.C., Subchapter I, §§ 6801-6809.

[47] The Fair Credit Reporting Act, 15 U.S.C. § 1681, *et seq.*

[48] The Health Insurance Portability and Accountability Act, 42 U.S.C. § 300(gg) and 29 U.S.C. § 1181, *et seq.*

[49] The Electronic Communications Privacy Act, 18 U.S.C. § 2510, *et seq.*

[50] The Children's Online Privacy Protection Act (COPPA), 15 U.S.C. § 6501, *et seq.*

[51] The Cable Communications Policy Act of 1984, 47 U.S.C. §§ 521, 551.

[52] The Telephone Consumer Protection Act of 1991, 47 U.S.C. § 227(b)(1)(A)(iii).

[53] The Telephone Records and Privacy Protection Act of 2006, 18 U.S.C. § 1039(a).

[54] The Telecommunications Act of 1996, 47 U.S.C. § 702.

[55] The Driver's Privacy Protection Act of 1994, 18 U.S.C. § 2721.

[56] Click-wrap agreements are discussed further in Chapter 20.

[57] Douglas Adams, *"The Hitchhiker's Guide to the Galaxy."*

[58] This is particularly important in a lawsuit where an individual may be suing a corporation with vast financial resources.

[59] Such as adoption records or other records concerning children, probate estate inventories, or records with personal financial data or Social Security numbers, for example.

[60] "Public Debates Online Access," Florida Bar News, December 15, 2004.

[61] Forrest Norman, "Florida Dept. of Law Enforcement Sued over Online Access to Juvenile Arrest Data," Daily Business Review, January 10, 2007.

[62] Fla. Stat. § 985.04(2) makes juvenile criminal records confidential unless the minor is arrested on a felony or has three or more misdemeanors.

[63] Cathy Corry, "We've Been Duped! — Juvenile Arrest Records Not Confidential…," Justice4Kids.org, April 29, 2005, *available at* www.justice4kids.org/duped.htm (accessed Mar. 23, 2012).

[64] Norman, fn. 61, *supra*.

[65] "Courts Keeping Records off Web to Shield Informants," Associated Press wire service report, July 25, 2007.

[66] *Remsburg v. Docusearch, Inc.*, 816 A.2d 1001 (N.H. 2003). (Included in the Cases Section on the Issues in Internet Law site, www.IssuesinInternetLaw.com).

[67] Since Youens knew where Boyer lived and had been stalking her for years, it is questionable how much of a factor the release of information by Docusearch was in her murder, since Youens could easily have followed her to or from work.

[68] www.amyboyer.org/mind.htm; this was a replica of Youens' site, displayed by Boyer's family to raise awareness of the circumstances surrounding their daughter's murder. As of September 21, 2005, the site was no longer available.

[69] *Preferred Nat'l Ins. Co. v. Docusearch, Inc.*, 829 A.2d 1068 (N.H. 2003). (Included in the Cases Section on the Issues in Internet Law site, www.IssuesinInternetLaw.com).

[70] New Hampshire Consumer Protection Act, RSA 358-A. After the court dismissed the claim for damages based on assault and battery, Boyer's family and Docusearch settled for $85,000 in March 2004.

[71] Janet Kornblum, "Social Web Sites Scrutinized," USA Today, February 12, 2006.

[72] *Available at* www.archive.org/Web/Web.php (accessed Mar. 23, 2012). The "Wayback Machine" is a reference to the time machine used by cartoon characters Sherman and Mr. Peabody (the talking dog) in the classic TV cartoon *The Rocky and Bullwinkle Show.*

[73] "Blog It Now, Regret It Later? Public Entries Intended for Friends Could Have Repercussions Later," Associated Press wire service report, July 10, 2005.

[74] "One in Five Bosses Screen Applicants' Web Lives: Poll," Reuters wire service report, September 11, 2008.

[75] David Lazarus, "Web Tours a Boon for Burglars," The San Francisco Chronicle, June 3, 2005.

[76] Nicholas Carlson, "Report: Facebook Users Loose with the Info," Internet.com, August 14, 2007.

[77] Daniel Terdiman, "Report: Foursquare Shuts off API for Girls Around Me App," CNET News.com, March 30, 2012. The "Creepy Factor" led Fourquare to terminate the app's access to its network, despite the fact it did nothing illegal by using public information that had been voluntarily disclosed.

[78] Carol J. Williams, "Jury Duty? You May Want to Edit Your Online Profile," The Los Angeles Times, September 29, 2008. *See also*, Brian Grow, "Internet v. Courts: Googling for the Perfect Juror," Reuters wire service report, February 17, 2011.

[79] Thomas B. Scheffey, "'Jane Doe' Status is Not Compromised by MySpace Postings," Connecticut Law Tribune, October 18, 2006.

[80] "Web Pics Come Back to Bite Defendants; Social Networking Sites Proving Fruitful for Prosecutors," Associated Press wire service report, July 18, 2008.

[81] *Ibid.*

[82] *Ibid.*

[83] "Canadian Woman Loses Benefits over Facebook Photo," Associated Press wire service report, November 22, 2009.

[84] Jan Pudlow, "On Facebook? FBBE May Be Planning a Visit," The Florida Bar News, September 1, 2009, p.1.

[85] Emily Nussbaum, "Kids, the Internet, and the End of Privacy: The Greatest Generation Gap Since Rock and Roll," New York Magazine, February 12, 2007.

[86] Belinda Goldsmith, "Burglars Using Facebook, Twitter to Find Targets — Report," Reuters wire service report, August 27, 2009.

[87] *Ibid.*

[88] *Ibid.*

[89] David Murphy, "Facebook Denies Involvement in $200K Worth of N.H. Burglaries," PCMag.com, September 12, 2010.

[90] M.G. Siegler, "Please Rob Me Makes Foursquare Super Useful For Burglars," Techcruch.com, February 17, 2010.

[91] *See* the discussion of the Electronic Communications Privacy Act in Chapter 9.

[92] *See* the discussion of data retention and data breaches in Chapter 8.

[93] Discussed in Chapters 14 and 15.

[94] The Privacy Act (R.S. 1985, c. P-21).

[95] The Personal Information Protection and Electronic Documents Act (2000, c. 5) *available at* http://laws.justice.gc.ca/en/P-8.6/index.html (accessed Mar. 23, 2012).

[96] Quebec, so far, is the only province deemed to have met this standard.

[97] Directive 95/46/EC of the European Parliament and of the Council of 24 October 1995 on the protection of individuals with regard to processing of personal data and the free movement of such data, Center for Democracy and Technology.

# CHAPTER

# 8

———

## DATA PRIVACY

> This chapter covers data collection, retention, and security, and the expectation of privacy in one's personally identifiable information collected and stored by third-parties.

*"An American has no sense of privacy. He does not know what it means. There is no such thing in the country."* — *George Bernard Shaw*

MOST WEB USERS SITTING behind their computers view their monitors as a one-way screen. But can the Web sites they visit "see" them? Are they leaving behind clues to their identities and could those clues be used to identify them? In many cases, the answer is yes. Many sites record each visitor's Internet Protocol (IP) address—the unique number assigned to everyone's computer to identify a user's location. Some acknowledge this in their privacy policies (see Chapter 10) but others do not. ISPs routinely log certain user activities. Although most delete these logs after a few days, some lawmakers want to require them to be retained for years or even permanently. Does a subscriber have a reasonable expectation of privacy for information held by his ISP? Does one using a screen name in a chat room have a reasonable expectation of privacy?

First, we will examine data collection, *i.e.*, how personal information is collected about online users, either by voluntary submission through account registration with ISPs, or search engine queries, or surreptitiously through cookies. Next, we will look at data retention, *i.e.*, how long data is kept and what is done with it. In the next chapter, we will discuss specific online activities and the expectation of privacy associated with them.

## Data Collection

An online privacy survey revealed most people want to know how they are being tracked online and to have more control over how their personal information, once collected, is used.[1] But online data collection practices often conflict with such privacy expectations. Even if one does not visit its site, Google collects data about a user when he or she browses the Web. Researchers have analyzed various companies' practices using Ghostery, a Firefox plug-in to detect **cookies**, **Web beacons** and other trackers that enable third-parties to collect visitors' data, often without their knowledge.[2]

Another Google-related privacy concern is the company's Web browser, Google Chrome. Privacy advocates fear it could allow Google to track more of users' online behavior and compose detailed user profiles. Chrome can collect a user's visited Web addresses, and thus track her journey through the Web. It collects 2 percent of all keystrokes (both search terms and URLs) typed into its combined search and address bar. Google may retain the collected data indefinitely to help refine its search engine, but has stated the **IP address** and cookie associated with the data are anonymized. [3]

Presumably anonymized data cannot be traced back to an individual, however that is not always the case. Computer science graduate student Latanya Sweeney proved how easily "anonymized" data could be "reidentified" when tied to other relevant bits of data. Massachusetts released data on state employee hospital visits after "scrubbing" the data of any personally identifiable information (*e.g.*, name, address, and SSN). Massachusetts Gov. William Weld assured the public individual privacy had been protected by deleting the personal identifiers. Sweeney decided to prove otherwise, by searching for the governor's hospital records in the released "anonymized" data. Aware Weld resided in Cambridge, a city of 54,000 with seven ZIP codes, Sweeney bought the complete voter rolls for $20 — a database of the name, address, ZIP code, birth date, and gender of every Cambridge voter. She cross-referenced it with the released data and found only six individuals in the city with Weld's birth date, half male, and only one living in his ZIP code. Presto! Sweeney sent the governor's health records (including diagnoses and prescriptions) to his office. [4]

Data alone might seem anonymous, but when coupled with other existing data, it is possible to reidentify the anonymous individual. Sweeney's later research showed 87 percent of Americans could be uniquely identified using only three pieces of data: ZIP code, birth date, and gender. [5] Google searches, Amazon book reviews, Netflix film subscriber lists, message board posts — the data composing a secret profile of your life — are out there, waiting to be linked. Law professor Paul Ohm stated: [6]

> For almost every person on earth, there is at least one fact about them stored
> in a computer database that an adversary could use to blackmail, discriminate
> against, harass, or steal the identity of him or her. I mean more than mere
> embarrassment or inconvenience; I mean legally cognizable harm. Perhaps it is
> a fact about past conduct, health, or family shame.

University of Texas researchers conducted a de-anonymization project using anonymized data released for a contest that contained movie recommendations and choices made by 500,000 Netflix customers, revealing users "apparent political preferences and other potentially sensitive information." [7] The researchers used contextual and background knowledge, combined with cross-correlation with publicly available databases like the Internet Movie Database to re-identify individual data records. The researcher concluded Netflix's privacy policy's statements pertaining to personally identifiable information and aggregate information were meaningless: "The simple-minded division of information into personal and non-personal is a false dichotomy." [8]

To the extent data privacy laws focus on restricting personally identifiable information, such laws need to be rethought in light of the prospect of reidentification. Unlike the United States, Europe considers IP addresses personal information because they can be traced back to an individual through the ISP (see the discussion of personally identifiable information in the Chapter 10).

## ISP Subscriber Information

An ISP may be asked to reveal a subscriber's identity for several reasons: to determine if the subscriber accessed illegal sites (*i.e.*, obscene sites such as those displaying child pornography), is stalking or harassing someone, or engaging in criminal or terrorist activities; and for *discovery* purposes, by a plaintiff in a civil suit, *e.g.*, a defamation action. Some courts have ruled an ISP can not release customer identities absent a valid subpoena. In a 2003 case, an anonymous harassing e-mail to a political campaign was turned over to the police, who filled out a search warrant but failed to get it signed by a judge — an illegible signature near the judge's signature line was actually a detectives' signature, invalidating the warrant. The police presented the invalid warrant to the ISP, demanding the sender's identity. The ISP (AOL) faxed them the subscriber's name, address, phone numbers, account status, membership information, software information, billing and account information, and his other AOL screen names. A Connecticut federal court held[9] AOL had violated the **ECPA** by releasing customer information that did not fall within its exceptions.[10] A similar result occurred when police secured a municipal court subpoena, instead of the necessary criminal grand jury subpoena, where a woman retaliated against her boss after an argument by changing his access codes to a supplier's Web site. A unanimous New Jersey Supreme Court held ISPs must not release personal information about users, even to police, without a valid subpoena, reinforcing a reasonable expectation of privacy for ISP subscribers.[11]

Nonetheless, a New Haven, Connecticut superior court, in a motion to suppress evidence, ruled by voluntarily giving subscriber information to an ISP, the subscriber had assumed the risk of it being turned over to a third-party.[12] (Although arguably, by issuing each subscriber a screen name to mask his identity, the ISP was creating an expectation of privacy). This case is not unique; where the issue of an Internet user's expectation of privacy in his subscriber information has arisen, many courts have found no Fourth Amendment protection. Here, a university traced a harassing e-mail's IP address to a student's ex-girlfriend.[13] Pursuant to a search warrant, police seized three computers from her house. She moved to suppress the evidence and recover the computers, but the court refused, stating "it is clear [plaintiffs] ceded any expectation of privacy in their underlying subscriber information, such as their residential address and other information, when they voluntarily entered into an agreement for [the ISP] to provide them with an Internet account servicing their home."[14]

Where a subpoena is issued to force an ISP to disclose a subscriber's identity because of alleged defamatory comments, courts must balance the speakers' privacy interest in his First Amendment right of anonymous free speech against the plaintiff's reputational interest as expressed in the defamation action. When a California appellate court reversed a ruling to allow a former executive to subpoena the names of anonymous critics on a Yahoo! message board, it held the messages were "unquestionably offensive and demeaning" but could not be considered defamation since they were not assertions of fact, and thus could not overcome the poster's First Amendment right to speak anonymously online.[15] Likewise, a former school board member's request for disclosure of anonymous online critics was denied by a state court finding the comments protected speech. A New York court ruled Google, the ISP hosting the blog, did not have to disclose the identities of the blogger or the anonymous users who posted the allegedly defamatory comments because they were on "a matter of interest to her religious community and the public in general" and not reasonably susceptible of a defamatory connotation.[16]

However, in one case, a federal court not only ordered Google to identify a subscriber but also to deactivate his e-mail account. [17] In a dumbfounding ruling, a federal district court judge compounded a bank blunder with his own overly broad and ill-considered decision. Rocky Mountain Bank accidentally e-mailed the names, addresses, SSNs, and loan information of more than 1,300 customers to a Gmail address. By itself, that was an egregious data breach and an unintentional disclosure of personally identifiable information harming the privacy of the bank customers. But the information was sent, unsolicited, to an innocent Gmail account holder. The bank e-mailed the Gmail account, advising of the error and requesting deletion of the data, but received no response. It then sought the account holder's identity and contact information from Google, who refused to release it without a court order (abiding by its stated privacy policy). The bank got the court order — and more. Once the account holder's identity was known, it would have been reasonable for either the bank to contact him by phone, mail, or fax, or for the court to enjoin the recipient from using or disclosing the data and to order him to destroy it. Instead, the judge ordered Google to deactivate the account holder's e-mail account. Remember, the Gmail account holder was an innocent party who had done nothing wrong; in fact, he had taken no action at all. The account holder was a passive recipient of an unsolicited e-mail who might never have received it at all if his spam filter deleted it first. Yet the judge ordered his e-mail account shut down, without any regard to the effect it might have on his business or personal life. The judge's order clearly violated the account holder's First Amendment rights to communicate online and his privacy rights. Five days later, the judge vacated his order at the joint request of Google and the bank, allowing Google to restore access to the account. [18] How stupid was the ruling? For three years, a Tennessee doctors' office accidentally sent patient information, including SSNs and medical histories, to an Indiana businessman's fax machine. [19] The court's order would be analogous to an order shutting off phone service to the doctor's office!

## Search Queries

Search engines *record and retain* every query in logs. Not only do they retain the typed phrase, but also the date and time of the search and the IP address from which it was entered. They also store a cookie containing a unique identifier on the searcher's computer that can be used to identify subsequent searches by the user. Even if the searcher logs on later with a different IP address, the search engine will still recognize the cookie identifier unless the searcher either deletes the cookie or uses another computer. Depending on the firm, some search engines record other information, such as browser type; native language; whether the search was for text, image, or video; and what links were clicked on the search results page. [20] With this data, a search firm could tell what phrases were searched from a specific IP address, or which IP addresses looked up certain phrases. Imagine the U.S. government in the 1950s being able to print out a list of everyone who had expressed interest in the phrase "Communist Party."

Search phrases may reveal personal information about an individual, such as he has a specific medical condition, is shopping for a divorce lawyer, is looking for a gay bar, or has unusual fetishes. Most believe what they type into a search engine cannot be connected to them personally; however, such data is logged by the search engine, though search firms have neither the time, manpower, or inclination to spy on users. Search firms usually strip out search terms that could be useful to advertisers and then delete old logs. But they do have the data and they know the IP address, which can be traced (by reverse

DNS lookup) to the ISP that issued it to the user. Whether by subpoena or voluntarily, the ISP could reveal who its logs reveal accessed the search engine at a specific time.

Likewise, if one is logged into an MSN or Yahoo! account and uses that firm's search engine, the firm might be able to correlate its search log data with the member's previously entered account registration information.[21] Google's "Web history" feature lets account holders "view and search across the full text of the pages you've visited, including Google searches, Web pages, images, videos and news stories", which means user's Web visits (not just searches) are being recorded and retained.[22] The potential for correlating data becomes enormous, given Google's 2008 acquisition of Internet ad firm DoubleClick, enabling it to track users' searches *and* Web site visits.

Bush administration federal prosecutors in 2006 attempted to force major search firms to surrender logs that would reveal information about customers' online searches.[23] Google, Microsoft, Yahoo! and AOL were subpoenaed and all but Google complied. The Bush administration asked a California federal court to force Google to comply with the subpoena. Google logs search terms used, sites visited, and the IP address and browser type of the computer for each search. While the information subpoenaed alone probably could not be used to identify a particular individual, the Bush administration claimed it needed the data about search patterns to bolster its case against anti-pornography filters. It had been defending the constitutionally-challenged **Child Online Protection Act** (COPA, discussed further in Chapter 17) arguing criminal prohibitions are more effective than technological filtering methods, and presumably wanted to use this data to support its claim. The federal court granted part of the administration's request for access to some of Google's index of Web sites but denied access to users' search queries.[24] The court voiced concerns about "perception by the public that this is subject to government scrutiny" when individuals type search terms, but added the government had demonstrated a "substantial need" for Google's random sampling data, although nonetheless admitting it had been vague about its purposes for studying the URL sampling.[25]

## Data Retention

As server space is limited, ISPs routinely delete log files they no longer need for business purposes (*e.g.*, network monitoring, fraud prevention, or billing disputes).[26] However, should a request be presented to an ISP from a law enforcement agency, the **Electronic Communication Transactional Records Act of 1996** (ECTRA) requires ISPs to retain any "record" in their possession for 90 days "upon the request of a governmental entity."[27] Wanting to go further, in 2006 the Bush administration sought to require ISPs to record and save logs of customers' online activities.[28] The proffered rationale for such a broad and invasive request stemmed from law enforcement agencies claims by the time they contact the ISPs, the records might have been routinely deleted. Under that rationale, although only a small percentage might be law enforcement targets, *all* ISPs' customer records would have to be retained, including the majority of "innocent" customers. The administration also expressed interest in legislation to require search engines to preserve logs.

A 2007 bill[29] would have required ISPs to track customers' online activities (*e.g.*, Web browsing, instant message exchanges, and e-mail) to aid police investigations, with fines and imprisonment for noncompliance.[30] The Internet Stopping Adults Facilitating the Exploitation of Today's Youth Act of 2007 (SAFETY Act) also would have allowed the U.S.

Justice Department to order companies to store such records forever and, under threat of imprisonment, required owners of sexually explicit sites to post warning labels.[31] The irony of the proposed SAFETY Act (besides bearing the same name as a 2006 bill[32] sponsored by Rep. Mark Foley, who resigned from Congress that year after the revelation he had sent sexually explicit instant messages to teenaged boys) is by mandating indefinite storage of customer data, it would subject even more individuals' private data to potential breaches by hackers.

Data retention, especially by American search engines, has been a topic of concern in Europe as well. The *European Union Data Retention Directive* requires communications providers in member countries retain subscriber data for a minimum of six months to two years (the precise period determined by each member state). While American search engines typically retain data from six months to two years as well, depending on the member state and the specific search engine, there could be a conflict. The Directive applies to the identity of the individual contacted by the subscriber; the date, time, and length of phone calls and Internet logins; and e-mails (but content is not supposed to be retained).[33] In the U.K., ISPs must retain customer traffic data for one year under the Directive.[34] Social networks are not covered by the Directive; however, the British Home Office security minister, in 2009, suggested the Directive did not go far enough and the government needs to monitor communications on social networks and instant messaging, as well.[35]

While most U.S. companies disclose their online data collection and retention practices in their site privacy policies (see Chapter 10), such policies tend to be about notice, not control—consumers rarely have a choice, other than to leave the site.[36] An example of lack of control over personal data was evident when a British Facebook user tried to close his account and delete data he had posted to the social network, only to discover while Facebook would allow him to "deactivate" his profile, most of his information, though not visible to others, would remain on its servers indefinitely. The U.K.'s Information Commissioner's Office, which oversees implementation of the *U.K. Data Protection Act*, said it would investigate whether Facebook's policy of keeping data after a user has deactivated his account violates the Act.[37] One study showed photographs deleted from social networks by users were only "unlinked", not deleted. The photographs disappeared immediately from the photo albums, but in many cases were still accessible by clicking on the direct URL link (the Web address where the image was stored).[38]

One reason the data retention period is so controversial is the longer data is retained, the greater the risk of it being stolen or misused. As of 2007, Google (except for its Web History feature and any backup data) and Microsoft had policies of removing identifying information from search logs after 18 months, while Yahoo! and AOL retained user data for 13 months.[39] Google announced in 2008 it would reduce its retention time for IP addresses to nine months.[40] Ask.com, the first search engine to address the issue of choice rather than control, offered users an option to block its search engine from recording search terms and IP addresses (although Ask's advertising partner Google received and could keep the data).[41] The EU rules would require:[42]

- Search engines based outside Europe comply with EU rules on how long an individual's IP address or search history is stored (*i.e.*, data retention)
- The individual must consent to his data being collected and be given the right to object or verify his information
- IP addresses generally be regarded as personal information

Essentially, the EU is pressing for shorter retention, American search engines want somewhat longer retention, and the Bush administration had advocated significantly longer or even permanent retention. Whether voluntarily or by legislative decree, data retention means companies will be storing large amounts of personal information about consumers. For example, the U.S. Treasury Department has proposed requiring online businesses to collect personal information about customers and report it to the Internal Revenue Service (IRS).[43] An entire underground economy has sprung up online, as ever-increasing numbers of people make their primary or secondary income from selling items on sites like eBay and Amazon.com. The U.S. Treasury Department would like a piece of this unreported small business income, but that would require a list of all the sellers and their SSNs. The initial proposal would only affect sellers who make more than 100 separate transactions of $5,000 or more; however from an administrative standpoint, most sites would simply collect personal data from all customers up-front. A Canadian court has already ruled eBay Canada must turn over contact information and gross sales data for high-volume sellers based in Canada to the Canada Revenue Agency, though the customer data is stored on servers in San Jose, California and owned by the U.S. parent company eBay. However, the court noted: "The information can be summoned up in Canada and for the usual business purposes of eBay Canada. The situation may be different if the information never had been used in Canada."[44]

## Data Breaches

The flip side of data retention is the risk of data breaches by hackers. Imagine a database with the names, addresses, and SSNs of every eBay seller — a hacker or phisher's dream! Increasingly, corporate and government databases, filled with personal information about every individual, are becoming accessible online. Sensitive customer data may reside not just on company workstations and servers, but on portable (and easily lost or stolen) devices, such as employee's smart phones, laptops, and tablets. Some individuals upload confidential data to third-party servers. *Cloud computing* allows software to be hosted on a remote server rather than on one's own computer, with the result data files are stored on the remote server — meaning that company has access to your data (*e.g.*, Google Docs allows Google access to your spreadsheets and documents) and it, not you, has control over how or if the data are protected. Many individuals manage their financial accounts on remote sites protected only by passwords, sweet targets for hackers. Cloud-based storage provider Dropbox, Inc. was sued for failing to secure users' private data or to notify them about a data breach.[45]

Even data in on a home computer may be at risk of exposure to roommates, spouses, family, burglars, police searches, and hackers. From our previous discussions of identity theft and phishing, it is apparent databases, holding the keys to one's identity, are virtual treasure troves for identity thieves. But rather than housed in Fort Knox, the data are often kept in the equivalent of a cardboard shoebox on a shelf. Identity thieves function technologically at state-of-the-art level, while most businesses are ill-equipped to provide adequate security for such data (witness the large number of data breaches in major corporations frequently reported in the news). Many entities — corporate, nonprofit, and government — are reluctant to report breaches for fear of losing customer or investor confidence, but of those that have, between 2005 and 2010, there were 1,565 data breaches made public, involving 488,382,525 breached records.[46] From 2009-2010 alone, data breaches were reported by major companies (including AT&T, Apple, Google, Equifax, and Monster.com); some of the nation's largest universities, credit unions, banks (including J.P. Morgan Chase, Bank of America, Wells Fargo, Capitol One, Charles Schwab, Wachovia, and Citigroup), and insurance companies (including AIG and Allstate); hospitals, medical offices, law offices, municipal governments, the U.S. Defense Department, the U.S. Army, the U.S. Postal Service, and the U.S. Consulate in Jerusalem.[47] Small businesses are even less equipped to protect data adequately. Perhaps the government should mandate set periods for data destruction, instead of data retention, if it is truly interested in protecting citizens.[48]

The threat of data breaches has spurred demand for so-called "cyber insurance" to protect against customer claims for data loss and identity theft. Customers whose data held by third-party businesses have been breached have sued for invasion of privacy, negligence (for breaching a duty to have adequate procedures in place to prevent unauthorized access), and breach of express and implied warranty of a reasonable expectation of privacy for stored customer data.[49] One insurer, Zurich American Insurance Company, asked a New York state court in 2011 to rule it did not have to defend or indemnify Sony Corporation of America against any legal claims related to a significant 2011 data breach.[50]

Encryption is an alternative to data deletion. About half of companies surveyed planned to use disk encryption software to protect information from data breaches.[51] Besides the obvious feature of making it more difficult to access stolen data, encrypted data is exempted from the data breach reporting requirements of many state privacy laws that do not require companies to report data breaches if the data were encrypted, sparing the company embarrassing publicity. A single file or an entire hard drive can be encrypted; however, if an encrypted drive fails, the data is unrecoverable.

## Types of Data Breaches

**Intrusion.** Occurs when, by hacking or malware, a third-party infiltrates the computer network and steals the data, as discussed above.

**Accidental Disclosure.** Occurs when sensitive information or personally identifiable information (*e.g.*, names and SSNs) are e-mailed (or faxed) to the wrong person, or posted on a Web site or included in metadata of distributed documents. A government spokeswoman blamed negligence for the disclosure of thousands of federal workers' personal information after a General Services Administration employee accidentally e-mailed the names and SSNs of all the agency's 12,000 employees to a private e-mail account in 2010.[52] A medical billing firm placed patient records — insurance forms, SSNs and doctors' notes — on a Web site for its employees to access, neglecting to password protect the site and code its HTML to instruct search engines not to index it, resulting in confidential patient medical histories appearing in Google search results.[53]

**Insider Breach.** Arises when an individual with legitimate access (*e.g.*, an employee or independent contractor) intentionally discloses information. A hospital employee with access to a patient's medical information allegedly posted it on his Facebook page to make fun of her and her medical condition, listing her name and adding: "Funny but this patient came in to cure her VD and get birth control."[54] In the U.K, there have been 23 reported cases of medical staff posting confidential medical information on Facebook, such as patient names, details about their medical condition, and one instance where a hospital medical staffer photographed a patient in bed and posted the picture on his Facebook page.[55]

**Portable Device Breach**. Occurs when a portable data device (*e.g.*, laptop, smart phone, flash drive, CD/DVD, or data tape) is lost, stolen, or discarded. For example, in 2006, a laptop with the personal information of 26.5 million veterans was stolen from a government employee's home.[56]

**Stationary Device Breach**. Certain stationary electronic devices, like computers and servers, may be stolen, or discarded with sensitive data remaining on the drive. In 2011, hard drives containing the medical histories, financial information, and SSNs of 1.9 million Health Net insurance customers were stolen from an office.[57]

**Hard Copy Loss**. Printed sensitive information can also be lost, stolen, or carelessly discarded (instead of shredded).

**Payment Card Fraud**. Another form of data breach occurs when skimming devices are attached to point-of-sale terminals or in handheld devices carried by sales clerks to record credit or debit cards information.

## Consequences of Data Breaches

As discussed later in this book, the Internet Generation has a lesser expectation of privacy, often volunteering personal information and details of their lives on publicly viewed social networks and might not appreciate the harm a data breach can cause.[58] Beside the obvious threat of hackers using stolen credit card information to purchase goods, misappropriated personally identifiable information might be used for identity theft, financial scams, blackmail, or public humiliation. In the case of accidental disclosure, once the information is publicly accessible on the Web, it might be used to the detriment of the individuals involved. For example, based on the revealed personal information, an employer might deny an applicant a job, or fire an employee; or an insurance company might deny coverage or payment of a claim, or raise premiums.

The consequences from data breaches will increase exponentially with enactment of the **American Recovery and Reinvestment Act** (ARRA)[59] a provision of which, the **Health Information Technology for Economic and Clinical Health** (HITECH) Act,[60] mandates all health records become electronic by 2014. One objection to adoption of electronic medical records has been concern over data breaches and patient privacy. These concerns are exacerbated by the fact an individual's medical records may be authorized to pass through multiple firms, and employees and contractors within them.

The **Health Insurance Portability and Accountability Act** (HIPAA)[61] was passed to protect patient privacy. One portion, the Security Rule, establishes security standards for "Electronic Protected Health Information". These are broken down into Administrative Safeguards (policies and procedures for health care provider compliance with **HIPAA**); Technical Safeguards (preventing unauthorized access to health care provider computer networks); and Physical Safeguards (protecting physical access to prevent misappropriation of patient information).

The **ARRA** includes civil fines for violations and gives patients the right to request all incidences where their health information has been released, copied or exchanged. Nonetheless, the ability to safeguard patient confidentiality and medical records remains highly questionable in light of incidents like the posting of patient medical records on Facebook by hospital employees[62] or discussions of specific patients by health workers on social networks.[63]

## Metadata

Metadata is often defined as "data about data" because it describes information about an electronic document. Computers and software create information about text files, spreadsheets, photographs, e-mails, and other electronic documents a computer user never sees and is probably unaware of. The information does not appear when a document is printed, nor does it show on a user's screen in normal settings. Invisibly embedded into the file, metadata can disclose how and when a document was created or revised and by whom. It may reveal earlier versions with changes and modifications made to text, including notes containing a culpable phrase later edited out, and in the case of photographs, it may hold geodata (information revealing physical location). Metadata can show who did what and when they did it, yielding a tactical advantage in business and legal settings, were a competitor or litigant to gain access to it. Under the amended Federal Rules of Civil Procedure, electronic data must be provided in a form in which it is ordinarily maintained or readily usable; however, the requesting party may specify the form of production.[64] This means electronic data in its original format (*e.g.*, the actual spreadsheet file and not a PDF reproduction) with its metadata (*e.g.,* file creator, creation date, and document changes; and in e-mails, routing details such as sender, recipients, and subject line) intact could end up in the hands of the opposing side in a lawsuit. State courts have only begun to address the issue dealing with metadata embedded in electronic evidence.[65]

So far, there have been two court decisions holding metadata subject to state public record statutes. The Supreme Court of Arizona held when a public entity maintains a public record in an electronic format, the electronic version, including any embedded metadata, is subject to disclosure under Arizona's public records statute.[66] Washington's supreme court ruled an e-mail's metadata (the "to," "from," "date," and "subject" fields; and the sender's IP address) attached to a public official's e-mail was subject to disclosure under the state's open records statute.[67]

---

### Chapter 8 Notes

[1] Miguel Helft, "Google is Top Tracker of Surfers in Study," The New York Times, June 2, 2009.

[2] The plug-in for Firefox browsers can be downloaded at www.ghostery.com (accessed Mar. 23, 2012).

[3] Ellen Nakashima, "Google Promises Privacy Fixes in its Chrome Browser," The Washington Post, September 9, 2008, p. D08.

[4] Nate Anderson, "Anonymized" Data Really isn't — and Here's Why Not," ArsTechnica.com, September 8, 2009.

[5] *Ibid.*

[6] *Ibid.*

[7] Steve Lohr, "Netflix Cancels Contest Plans and Settles Suit," The New York Times, March 12, 2010.

[8] *See* Arvind Narayanan and Vitaly Shmatikov, "Robust De-anonymization of Large Datasets (How to Break Anonymity of the Netflix Prize Dataset)," February 2008, *available at* http://arxiv.org/PS_cache/cs/pdf/0610/0610105v2.pdf.

[9] *Freedman v. Am. Online, Inc.*, 325 F. Supp. 2d 638 (E.D. Va. 2004), reh'g denied 329 F. Supp. 2d 745.

[10] The Electronic Communications Privacy Act, 18 U.S.C. § 2510, *et seq.* Exceptions are listed in §§ 2702-03.

[11] Jeffrey Gold, "New Jersey Court Requires Subpoena for Internet Subscriber Records," Associated Press wire service report, April 21, 2008.

[12] Lisa Siegel, "Online Service Provider Rats Out User," The Connecticut Law Tribune, January 25, 2006.

[13] *Ibid.*

[14] *Ibid.*

[15] Gina Keating, "California Court Bars Unmasking of Web Critic," Reuters wire service report, February 6, 2008.

[16] *Greenbaum v. Google, Inc.,* 845 N.Y.S. 2d 695 (N.Y. Sup. Ct. 2007).

[17] Wendy Davis, "Judge Orders Google to Deactivate User's Gmail Account," Online Media Daily, September 24, 2009.

[18] Wendy Davis, "Judge Allows Google to Restore Gmail Account That Received Misdirected Email," MediaPost.com, September 29, 2009, *available at* www.mediapost.com/publications/index.cfm?fa=Articles.showArticle&art_aid=114513#comments (accessed Mar. 23, 2012).

[19] "Tennessean: Doctors Mistakenly Fax Patients' Data to Indiana Company," PrivacyLives.com, September 30, 2009, *available at* www.privacylives.com/tennessean-doctors-mistakenly-fax-patients-data-to-indiana-company/2009/09/30/#more-4106 (accessed Mar. 23, 2012).

[20] "Mary Brandel, "What Search Engines Store about You," Computerworld, July 10, 2007.

[21] *Ibid.*

[22] Google Web History page, *available at* https://www.google.com/accounts/ServiceLogin?hl=en&continue=http://www.google.com/psearch&nui=1&service=hist (accessed Mar. 23, 2012).

[23] Declan McCullagh and Elinor Mills, "Feds Take Porn Fight to Google," CNET News.com, January 19, 2006.

[24] Anne Broache, "Judge: Google Must Give Feds Limited Access to Records," CNET News.com, March 17, 2006.

[25] *Ibid.*

[26] Google retains search data for a certain period to assist in improving services and fighting computer attacks and fraud, however the search engine has refused to disclose the length of time it retains such data. *See* Anick Jesdanun, "Control over Online Data Rests with Companies—Consumers' Only Option for Privacy is Often Logging off," Associated Press wire service report, October 16, 2006.

[27] The Electronic Communication Transactional Records Act, 18 U.S.C. § 2703(f).

[28] Jesdanun, fn. 26, *supra.*

[29] A bill must be passed by both the House and Senate and then signed by the president before it becomes law. At the end of each session, any bills not passed into law are cleared from the books.

[30] Declan McCullagh, "GOP Revives ISP-tracking Legislation," CNET News.com, February 6, 2007, and Beth Pariseau, "ISPs Fear SAFETY Act Retention Requirements," SearchStorage.com, March 2007.

[31] H.R. 837 [110th Congress]: Internet Stopping Adults Facilitating the Exploitation of Today's Youth Act (SAFETY) of 2007, introduced on February 6, 2007 by Rep. Lamar Smith [R-TX].

[32] H.R. 5749 [109th Congress]: Internet Stopping Adults Facilitating the Exploitation of Today's Youth Act (SAFETY) of 2006, introduced on July 10, 2006 by Rep. Mark Foley [R-FL].

[33] Directive on Mandatory Retention of Communications Traffic Data: Directive 2006/24/EC of the European Parliament and of the Council of 15 March 2006 on the retention of data generated or processed in connection with the provision of publicly available electronic communications services or of public communications networks and amending Directive 2002/58/EC, *available at* http://eur-lex.europa.eu/LexUriServ/LexUriServ.do?uri=CELEX:32006L0024:EN:NOT (accessed Mar. 23, 2012).

[34] Tom Espiner, "Gov't May Track All UK Facebook Traffic," ZDNet.uk, March 18, 2009.

[35] *Ibid.*

[36] Jesdanun, fn. 26, *supra.*

[37] Ben King, "Facebook Data Protection Row," Channel Four News, November 17, 2007.

[38] "Websites 'Keeping Deleted Photos'," BBC News, May 21, 2009.

[39] Margaret Kane, "Google Cuts Data Retention Time in Half," CNET News.com, September 9, 2008.

[40] Catherine Rampell, "Google Calls for International Standards on Internet Privacy," The Washington Post, September 15, 2007, p. D01.

[41] "Search Engine Ask to Stop Keeping Search Data upon Request," Associated Press wire service report, July 20, 2007.

[42] "EU Data Privacy Regulators Say Internet Search Engines Must Follow EU Rules," Associated Press wire service report, February 21, 2008. *See also* Anne Broache, "Europeans Warn Search Engines: Delete User Data Sooner," CNET News.com, April 7, 2008.

[43] Jaikumar Vijayan, "IRS Wants Data on Users from Internet Firms," Computerworld, May 08, 2007.

[44] Ian Austen, "Canadian Court Opens up eBay Data to Tax Agency," The New York Times, October 1, 2007.

[45] *Wong v. Dropbox, Inc.*, Case No. 113092, (N.D. Cal. filed Jun. 22, 2011).

[46] "Chronology of Data Breaches, Security Breaches 2005 — Present," Privacy Rights Web site, *available at* www.privacyrights.org/data-breach (accessed Mar. 23, 2012).

[47] *Ibid.*

[48] In 2006, Rep. Edward Markey [D-MA] sponsored a bill, H.R. 4731 [109th Congress]: Eliminate Warehousing of Consumer Internet Data Act of 2006. It proposed mandating Web site owners destroy obsolete personally identifiable data such as credit card numbers, bank numbers, and birth dates, home address, and SSNs. The bill did not become a law.

[49] Whether unauthorized disclosure of personal information through a data breach is covered by a general liability insurance policy's "invasion of privacy" provisions is a subject of debate within the insurance industry. One might also question if a data breach by a hacker can support an invasion of privacy cause of action against the data holder, rather than the hacker. A data breach might support causes of action by the affected individuals for negligence, breach of express and implied warranty, or possibly breach of an implied fiduciary duty (in cases where a company is entrusted with sensitive financial or medical data), but since the breached companies have not engaged in any affirmative act, such as publication (a necessary element of the tort) of the data, the only support for a claim of invasion of privacy would appear to stem from their inaction, *i.e.*, their failure to take appropriate steps to safeguard the data. In other words, if an individual voluntarily provides personal information to a company, and the company has not disclosed that data, if the data is stolen, has the company committed the tort of invasion of privacy or is the hacker the one who has? If the company has a legal duty to safeguard the data, then it would be more logical for a plaintiff to sue based on the cause of action from which that legal duty arose, *e.g.*, an express or implied breach of contract.

[50] *Zurich Am. Ins. Co. v. Sony Corp. of Am.*, Case No. 651982/2011 (N.Y. Sup. Jul. 20, 2011). Zurich sued Sony over coverage for Sony's insurance claim after hackers reportedly stole nearly 100 million Sony Playstation users' account data, compromising more than 12 million credit and debit cards.

[51] Heather Clancy, "Encrypting Data Can Save You Lots of Heartache. How Should You Do It?" U.S. News & World Report, September 19, 2008.

[52] Ed O'Keefe, "Personal Data of Thousands of GSA Employees at Risk," The Washington Post, November 9, 2010.

[53] Jordan Robertson, "New Data Spill Shows Risk of Online Health Records," Associated Press wire service report, August 22, 2011.

[54] Susan Abram, "Hospital Employee Allegedly Makes Fun of Patient's Medical Condition on Facebook; Officials Investigating," The Los Angeles Daily News, December 29, 2011.

[55] Sarah Rainey, "Nurses Discuss Ill Patients on Facebook, Study Finds," The (U.K.) Telegraph, October 28, 2011.

[56] Robertson, fn. 53, *supra*.

[57] *Ibid.*

[58] The hospital staffer who posted a patient's name and medical condition, *see* fn. 54, *supra*, replied to criticism on his Facebook page: "People, it's just Facebook…Not reality. Hello? Again…It's just a name out of millions and millions of names. If some people can't appreciate my humor than tough. And if you don't like it too bad because it's my wall and I'll post what I want to. Cheers!"

[59] The American Recovery and Reinvestment Act of 2009 (ARRA), Pub. L. 111-5, 123 Stat 115.

[60] The Health Information Technology for Economic and Clinical Health (HITECH) Act, 42 U.S.C. Chapter 156 — Health Information Technology.

[61] The Health Insurance Portability and Accountability Act of 1996 (HIPAA), Pub. L. 104-191, 110 Stat. 1936.

[62] Abram, fn. 54, *supra*.

[63] Rainey, fn. 55, *supra*.

[64] Fed. R. Civ. P. 34(b).

[65] *See* David Hrick and Chase Edward Scott, "Metadata: The Ghosts Haunting e-Documents," Georgia Bar Journal, February 2008, Vol. 13, N.8, p. 16; *see also* David Hrick and Chase Edward Scott, "Metadata: Ethical Obligations of the Witting and Unwitting Recipient," Georgia Bar Journal, April 2008, Vol. 13, N.9, p. 30.

[66] *Lake v. City of Phoenix*, 207 P.3d 725 (Ariz. App. Div. 1, 2009).

[67] *O'Neill v. City of Shoreline*, 240 P.3d 1149 (Wash. 2010) aff'g 187 P.3d 822 (Wash. App. 2008).

# CHAPTER

# 9

---

## THE EXPECTATION OF PRIVACY

This chapter covers the expectation of privacy in chat, e-mail, and on the World Wide Web, e-mail privacy, employer monitoring, ISP monitoring, the Electronic Communications Privacy Act, and the 2006 amendments to the Federal Rules of Civil Procedure affecting electronic discovery, with emphasis on the First, Fourth, and Fifth Amendments.

*"The critical point is that the Constitution places the right of silence beyond the reach of government." — Justice William O. Douglas*

WE HAVE DISCUSSED THE electronic trail, how ISPs and Web sites collect data, often surreptitiously, about Web users, the concept of privacy, and the Internet Generation's lessened expectation of privacy. What degree of privacy should an individual expect for information residing on her computer or in her interactions online? What constitutes a reasonable expectation of privacy?

## Expectation of Privacy In Chat Rooms

An Internet *"chat room"* is a Web page using chat software to display typed messages in *real time*. This differs from a message board or forum where messages are posted on a page and maintained in static form indefinitely, often permanently archived and searchable. In chat, messages scroll down the page and eventually disappear from view. When several individuals are logged onto the same chat page, each can type brief messages, often with standardized abbreviations or emoticons (*e.g.*, smiley faces), onto the page. Each message, as well as replies from others in the chat room, are immediately visible to all participants as sequential lines beginning with the identification of the author, a nickname or "screen name" created for the session. Obviously, since everyone logged onto the page can view the "conversation", there can be no expectation of privacy in a public chat room. Additionally, anyone can print a transcript of the chat or save it to a file. The chat may also be logged and archived by the chat site, or any participant.

Another chat feature is the private message (PM) or instant message (IM), which allows exchange of messages between two parties. They may carry on a private text conversation while still in the main chat room, but do not necessarily need to be in a chat room to use the IM function. Each knows only the other party can see what is typed in the IM. Does this create an expectation of privacy for IMs? What if one party copies the IM conversation and pastes it into the main chat room? Or if one party saves the IM conversation to a file and later e-mails it to a third-party? What if law enforcement use special electronic eavesdropping software to read an IM sent from one person to another?

One attorney argued a chat room transcript should not be admitted into evidence because it was an *illegal eavesdropping* by police. The state (Illinois) law defined eavesdropping as "using any device capable of retaining or transcribing conversations or electronic communications without the consent of all parties involved in the communication." The attorney argued the police computer was a device capable of retaining or transcribing electronic communication. A 43-year-old lawyer had arranged through chat to meet a 14-year-old girl for sex.[1] However, the "14-year-old girl" was, in reality, an undercover police officer. Police had created the imaginary girl's chat profile using a picture of a real 14-year-old from the police department's youth program. Since the defendant entered into a plea bargain to avoid prison, the illegal eavesdropping issue was never ruled on, so it remains a viable legal argument.

In a fact pattern similar to the Illinois case, a New Hampshire judge threw out chat log evidence against an alleged pedophile.[2] A police detective had logged onto a chat room disguised as a 14-year-old girl. A man then solicited the "girl" for sex. The detective used screen capture software to record the chat session. The defense moved to suppress the recorded conversation as a violation of the state wiretap statute, which required all parties to a conversation *consent* before it could be intercepted or recorded.[3] The court ruled the log was an unlawful wiretap and inadmissible. While it was legal for the detective to pose as a 14-year-old girl and chat with the suspect because U.S. law allows law enforcement agents to deceive, defraud, and lie in criminal investigations;[4] the detective ran afoul of the law by recording the chat without consent of the other party (the suspect). The decision, the first of its kind to apply that standard to online chats, struck down a technique routinely used by law enforcement, employers, and ISPs. New Hampshire, like California, Connecticut, Delaware, Florida, Illinois, Maryland, Massachusetts, Michigan, Montana, New Hampshire Pennsylvania, and Washington, require *all* parties to the communication to consent to a recording.

However, a Washington court allowed a chat transcript admitted as evidence where a man solicited a "girl" who was an undercover detective.[5] The detective created the identity of "Amber", a 13-year-old with a Hotmail account and a chat screen name "ambergirl87." He approached a 26-year-old man in a chat room and, after a series of e-mails and chats, the man agreed to meet "Amber" at a local hotel, where he was charged with attempted rape of a minor. The difference here was the chat software, ICQ, had a *default setting* to make a permanent record of the conversation. The appellate court noted ICQ expressly advised users: "Some versions of the software allow any party to an ICQ session to record the content of the session (messages, chat, URL, chat request, and other events). The ICQ program default in some versions is set to record message and other event dialog and traffic."[6] Using a combination of *imputed knowledge* and *implied consent*, the court reasoned the defendant should have known about the default setting, and effectively consented to the recording under Washington's "both party" consent statute. "By using the ICQ client–to–client communications, [he] impliedly consented to recording of the communications by the intended recipient."[7] The appellate court ruled the e-mail and ICQ messages private communications protected by the Washington **Privacy Act** but "because [he] impliedly consented to the recording of the messages, there was no violation. The trial court correctly concluded the messages admissible."[8]

Imputing knowledge of all features of a software program may be a large leap. Here, the default was to archive all conversations. What if the software has archiving capability but the default is set to not archive? Does the mere capability of archiving in the software eliminate any reasonable expectation of privacy and imply consent to recording of the conversation? If so, how does that differ from knowledge of the existence of external tools, like screen capture software, which can be used to record IM conversations?

One common feature in the three cases above was all the defendants were charged with using Internet chat to solicit sex from minors who were in reality not minors but police officers. This raises the interesting issue of whether one can be charged with a crime against a minor when there is no minor involved. While such a scenario may appear a form of entrapment, courts have focused on the defendant's *mens rea* or "state of mind". They look at whether the defendant had a guilty mind and took steps toward bringing about the criminal act, such as showing up at an agreed on location to meet the "minor." For example, the Connecticut Supreme Court upheld an attempted sexual assault conviction in a police sting where a man had arranged to meet what he believed was a 13-year-old girl from a chat room; but "Danuta333" was a police officer who arrested him when he showed up to meet the nonexistent girl at a shopping mall.[9]

Even use of a commercial spyware program may be deemed an illegal "wiretap."[10] A woman was convicted of violating Florida's wiretapping statute after she installed spyware on her husband's computer to catch him chatting with his lover.[11] The court found she had "intercepted the electronic communication contemporaneously with transmission" in violation of the state's wiretap act when she obtained the online transcript of a Yahoo! Dominoes chat game between her husband and his lover. Adding to the wife's troubles, the court also ruled she could not reveal or use the illegally obtained conversations in the couple's pending divorce case.

## Expectation of Privacy In E-mail

You may think your e-mail is private. But in this section, we'll look at who else may see your e-mail besides its intended recipient, whether through interception, under false pretenses, or after your death.

What happens in Vegas might stay in Vegas, but what happens in your e-mail may travel around. Consider who else, besides the intended recipient, might be perusing it—employers, hackers, mistaken recipients, ISPs, law enforcement officials, or a party in a lawsuit.

### In the Workplace

Most employees now communicate through e-mail, IMs, or intranets; an estimated 90 million U.S. workers send 1.5 billion e-mails daily. The Internet has become an integral office fixture and computers are the 21st century filing cabinets—90 percent of business documents are not printed and filed, but instead stored electronically.[12] But employers must be mindful e-mails might present great financial and legal jeopardy for the firm. Outgoing e-mails may reveal trade secrets or confidential proprietary information, while internal office e-mails might provide evidence for employees claiming discrimination, harassment, or retaliation, or for customers seeking to sue the firm. At brokerage firm Merrill Lynch, e-mails from investment analyst Henry Blodget were revealed to contain words such as "junk", "disaster", and "crap" to describe stocks the firm was recommending to clients.[13] Such interoffice e-mails can be subpoenaed through the *discovery* process in a lawsuit.[14] In fact, under 2006 amendments to the Federal Rules of Civil Procedure (FRCP) discussed below, such electronic data *must* be disclosed "without awaiting a discovery request."[15]

Employees often think of e-mail as private correspondence that ends after the message is sent, but e-mails, and back-ups of e-mails, exist on computer workstations, company servers, and ISP servers indefinitely. Employees' e-mail also reside indefinitely in backup media of corporate computer systems. Many businesses do not regularly purge old backups, and archived e-mail can be a treasure trove for attorneys suing the company. Courts do not consider destruction of e-mail and records pursuant to a fair and consistent business policy to be destruction of evidence, and the amended FRCP provide a safe harbor to protect companies from sanctions for deleting e-mail as part of "routine, good-faith operation."[16]

Your boss might be reading your e-mail to your boyfriend or the résumé you sent a competing firm. Is such snooping legal and why would an employer read employees' e-mail? Typically, employers only look at e-mails sent using the firm's computers, not from an employee's personal laptop, or smart phone; but in situations where the company supplies or pays for the desktop computer, laptop, or phone, employers often feel they have a right to access anything stored on the device.[17] They not only believe they have a right of access, but a strong need to know what employees are communicating to others. Employers are concerned about:

- **Business confidentiality.** Employees leaking (intentionally or not) trade secrets or confidential business information, *e.g.*, new products in development, names of customers or suppliers, pending deals or contract negotiations, or threatened lawsuits.

- **Client confidentiality.** Employees leaking sensitive client information entrusted to the firm, *e.g.*, financial or medical information, or details about a client's business or personal life. An employee may overhear, or have access in the course of her work to, private information about the client or his business not meant to be shared with the world or friends and family. This is particularly true in industries where professional ethics codes create a fiduciary duty between the firm and the client, as with attorneys, doctors, and accountants.

- **Legal privacy compliance.** Firms must comply with federal laws and regulations regarding confidentiality of clients' personal, financial, and health care information. Some privacy regulations, such as the **Health Insurance Portability and Accountability Act** (HIPAA), are discussed in Chapter 12.

- **Legal securities compliance.** Federal securities laws prohibit public companies (and their employees) from discussing certain matters at certain times. During the *"Quiet Period"* — from the time a company files a registration statement with the SEC for a public offering until the SEC declares the registration effective — federal securities laws limit what it and related parties can publicly release. Any disclosure — even inadvertently through an e-mail — could force the offering's postponement. Employees leaking unannounced financial results of their publicly-traded employers can also be problematic.

- **Illegal misrepresentation of false claims.** A company can be in enormous trouble with federal regulators if an employee e-mails false claims to clients, *e.g.*, claims a product has FDA approval (if it has not); claims a product will perform in a certain way (if it does not); or stockbroker claims guaranteeing a stock will increase in value. Firms face fines and other penalties for such statements under the FTC Truth in Advertising laws and the federal securities laws, respectively.

- **Prevention of sexual harassment lawsuits.** While many workplaces once merely displayed the ubiquitous nude calendar, the Internet has increased the opportunity for pornography to enter the workplace. Courts have held exposure to pornography in the workplace can create a "hostile work environment" that can be a form of sexual harassment. Sexually explicit e-mail attachments, screen savers, wallpaper, or files on a company computer may be factors deemed to create a hostile work environment. While a single offensive e-mail to a co-worker may not be enough to establish a hostile work environment, it might establish a pattern, which can be used as the basis for a sexual harassment claim.

- **Company image.** All companies are concerned about their image, and most devote substantial revenue establishing and maintaining it. A leaked employee's e-mail, containing racist or anti-Semitic comments, or admitting the employee would never use her company's product, could tarnish or irreparably damage that image.

These concerns have led companies to implement an (often unstated) policy of monitoring e-mail. Thirty percent of all firms and 43 percent of those with more than 20,000 employees hire staff to monitor and read outbound e-mail.[18] One study revealed 25 percent of employers have fired employees for misusing office e-mail.[19] While employers might feel justified monitoring e-mail and Internet use to avoid or curtail liability from discrimination or harassment suits, or disclosure of proprietary or confidential information, restrictions on personal e-mail and awareness their every move is watched may result in resentment and low employee morale. Nonetheless, more than three-quarters of employers electronically monitor employees.[20] Such monitoring includes e-mail, Internet use, videotaped camera surveillance and recording, and logging phone calls. Half of all companies store and review employees' computer files.[21] The test for whether such monitoring is legal or an impermissible invasion of privacy hinges on whether there is a *"reasonable expectation of privacy."* The trend has been for courts to find no reasonable expectation of privacy for e-mail in the workplace.

In *Shoars v. Epson America, Inc.*,[22] Alana Shoars ran the e-mail system at a California Epson plant. After assuring employees their e-mail was private, she discovered her boss was reading all employee e-mail. When she refused to go along with the monitoring, she was fired. She sued for wrongful termination, based on a state law prohibiting electronic surveillance, but the court held the statute's protections applied only to telephone communications, not e-mail. It found employees lacked a reasonable expectation of privacy in their business e-mail used primarily for business purposes.

In *Smyth v. Pillsbury Company*, despite assurance employees' e-mails would be confidential, not intercepted, or used as grounds for termination, Michael Smyth was fired for "unprofessional use" of Pillsbury's e-mail system,[23] after his employer found a printout of an e-mail to his supervisor sent from his home computer, calling sales managers "backstabbing bastards." Smyth sued for wrongful discharge. The court found Pillsbury's interest in preventing inappropriate and unprofessional comments on its network precluded any reasonable expectation of privacy.

In *Bourke v. Nissan Motors Corp.*, plaintiffs Bonita Bourke and Rhonda Hall were car dealership customer service representatives. [24] During a demonstration of the company's e-mail system, Bourke's randomly selected e-mail turned out to be of a sexual nature. A management review revealed more sexual e-mails from both. Bourke resigned and Hall was fired. Both sued for wrongful termination, claiming invasion of privacy, but the court ruled they had no reasonable expectation of privacy because they had signed an employment agreement that restricted e-mail use to company business and knew their employer sometimes monitored e-mail.

Ideally, an employer should have a policy manual addressing employee privacy the employee is required to read and sign when hired. But, once an employer has a policy, it must adhere to it. In a Ninth Circuit case, a police department had a formal policy stating employees should have no expectation of privacy in their use of computers, the Internet, and e-mail. However, it had an informal policy of not monitoring police officers' text messages. An officer texted sexually explicit messages to his girlfriend on an employer-provided mobile phone. The court found the informal policy was actually the operational policy, creating a reasonable expectation of privacy for messages, despite the formal policy's existence. [25] Thus, an employer must follow its policy in practice or possibly lose the right to rely on it.

As the trend has been for courts to find no reasonable expectation of privacy for e-mail in the workplace, employees might be advised to limit personal e-mails to their own computers and not company-owned computers or e-mail systems. However, employees do use e-mail to communicate with co-workers. Labor unions have argued employees should be allowed to e-mail co-workers to discuss work-related matters of mutual concern. If an employer allows personal use of e-mail at the workplace, can it then ban employees from using e-mail to discuss union organizing, or concerns about compensation, working conditions or other terms of employment?

Suzi Prozanski, an employee of *The Register-Guard*, an Oregon newspaper, and also president of her local newspaper guild's union, e-mailed co-workers from her office computer on a break, reminding them of a union rally that day. The company admonished her for violating its written communications system policy by using the company-owned e-mail system. She later sent two e-mails from her personal computer — one urged employees to wear green in support of the union and the other urged participation in the union's local parade entry. The employer again warned her in writing. Her union filed an unfair labor practice complaint alleging the policy was unlawful and discriminatorily enforced against her. [26] Earlier National Labor Relations Board (NLRB) decisions had held if an employer let employees use communications equipment for nonwork-related purposes, it could not prohibit use for union purposes. [27] But in this case, the board effectively reversed that decision, ruling employers can allow workers to use e-mail for personal communications while barring organizational-related use. The NLRB held an employer could discipline an employee for union-related e-mails, even if it permitted other non-business and personal use of e-mail, so long as the ban applied to solicitations of all groups and organizations. [28] In a 3–to–2 decision, the board ruled employees have no right under the **NLRA** to conduct union business on an employer's e-mail system: "An employer has a 'basic property right' to regulate and restrict employee use of company property." [29] However, on appeal, the D.C. Circuit rejected that rationale, stating the NLRB's distinctions between personal and organizational solicitations had no basis in either the employer's communications policy nor its past enforcement. [30] On remand, the NLRB found the employer's discipline of Prozanski for union-related e-mail use, given it allowed widespread personal e-mail use by employees, to be a violation of § 7 of the **NLRA**, which governs employer enforcement of employee communications policies in both union and nonunion situations.[31] Thus, if an employer permits personal e-mail use and social media use in the workplace, it might run afoul of § 7 by disciplining union-related communications or discussions of workplace grievances and concerns.

Employees often use portable communications equipment (*e.g.*, laptops and smart phones). The level of privacy they might reasonably expect may depend, in part, on who owns or pays for it. An employee has a lessened privacy expectation where the employer owns it and conversely, a greater expectation where the employee owns it. Each case will turn on the individual facts and jurisdictional law, but six factors for a court to consider are:

- **Employer Policy.** How do the employer's privacy policy, Internet usage policy, employee manual provisions, written or oral employment agreements, and communications to employees (*e.g.*, e-mails, memos) address monitoring, privacy, and use of electronics devices?
- **Practices.** How do the employer's past and current practices differ from stated policies? Is there an informal policy followed at odds with the formal policy? Absent a stated policy, the court may infer one from the employer's practices.
- **State Tort Law.** How did the employer obtain the information? Was there an invasion of privacy (*i.e.*, intrusion upon seclusion; see Chapter 12), trespass to chattels, or conversion by the employer?
- **State Statutes.** Does the state have any applicable statutes governing communications and/or privacy ?
- **Electronics Communications Privacy Act (ECPA).** Does the **ECPA** allow or prohibit employers reading and disclosing the contents of employee messages?[32]
- **Fourth Amendment.** Is a public or quasi-public entity employee involved? The U.S. Constitution's Fourth Amendment protects government employees from "unreasonable searches and seizures" by the government, while employees of private, non-governmental entities have no such protection from employer searches.[33]

E-mail monitoring is part of the employee monitoring process in America.[34] More than $140 million of employee surveillance software is sold annually and the extent and degree of such monitoring is mind-boggling.[35] Keystroke loggers can recreate what an employee typed and software can take screenshots of employee's computers,[36] scan e-mail attachments for images resembling human flesh,[37] notice when certain phrases are typed in documents or Web forms and warn users they are violating company policy or block the action.[38] Proofpoint hospital software scans outgoing e-mail for confidential data (*e.g.*, patient names, prescription histories, and Social Security numbers) automatically encrypting the message.[39] Monitoring may reveal which employees are sending e-mail with "résumé attached" subject lines. "Smart" ID cards track an employee's location as she walks through the workplace.[40] As monitoring software proliferates, the question *Qui custodiet ipsos custodes?* ('Who watches the watchmen?') arises. One prescient article suggests the ultimate creation of a new corporate position of information compliance officer to oversee "who in an organization can send what kind of data where."[41]

Monitoring has risks, such as *false inferences* derived from the data. An employee might accidentally visit www.whitehouse.com, a pornographic site, while attempting to access www.whitehouse.gov, the White House's Web site. While monitoring software can detect access to an inappropriate Web site, it cannot determine the employee's intent in accessing the site.

Firms are concerned with employees accessing pornographic sites not just because of lost productivity but also due to a fear of sexual harassment lawsuits stemming from creation of a "hostile work environment." That fear has been exacerbated by the rise of wireless devices entering the workplace.[42] Such devices allow easy access to pornography and employers can only use blocking software if they have provided the devices to employees. Some restrict employees use of their own smart phones and laptops at work.[43]

Government employees may also be subject to monitoring. In some situations, the public can access their e-mails under freedom of information laws. Almost all states have such laws, referred to as Public Records, Open Records, Open Meetings, Open Government, or Sunshine Laws.[44] State laws differ on how long e-mails are retained and which can be released.[45] The federal **Freedom of Information Act** (FOIA) provides anyone the right to request access to federal agency records or information. It applies only to federal agencies and does not create a right of access to records held by Congress, the courts, or state or local governments. The **FOIA** mandates a response within 20 days of receipt of a request. All requests become a matter of public record, with requesters' personal information omitted. The **FOIA** was amended by the **Electronic Freedom of Information Act Amendments of 1996**, which mandated creation of "electronic reading rooms" to enhance public access to records and required federal agencies to create an online index of frequently requested material. Despite the ubiquitous presence of e-mail and text messaging in both the private sector and government, city, state, and federal governments have been reluctant to let the public see e-mails and text messages, claiming state or federal laws do not cover those sent from (1) personally-owned computers, mobile phones, or devices not purchased with public funds, or (2) officials' home instead of their public office.[46] While these debates are only beginning to reach courts, it would seem a more logical analysis would base public access on whether the message content was related to the public office, rather than the means or method of transmission. Otherwise, a public official could evade sunshine laws or **FOIA** requests by hanging up the office phone and continuing the discussion on a mobile phone.

When a CIA employee used a government computer to download pornography, the FBI impounded and searched it and the e-mails on it.[47] The court ruled because the government had a long-standing policy allowing hard drives audits, the employee had no expectation of privacy. Even the U.S. judiciary is not immune from employee monitoring. In 2001, U.S. federal judges discovered court administrators monitoring their Internet communications. Concerned about privacy and confidentiality issues raised by the monitoring (at least as it applied to them), the Ninth Circuit judges disabled the monitoring systems. The administrators sought to reinstate it with a policy of no expectation of privacy in the workplace for federal judges and their staffs. The judges argued monitoring would threaten judicial independence. The Judicial Conference of the United States, the federal judiciary's policy-making body, settled the dispute, rejecting the administrators' "no expectation of privacy" policy and ending e-mail monitoring, but allowing limited Internet use monitoring and banning some file-sharing programs.[48]

As seen from examples in this section, most claims against employer monitoring fall under invasion of privacy, and most cases have allowed employers to monitor e-mail and Internet use, finding no reasonable expectation of privacy for e-mail in the workplace. Often, the key factor is whether employees were *informed in advance* e-mail and other Internet use were subject to monitoring. However, where the employee's e-mail is stored in a personal e-mail account on a third-party server, such as Yahoo! or Hotmail, the employer cannot legally access it. In a case where an employer accessed a former employee's personal e-mail stored on AOL's server, the Fourth Circuit found him liable for punitive damages and attorneys' fees under the **Stored Communications Act**, even without proof of actual damages. [49]

Co-workers might have access to your e-mail, including system administrators and any employees designated to read employee e-mail (as in the *Shoars* case, discussed above). If your company employs a Web designer to maintain its site and you use the site's Web-based e-mail, then the designer might be able to read your e-mail.

## Hackers

Hackers using "sniffer" programs that look for keywords in e-mails can intercept e-mails and read them. In one case, a hacker allegedly configured the "copy and forward" function of a torrent company's server so he could receive copies of company e-mail, which he allegedly forwarded to an MPAA executive. [50]

## Mistaken Recipients

A typographical error in the address line can easily result in a confidential e-mail being sent to an unintended recipient. When the University of Kansas e-mailed 119 students who had failed their classes to inform them they were at risk of losing financial aid, [51] the e-mail address list included the names of all 119 students, so everyone on the list could see each other's names, *i.e.*, the header used a carbon copy (cc:) instead of a blind carbon copy (bcc:). [52] Likewise, clicking the "Reply All" button instead of the "Reply" button on an e-mail program will forward the reply not just to the named recipient but to everyone carbon copied (cc:) in the original e-mail. In 2009, the Rocky Mountain Bank erroneously e-mailed the names, addresses, Social Security numbers, and loan information of more than 1,300 of its customers to the wrong e-mail address. [53]

## Internet Service Providers

Your Internet Service Provider (ISP), its employees, and anyone it gives access to — including any backbone provider that routes the e-mail from the sender to you — can read all your e-mails. The **ECPA** lets an ISP look through stored messages, including unopened e-mail, in a user's mailbox or recently sent and received mail. [54] Most ISPs temporarily store messages that pass through their system. The **ECPA** does not directly refer to the Internet, but instead governs "wire, oral, or electronic communications." [55] It contains a "Service Provider Exemption", which allows ISPs access to *stored communication messages*. Some courts have used this exemption to permit a company providing hardware and software to access employees' e-mail.

The **ECPA** governs unauthorized interception of communications. [56] The Act, written before the Internet became a ubiquitous part of daily life, may not be adequate to address modern communications. As the following case makes clear, it has failed to adapt to the realities of Internet communications and must be updated to protect online privacy. [57] E-mail privacy was set back in *United States v. Councilman* when a federal appellate panel ruled 2–to–1 an e-mail provider did not break the law by reading its customers' e-mails without consent. [58]

A bookseller offered e-mail accounts through its Web site to book dealer customers but secretly installed programming code to intercept and copy e-mails its competitor, Amazon.com. It read thousands of messages to learn which books its customers sought and gain a commercial advantage. The court held it did not violate the **ECPA** because the e-mails were already in the RAM of the defendant's computer when copied and therefore the bookseller did not intercept them while in transit over wires, even though it copied the messages before the intended recipients read them. The court ruled the messages were in *storage* rather than transit and thus fell under the **ECPA**'s service provider exemption. The dissent, which contained a fascinating, detailed description of how e-mail works, argued Congress never intended e-mail temporarily stored in the transmission process to have less privacy than messages in transit. However, the majority ruled the **ECPA**'s application turns on the issue of *whether e-mail is "in transit" or "in storage."* In the view of this book's author, if an e-mail has not reached its final destination, *i.e.*, the addressed recipient, then even in temporary storage, it should still be deemed in transit and the Act should apply.

As a result of <u>Councilman</u>, the *E-mail Privacy Act* was introduced in Congress in 2004.[59] This proposal would have altered the **ECPA** to prohibit the form of e-mail eavesdropping in <u>Councilman</u>, by providing ISPs may intercept e-mail only "to the extent access is a necessary incident to rendition of service, protection of rights or property of the service provider or to honor a government request", and giving e-mail intercepted in real-time transmission privacy protection under the **ECPA**. A similar bill was introduced in the Senate in 2005, but neither was enacted. In October 2004, in response to a U.S. Justice Department request, the First Circuit agreed to rehear <u>Councilman</u> **en banc**. Appellate courts sometimes grant a rehearing by all the court's judges to reconsider a panel decision where the case concerns a matter of exceptional public importance or conflicts with an earlier decision. In August 2005, the full appellate court, in a 5–to–2 decision, reversed, holding interception of an e-mail communication in "transient" electronic storage violates the **ECPA**, and remanding the case.[60]

In 2007, the Central District Court of California ruled an alleged hacker had not intercepted e-mails in violation of the **ECPA** because they were technically in storage, if only for a few nanoseconds, rather than in transmission. The case was pending in the Ninth Circuit Court of Appeals at time of publication.[61]

The issue of ISP e-mail monitoring was raised again when Google launched "Gmail", a free e-mail service. Google's computers scanned the e-mails (*i.e.*, sniffing) for keywords to use in sending targeted ads to Gmail users. Google would also keep copies of the e-mails *even after customers had deleted them*. Google's Gmail raised privacy concerns worldwide, due to both the retention of e-mails and the sniffing for keywords. Gmail might violate Europe's privacy laws because it stores messages where users cannot permanently delete them. Even if the Gmail account holder is aware of, and consents to, the sniffing, consent can only be given by the Gmail account holder; those who send e-mail to a Gmail customer have no opportunity to consent to having their e-mail read for keywords.

## Law Enforcement Officials

Armed with proper warrants or administrative subpoenas, state and federal law enforcement agents can legally gain access to an individual's e-mail.[62] While ISPs usually delete logs no longer needed for business purposes (*e.g.*, network monitoring, fraud prevention, or billing disputes), the **Electronic Communication Transactional Records Act of 1996** requires ISPs to retain any "record" for 90 days on "request of a governmental entity."[63] (See Chapter 8's discussion on data retention). One does not have to be the subject of a government investigation (or even a properly issued subpoena) for the government to read one's e-mail. In 2006, the Foreign Intelligence Surveillance Court (FISC) approved a warrant for surveillance of a single e-mail address, but the FBI admitted two years later the ISP it was served on "misinterpreted" it as a warrant for the entire network! The FBI blamed the mistaken mass surveillance on "human error."[64]

In a criminal appeal, the Sixth Circuit held the government must have a search warrant before it can seize and search e-mails stored by ISPs, finding e-mail users have the same reasonable expectation of privacy in stored e-mail as in their phone calls and postal mail.[65] The decision struck down part of the **Stored Communications Act** (Title II of the **ECPA**). Under the Act, law enforcement agents needed a warrant to obtain e-mails up to 180 days old, but could obtain older ones with only an administrative subpoena or an SCA 2703(d) order, both lacking a warrant's probable cause requirement.

## A Party in a Lawsuit

A party in a lawsuit may access e-mails through the legal process known as "*discovery*." If a company is sued, all e-mails, sent or received, archived on its computers may be subpoenaed for review. The rationale is, unlike formal written letters, e-mails and instant messages are composed "off-the-cuff" and in the heat of the moment individuals tend to be blunt and therefore more honest in what they write (as in the Merrill Lynch e-mails, discussed above). As a result, e-mail is subpoenaed as evidence in almost all workplace lawsuits.[66] This might suggest the safest course, if a lawsuit is anticipated, would be routinely to delete e-mails and archives of e-mails and instant messages. However, in one Florida case, that approach proved costly to the defendant.[67] When billionaire investor Ron Perelman sued investment firm Morgan Stanley for fraud, he repeatedly requested Morgan Stanley's internal e-mails, but the investment banker failed to preserve them. At the plaintiff's request, the court instructed the jury, since the defendant had failed to preserve them, it might infer the e-mails revealed a scheme to defraud him. The jury returned a verdict of $604.3 million in actual damages and $850 million in punitive damages — with interest and attorney fees, the verdict topped $1.58 billion! (On appeal, the compensatory and punitive damage awards were reversed and the case remanded with directions to enter judgment for Morgan Stanley; Perelman stated he would appeal).[68]

The issue of whether the duty to preserve electronic evidence (*e.g.*, e-mails and IMs) arises when a potential lawsuit is reasonably foreseeable, or on the actual filing of such a suit, remains unclear at both federal and state levels. Some federal courts have held the duty arises as soon as the company has a reasonable belief it may be subject to pending litigation.[69] While the Fourth Circuit has found the duty arises "when a party should reasonably know the evidence may be relevant to an anticipated litigation",[70] the First Circuit has determined it arises after persistent attempts to obtain the electronic evidence prior to filing suit.[71] In some states, such as Florida, site of the Morgan Stanley case, the duty does not arise until the actual filing. Of course, deliberately deleting electronic data after receipt of a subpoena would be the crime of destruction of evidence, referred to as spoilation.

*Spoilation* is a bad faith destruction of evidence. In the _Howell_ case from Chapter 3, the court found for the plaintiff after the defendants willfully and intentionally destroyed evidence related to his P2P activities on notification of a pending RIAA lawsuit.[72] The defendants allegedly uninstalled P2P software and reformatted the hard drive to remove evidence of file-sharing. In _Columbia Pictures, Inc. v. Bunnell_, a federal judge ruled the defendants had willfully despoiled evidence to such an extent it warranted termination of the case, stating, "Defendants' conduct during discovery in this case has been obstreperous. They have engaged in widespread and systematic efforts to destroy evidence and have provided false testimony under oath in an effort to hide evidence of such destruction."[73]

As discussed further in Chapter 19, the 2006 amendments to the FRCP have changed the nature of e-discovery. The FRCP are important because they affect anyone — individuals, businesses, and organizations — who becomes a party in a federal lawsuit. (State courts have their own rules of civil procedure). Companies should institute "*litigation hold*" procedures to provide notice to all relevant individuals within the firm as to *what* data must be kept and for *how long*. As soon as a lawsuit is anticipated, a company must use its litigation hold procedures and not wait to be subpoenaed.[74] A party must now identify the existence of electronic data it has not searched for or produced because of the costs and burdens of accessing it (*e.g.*, deleted files, backup tapes, data stored on systems no longer in use). If the other party insists on seeing this data, the party holding it has the burden of proving to the court the information is not reasonably accessible.[75] The amended FRCP have an exception for data privileged or subject to protection as trial preparation material.[76] The electronic data must be provided in a form in which ordinarily maintained or readily usable; however, the requesting party may specify the form of production.[77] This is important because it might include electronic data in its original format (*e.g.*, the actual spreadsheet file and not a PDF reproduction) with its *metadata* (*e.g.*, file creator, creation date, and document changes; and in e-mails, routing details such as sender, receivers, and subject line) intact.

So, many more people — employers, hackers, mistaken recipients, ISPs, law enforcement officials, and parties in a lawsuit — might possibly read your e-mail than you imagined when first typing it. The only way to ensure a high degree of privacy for e-mail messages is to encrypt them. The current encryption standard for e-mail is a software program called Pretty Good Privacy ("PGP"), based on "RSA encryption", which uses a "public key/ private key" system. The sender encrypts his e-mail with his private key (known only to him) and delivers it to the recipient, who can decrypt the message using the sender's public key (which is available to everyone).

## False Pretenses

Does volunteering personal information in a private context waive your privacy rights? This issue was raised when a man posted a raunchy sex classified ad on Craigslist, an online classifieds site. Posing as a submissive 27-year-old woman seeking a dominant man to humiliate and abuse her, the 30-year-old male from Seattle, Washington collected replies and posted them on Encyclopedia Dramatica, a Web site devoted to parodies and satires.[78] The result: 178 responses with 145 photos of men, including nude photographs of respondents and their genitalia, their names, e-mail addresses, phone numbers, IM accounts, and other contact information.[79] He also collected and posted voice messages. Most replies contained detailed descriptions of deviant sex acts. One wrote, "I'm married and looking to fill the needs not being done at home", followed by his name, mobile phone number, e-mail, and four photographs.[80] How long before someone recognized him and tipped off his wife is open to speculation, but the potential harm the respondents could suffer from public exposure of what they believed private communications is evident.

Craigslist said the perpetrator's actions violated its Terms of Use.[81] The **CDA** § 230, protects Craigslist, as a service provider, from liability for certain posts by users. The perpetrator faced civil liability for invasion of privacy.[82] As discussed in Chapter 7, one form is the tort known as *public disclosure of private facts*. The elements of this tort are: (1) the disclosure must be public, (2) the facts must be private, (3) the plaintiff must be identified, (4) the publication must be "highly offensive", and (5) there must be an "absence of legitimate concern to the public" with respect to the publication.[83] This is an example where all the elements for this invasion of privacy tort appear to have been met.

## After Death

Absent a court order, most ISPs vigorously protect subscribers' privacy. This makes sense. The subscriber is the ISP's customer and it is bad business to divulge a customer's private matters. Few would remain with an ISP that routinely disclosed e-mails and files to any who asked. Therefore, there is an expectation of privacy and nondisclosure, either implied or often expressed in the service contracts with ISPs. But what if the customer dies? What happens to customer data (*e.g.*, e-mail or files) on the ISP's server? Can, or should, the ISP delete data to protect the deceased's privacy? Or can, or should, the ISP release it to an estate administrator, spouse, or other relative? If so, what constitutes a relative for this purpose (*e.g.*, a child, a parent, a cousin, an unmarried common law spouse, or a homosexual partner)? Who decides where the line is drawn? Do the digital data become part of the deceased's estate, giving his heirs a property right in the data? Or are the data subject to the terms of the contract the decedent entered into with the ISP?

In 2004, 20-year-old Marine Lance Cpl. Justin Ellsworth was killed in Iraq. Under the Marines' policy of returning personal items to families and next-of-kin, the Ellsworth family would receive any personal possessions he had left at Camp Pendleton, California before shipping out to Iraq. All letters destined for mail are sent to their recipients and received mail, including opened letters, are sent to the families. Since the government does not provide e-mail accounts to soldiers on the front line, many use commercial ISPs like AOL, MSN, or Yahoo! for e-mail.[84] Ellsworth's father sought access to his late son's Yahoo! e-mail account but did not know his password. Yahoo! refused to reveal it to his father, citing its privacy policy in its Terms of Use agreement with Ellsworth.[85] Yahoo! also has a policy of deleting e-mail accounts after 90 days of inactivity. This created a public relations nightmare for Yahoo! which was in the position of announcing its intention to delete the last words of a dying son without allowing a mourning father to read them. Yahoo!'s justification was it was protecting the privacy rights of the deceased and those with whom he had corresponded. Its position is understandable. Senders of e-mail in Ellsworth's account believed it would only be read by Ellsworth; should not their privacy interests be protected? Conversely, Ellsworth wrote to the intended recipients of those e-mails residing in his account with the expectation his words were meant to be read only by them. Suppose there was something within those e-mails he did not want anyone else, even his family, to see? Should not his privacy interests be respected and protected? Yahoo! might well respond if Ellsworth had wanted his father to read his mail, then he would have forwarded it to him. On the other hand, soldiers killed in action might have important information in their e-mail accounts that could assist families in resolving personal matters.

The issue becomes one of balancing the privacy interests of the decedent and his correspondents with the presumed property interest of the decedent's family or heirs. On an episode of the TV series *"Married With Children"*, Peggy Bundy asked her husband Al "What are you thinking?" to which he replied, "If I wanted you to know what I was thinking, I would be talking." To paraphrase, if I wanted you to read my e-mail/files, I would have sent it to you (or given you the password). Would the average person want his parents to read her e-mail correspondence or diary? Perhaps a decedent would want his or her gay lover to have access to the account; on the other hand, the same decedent might not want a parent or child to see messages relating to a heretofore unrevealed lifestyle. Also at risk would be the privacy of third parties discussed in the e-mails. The easiest solution would be for subscribers to share passwords with those individuals they wish to have access (perhaps leave the password in a safe deposit box with a will) and for ISPs to have clear, stated policies. AOL, for example, permits next-of-kin to access e-mail accounts after submitting documents proving the relationship and faxing a copy of the death certificate. [86] ISPs could ask subscribers to designate an "account beneficiary" to be allowed access in event of the subscriber's death, similar to naming a beneficiary on an insurance policy. The issue of **digital estate planning** is discussed further in Chapter 21.

In the Ellsworth case, Yahoo!'s Terms of Use had a clause that read: "You agree that your Yahoo! account is nontransferable and any rights to your…contents…terminate upon your death." Setting aside the situation's emotional impact, from a legal standpoint this would appear to support Yahoo!'s refusal to release the e-mails. [87] However, a California probate judge ordered Yahoo! to release the account contents to Ellsworth's parents. [88] Yahoo! gave the family a CD with more than 10,000 pages of material (presumably a large amount of undeleted spam the account had received) and a hard copy printout. Yahoo! chose not to appeal, taking the opportunity to end the negative publicity while remaining true to its policy to protect user privacy (unless compelled by court order), but leaving the legal status of the issue unsettled.

## Expectation of Privacy on Social Networks

Social networks are all about sharing: sharing photographs of drunken college parties, sharing blogs about one's day at work; sharing videos of friends and family; sharing journal entries of the most intimate details of one's life…so one might imagine a rather diminished expectation of privacy on a social network. But there appear limits to the Internet Generation's laid back attitudes toward privacy, even within the "anything goes" environment of social networks. In November 2007, Facebook unveiled its "Beacon" program. The concept was simple: whenever a Facebook user bought an item on an affiliated Web site, all his or her Facebook friends would receive an immediate notification of the purchase. Bought your boyfriend a birthday gift online? Better hope he hasn't logged into his Facebook page or there goes the surprise! And that *"Cheerleaders in Bondage"* DVD you ordered online? Expect some strange looks from your Facebook friends. And how long do you think it will be before your girlfriend figures out that negligee Facebook told her you ordered online wasn't for her? Needless to say, Beacon went over about as well as the introduction of the Edsel. Within days of Beacon's launch, Facebook had received 50,000 user complaints over the invasion of privacy implications. Facebook founder Mark Zuckerberg, in full damage control mode, scurried to revamp Beacon into something more palatable to his users, adding an opt-out provision and apologizing.[89] Facebook users in Texas filed a class action against Blockbuster,[90] while California Facebook users filed a class action against Facebook, claiming sharing the list of videos they had rented violated the **Video Privacy Protection Act**.[91] In 2010, a federal court approved a $9.5 million settlement in the California class action challenging Facebook's Beacon program.[92]

In theory, the Beacon concept made sense. Advertisers would be willing to pay to have friends share their purchases with other friends; what better advertising than to have customers immediately tell all their friends they just bought a new widget from Joe's Widget Shop. It validates both product and merchant, as a purchase recommendation from a trusted friend carries far more weight than a banner ad. But the path from theory to practice can be a bumpy road. The lesson appears while social network users have a lower expectation of privacy, they want control of what personal information they make public and share with their network.

## Expectation of Privacy in One's Own Hard Drive

The Fourth Amendment to the U.S. Constitution guarantees protection from unreasonable search and seizure by the government. It reads:[93]

> The right of the people to be secure in their persons, houses, papers, and effects, against unreasonable searches and seizures, shall not be violated, and no Warrants shall issue, but upon probable cause, supported by Oath or affirmation, and particularly describing the place to be searched, and the persons or things to be seized.

Should one have a reasonable expectation of privacy for contents of one's computer hard drive? There may be little or no such expectation at one's office workstation, but are files on a home computer or a laptop private? Four 2008 cases shed light on this issue.

**Case no. 1:** Edison Chen, a well-known actor and singer in Hong Kong, brought his computer into a repair shop. The technician found photos on it of the actor in bed with various starlets. Copies of the photos then circulated on the Internet. Hong Kong police arrested eight technicians from the shop and announced 1,300 "private" photos of celebrities had been stolen from Chen's computer. A Hong Kong newspaper added some were nude photos of female celebrities.[94] Did the technician have a right to:

- Examine the computer's contents?
- Open specific files?
- Copy files?
- Disseminate those file on the Internet?
- And did the actor have a right to privacy that was violated?

Obviously, the actor granted the technician the right to examine the computer as a prerequisite to repairing it. Perhaps he even needed to open random files to test the functioning of the computer. But he did not have a right to steal the files (theft) or to disseminate them online (copyright infringement).

**Case no. 2:** Kenneth Sodomsky brought his computer to a Circuit City store to have a DVD burner installed. After installing it, the technician searched the computer for video files to test the burner. Some file names appeared pornographic. He opened one and observed a video of "the lower torso of an unclothed male."[95] The technician called the police. At trial, he admitted he hoped to enter law enforcement and had been told by a police officer to contact them if he encountered child pornography. [96] Police seized Sodomsky's computer and arrested him when he arrived to pick it up. Police later got a search warrant and discovered child pornography. The issue of Sodomsky's expectation of privacy was paramount, because if he had a legitimate expectation of privacy when he dropped off the computer, then the allegedly incriminating files could be suppressed; otherwise they could be used as evidence. Did Sodomsky have a reasonable expectation of privacy as to the contents of his computer when he brought it in to have hardware installed?

- The technician stated he needed to play a video file on the hard drive to test if the DVD burner had been properly installed. Would not one test a DVD burner by inserting a DVD into it rather than searching the hard drive for files to play? [97] If there were no valid reason for the technician to search the drive, would that affect Sodomsky's reasonable expectation of privacy as to its contents?

- The technician admitted he wanted a career in law enforcement and had been told by police to report any child pornography he found on his job. If he had been searching the computer for that purpose, and not for a valid reason relating to installation of the burner, would that affect Sodomsky's reasonable expectation of privacy as to his computer's contents?

- Did the technician have the right to choose any file on the drive to open? Did Sodomsky relinquish the privacy interest in every file on his computer? Would Sodomsky have a reasonable expectation of privacy in assuming the technician would not open his financial software or his medical records? Or were all files 'fair game'? Do computer repair shops not have test DVDs for that purpose?

- When the police arrived, they viewed the same clip of "the lower torso of an unclothed male." They then sought a warrant to view the rest of the files. That description might be considered pornographic but it is not obscene. Unlike obscenity, pornography is protected by the First Amendment. How did the mere title of this clip justify issuance of a search warrant?

- The police confiscated the computer and days later obtained a warrant to search the drive. Should they have been allowed to seize the computer without a warrant?

The lower court granted Sodomsky's request to suppress the evidence but the appellate court reversed, allowing it to be introduced and remanded the case. The court rationalized by "abandoning" the computer Sodomsky had abandoned control over the property and could not object to a subsequent lawful police search, and such abandonment meant he had no reasonable expectation of privacy: [98]

> [...] appellee knowingly exposed to the public, the Circuit City employees, the contents of his video files. It is clear that Circuit City employees were members of the public; hence, if appellee knowingly exposed the contents of his video files to them, as members of the public, he no longer retained an expectation of privacy in those videos nor could he expect that they would not be distributed to other people, including police.

The court noted had Sodomsky wanted to maintain his privacy, he had three options: (1) not bring the computer to the repair shop, (2) remove the files before bringing it in, or (3) encrypt the files. Pragmatically, if he needed a computer repair or upgrade, unless he had the technical skill to do it himself, the first option is not realistic. Likewise, had the computer needed repair and not merely an upgrade, it might not have been possible for him to access, let alone remove, the files. So, this court appears to propose if one wants a reasonable expectation of privacy, then one should encrypt the computer files. Is that a valid proposition? The fourth case below deals with a situation where the computer owner, as this court suggests, has encrypted his files.

**Case no. 3:** Michael Arnold, returning to the United States from the Philippines, was asked by a Customs agent inspecting his luggage to start his laptop. The agent browsed through two folders on the computer's desktop labeled "Kodak Pictures" and "Kodak Memories." After finding a photo of two nude women (not minors), the search continued for several hours, resulting in the discovery of alleged child pornography on the laptop and several storage devices Arnold was carrying. Arnold's laptop was seized and he was arrested. Two weeks later, the government received a warrant to search the laptop and storage devices.[99] At trial, Arnold moved to suppress the evidence on the grounds the search violated the Fourth Amendment. The district court ruled the Fourth Amendment required reasonable suspicion for Customs agents to have searched the contents of Arnold's computer.[100] The government filed an interlocutory appeal. The issue was whether the search of the computer and storage devices by Customs agents without reasonable suspicion should have been barred by the Fourth Amendment prohibition against unreasonable search and seizure. A three-judge panel of the Ninth Circuit reversed, holding reasonable suspicion unnecessary to check laptops or other electronic devices at border checkpoints.[101] The ruling means U.S. Customs and Border Patrol officers can open every single file on anyone's laptop on a whim, without any reasonable suspicion for doing so. The panel rejected the lower court's argument a higher level of suspicion was needed for computer searches at the border because of the risk of "expressive material" being exposed in such searches. The trial court had noted:[102]

> Technological advances permit individuals and businesses to store vast amounts of private, personal and valuable information within a myriad of portable electronic storage devices including laptop computers, personal organizers, CDs, and cellular telephones.

The lower court reasoned such electronic storage devices — because "they are capable of storing our thoughts, ranging from the most whimsical to the most profound" — function as an extension of our memory and should not be subject to an "intrusion into the dignity and privacy interests of a person" without at least a reasonable suspicion.[103] The panel rejected this reasoning, likening laptop searches to searches of other "closed containers" such as a briefcases, purses, and wallets routinely examined without cause by border agents. This "container model" sees no distinction in whether the container holds thoughts, ideas, and expressions or merely soiled vacation clothing.

On February 23, 2009, the U.S. Supreme Court refused Arnold's appeal from the Ninth Circuit.[104] Two days later, he committed suicide.[105] The case raises some interesting points:

• Is there a distinction as to reasonableness between simply picking up or switching on a device (presumably to determine it is what it appears, and not a disguised weapon, like a bomb) and conducting a comprehensive review of its contents?[106]

• Under this decision, laptops and other electronic devices can be seized without reason, their contents copied, and the device returned hours or even weeks later. Should the government, without reasonable suspicion, be allowed to copy and retain the entire contents of a drive, considering laptops may contain:

  ▶ Personal and professional communications
  ▶ Financial information (bank accounts, tax documents)
  ▶ Legal information

> ▶ Medical information
> ▶ Personal photographs
> ▶ Journalists' communications with confidential sources (In February 2008, a reporter's laptop was impounded for two weeks by customs agents at Dulles International Airport (Washington, DC), who also removed and inspected the memory card from his digital camera) [107]
> ▶ Attorneys' notes protected by the attorney-client privilege [108]
> ▶ Sensitive business documents and trade secrets (For a business traveler, impounding his computer deprives him of the data — and revenue — that was the purpose of his business trip, as many laptops have been held for months) [109]
> ▶ Diaries, letters, and e-mails
> ▶ Stored passwords

- An *amicus curiae* brief reasoned this is "electronic surveillance after the fact": [110] Under the government's reasoning, border authorities could systematically collect all of the information contained on every laptop computer, smart phone, or other electronic device carried across our national borders by every traveler, American or foreign. As Marc Rotenberg, executive director of the Electronic Privacy Information Center, has said, Customs agents typically do not search briefcases to copy business records they contain. [111]

- Another concern is if laptops and electronic devices can be seized without reason and returned hours, weeks, or months later, the government would be able to install spyware in the device while it has physical possession.

**Case no. 4:** Customs agents stopped Sebastien Boucher at the U.S. – Canada border. They found child pornography on his laptop, confiscated it, and copied the hard drive but it was protected by PGP (Pretty Good Privacy) encryption. When they tried to restart the computer, they could not access the encrypted drive. A grand jury subpoenaed Boucher for the password. He moved to quash the subpoena as violative of his Fifth Amendment right against self-incrimination, which guarantees: "no person * * * shall be compelled in any criminal case to be a witness against himself, nor be deprived of life, liberty, or property, without due process of law." The district court granted the motion, reasoning compelling him to give up the password would "convey the contents of one's mind," a "testimonial" act protected by the Fifth Amendment. [112] But an appellate court reversed and directed Boucher provide an unencrypted version of the drive. [113]

The issue of whether compelling revelation of the steps needed to decrypt a PGP-encrypted hard drive violates the Fifth Amendment privilege against self-incrimination was raised in <u>United States v. Fricosu</u>. [114] Ramona Fricosu was charged with bank fraud and the prosecution's case rested on the contents of Friscou's encrypted computer. Prosecutors believed Fricosu's hard drive might contain evidence against her based on a recorded jailhouse conversation between her and a co-defendant. The Supreme Court has said a witness may be compelled to produce a key to a lock, since it implies only possession of the key, but not the combination to a locked safe, since that implies ownership and control. The prosecution argued the encryption password is like a key, but the defense argued it is more like the combination to a lock, since it resides in the defendant's mind. In 2012, a federal judge ruled she must unlock her computer and set a deadline for her compliance. [115] The court held Fricosu could not claim a Fifth Amendment privilege against self incrimination because the government had met its burden of proof by demonstrating it knew of the relevant computer files' existence and location and that she was the laptop's sole or primary user, and because the government had offered her immunity under which it could not use the unencrypted contents against her. The 10th Circuit declined to rule on the trial court's order before the case was tried. Fricosu refused to reveal the password but on the day of the deadline, prosecutors announced they had decrypted the laptop, mooting the issue.[116]

In February 2012, at the same time the _Fricosu_ case was unfolding in the 10th Circuit, the 11th Circuit faced a similar situation. Police had seized several drives and laptops suspected of containing child pornography. The defendant had refused a grand jury's orders to decrypt the data under the prosecution's offer of limited immunity. The trial court found him in civil contempt and sent him to jail. The appellate court ordered him released after hearing an oral argument and later held the district court had erred in concluding the defendant's act of decryption and production would not constitute testimony. The court said:[117]

> First, the decryption and production of the hard drives would require the use of the contents of Doe's mind and could not be fairly characterized to a physical act that would be non-testimonial in nature. We conclude that the decryption and production would be tantamount to testimony by Doe of his knowledge of the existence and location of potentially incriminating files; of his possession, control and access to the encrypted portions of the drives; and of his capability to decrypt the files.  *  *  *  Requiring Does to use a decryption password is most certainly more akin to requiring the production of a combination because both demand the use of the contents of the mind, and the production is accompanied by the implied factual statements noted above that could prove to be incriminatory.

The appellate court also found the trial court had erred by limiting his immunity to the government's use of his act of decryption and production but allowing it to use  any evidence his act might disclose:[118]

> [W]e hold that Doe's decryption and production of the hard drives' contents would trigger Fifth Amendment protection because it would be testimonial, and that such protection would extend to the Government's use of the drives' contents. The district court therefore erred in two respects. First, it erred in concluding that Doe's act of decryption and production would not constitute testimony. Second, in granting Doe immunity, it erred in limiting his immunity  *  *  *  to the Government's use of his act of decryption and production, but allowing the Government derivative use of the evidence such act disclosed.

The court distinguished _Fricosu_ by noting in that case the government knew the evidence was on the drive because the defendant had admitted that fact in a taped phone call (_i.e.,_ the "_foregone conclusion" doctrine_), whereas in this case, "the Government does not know whether any files are present on the encrypted drive; if any, what their location on the drive may be; whether Doe has access and control to the encrypted drives; and whether Doe is capable of decryption."[119] The ruling was the first federal appellate decision to hold an individual has a Fifth Amendment privilege to withhold encryption codes or passwords in a criminal investigation.

A 2010 case may represent the most egregious invasion of privacy emanating from one's own hard drive. The Lower Merion, (PA) School District (LMSD) assigned each of its 2,300 high school students a school-owned laptop and allowed them to bring it home. LMSD failed to disclose, in either the program promotion or individual contracts students signed, it had installed spyware in each laptop, without the students' or their parents' knowledge or authorization. [120] The spyware used the laptop's MAC address to pinpoint its location. [121] It also allegedly captured screen shots of Web sites students visited and excerpts of their online chats, [122] as well as secretly taking 56,000 photographs of students, including pictures of them sleeping and in various states of undress, through the Webcam embedded in each laptop. [123] Blake Robbins, a 15-year-old student at Harriton High School, sued LMSD, alleging it spied on students in their homes using remote activation of the laptop Webcams. [124] Robbins alleged an assistant principal showed him a Webcam photo of him in his bedroom appearing to ingest pills and accused him of selling drugs. [125] Robbins claimed the photo showed him eating a handful of Mike & Ike candies (capsule-shaped jelly beans). [126] His parents said the assistant principal told them their son was "engaged in improper behavior in his home," showed them the photo, and explained the remote monitoring capability of the school-issued laptops. They claimed that was the first knowledge they had of the monitoring program. [127] Robbins' suit alleged LMSD collected more than 400 surreptitious photos of him. [128] He sought punitive damages for invasion of privacy, theft of private information, unlawful interception and access of electronic communications in violation of federal and state laws, and an unconstitutional search in violation of the Fourth Amendment. [129] LMSD contended the remote Webcam was an antitheft measure, only turned on if a laptop was reported stolen or missing. [130] It claimed to have activated the Webcams remotely 42 times over a 14-month period, and then only to find missing laptops, never to spy on students. [131] On remote activation, once the laptop was opened, the Webcam would automatically photograph whatever was in front of it, every 15 minutes. [132] The district conducted its own investigation and determined LMSD employees had activated the Webcams and tracking software about 80 times over a two-year period and photographed 56,000 images of students, the interior of their homes, and screen shots of open files and programs running on their laptop screens. [133] The FBI investigated whether LMSD had violated federal wiretap or computer intrusion laws but the U.S. Justice Department declined to file criminal charges, citing no evidence of criminal intent. [134] The case was settled in October 2011, with LMSD agreeing to pay $175,000 in damages and $425,000 in attorney fees; however, other students filed similar cases against the school district. [135]

This is not the only instance of laptop Webcams being commandeered to spy on their owners. A Wyoming couple sued furniture rental chain Aaron's, Inc. for violations of the **CFAA** and the **ECPA**, alleging it rented customers computers that enabled it to track keystrokes, take screenshots, and snap photographs as they used the computer. The plaintiffs claimed they were unaware of the spy camera until a store manager showed them a photograph of the husband using the computer. [136]

A computer repairman in Southern California allegedly installed spyware on his customers' laptops, allowing him to use their Webcams to shoot and download photographs of women showering and undressing in their homes. [137] The software would deliver false error messages advising users "fix their internal sensor soon," and "try putting your laptop near hot steam for several minutes to clean the sensor," leading some users to take their laptops into the bathroom as they showered. Many victims were students at a nearby university. Police recovered hundreds of thousands of photographs and videos from his computer.

Another hidden Webcam incident led to a fatal result after Rutgers University student Dharun Ravi surreptitiously streamed his roommate's homosexual encounter to a friend's laptop and IMed and tweeted about it. Three days later, 18-year-old freshman Tyler

Clementi committed suicide by jumping off the George Washington Bridge. His roommate, Ravi, was convicted of 15 counts including invasion of privacy, evidence tampering for deleting relevant tweets and text messages, and a hate crime and sentenced to 10 years in prison.[138]

A final thought to consider about the expectation of privacy in one's own hard drive: if your employer or client becomes a party to a lawsuit, computers will likely be subject to the discovery process. If you have used your personal computer for business use, it might be confiscated and the hard drive's contents exposed to the litigants, their lawyers, and the attorneys' support staffs. Any personal information on it (financial, medical, SSN, documents, and photos) would be seen by many eyes.

## Expectation of Privacy in Web Posts

Should one have a reasonable expectation of privacy in one's online posts? One might assume there should be no reasonable expectation of privacy for anything posted on the Web, since it is a global medium. But what if a post is restricted to a select group of individuals based on user privacy settings? Or if a user deletes a post, should she have a reasonable expectation it will not be resurrected? A New York court held a woman had no reasonable expectation of privacy for her Facebook and MySpace posts, even if restricted to friends and if later deleted.[139] It ruled the deleted posts subject to discovery, since they might contradict her claims about injuries preventing her from living an active lifestyle.

Is there a reasonable expectation of privacy in personal information held by third parties sufficient to subject government searches to Fourth Amendment scrutiny? The U.S. Supreme Court has held a bank did not have to notify a customer when it gave his records to the government and the Fourth Amendment did not apply because the records were bank property in which he had no legitimate "expectation of privacy."[140] How would this rationale affect personal information held by social networks on their servers (whether or not deleted from user profiles)?

Courts, since 2008, have authorized at least two dozen warrants allowing U.S. law enforcement agencies to search Facebook accounts of individuals, often without their knowledge, according to a Reuters investigation.[141] The personal information searched includes messages, status updates, links to videos and photographs, calendars of future and past events, "wall" posts, and rejected friend requests. Neither Facebook nor the government is legally required to notify a user of the search. The warrants also ask for a user's "Neoprint" and "Photoprint" — a detailed package of profile and photo information not available to users themselves.

## Spyware

Although detailed at greater length in Chapter 6 in the discussion of cybercrimes, *spyware* deserves mention here as well, as it is an obvious invasion of privacy. Online advertisers in concert with certain file-sharing networks place spyware on users' computers to monitor activity or use their computers' processors. Many users are *unaware* they are being monitored for commercial purposes. Though some spyware may violate communications and computer trespass laws, many programs are protected by agreements buried in long, detailed disclosures users click when downloading other programs. Besides being intrusive and an invasion of privacy, spyware can crash computers or slow their performance and be difficult to find and remove.

## Government Intrusion into Individual Privacy

With technological advances, government has new capabilities to invade individuals' privacy in subtler ways. Today, the new technology is the Internet, but a century earlier the telephone was the innovative communications technology. The Supreme Court was called on to address the question of whether by tapping the phone wires of a suspect, the government had violated the Fourth Amendment. Evidence obtained in violation of the Fourth Amendment is inadmissible in court (the *"Exclusionary Rule"*).[142] The Fourth Amendment to the U.S. Constitution protects citizens from unreasonable "search and seizure" by the government. It embodies the concept one should feel secure in one's home and in one's person and that individuals exist within a sphere of privacy, which government should not intrude on without a compelling interest. The notion may be best summarized by Justice Brandeis, in his dissenting opinion, after the Court held wiretapping was not a violation of the Fourth amendment:[143]

> The right to be let alone — the most comprehensive of rights and the right most valued by civilized men. To protect that right, every unjustifiable intrusion by the government upon the privacy of the individual, whatever the means employed, must be deemed a violation of the Fourth Amendment.

In 1967, the Court reversed its ruling, holding recording by police of conversation in a public phone booth violated the Fourth Amendment because the speaker had a reasonable expectation of privacy in the booth.[144] The Court has established the principle a "Fourth Amendment search occurs when the government violates a subjective expectation of privacy that society recognizes as reasonable."[145] Generally, government agents must have a valid search warrant for the search to be constitutionally permissible, but there are exceptions: when the property owner gives consent; when an individual does not possess a "reasonable expectation of privacy"; when "exigent circumstances" exist (*e.g.*, the evidence may be destroyed, the public is endangered, or police are in "hot pursuit" of a suspect), so long as there is probable cause; or during an investigatory stop or incident to an arrest. The government must establish probable cause and describe with specificity the place to be searched and the materials to be seized before a court will issue a warrant. While an individual has no ability to contest a search and seizure pursuant to a properly issued warrant, he may be able to contest its admissibility at trial.

In 1976, the Supreme Court reaffirmed customer account records held by a bank are the bank's property, not the customer's.[146] This has come to stand for the proposition that when an individual's records are held by a third-party, the individual lacks a proprietary interest or a "legitimate expectation of privacy" in them and has no legal right to challenge access to those records by the government or anyone else. Absent a specific statute to the contrary, the government can demand those records from a third-party custodian with only a subpoena instead of a warrant.[147] A subpoena is subject to a much lower standard than a warrant. Under FRCRP Rule 17, a subpoena requires the government show the requested information is evidentiary, relevant, necessary for the case, and made in good faith. A warrant requires a showing of probable cause. A subpoena may demand specific items but, unlike a warrant, is not an authority to conduct a search. Many administrative agencies have been granted the power to issue subpoenas by statutes. Third parties institutions (*e.g.*, banks, brokerage firms, hospitals, schools, and employers) maintain many records—most digitalized—documenting various activities of a given individual. Often they must disclose records about an individual to the government without obtaining the individual's approval. In some cases, the individual may never know the government accessed his records. Except in a limited circumstances, or where mandated by statute, neither the record holder nor the government is required to notify an individual his records were examined by the government.

In the classic dystopian novel "*1984*", George Orwell described a totalitarian state where the government monitored and controlled the thoughts and actions of its citizenry. "Big Brother" spied on citizens through cameras and hidden microphones because in 1948, when Orwell wrote the book, the concept of the Internet was unimaginable. ENIAC (Electronic Numerical Integrator And Computer), the first computer, which was so large it filled a room, had only been turned on two years earlier, and it would be 21 more years before ARPANET, the forerunner to the Internet, appeared on the scene. The rise of databases filled with personal information, combined with the development of the personal computer and the Internet has created a tool of unimaginable power and scope for governmental intrusion into individual privacy. While totalitarian regimes like China have been quick to use the Internet to spy on its citizens (see Chapter 18), it wasn't until the September 11th attacks that the United States launched a massive domestic spying operation, beginning with passage of the **USA PATRIOT Act**. [148]

Prior to the Act's passage, a crime had to have been committed before the federal government could intercept electronic messages, but the **USA PATRIOT Act** permits interception of all messages "relevant to an ongoing criminal investigation", and its guidelines apply to all surveillance cases, not just suspected terrorists. It expanded the government's reach by allowing it to collect addressing and routing information in wiretaps, despite the fact content might be swept up in its net. For example, a data packet with an e-mail header also contains the rest of the e-mail message, making it unlikely the FBI would not read the message. Routing data might also include information on other ISP customers, resulting in the privacy rights of persons unrelated to the investigation being compromised. The amendment added customer credit card and bank account numbers to the list of personal information the government could subpoena from ISPs (in addition to customer's name, address, length of service, and method of payment). The Act provides ISPs may voluntarily reveal customer records and content of electronic transmissions to the government "if the provider reasonably believes that an emergency involving immediate danger of death or serious physical injury to any person justifies disclosure of the information." While reasonable where the ISP believe a customer intends to harm himself or others, read broadly it can be construed to apply to harm from any potential terrorist—terrorism by its nature implies a constant state of emergency involving immediate danger of death or serious physical injury. By labeling a suspect a terror suspect, the government could request ISP customer records and e-mails without a subpoena (although, an ISP could refuse the request). Another provision introduced the "sneak and peek" search warrant, where the government can search a home or business without immediately notifying the target of the investigation, eliminating the traditional notice requirement. Prior to the Act, the Supreme Court had held law enforcement officials must obtain a search warrant and provide notice to any party whose property is to be searched before the search is conducted, for it to be valid under the Fourth Amendment. The Act allows sneak and peek warrants to be used for minor crimes, not only terror and spy cases.

The Act modified **FISA** to allow the FBI, the Defense Department, and other government agencies, secretly to demand information from ISPs without a court order by issuing secret "*National Security Letters*" (NSLs). These NSLs demand information about subscribers, such as home addresses, phone calls placed, e-mail subject lines, and logs of sites visited. NSLs had been around since 1978, but the **ECPA** had restricted the FBI from issuing them to telecommunications firms except in relation to an investigation of "an agent of a foreign power." Formerly a tool to investigate suspected terrorists and spies, NSLs became an all-purpose cudgel — the FBI need only say an NSL may be "relevant" to a terrorist-related investigation and no court approval is required. The FBI issues more than 30,000 NSLs annually, and not just to ISPs. Librarians have been served, demanding they turn over "all subscriber information, billing information and access logs" of patrons who used library computers. Unlike subpoenas, NSLs do not require approval by a judge, grand jury, or prosecutor, but are instead need only be signed by FBI field supervisors. The **USA PATRIOT Act** forbids anyone served with an NSL from ever disclosing its existence "to any person." A federal court ruled that mandatory gag order was an "unconstitutional prior restraint of speech in violation of the First Amendment" (*Prior restraint* is discussed in detail in Chapter 18) and struck down that and other provisions as unconstitutional. [149] The ACLU sued on behalf of an ISP that received an NSL, challenging the constitutionality of one statute amended by the Act, requiring ISPs to comply with FBI requests for subscriber information and forbidding disclosure of the order to anyone. The court addressed the overbreadth of the statute, concerned the NSLs could force disclosure of "vast amounts of anonymous speech and associational activity," including "email addresses with whom a subscriber has corresponded and the Web pages that a subscriber visits" and enable the government "to specifically identify someone who has written anonymously on the internet." A federal court in Connecticut subsequently enjoined the government from enforcing an NSL gag order on a library. Both cases were combined, but while pending on appeal, Congress renewed the **USA PATRIOT Act** with minor changes in 2006. [150] In response to the court's decision, Congress amended the Act to allow for judicial review of an NSL after receipt and allowed an NSL recipient to inform his attorney of his receipt of the NSL. Based on those changes, the Second Circuit remanded the first case and dismissed the second as moot. The lower court held, despite the revisions, the NSL's gag order provision violated First Amendment free speech rights, as both a prior restraint on speech and a content-based ban. But FBI agents can still use other means to obtain information from ISPs, including a subpoena, warrant, or court order. The Sixth Circuit, meanwhile, held e-mail users have a reasonable expectation of privacy in the contents of their e-mail accounts under the Fourth Amendment and to the extent any **USA PATRIOT Act** modifications to the **Stored Communications Act** allow the government to obtain such e-mails without a warrant, those provisions of the **SCA** are unconstitutional. [151]

Under FISA, wiretapping of U.S. citizens by the National Security Agency (NSA) required a warrant from a three-judge **FISA** court. President Bush issued an executive order authorizing the NSA to implement an electronic surveillance program to monitor — without search warrants — phone calls, Internet activity (Web browsing and e-mail), text messaging, and other communication involving any party the NSA believed to be outside the country, even if the other party being communicated with was in the United States. Bush based the authority to issue the executive order, which effectively did an end run around the **FISA** court, on the **Authorization for Use of Military Force** (AUMF), a joint resolution passed by Congress on September 18, 2001, authorizing the president to use all "necessary and appropriate force" against those whom he determined "planned, authorized, committed or aided" the September 11th attacks, or who harbored said persons or groups. [152] The NSA was given complete, unsupervised access to all fiber-optic communications of some of the nation's largest telecommunication companies. The surveillance encompassed phone conversations, e-mail, web browsing, and corporate private network traffic of presumably millions of American citizens. Critics assailed the action as unconstitutional. Dozens of lawsuits were filed against the government and the telecommunications firms, including a class action against AT&T. [153] The government argued the telecom firms should be granted immunity because the lawsuits would bankrupt them. [154] **The Protect America Act of 2007**, passed as an amendment to **FISA**, removed the warrant requirement for government surveillance of foreign intelligence targets "reasonably believed" to be outside of the United States. [155] The following year, Congress passed and Bush signed into law, the **FISA Amendments Act**, which repealed the **Protect America Act** but replaced it with similar provisions and granted retroactive immunity to telecommunications companies for past violations of **FISA**. [156]

The Terrorism Information Awareness Project was a controversial Pentagon anti-terrorism plan to compile computerized dossiers on American citizens linking databases from credit card companies, medical insurers, and motor vehicle departments. While providing a tool for law enforcement to track terrorist suspects, the scope and breadth of the project represented the greatest governmental invasion of privacy to date. In 2003, the U.S. House of Representatives ended its funding, effectively terminating the project.

Prior to 2005, the FBI intercepted e-mail through an Internet surveillance program code-named "Carnivore". [157] The program could capture all e-mail to and from a user's account and all network traffic to and from a user or IP address, as well as headers and addresses to and from an e-mail account, but not the contents or subject line. Carnivore could list the servers the user accessed, track everyone who accessed a specific Web page or FTP file and track all Web pages or FTP files accessed by a user. Critics claimed it lacked safeguards to prevent misuse and may have violated individual the Fourth Amendment. In January 2005, the FBI announced it was replacing Carnivore with commercial software to eavesdrop on computer traffic, reported to be more effective and less expensive than the estimated $6–to–$15 million Carnivore.

In 2006, Bush administration federal prosecutors tried to compel the nation's major search firms to turn over their logs that would reveal information about customers' online search queries. [158] Prosecutors subpoenaed Google, Microsoft, Yahoo! and AOL. Unlike the others, Google refused to comply with the subpoena. The Bush administration asked a California federal court to force Google's compliance but received a mixed result. It granted part of the administration's request for access to a portion of Google's index of Web sites but denied access to users' search queries. [159] The Bush administration also sought to require ISPs to record and retain logs of customers' online activities. [160] Congress attempted to intrude on individual privacy in 2007, when it considered, but did not pass, a bill that would have required ISPs to track customers' online activities (*e.g.*, Web browsing, instant message exchanges, and e-mail) and permitted the Justice Department to order companies to store such records forever. [161]

In 2008, the Ninth Circuit ruled the Fourth Amendment does not require government agents to have reasonable suspicion before searching laptops or other digital devices at U.S. border stations, including international airports. [162]

The FBI's plans to develop a Web application to provide continuous real-time monitoring of social networks (specifically Facebook, Twitter, and Myspace) and news organizations' RSS feeds were inadvertently leaked by the FBI's Strategic Information and Operations Center in a solicitation for a "Social Media Application" in 2012. The FBI was seeking companies to help it build the new monitoring system. The FBI wanted the app to store cached information, as well as real time data, and allow that information to be linked to specific locations and easily shared. [163]

**Chapter 9 Notes**

[1] "Legality of Internet-Based Arrest Draws Challenge," Belleville News Democrat, March 10, 2004.

[2] Mark Rasch, "Chat, Copy, Paste, Prison," Security Focus, April 12, 2004, *available at* www.securityfocus. com/columnists/233 (accessed Mar. 23, 2012).

[3] New Hampshire Revised Statutes Chap. 570-A: Wiretapping and Eavesdropping.

[4] Law enforcement officers routinely pose as minors in chat rooms to arrest potential sex offenders, but Maryland's highest court (known as the Maryland Court of Appeals) has held unanimously an individual could not be found guilty of committing a crime with a nonexistent victim (*i.e.*, a "minor" who in reality is a legal adult). *See* Fredrick Kunkle, "Court Overturns Child Porn Conviction — MD Ruling Squelches Tactic Used to Find Potential Molesters," The Washington Post," September 8, 2005, p. B02.

[5] *State v. Townsend*, Case No. 19304-7-III (Wash. Ct. App. 2001), Keene, New Hampshire city site, *was available at* www.ci.keene.nh.us/police/Townsend.html but is no longer available.

[6] *Ibid.*

[7] *Ibid.*

[8] *Ibid.*

[9] Belinda Yu, "Connecticut Rules against Internet Sex Predator," Reuters wire service report, February 2, 2006.

[10] However, at least one federal court in California has held keystroke logging devices do not violate the federal **Wiretap Act**, since there is not necessarily any "transmission in interstate commerce" when keystrokes are logged. *United States v. Ropp*, 347 F. Supp. 2d 831 (C.D. Cal. 2004), where, allegedly attempting to collect evidence of his employer's wrongdoing, a disgruntled employee installed a keystroke logging device on a cable connecting his employer's computer to the keyboard. Prosecutors had argued the **Wiretap Act** was applicable since outgoing e-mails were also logged by the device.

[11] Lester Haines, "Cheated Wife on Spyware Wiretap Rap," The Register, February 16, 2005.

[12] Howard Mankoff, Electronic Discovery: The Final Frontier," *was available at* www.marshalldennehey. com/CM/DefenseDigest/DefenseDigest294.asp but is no longer available as of July 1, 2009.

[13] NOW with Bill Moyers, May 31, 2002, *available at* www.pbs.org/now/politics/wallstreet.html (accessed Mar. 23, 2012).

[14] During the **discovery** process, prior to the start of a civil trial, both the plaintiff and defendant can use civil procedural tools such as interrogatories, depositions, requests for production, and subpoenas to compel the production of evidence, in preparation for the upcoming trial.

[15] Fed. R. Civ. P. 26(a)(1).

[16] Fed. R. Civ. P. 37(f). However, the Rules do not define "routine, good-faith operation."

[17] *See Quon v. Arch Wireless Operating Co.*, fn. 14, *infra*, discussed later in this chapter.

[18] "Survey: 40% of Large Companies Read Employees' Outbound E-mail," Cincinnati Business Courier, July 12, 2004.

[19] Study by the American Management Association and the ePolicy Institute. *See* Frauenheim, fn. 20, *infra*.

[20] Ed Frauenheim, "Is Your Boss Monitoring Your E-mail?" CNET News.com, May 18, 2005.

[21] *Ibid.*

[22] *Shoars v. Epson Am., Inc.*, Case No. B073243 (Cal. Ct. App. 1994), rev. denied, Case No. S040065, 1994 Cal. LEXIS 3670 (1994).

[23] *Smyth v. Pillsbury Co.*, 914 F. Supp. 97 (E.D. Pa. 1996).

[24] *Bourke v. Nissan Motors Corp.*, Case No. B068705 (Cal. Ct. App. 1993). (Included in the Cases Section on the Issues in Internet Law site, www.IssuesinInternetLaw.com).

[25] *Quon v. Arch Wireless Operating Co.*, 529 F.3d 892, 906-07 (9th Cir. 2008). However, in this particular case, the U.S. Supreme Court reversed, holding while Quon had a reasonable expectation of privacy in the text messages sent on the pager provided by the city, his employer's review of the transcript constituted a permissible search under the Fourth Amendment because it was analogous to a government employer's search of an employee's physical office. *See City of Ontario v. Quon*, 560 U. S. ___ (2010). The court noted this case should be narrowly construed: "Prudence counsels caution before the facts in this case are used to establish far-reaching premises that define the existence, and extent, of privacy expectations of employees using employer-provided communication devices."

[26] *The Guard Publ'g Co. d/b/a The Register Guard & Eugene Newspaper Guild*, CWA Local 37194, 351 NLRB No. 70 (2007).

[27] *Fleming Co.*, 336 NLRB 192 (2001), enf. denied 349 F.3d 968 (7th Cir. 2003).

[28] *The Guard Publ'g Co.*, 351 NLRB No. 70.

[29] *Ibid.*

[30] *The Register Guard*, 351 NLRB 1110 (2007), enf. denied in part 571 F. 3d 53 (D.C. Cir. 2009). Previous editions of this book stated, in regard to the 2007 decision:

The *Guard Publ'g Co.* (Prozanski case) decision is important for four reasons:

1. It affects every employer that provides company e-mail access to its employees
2. It is a case of first impression on the issue of whether employees have a specific right under the NLRA to use an employer's e-mail system for union activity,
3. Courts are required to defer to NLRB interpretations of the NLRA when the Act is ambiguous, (provided that interpretation is reasonable), and
4. It is a textbook example of reaching a politically motivated result and then working backwards using tortured reasoning in a misguided attempt to justify that result.

Reading between the lines of the 30-page decision, it effectively says an employer can authorize a policy of employee use of its e-mail system for "any purposes except union activities"; a conclusion that should de facto violate the NLRA. The specious distinction between "non-job-related solicitations" and "non-job-related communications" is disingenuous. The five members of the NLRB are appointed by the president of the United States. The board members who decided this case by a 3–to–2 vote consisted of three Republicans and two Democrats. Traditionally, Republicans are considered pro-business and Democrats pro-labor. It is also disingenuous to cast the issue as revolving around the employer's ownership of the workplace computers, as two of the three e-mails were not sent from workplace computers. Likely, the real concern was the recipient list, *i.e.*, an *electronic mailing list* that would allow a union organizer to reach all of a company's employees with one mouse click. Arguably, also employer property, it would only be of greater value in cases where the union had little or no presence in the company and was trying to initiate contact with employees to form a union; where most employees already belong to the union, the union would be in a position simply to collect their nonwork e-mail addresses. Besides, presumably a union would prefer to contact members through their private e-mails, than employer-monitored e-mails. Nonetheless, the decision stands as the current law on the issue. Fortunately, shifting majorities on the NLRB are able to change the board's interpretation of the law (*see Chevron USA, Inc. v. Natural Res. Def. Council, Inc.*, 467 U.S. 837 (1984)), so this decision may be "clarified" or reversed with the incoming Democratic administration. Ironically, the *Guard Publ'g Co.* ruling was the last board decision before the terms of three of its five members expired. As of the first half of 2008, the NLRB had three vacancies on its five-member board, making it questionable whether the board could take any further action as it lacked a quorum.

[31] *Guard Publ'g Co. d/b/a The Register Guard*, 357 NLRB No. 27 (2011) [*Register Guard II*].

[32] The Electronic Communications Privacy Act, Title I, 18 U.S.C. § 2510, *et seq.* ("Wiretap Act") deals with interception and disclosure of electronic communications and Title II, 18 U.S.C. § 2510, *et seq.* ("Stored Communications Act") deals with stored communications (*e.g.*, e-mail on a server). Some courts have held the ECPA allows employers to read and disclose employees' stored communications, but in *Quon*, fn. 25 *supra*, the Ninth Circuit held the Stored Communications Act prohibits third-party service providers (*e.g.*, text message services and ISPs) from disclosing stored electronic communications without consent of the employee who sends or receives the communication, even if the employee is using employer-provided equipment and the employer pays for the service.

[33] U.S. Const., Fourth Amendment: "The right of the people to be secure in their persons, houses, papers, and effects, against unreasonable searches and seizures, shall not be violated, and no warrants shall issue, but upon probable cause, supported by oath or affirmation, and particularly describing the place to be searched, and the persons or things to be seized." But *see Quon*, fn. 25, *supra*.

[34] By contrast, Germany's Nazi past has made it cautious where individual privacy is concerned. German employers filming employees and reading their e-mails has led to public outrage and calls for laws prohibiting surreptitious workplace videotaping and criminalizing prospective employers spying on applicants' private social network posts. *See* Verena Schmitt-Roschmann, "Germany May Prevent Employer Facebook Checks," Associated Press wire service report, August 15, 2010.

[35] Privacy Foundation Study, Linda Rosencrance, "Study: Monitoring of Employee E-mail Escalates," CNN. com, July 9, 2001, *available at* http://archives.cnn.com/2001/TECH/internet/07/09/employee.monitoring.idg (accessed Mar. 23, 2012).

[36] Frauenheim, fn. 20, *supra*.

[37] "Pornsweeper," manufactured by ZiBiz, Inc., *available at* www.zibiz.com/solutions/mime-sweep (accessed Mar. 23, 2012).

[38] "Orchestria," *was available at* http://monitrax.com/company/about (accessed July 23, 2010) but no longer available.

[39] Brian Bergstein, "Software Makes Office Computer Monitoring More Sophisticated," Associated Press wire service report, August 19, 2007.

[40] Phillip J. Trobaugh, Mansfield, Tanick & Cohen, P.A. site, "The Workplace Panopticon: Minnesota Privacy Law at Work," *available at* www.mansfieldtanick.com/CM/Articles/The-Workplace-Panopticon. asp (accessed Mar. 23, 2012).

[41] Bergstein, fn. 39, *supra*.

[42] Stephanie Armour, "Technology Makes Porn Easier to Access at Work," USA Today, October 24, 2007.

[43] *Ibid.*

[44] For a list of state freedom of information laws, *see* www.pbs.org/now/politics/foiamap.html (accessed Mar. 23, 2012).

[45] Tom Hester Jr., "State Officials Keep E-Mail from View," Associated Press wire service report, March 15, 2008.

[46] *Ibid. See also* Ledyard King, "Text Messages Enter Public-Records Debate," USA Today, March 15, 2008.

[47] *United States v. Simons*, 29 F. Supp. 2d 324 (E.D. Va. 1998).

[48] Report of the Judicial Conference Committee on Automation and Technology (September 2001).

[49] *Van Alstyne v. Elec. Scriptorium, Ltd,* 560 F.3d 199 (4th Cir. 2009).

[50] *Bunnell v. Motion Picture Ass'n of Am.*, Case No. 07-56640 (9th Cir. filed 2008).

[51] "119 Students Who Failed Courses Get Group E-mail," Associated Press wire service report, June 17, 2005.

[52] A commentator on TechDirt.com opined, presumably with tongue-in-cheek: "Even so, the mistake might not be all bad. After all, it was limited just to people who failed all their classes, so they simply discovered who their peers are. It's like social networking for failures. FlunkedIn, anyone?" (An allusion to the social network 'LinkedIn'), *available at* www.techdirt.com/articles/20050617/1340223_F.shtml (accessed Mar. 23, 2012).

[53] Wendy Davis, "Judge Orders Google to Deactivate User's Gmail Account," Online Media Daily, September 24, 2009.

[54] The Electronic Communications Privacy Act (ECPA), Title II, 18 U.S.C. § 2510, *et seq.* ("Stored Communications Act").

[55] *Ibid.*

[56] The ECPA, Title I, 18 U.S.C. § 2510, *et seq.* ("Wiretap Act"). Interception and Disclosure of Wire, Oral, or Electronic Communications Prohibited.

[57] *United States v. Councilman*, 418 F.3d 67 (1st Cir. 2004). Councilman, as vice president of Interloc, the online bookseller specializing in rare books, managed Interloc's ISP activities. By providing customers with e-mail addresses ending with "@interloc.com", Interloc was acting as an ISP.

[58] *Ibid.*

[59] The E-mail Privacy Act of 2004 (HR 4956).

[60] *Councilman*, 418 F.3d 67, 79.

[61] *Bunnell*, fn. 50, *supra*. The case involved an alleged hacker charged with breaking into a file-sharing company's server and obtaining copies of company e-mails as they were being transmitted, which he allegedly forwarded to an MPAA executive in exchange for $15,000.

[62] *See* the discussion in Chapter 6 about the FBI's Carnivore software, and the USA PATRIOT Act (Pub. L. No. 107-56), which allows the government to issue NSLs to ISPs to view all the e-mail subject headers in a target's e-mail account.

[63] The Electronic Communication Transactional Records Act (ECTRA), 18 U.S.C. § 2703(f).

[64] According to Nancy Flynn, executive director of the ePolicy Institute, "In almost every workplace lawsuit being filed today, e-mail is being subpoenaed as evidence." *See* Burke Hansen, "FBI Screwed Up, Spied on Entire Email Network," The Register, February 18, 2008.

[65] *United States v. Warshak*, 631 F.3d 266 (6th Cir. 2010), reh'g and reh'g *en banc* denied (2011).

[66] Dawn Kawamoto, "Mind Those IMs — Your Cubicle's Walls Have Eyes," CNET News.com, October 25, 2004.

[67] *Coleman Holdings, Inc. v. Morgan Stanley & Co.*, 2005 WL 679071 (Fla. 15th Cir. 2005).

[68] *Morgan Stanley & Co. v. Coleman Holdings Inc.*, 955 So. 2d 1124 (2007), reversing the compensatory and punitive damage awards and remanding, with directions to enter judgment for Morgan Stanley. *See also*, "Morgan Stanley–Perelman Judgment Flipped," Associated Press wire service report, March 21, 2007.

[69] *Stevenson v. Union Pacific R.R. Co.*, 354 F.3d 739 (8th Cir. 2004).

[70] *Silvestri v. Gen. Motors Corp.*, 271 F.3d 583, 591 (4th Cir. 2001).

[71] *Blinzler v. Marriott Int'l, Inc.*, 81 F.3d 1148, 1159 (1st Cir. 1996).

[72] *Atlantic Recording Corp. v. Howell*, 554 F. Supp. 2d 976 (D. Ariz. 2008).

[73] *Columbia Pictures, Inc. v. Bunnell*, 85 U.S.P.Q.2D (BNA) 1448, (C.D. Cal. 2008). The judge awarded $111 million to the Motion Picture Association of America against defendants involved with the TorrentSpy P2P network, finding them guilty of contributory, vicarious, and induced copyright infringement in connection with file-sharing of copyrighted movies by the network's users.

[74] Fed. R. Civ. P. 26(a)(1).

[75] Fed. R. Civ. P. 26(b)(2).

[76] Fed. R. Civ. P. 26(b)(5).

[77] Fed. R. Civ. P. 34(b).

[78] *Available at http://encyclopediadramatica.ch/Main_Page* (accessed Mar. 23, 2012).

[79] Anick Jesdanun, "Legal Concerns Raised over Exposing Replies to Online Sex Ad," Associated Press wire service report, September 12, 2006.

[80] *Available at http://encyclopediadramatica.ch/RFJason_Craigslist_Experiment* (accessed Mar. 23, 2012).

[81] Craigslist's Terms of Use policies include the following provisions:

> You agree not to post, email, or otherwise make available Content:
>
> a) that is unlawful, harmful, threatening, abusive, harassing, defamatory, libelous, invasive of another's privacy, or is harmful to minors in any way;
>
> b) that is pornographic or depicts a human being engaged in actual sexual conduct including but not limited to (i) sexual intercourse, including genital-genital, oral-genital, anal-genital, or oral-anal, whether between persons of the same or opposite sex, or (ii) bestiality, or (iii) masturbation, or (iv) sadistic or masochistic abuse, or (v) lascivious exhibition of the genitals or pubic area of any person; * * *
>
> h) that includes personal or identifying information about another person without that person's explicit consent;
>
> i) that is false, deceptive, misleading, deceitful, misinformative, or constitutes "bait and switch" * * *
>
> t) collect personal data about other users for commercial or unlawful purposes;

*see* www.craigslist.org/about/terms.of.use.html (accessed Mar. 23, 2012).

[82] At least one "prank" victim sued the perpetrator, not for invasion of privacy but for copyright infringement. *Doe v. Fortuny*, Case No. 1:2008-cv-01050 (N.D. Ill. 2009). On April 9, 2009, the court entered a default judgment against Fortuny for $74,252.56.

[83] Restatement (Second) of Torts § 625(e) (1977).

[84] Only officers outside the front lines are issued official Marine e-mail accounts. If an officer is killed, the Marines delete the account after retrieving military-related messages. *See* Jim Hu, "Yahoo! Denies Family Access to Dead Marine's E-mail," CNET News.com, December 21, 2004.

[85] Yahoo!'s policy is to release the account to family members only after they go through the courts to verify their identity and relationship with the deceased. *Ibid.* However, Yahoo!'s policy of deleting inactive accounts after 90 days might result in the account and all e-mails being deleted before the matter could be adjudicated.

[86] Earthlink and Microsoft's MSN Hotmail have similar policies.

[87] The Ellsworth case is not unique. Parents of the late Marine Corps reservist Karl Linn complained ISP Mailbank.com, Inc. would not release their son's digital data after his death. Mailbank, like Yahoo! cited clients' privacy interests as the reason for its refusal. Army Spc. Michael J. Smith's family met the same resistance when trying to obtain private portions of their late son's online journal on LiveJournal.com.

Ariana Eunjung Cha, "After Death, a Struggle for Their Digital Memories," The Washington Post, February 3, 2005.

[88] "Yahoo! Provides Family with E-mail Account of Marine Killed in Iraq," Associated Press wire service report, April 21, 2005.

[89] Louise Story and Brad Stone, "Facebook Retreats on Online Tracking," The New York Times, November 30, 2007; *see also* Jim Hopkins, "Facebook's Zuckerberg: Sorry about 'Beacon'" USA Today, December 5, 2007. *See also* Caroline McCarthy, "Blockbuster Sued over Role in Facebook's Beacon Ad Program," CNET News.com, April 17, 2008.

[90] *See Harris v. Blockbuster, Inc.*, 622 F. Supp. 2d 396 (N.D. Tex. 2009). The case was reportedly settled for $50,000.

[91] The Video Privacy Protection Act (18 U.S.C. 2710), which prohibits a videotape service provider from disclosing personally identifiable information about a customer unless given informed, written consent at the time the disclosure is sought. The Act provides for liquidated damages of $2,500 for each violation.

[92] *Lane v. Facebook, Inc.*, Case No. 08-3845 RS (N.D. Cal. Mar. 17, 2010). The lead plaintiff's wife learned on Facebook, along with all her husband's friends, he planned to surprise her with a diamond ring purchased from Overstock.com.

[93] U.S. Const., Fourth Amendment.

[94] *See* "Nude Pictures Copied from HK Star's Computer," Reuters wire service report, February 4, 2008; *and* Ed Flannigan, "Sex Scandal Rocks Hong Kong," MSNBC.com, February 14, 2008.

[95] Amaris Elliott-Engel, "Court Reissues Opinion in Case Involving Seizure of Porn Defendant's Computer from Circuit City," The Legal Intelligencer, January 10, 2008.

[96] *Ibid.*

[97] Nate Anderson, "Court: Privacy No Defense when Circuit City Finds Child Porn," ArsTechnica.com, December 18, 2007: "Unanswered by the opinion is the question of what, exactly, the Circuit City techs thought they were testing. According to the court, 'the playing of videos already in the computer was a manner of ensuring that the burner was functioning properly.' Note, the techs weren't burning a disc, nor reading from a disc; they were playing a video file from the hard drive. How this proves a DVD burner is installed correctly is unclear."

[98] *Commonwealth v. Sodomsky*, 939 A.2d 363 (Pa. Super. Ct. 2007), cert. denied (2009).

[99] *See* Adam Tanner, "Court Says Search of Laptop with Porn is Legal," Reuters wire service report, April 21, 2008; "Full Appeals Court Hearing Sought in Laptop Search Case," CIO World News, June 3, 2008; Nate Anderson, "Laptop Searches at the Border: No Reason? No Problem," ArsTechnica.com, April 23, 2008; Jacqui Cheng, "EFF, Others Fighting Privacy-invading Border Laptop Searches," ArsTechnica.com, June 13, 2008; *and* Richard Koman, "Customs Can Search All Files on a Laptop, Court Rules," Enterprise-Security-Today.com, April 23, 2008.

[100] *United States v. Arnold*, 454 F. Supp. 2d 999 (C.D. Cal. 2006).

[101] *United States v. Arnold*, 523 F.3d 941 (9th Cir. 2008).

[102] *Arnold*, 454 F. Supp. 2d 999.

[103] *Ibid.*

[104] *Arnold v. United States*, 08-6708 (U.S. Supreme Court, docketed Oct. 9, 2008), denying Arnold's petition for a writ of *certiorari*.

[105] *United States v. Arnold*, Appellee Arnold's Motion to De-Publish Opinion (Mar. 3, 2009).

[106] See also, *United States v. Cotterman*, Case No. No. 09-10139 (9th Cir. Mar. 30, 2011), holding customs agents at the U.S. border may seize laptops and other electronic devices without a warrant and send them to a secondary site for forensic inspection. Agents found no incriminating data in their initial inspection of Cotterman's computers and digital camera, but since many files were password protected, they decided to send them to a forensics lab 170 miles away. The lower court had held the government needed a specific suspicion to conduct such an extended search but the Ninth Circuit found all border searches are reasonable because they occur at the border.

[107] Alex Kingsbury "Seizing Laptops and Cameras without Cause: A Controversial Customs Practice Creates a Legal Backlash," U.S. News & World Report, June 24, 2008.

[108] The National Association of Criminal Defense Lawyers (NACDL), along with the National Press Photographers Association, filed a Complaint for Declaratory and Injunctive Relief challenging the constitutionality of the Department of Homeland Security policies that authorize suspicionless searches

of contents of Americans' laptops, cell phones, cameras and other electronic devices at the international border. *Abidor v. Napolitano*, Case No. cv 10-4059 (E.D.N.Y. filed Sept. 7, 2010). Lisa Wayne, then president-elect of the NACDL, had her laptop taken out of her sight for 30 minutes and searched without cause, by a customs agent at the Houston airport. According to the complaint, 3,000 Americans had their electronic devices searched as they crossed U.S. border from October 2008 to June 2010. *See* "Defense Lawyers Sue to Limit Laptop, Phone Searches at Airports," BLT: The Blog of LegalTimes, September 07, 2010, *available at* http://legaltimes.typepad.com/blt/2010/09/defense-lawyers-sue-to-limit-laptop-phone-searches-at-airports.html (accessed Mar. 23, 2012).

[109] *Ibid.*

[110] Filed by the Association of Corporate Travel Executives and the Electronic Frontier Foundation.

[111] Kingsbury, fn. 107, *supra.*

[112] *In re Grand Jury Subpoena (Boucher)*, 2007 U.S. Dist. LEXIS 87951 (2007).

[113] *In re Grand Jury Subpoena (Boucher)*, 2009 WL 424718 (D. Vt. 2009). *But cf. United States v. Kirschner*, Case No. 09-MC-50872 (E.D. Mich. Mar. 30, 2010), holding Thomas Kirschner, facing charges of receiving child pornography, did not have to surrender his password.

[114] *United States v. Fricosu*, Case No. 10-cr-00509-REB-02, 2012 WL 182121 (D. Colo. Jan. 23, 2012).

[115] *Ibid.*

[116] David Kravets, "Constitutional Showdown Voided: Feds Decrypt Laptop without Defendant's Help," Wired.com, February 29, 2012.

[117] *In Re Grand Jury Subpoena Duces Tecum Dated March 25, 2011*, No. 11-12268 & 11-15421, D.C. Dkt. No. 3:11-mc-00041-LAC (11th Cir. Feb. 23, 2012).

[118] *Ibid.* at note 27.

[119] *Ibid.*

[120] Complaint, p.6, *Robbins v. Lower Merion Sch. Dist.*, Case No. 2:2010-cv-00665 (E.D. Pa. filed Feb. 16, 2010); *see also,* Dan Hardy, Derrick Nunnally, and John Shiffman, "School Laptop Camera Snapped Away in One Classroom," The Philadelphia Inquirer, February 22, 2010.

[121] John P. Martin, "Lower Merion Report: Web Cams Snapped 56,000 Images," The Philadelphia Inquirer, April 19, 2010.

[122] John P. Martin, "Lower Merion Schools: Number of Webcam Photos "Substantial," The Philadelphia Inquirer, April 16, 2010.

[123] Martin, fn. 121, *supra.*

[124] Complaint, *Robbins*, fn. 120, *supra.*

[125] Chris Matyszczyk, "School District: Spy Webcams Activated 42 Times," CNET News.com, February 10, 2010.

[126] Martin, fn. 121, *supra.*

[127] Complaint pp. 6-7, *Robbins*, fn. 120, *supra*; *see also*, Martin, fn. 122, *supra.*

[128] Martin, fn. 121, *supra.*

[129] The complaint alleged violations of the Electronic Communications Privacy Act (ECPA), 18 U.S.C. § 2511; the Computer Fraud Abuse Act (CFAA), 18 U.S.C. § 1030; the Stored Communications Act (SCA), 18 U.S.C. § 2701; § 1983 of the Civil Rights Act, 42 U.S.C. § 1983; the Pennsylvania Wiretapping and Electronic Surveillance Act, 18 Pa. C.S.A. § 5701; and Pennsylvania common law.

[130] Barry Levine, "School District Sued for Spying on Students with Webcam," newsfactor.com, February 19, 2010.

[131] Matyszczyk, fn. 125, *supra.*

[132] According to an attorney representing one of the district's two IT employees who oversaw the program. *See* Larry Magid, "Police Get Webcam Pictures in School Spy Case," CNET News.com, March 6, 2010.

[133] According to the district report, in most instances the spyware was activated when a laptop was reported missing and deactivated when found, but in at least five cases, school employees allowed the cameras to run for days or weeks after recovery of the laptops; and in 15 other cases, investigators were unable to determine why a laptop was monitored. The report also claimed about 38,500 images came from six stolen laptops later recovered. *See* Martin, fn. 116, *supra.*

[134] Jaikumar Vijayan, "Update: School District Settles Webcam Spying Suit for $610,000," Computerworld, October 12, 2010.

[135] LMSD settled with student Jalil Hasan for $10,000 in 2010 and was sued in June 2011 by Joshua Levin, a former Harriton High School student. *See* Gregg Keizer, "Penn. School District Hit With New Mac Spying Lawsuit," Computerworld, June 8, 2011.

[136] Joe Mandak, "Lawsuit: Furniture Rental Company Spies on PC Users," Associated Press wire service report, May 4, 2011.

[137] "Cops Arrest Alleged High-Tech Peeping Tom," Associated Press wire service report, June 9, 2011.

[138] Megan DeMarco, "Dharun Ravi Found Guilty In Rutgers Webcam Spying Trial," The New Jersey Star-Ledger, March 16, 2012.

[139] Dan Goodin, "Judge Orders Turnover of Woman's Deleted Facebook Posts," The Register, September 29, 2010.

[140] *United States v. Miller*, 425 U.S. 435 (1976).

[141] Jeff John Roberts, "A New U.S. Law-Enforcement Tool: Facebook Searches," Reuters wire service report, July 12, 2011.

[142] The Exclusionary Rule was enunciated in *Weeks v. United States*, 232 U.S. 383 (1914) for federal courts but was not applied to the states through the Due Process clause of the Fourteenth Amendment until *Mapp v. Ohio*, 367 U.S. 643 (1961).

[143] *Olmstead v. United States*, 277 U.S. 438, 478 (1928) (Brandeis, J., dissenting).

[144] *Katz v. United States*, 389 U.S. 347, 350 (1967).

[145] *Kyllo v. United States*, 533 U.S. 27, 33 (2001) (citing *California v. Ciraolo*, 476 U.S. 207, 211 (1986)) (Harlan, J., concurring).

[146] *United States v. Miller*, 425 U.S. 435 (1976).

[147] For example, the Right to Financial Privacy Act, 12 U.S.C. § 3401-13 establishes a due process requirement, mandating government agencies provide notice and an opportunity to object before a bank or other institution can disclose an individuals' personal financial information to a government agency (with exceptions for the IRS and matters involving drug trafficking or espionage).

[148] The USA PATRIOT Act, (Pub. L. No. 107-56).

[149] *Doe v. Gonzales*, 386 F. Supp. 2d 66, 82 (D. Conn. 2005).

[150] The USA PATRIOT Improvement and Reauthorization Act of 2005, Pub. L. No. 109-177, 120 Stat. 192 (March 9, 2006).

[151] *United States v. Warshak*, 631 F.3d 266 (6th Cir. 2010).

[152] The Authorization for Use of Military Force (AUMF), 115 Stat. 224 Pub. L. 107–40 (Sept. 18, 2001).

[153] *Hepting v. AT&T Corp.*, Dkt. No. 09-16676 (9th Cir. 2011).

[154] Director of National Intelligence Mike McConnell commenting in an August 14, 2007 interview with the El Paso Times.

[155] The Protect America Act of 2007 (PAA), Pub. L. 110-55, 121 Stat. 552.

[156] The FISA Amendments Act, Pub. L. No. 110-261, 122 Stat. 2436 (2008).

[157] "FBI Tosses Carnivore to the Dogs," Associated Press wire service report, January 18, 2005.

[158] Declan McCullagh and Elinor Mills, "Feds Take Porn Fight to Google," CNET News.com, January 19, 2006.

[159] Anne Broache, "Judge: Google Must Give Feds Limited Access to Records," CNET News.com, March 17, 2006.

[160] Anick Jesdanun, "Control over Online Data Rests with Companies—Consumers' Only Option for Privacy is Often Logging off," Associated Press wire service report, October 16, 2006.

[161] H.R. 837 [110th Congress]: Internet Stopping Adults Facilitating the Exploitation of Today's Youth Act (SAFETY) of 2007, introduced on February 6, 2007 by Rep. Lamar Smith [R-TX].

[162] *United States v. Arnold*, 523 F.3d 941 (9th Cir. 2008).

[163] Dominic Rushe, "FBI to Step up Monitoring of Social Media Sites Amid Privacy Concerns," The (U.K.) Guardian, January 26, 2012.

# CHAPTER

# 10

---

# PRIVACY POLICIES AND BEHAVIORAL MARKETING

This chapter discusses Web site privacy policies, focusing on the elements of a good privacy policy. It also examines the California Online Privacy Protection Act, and the practice of behavioral marketing.

*"There are two kinds of light — the glow that illuminates, and the glare that obscures." — James Thurber*

A MAJORITY OF AMERICANS believe when they browse the Web their online activities are private, not shared without permission, and Web firms must identify themselves, explain why they are collecting data and if they plan to share it, according to one poll. Nearly as many believe companies must obtain consent before using any personal information they have collected.[1] They are wrong. Both Web firms and ISPs monitor Web browsers' online activities. Web firms need not explain their data collection or data retention policies unless they choose to have a privacy policy. Companies can and do use personal information they have collected without consent (except in the case of children under age 13, where the **Children's Online Privacy Protection Act of 1998** (COPPA) requires parental consent to collect personal information from them).[2] The greatest restriction on a firm's collection of data is not the law, but its own privacy policy.

In this chapter, we will discuss why firms choose to have a privacy policy and how they are bound by it, what the policy should contain, and how it discloses the firm's behavioral marketing procedures.

## Define "Never"

A "homesteader" was a 19$^{th}$ century man who, for a nominal fee, acquired and settled on U.S. public land. Nearly two centuries later, GeoCities revived the "homesteading" concept, revamped for the Internet, by allowing customers to build free Web pages on its servers. GeoCities made money placing banner ads on customers' pages, but had other ideas on how to profit from its customers. GeoCities homesteaders were required to fill out an application with their first and last name, e-mail address, zip code, gender, birth date, and member name. It also asked for, but did not require, education level, marital status, occupation, and interests. Marketers find such information from millions of customers highly lucrative and desirable. GeoCities asked if they wanted to receive "special offers" from advertisers; presumably, if they declined, it would not share their personal information. To encourage people to complete the form, it included a privacy statement that read, "… we will never give your information to anyone without your permission." However, according to an FTC complaint, it "sold, rented, marketed, disclosed" the information, including from children, to marketers.[3] The FTC charged GeoCities with misrepresenting why it collected personal information from adults and children. GeoCities agreed to a settlement with the FTC.

Toysmart, an online toy retailer, also stated in its privacy policy it would never disclose customer data[4] Although it had promised customers it would never sell personal information it solicited from them, after it filed for bankruptcy, its customer information became a bankruptcy estate asset, and a valuable one at that. The bankruptcy estate had a duty to liquidate the firm's assets to pay creditors. This created a conflict between the firm's obligation to adhere to its promise not to sell its database of personal information and the bankruptcy trustee's obligation to liquidate the firm's assets for the benefit of its creditors. Toysmart tried to sell its database to the highest bidder, advertising its customer list in The Wall Street Journal, despite the privacy policy promise. The FTC claimed the attempted sale violated § 5 of the **Federal Trade Commission Act**,[5] prohibiting unfair or deceptive acts, and **COPPA**, prohibiting collection of personal information from children without parental consent.[6]

Geocities *chose* to ignore its stated privacy policy; Toysmart had *no choice*: its database was a company asset, and in bankruptcy all assets must be sold to pay creditors. Toysmart was placed in a "no-win" situation by virtue of its circumstances. One solution might have been for the buyer to take the database subject to the privacy policy terms. Alternatively, the Bankruptcy Court could have declared it was not an asset and order it destroyed (although a customer list is a valuable asset). Ideally, Congress should amend the Bankruptcy Act to deal with this conflict. The database was ultimately destroyed with the approval of the United States Bankruptcy Court.[7]

*XY Magazine*, started in 1996, was a print magazine with an online counterpart, XY.com, whose target audience was gay teens between 13 and 17 years old.[8] The magazine folded in 2007, followed by the demise of the site in 2009. According to the FTC, the magazine had 100,000 subscribers, 3,000 of whom contributed articles and photographs, while the site had up to 1 million users who had submitted their names, street addresses, e-mail addresses, photos, personal stories, online personal profiles, and, in the case of XY subscribers, bank card account information.[9] The site's privacy policy stated: "We never give your info to anybody" and "[O]ur privacy policy is simple: we never share your information with anybody." The *XY Magazine* subscription form stated: "Privacy Policy: XY never sells its list to anybody." Those submitting online profile information were told such information "will not be published. [W]e keep it secret."[10] When the site's founder filed personal bankruptcy in 2010, that personally identifiable information was at risk of being turned over to creditors. The founder, a graduate student, listed XY's "customer list, personal data, and editorial and back issue files of XY Mag and XY.com" as his only significant asset. XY's creditors sought to obtain that asset.[11] The FTC wrote to the creditors, stating "any sale, transfer, or use" of XY's personal information "raises serious privacy issues and could violate" federal law.[12] The FTC took the position, because of the statement in the privacy policy, the personal information should be destroyed. The creditors indicated an intent to use the subscriber database to restart the magazine and Web site.[13] In *Toysmart*, the FTC had said use of the information might be permissible under limited circumstances consistent with the original purpose for which it was provided. [14] Here, however, the FTC was concerned many subscribers were minors, living with family members unaware of their homosexuality; any attempt to market to them at the street addresses they provided XY years ago, especially if they had moved from home, might reveal their sexual orientation to those residing at their former addresses. In this situation, the personal information was more sensitive than in *Toysmart*. A law firm representing the court-appointed bankruptcy trustee reportedly stated its intent to administer any assets listed on the debtor's bankruptcy petition for the benefit of creditors, pitting the bankruptcy trustee against consumer privacy interests, presumably protected by the **FTC Act**'s prohibition against deceptive business practices. [15] In 2010, XY Magazine's publisher agreed to destroy the personal information. [16]

If a privacy policy states the site will never give information to third-parties but it later modifies its policy, does the change apply retroactively to previously collected information? Gateway Learning Corp., maker of the "Hooked on Phonics" products, subsequently modified its policy to let it share information. [17] The FTC considered that a deceptive and unfair practice in violation of § 5 of the **FTC Act**. Under the consent agreement, Gateway was prohibited from sharing previously collected customer information without obtaining express "opt-in" consent from customers, and in the future Gateway could not retroactively apply material changes to its privacy policy without first obtaining customer consent.

## Web Site Privacy Policies

The concept of privacy entails the right to control information about oneself. E-commerce sites collect personal information from customers, sometimes out of necessity and sometimes for marketing purposes. Personal identifiable information, such as name, address, birth date, occupation, income, age, gender, and hobbies, is highly valued by marketers to reach *targeted* audiences. People want a sense of control over their personal information. When they share it with a site, they want to know what it plans to do with the information. They also want assurance it will be stored safely, inaccessible to hackers or other inappropriate parties.

Who has access to personally identifiable information once it has been collected is of major importance to the Web site visitor. For example, Beverly Dennis, a 47-year-old Ohio woman, began receiving sexually explicit letters from a convicted rapist and burglar in a Texas maximum security prison. Although he was a complete stranger, the letters were filled with personal details he seemed to know: her birthday; that she was divorced; her salary, her preferences for bath soap and magazines, and even details about her use of a particular hemorrhoid medicine. The lengthy handwritten letters were not only filled with sexual fantasies but also threats, which he promised to carry out on his release from prison. Dennis had filled out a marketing survey with her name, address, sex, age, medical conditions, and buying habits in exchange for discount coupons and free products. The marketer, Metromail, had hired a third-party contractor to input the collected consumer survey data into a computer. The contractor farmed the job out to the Texas prison system, where hundreds of unpaid inmates, including sex offenders, were responsible for data entry of the collected personal information, such as the 25-page file Metromail had compiled on Dennis. [18]

Web visitors want assurance a site will not promise to use their collected personal information for a stated purposes but later market it to other companies. To address this concern, many e-commerce sites post privacy policies explaining how they collect information and what they do with it. But, as seen in the _GeoCities_ and _Toysmart_ cases, once a firm has a stated privacy policy, it must abide by it. A stated privacy policy is the greatest restriction on a site's ability to collect and use customer information. With certain exceptions, discussed below, a site is not required to have a privacy policy. Some lawyers advise clients _not_ to have one, on the theory one cannot violate what one does not have. So why have a privacy policy? Most e-commerce sites choose to have privacy policies because they make sites appear _trustworthy_.

Some sites are required by law to post privacy policies if they collect information from California residents, children under 13, or European customers. California requires any commercial site or online service operator collecting personally identifiable information about California residents provide notice of its privacy policies. The California **Online Privacy Protection Act**[19] requires sites: (1) identify categories of personally identifiable information collected and categories of third-parties with whom it may be shared; (2) describe how to review and change such information, if the site allows review and changes; (3) describe how to learn of policy changes; and (4) state its effective date. It defines "_personally identifiable information_" as: first and last name, home or other physical address, e-mail address, phone number, SSN, and "any other identifier that permits the physical or online contacting of a specific individual", as well as any other information collected by the site. The Act also requires a link from the main page to the privacy policy. Sites that collect personal information from, or are aimed at, children are subject to **COPPA**, discussed at length in the next chapter. Sites with customers or business operations in the European Union (EU) are subject to the EU's **_Data Protection Directive_**, which requires them to inform users their data may be collected and used for direct marketing, and to provide a right to object (_i.e._, an "opt-out" provision). The Directive prohibits transfer of personal data to non-EU nations that do not meet its "adequacy standard" for privacy protection. The U.S. Commerce Department and the European Commission have devised a "_safe harbor_" framework of data protection principles to enable U.S. businesses to satisfy the EU's requirement of adequate data protection for personally identifiable information transferred from the EU to America.

## Ingredients for a Good Privacy Policy

If a Webmaster either needs or chooses to have a privacy policy, it should be simple and straight-forward. A good policy should be easily understandable by site visitors, not filled with indecipherable legalese. It should be reviewed periodically and updated as necessary. Employees should be familiar with it, both so they can respond to questions about it and so they do not violate it.

Site visitors need to understand the privacy policy. Web sites collect two kinds of data: personally identifiable information and aggregate information. _Personally identifiable information_ is identifiable to a specific individual, _e.g._, name, e-mail address, phone number, home or other address, school attended or business employer, SSN, credit card number, bank account number, or any other information that tells who the person is. _Aggregate information_ is general demographic information that does not identify any individual.

### General Elements

The necessary elements of a privacy policy should include:

- *What* personally identifiable information is collected
- *Who* collects the information
- *How* information is used
- *With whom* information may be shared
- What *choices* visitors have about collection, use, and distribution of information
- What *security procedures* are used to protect against loss, misuse, or alteration of information (*i.e.,* data breaches, hacking, employee data theft)
- How visitors can *correct inaccuracies* or update information

## Specific Elements

- Contact information: the company's name, address (main office, possibly branches too), phone numbers, e-mail address, and the privacy policy's effective date
- What information (*e.g.,* IP addresses, browser type, ISP, referring/exit pages, operating system, date/time stamp, and clickstream data) is automatically logged
- If the site collects any of the following (and if so, how long is it retained?):
  - ▶ Site visitor e-mail address
  - ▶ e-mail address of visitors referred to the site by previous visitors
  - ▶ The referring URL of site visitors
  - ▶ e-mail address of individuals who send or receive e-mail through the site
  - ▶ e-mail address of visitors who post messages to the message board
  - ▶ e-mail address of visitors who post in the chat room
  - ▶ Logs of chat room conversations
  - ▶ Information on which pages visitors access (and if such information is general or user-specific)
  - ▶ Information voluntarily submitted by visitors
  - ▶ Payment information (*e.g.,* name, billing addresses, phone number, e-mail address, bank account number, credit card number and expiration date)
  - ▶ Transaction information (*e.g.,* purchase dates, dollar amounts, quantities, and item descriptions)
- The disposition of collected information
  - ▶ Used to improve the site content
  - ▶ Used to analyze trends, administer the site, track users' movements around the site, and gather demographic data
  - ▶ Used to notify visitors about site updates
  - ▶ Used to contact visitors for marketing purposes (*i.e.,* targeted marketing)
  - ▶ Shared with third-parties for marketing purposes (*i.e.,* targeted marketing)
  - ▶ Shared in the aggregate (nonuser-specific) with third-parties for marketing purposes (*i.e.,* demographics, aggregate reports, and market research)
  - ▶ Not shared with anyone for any purpose
  - ▶ Disclosed when legally *required* to do so by law enforcement or government agencies (*i.e.,* when subpoenaed)
  - ▶ Disclosed when *requested* to do so by law enforcement or government agencies (*i.e.,* without a subpoena)
  - ▶ To protect against misuse or unauthorized use of the site, or violation of the Terms of Use policy

▶ To a successor entity in the event of sale of the business, merger, bankruptcy, or other ownership change

▶ Used to create a user "profile" based on information collected through cookies, log files, and *Web beacons*, that is then tied to the user's personally identifiable information and purchasing history

• The length of time information is retained, if at all

• Whether the site sets a *cookie* (a small text file stored on a user's computer to allow the site to authenticate the user's identity, speed up transactions, monitor user behavior, and personalize the presentation) on the visitor's computer and if so, for what specific purposes

▶ Whether the site links the information it stores in cookies to personally identifiable information submitted by the user

▶ Whether the site uses both *session ID cookies* (that expire when the browser is closed) and *persistent cookies* (that remain on the user's hard drive)

▶ Whether the session ID cookies and persistent cookies are encrypted

▶ Whether any cookies are set by third-party content or service providers

• Whether the site uses *Web beacons* or "*clear GIFs*" (small one pixel GIF files embedded invisibly in a Web page to track visitors' online movements)

▶ Whether data collected by Web beacons is tied to personally identifiable information

▶ Whether Web beacons are used in HTML-based e-mails sent to visitors

• If Web visitors must register as members (*i.e.*, create a user name and password) what information must they provide during registration?

▶ How long will it be retained?

▶ Will it be shared with third-party advertisers?

• If Web visitors must register to participate in a survey or contest, what information must they provide?

▶ How long will it be retained?

▶ Will it be shared with third-party advertisers?

• Instructions on how to opt-out of having personally identifiable information used to deliver marketing offers through e-mail. (For Webmasters, it is better to offer an opt-in option than to send e-mail automatically to the addresses collected, as that might be considered unsolicited bulk e-mailing, *i.e.*, spamming.)

• Whether affiliated ad servers, if any, may collect information such as the visitor's domain type, IP address, and *clickstream data* (*e.g.*, a record of all pages on the site visited, number of times an ad is viewed)

• What methods, if any, are available for a visitor to correct errors in previously collected information or update or delete that information

• If, and under what circumstances, visitors are redirected to a secure server to transfer sensitive information, using secure socket layer technology (SSL) to encrypt it

• How the user is notified of changes to the privacy policy

• If there are links to third-party sites that do not follow this privacy policy

## If No One Heard the Tree Fall, Did It Make A Noise?

Are privacy policy terms enforceable if never read? In *In re Northwest Airlines Privacy Litigation*, the plaintiffs alleged the airline had violated laws and its privacy policy by giving passenger name records, flight numbers, credit card information, hotel and car rental reservations, and names of travel companions to NASA for research on improving airline security following the September 11th terrorist attacks. [20] The court found the suits meritless, in part because the privacy policy posted on the airline's site was unenforceable *unless plaintiffs claimed to have read it*. Since they did not actually read it before providing Northwest personal information, their "expectation of privacy was low," the court reasoned. Privacy advocates argue rather than focus on what the plaintiffs actually read, the focus should be on what the company promised.

In a similar case, JetBlue Airways was sued by customers after it disclosed passenger name records to the U.S. Defense Department, which turned over the records to a data mining company hired to analyze the personal characteristics of individuals seeking access to military installations to predict which ones posed security risks. [21] One claim was breach of contract. Unlike <u>Northwest Airlines</u>, this court found JetBlue's privacy policy formed a valid contract between JetBlue and site visitors. The court made no distinction between those who had read the policy and those who had not. However, it nonetheless dismissed the contract claims because the plaintiffs were unable to show any economic damages; only damages for loss of privacy, which are unrecoverable for breach of contract under New York law.

## Behavioral Marketing

Online marketing can be divided into contextual marketing and behavioral marketing. Delivering relevant ads based on content, as you may recall from our discussion of **keyword advertising** in Chapter 5, is an example of **contextual marketing**. When a user types a keyword into a search engine, in addition to search results, targeted ads related to the keyword appear on the page. **Behavioral marketing** targets consumers based on their behavior on sites, instead of by the content of pages they visit. Behavioral marketing uses clickstream data to track sites a consumer visits, creating a profile of what products interest him and delivering related targeted advertising. A **clickstream** is a sequential server log of a user's online activity. **Clickstream data** include what Web page or Web site the user visited; how long the user was on a page or site; in what order the user viewed the pages; newsgroups the user participated in; keywords typed into search engines; and addresses of incoming and outgoing e-mail. Both Web sites and ISPs track clickstream data. By using clickstream data and IP addresses, advertisers can follow the trail of an individual's online activities and deliver targeted ads based on that information.

Cookie-based tracking is the most common method of behavioral marketing. A **cookie** allows a site's server to place information about a user's visit on the user's hard drive in a small file readable only by that site. The information is then sent back to the server each time the browser requests a page. The server can use it to personalize the page it sends to the browser. Marketing companies use **third-party cookies** set by a site other than the one the user is currently visiting. Most browser privacy settings default to accept regular cookies but allow users to accept or decline third-party cookies.

Users can manage most cookies by changing privacy settings in their Web browser, but Flash cookies (based on Adobe's Flash software) are stored in a separate directory many users do not know about and they may not know how to control them. Flash cookies are difficult to delete and some reinstate regular cookies a user has deleted, a process called "re-spawning". Flash cookies are a privacy concern because they may enable companies to create detailed profiles of users without their knowledge.

Cookies are not the only way personal information can be transferred to Web firms. Personally identifiable information, such as name, user name, or e-mail address, may be embedded in the Uniform Resource Locator (URL) created when a user logs on to a site, and then sent to third-party advertisers who deliver ads and other content on the page. [22]

Facebook has been sued by users for embedding a tracking cookie that records Web browsing history after logging off the social network, enabling it to compile a running log of all Web sites the user has visited in the past 90 days. [23] Facebook plants two different kinds of tracking cookies in members' browser: a session cookie and a browser cookie. [24] Nonmembers who land on the site and move on only receive the browser cookie. If a member is logged on to her Facebook account and surfs the Web, her session cookie will record her name, e-mail address, friends, IP address, time stamp, and all data associated with her profile. If a member is logged off and surfing the Web, or if the user is a nonmember landing on the site, the browser cookie will log the IP address and time stamp. Facebook could track where members go on the Web after they have logged off by matching data from the session cookie and the browser cookie. Facebook makes most of its profits from advertising, which means users are not its customers but products it offers to advertisers. The more data it can collect, the better it can target its advertising, which means more revenue.

Online advertising is estimated to be a $45 billion-a-year industry. [25] U.S. firms spent $575 million on behavioral marketing in 2007, with behavioral marketing expected to account for $3.8 billion of online ads by 2011. [26] The trend in online advertising is away from contextual marketing and toward behavioral marketing — targeted advertising based on what individuals say and do. That means gathering more information about consumers, which raises privacy concerns. Already, advertisers increasingly select Web venues for ads based on how much a site know about its users. [27] In the World Wide Web's early days, companies could only monitor customers' actions on their own sites, but now, using third-party *widgets* to place ads on thousands of sites, they can follow customers' activities on those sites, as well.

There has not yet been a public outcry against behavioral marketing; likely because most Web users do not realize they are being monitored as they traverse the Web. Often details of a company's behavioral marketing are buried deep in a long privacy policy most users do not bother to read. However, when they do become aware of such tracking, as with Facebook's Beacon program (discussed in Chapter 9), the reaction can be decidedly negative. [28] No one likes to be stalked online. A Harris survey found 60 percent of respondents "uncomfortable" when sites used their personal information to tailor advertising or content; and in a Zogby International poll, 81 percent were "somewhat" or "very" concerned about companies tracking their browsing habits for marketing purposes and 88 percent labeled it an "unfair" corporate practice if done without the user's permission. [29] People complain of the "Creepy Factor", akin to phoning in a pizza order and realizing the unknown voice at the other end already knows your name and where you live, thanks to computerized caller ID databases. The Creepy Factor sets in as Web users realize how much of their personal information has been collected, retained, and used to target them with personalized ads. As discussed in the next chapter, younger people (the Internet Generation) have a diminished expectation of privacy, so it is not surprising younger Web users are more comfortable with customized Web content. [30]

The "Creepy Factor" may have reached its zenith when it was revealed Target had a pervasive behavioral marketing scheme in play that enabled it to send coupons for baby items to customers according to their "pregnancy scores" — in one case, alerting a father his high school daughter was pregnant. Target assigns each customer a "Guest ID number" tied to her credit card, and supplemented by purchased customer data, that tracks every purchase. It discovered newly pregnant women tended to buy specific items, so it mailed them fliers for baby products. A Target statistician stated, "If we send someone a catalog and say, 'Congratulations on your first child!' and they've never told us they're pregnant, that's going to make some people uncomfortable. We are very conservative about compliance with all privacy laws. But even if you're following the law, you can do things where people get queasy." [31] Target learned to mix the baby ads with generic items like lawn mowers so the women would think they had been randomly sent the fliers, so as not to "spook" them. The data mining begins with the Guest ID number. Visit the Web site, open an e-mail from the store, charge a purchase, complete a survey, or mail in a refund, and Target assigns a Guest ID number. Target can buy marketing data to add to the Guest ID number, such as product brands purchased, job history, political leanings, college, bankruptcy, marital status, reading habits, ethnicity, and Web sites visited. It can complete the profile with demographic data, such as age, neighborhood, and estimated salary. [32]

Once Web users become aware of behavioral marketing, there is a way they can opt-out. The Network Advertising Initiative (NAI), an industry trade association of major online ad companies, including Yahoo! and DoubleClick, offers a cookie users can place on their computers instructing advertisers not to deliver behaviorally targeted ads. The only problem is the cookie may be deleted by browser privacy controls and anti-spyware software that routinely delete cookies. [33]

In addition to the privacy concern behavioral marketing is being done without consumer knowledge or consent, another concern is too little is known about if or how companies adequately protect personal information. [34] Firms claim customers' privacy is protected because no personally identifying details are released. AOL offers the choice to opt-out of certain targeted advertising; Google allows users to edit search histories linked to their user names; and Microsoft claims it does not link visitors' behavior to user names. [35] Yet Google stores a user's IP address with searches made from it, and its Gmail serves ads based on keywords found in users' e-mails. [36]

So far, the FTC approach toward behavioral marketing has been to favor industry self-regulation, releasing a set of "guidelines", suggesting: [37]

1. Every site where data is collected for behavioral advertising should provide a clear, consumer-friendly, and prominent statement data is being collected to provide ads targeted to consumer and let them choose whether or not to have their information collected.

2. Any company that collects or stores consumer data for behavioral advertising should provide reasonable security for it and retain it only as long as necessary to fulfill a legitimate business or law enforcement need.

3. Companies should get consumers' affirmative express consent before using data in a materially different way from promises made when collecting it.

4. Companies should only collect sensitive data for behavioral advertising if they get consumers' affirmative express consent to receive such advertising.

But what is a "clear" statement? Is it clear if buried in a lengthy privacy policy or written in legalese or "tech-speak"? What qualifies as "reasonable security" when it comes to protecting against data breaches? What steps must a company take to obtain "affirmative express consent"? And what qualifies as "sensitive data"? Critics contend the proposed FTC guidelines have been outpaced by technology and do not address evolving aspects of behavioral marketing. [38]

In 2009, Google announced behavioral marketing plans to use stored browsing histories to trigger ads, on the idea site visitors will want to buy things based on the type of sites they have visited. Google earns most of its revenue from ads that appear next to search results, tied to the browser's interest in a topic or products. By targeting display ads to browser's interests, Google will have an opportunity to increase its two percent share in the $8 billion display ad market.[39]

## Deep Packet Inspection

ISPs want a piece of the advertising dollar Web firms like Google and Yahoo! are digging into by tracking Web visitors and displaying relevant ads. ISPs actively monitor every click and keystroke of American Web users, and have the ability to harvest the data stream to identify customers' interests and sell that information to advertisers for target marketing.[40] Three of the four largest U.S. ISPs — AT&T, Time Warner Cable, and Verizon — testified before a U.S. Senate committee they presently do not engage in behavioral marketing methods targeting their subscribers' Web activities to deliver contextual ads.[41] But that may change. The ISPs promised to adopt policies requiring informed customer consent before tracking online activities and collecting their data.

ISPs have a greater ability than Web firms like Google to track, monitor, and profile user behavior. The major privacy concern is if ISPs begin targeting ads for behavioral marketing, they may employ a practice known as "*deep packet inspection*" (DPI). Instead of a site using a cookie to track a visitor on its site, DPI is employed at the ISP level, allowing it an almost unlimited reach, as the ISP can track every page visited on every site, every e-mail sent, and every search phrase entered by a user. DPI can monitor everything an ISP customer does online, which alarms privacy advocates. ISPs who use DPI — and the number who do is uncertain because they do not publicize their use[42] — tout it as beneficial for all concerned: advertisers can target consumers interested in their products and services; consumers can view more relevant ads; ISPs can profit from sharing customer data; and Web sites can increase online ad revenues.[43] Some ISPs have modified their user agreements to allow DPI, describing it as a "preference advertising service" or "working with third-party advertising."[44]

ISPs could substantially increase revenue by monetizing DPI-derived customer data and selling it to behavioral advertising firms. But there are questions about the legality of what ISPs can do with DPI-derived data. Do they legally own the information, and if so, are there legal restrictions on its use or sale (not just to online advertisers, but offline, to prospective employers, landlords, insurance companies, or credit agencies)? Broadband ISPs may risk violating state and federal wiretapping laws if they intercept customers' Web browsing and review the packets' contents (each bit of data is divided into packets whose content can be accessed and analyzed).[45] **The Communications Act of 1934** (as amended by the **Telecommunications Act of 1996**) states companies engaged in "transmitting" communications shall not "divulge" those contents.[46] While ISPs can track customer usage for routine maintenance or billing purposes, tracking the content of what users do and selling that information might be considered a violation. The **Electronic Communications Privacy Act of 1986** (ECPA), enacted to extend restrictions on wiretaps to include transmissions of electronic data by computer, provides:[47]

> A person or entity providing remote computing service to the public shall not
> knowingly divulge to any person or entity the contents of any communication
> which is carried or maintained on that service * * * on behalf of, and received
> by means of electronic transmission from * * * a subscriber or customer

of such service * * * Exceptions * * * A provider * * * may divulge the contents of a communication * * * with the lawful consent of the originator or an addressee or intended recipient of such communication, or the subscriber.

The **ECPA** could be interpreted to prohibit DPI without the subscriber's consent. While it applies to all ISPs, the most restrictive statute applies solely to cable broadband providers, placing them at a competitive disadvantage in relation to the phone company ISPs. The **Cable TV Privacy Act of 1984** states a "cable operator shall not disclose personally identifiable information concerning any subscriber without the prior written or electronic consent of the subscriber".[48] This means cable ISPs must obtain express consent before collecting personally identifiable information and must provide notice to customers before disclosing that information. These three U.S. federal statutes bring into question the legality of DPI.[49]

DPI may also violate the U.K.'s Regulation of Investigatory Powers Act of 2000 (RIPA) and the Data Protection Act (DPA). RIPA makes it illegal to monitor communications between two entities without consent, and the DPA prohibits processing personal data without consent. Ironically, in 2008, the U.K. government proposed "The Intercept Modernisation Programme" to conduct mass monitoring of traffic data as an anti-terrorism tool by using DPI to monitor the Web communications of all U.K. citizens and retain the traffic data in a centralized government database.[50] Under the Bush Administration, ISPs were pressured by the federal government to configure their networks in ways to assist monitoring by law enforcement agencies. Web firms and governments may be slow to setup their own DPI monitoring due to the substantial cost involved in installing DPI filtering and analysis technologies.

ISPs may have additional motivations to use DPI besides behavioral marketing. As discussed in Chapter 3, copyright holders like the RIAA members are eager to work with ISPs to track file-sharing infringers, and DPI would be an effective monitoring method.

In Chapter 8, we discussed Web firms and ISPs collecting and retaining data, much of it personally identifiable information. Marketers want to use this information to target consumers, and firms and ISPs who have it realize they have a valuable asset. In the case of ISPs, some information may come from monitoring customers. The federal **Wiretap Act**, which governs unauthorized interception of communications, would prevent an ISP from using such data for behavioral marketing purposes without first obtaining "express informed consent". But Web firms like Google might acquire personally identifiable information by means other than interception, thus not falling under the **Wiretap Act**. One unresolved issue is whether courts will equate a visitor's implied consent (to monitoring his Web movements) — by use of a site where the monitoring is disclosed in a privacy policy — to expressed informed consent.

A class action targeting behavioral marketing filed in 2009 alleged an ISP installed spyware devices on its broadband networks to divert Internet traffic, including users' personal information, to NebuAd, a now-defunct behavioral marketing firm.[51] NebuAd provided the device to ISPs to install inside their network. Each device monitored up to 50,000 users, and tied the content to the user's IP address using DPI.[52] The complaint alleged it had monitored 330,000 high-speed Internet customer accounts.[53]

## Behavioral Marketing and Privacy Policies

A Web site privacy policy should disclose its policy regarding, and use of, behavioral marketing. A cookie does not usually identify a specific individual but when combined with registration data supplied by the visitor, the merged data may be used to build a profile of the specific visitor. Although the NAI-issued guidelines bar collection of personally identifiable data about Internet users and restrict Web marketers from merging online data with personally identifiable data from offline databases, there is no assurance marketers will adhere to these guidelines. Some sites offer visitors a choice of receiving either the same ads as everyone else or a selection tailored to their interests, based on its behavioral marketing results. A site's behavioral marketing practices may or may not be revealed in its privacy policy, although the NAI guidelines require disclosure in a posted privacy policy, along with "a clear and conspicuous link to opt-out of the use of their information." [54]

Failure to disclose use of Web beacons and clear GIFs by a third-party contractor in its privacy policy cost Toys "R" Us $900,000 and its contractor almost half that much. Toys "R" Us hired Coremetrics, who used cookies, Web beacons, and clear GIFs on the Toys "R" Us Web site and linked the information obtained to personally identifiable visitor information. However, Toys "R" Us stated in its privacy policy it did not share "any" personally identifying data with "anyone outside of Toysrus.com, its parents, affiliates, subsidiaries, operating companies and other related entities." [55] Privacy policies must clearly explain the site's use of cookies, clear GIFs, or other features that might result in linking browsing information with personally identifiable information.

## Society, Technology, and the Law

The current approach to protecting online privacy is one of "notice and choice," in which sites post notices of their privacy policies and visitors can choose which to visit based on the level of privacy offered. But this approach is flawed, because privacy policies are:
- Lengthy written notices and therefore seldom read in their entirety
- Often confusing, possibly written in "legalese" or pasted together with contradictory clauses and undefined phrases
- Disingenuous about the complexity of modern data harvesting practices, as when they "disclose" DPI as "working with third-party marketers".

As with most Internet issues, the solution must be addressed by society, technology, and the law. Society needs to educate itself about the use of behavioral marketing and if it finds it objectionable, complain to ISPs, web firms, and lawmakers. People also need to become savvy about social engineering techniques. Technology must be employed to re-engineer the Web browser for greater privacy. Browser manufacturers have taken the first step by adding "private browsing" modes in the latest crop of browsers, but the degree of privacy offered is minimal and there is an inherent conflict of interest when many firms making the browsers, like Google and Microsoft, also have a vested interest in selling marketing data to advertisers. The law can be effective through greater regulation to protect consumers. Both Congress and the FTC have regulatory authority; the former through lawmaking and the later through promulgation of rules and regulations.

**Chapter 10 Notes**

[1] Grant Gross, "Large ISPs Endorse Customer Opt-in for Web Tracking," IDG News Service, September 25, 2008. According to a Consumer Reports National Research Center poll, 61 percent "are confident their online activities are private and not shared without permission"; 57 percent think firms must identify them-

selves, indicate the purpose of their data collection and if they plan to share it; and 48 percent think consent is necessary for firms to use the data they collect.

² The Children's Online Privacy Protection Act (COPPA), 15 U.S.C. § 6501, *et seq.*

³ Complaint *In re GeoCities*, File No. 9823015 (Fed. Trade Comm'n Aug. 13, 1998), *available at* www.ftc.gov/os/1998/08/geo-cmpl.htm (accessed Mar. 23, 2012). (Included in the Cases Section on the Issues in Internet Law site, www.IssuesinInternetLaw.com); *Geocities*, FTC Dkt. No. C-3849 (Final Order Feb. 12, 1999).

⁴ *FTC v. Toysmart.com, LLC*, Civil Action No. 00-11341-RGS (D. Mass. filed Jul. 10, 2000, amended Jul. 21, 2000).

⁵ The Federal Trade Commission Act of 1914, 15 U.S.C. §§ 41-58, as amended.

⁶ The Children's Online Privacy Protection Act (COPPA), 15 U.S.C. § 6501, *et seq.*

⁷ Greg Sandoval, "Judge OKs Destruction of Toysmart List," CNET News.com, January 31, 2001.

⁸ COPPA applies to commercial sites directed at children under 13 (preteens); however, it does not apply to those in their teen years, 13–to–17. This "COPPA Gap" may put teens at even greater risk than younger children because neither the collection of their personal information nor its disclosure is regulated or protected. These teens' privacy rests solely on the particular Web site's privacy policy and on their own judgment in what they disclose online. Highlighting XY's target teenage audience and their unique privacy concerns, the XY.com site published the following FAQ: "[Q:] Will my mom figure out what I'm getting in the mail? [A:] Subscription copies of XY are mailed in plain, shrink-wrapped black plastic, with no mention of XY on the mailing label."

⁹ FTC letter to Peter Larson and Martin E. Shmagin, July 10, 2010, included in the Cases Section on the Issues in Internet Law site (www.IssuesinInternetLaw.com).

¹⁰ *Ibid.*

¹¹ *In re Peter Ian Cummings*, Case No. 10-14433 (Bankr. D.N.J.). One important issue is how the site owner ended up as the "owner" of the subscribers' personal information. The press reports do not indicate what type of business entity XY was, although they do state at least two other individuals were involved. If the entity was a corporation or partnership, unless dissolved and the assets distributed to him as an owner (or if operated as a sole proprietorship), there may be an issue as to whether the subscribers' personal information should have been listed in his personal bankruptcy petition.

¹² FTC letter, fn. 9, *supra*. The FTC has brought several cases alleging failure to adhere to promises about information privacy constitute a deceptive practice under the FTC Act.

¹³ *Ibid.*

¹⁴ *FTC v. Toysmart.com, LLC*, Stipulated Consent Agreement and Final Order, Case No. 00-1 J341-RGS (D. Mass. Jul. 21, 2000), *available at* www.ftc.gov/os/2000/07/toysmartconsent.htm (accessed Mar. 23, 2012).

¹⁵ Declan McCullagh, "End of Gay Teen Web Site Sparks Privacy Concerns," CNET News.com, July 12, 2010.

¹⁶ Steve Smith, "XY Mag to Destroy Rather Than Share Personal User Info," Min Online, August 16, 2010, *available at* www.minonline.com/news/XY-Mag-to-Destroy-Rather-Than-Share-Personal-User-Info_15008.html (accessed Mar. 23, 2012).

¹⁷ *In re Matter of Gateway Learning Corp.*, FTC Dkt. No. C-4120 (2004).

¹⁸ *Dennis v. Metromail Corp.*, Case No. 96-04451, (Tex. Dist. Ct. 1996). *See also* Nina Bernstein, "Personal Files via Computer Offer Money and Pose Threat," The New York Times, June 12, 1997.

¹⁹ The California Online Privacy Protection Act, California Business and Professions Code § 22575-22579.

²⁰ *In re Nw. Airlines Privacy Litig.*, Civil File No. 04-216, 2004 US Dist. Lexis 10580 (D. Minn. 2004). *See also Feldman v. Google, Inc.*, 513 F. Supp. 2d 229 (E.D. Pa. 2007) holding a click-wrap agreement enforceable even though the plaintiff claimed he had never read the terms, because a "reasonably prudent Internet user" would have been on notice of the terms, which were of reasonable length and clearly presented in readable text despite being in a window that required scrolling, and the user was required to click an "I agree" button to assent. *See also DeJohn v. The .TV Corp.*, 245 F. Supp. 2d 913 (N.D. Ill. 2003) holding a click-wrap agreement legally binding even when the terms are not prominently displayed, so long as the user has an opportunity to review them by clicking a link.

²¹ *In re JetBlue Airways Corp. Privacy Litig.*, 379 F. Supp. 2d 299 (E.D.N.Y. 2005).

²² Jim Puzzanghera and Jessica Guynn, "Websites Share User Data More Often Than Previously Thought," The Los Angeles Times, October 12, 2011.

²³ "Kansas Man Sues Facebook over Privacy Breach," Associated Press wire service report, October 06, 2011.

²⁴ Byron Acohido, "Facebook Tracking is under Scrutiny," USA Today, November 16, 2011.

[25] Declan McCullagh, Anne Broache "Web Monitoring for Ads? It May Be Illegal," CNET News.com, May 19, 2008.

[26] Michele Gershberg , "Where Were You Online? Advertisers Know," Reuters wire service report, June 20, 2007.

[27] Louise Story, "To Aim Ads, Web is Keeping Closer Eye on You," The New York Times, March 10, 2008.

[28] Discussed in Chapter 12.

[29] See Lara Hertel, "People Uneasy with Web Sites Using Personal Details: Poll," Reuters wire service report, April 11, 2008 and Juliana Gruenwald, "Poll Finds Public Concern over Online Privacy," The National Journal, June 8, 2010.

[30] Hertel, ibid., according to a Harris Interactive poll that found younger users more comfortable with the customized Web content, especially in the 18–to–43 age range.

[31] Charles Duhigg, "How Companies Learn Your Secrets," The New York Times, February 16, 2012.

[32] Ibid.

[33] Jim Puzzanghera, "Tough Cookies for Web Surfers Seeking Privacy," The Los Angeles Times, April 19, 2008.

[34] Peter Whoriskey, "Every Click You Make; Internet Providers Quietly Test Expanded Tracking of Web Use to Target Advertising," The Washington Post, p. D01, April 4, 2008.

[35] Story, fn. 27, supra.

[36] Whoriskey, fn. 34, supra.

[37] FTC Press Release, "FTC Staff Proposes Online Behavioral Advertising Privacy Principles," December 20, 2007.

[38] Whoriskey, fn. 34, supra.

[39] Robert D. Hof, "Behavioral Targeting: Google Pulls out the Stops," Business Week, March 11, 2009.

[40] Ellen Nakashima, "Lawmakers Probe Web Tracking: Panel Examining Ad Technology for Privacy Concerns," The Washington Post, p. D01, July 17, 2008.

[41] Grant Gross, "Large ISPs Endorse Customer Opt-in for Web Tracking," IDG News Service, September 25, 2008.

[42] McCullagh, fn. 25, supra.

[43] Whoriskey, fn. 34, supra.

[44] Ibid.

[45] McCullagh, fn. 25, supra.

[46] The Communications Act of 1934, 47 U.S.C. § 605 states, in part: "…no person receiving, assisting in receiving, transmitting, or assisting in transmitting, any interstate or foreign communication by wire or radio shall divulge or publish the existence, contents, substance, purport, effect, or meaning thereof, except through authorized channels of transmission or reception." Section 605(a)(6) addresses intercepted radio transmissions and adds "… or use such communication (or any information therein contained) for his own benefit or for the benefit of another not entitled thereto." While this provision applies to radio and not the Internet, it was clearly Congress' intent not to allow any third-party (including provider employees) to intercept and divulge for gain any content transmitted through the major communication systems of the day. In 1934, when the Act was passed, radio, telegraph, and telephone were the major communication systems; today the Internet is arguably the major communication system. It is conceivable a court might interpret the statute in light of both the legislative intent and changes in technology; even when Congress amended the Act in 1996, it did not contemplate the technological advances that would enable behavioral marketing and DPI. It is also possible Congress might amend the Act again to protect consumer privacy if there is a public outcry as public awareness of behavioral marketing increases.

[47] The Electronic Communications Privacy Act of 1986, 18 U.S.C. § 2702 ("Stored Communications Act").

[48] The Cable TV Privacy Act of 1984, 47 U.S.C. § 551.

[49] McCullagh, fn. 25, supra.

[50] Tom Espiner, "Gov't May Track All UK Facebook Traffic," March 18, 2009.

[51] Valentine v. WideOpenWest Fin., LLC, No. 1:09-cv-07653 (N.D. Ill. 2009). An earlier class action by the same lead plaintiff, Valentine v. NebuAd, Inc., No. 3:08-cv 05113 (N.D. Cal. 2009), was dismissed for lack of jurisdiction.

[52] Saul Hansell, "NebuAd Observes 'Useful, But Innocuous' Web Browsing," The New York Times," April 7, 2008.

[53] WideOpenWest Fin., LLC, fn. 51, supra.

[54] D. Reed Freeman, Jr., "Privacy and the Future of Behavioral Marketing," December 15, 2004, available at www.imediaconnection.com/content/4791.asp (accessed Mar. 23, 2012).

[55] In re Toys R Us, Inc., Privacy Litigation, MDL No. M-00-1381-MMC (N.D. Cal. 2001).

# CHAPTER

# 11

---

## PRIVACY AND CHILDREN

This chapter explores privacy on the Internet as it relates to children and their social interaction in the cyber-environment, with particular attention to FTC regulation and the Children's Online Privacy Protection Act.

*"The test of the morality of a society is what it does for its children." — Dietrich Bonhoeffer*

## Soupy Sales ... and the Naiveté of Kids

I N 1965, SOUPY SALES, so the story goes, was perturbed at having to work on New Year's Day. With a few minutes left at the end of the live broadcast of his children's TV show, he looked into the camera and ad-libbed, "Hey kids, I want you to tiptoe into your parents' bedroom, look in their pockets for all the green pieces of paper with the pictures of the guys in beards, and send them to your old pal, Soupy, at Channel 5 in New York."[1] Shortly thereafter, cash-filled envelopes trickled into the studio, as did complaints from outraged parents. Sales was suspended for a week for his prank, but it serves as a classic example of the ease with which the naiveté of children can be exploited by the power of a mass medium like television or the Internet.

## Protecting Children from Marketers and Other Predators

Imagine what Soupy Sales could have done on the Internet! Studies have shown children are less able to appreciate the ramifications of disclosing personal information online. One psychiatrist told an FTC privacy workshop children do not understand what personal information is, look up to fictional characters, and tend to do what they ask of them.[2] Some countries and provinces, recognizing the seriousness of the threat to children, restrict marketing targeted at them. Quebec prohibits print and broadcast advertising targeting children under 13, while for Sweden the cutoff age is 12.[3] But the United States has never had a law that prevented marketing to children; to the contrary, historically, marketers specifically targeted children. Examples include cereal and toy commercials, magazine subscriptions in children's names, sponsored radio and TV show (*e.g.*, Superman hawking Cheerios in commercials on the

*Adventures of Superman* radio and television shows), and the classic Johnson and Smith comic book novelty ads (*e.g.*, x-ray glasses and sea monkeys).[4] A walk down the supermarket cereal aisle reveals how products are heavily marketed to children. Movies now have "tie-in" products aimed at children; see the Spider-Man movie, then buy Spider-Man ravioli and a Spider-Man toothbrush before getting into Spider-Man pajamas and crawling under the Spider-Man sheets (and remember to turn on the Spider-Man nightlight!). Marketers' goal is to get kids to nag parents until they give in and buy the products. Mom may not have intended to buy ravioli tonight, but ultimately she will succumb to her kids' nagging prompted by the picture of Spider-Man on the can.

American children spend more time watching TV than in the classroom.[5] The average U.S. child sees 40,000 commercials a year.[6] Many school districts broadcast the commercial-filled Channel One News to a captive student audience.[7] How pervasive is advertising? U.S. adults and children are exposed to countless ads all day long on TV, radio, billboards, bus benches, store floors, gas pumps, and in magazines, newspapers, and movie theaters — before the feature film starts and during movies through product placement. One enterprising marketer has proposed placing ads on egg shells![8]

America has 4.5 percent of the world's population, but buys 45 percent of global toy production.[9] In 2004, U.S. children spent $35 billion of their own "pocket money" but influenced $670 billion of parental purchases.[10] Advertisers spend $15 billion annually marketing to children.[11] Children comprise three distinct market segments: (1) their own disposable income (*e.g.*, from allowances and after-school jobs), (2) influencing parents' income (*i.e.*, the "nag" factor"), and (3) future spending as they mature into adulthood (*i.e.*, creating brand loyalty now yields loyal customers tomorrow). Toyota paid for product placement of its Scion automobile in a social network aimed at 8–to–15-year-olds.[12] While obviously not planning to buy a Scion with their paper route earnings, these children could influence parents' decisions when it came time to buy the new family car and might become predisposed to Toyota's brand by the time they start driving.

Kids want to be seen as "cool." Since "coolness" is defined by peer pressure, advertisers use "*buzz marketing*" to get the coolest kids in a community (at school or online) to use or wear their product, creating a buzz about it among the target adolescent market. Online, this can take the form of posts in newsgroups, chat rooms, blogs, and social networks like Twitter.[13] Children and young adults of the Internet Generation, most of whom grew up playing interactive video games, are especially drawn to the Internet, not only because of its graphics, but because of its interactivity as contrasted with the unilateral experience of passively viewing TV. Savvy marketers create Web sites with interactive features, such as polls and Adobe Flash-based games to attract children while simultaneously marketing to them. Many games are product advertisements that reinforce logos and characters associated with the products, and the polls are used to elicit personal information from children for marketing purposes.[14] Some games tie product purchases into the game, *e.g.*, where a cereal company places coded coupons in specially marked boxes — the codes can then be used in the online games to provide a shield or weapon to a character.[15]

This shows children are a major market for advertisers, especially the Internet Generation, for whom screen time has replaced playtime. Advertisers crave data to target the kid market, whose naiveté combined with the power of a mass medium like the Internet poses the prospect of abusive collection and use of children's private information.

## Children's Online Privacy Protection Act (COPPA)

To address this issue, Congress passed the **Children's Online Privacy Protection Act (COPPA)**,[16] to regulate how sites collect and maintain children's personal information. **COPPA** applies to a site if it is "directed at children" or that "knows it is collecting information from children." The Act defines a "child" as under age 13, which leaves open the door for data collection from teens 13–to–17 years old. The only Internet-specific U.S. federal privacy law, **COPPA** applies only to commercial sites and not to nonprofit sites. It requires the site:

- Provide parents with notice of its information practices: *what* information is collected, *how* it is used, and *to whom* it may be disclosed
- Obtain prior verifiable parental consent to collect, use, or disclose personal information *before* collecting it from a child
- Provide parents, on request, a right to *view* information submitted by the child
- Provide parents the opportunity to *refuse to permit further use*, maintenance, or future collection of the child's personal information
- Limit personal information collection required to partake in games or prize offers
- Provide reasonable procedures to protect the confidentiality, security, and integrity of personal information received

Under **COPPA**, a site must provide notice of information collection practices, linked from its home page and on each page where information from children is collected. It must get verifiable parental consent before collecting, using, or disclosing any child's information. In addition to collecting information from online forms, under **COPPA** "collection" also encompasses permitting children to post messages in a chat room or on a message board, and providing them with e-mail accounts or instant messaging.

Companies have been fined by the FTC for **COPPA** violations.[17] Mrs. Fields Cookies was fined $100,000 for knowingly collecting personal information from more than 84,000 children under age 13 without obtaining parental consent.[18] The company had set up a site aimed at children by promoting birthday clubs and had stated "only children 12 years old or younger may participate."[19] On joining, children were mailed a birthday greeting and a coupon for a free pretzel or cookie.

Should children's Social Security numbers be required for an art contest? Google required children entering its Doodle-4-Google competition to include a parental consent form that asked for the child's date and place of birth, details about the parents, and the last four digits of the child's SSN.[20] Google removed the four-digit requirement from the consent form after a complaint to the FTC.

Some sites have stopped collecting information from children, citing **COPPA** compliance as too burdensome; but sites do not need verifiable parental consent if responding directly on a one-time basis to a child and not retaining the information, or if reasonably necessary to protect a child's safety or the site's security and integrity.

## COPPA and COPA

**COPPA** should not be confused with **COPA**. **COPPA**, the **Children's Online Privacy Protection Act**, is valid and enforced by the FTC, as you may recall from Chapter 10, where the FTC claimed Toysmart had violated **COPPA** by collecting children's personal information without parental consent. **COPA** is the **Child Online Protection Act**, which makes it a federal crime to use the Web to communicate for "commercial purposes" material "harmful to minors."[21] The Third Circuit ruled **COPA** violated the First Amendment; the U.S. Supreme Court did not go that far, but has blocked **COPA** from being applied.[22] **COPA** is discussed in greater detail in Chapter 17.

### To Catch A Predator

There is a predator behind every keyboard and monitor, intent on luring every innocent child online to an offline rendezvous for nefarious sexual encounter, if one believes the spate of TV and newspaper reports. It is sensational, it is shocking, it is horrifying — it is also not true. That is not to say there might not be isolated instances, but studies and experts agree on two points: today's kids are not naive when it comes to the threat of online sexual predators, and most child abductions occur offline not by strangers but by one who knows the victim (often a relative).[23] TV shows like Dateline NBC's "*To Catch a Predator*" have fueled the flames of "predator panic" but the reality is any widespread threat of online sexual predators is greatly exaggerated. Rachel Dretzin, co-producer, co-director, and writer of the 2008 PBS documentary "*Growing Up Online*", reported children of the Internet Generation are savvy when it comes to predators. She related her film crew's experience, finding kids were highly suspicious and hesitant to talk to unknown adults online and would not contemplate "real world" contact with online strangers.[24]

On rare occasions when a minor is sexually abused by someone she met online, parents usually seek to sue the Web site or social network that facilitated the introduction. In 2008, MySpace was sued by a girl and her mother who claimed it should be liable for a sexual assault on the daughter by a 19-year-old man she met on MySpace. The plaintiffs argued MySpace should have had a technology in place to prevent minors from creating profiles on the social network. The court correctly held there was such a technology already in place, called "parents." It noted although MySpace's Terms and Conditions limited site use to persons over 14, automatically defaulted profiles of users ages 14–to–15 to "private", and used a computer program to weed out underage members who lied about their age, ultimately responsibility for supervising and controlling children's actions rested with parents.[25] Here, the 13-year-old had lied about her age on her profile, stating she was 18, enabling her to circumvent all the site safety features; so while MySpace did have safety features in place, it was the plaintiff's own actions that rendered them ineffective. As reported in the trial court transcript:[26]

> THE COURT: I want to get this straight. You have a 13-year-old girl who lies, disobeys all of the instructions, later on disobeys the warning not to give personal information, obviously, [and] does not communicate with the parent. More important, the parent does not exercise the parental control over the minor. The minor gets sexually abused, and you want somebody else to pay for it? This is the lawsuit that you filed?

Age verification is an important factor in protecting children online, but as seen in the MySpace example, many age-related safeguards can be bypassed by a crafty kid who lies about her age. The FTC has said it will not hold site owners liable under **COPPA** unless they could have determined the child was under 13 from other factors. Some sites require a credit card number for access, but this is a flawed approach because (1) some adults lack credit cards; (2) in some countries, credit cards are issued to individuals under 18; and (3) if a social network targets ages 13–up (assuming it excludes those under 13 to avoid **COPPA** issues), the 13–to–17 market segment will not have credit cards. Dozens of age verification firms have formed, but privacy advocates charge they collect children's personal information (*e.g.*, birth date, address, school, and gender) not merely for age verification but also to help Web firms tailor ads directed to children (discussed below).[27]

## Web Monitoring Software

Some parents wishing to keep tabs on children's online lives, discreetly, have turned to monitoring software — spyware they can install to record their kids' chats on Yahoo!, MSN, AOL and other chat services. EchoMetrix's Sentry software even records private chats and instant messages. But is the fox guarding the henhouse? What parents using Sentry did not know — because EchoMetrix did not directly tell them — was its spyware sent back data on what kids were saying to them as well, which they sold to marketers to tailor ads to kids.[28] EchoMetrix claimed compliance with **COPPA** by stating in its Terms of Use agreement it has "a parent's permission to share the information if the user is a child under age 13." So, by using the software, the parent is assumed to have read and agreed to the Terms of Use, which allow sharing the information collected with… whom? A parent might assume the language refers to EchoMetrix sharing the data with them. But EchoMetrix is referring, presumably, to its data-mining service called Pulse that mines the teen chatter collected by Sentry. Pulse snoops on private chats and collects snippets from instant messages, blogs, social networks, message boards, and chat rooms.[29] EchoMetrix amassed a database of more than 132 million teen conversations.[30] On the other side, client corporations enter keywords (like their products) and get back a "word cloud" display of frequently used phrases and snippets of chats. This tells them what the buzz is among teens about new products, upcoming movies, games or fashion trends.[31] In 2010, EchoMetrix settled with the FTC over charges it failed to inform parents information it was collecting about their children would be disclosed to third-party marketers.[32]

In Chapter 10, we discussed Web sites using cookies and Web beacons to track visitors for behavioral marketing purposes. An investigative report revealed children's Web sites may install far more tracking software than sites whose content is aimed at adults.[33] The survey found they employed 30 percent more *cookies* and *Web beacons* on popular children's sites. The FTC is reviewing **COPPA** and some changes under consideration are expanding the definition of "personal information" to include data "collected in connection with online behavioral advertising" and changing a portion of the definition of "collects or collection" to include "passive tracking of a child online."[34]

## Inappropriate Misappropriation?

A trend has emerged where commercial sites engage minors (often preteens) to model skimpy swimsuits, ostensibly to pander to pedophiles. These sites stay within the law by not allowing nudity, although they feature young boys in bikini briefs and girls wearing thongs, often posing provocatively. Some sites have taken this a step further, dispensing with paying for models and simply photographing their subjects in public places. One example is the news report of a California woman who complained a photograph of her 13-year-old son in a tight-fitting bikini brief style swimsuit appeared on an adult Web site filled with "lewd comments."[35] This might raise questions of obscenity or misappropriation, but such images are not obscene, and if shot at a public place or event, they are protected by the First Amendment. A similar situation arose when high school pole-vaulter Allison Stokke, of Orange County, California, received a torrent of unwanted publicity, becoming an Internet sensation after many blogs and Web sites posted photographs, without her consent, of her competing in a spandex uniform with bare midriff. A Yahoo! search query returned 310,000 results for her name, her MySpace page received more than 1,000 new messages after the first picture appeared, and a three-minute YouTube video of Stokke commenting on her performance after a meet was viewed 150,000 times (up to 2.1 million views at the time of this book's writing).[36] Stokke had not sought the publicity and reportedly resented the prurient nature of it, as it focused more on her physical attractiveness than on her abilities as a pole vaulter.

## Social Interaction in the Cyber-Environment

The World Wide Web was created as a cyber-environment for the exchange of ideas, communication, and eventually for entertainment and commerce. But with the rise of topic-specific forums, and later, social networks, complete strangers connected with one another, forming "cyberfriendships", often with deep emotional bonds. These friendships were formed within the framework of a cybercommunity, either though a forum where members shared a common interest (*e.g.*, pet lovers; support group) or a social network of similar persons (*e.g.*, students). One survey found more than 40 percent rated their cyberfriends equally as important as their real world friends.[37] This makes sense when one pictures the cyberfriend as a real person sitting in front of a computer somewhere far away. However, a more cynical observer would argue a cyberfriend is a cipher; without having personally met the cyberfriend, everything one knows about the friend could be false, since the only source of information comes from the cyberfriend himself.

With the advent of Massively Multiplayer Online (MMO) games, (*e.g.*, "Second Life") a new level has been added to the cyber-environment. Players choose avatars to represent them in interactive pseudo-lifelike games in vivid fantasy worlds where they, through avatars, often engage in violent or socially objectionable behavior. Psychologists disagree on whether this encourages similar behavior in real life; some argue it has no effect and others contend it may serve as a positive way to let off steam and aggressive feelings.[38]

It is against this backdrop children's online social interactions must be viewed. Often, they view their audience not as complete strangers, but as intimate friends, even part of their own support network. And after all, you can tell your friends everything, right?

### "Show And Tell" on the Internet

COPPA applies to commercial sites directed at children under 13 (preteens). That is why social networks aimed at teenagers and young adults prohibit members under 13. However, COPPA does not apply to those in their teen years, 13–to–17 (the "COPPA Gap"). That may put teens at even greater risk than younger children, because neither the collection of their personal information nor its disclosure is regulated or protected. These teens' privacy rests solely on the particular Web site's privacy policy and on their own judgment in what they disclose online (Recall the XY Magazine case in Chapter 10).

In grade school, "Show and Tell" was a daily ritual where students shared intimate details of their personal or home lives with classmates, often accompanied by the occasional prop (*e.g.*, a stuffed animal, favorite toy, or science project gone awry). Today, "Show and Tell" has moved from the classroom to the Web and the audience has become anyone in the world who wishes to tune in. Andy Warhol's promise of "15 minutes of fame" seems outdated in our culture of Web pages, uploadable photos, Webcams, blogs, vlogs, Facebook, YouTube, and Twitter. Children voluntarily post a wide array of personal information for all to see. Often, they do not stop to think others besides their intended friends will be able to view this information; or they may not care who views it. On the following pages, we will review what they are posting, where they are posting it, and whether this is a good or bad thing.

### What Kids are Posting

Children, as any parent will attest, have a weird view of privacy. They will pen their most intimate thoughts in a poem and bring it to school to read before classmates, but should their mother stumble across it while cleaning their bedroom, outraged teenaged cries of "how dare you invade my privacy" will reverberate throughout the neighborhood. The same teens who hide their diaries under the mattress, lest their darkest secrets and teen angst be revealed to the eyes of prying parents, routinely publish the same words on their blogs for the whole world — friends and strangers — to read. As John Maggio, co-producer and co-director of the 2008 PBS documentary *Growing Up Online*" has said, we live in an era where it is now culturally acceptable for teens to pour their most private selves out into an anonymous universe.[39] For example, the following excerpts from various teenage blogs:[40]

> ["I'm 14 and I'm gay. I'm out to everyone, except my parents."] ... ["Looking for 420-friendly[41] friends"] ... ["That was close! His mom almost walked in while I was giving him a blow job!"] ... ["I tried to kill myself last night. Guess I didn't take enough pills because I'm still here, lol."] ... ["Well, this is the first time I have admitted in public that I am bi. I wonder if my parents will find out and if they will be upset. I guess I don't care — I am who I am."] ... ["I had a horrible day. I was asked to leave (name deleted) Christian Academy. You know why, because I am a faggot. Yeah isn't that the sickest thing you have ever heard. You know what the most fucked up part about it is? They found out from my Myspace profile."]

Teens are active bloggers and heavy users of social networks, often posting their names, addresses, phone numbers, school names, and even their school schedules. Personally identifiable information is not all they reveal; they also post photographs of themselves — girls wearing thongs and bikinis in provocative poses and shirtless boys in boxers or bikini briefs, with sexually-charged captions. Some profiles have more cleavage and crotches than a Victoria's Secret catalog. Many parents do not know their children belong to social networks. An MSNBC reporter interviewed one who, after discovering her daughter's MySpace profile, said, "I sat my daughter down and said, 'Do you realize how inappropriate and how dangerous this is? Here's your face. Here's the town you come from. Do you realize how many sick people are out there?'"[42]

Many teenagers are natural exhibitionists craving attention and a voyeuristic aspect to the Web draws teens to seek out and view their peers. But can this go too far? Justin.tv is a site where users broadcast live video from their Webcams to the Internet. In late 2008, a 19-year-old, egged on by chat room posters, committed suicide while broadcasting himself on Justin. tv. The Ft. Lauderdale, Florida teen overdosed on pills on camera, as he was mocked by some viewers. One viewer contacted the police, who broke into the teen's room and found his body. [43]

The latest exhibitionist craze among teens, in addition to undressing and performing sex acts on their Webcams on chat sites like Stikam, is *sexting*, a play on the phrase "texting". Instead of sending text messages on their mobile phones, teens now snap and send nude or semi-nude photographs of themselves to other teens, sometimes to flirt and other times to harass (see the discussion of cyberbullying in Chapter 18). With the growth of social networks and the ubiquitousness of mobile phones with cameras, sexting has become a concern for parents and schools. Impulsively, teens often neglect to consider the consequences of their actions; once the "send" button is pressed, the photo is passed on to other hands, who can copy and resend it, as can all the recipients, indefinitely. Once disseminated, the photo cannot be retrieved and copies may always exist, poised to resurface at any time in the future, damaging careers or relationships.

Children as young as 13 have engaged in sexting. A survey found 20 percent of U.S. teens admitted sexting nude or semi-nude self-photos to others; 39 percent sent sexually suggestive messages; and 48 percent had received such messages. [44] Most send photos to boyfriends or girlfriends, but they risk the photograph being passed along to others, especially after a breakup. Even "High School Musical" star and teen actress Vanessa Hudgens' self-taken nude photos, meant for her boyfriend, found their way online. [45]

Sexting has attracted state prosecutors' attention, who have filed child pornography charges against both teens who sent their nude photos and teenage recipients. The charge is a serious felony that could append the phrase "sex offender" to a juvenile's official record or list them in a state's sex offenders registry. In Fort Wayne, Indiana, a teen who allegedly sexted a photograph of his genitalia faced felony obscenity charges, while in Newark, Ohio, a 15-year-old girl was charged child pornography for allegedly sexting her photo from her mobile phone to classmates (the charges were later dropped when she entered a juvenile program); and in Greensboro, Pennsylvania, prosecutors charged three high school girls who allegedly sexted semi-nude photos, and four boys who allegedly received them, with child pornography (reduced to a misdemeanor charge for all but one). [46] In Massachusetts, six teens — one only 13 — faced felony charges for allegedly sending and receiving a photo of a female classmate exposing her breast. [47] New Jersey prosecutors charged a 14-year-old girl who posted sexually explicit photographs of herself on MySpace with possession and distribution of child pornography. [48] Two 18-year-olds, one in Iowa and the other in Florida, were placed on state sex offenders registries for sexting. [49] The Iowa teen was convicted of distributing obscene materials to a minor after sexting a photograph of his penis to a 14-year-old female friend who had requested it. The Florida teen was charged with distributing child pornography, after breaking up with his 16-year-old girlfriend, and sexting her nude photos to dozens of friends and her parents.

Should minors be charged with felony child pornography for sending semi-nude and nude photos of themselves to their friends? Should a surprised recipient of unsolicited photos be charged with possession of child pornography? Should teens with poor judgment be treated as sex offenders? Is the criminal justice system the best venue for these cases or is this a case of society and the law not keeping pace with technology? Nebraska, Utah, and Vermont have reduced penalties for teens who engage in sexting.[50] In 2009, a federal appellate court ruled a district attorney could not file criminal charges against three girls in a sexting case. The prosecutor had threatened to charge children as young as 11, who appeared "scantily clothed" (including two girls, ages 12 and 13, wearing bras at a slumber party) in the photos but did not send or receive them.[51]

One girl in that case sued the Scranton, Pennsylvania high school, the school district, county, prosecutors, and a detective. Allegedly, the 17-year-old was in class, debating whether to sext her photo to her boyfriend when a teacher confiscated her phone. The lawsuit alleged the principal illegally searched her phone, found nude photos she had taken of herself, and turned the phone over to prosecutors. There is no evidence the photos were ever sent or received. The plaintiff noted with irony the only "distribution" of the photos occurred when they were printed out and passed around by school officials and the prosecutor, stating in her complaint: "I was absolutely horrified and humiliated to learn that school officials, men in the DA's office, and police had seen naked pictures of me."[52] One press report describes the prosecutor lining up the teens and their parents to view the photos, printed onto index cards, and the 17-year-old's realization the prosecutor and other investigators had seen them, as might the crowd around her. The report quotes her saying, "I think the worst punishment is knowing that all you old guys saw me naked. I just think you guys are all just perverts."[53]      The photos merely resided in storage on the mobile phone, as they might on a student's laptop. The case raises a Fourth Amendment issue of whether school officials can confiscate and search through a student's phone or laptop. Does the student have a reasonable expectation of privacy in an electronic device, or is this akin to a school searching student lockers? (Note, lockers, while used by students, are school property, whereas the electronic devices are the students' property. Also, it may be more reasonable to condone a search of a physical container for contraband such as drugs or guns, than a search of a phone or camera.). The ACLU contended school officials aare mistaken in their belief they have the right to search through mobile phones whenever a student misuses one, arguing schools have the right to confiscate but not search it.[54] The plaintiff's complaint argued mobile phones "have become one of the most important storage devices for private material" and "phones belonging to high school students cannot be searched without 'reasonable suspicion'."[55] However, that proposition may be questionable in light of _United States v. Arnold_, allowing customs searches of laptops without reasonable suspicion, discussed earlier in Chapter 9.[56]

One of the biggest dangers of sexting is loss of control over the photographs once they have been sent. The photo could end up in an unlimited number of hands and circulate on the Internet forever. A 16-year-old Wisconsin girl learned this when her ex-boyfriend allegedly posted nude mobile phone photos she had sent him on his MySpace page. The 17-year-old boy was charged with child pornography, sexual exploitation of a child, and defamation.[57] Some Syracuse, New York teenagers sent nude mobile phone photos to their boyfriends and later discovered another enterprising boy had downloaded them and was trying to sell them as a DVD collection.[58] Jessica Logan, an 18-year-old Cincinnati, Ohio teen, had sent nude self-photos to her boyfriend; after they broke up, he allegedly circulated them to other girls at their high school. These girls began harassing and taunting her, until she became deeply depressed and killed herself.[59] In 2009, in Tampa, Florida, 13-year-old Hope Witsell hanged herself after taunting by classmates. She had sent her nude photo to a boy she liked, and a girl used his phone to forward it to other students.[60]

Authorities are concerned about a side effect of sexting: online sexual extortion. Sexting teens are being contacted by blackmailers who threaten to expose their behavior to friends and family unless they pose for more explicit photographs or videos. Some have labeled this "sextortion." Several recent high-profile examples include an Alabama man convicted of sending threatening e-mails on Facebook and MySpace extorting nude photographs from more than 50 young women in Alabama, Pennsylvania, and Missouri; an 18-year-old Wisconsin man was convicted of posing as a girl on Facebook, tricking 31 male high school classmates into sending him nude photos of themselves, and then threatening to post them online and send them to their Facebook friends unless they performed sex acts on him; and a California man was charged with extortion after allegedly hacking into more than 200 computers and threatening to expose nude photographs he had found unless their owners (44 of whom were minors) posed for sexually explicit videos. Prosecutors said he also remotely activated some victims' Webcams without their knowledge and recorded them undressing or having sex. [61]

The law can only be expected to do so much. Parents have to take a proactive role by examining children's online profiles to see if they are too detailed or if their photographs are provocative. Rather than insisting legislators over-regulate the Internet with potentially unconstitutional laws aimed at protecting children, parents should discover who their children's cyberfriends are. To whom are they talking and what are they disclosing? Just as parents lock their house to keep strangers out, they should instruct their children to "lock" their profiles to keep strangers out; most social networks allow users to set profiles to "private" to control viewing access.

## Where Kids are Posting

While some kids set up Web pages, either through their own URLs or a free service like Yahoo!, most use *blogs* or social networks. Popular blogging sites like LiveJournal, Xanga, Blogspot, and Blogger are basically online diaries with a global audience, although some have a feature to limit readers to preselected "friends." One study showed 51.5 percent of blogs were written by teenagers (ages 13 – 19) and described the typical blogger as a teenage girl blogging "twice a month to update her friends and classmates on happenings in her life." [62]

*Social networks* popular with teens include MySpace, Facebook, Twitter, Formspring, and Bebo (in the U.K.). [63] Whereas a blog is merely an online diary, a social network offers a personalized Web page with a user profile that may contain not only a blog but personal information (*e.g.*, name, nicknames, screen names, age, birth date, birthplace, current city and state, schools attended, hobbies and interests, brief biographies, instant messaging contact information, and e-mail addresses), uploaded photographs, links to friends' profiles, and comments by friends. A popular student's profile may have links to her entire class. Even if a teenager is careful not to include personally identifiable information on his profile, friends may inadvertently reveal such information in comments they post to his page. For example, "Happy Birthday today, David, how's it feel to be 15? I hear you're going to celebrate at Fisherman's Wharf tonight!" We now know the student is a 15-year-old boy named David, whose birth date was 15 years ago this day, and he lives in San Francisco, California. A click on the poster's name opens his profile, revealing him as a classmate of "David's" at Pope Pius IX High School. So we can now extrapolate the neighborhood David lives in, the school he attends, and his religion. Think what a stranger could learn from a few more comments like this.

## Is it a Good or Bad Thing?

While some studies contend teenagers reveal too much personal information on blogs and social networks, fears of an army of child predators ensconced on sites like MySpace may be more media-fueled mass hysteria than truth. Even the MSNBC report above admits the "article could not cite a single case of a child predator hunting for and finding a child through a blog."[64] Not to say at some point, somewhere, there will not be such a situation; it is equally likely a determined predator would find such information in a school newspaper, yearbook, or other offline source.

There are positive aspects to teenage social networking. Shy children often develop new friends more easily online than offline. Socially outcast teens, considered nerds or geeks at school, form meaningful friendships online with others like themselves. A gay teen in a small rural conservative town may find solace and support from a sympathetic gay teen in a liberal city across the country. Students at all-girls and all-boys schools can create a virtual coed environment and develop friends of the opposite gender that would not be possible in their school social settings. Blogs and social networks can play an important role by connecting teens and helping them learn to express themselves. Teens often debate current events, on topics as diverse as religion, homosexuality, war, and politics. By conversing with peers from all walks of life and from literally the four corners of the globe, teenagers are exposed to differing views and perspectives and challenged to think and re-evaluate their own views.

Surprisingly, social networks can serve as an outlet for collective group grief. More than ever, teens are encountering peer loss, whether through suicide, drunk driving, school shootings, gang violence, AIDS, drug overdoses, or accidents. When a teen skateboarder was killed by a drunk driver, his classmates created a photo montage of him set to music in a video, uploaded it to YouTube, and then linked the video memorial to play from each of their MySpace profiles.[65] They also posted "farewell" comments on the student's own profile, turning his MySpace page into a highly emotional shrine to the memory of their deceased friend — and serving as a mass cathartic outlet for teens sharing, and trying to cope with, a common grief.[66]

**Chapter 11 Notes**

[1] Benjamin Svetkey, "Soupy's Greenmail Scandal," Entertainment Weekly, January 8, 1993.

[2] Michael Brody, spokesperson for the American Academy of Child and Adolescent Psychiatry. *See* Susan Gregory Thomas, "Pushing Products to Young Consumers," U.S. News & World Report, June 23, 1997).

[3] "Special Issues for Young Children," *available at* www.media-awareness.ca/english/parents/marketing/issues_kids_marketing.cfm (accessed Mar. 23, 2012).

[4] The "sea monkeys" were actually brine shrimp.

[5] American Academy of Pediatrics and surveys by the nonprofit Kaiser Family Foundation.

[6] Richard Zoglin, "Is TV Ruining Our Children?" Time magazine, October 15, 1990.

[7] Donnell Alexander and Aliza Dichter, "Ads and Kids: How Young is Too Young?" *was available at* www.mediachannel.org/atissue/consumingkids/index.shtml (accessed July 1, 2009) but no longer available.

[8] Renuka Rayasam, "They'll Pay to Have Ads Put on Shells? Egg-cellent!" U.S. News & World Report, November 5, 2006.

[9] Juliet B. Schor, "Born to Buy: The Commercialized Child and the New Consumer Culture" (Scribner 2004).

[10] *Ibid.*

[11] *Ibid.*

[12] Julie Bosman, "Hey, Kid, You Want to Buy a Toyota Scion?" The New York Times, June 14, 2006.

[13] "How Marketers Target Kids," Media Awareness Network, *available at* www.media-awareness.ca/english/parents/marketing/marketers_target_kids.cfm (accessed Mar. 23, 2012).

[14] Adrian Humphreys, "Internet Marketing Targets Children," The Edmonton Journal, July 3, 1997.

[15] Marni Goldberg, "Is It a Game or an Advertisement?" The Chicago Tribune, July 20, 2006. *See also* Janet Raloff, "How Advertising is Becoming Child's Play," Science News Online, July 29, 2006, *available at* www.commercialexploitation.org/news/advertisingischildsplay.htm (accessed Mar. 23, 2012).

[16] The Children's Online Privacy Protection Act (COPPA), 15 U.S.C. § 6501, *et seq.*

[17] *See United States v. Lisa Frank, Inc.*, No. 01-1516-A (E.D. Va. 2001) ($30,000 civil penalty — site targeted girls under age 13 and collected registration information including name, birth date, and favorite color); *United States v. BigMailbox.com, Inc.*, No. 01-605-A (E.D. Va. 2001) (consent decree for $35,000 civil penalty); *United States v. Looksmart, Ltd.*, No. 01-606-A (E.D. Va. 2001) (consent decree for $35,000 civil penalty); and *United States v. The Ohio Art Co.*, No. 027203 (N.D. Ohio 2002) (consent decree for $35,000 civil penalty).

[18] FTC press release, February 27, 2003, *available at* www.ftc.gov/opa/2003/02/hersheyfield.htm (accessed Mar. 23, 2012).

[19] *United States v. Mrs. Fields Famous Brands, Inc.*, Civ. Action No. 2:03 cv205 (D. Ut. 2003).

[20] The nine-digit SSN consists of three parts: area numbers (the first three digits), group numbers (the next two digits), and serial numbers (the last four digits). Prior to 1982, the area numbers represented the state in which a person first applied for a Social Security card. Since 1972, the SSA has assigned area numbers using the ZIP code provided by the applicant. While the area number state might not be the same as the state of birth, it often is, meaning an individual's place and year of birth together with the last four digits of the SSN might yield a complete SSN. *See* Bob Bowdon, "Why Has Google Been Collecting Kids' Social Security Numbers under the Guise of an Art Contest?" The Huffington Post, February 22, 2011, *available at* www.huffingtonpost.com/bob-bowdon/why-has-google-been-colle_b_825754.html (accessed Mar. 23, 2012) *and* Chris Matyszczyk, "Why Did Google Ask for Kids' Social Security Numbers?" CNET News.com, February 22, 2011. The original form is *available at* www.bowdonmedia.com/doc/Doodle4Google_ConsentRules_2011original.pdf (accessed Mar. 23, 2012).

[21] The Child Online Protection Act (COPA), 47 U.S.C. § 223, *et seq.*

[22] *ACLU v. Reno*, 31 F. Supp. 2d 473 (E.D. Pa. 1999), aff'd 217 F.3d 162 (3ᵈ Cir. 2000), vacated and remanded *Ashcroft v. ACLU*, 533 U.S. 564 (2002), aff'd *ACLU v. Ashcroft*, 322 F.3d 240 (2003), aff'd *Ashcroft v. ACLU*, 542 U.S. 656, on remand *ACLU v. Gonzales*, Case No. 98-559 (E.D. Pa. 2007), aff'd *ACLU v. Mukasey*, Case No. 07-2539 (3ᵈ Cir. 2008).

[23] Janet Kornblum, "The Net is a Circuit of Safety Concerns," USA Today, November 8, 2007; *see also* Helen A.S. Popkin, "The Secret Lives of Your Kids Online: New Technology Serves Impetuous Youth, Much to the Chagrin of Parents," MSNBC, September 17, 2008.

[24] Rachel Dretzin, *"Growing Up Online"*, *available at* www.pbs.org/wgbh/pages/frontline/kidsonline/etc/notebook.html (accessed Mar. 23, 2012). Rachel Dretzin is the co-producer, co-director, and writer of the 2008 PBS documentary *"Growing Up Online"* about how the Internet is transforming childhood. The documentary can be viewed on the site or ordered as a DVD.

[25] *Doe v. MySpace Inc.*, 528 F.3d 413 (5ᵗʰ Cir. 2008).

[26] *Ibid.* The court ruled the plaintiffs' negligence and gross negligence claims were barred by the Communications Decency Act (discussed at length in Chapter 14).

[27] Brad Stone, "Online Age Verification for Children Brings Privacy Worries," The New York Times, November 16, 2008, p. BU4.

[28] Juliana Gruenwald, "FTC Reaches Settlement with Firm over Use of Children's Data," The National Journal, November 30, 2010.

[29] Deborah Yao, "Web-monitoring Software Gathers Data on Kid Chats," Associated Press wire service report, September 4, 2009.

[30] Shannon Proudfoot, "Pulse of Teen Online Habits Makes Marketers' Dreams Come True," Canwest News Service, July 5, 2009.

[31] Yao, fn. 29, *supra.*

[32] Gruenwald, fn. 28, *supra.*

[33] According to a *Wall Street Journal* report. *See* Steve Stecklow, "On the Web, Children Face Intensive Tracking," The Wall Street Journal, September 17, 2010.

[34] Federal Registrar, "Children's Online Privacy Protection Rule: A Proposed Rule by the Federal Trade Commission on 09/27/2011," *available at* www.federalregister.gov/articles/2011/09/27/2011-24314/childrens-online-privacy-protection-rule#p-92 (accessed Mar. 23, 2012).

[35] Jim Sanders, "Law is Little Help to Parents Fighting Use of Children's Photos on Web," The Sacramento Bee, March 17, 2008.

[36] Eli Saslow, "Teen Tests Internet's Lewd Track Record," The Washington Post, p. A01, May 29, 2007. Video *available at* www.youtube.com/watch?v=zasPlQYZEHw (accessed Mar. 23, 2012).

[37] Annenberg School Center for the Digital Future at the University of Southern California survey. *See* Bernadine Healy, "Alone in a Parallel Life," U.S. News & World Report, May 21, 2007, p. 66.

[38] *Ibid.*

[39] John Maggio, *"Growing Up Online",* available at www.pbs.org/wgbh/pages/frontline/kidsonline/etc/notebook.html (accessed Mar. 23, 2012). *See* fn 24, *supra.*

[40] These quotes from teenage blogs, unlike all of the other quotes throughout this book, are deliberately unattributed to protect the identity of the minors who wrote them.

[41] Slang for pot smoking.

[42] Bob Sullivan, "Kids, Blogs and Too Much Information: Children Reveal More Online Than Parents Know," MSNBC, April 29, 2005, *available at* http://msnbc.msn.com/id/7668788 (accessed Mar. 23, 2012).

[43] Greg Sandoval, "Teen Commits Suicide on Justin.tv," CNET News.com, November 20, 2008.

[44] Belinda Goldsmith, "Safe" Sexting? No Such Thing, Teens Warned," Reuters wire service, May 4, 2009. The survey was commissioned by the National Campaign to Prevent Teen and Unplanned Pregnancy and CosmoGirl.com. The survey percentages included photographs uploaded to the Web, but that would account for a small number since most would be immediately deleted as violations of site Terms of Use agreements. The survey included text messages, IMs, and e-mail. A total of 1,280 teens (13-19) and young adults (20-26) were surveyed; 653 were teens and 627 were young adults, but the results were broken out separately. The survey is *available at* www.thenationalcampaign.org/sextech/PDF/SexTech_Summary.pdf (accessed Mar. 23, 2012).

[45] "Vanessa Hudgens Apologizes for Nude Photo," Associated Press wire service report, September 7, 2007.

[46] Martha Irvine, "Teens Who 'Sext' Racy Photos Charged with Porn," Associated Press wire service report, February 4, 2009.

[47] Emily Friedman, "'Sexting' Teens May Face Child Porn Charges," ABCNews.com, February 12, 2009.

[48] Tamar Lewis, "Rethinking Sex Offender Laws for Youth Texting," The New York Times, March 20, 2010.

[49] *Ibid.*

[50] *Ibid.*

[51] Dionne Searcey, "A Lawyer, Some Teens and a Fight over 'Sexting'," The Wall Street Journal, April 21, 2009.

[52] Shannon P. Duffy, "Student's Privacy Rights Violated in Pa. 'Sexting' Case, ACLU Suit Says," The Legal Intelligencer, May 21, 2010.

[53] Searcey, fn. 51, *supra.*

[54] Duffy, fn. 52, *supra.*

[55] *Ibid.*

[56] *United States v. Arnold*, 523 F.3d 941 (9th Cir. 2008).

[57] Stephanie Reitz, "Teens Sending Nude Photos via Cell Phones: Pictures Meant for Boyfriend or Girlfriend are Ending up on the Internet," Associated Press wire service report, June 4, 2008.

[58] *Ibid.*

[59] Mike Celizic, "Her Teen Committed Suicide over 'Sexting'," MSNBC.com, March 6, 2009.

[60] Libby Quaid, "Poll Finds Sexting Common among Young People," Associated Press wire service report, December 3, 2009.

[61] Charles Wilson, "Feds: Online 'Sextortion' of Teens on the Rise," Associated Press wire service report, August 15, 2010. *See also,* "Teen Accused of Sex Assaults in Facebook Scam," Associated Press wire service report, February 5, 2009.

[62] According to a Perseus Development Corp. 2003 study, "The Blogging Iceberg," Perseus Development Corp., *was available at* http://perseus.com/survey/resources/perseus_blogging_iceberg.pdf but no longer available.

[63] One survey found 20 percent of teens abandoning Facebook, ironically citing as one reason the presence of their parents on the social network. *See* Jennifer Van Grove, "Teens Experiencing Facebook Fatigue [STUDY]," Mashable.com, June 30, 2010, *available at* http://mashable.com/2010/06/30/teens-social-networks-study/ (accessed Mar. 23, 2012).

[64] MSNBC cited a Children's Digital Media Center study at Georgetown University; *see* Sullivan, fn. 38, *supra*.

[65] *Available at* http://youtube.com/watch?v=wls5zwHb1-s (accessed Mar. 23, 2012).

[66] *Available at* www.myspace.com/tylerlitton01 (accessed Mar. 23, 2012).

# CHAPTER

# 12

## SOCIAL NETWORKS

> This chapter looks at Social Networks, Reputation Management, and Social Media Monitoring.

*"When I took office, only high energy physicists had ever heard of what is called the World Wide Web. Now, even my cat has its own page." — President Bill Clinton*

The rise of social networks has led to concerns over defamation, privacy, safety of children, and marketing techniques. In 2011, there were 2.4 billion social networking accounts worldwide.[1] As the number and variety of social networks expand exponentially, new fields such as Reputation Management and Social Media Monitoring are taking on increasing importance.

## Social Networks

In the mid-1990s, three college students devised a game called *"Six Degrees of Kevin Bacon"* showing every actor could be linked to actor Kevin Bacon within six steps.[2] The game was based on the John Guare play and movie adaptation *"Six Degrees of Separation"*, which theorized every individual is connected by six or fewer stages of circumstance or acquaintance. The idea relationships between individuals can be mapped like an infinitely expansive geometric progression was the basis for the establishment of social networking sites. If "A" has a circle of 10 friends or "contacts" (let us call them $B_1$ through $B_{10}$) as does each of the 10 "B"s (let us call them $C_1$ through $C_{100}$) then that means "A" now has 100 "friend of a friend" contacts. By trading on her own relationship with "B", "A" can gain instant credibility with 100 individuals who would otherwise be strangers. From a business perspective, this network creates instant entrée for "A" among any of the "C"s, as a close friend or business associate of one of their own close friends or business associates. One is more likely to do business with someone who knows or is referred by a mutual acquaintance than with a stranger. In a social environment, many individuals feel more at ease dating a "friend of a friend" than a complete stranger. Thus, by listing only 10 contacts, "A"'s business or social network of three degrees contains 110 contacts

(10 "B"s and 100 "C"s). Now if each "C" were to add 10 names (let us call them $D_1$ through $D_{1000}$) to the network, the size of the network would increase exponentially to 1,110 contacts (10 "B"s and 100 "C"s and 1,000 "D"s). Extending this concept to five degrees increases the contact list to 11,110 (10 "B"s, 100 "C"s, 1,000 "D"s, and 10,000 "E"s) and going to the full six degrees yields 111,110 contacts in A's social network (10 "B"s, 100 "C"s, 1,000 "D"s, 10,000 "E"s, and 100,000 "F"s). Of course, this is based on 10 names per person; a greater number would produce an even larger exponential result.

A number of Web firms realized the tremendous advantage to social networking and established sites, such as Friendster and LinkedIn, where individuals could start their own social networks by inviting contacts to register through the site. Then, individuals related by varying degrees within the common network could see and contact each other, though most were strangers to each other.

What possible liability might ensue, if any, from the creation of such social networks? In our litigious society, it is not hard to imagine a scenario where, regardless of the legal validity of such a lawsuit, a claim could arise where "$B_{10}$" through a social network meets and is date-raped by "$E_{27}$" or where "$C_{78}$" hires "$F_{1212}$" who ends up embezzling from "$C_{78}$." Or perhaps the Web site would also be named as a party in such a lawsuit. While the legal foundation for such liability would appear shaky (indeed, seismically so), it would not be the first time a specious lawsuit made its way through the court system draining thousands of dollars from defendants forced to defend against such claims.[3]

The most successful social networks have carved out a niche. The preteen set can play games at Club Penguin; migrate to Xanga during junior high; switch to MySpace in high school; join the college crowd at Facebook; and after graduation, network with their peers at LinkedIn. A 2005 survey showed MySpace had the broadest appeal across all age ranges: a quarter of its users were teens (12-to-17) but a year later that percentage had dropped by more than half, while adult (35-to-54) membership had risen to comprise 40 percent.[4] According to a 2006 survey of four social networks (MySpace, Facebook, Xanga, and Friendster), the largest member age group was 35-to-54 years old, making up between 33.5-to-40.6 percent of the sites' membership. The 12-to-17 age range accounted for 9.6 percent of all Internet users but a huge 20.3 percent of Xanga membership. The 18-to-24 age range accounted for 11.3 percent of all Internet users but a significant 34 percent of Facebook. The 24-to-34 age range accounted for 14.5 percent of all Internet users but a sizable 28.2 percent of Friendster. The 35-to-54 age range accounted for 38.5 percent of Internet users and was evenly distributed across all of the sites. The over-55 age range accounted for 18 percent of Internet users but single digit membership in most of the studied social networks.[5]

Contrary to popular belief, social networks are not primarily the stomping grounds of kids. They are used to a greater degree by adults, often as a business networking tool. However, some businesses complain about lost worker productivity due to employees spending too much time on Facebook. An Australian study found Facebook users potentially cost employers up to $4 billion annually.[6]

But there are social networks specifically aimed at kids. Club Penguin, a 12 million member site targeting the 8-to-14 age range, blends interactive gaming with social networking. Children joining Club Penguin interact through a customized penguin avatar. The site, launched in 2005, is child safety-oriented, employing filtering software to prevent children

## List of Social Networks

- ANobii (Books)
- Bebo (United Kingdom)
- BlackPlanet (African-American)
- Blogster (Blogging)
- Buzznet (Music and Pop Culture)
- Club Penguin (MMO for Kids)
- CouchSurfing (Travelers)
- CyWorld (South Korean)
- Delicious (Social Bookmarking)
- deviantART (Artists)
- Daily Motion (Video)
- Digg (Social Bookmarking)
- Eons (Baby Boomers)
- Facebook (General)
- Flickr (Photo sharing)
- Formspring (Social Q-and-A Site for Teens)
- Foursquare (Location-based Mobile)
- Friendster (redesigned as a Social Gaming Network in June 2011)
- FuBar (Dating)
- Goodreads (Books)
- Habbo (Teens)
- hi5 (Latin American)
- Hyves (Dutch)
- LibraryThing (Books)
- LinkedIn (Business and Professional Networking)
- Live Journal (Blogging)
- Mixi (Japanese)
- MySpace (General)
- Ning (User-created Networking)
- Orkut (Brazilian site owned by Google)
- Plaxo (Business and Professional Networking)
- Qzone (China)
- Renren (Chinese network formerly known as Xiaonei)
- Second Life (Virtual World Gaming)
- Shelfari (Books)
- Skyrock (French)
- Stikam (Live Video Streaming and Chat)
- StudiVZ (German)
- Tuenti (Spain-based, Invitation-only Private Network for Students)
- Twitter (Micro-blogging)
- WeRead (Books)
- Xanga (Blogging)
- YouTube (Video)

Figure 16-1

from disclosing e-mail addresses and phone numbers, or using profanity. Members inhabit an arctic virtual world where they play games, chat, or ski with other penguins in a "virtual sandbox." Penguins chat through word balloons above their heads, using either a list of pre-approved phrases or filtered chat software. They can ask another penguin "boy or girl?" and exchange virtual hearts or flowers in hope of attracting a little penguin boyfriend or girlfriend.[7] Club Penguin members play arcade style games, where they can win "coins" to buy accessories (*e.g.*, clothes, pets, or furniture) for their penguin or igloo (all penguins get a virtual igloo on their home page). In preparation for real life, the more toys a penguin has, the more popular he becomes with other penguins. A penguin clothed in attire no longer available for purchase can expect to be flooded with "friend requests" and virtual "postcards." Club Penguin makes money through subscriptions rather than advertising. Only subscribers can buy clothing or furniture; nonsubscribers can only have blue or red penguins (out of 13 possible colors).[8]

Most other social networks targeting children follow an advertising-based business model. One let advertisers do product placement in its virtual world, offering kids a chance to drive virtual Toyota Scions or append a mermaid tail to their avatar's body in advance of a "*Walt Disney's The Little Mermaid*" promotion (see Chapter 11).

Facebook had 800 million users worldwide in 2011,[9] having taken away significant market share from competing social networks based in markets outside the United States.[10] Bebo, with 117 million members as of 2010,[11] is Facebook's U.K. competitor, while across the Channel in France, Skyrock is battling the American social networking giant, having lost a third of its users to Facebook.[12] Skyrock had about 11 million members in 2010, about half of Facebook's share of the French market.[13] With 56 million users, hi5 is the number one social network in 25 countries across Latin America, Europe, Asia and Africa, and is available in 24 languages[14] German network StudiVZ, with 16.5 million users as of 2010, the once premier social network in Germany, Austria, and Switzerland, has ceded its reign to Facebook.[15] StudiVZ is a collection of three networks, including one for students and another for nonstudents. The fact its name identifies it as a student social network, along with outdated technology and a German language interface account for its continuing market share loss to rival Facebook. StudiVZ was sued by Facebook for intellectual property theft. Facebook claimed it had infringed on its design, features, and services and stolen its PHP source code, but a German court ruled against it.[16] The German network settled a suit filed by Facebook in America alleging StudiVZ had copied Facebook's look, feel, features, and services.[17] Facebook has overtaken Spain's social network, with 10.5 million members versus 6.8 million for Tuenti in 2010.[18] However, Dutch social network Hyves maintained its lead against Facebook in the contest for market share in the Netherlands, pulling in 7.5 million Dutch users to Facebook's 3.3 million in 2010.[19]

Mixi is Japan's largest social network, with 15 million users as of 2009.[20] Mixi differs from Facebook and MySpace in that it is an invitation-only service open only to Japanese, and, unlike MySpace, it does not allow members to edit their page layout. Mixi also differs from its American counterparts because of the Japanese culture's penchant for anonymity. Japanese users seldom post their names or photographs, and Mixi has been called the social network "where you're unlikely to meet anyone you don't know already".[21] Japanese society emphasizes community over the individual, and security is a prominent concern of Japanese life. These cultural distinctions are why Mixi is the flip side of a social network like Facebook, which prides itself on a user base of profiles containing real names and photos. Japanese prefer the safety and anonymity of an invitation-based social network like Mixi. Fewer than 5 percent of its members use their real names on the site. [22] Membership is highly restricted: Mixi is only available in Japan and members must be 15 or older. Membership requires an invitation from an existing member and a Japanese mobile phone's e-mail address for identity confirmation. Mixi is also maximized for mobile phone access; about 60 percent of members access it from their mobile phones while only 40 percent log in from computers. [23]

CyWorld (short for CyberWorld), a South Korean social network, features photo galleries, message boards, and friends lists but also provides each member with a virtual room inhabited by an avatar of her choice. To say CyWorld has taken South Korea by storm would be an understatement — 22 million people [24] are members and among those in their late teens and early twenties that number rises to 90 percent. [25] CyWorld briefly entered the U.S. market, but closed its American site in 2010. [26]

China's leading social network, Qzone, has 376 million members, mainly teenagers. [27] The second most popular social network in China — 51.com, with 130 million users — targets rural, working class adults. [28] Nearly 40 million Chinese students belong to Renren. [29] Renren, formerly called Xiaonei, openly encourages users to share music and movies; understandable, given China is one of the world's main sources of intellectual property piracy. [30] As discussed in Chapter 18, Chinese Internet sites and users are subject to censorship and filtering.

Social networks provide unique opportunities for criminals. As seen in Chapter 6, criminals use social engineering techniques to obtain personally identifiable information for identity theft or other crimes. Given the vast amount of personal information people share on social networks — details about their lives, romances, jobs, hobbies, friends, and families they would not share with a stranger in person but expose to the online world — such sites are a treasure trove for social engineering. Just names of co-workers may give criminals enough knowledge to launch a social engineering attack, by posing as a co-worker or business associate, to trick employees into revealing information. Criminals also use social networks to network with peers. In Brazil, drug dealers set up a "members-only" group on Google's "Orkut" social network and used it to facilitate drug transactions, with group members buying and selling ecstasy and marijuana. [31] In Japan, a "crime mates" social network matches up potential partners in crime. The site came to light after three men were arrested for allegedly meeting and conspiring online to kidnap and murder a woman. She was kidnapped on her way home from work, robbed of $600, beaten to death, and her body dumped in a forest west of Tokyo, Japan. The alleged online conspirators reportedly never even told each other their names. [32] Three U.K. teens were convicted of creating and operating one of the world's largest English-language Internet crime forums. Gh0stMarket.net had 8,000 members and the court dubbed it a "Crimebook" social network. It allowed hackers and fraudsters to trade breached databases anonymously, exchanging personal information including account numbers, pins and passwords. The site published manuals titled "14 Ways of Hacking Credit Cards" and "Running Cards on eBay", sold hacking software, and offered instructions on manufacturing crystal meth and explosives. Police estimated the network cost credit cardholders $26.37 million. [33]

Social networking can backfire on criminals. Police captured a California parole violator after TV viewers recognized his photo from his MySpace page. [34] A young woman plotting the murder of her ex-boyfriend's new girlfriend turned to his MySpace page to get all the information she needed — including a photo of her intended victim — to recruit a hit man.

(Recall the discussion in Chapter 12, about the dangers of voluntary disclosure of personal information on the Internet, and how a personal profile page on a social network can be a gold mine of information waiting to fall into the wrong hands.) Fortunately the "hit man" turned out to be an undercover cop. [35]

As social networks present opportunities for criminals, they also pose challenges for police departments. Nationwide, departments are scrambling to develop rules for what officers can and cannot do online, in the wake of a series of embarrassing posts on social networks. An Albuquerque police officer listed his occupation on his Facebook as "human waste disposal"; an Arkansas officer's character was questioned in court after he posted photographs on MySpace of him pointing a gun at the camera beside symbols of the Marvel Comics vigilante character, the Punisher; a New York jury dismissed a weapons charge against a defendant on learning the arresting officer had listed his mood on MySpace as "devious"; an Indiana state trooper posted photographs of his drunken revels on his MySpace page and commented about a homeless man beaten by police officers: "These people should have died when they were young, anyway, I'm just doing them a favor"; and a police recruit was rejected after posting on Facebook: "Just returned from the interview with the Southfield Police Department and I can't wait to get a gun and kick some ass." [36] Media coverage is often what stirs police departments into developing social media policies. Another factor is they know defense attorneys search social networks for evidence to impeach police testimony. The problem should not be how to hide bigotry, ego mania, and power trips of individual officers but rather that such attitudes and behavior exist and proper screening procedures should be instituted to keep such individuals from becoming armed police officers.

School districts, as a result of scandals and complaints about teachers misusing social media, are implementing policies to prohibit social media contact between teachers and their students. The new rules are a response to teachers posting inappropriate comments or photographs (often involving sex or alcohol) on social networks; having inappropriate contact with students; and being arrested on sexual abuse and assault charges after relationships with students that started online. [37] Educational administrators also worry teachers may share too much of their private lives with their students. The results can come back into the classroom, like the New York principal who posted a racy photograph on her Facebook page and found it subsequently reposted in her school hallways. Some teachers argue the restrictive policies take away an effective method of engaging Internet Generation students, who have grown up using social media to communicate. They complain the policies ignore the technology's usefulness as a teaching aid. A Missouri teachers' union used a free speech argument to convince a court to find a statute prohibiting electronic communication between teachers and students unconstitutional. [38]

Social networks present other challenges. A Staten Island family court ruled a MySpace "friend request" can constitute a violation of a temporary protection order. It had barred a 16-year-old girl from contacting a woman who had dated her father and her two minor daughters. She allegedly sent separate MySpace friend requests to them. The girl was charged with three counts of second degree criminal contempt. The court denied her motion to dismiss, stating, "While it is true that the person who received the 'friend request' could simply deny the request to become 'friends,' [it] was still a contact, and 'no contact' was allowed by the order of protection." [39] A North Carolina woman was arrested for violating a protection order banning "telephoning, contacting or otherwise communicating with the petitioner" after virtually "poking" someone on Facebook.[40] Similarly, in the United Kingdom, a man was sentenced to 10 days in jail for violating an order prohibiting contact with his wife, after sending her a Facebook friend request.[41] A Florida man was dismissed as a juror in a civil trial after trying to "friend" a defendant on Facebook.[42] The dismissed juror later gloated on Facebook he had gotten out of jury duty by following advice from friends. A juror in a London, England drug trial was charged with contempt of court after she contacted a defendant on Facebook.[43] The defendant had been acquitted but his co-defendants were still on trial, causing the judge to discharge the jury. The juror discussed the case while the jury was deliberating and revealed details of the jury's deliberations. A juror's tweets led the Arkansas Supreme Court to reverse a jury's guilty verdict, finding they caused a convicted murderer not to receive a fair trial.[44] California jurors who tweet during a trial can be sentenced to up to six months in jail under a law that went into effect in 2012.[45]

However, courts are turning to social networks, as well. In 2012, the Judicial Office for England and Wales said a judge at England's High Court allowed lawyers to serve legal claims through Facebook.[46] The previous year, a British judge filed an injunction against Occupy protesters in London using a text message.[47]

Many businesses now use social media as an integral part of their marketing strategy. When an employee blogs on a social network, is she building her own brand or the company's by establishing a social media profile? Consider the case where a mobile phone company sued a social media specialist it had hired over ownership of a Twitter account and its 17,000 followers.[48] Noah Kravitz claimed PhoneDog told him he could keep his Twitter account after leaving the firm in exchange for posting on it occasionally. But eight months after Kravitz changed his account name from "@Phonedog_Noah" to "@NoahKravitz," Phonedog sued him for $340,000 (valuing each follower at $2.50 per month, and multiplying $2.50 x 8 months x 17,000 followers) arguing the Twitter followers were a company asset, acquired during the period he worked for the firm.[49] The case raises the issue — in the absence of germane contractual agreements or a pre-existing social media policy — whether a company claim ownership of an employee's social media account, *i.e.*, whether an employee is building his own brand or the company's by establishing a social media profile. While the case was pending at publication and thus undecided, one can speculate on factors a court might use to determine ownership, such as how the account is used and why followers are drawn to it. If the social media appears more like an organ of the company, used to address customer inquiries and complaints, then it might be deemed the company's property. But if it appears followers are attracted to it by the thoughts and insights of a specific writer, then it might be seen as the writer's property.[50] Of course, it is ultimately the follower's decision whom to follow. While ownership of social media should be addressed in employment agreements or social media policies, there is no reason why a company and a former employee cannot each maintain a social media presence and leave it to followers to decide to follower one or both.

Conversely, when the marketing director of a Chicago interior design firm was hospitalized after an automobile accident, other employees took over posting on the company Facebook and Twitter accounts she had created, as well as posting on her personal Twitter account, which had amassed 1,250 followers, to promote the company with posts claiming to be from her. When the firm refused to cease using her personal account, she sued under the **Illinois Right to Publicity Act** and the **Lanham Act** for using her identity to endorse its services.[51]

## Caches, Like Diamonds, are Forever

Society can expect an array of Internet-spawned issues unimaginable a mere 20 years ago. Among these, privacy and reputation management are perhaps the most vexing and exponentially growing concerns. The Internet provides the means for any*one*, any*where*, to say any*thing* about an individual to a worldwide audience. The statements may be false and thereby libelous, or true but nonetheless damaging, such as public disclosure of private facts (an invasion of privacy). The individual may be falsely accused of immoral or criminal behavior, subjected to public embarrassment or humiliation, or placed in danger of identity theft or stalking. Disclosure of personally identifiable information poses serious risks, including identity theft and stalking. Recognizing these risks, the European Union, Canada, and the state of California have enacted strict laws regulating how Web sites collect, maintain, and disclose personally identifiable data. When such personal data about an individual are posted on the Web, the data reach a nearly unlimited audience instantaneously. Additionally, the viewing audience may never see any subsequent retraction. Finally, due to the Web's viral nature, the damaging information may be reposted infinitely on other sites and stored in searchable online repositories.

As discussed in earlier chapters, employers often search the Web to learn about job candidates. We have already discussed you should bear in mind how a prospective employer might view what you have posted online, but what about what others have posted about you? Did a competitor make a damaging comment about you? Did your friends post photos of you at that night of drunken revelry? Did someone post false or erroneous statements about you? Has a disgruntled customer set up a gripe site about your business? Did an ex-girlfriend maliciously list you on DontDateHimGirl.com?

## Reputation Management

*"To build may have to be the slow and laborious task of years. To destroy can be the thoughtless act of a single day."* — *Sir Winston Churchill*

Your reputation is important, so you must frequently engage in reputation management. The first step in damage control is to assess the damage. Search for your own name in all the major search engines and see what pops up. If there is nothing negative, congratulations! The next step is prevention. Subscribe to Google Alerts to receive regular updates when your name is used on the Web. Be proactive: reserve your name on social networks and professional Web sites. If you have a profile or listing in your name, an impersonator will not be able to pretend to be you. If you have a common name, like John Smith, use your middle initial or your full name to differentiate yourself, *e.g.*, "John Q. Smith" or "John Aloysius Smith". Another reason to create online profiles is you can fill them with the positive information you want known about yourself, and they will crowd out negative pages about you in search engine returns. Familiarize yourself with the privacy settings on each social network you join so you can control what and how much information you share. You can post book reviews on Amazon.com on subjects about which you wish to appear knowledgeable, as they will show up in searches too.

But suppose you have been libeled on the World Wide Web, or someone has posted your personally identifiable information or disclosed private facts about you online. Your attorney dutifully dashes off a cease and desist letter demanding removal of the offending material; the offender promptly removes the material from the Web and the attorney informs you the matter has been resolved. But has it really, or is this the start of a never-ending nightmare? Where else, besides the offender's own site, might the information appear online? Has it been reposted on a mirrored site, or on another individual's blog, or worse, syndicated throughout the blogosphere? If so, you will have to contact the site owner, the blogger, and the ISP to seek its removal. While many ISPs might comply voluntarily with a cease and desist letter, some may believe they fall within the expansive safe harbor of the **CDA** § 230 and refuse to remove the offending content. [52]

Several Internet entities routinely archive copies of Web pages. The Wayback Machine hosts "85 billion Web pages archived from 1996 to [the present]." [53] Google, the pre-eminent Internet search engine, typically caches (*i.e.*, indefinitely archives) every page it crawls, as it explains on its site: [54]

> Practically every search result includes a Cached link. Clicking on that link takes you to the Google cached version of that Web page, instead of the current version of the page. This is useful if the original page is unavailable because of:
> - Internet congestion
> - A down, overloaded, or just slow Web site
> - The owner's recently removing the page from the Web

This means even after the offending page has been removed by the Web site owner, it may still be visible in its entirety through the cached copy. Worse, the deleted page may still appear in search engine results, along with a *snippet* (*i.e.*, descriptive text about the link) and a link to the cached page.

Google offers a "Web Removal Tool" on its site that allows users to submit URLs for review by Google for possible deletion from its cache; however, the removal process is not automatic but subjective, and the stated reason for requesting removal must fall into one of four categories. [55] Google states it will only remove cached pages if the original Web page (1) is outdated or missing and returns a "404 not found" error in Google search results; (2) has been either modified, removed from the Web, or blocked from indexing by the site owner; (3) contains a Social Security or government ID number, bank account or credit card number, an image of a signature, or "your full name or the name of your business appearing on an adult content site that's spamming Google's search results", and the site owner has been uncooperative; or (4) contains inappropriate content that appears in Google's "SafeSearch" filtered results (note this would appear to exclude from consideration removal of inappropriate content appearing in unfiltered search results). [56] Additionally, the user must first set up a Google account to use the Web Removal Tool. If the removal request is approved, the URL will be removed from Google Web Search and Image Search results and subsequently excluded from Google search results for six months. [57]

If any offending material is copyrighted, your attorney may yet have another arrow in his legal quiver, in the form of the **DMCA**'s safe harbor provision, which provides protection from liability for copyrighted content illegally posted by users only so long such content is removed "expeditiously" on notification of the infringement. As a practical matter, most online service providers (OSPs) are likely to respond to takedown notices by immediately removing the material without an independent investigation of whether it was indeed a copyright infringement. So, where copyrighted material appears without authorization on the offending Web page, a **DMCA** takedown notice served on the party hosting the cached page should result in immediate compliance.

If the OSP fails to comply with the takedown notice, then you could sue for copyright infringement. However, in one case, a court found Google's caching was not copyright infringement.[58] In that case, since the plaintiff was the site creator, the court based its decision on the fact he could have taken acts to prevent Google or other search engines from caching the page. A site creator may place a code in meta tags within the HTML instructing search engines not to index or cache the page, or upload a separate robots.txt file to the server with similar instructions. Because of the Web page creator's control over whether search engines can index or cache the page, the court reasoned by failing to instruct search engines not to cache it, the plaintiff had granted Google an implied license to do so and he was estopped from asserting a copyright claim.[59] However, the implied license and estoppel rationales would not be relevant where the copyright holder was not the Web page creator; in that case, the copyright holder would lack control over the meta tags or the robots.txt file.

## Social Media Monitoring

Potential employers are not the only ones snooping on your online presence — lenders may be watching too, and checking out who your online friends are. When you get turned down for a job, credit card, or loan, it might be because of who your social network friends are, or whom you are mistaken for online. Lenders and other firms are turning to companies that specialize in using any other aggregate of an individual's online presence to compile a consumer profile called a *social graph*. Such *Social Media Monitoring* (SMM) firms search the Internet to find your various social network pages — MySpace, Facebook, LinkedIn, Twitter, Flickr, and others — and collate the information on them. They read your Facebook status updates, Twitter "tweets", online organizations you join, sites you link to, and comments you have posted. Put it all together and the resulting social graph reveals your behavior patterns, your likes and wants, and dislikes — a marketer's gold mine. For example, Facebook's "Friends of Connections" enables companies to serve ads to friends of users who have signed on as "fans" of that company's Facebook page.[60]

But this information is valuable to more than just marketers. Your online reputation may be weighed by employers considering you for a job or lenders evaluating your credit card or loan application.[61] A bank may look at your Facebook friends and if any are also bank customers, it may analyze their payment history and credit stability to extrapolate what sort of risk you might be (guilt by association, so to speak). If a lot of your friends are bad risks, the bank might assume you are, too. Earlier, we discussed ways to protect and preserve your online reputation. In addition to searching your own name, you can see what Facebook information on your account is shared publicly at Reclaimprivacy.org and view your social graph at Rapleaf. com. You can also use the Google Privacy Dashboard to see an overview of what information Google has about you based on the Google products you use. Google Privacy Dashboard tracks the following Google products: Account & Profile; Web-history; Gmail; Docs; Calendar; YouTube; Blogger; iGoogle; Latitude; Reader; Talk; Health; Orkut; Picasa; Shopping List; Voice; Contacts; Alerts; Finance; Friend Connect; Tasks; Custom search engines; and Mobile Sync.

## Chapter 12 Notes

[1] "Internet 2011 in Numbers," Pingdom.com, *available at* http://royal.pingdom.com/2012/01/17/internet-2011-in-numbers (accessed Mar. 23, 2012).

[2] Some credit the theory to Hungarian writer Frigyes Karinthy's 1829 short story "*Chains.*"

[3] Perhaps not so farfetched. In *Doe v. Sexsearch.com*, 502 F. Supp. 2d 719 (N.D. Ohio 2007), an online dating service was sued by a member after he was introduced to, and had sex with, an underage female, leading to criminal proceedings against him. The site was shielded from liability by the CDA § 230 because it had not exercised control over the female member's profile.

[4] ComScore Media Metrix, October 2006, *was available at* www.comscore.com/press/release.asp?press=1019 but is no longer available.

[5] *Ibid.*

[6] "Facebook Surfers Cost Their Bosses Billions," Reuters wire service report, August 20, 2007.

[7] Elizabeth Weiss Green, "Clique on to Penguin: How a Virtual World is Changing Social Dynamics in Fifth-Grade Classrooms across the Country," U.S. News & World Report, pp. 31-32, March 19, 2007.

[8] *Ibid.*

[9] "Internet 2011 in Numbers," fn. 1, *supra.*

[10] Maija Palmer, "A Future Alongside Facebook," Financial Times (London), February 24, 2010.

[11] Ben Worthen, "Meet the New Bebo," The Wall Street Journal, July 13, 2010.

[12] Palmer, fn. 10, *supra.*

[13] *Ibid.*

[14] Social Media Statistics, *available at* http://socialmediastatistics.wikidot.com/hi5 (accessed Mar. 23, 2012).

[15] Martin U. Müller, "Facebook LOL as Germany's StudiVZ Loses Ground," Der Spiegel, May 20, 2010.

[16] *Facebook, Inc. v. StudiVZ, Ltd.*, Case No. 33 O 374/08 (Dist. Ct. of Cologne Jun. 6, 2009). *See also* Serkan Toto, "Facebook Loses Lawsuit against German Clone StudiVZ, Gets Criticized for Sloppy Preparation," TechCrunch June 16, 2009, *available at* www.techcrunch.com/2009/06/16/facebook-loses-lawsuit-against-german-clone-studivz (accessed Mar. 23, 2012).

[17] *Facebook, Inc. v. StudiVz, Ltd.*, Case No. 08-03468 (N.D. Cal. 2009)

[18] Palmer, fn. 10, *supra.*

[19] *Ibid.*

[20] Kenji Hall, "Japan's Mixi Tops Facebook and MySpace," Business Week, August 26, 2008.

[21] Jay Alabaster, "Japan's Online Social Scene isn't So Social," Sydney Morning Herald, September 27, 2008.

[22] Social Media Statistics, *available at* http://socialmediastatistics.wikidot.com/mixi (accessed Mar. 23, 2012).

[23] *Ibid.*

[24] "Social Networking Embracing Search Engines, Games," Korea Times, May 19, 2008.

[25] "E-Society: My World is Cyworld," Business Week magazine, September 26, 2005.

[26] The U.S. version was *available at* http://us.cyworld.com, but Cyworld ceased its U.S. operations as of February 19, 2010.

[27] "Chinese Social Networks 'Virtually' Out-Earn Facebook and MySpace: a Market Analysis," TechCrunch, April 5, 2009 *available at* http://techcrunch.com/2009/04/05/chinese-social-networks-virtually-out-earn-facebook-and-myspace-a-market-analysis/ (accessed Mar. 23, 2012).

[28] *Ibid.*

[29] *Ibid.*

[30] Don Reisinger, "5 International Social Networks to Keep an Eye on," CNET News.com, December 18, 2008.

[31] Gregg Keizer, "Brazilian Police Bust Dope Ring Built around Google's Orkut," Informationweek.com, July 21, 2005, *available at* www.informationweek.com/news/management/showArticle.jhtml?articleID=166401653 (accessed Mar. 23, 2012).

[32] "Internet 'Crime Mates' Arrested after Japan Killing," Reuters wire service report, August 27, 2007.

[33] Emil Protalinski, "Teenagers Jailed for Running "Criminal Equivalent of Facebook," ZDNet.com, March 3, 2011.

[34] Sandra Gonzales, "Profile on MySpace Proves to Be S. J. Fugitive's Undoing," San Jose Mercury News, August 9, 2006.

[35] Tracey Christensen, "Police Foil MySpace Murder Plot," 11alive.com, October 10, 2006, *was available at* www.11alive.com/includes/tools/print.aspx?storyid=85876 (accessed July 23, 2010) but no longer available.

[36] Erica Goode, "Police Lesson: Social Network Tools Have Two Edges," The New York Times, April 6, 2011.

[37] Statesboro, Georgia schools banned private electronic communications between teachers and students after revelation of an affair between an eighth-grade teacher and her 14-year-old student that began with Facebook and text messages. An Illinois teacher was found guilty of sexual abuse and assault of a 17-year-old student with whom he had texted 700 messages. A California high school band director pleaded guilty to sexual misconduct with a 16-year-old student after 1,200 private messages from him on her Facebook page came to light. In Pennsylvania, a high school athletic director pleaded guilty to attempted corruption of a minor after offering an ex-student gifts for sex. *See* Jennifer Preston, "Rules to Stop Pupil and Teacher from Getting Too Social Online," The New York Times, p. A1, December 18, 2011.

[38] *Ibid.*

[39] *People v. Fernino*, 851 NYS2d 339 (N.Y. City Crim. Ct. 2008).

[40] Eric Miller, "Facebook 'Poke' Leads to Woman's Arrest," Hendersonville (NC) Star News, October 8, 2009.

[41] Laura Clout, "Man Jailed over Facebook Message," The (London) Telegraph, October 5, 2007.

[42] "Juror Booted for Facebook-Friending Defendant," Forbes, January 4, 2012.

[43] "Juror Admits Contempt of Court over Facebook Contact," BBC News, June 14, 2011.

[44] Martha Neil, "Convicted Murder Defendant Sentenced to Death Gets New Trial over Juror's Tweets," ABA Journal, December 8, 2011.

[45] Stephanie Francis Ward "Tweeting Jurors to Face Jail Time With New California Law," ABA Journal, August 8, 2011.

[46] "UK Court OKs Legal Claim to be Served Via Facebook," Associated Press wire service report, February 22, 2012.

[47] *Ibid.*

[48] *PhoneDog v. Kravitz*, Case No. C 11-03474 MEJ (N.D. Cal. filed 2011).

[49] Dan Schawbel, "When is Your Twitter Account Not Your Twitter Account?" Time Magazine, January 4, 2012.

[50] Recall the discussion in Chapter 5, *supra*, of the Barack Obama campaign page created by Joe Anthony on MySpace and CNN's attempt to gained control over the URL Twitter.com/CNNBrk from a CNN fan who had amassed 1.5 million followers on his Twitter account. In the Obama case, MySpace gave the subdomain to the campaign but, recognizing Anthony's effort in gaining the followers, allowed him to retain them.

[51] The district court refused to dismiss the case or grant a motion for summary judgment. *Maremont v. Susan Fredman Design Grp., Ltd.*, Case No. 10 C 7811 (N.D. Ill. Dec. 7, 2011).

[52] However the CDA § 230 has been found by courts to protect online service providers (such as ISPs) from defamation liability from third-party posts. Subsequent decisions have interpreted this phrase to encompass ISPs, blogs, forums, electronic mailing lists, and Web 2.0 interactive content providers (*e.g.*, Amazon.com reviews, eBay feedback, YouTube videos, and social networks like MySpace).

[53] *Available at* www.archive.org/web/web.php (accessed Mar. 23, 2012).

[54] *Available at* www.googleguide.com/cached_pages.html (accessed Mar. 23, 2012).

[55] *Available at* http://support.google.com/webmasters/bin/answer.py?hl=en&answer=164734 (accessed Mar. 23, 2012).

[56] Google does not define "inappropriate content" nor indicate if the phrase is subject to a contextual standard, *e.g.*, if nudity and hate propaganda were considered inappropriate content, would a Web page discussing breast cancer featuring photographs of naked breasts or a Web page examining hate crimes containing a picture of a swastika be considered inappropriate when viewed in that context?

[57] *Ibid.* At the end of the six-month period, it might be prudent to search through Google periodically to see if the URL has reappeared in search results. If the original (uncached) page has been removed, then theoretically there should be no page for Google's spiders to recache.

[58] *Field v. Google, Inc.*, 412 F. Supp. 2d 1106 (D. Nev. 2006).

[59] *Ibid.*

[60] Mark Walsh, "Facebook Targeting Fans' 'Connections'," Media Post News, November 12, 2009.

[61] *See* Tony Bradley, "What You Don't Know about Your Online Reputation Can Hurt You," PC World, May 29, 2010; and Lucas Conley, "How Rapleaf is Data-Mining Your Friend Lists to Predict Your Credit Risk," fastcompany.com, November 16, 2009.

# CHAPTER

# 13

___

## FREE SPEECH

> This chapter examines the First Amendment guarantee of Free Speech, the various categories of speech, strict scrutiny, intermediate scrutiny, content-neutral laws and content-based speech, and unprotected speech.

*"In a free state there should be freedom of speech and thought." — Emperor Tiberius*

THE FIRST AMENDMENT IS very short—only a single sentence—yet it represents perhaps the greatest restraint ever placed on any government in history. It reads:[1]

> Congress shall make no law respecting an establishment of religion, or prohibiting the free exercise thereof; or abridging the freedom of speech, or of the press; or the right of the people peaceably to assemble, and to petition the government for a redress of grievances.

The Supreme Court has interpreted the First Amendment to apply not only to the federal government, but to state legislatures as well, through application of the Due Process clause of the Fourteenth Amendment. The relevant portion for this discussion are the words "Congress shall make no law...abridging the freedom of speech, or of the press." Justice Hugo Black applied a strict constructionist view to that language, stating no law means no law, period. "An unconditional right to say what one pleases about public affairs is what I consider to be the minimum guarantee of the First Amendment."[2] Justice Black believed so passionately in the right of individuals to express their thoughts, he maintained all libel laws violate the First Amendment. "The only sure way to protect speech and press against these threats is to recognize that libel laws are abridgments of speech and press and therefore are barred in both federal and state courts by the First and Fourteenth Amendments."[3]

Justice Black espoused the notion free speech was paramount as an individual right and to the safety of a democracy. However, free speech is not always accurate; it may be incorrect, misleading, distorted, or false. Words can be used to spread lies and destroy reputations. What redress should the victims of such attacks have? One approach is the *Marketplace of Ideas* concept that argues, like cream, the truth shall rise to the surface in an open exchange of speech. U.S. Supreme Court Justice Oliver Wendell Holmes first enunciated the "marketplace of ideas" metaphor in his dissent in <u>Abrams v. United States</u> in 1919.[4] The concept behind his metaphor is ideas compete for acceptance against each other — with the underlying faith the truth will prevail in such an open encounter. Applying this concept to the Internet, the injured party can counter the damaging effects of online posts by rebutting them in same forum. However, there is the time factor until a rebuttal can be made to be considered. An individual may not learn of a defamatory posting until long after many people have seen it. While a rebuttal can be made almost instantaneously on the Internet, so too can a defamatory comment be seen or reposted instantaneously. The rebuttal must also avoid defamatory comments itself. One problem with this approach is, in defamation cases, it merely reinforces the defamation by repeating it and adding another layer to the cached and searchable content existing online. In cases where a public company seeks to rebut a defamatory statement, there may be securities laws restrictions on what public statements it can make and when it can make them.

What if one speaker has significantly greater resources? Can a wealthy corporation or a Super PAC (a form of political action committee allowed to raise unlimited funds) purchase enough advertising to promote its view as the truth and drown out competing speech? Joseph Goebbels said, "If you tell a lie big enough and keep repeating it, people will eventually come to believe it."

Our judicial system provides redress against defamation, allowing lawsuits for *libel* (written or broadcast) or *slander* (transitory or spoken). It also identifies situations where government may restrict time, place, and manner of speech and in rare instances, such as national security concerns, prohibit it. It classifies speech as content-neutral or content-based. The constitutionality of content-neutral laws is determined by the time, place, and manner of restrictions imposed on speech. Courts will subject a content-neutral statute or policy to "intermediate scrutiny", applying a five-prong test:[5]

- Is the restriction within the government's constitutional power?
- Does the restriction further an important or substantial governmental interest?
- Is the governmental interest unrelated to the suppression of free expression?
- Is the restriction narrowly tailored, *i.e.*, no greater than necessary to achieve that interest?
- Does the restriction leave open ample opportunities of communication?

Content-neutral laws do not target speech directly but have a substantial impact on the message. If they prohibit the message, rather than merely restricting the time, place, and manner in which it is conveyed, then the law will not stand up to intermediate scrutiny and will be struck down as unconstitutional.

Content-based speech is categorized as political speech, commercial speech, expressive conduct, speech subject to restrictions based on the role of the state, and unprotected speech.

## Political Speech

Recognizing the importance of political speech to a democracy, courts will apply *strict scrutiny* to restrictions on it. The three-prong strict scrutiny analysis demands:
- There must be a compelling government interest in prohibiting the speech
- The law must be narrowly tailored to achieve that interest
- The law must be the least restrictive possible in order to achieve that interest

## Commercial Speech

Commercial speech, while afforded First Amendment protection, is considered to have "diminished protection". Advertising can be restricted (*e.g.*, cigarette ads no longer allowed on television) and the government can punish false or misleading ads (*e.g.*, the **Federal Trade Commission Act**). Restrictions on profit-motivated speech are subject to a four-element intermediate scrutiny analysis:[6]

> At the outset, we must determine whether the expression is protected by the First Amendment. For commercial speech to come within that provision, it at least must concern lawful activity and not be misleading. Next, we ask whether the asserted governmental interest is substantial. If both inquiries yield positive answers, we must determine whether the regulation directly advances the governmental interest asserted, and whether it is not more extensive than is necessary to serve that interest.

## Expressive Conduct

Speech, *i.e.*, the communication of ideas and opinions, may be expressed through action instead of words, *e.g.*, the wearing of armbands[7] or T-shirts.[8] The bellwether case is _Texas v. Johnson_, where the Supreme Court ruled burning the American flag was a protected form of expressive speech.[9] However, one federal court has held "liking" a candidate's Facebook page was not speech protected by the First Amendment.[10] The plaintiff, a sheriff's department employee, expressed support for a candidate opposing the incumbent sheriff by clicking the "like" button on the Facebook page. The sheriff was re-elected and the employee was fired. The plaintiff contended his termination violated his First Amendment rights. The court rationalized its decision stating the plaintiff had not made any specific statements on the page: "It is the court's conclusion that merely "liking" a Facebook page is insufficient speech to merit constitutional protection. In cases where courts have found that constitutional speech protections extended to Facebook posts, actual statements existed within the record." This anomalous decision ignores voluminous case law holding such conduct to be both expressive conduct and political speech. Endorsing a political candidate is fundamental to the First Amendment and was one of the very reasons it was drafted.

While the state may not prohibit an individual from expressing his ideas and opinions in the public square, it may restrict him from doing so at 3 a.m. with a bullhorn in a residential suburb. Recall the Occupy Wall Street protests of 2011, where local authorities allowed the protests but banned the use of megaphones; protesters responded by repeating in unison what the speaker had said, chanting sentence by sentence so those farthest away could hear the message. Expressive conduct may be subject to "Time, Place, and Manner" restrictions, so long as they are "content neutral", *i.e.*, not used to suppress a particular idea, and applied equally to all speakers, and narrowly tailored to achieve significant government interest.

## Speech Subject to Restrictions Based on the Role of the State

The First Amendment is a prohibition against government action; it applies only to the state, not to private individuals or businesses. But sometimes government may act in a capacity that allows it to regulate speech within the confines of the First Amendment. These capacities include employer, educator through the public school system, prison warden, military, state bar regulator, and regulator of the airwaves.

## Employer

Government employees have a First Amendment right to speak on issues of public concern and cannot be fired for doing so;[11] however, the First Amendment does not protect statements made by public employees pursuant to their official duties.[12]

## Educator Through the Public School System

The Supreme Court has held public school students have First Amendment protection unless there is "substantial interference with school discipline or the rights of others".[13] Subsequent court decisions have narrowed this protection.[14] The subject of student speech is discussed in greater detail in Chapter 15.

## Prison Warden

The government runs the nations' prisons and has broad powers to restrict inmates' speech. The Supreme Court has ruled regulations are "valid if reasonably related to legitimate penological interests"[15] and that "Prison officials are due considerable deference in regulating the delicate balance between prison order and security and the legitimate demands of 'outsiders' who seek to enter the prison environment."[16]

State and federal inmates do not have direct access to computers and are not allowed to access the Internet directly. The rationales for this policy include: prisoners might download instructions on making weapons, like pipe bombs; prisoners might harass their victims or victims' families online; and prisoners forfeit their rights when convicted. There are two primary free speech issues concerning inmates. Should inmates have direct access to computers or the Internet? If not, should inmates be allowed to receive correspondence or material from the Internet indirectly? Family, friends, and prisoner advocacy groups often attempt to mail inmates material they have downloaded, arguing the First Amendment protects the inmates' rights to receive downloaded material. An argument can be made inmates should be allowed to avail themselves of the Internet to communicate with the outside world or to do legal research; many file their own appeals *pro se* from their prison cells. Some — through family and friends — have created Web sites and opened e-mail accounts to voice grievances, seek legal aid, and express political views.[17]

Some states not only deny prisoners direct Internet access but indirect access as well. Georgia prison guards confiscated a package containing legal research downloaded by a prisoner's girlfriend, following the Georgia Department of Corrections' policy prohibiting inmates from receiving downloaded printed material. In 2005, the inmate sued in federal court to challenge the policy.[18] The trend has favored prisoners. A federal appeals court in California ruled against a state policy preventing inmates from receiving mail with Internet-generated information.[19] In Colorado, a district court ruled against a similar prison policy.[20] And an Arizona court declared a state law prohibiting inmates from exchanging written mail with ISPs or creating profiles on Web sites via outside contacts unconstitutional.[21]

Many inmates have social network profiles, created either prior to their incarceration or by family or friends during their imprisonment. At least 30 Texas death row inmates have MySpace pages.[22] While MySpace does not want to be known as the cyberhaunt where kids meet killers, the company has stated it will only remove prisoner profiles that violate its terms of service. [23] Facebook, however, announced it would disable inmate accounts if used while the prisoner is incarcerated. The social network was responding to a problem that has grown with the advent of smart phones and social media. In 2005, California prisons confiscated 261 smuggled phones but that number ballooned to 10,760 in 2011 and 7,284 in the first half of 2012. Prison officials reported prisoners have used Facebook to stalk victims of their crimes and direct criminal activity outside the prison walls. [24]

### Military

The federal government has broad power to restrict the speech of members of the military. The Supreme Court upheld the court-martial of a soldier who suggested enlisted men refuse orders to go to Vietnam and called Special Forces soldiers "liars and thieves", "killers of peasants", and "murderers of women and children". [25] The soldier had argued the **Uniform Code of Military Justice** (UCMJ) articles he was tried under violated his First Amendment right to free speech. The Supreme Court held "while military personnel are not excluded from First Amendment protection, the fundamental necessity for obedience, and the consequent necessity for discipline, may render permissible within the military that which would be constitutionally impermissible outside it." [26] The Court noted, "Because of the factors differentiating military from civilian society, Congress is permitted to legislate with greater breadth and flexibility when prescribing rules". [27]

The Iraq War has put a new spin on blogging. Many soldiers eschew old-fashioned letters to the homefront in favor of blogs. These *milbloggers (i.e.,* military bloggers) offer war details that do not make it into most hometown newspapers. Raw war reporting with varied themes, including photographs snapped by the soldiers and diary entries fill the milblogs. Some are political; some question the war while others enthusiastically embrace it. Many milblogs are filled with examples of military absurdity, the 21$^{st}$ century "e-version" of Joseph Heller's "*Catch-22*" novel. [28]

Milbloggers must be careful not to reveal information, such as names and locations, that might be useful to enemies. What may seem harmless, such as soldiers posting photographs of the scene of an enemy attack, might unwittingly provide the enemy with valuable damage assessment data. Such revelations could not only be harmful to troops but also subject the milbloggers to punishment under Article 15 of the **UCMJ**. During the Iraq war, an Arizona National Guardsman on active duty in Baghdad was demoted and fined after a military tribunal concluded he had revealed classified information in his milblog. [29] The **UCMJ** prohibits soldiers from disclosing or "encouraging widespread publication" of classified or specific information about troop movement and location, military strategy and tactics, and soldiers wounded or killed. [30] The latter restriction, which also includes photographs of casualties, is to prevent families from learning of a loved one's injury or death before official notification by the military. Additionally, milbloggers are forbidden from disclosing planned raids, senior leaders' itineraries, photographs of new technology, or details that could compromise their location. [31]

While most are cautious not to reveal information, some milbloggers have been shut down by commanding officers. A Defense Department spokesperson told the Associated Press in 2004: [32]

> [The Pentagon has] no specific guidelines on blogging per se ... Generally, they can do it if they are writing their blogs not on government time and not on a government computer. They have every right under the First Amendment to say any darn thing they want to say unless they reveal classified information, and then it becomes an issue as a security violation.

Despite that assurance, servicemen reported being ordered to shut down milblogs for non-security reasons. Beginning in April 2005, all military personnel in Iraq were required to register their blogs, which became subject to quarterly monitoring by commanding officers to ensure they did not violate operational security and privacy restrictions.[33] Unit commanders were authorized to establish more restrictive requirements if necessary, such as reviewing individual blog posts.

Both the U.S. Army and Defense Department have programs to monitor blogs and Web sites. The Army Web Risk Assessment Cell (AWRAC) in Virginia monitors official and unofficial blogs and sites for security threats, *e.g.,* official documents, personal contact information, and photographs of weapons or camp entrances.[34] The Defense Department's Joint Web Risk Assessment Cell only monitors official military sites. Procedurally, the AWRAC first contacts a soldier to remove objectionable content; if he does not, then it contacts his commanding officer. An Army investigative report showed official Army sites violated operational security more than milbloggers.[35] AWRAC audits revealed at least 1,813 operational security violations on 878 official military sites, as opposed to 28 on 594 milblogs (from January 2006 to January 2007).[36] While likely the military will promulgate guidelines on milblogging, boundaries between the military employer's need to control speech for security purposes and servicemen's First Amendment right to free speech through milblogging have not yet been defined.[37]

## Regulator of the State Bar

State bar associations regulate attorneys' conduct and speech. They may require lawyers to submit advertising in advance for approval and restrict what lawyers say in ads and even on their letterhead. Many lawyers blog, either as a marketing tool or simply to discuss a wide range of legal topics regularly with clients. This raises the issue of whether lawyer blogs fall under advertising (regulated by state bar associations) or political free speech. State bars are revising attorney advertising and ethics rules to address the issue. Most regulate all advertising by their attorneys, but the scope of what is considered "advertising" can encompass business cards, letterheads, print ads, radio and television commercials, direct mail, and the Internet. When does an attorney blog cross from free speech to regulated advertising? Lawyers may blog about current court decisions, political events, or subjects within their practice (*e.g.,* criminal law, bankruptcy, personal injury, litigation) or their blogs may be more personal in nature, such as discussing their last family vacation. As with most blogs, readers may be permitted to post comments. But these seemingly innocuous topics may be viewed by state bars as marketing focused with the purpose of attracting or retaining clients. To fend off state bar criticism, some attorneys attach a disclaimer identifying the blog's purpose, *e.g.,* it is not intended as advertising and does not represent the firm's views. However, it is likely content rather than disclaimers will sway bar associations in their determinations. Does requiring attorneys to submit blogs for review by a bar committee stifle blog discussions? There is an inherent contradiction between the spontaneity and immediacy of blogging and the red tape of review committees.

Lawyers' freedom to blog is limited by professional codes of conduct.[38] As "officers of the court", attorneys sacrifice some freedom to criticize it. Free speech issues are inevitable, as the Internet Generation, in this era of blogs and social media, enters a profession mired in centuries-old tradition. A Florida lawyer was reprimanded and fined by the state bar after blogging a local judge was an "evil, unfair witch."[39] An Illinois attorney was fired from her assistant public defender position of 19 years after her blog referred to a judge as "Judge Clueless" and discussed client identities and confidential details of a case.[40] A San Diego lawyer was fired when he blogged about a case he served on as a juror.[41] The defendant's criminal conviction had to be set aside and the case remanded. Jurors who blog about trial details risks civil contempt charges, but lawyers can also face professional penalties. Astonishingly, the lawyer was quoted as saying he did not think the judge's admonition against discussing the case included blogging![42]

The Florida Judicial Ethics Advisory Committee ruled judges may not permit lawyers who might appear before them to be identified as "friends" on the judge's social network profiles, because it might convey "to others the impression that these lawyer 'friends' are in a special position to influence the judge."[43] Some committee members dissented, arguing a social "friend" is a contact or acquaintance; and not a "friend" in the traditional sense. The committee stated it was acceptable for judges to have nonlawyer friends on social networks or list as 'friends' lawyers who do not appear before the judge. Surprisingly, the same opinion allowed lawyers who may practice before the judge to designate themselves as "fans" or supporters of a judge's candidacy on the judge's social network campaign page.

Another issue is whether comments could run afoul of lawyers' professional liability insurance coverage guidelines. One of the largest legal professional liability carriers, Chubb Group of Insurance Companies, stated its policy would be to insure blogging by attorneys, so long as the blog fell within certain parameters.[44] The insurer differentiated "informational blogs" that inform about the law and pose minimal risk from "advisory blogs" that might be construed as offering legal advice. Whether a Q-and-A format blog would be equivalent to offering legal advice, or establish an attorney-client relationship (and hence potential malpractice liability) is subject to debate. Most attorneys would argue to have an attorney-client relationship, the attorney must first meet his client.

## Regulator of the Airwaves

The federal government, through the FCC, licenses and regulates broadcast radio and television stations. To be consistent with the First Amendment, its regulations must be narrowly tailored and further a substantial government interest. The FCC prohibits the airing of obscene programming and restricts airing of indecent programming or profane language to specific hours. It may revoke a station's license, impose a fine, or issue a warning. The FCC defines broadcast indecency as "language or material that, in context, depicts or describes, in terms patently offensive as measured by contemporary community standards for the broadcast medium, sexual or excretory organs or activities."[45] Indecent or profane material is constitutionally protected but the FCC may restrict its broadcast to hours when children are less likely to view it (determined to be between 10 pm and 6 am, per FCC rules). In 1978, the Supreme Court ruled the government could restrict George Carlin's famous "seven dirty words" monologue, which had been aired on the radio during the afternoon, finding the government had a compelling interest in "shielding children from patently offensive material, and ensuring that unwanted speech does not enter one's home."[46]

The Court noted broadcasting's "uniquely pervasive presence" and that "broadcasting is uniquely accessible to children". The Supreme Court reviewed the FCC's indecency standards in *FCC v. Fox Television Stations*, involving the broadcast of brief expletives by celebrities on awards shows on the Fox television network and partial nudity on the ABC TV police drama "*NYPD Blue*".[47]

# Unprotected Speech

The Supreme Court has ruled certain speech is not entitled to First Amendment protection. This includes:

**Incitement**. Advocacy of the use of force directed toward inciting or producing imminent lawless action and likely to incite or produce such action. [48]

**Fighting Words**. Words expressed to incite hatred or violence from their target. [49]

**"True Threats."** Threats of violence, directed at a specific person and not hyperbole. A young man who had just been drafted stated at a protest against the Vietnam war in Washington, DC, "If they ever make me carry a rifle the first man I want to get in my sights is L.B.J." [50] He was convicted of violating a federal law that prohibits threats against the president. The Supreme Court reversed his felony conviction, ruling his statement was political hyperbole rather than a true threat. Justice Sandra Day O'Connor defined true threats: [51]

> 'True threats' encompass those statements where the speaker means to communicate a serious expression of an intent to commit an act of unlawful violence to a particular individual or group of individuals. The speaker need not actually intend to carry out the threat. Rather, a prohibition on true threats protect[s] individuals from the fear of violence and from the disruption that fear engenders, in addition to protecting people from the possibility that the threatened violence will occur.

**National Security**. Classified documents, military secrets, troop movements in wartime, and information pertaining to the development of nuclear, biological, or other weapons of mass destruction all fall under the heading of national security. (See the discussion of prior restraint in Chapter 18). National Security is a governmental concern that has conflicted with the First Amendment many times since the nation's founding. President John Adams signed the **Sedition Act of 1798** giving federal authorities the right to prosecute anyone suspected of plotting against the government. The Act also made it illegal to speak or write "with the intent to defame" the president or Congress or to bring either "into contempt or disrepute." During World War I, Congress passed the **Sedition Act of 1918,** which made it a federal offense to speak out against the government or the war, or to discourage men from enlisting. It also empowered the postmaster general to ban from the U.S. mail any publication considered unfavorable to the war effort. The Act was repealed in 1920. The **Sedition Act of 1918** was an amendment to the **Espionage Act of 1917**, which has not been repealed. [52] The **Espionage Act** made it a crime to write or say anything that might encourage disloyalty or interfere with military conscription or military operations, promote insubordination in the military, or support enemies during wartime. A unanimous Supreme Court ruled the **Espionage Act** was constitutional. [53] When a former CIA agent published a book containing unclassified information without first submitting it for approval to the CIA per a secrecy agreement he had signed with the agency, the Supreme Court rejected his First Amendment argument that prohibiting him from publishing unclassified information was an impermissible prior restraint on speech. The Court held "[G]overnment has a compelling interest in protecting both the secrecy of information important to our national security and the appearance of confidentiality so essential to the effective operation of our foreign intelligence service." [54]

**Obscenity**. Obscenity is completely without First Amendment protection. Obscenity is discussed in detail in Chapter 17.

**Child Pornography**. Child pornography, also covered in Chapter 17, is another category devoid of First Amendment protection.

## Social Boundaries of Free Speech

The First Amendment prevents the government from interfering with free speech. The U.S. Supreme Court has held protection is not absolute; certain categories of speech have lesser protection or no protection, and circumstances affect how speech is protected. Commercial speech has a lesser degree of protection than political speech. Obscenity is not protected by the First Amendment (although non-obscene pornography is protected, but child pornography is not). One cannot yell "Fire" in a crowded theater (unless there is actually a fire) but one can yell "Fire" on a target range.

Criminal conduct is not protected by First Amendment free speech guarantees. In a case where a site sold material to teach people how to avoid paying taxes (allegedly) legally, a federal court held the First Amendment did not protect the two organizations that operated the site, or their founder, because the site incited criminal conduct by "instructing others how to engage in illegal activity and [supplying] the means to do so." [55] (Ironically, the organizations had solicited donations it claimed were tax deductible). [56]

What about speech that society may find offensive, and may be illegal in some but not all jurisdictions? Since the Internet extends across all jurisdictions, how should such cases be handled? In 2007, cockfighting was illegal in every U.S. state except Louisiana. Amazon. com offered subscriptions to two cockfighting magazines, *The Feathered Warrior* and *The Gamecock.* The Humane Society sued Amazon, claiming it was violating animal cruelty laws by selling magazines promoting illegal behavior, and the magazines were effectively catalogs for illegal goods since they carried ads for blades that attached to birds' legs. [57] There is no doubt that cockfighting is a form of animal cruelty and a reprehensible "sport." But Amazon contended since the magazines themselves were legal to sell, it should not be cast in the role of a censor simply because some individuals object to the content. YouTube reportedly hosted video clips of a 1940 anti-Semitic propaganda film and music videos of a banned far-right German rock band that contained scenes of World War II Nazi military operations. [58] Such material would be illegal under German laws prohibiting expression of pro-Nazi sentiments and the production of pro-Nazi materials; in the United States there are no corresponding laws. In both instances, the speech and the underlying activities (illegal in some jurisdictions) are abhorrent, yet under U.S. laws would be considered protected speech.

A California man was jailed after sending an unyielding barrage of tweets targeting a Buddhist leader in Maryland, posing yet another new issue in Internet law: Is a public message on Twitter comparable to speaking from a soapbox in the public square or is it a means of direct personal communication, analogous to a letter or phone call? The case calls into question the issue of what can be said *about* an individual as opposed to what can be said *to* an individual. Using a number of aliases, the defendant allegedly published 8,000 tweets about the victim and was charged with cyberstalking. Tweets have been the subject of civil defamation suits but this was a criminal case, weighing free expression against individual safety. According to published reports, the tweets caused the victim "substantial emotional distress" and put her in such fear for her safety she hired armed guards and did not leave her home for 18 months. Her fear was not without a basis: the defendant had a criminal record of assault, arson, domestic violence, and carrying a "dangerous weapon" onto a plane. [59] Another wrinkle in the case was the victim was a public figure, with 23,000 Twitter followers. Should one who shines the public spotlight on oneself expect to attract a certain number of kooks? Would it be more egregious if the victim were not a celebrity, but an ordinary private individual?

In 2012, a federal court found the Internet to be so pervasive in people's daily lives that a state law barring sex offenders from social networks like Facebook was an unreasonable restriction on free protected speech. It ruled unconstitutional a Louisiana statute that made it a crime for anyone convicted of video voyeurism or a sex offense against a minor to use social networks, chat rooms, and P2P networks. Finding the ban too broad, the court said: [60]

> Although the act is intended to promote the legitimate and compelling state
> interest of protecting minors from Internet predators, the near total ban on
> Internet access imposed by the act unreasonably restricts many ordinary
> activities that have become important to everyday life in today's world.

The ACLU claimed the statute's terms barred the offenders from browsing everything from news sites to job search sites. The judge noted the statute might prevent the sex offenders from using the federal court Web site. [61]

One of this book's central themes is the necessity for the law to adapt to and address societal issues raised by the advent of new technology, as the Internet continues to bring new ways for people to communicate with each other and the world at large. Just as federal authorities used a cyberstalking statute to deal with harassing communication, courts have applied other existing statutes in innovative ways to deal with abusive behavior. California prosecutors used a felony identity theft law to prosecute a boy who hacked into another student's Facebook account using her password, which someone had texted to him unsolicited, to deface her profile with profanity and sexual innuendo. [62] A Nebraska student who harassed his political science professor with a series of 18 e-mails on political topics (described by the appellate court as "rants often laced with profanity and invective") was convicted of violating a state statute against disturbing the peace and the conviction was upheld on appeal. The appellate court found the e-mails constituted "fighting words" but, in overturning the conviction, the Nebraska Supreme Court ruled they were not fighting words because, having been exchanged over a period of six months, they were unlikely to provoke an immediate breach of the peace. [63]

## Chapter 13 Notes

[1] U.S. Const., First Amendment.

[2] *New York Times Co. v. Sullivan*, 376 U.S. 254 (1964) (Black, J., concurring).

[3] *Rosenblatt v. Baer*, 383 U.S. 75 (1966) (Black, J., concurring in part and dissenting in part).

[4] *Abrams v. United States*, 250 U.S. 616 (1919).

[5] The first four prongs were enunciated in *United States v. O'Brien*, 391 U.S. 367 (1968); the last prong was added in *Ladue v. Gilleo*, 512 U.S. 43 (1994).

[6] *Central Hudson Gas & Elec. Corp. v. Pub. Serv. Comm'n*, 447 U.S. 557 (1980).

[7] *Tinker v. Des Moines Indep. Cmty. Sch. Dist.*, 393 U.S. 503 (1969).

[8] *Cohen v. California*, 403 U.S. 15 (1971).

[9] *Texas v. Johnson*, 491 U.S. 397 (1989).

[10] *Bland v. Roberts*, Case No. 4-11cv45 (E.D. Va.; Apr. 24, 2012).

[11] *Pickering v. Bd. of Educ.*, 391 U.S. 563 (1968), teacher fired after writing a letter to a local newspaper critical of the board of education and the district superintendent.

[12] "When employees make statements pursuant to their official duties, the employees are not speaking as citizens for First Amendment purposes and the Constitution does not insulate their communications from employer discipline." *Garcetti v. Ceballos*, 547 U.S. 410 (2006), where a district attorney claimed he had been passed up for a promotion for criticizing a warrant's legitimacy, the Court ruled 5-to-4 the First

Amendment did not protect his speech because his statements were made pursuant to his position as a public employee, and not as a private citizen.

[13]*Tinker v. Des Moines Indep. Cmty. Sch. Dist.*, 393 U.S. 503 (1969).

[14] *See Bethel Sch. Dist. v. Fraser*, 478 U.S. 675 (1986) upholding disciplinary action against a student who presented a speech laced with sexual innuendo, *Hazelwood v. Kuhlmeier*, 484 U.S. 260 (1988), holding public school officials may restrict content in school-sponsored student publications, and *Morse v. Frederick*, 551 U.S. 393 (2007), upholding a student's suspension for holding a banner reading "Bong Hits 4 Jesus" at a school-supervised event outside school grounds.

[15] *Turner v. Safley*, 482 U. S. 78 (1987).

[16] *Thornburgh v. Abbott*, 490 U.S. 401 (1989), where inmates and publishers contested prison regulations prohibiting inmates from receiving certain periodicals as a violation of their First Amendment rights.

[17] *See* Kevin Johnson, "Inmates Go to Court to Seek Right to Use the Internet," USA Today, November 23, 2006 and *see also* Vesna Jaksic, "Prisoners' Right to Internet Materials Contested," The National Law Journal, December 26, 2006.

[18] *Williams v. Donald*, Case No. 5:01-cv-292-2, 2007 U.S. Dist. LEXIS 89079 (M.D. Ga. 2007), appealed *Williams v. Donald*, 322 Fed. Appx. 876 (11th Cir. Apr. 10, 2009), vacating summary judgment for defendants and remanding to the district court to be dismissed as moot.

[19] *Clement v. Cal. Dept. of Corrs.*, 364 F.3d 1148 (9th Cir. 2004).

[20] *Jordan v. Hood*, Case No. 03-cv-02320 (D. Colo. 2004).

[21] *Canadian Coal. Against the Death Penalty v. Ryan*, 269 F. Supp. 2d 1199 (D. Ariz. 2003).

[22] Andy Cerota, "Dozens of Condemned Killers Have MySpace.com Accounts," ABC13.com, November 11, 2006.

[23] Johnson, fn. 17, *supra*.

[24] Don Thompson, "Calif. Says Facebook Will Remove Inmates' Pages," Associated Press wire service report, August 8, 2011.

[25] *Parker v. Levy*, 417 U.S. 733 (1974).

[26] *Ibid.*, at 758-759.

[27] *Ibid.*, at 756-757.

[28] The phrase "Catch-22", derived from the 1961 novel of the same name by Joseph Heller about the madness of war, has evolved into common use to mean a cyclical conundrum.

[29] *United States v. Clark* (U.S. Army Ct. Martial 2005). *See also* "Private First Class Leonard Clark Press Release," CENTCOM press release, July 2005. Leonard Clark was charged with violating UCMJ Article 92:

> (Failure to obey order), 11 specifications; by releasing classified information regarding unit soldiers and convoys being attacked or hit by an improvised explosive devices on various dates, discussing troop movements on various dates, releasing Tactics, Techniques, and Procedures and Rules of Engagement used by the unit on various dates, in violation of a lawful general order prohibiting the release of such information and Article 134 (Reckless endangerment), 2 specifications, by releasing specific information, on various dates regarding Tactics, Techniques, and Procedures and Rules of Engagement used by his unit and encouraging its widespread publication, such that the enemy forces could foreseeably access the information, such that with that information it was likely that the enemy forces could cause death or serious bodily harm to U.S. forces engaged in the same or similar mission.

[30] *Ibid.*

[31] "Soldier Bloggers Told to Guard Information," Associated Press wire service report, May 2, 2007.

[32] Associated Press wire service report, September 27, 2004.

[33] Martha Brant, "Soldiers: War on 'Milblogs,'" Newsweek magazine, August 8, 2005.

[34] Michael Felberbaum, "Army Monitors Soldiers' Blogs, Web Sites," Associated Press wire service report, October 30, 2006.

[35] Robert Weller, "Report: Official Sites, Not Bloggers, Breaching Army Security," Associated Press wire service report, August 22, 2007.

[36] *Ibid.*

[37] In May 2007, the Pentagon banned military personnel from using military computers to access certain sites that allow video uploads, including video-sharing sites (YouTube, Metacafe, IFilm, FileCabi, and StupidVideos); social networks (MySpace, BlackPlanet, and Hi5); music sites (Pandora, MTV, 1.fm, and live365); and the photo-sharing site Photobucket. The ban did not apply to private Iraqi Internet cafés. Ironically, the Defense department routinely uploaded videos of American soldiers in Iraq to some of the banned sites as a recruitment tool. *See* "Military Puts MySpace, Other Sites off Limits," Associated Press wire

service report, May 14, 2007, *and* Sam Diaz, "Military Says Bandwidth Alone Forced Web Site Blocking," The Washington Post, p. D01, May 18, 2007. In 2008, the U.S. military launched TroopTube, a video-sharing site for troops and their families. Pentagon employees screen uploaded videos for taste, copyright violations, and national security issues. *See* "Military Bans YouTube, Launches TroopTube," Associated Press wire service report, November 11, 2008.

[38] Lawyers are not the only ones whose blogging is subject to professional conduct codes. Several National Basketball Association players and coaches were fined in 2010 for publicly criticizing game officials in their blogs. NBA Commissioner David Stern said he would fine and possibly suspend players or coaches from playoff games for speaking negatively about referees. *See* Frank Pingue, "Magic's Howard Fined $35,000 for Blog Rant at Refs," Reuters wire service, April 29, 2010.

[39] John Schwartz, "A Legal Battle: Online Attitude vs. Rules of the Bar," The New York Times, September 12, 2009.

[40] *Ibid.*

[41] *Ibid.*

[42] *Ibid.* Presumably, he thought the judge meant it was all right to tell the world at large, just not anyone he knew, which of course, makes no sense. *See also,* the discussion of jurors blogging in Chapter 12.

[43] Florida Judicial Ethics Advisory Committee Opinion No. 2009-20.

[44] Lisa Brennan, "'Dear Abby' Law Firm Blogs a No-No, Insurance Carrier Says," New Jersey Law Journal, April 17, 2007.

[45] FCC Web site, *available at* www.fcc.gov/guides/obscenity-indecency-and-profanity (accessed Mar. 23, 2012).

[46] *FCC v. Pacifica Found.,* 438 U.S. 726 (1978).

[47] *FCC v. Fox Television Stations,* No. 10-1293 (2012).

[48] *Brandenburg v. Ohio,* 395 U.S. 444 (1969).

[49] *Chaplinsky v. New Hampshire,* 315 U.S. 568 (1942).

[50] *Watts v. United States,* 394 U.S. 705 (1969).

[51] *Virginia v. Black,* 538 U.S. 343 (2003) (O'Conner, J., plurality opinion).

[52] Espionage Act of 1917 (Pub. L. 65-24, 40 Stat. 217, enacted June 15, 1917) 18 U.S.C. § 792, *et seq.*

[53] *Schenck v. United States,* 249 U.S. 47 (1919).

[54] *Snepp v. United States,* 444 U.S. 507 (1980).

[55] *United States v. Schulz,* 101 A.F.T.R.2d (RIA) 2436 (N.D.N.Y. 2007). Of course, the free speech issue could have been avoided had the site been shut down under anti-fraud laws.

[56] David Cay Johnston, "Judge Orders a Web Site Selling Tax-Evasion Advice to Close," The New York Times, August 30, 2007. The Times article reported the judge also ordered the names, addresses, telephone numbers, e-mail addresses, and SSNs of every person who merely received materials from the site be turned over to the government so the Internal Revenue Service could identify them and the Justice Department could prosecute them for tax crimes. One wonders if persons ordering material marketed as "How to LEGALLY Avoid Paying Taxes" would have the demonstrated requisite criminal intent to be prosecuted if they honestly believed they were receiving information on some sort of legal tax shelter.

[57] Andrew Adam Newman, "Humane Society Has Its Sights on Amazon.com," The New York Times, August 27, 2007.

[58] Nicola Leske, "YouTube Criticized over Neo-Nazi Clips," Reuters wire service report, August 27, 2007.

[59] *United States v. Cassidy,* Case No. RWT 11-091 (D. Md. 2012). The court dismissed the case, saying the tweets were "protected speech: anonymous, uncomfortable Internet speech addressing religious matters." At least one commentator has suggested the judge misunderstood the nature of Twitter, noting while possible to block individuals on Twitter, a stalker could create a new account and continuing the harassment. *See* Annie Urban, "Shocking Twitter Stalking Case Dismissed as 'Free Speech'," December 16, 2011 *available at* www.care2.com/causes/shocking-twitter-stalking-case-dismissed-as-free-speech.html (accessed Mar. 23, 2012).

[60] Melinda Deslatte, "Judge Throws out La. Facebook Ban on Sex Offenders," Associated Press wire service report, February 16, 2012.

[61] *Ibid.*

[62] *People v. Rolando S.,* Case No. F061153 (Calif. 5th App. Dist. 2011).

[63] *Nebraska v. Drahota,* 17 Neb. App. 678 (Neb. App. Ct. 2009), rev'd 280 Neb. 627 (2010).

# CHAPTER

# 14

---

# DEFAMATION, THE CDA, AND ANONYMOUS SPEECH

> This chapter examines the tort of defamation and its application to the Internet; the Communications Decency Act § 230 and the protection it may provide in certain circumstances; and the right of anonymous free speech.

*"The liberty of the press is a blessing when we are inclined to write against others, and a calamity when we find ourselves overborne by the multitude of our assailants." — Samuel Johnson*

THE FIRST AMENDMENT TO the U.S. Constitution guarantees the right of freedom of speech. But freedom of speech is not absolute; it can be subject to reasonable restrictions on time, place, and manner, and in rare instances, prohibited. Standards for speech may differ if the speaker is a student, a prisoner, or an employee. Speech may provoke a lawsuit, but to sue, a plaintiff needs a valid cause of action, *i.e.*, legal "grounds" for the suit. Primary causes of action include: defamation, breach of contract, tortious interference with business, disclosure of trade secrets or confidential business information, and securities fraud. In this chapter, we will examine the tort of defamation and common law defenses. We will also discuss how defamation applies to the Internet and examine the **Communications Decency Act** as a defense to online defamation claims. The issue of defamation arises throughout the next chapters that comprise the free speech section of this book.

## Defamation

*"My initial response was to sue her for defamation of character, but then I realized that I had no character." — Charles Barkley*

Defamation is a creature of state law. As such, both the elements comprising the tort, and defenses to it, vary in each jurisdiction, depending on the applicable state's statute. Generally, most statutes will define defamation along the lines of an unprivileged, published false statement of fact communicated to an identifiable third-party, that injures the reputation of another. The definition will include the elements of the tort the plaintiff must prove at trial to establish defamation:

**Unprivileged.** The statement cannot be covered by an absolute or qualified privilege.

**Publication.** "Published" in this context means the defamatory statement was communicated to a third-party other than the plaintiff. If made only to the defamed person, it has not been "published", unless reasonable to expect others would see it. On the Internet, the publication element is always met, as the statement is seen by more individuals than the target.

**A false statement of fact.** A fact is objective information that can be proved to be true, as contrasted with an opinion, which is subjective.

**Identifiable.** The statement must clearly identify the defamed party. It need not identify the plaintiff by name, so long as it is clear that the plaintiff is the one being defamed. If the plaintiff were described only as "the pipe-smoking detective in the trench coat and deerskin cap, wielding a magnifying glass, who lives at 221B Baker Street in London" even unnamed, Sherlock Holmes would be clearly identifiable. A plaintiff may even be defamed in a work of fiction if a reasonable person would infer a particular fictitious character actually referred to the plaintiff. This is true even if the author states in a disclaimer the work is fictional. An author wrote a short story published in *Seventeen* magazine based on a conflict between the narrator and "Bryson", her promiscuous classmate. A former classmate of the author, named Kimberly Bryson, sued *Seventeen* for defamation. The court held the disclaimer labeling the story as fiction was not dispositive: "The fact that the author used the plaintiff's actual name makes it reasonable that third persons would interpret the story as referring to the plaintiff despite the fictional label."[1] Haywood Smith, author of the book *The Red Hat Club*, and his publishers were sued for defamation by a woman who claimed a character in the novel resembled her too closely.[2] The fictional character, a sexually promiscuous alcoholic, shared more than 30 similarities with the plaintiff. A jury awarded the plaintiff $100,000 in damages. (Notably, it chose not to award attorneys fees and the cost of the five-year legal battle probably exceeded the award).

**Tends to injure the reputation of another.** The reputation may be that of an individual or a corporation, organization or other entity. In most states, damage to reputation is presumed where the statement is *defamation per se* (*i.e.*, obviously defamatory statements), but a plaintiff must generally prove "special damages" (*i.e.*, a monetary loss caused by the statement) in cases of *defamation per quod* (*i.e.*, not obviously defamatory, but becomes so when extrinsic facts are known). Under common law, a statement was considered defamation per se if it:

- Accused the plaintiff of criminal conduct, or
- Alleged incompetence in the plaintiff's trade, business, or profession, or
- Alleged the plaintiff had a loathsome disease, or
- Alleged unchastity in a woman

In cases of defamation per quod, the burden of proof remains on the plaintiff to prove the statement damaged his reputation.

Intent may be an element of defamation:[3]

- Under certain state statutes
- Under criminal defamation statutes
- In certain matters related to employment

Often the intent element is expressed in common law terms as "fault", and if the defamatory matter is of public concern, mere negligence on the publisher's part can suffice as "fault."

Where the defendant is a media defendant, negligence can sustain a defamation cause of action. The requisite fault depends on the status of the plaintiff. Where the plaintiff is a public official or public figure, he must prove "knowledge of falsity or reckless disregard of the truth" (the *New York Times "actual malice"* standard).[4] Newspapers (and other news media) exist as publishers of matters of public concern and as such have an implied duty to report on matters accurately and truthfully. The breach of such duty is negligence. The elements of a cause of action for negligence are:[5]

1. Duty requiring conformity to a certain standard of conduct;
2. Breach of that duty (failure to conform to the standard);
3. Proximate cause (but for the breach, the result would not have occurred); and
4. Actual harm / damages (financial loss, which may include pain and suffering).

Defamation includes both *libel* (a statement that has permanent form, *e.g.*, written in a letter or book) and *slander* (*i.e.*, comprised of spoken words or gestures and transient, lacking permanent form). An entity that republishes a defamatory statement is equally liable as the original publisher, if the entity knew or had reason to know the defamatory nature of the statement.

## Defenses to Defamation

There are several recognized defenses to a defamation claim:

- **Truth.** An absolute defense to a defamation action. However, since defamation is a creature of state law, a state statute can change that general rule. Case in point: Massachusetts has never recognized an "absolute" truth-based defense, instead adhering to colonial English law principles truthful statements made with "*actual malice*" (*i.e.*, "hatred and ill-will") may constitute defamation. Note, this common law definition of "actual malice" differs from the U.S. Supreme Court definition crafted in <u>New York Times Co. v. Sullivan</u> — "knowledge of falsity or reckless disregard of the truth" ("***Times Malice***").[6] Many do not understand elements of, and defenses to, defamation are derived from state law, so when a Massachusetts court held truth was not a defense to defamation in <u>Noonan v. Staples, Inc.</u>,[7] legal bloggers, who should have known better, dubbed it a "dangerous precedent" and "the most dangerous libel decision in decades".[8] Of course, the case was only a precedent in Massachusetts — the state with the statute — and then, subject to the facts of that case (*i.e.*, had the plaintiff been a public figure, the <u>Times</u> Malice standard would have applied). In <u>Noonan</u>, a traveling salesman claimed his office supply chain employer defamed him and violated several employment agreements after firing him for allegedly padding his expense account (he stated his expense claim of $1,129 for a Big Mac resulted from a misplaced decimal point on his $11.29 McDonald's lunch reimbursement form).[9] Staples e-mailed its 1,500 employees, telling them of Noonan's termination: "A thorough investigation determined that Alan was not in compliance with our [travel and expense] policies."[10] The federal district court granted summary judgment (dismissing the claim), stating truth is an absolute defense to defamation under Massachusetts law. The plaintiff appealed. A three-member panel for the First Circuit upheld the decision, but later reversed itself on the libel claim, ruling the plaintiff could pursue it because of a 1902 state law that says truth is a defense against libel unless the plaintiff can show "actual malice" by the person publishing the statement.[11] It decided the term "actual malice" should be given the common law meaning it had when written into the Massachusetts statute in 1902, not the *Times* Malice meaning of actual malice established in the landmark 1964 U.S. Supreme Court decision. [12]

- **Absolute Privilege.** A complete defense for individuals with a public duty to speak out, absolute privilege is a legal concept protecting statements in court by witnesses, attorneys, or judges; or made on the floor of a legislative body

- **Qualified Privilege.** This is a limited (*i.e.*, not absolute) privilege that protects a statement that would otherwise be defamatory, if made in good faith, without malice, to a person with a corresponding interest or duty, on a matter in which the speaker/writer has an interest or duty (*e.g.*, an employer giving an employee reference). Qualified privilege protects expression made in the public interest unless the statements are made with malice.

- **Fair Comment.** A statement of opinion, as opposed to fact, on a matter of public interest, is not actionable as defamation (*e.g.*, a restaurant or book review).

- **Opinion.** Many state courts have found a privilege for opinion based on their own state constitutions. However, the U.S. Supreme Court has declined "to create a wholesale defamation exemption for anything that might be labeled 'opinion'" because "expressions of 'opinion' may often imply an assertion of objective fact."[13] A statement that contains a fact or can be reasonably interpreted as stating actual facts will not be protected as opinion just because one phrases it as his opinion. "Simply couching such statements in terms of opinion does not dispel [the defamatory] implications; and the statement, 'In my opinion Jones is a liar,' can cause as much damage to reputation as the statement, "Jones is a liar.'"[14] However, statements that cannot reasonably be interpreted as stating actual facts about a person may be protected, as *opinion*, **parody**,[15] or *rhetorical hyperbole*.[16]

- **Consent.** A rather uncommon defense, but it may arise where the defamed individual has signed a waiver of liability prior to the statement.

Most plaintiffs need prove only negligence but public officials and public figures must prove "actual malice" as defined by the U.S. Supreme Court in <u>*New York Times Co. v. Sullivan*</u>. This standard, also referred to as "*Times* Malice," places the burden of proof on the plaintiff to show the defendant acted with "knowledge of falsity or reckless disregard of the truth."

Many other nations follow the "reasonableness" standard established by the High Court of Australia in <u>*Theophanous v. H & W Times*</u>, which adopted a modified version of the *Times* Malice standard.[17] The three-prong "reasonableness" test places the burden of proof on the defendant, who must prove it did not know the information was false, it did not publish recklessly, and its decision to publish was justifiable. Unlike American law, the test applies not to people (*i.e.*, whether the plaintiff is a public figure or private individual), but to subject matter (*i.e.*, discussions of government or political matters, or discussions regarding the suitability and performance of governmental officials").

## Forums for Potential Defamation

There are several possible venues for online defamation. Real time venues include chat rooms and instant messages. These posts disappear shortly after made, but can be preserved by archiving or screenshot programs. Static forums include Web sites, blogs, e-mail, message boards or forums, electronic mailing lists (e-mailed compilations of newsgroup or forum posts), Usenet newsgroups, and archived newsgroups (*e.g.*, Google Groups). Keep in mind, any of these can be archived and/or printed out.

Participants in message boards and chat rooms, besides posting defamatory statements, might post confidential, false, or misleading information about businesses or financial securities, including disclosure of business or trade secrets or falsehoods designed to affect a company's stock price. While chat room posts disappear shortly after posting, message boards often stay archived indefinitely and search engines add permanence to such statements. The fact most forum, message board, and chat room posters use screen names or aliases makes identification of the individual who posted the comment difficult.

## § 230 of the Communications Decency Act

Once a defamation cause of action has been established, the issue becomes: Who is liable? The author? The site owner or Webmaster on whose site the words appeared? The Online Service Provider (OSP) of the interactive content (*e.g.*, Amazon reviews, eBay feedback, YouTube videos)? The firm whose server hosts the site? Or the ISP that distributed the content?

### Common Law Approach

Under common law, courts distinguish between publishers and distributors. If an author's defamatory comment appears in print (*e.g.*, newspapers, magazines, books), then not only the author but the publisher can be liable. The publisher's liability rests on the theory it is in a position to have the knowledge, opportunity, and ability to exercise editorial control over the publication's content. Distributors — such as newsstands, bookstores, and libraries — are usually not subject to liability for an author's defamation on the theory it would not be practical to expect distributors to read every newspaper, magazine, and book they stock. The concept is one sues the newspaper, not the newsboy. Distributors are viewed as mere conduits of the information.

CompuServe, an Internet Service Provider (ISP), allowed subscribers to create bulletin board forums (*i.e.*, message boards). One subscriber published a daily newsletter about the journalism industry on CompuServe's "Journalism Forum." Cubby, a company with a competing news source, claimed it ha been defamed by the subscriber's forum remarks. Cubby sued not only the subscriber, but CompuServe, the latter a far better "deep pocket" defendant. Following common law theory, Cubby alleged CompuServe was liable as a "publisher" of the subscriber's remarks. The federal district court in New York disagreed, holding an ISP more akin to a distributor than a publisher:[18]

> CompuServe has no more editorial control over such a publication than does a public library, book store, or newsstand, and it would be no more feasible for [it] to examine every publication it carries for potentially defamatory statements than * * * for any other distributor to do so.

But four years later, a New York state court reached the opposite result in *Stratton Oakmont v. Prodigy*.[19] An anonymous poster on Prodigy's "Money Talk" forum stated securities firm Stratton Oakmont, Inc., and its president, Daniel Porush, had committed criminal and fraudulent acts in an initial public offering. Stratton and Porush sued

Prodigy, the ISP, for defamation. The court found by using software to filter offensive language and forum moderators to enforce content guidelines, the ISP exercised editorial control over the content of messages, acting more as a publisher than a distributor. By screening and editing messages on its forum, Prodigy was now liable as a publisher.

## Enactment

Ironically, the result of _Cubby_ and _Stratton Oakmont_ made it safer for an ISP to do nothing than attempt to edit or moderate user-posted content. After _Stratton Oakmont_, ISPs were left with two choices: not remove offensive material, lest they be deemed a publisher and subject to liability; or not allow third-party posts. This decision was seen to have the potential to stifle the growth of the Internet and Congress realized what worked for print media might not be appropriate for the Internet. It enacted § 230 of the **Communications Decency Act** (CDA), as a response to _Stratton Oakmont_.[20] Titled "Protection for 'Good Samaritan' Blocking and Screening of Offensive Material", § 230 provides:[21]

> No provider or user of an interactive computer service shall be treated as publisher or speaker of any information provided by another information content provider.

Section 230 established the most important legal protection for ISPs and others who publish online content by overriding traditional treatment of publishers, distributors, and speakers under statutory and common law. The rationale for immunizing ISPs is they are merely conduits (_i.e._, distributors of content) providing a connection to the Internet. Some ISPs act as hosting companies, storing site content on their servers. ISPs may have hundreds of thousands, or even millions of customers; it is impractical to assume they could constantly monitor all content customers post. As a matter of public policy, Congress decided not to treat providers of interactive computer services like other information providers, (_e.g._, newspapers, magazines, TV, and radio), all which may be liable for publishing defamatory material written or prepared by others.

Attempting to rectify the anomalous result of _Stratton Oakmont_, where an ISP is penalized for screening content, § 230 further provides:[22]

> No _provider or user_ of an _interactive computer service_ shall be held liable on account of —
>
> (A) any action voluntarily taken in good faith to restrict access to or availability of material that the provider or user considers to be obscene, lewd, lascivious, filthy, excessively violent, harassing, or otherwise objectionable, whether or not such material is constitutionally protected; or
>
> (B) any action taken to enable or make available to information content providers or others the technical means to restrict access to material described [above].

What is an Interactive Computer Service? The **CDA** defines an it as:[23]

> The term "interactive computer service" means any information service, system, or access software provider that provides or enables computer access by multiple users to a computer server, including specifically a service or system that provides access to the Internet and such systems operated or services offered by libraries or educational institutions.

Subsequent court decisions have interpreted this phrase to include ISPs, blogs, forums, electronic mailing lists, and Web 2.0 interactive content providers (_e.g._, Amazon reviews, eBay feedback, YouTube videos, and social networks) based on the distributor rationale. This makes sense considering the sheer volume of products on Amazon and eBay, and videos on YouTube; self-policing to screen out defamatory material is too manpower intensive to be practical.

Section 230 has also been held to apply to torts besides defamation, such as invasion of privacy. However, the statute exempts from coverage federal criminal statutes and the **Electronic Communications Privacy Act of 1986** (ECPA).[24] It also does not preempt state laws consistent with it and does not "limit or expand any law pertaining to intellectual property." Thus, § 230 does not bar intellectual property (i.e., copyright, trademark,[25] patent, trade secrets) claims against an ISP or site operator, although they may find protection from infringement allegations under the safe harbor provisions of the **Digital Millennium Copyright Act** (DMCA).[26]

Recall from earlier chapters on intellectual property, trademarks can be issued by both states and the federal government, and trade secrets are governed almost exclusively by state law. A debate has arisen over whether the § 230 intellectual property exemption applies to state laws. The Ninth Circuit, in *Perfect 10 v. CCBill*, held it applies to federal intellectual property claims, not state claims.[27] However, the First Circuit indicated § 230 was not limited to federal claims.[28] A broad reading of the statute, like the First Circuit's, would allow state intellectual property claims against ISPs and Web site operators, whereas a narrow interpretation like the Ninth Circuit's would prohibit such claims (i.e., granting immunity to providers of interactive computer services from suit under state law intellectual property claims arising from third-party generated content).

While § 230 may shield the ISP or site operator from liability, the statute does not immunize the alleged defamation's author, who remains liable for his statements.

## No Takedown Provision

Unlike the **DMCA**, § 230 does not have a takedown requirement, though arguably it should.[29] Not only are providers and interactive computer services users immune under § 230 from defamation suits arising from third-party posts—they do not have to remove the defamatory comment after receiving notice of it! In *Zeran v. America Online*, messages on an AOL bulletin board offered T-shirts with "offensive and tasteless slogans" about the Oklahoma City bombing and listed Zeran's contact information. Zeran had not posted them, but received abusive phone calls and death threats. Despite repeated demands AOL remove the messages, they remained on the forum until he sued. The court held § 230 protected AOL and even when notified of defamatory material, ISPs face no liability for failing to remove it.[30]

In *Barrett v. Clark*, Dr. Stephen Barrett, a retired psychiatrist and medical journalist, ran Quackwatch.com, a guide to health fraud and quackery.[31] He had written 48 books, 10 textbook chapters, and "hundreds of articles" in lay and scientific publications.[32] The defendants were "alternative medicine" advocates—Hulda Clark, an unlicensed naturopath operating clinics in California and Mexico, who claimed "all cancers are caused by parasites, toxins, and pollutants" and "can be cured within a few days by herbs and administration of low-voltage electric current" from a battery-operated "zapper" she sold, and Ilena Rosenthal, an online newsgroup moderator.[33] Clark hired Tim Bolen to handle her public relations. Bolen wrote a letter accusing Dr. Terry Polevoy (one of the plaintiffs) of stalking a woman. Rosenthal republished Bolen's letter in her Usenet newsgroup. Barrett and Polevoy sued Clark and Rosenthal for libel. Rosenthal argued she should not be held liable for libelous comments she had not written but merely reposted. Despite the fact print and broadcast media are liable for *republication of libel* because they exercise editorial control over their communications, the trial court held a newsgroup poster of a libelous message written by another immune because she was not the "publisher", only the poster: "As a user of an interactive computer service, that is, a newsgroup, Rosenthal is not the publisher or speaker of Bolen's piece. Thus, she cannot be civilly liable for posting it on the Internet. She is immune."[34] Since the ISP transmitting the newsgroup also has § 230 immunity, the result is a *free pass to libel*. While the plaintiff could have sued the original author (Bolen), he was left with no recourse against others who, like Rosenthal, might republish the comments. In effect, the decision let individuals to republish defamatory content online even if notified it is defamatory. Even the court was not totally at ease with its decision, stating:[35]

> We acknowledge that recognizing broad immunity for defamatory republications on the Internet has some troubling consequences. Until Congress chooses to revise the settled law in this area, however, plaintiffs who contend they were defamed in an Internet posting may only seek recovery from the original source of the statement.

Should Congress follow the court's suggestion and amend the statute, it might draft a safe harbor provision similar to the **DMCA**'s, which requires removal of offending content on notice to the ISP. While reasonable to provide protection for third-parties who republish content, on notification such content is defamatory it makes no sense to allow the third-party to continue to distribute what it knows or has reason to suspect is defamatory content.

### No Recourse?

Some blogs and message boards seem to invite libel from posters; they are the new "bathroom walls" of the Web. Disgruntled waitresses can name bad tippers at bitterwaitress. com — a cursory review reveals "cheapskate" is one of the nicer epithets a tightwad tipper may expect to see next to his name. That pales by comparison to comments on DontDateHimGirl.com, where women post bad date reviews identifying their dates by name and label them as rapists, pedophiles, or carriers of sexually-transmitted diseases, with no concern for the veracity of their statements.

As blogger Kim Ficera succinctly commented:[36]

> Scorned women no longer need to waste time and energy boiling pet rabbits; they can now simply log in to DontDateHimGirl.com, post their exes' pictures and names, and begin destroying the reputations of the men who've done them wrong, all in the name of revenge and in the comfort of anonymity.

Therein lies the problem: assured of anonymity, posters fear no consequences from their comments. Truth becomes the first casualty of the lack of accountability. A criminal defense lawyer sued DontDateHim.com for libel, after several posts allegedly from women he had dated, appeared on the site with his photograph. One claimed he had herpes; another alleged he had infected a woman with a sexually transmitted disease; a third said he was gay.[37] The plaintiff argued the site operator was liable because the site solicited negative comments but did not screen them for truthfulness. The site sought to fall under the **CDA**'s safe harbor, but would the **CDA** leave no recourse to a plaintiff defamed by a message board that literally invited and solicited potentially libelous comments? The public policy rationale the **CDA** should provide a site, message board, or blog with safe harbor for comments made in the heat of debate on topics of public interest is understandable. But where the forum's sole purpose is to solicit "talk trash" about specific individuals without regard to the truth or falsity of their comments, would it not be both inequitable and legally reckless to grant such forums safe harbor?[38] Separate from the defamation issue is a privacy issue. Assuming arguendo the allegations were true, would not posting such personal details on the Web for the whole world to see be an invasion of privacy (*i.e.*, public disclosure of private facts)? What about a post revealing a man was HIV positive, had served time in prison, or had been sexually abused as a child? The technology of the Internet, through instant access to a worldwide audience, enables a single individual to destroy the reputation of another, either through false statements or revelation of private matters. As a society, we must ensure our laws protect against both threats while not chilling legitimate free speech.

This type of site can be defined as a ***personal attack Web site***, *i.e.*, a site that solicits online posts containing personal attacks and offensive content, archived indefinitely, and easily accessed through search engine queries. Usually, these sites take the form of message boards or forums where users start a thread and post comments to it. The sites are archived by search engines, so names posted on the boards will show in search query results. As discussed in Chapter 7, an increasing number of employers conduct Google searches on job applicants. Suppose such a search turned up negative or potentially defamatory comments on a personal attack Web site? A potential employer might reject an applicant solely based on such defamatory comments, without the applicant having the opportunity to dispute the falsehoods.

One woman claimed that happened to her. The Yale law student interviewed for a summer job with 16 firms but failed to receive a single offer, which she attributed to posts about her on a law school-related message board. The Phi Beta Kappa student had been the topic of derogatory posts on AutoAdmit.com, a board for law students run by a third-year law student at the University of Pennsylvania (the site was not operated with school resources) and a 23-year-old insurance agent.[39] Users posted anonymously with no accountability for comments, which were often violent homophobic, racist, anti-Semitic, sexist, and misogynistic, as well as targeted attacks on specific female students.[40] The personal attacks were at times accompanied by the victim's photo, stolen from social networks like Facebook and photo archiving sites like Flickr, increasing the victim's sense of personal violation. (Note, copying one's photographs and republishing them without permission is copyright infringement). One poster reportedly threatened "to sexually violate" the Yale student, while another posed as her on the board to make it look as if she were participating in the chat.[41] A student, whose photograph and breasts were discussed explicitly on the board, said she feared to venture outside, after posters encouraged her classmates to stalk her with their mobile phone cameras and upload her photos. The message board operators were quoted saying the women invited attention by posting their photographs on social networks — a comment wrong on so many levels it bears repeating, if only to offer a glimpse into the mindset of those who run personal attack boards.[42] Ironically, the operators were quoted saying their users posted anonymously because they did not want to "worry about employers pulling up information on them", showing they and their users were (hypocritically) aware of the negative consequences posed by prospective employers conducting Google searches on the victims.[43] More ironically, after the situation was reported in *The Washington Post*, one of the site operators complained of losing a $160,000 job offer from a Boston law firm in the wake of the negative publicity.[44]

If DontDateHimGirl.com attracted venomous posts from women and AutoAdmit.com was filled with misogynistic posts from men, then JuicyCampus.com might be considered as an equal opportunity rumor mill. The site allowed students to comment anonymously about anyone, claiming it assured posters' anonymity by logging IP addresses but not associating them with specific posts. [45] Both male and female students logged on to find anonymous posts purporting to disclose intimate details of their sex lives. Discussion topics included "Who is the biggest slut on campus?" where posters would list female students by name. Students reported worries over how appearing on the site might impact their reputations and job prospects; one expressed concern over what his preteen sister would think if she stumbled across a post of his alleged sexual exploits at college. [46] In one egregious case, a 20-year-old student discovered her deepest secret — having been raped by a homeless vagrant as she walked back to campus from a coffee shop — had been exposed to the world on JuicyCampus.com by an anonymous poster under a heading with her full name followed by the words "deserved it." [47] Launched on seven campuses in 2007, JuicyCampus spread nationwide, getting more than one million unique monthly visitors before shuttering its site in February 2009. [48] Although New Jersey prosecutors investigated whether the site violated the state's **Consumer Fraud Act**, no charges were filed. The site owner blamed the closing on ad revenue and venture capital drying up, no doubt due in part to negative publicity and the threatened investigation deterring advertisers and investors. JuicyCampus' anonymity brought out the worst in people. As one educator noted, freedom of speech "also requires you to be held responsible for what you say," highlighting the problem that anonymous speech can remove accountability. [49]

Although the **CDA** immunizes personal attack sites from liability for third parties posts, nothing prevents such sites from removing offensive content once notified of its existence. But, from anecdotal experience, most do not remove the material. While theoretically the poster could be sued for defamation, it is not always easy to uncover his identity; should the site refuse to reveal it, it would need to be subpoenaed and, as discussed below, such subpoenas are not necessarily issued due to the poster's anonymous free speech rights. There is a difference between protecting a site operator when, unbeknownst to him, one posts a defamatory comment and protecting sites created to propagate gossip and defamation. While the **CDA**'s drafters did not contemplate this distinction and courts have yet to address it, public policy may require judicial creation of a "sliding scale" to balance anonymous free speech against individuals' reputational and privacy interests. While there is a clear need to protect anonymous free speech for whistleblowers and political speech (which both serve the public good), an obvious societal need exists to protect individuals from assaults on their reputations and privacy by personal attack Web sites (which serve no public good).

Also, the damage has been done by the initial posting, its continued presence on the site, and the fact the defamatory comments will be searchable forever through archived caches. Some misguided free speech advocates contend the solution is to counter the defamatory speech with more speech, *i.e.* a rebuttal (the "***Marketplace of Ideas***", as discussed in Chapter 13). The problem with this approach is, in defamation cases, it merely reinforces the defamation by repeating it and adding another layer to the cached and searchable content. Suppose an anonymous poster writes John Smith is a child molester, and Smith writes back "I am not a child molester." Five years later, after a job interview, a prospective employer conducts a Google search on John Smith's name and finds his statement "I am not a child molester." The employer may think "Why would someone write that?" draw his own inferences, and not bother to search further.

## Limitations on § 230 Immunity

As seen in _Barrett v. Clark_, a broad grant of immunity to every site with third-party comments (especially where anonymous) can become a license to libel. Some sites, hiding behind the **CDA's** skirt, actively solicit potentially defamatory comments. The Ninth Circuit has stepped further into the breach, holding § 230 can immunize ISPs where their users have violated state laws, such as right of publicity and trademark statutes.[50]

As discussed below, at least two courts have begun to step back from an absolute grant of immunity, holding immunity applies only for information the site transmitted but did not create.[51] The question of what constitutes "creation" is subjective, however. Screening objectionable content prior to publication is allowed under § 230, as is correcting, editing, or removing content, so long as the meaning is not substantially altered. At some point, courts may determine editing has crossed a line and become equivalent to control over that content, making the site a content producer rather than merely a conduit.

In _Ramey v. Darkside_, a nude dancer sued a site after one of its advertisers used her photograph on the site without her permission.[52] The court ruled online publishers are not responsible for ad content created by others, finding Darkside did not lose **CDA** § 230 immunity by making "minor alterations" to the ad, such as putting its own Web address and a watermark on images. (Note, the dancer might have an appropriation claim against the advertiser directly [_i.e._, the right of publicity, discussed in Chapter 7],[53] and depending on how it obtained the photograph, possibly copyright infringement.)

The idea of limitations on § 230 immunity has manifested itself in litigation involving the **Fair Housing Act** (FHA).[54] In 2004, the U.S. Justice Department sued Spyder Web Enterprises, alleging it published notices and ads on its sites that discriminated based on race, gender, family status, religion, and national origin, in violation of the **FHA**.[55] The government argued since the Internet was a growing source of information for home buyers, it was important sites posting housing listings abide by federal anti-discrimination laws. No binding legal precedent was established, as the case was settled by **consent decree**, _i.e._, the defendant agreed to abide by the law. The issue, however, would not go away. Section 230's immunity for most third-party posts conflicts with another federal statute, the **FHA** and its discrimination prohibitions. If a third-party posts a discriminatory ad on a housing Web site, which federal statute prevails? Both the interest in prohibiting discrimination and the interest in not placing an impossible oversight burden on sites are legitimate concerns. Further, an advertiser could argue a First Amendment freedom of association right in placing an ad, such as for a home "close to synagogues" or stating a roommate preference. While offensive to read an ad stating "no (fill in the blank)", an ad stating "lesbian preferred" might be helpful to both the advertiser and prospective roommate. Two subsequent cases have addressed these issues.

A public interest law group sued Craigslist, an online version of a newspaper classifieds section, charging **FHA** violations by third-party posts with discriminatory language such as "no minorities" on its Chicago site.[56] It cited more than 200 instances of alleged illegal discriminatory language, although Craigslist called the examples "rare" in light of the 10 million housing ads it received monthly.[57] The plaintiff argued Craigslist should be held to the same standards as newspapers and other publications rather than fall under **CDA** § 230's safe harbor. But Congress enacted § 230 because, unlike newspapers, Web sites are often composed of content submitted by visitors without intervention by an editor. The safe harbor provisions have shielded such sites from traditional tort liability (but not criminal or intellectual property claims). Craigslist informed users on every housing listing page discriminatory posts are illegal under federal law and asked readers to contact the site if they saw offending posts, which would then be immediately removed. The Chicago federal district court dismissed the suit based on Craigslist's compliance with the safe harbor provisions. [58] The appellate court upheld the dismissal, noting while the plaintiffs were barred by § 230 from suing Craigslist, they could still "collect damages from any landlord or owner who engages in discrimination." [59] However, veering from a growing body of case law that finds § 230 confers a broad grant of immunity, the court held such immunity exists only where the site has not altered third-party content and caused injury. Drawing on the distinction between a "conduit of information" and a "publisher", the court held ISPs and site operators are immune only for information they transmitted but did not create.

The Ninth Circuit decision by a three-judge panel in _Fair Housing Council of San Fernando Valley v. Roommates.com,_ [60] would seem to follow this narrower interpretation of § 230's grant of immunity. Roommates.com had users fill out a roommate preferences form asking them to choose by gender, sexual orientation, or families (_i.e._, children). On a practical level, the form makes perfect sense. Individuals not only have a legitimate interest in with whom they choose to share (or not share) an apartment or even a bedroom, but also a legal right under the First Amendment to choose with whom they wish to associate. Does it not make more sense for a single woman to state up front she wishes to share her small Manhattan apartment with another woman, rather than have to fend off hundreds of responses from single men? Unfortunately, in a valiant but perhaps misplaced effort to prevent discrimination, the **FHA** precludes such forthrightness in advertising. While the **FHA** prohibits housing discrimination on the basis of race, gender, family status, religion, and national origin (note sexual orientation is not included in that list as a protected class), there is an **FHA** exception allowing discrimination by roommates in shared-housing situations — although _advertising_ those discriminatory preferences is not allowed. [61] This would seem to put an incredible burden on roommate seekers, who must follow up on every ad without the ability to weed out the unsuitable ones.

Roommates.com argued, though legally its form ran counter to the **FHA**, it was protected by the **CDA** § 230 and the trial court agreed, granting the defendant **summary judgment** (meaning there was no genuine issue of material fact). But a Ninth Circuit three-judge appellate panel reversed, stating it was improper to grant summary judgment because it believed there was an issue of fact as to the applicability of the **CDA** § 230 safe harbor. The panel focused on the facts both the search menu and the roommate selection form used drop-down menus specifying gender, sexual orientation, and children options, and the site e-mailed users listings based on those same selected profile preferences. The panel appeared unsure whether the site was a "conduit of information", or a "publisher" because it created a drop-down menu of choices to be selected by the user. Was it merely transmitting the information or, by shaping it, actually creating it? That would be a question of fact for the lower court to decide, as the appellate court _remanded_ the case. One issue the panel debated was whether the form's "additional comments" portion in which users could type remarks in their own words would qualify for § 230 immunity. Two judges said it would, since the site was merely transmitting language created by the user; however, the third judge disagreed, arguing this was where the most objectionable comments had appeared and the site should be judged as a whole. On _en banc_ rehearing, the Ninth Circuit agreed the "additional comments" section qualified for § 230 immunity, as it was not written by Roommates.com, even if the comments themselves were otherwise impermissible. But it found no immunity for publication of users' gender and family status, and use of this information to "channel subscribers away from listings where the individual offering housing has expressed preferences that are incompatible with the subscriber's answers",[62] stating:[63]

> [T]he information about sex, family status and sexual orientation — is provided by subscribers in response to Roommate's questions, which they cannot refuse to answer if they want to use defendant's services. By requiring subscribers to provide the information as a condition of accessing its service, and by providing a limited set of prepopulated answers, [Roommates.com] becomes much more than a passive transmitter of information provided by others; it becomes the developer, at least in part, of that information. And section 230 provides immunity only if the interactive computer service does not "creat[e] or develop" the information "in whole or in part."

Here, the court said by choosing both the questions and choice of answers through use of a drop-down menu in its form, the site exercised control over content — much as a newspaper editor — and was not just a conduit but liable as a publisher of the information. It will be interesting to see if, and how, other courts respond to these two decisions.

## Summary of CDA § 230

The **CDA** § 230 has been interpreted to grant site owners immunity from suits based on content posted by third-parties. This statute preempts all state and local laws that may conflict with it. Where the site is an Internet Content Service (ICS) passively displaying information it is immune from liability. But a site remains liable for content it created or developed, in which case it is acting as an Internet Content Provider (ICP). A site can be an ICS, as well as an ICP liable for content it creates or develops.[64] RSS feeds are "information provided by another content provider" and the site has no liability for that content, but immunity is lost if the site (or blogger) adds its own comments to the feed.[65] **CDA** § 230 has been broadly interpreted, as courts have applied it to an expansive definition of ICSs by extending immunity beyond ISPs to Web sites, message boards, social networks, and blogs. An ICS will not lose immunity by exercising editorial (*e.g.*, changes to spelling, grammar, and length)[66] and self-regulatory functions (*e.g.*, screening out obscenity, profanity, and libel) on the third-party content. Having policies, procedures, or contract provisions to police its site will not make the site owner liable for failing to remove offending third-party content. But an ICS can be liable if:

- It creates or develops the objectionable content
- Promises to remove unauthorized material and fails to keep its promise[67]
- Makes significant changes to third-party content or adds its own comments or other defamatory content, transforming it into an "ICP" (For example, in one case, where a site hosted a consumer complaint forum with defamatory messages about the plaintiff, the court held the **CDA** § 230 did not bar the plaintiff's claim because the site had created the alleged false and defamatory report titles, headings, and other editorial content framing the third-party content.)[68]
- It receives information or e-mail (*e.g.*, "regular U.S. mail" or "private e-mail") it does not believe the sender meant for posting online but makes an affirmative decision to publish it on the site[69]

Courts have found **CDA** § 230 immunity where:

- The site, after notification, failed to remove the defamatory material posted by the third-party—even where, rather than the allegedly defamed party, the actual author requests removal. In one case, gemstone investment firm Global sued Xcentric, owner of the Ripoff Report gripe site, when a third-party posted three allegedly defamatory comments about Global.[70] The poster later asked the site to remove his posts, but it refused, citing its policy against removing reports. The court held "the **CDA** is a complete bar to suit against a Web site operator for its 'exercise of a publisher's traditional editorial functions—such as deciding whether or not to publish, withdraw, postpone or alter content.'"[71]

- The site bought, or was paid to post, third-party content. For example, a court ruled despite being paid auction listing fees, eBay was shielded by the **CDA** § 230 for allowing a third-party to post allegedly fraudulent auction listings.[72]

- The site provided "neutral tools" to create content (*e.g.*, chat rooms, search engines, or social networks with user-created profiles), even if it is aware of a third-party's use of such tools to create defamatory content.[73] However, the site would lose immunity if it "contributed materially" to the illegal or defamatory content.[74]

Two federal appellate decisions point toward a possible emerging trend to restrict application of **CDA** § 230 immunity. Critics have decried the potential for abuse, arguing a broad grant of statutory immunity is unnecessary, potentially harmful, and should be replaced by reliance on defamation law. The trend may be a response to injured parties denied adequate recourse by **CDA** § 230 immunity, after suffering abuse on personal attack Web sites, like those discussed in this chapter, which actively solicit defamatory or privacy invasive comments. A federal court in New Hampshire ruled **CDA** § 230 immunity does not bar state intellectual property claims, including "right of publicity" claims.[75] The decision conflicts with a Ninth Circuit holding the **CDA** § 230 exempts only federal intellectual property claims but would preclude a state claim.[76] Whether a right of publicity claim is an intellectual property claim or a privacy claim (the latter not exempt from **CDA** § 230's coverage) is also an unsettled issue.

## The Fake Profile Cases

In many cases, an individual has created and uploaded a fake profile of another (*e.g.*, a friend, enemy, or celebrity) to a dating site or social network. As discussed in Chapter 15, students have created disparaging MySpace and Facebook profiles of teachers and principals. Such posters may face liability, but the site and ISP are generally shielded by § 230. In *Carafano v. Metrosplash.com, Inc.*, the Ninth Circuit held Matchmaker.com protected from an actress' claims of invasion of privacy, misappropriation, defamation, and negligence after an individual uploaded a fake profile to the dating site.[77] It stated she was "looking for a one-night stand" and listed her home address, with a fake e-mail "which, when contacted, produced an automatic e-mail reply stating, 'You think you are the right one? Proof [sic] it!!', and providing her home address and phone number."[78] She received sexually explicit messages and threats, causing her to move with her son from her home to a hotel for months. The court stated:[79]

> [C]ourts have treated § 230(c) immunity as quite robust, adopting a relatively expansive definition of "interactive computer service" and a relatively restrictive definition of "information content provider." Under the statutory scheme, an "interactive computer service" qualifies for immunity so long as it

does not also function as an "information content provider" for the portion of the statement or publication at issue.

In 2001, Oregon district attorney candidate Jim Carpenter created a Classmates.com account under a former high school acquaintance's name.[80] Classmates.com is a commercial site where individuals can find and reunite with former classmates. The acquaintance, now a high school teacher, had been rumored to have had an extramarital affair with a student. Carpenter, impersonating him, "confessed" to sex with female students. After his message appeared, a copy with an angry letter was sent to the school principal, superintendent, and school board. The teacher denied having posted the message and its content. The principal told him to discover who had posted it. Classmates.com refused to disclose the account creator's identity, so the teacher turned to the police, who subpoenaed the site's records and learned Carpenter had created it. Carpenter apologized and dropped out of the district attorney's race after a local newspaper learned of the incident. The Oregon Bar Association, the state's regulatory body for attorneys, filed a formal complaint against him and the Oregon Supreme Court reprimanded him, questioning his "trustworthiness and integrity" to practice law.[81]

## Defamation in a Blog

There was a time, in pre-Internet days, when one wrote one's inner-most thoughts and feelings in a diary — a small book, usually hidden under lock and key in a desk drawer. Today, many individuals bare their souls in online diaries, called blogs (short for "Web logs"). Unlike locked diaries, blogs are accessible by the entire world, yet often their authors, called "bloggers", forget their words may be read by anyone and everyone and carry consequences. A remark that lies unread in a locked diary is harmless, but an offensive remark broadcast to the world-at-large may be actionable as defamation, breach of contract, or grounds for dismissal from employment. When an individual types words into her blog, she may feel as though she is writing in her diary, but her words potentially may be seen by thousands of readers. Many blogs are rife with defamatory comments the writer might not otherwise have published in a more traditional, less spontaneous medium. Some blogs purport to be news or social commentaries, but, unlike professional journalists trained to avoid libel lawsuits by labeling opinions as such and substantiating and verifying facts before presenting comments as true, bloggers "shoot from the hip", often without regard to the consequences (see the discussion in Chapter 16).

Three months short of the 2004 election, a Republican congressman dropped his re-election bid after a blogger posted an audio file purporting to be the Virginia representative's voice requesting homosexual encounters.[82] The blogger offered no proof for his claims or that the voice was the congressman's, although there had been rumors for years the congressman was gay. Nor did anyone substantiate the claim and the congressman did not comment on it. However, in just 11 days, its posting on the blog was enough to lead to the congressman's withdrawal. While no defamation suit was filed, this example illustrates the ease with which an unsubstantiated rumor can be disseminated to large numbers quickly via the Web and the potential damage to reputations and careers that can result.

Defamation can occur on a Web site, in a blog or on a message board. When a professor posted a student essay on the school's site, both the university and the professor were sued for libel.[83] In the allegedly libelous essay on business ethics, the student recounted being urged by his employer to steal software from a former employer. The current employer insisted the school remove the paper from its site and publish a retraction; the university did the former but refused the latter. He sued for libel, and although a lower court granted *summary judgment* to the defendants,[84] the Michigan Appeals Court reversed,[85] finding the professor negligent in not having read the paper closely before posting it "given (his) education as a lawyer, his position as a professor of business law and that he teaches defamation in the course at issue."[86]

Judging from a survey of articles, confusion exists among commentators (and presumably bloggers) about applicability of libel laws to bloggers. One article describes "a mindset that has long surrounded blogging: that most bloggers essentially are 'judgment-proof' because they—unlike traditional media such as newspapers, magazines, and television outlets—often are ordinary citizens who don't have a lot of money."[87] Any blogger who believes this is in for a rude awakening. Being poor does not grant one a license to libel. As seen from the cases below, anyone from students[88] to homeless hurricane victims[89] can be sued for defamation. While most bloggers "shoot from the hip", unlike a speaker who, too late, wishes she could stuff the spoken words back into her mouth, a blogger still has time to reread and edit comments before posting. This is the point at which the blogger must shift her brain out of neutral and ask: "Did I just type something that might cause me to be sued?"

Money is not always the primary motivator of a defamation suit. The plaintiff may feel a need for vindication and sue even if there is no hope of economic recovery. In 2006, a Florida jury awarded against an impoverished defendant what may be the largest judgment over blog or message board posts.[90] Louisiana resident Carey Bock had a dispute with Florida resident Sue Scheff and posted critical messages about her on a site. Scheff sued for defamation. Bock retained an attorney but, when she could no longer could afford his fees, was left unrepresented. Then, Hurricane Katrina devastated Louisiana in August 2005 — Bock's house was flooded and she was forced to relocate temporarily to Texas, returning to Louisiana in June 2006. During her absence, according to court records, copies of pleadings (and presumably subsequent notice of trial) mailed to her destroyed home in the disaster area were returned by the post office. Bock's Mandeville, Louisiana home was less than 35 miles north of the flooded-ravaged New Orleans, separated only by Lake Pontchatrain. She had stated, on returning to her home, she knew the trial was pending but not when, and in any event could not afford an attorney. When she did not appear at the trial, the judge entered a *default judgment* for the plaintiff. Damages were left to a jury, which returned a verdict of $11.3 million ($6.3 million in compensatory and $5 million in punitive damages).[91] The defendant had posted messages calling the plaintiff a "crook", a "con artist", and a "fraud."[92] She probably did not receive proper notice. She could not afford legal counsel and was not represented at, nor did she attend, the trial. As a result, she had an $11.3 million judgment entered against her. The defendant moved to set aside the verdict and vacate the final judgment, but the court refused; she appealed, but lost.[93] If nothing else, this case should put to rest the mindset judgment-proof bloggers cannot be sued.[94]

Another misconception is, since false posts online can be edited and replaced instantly, reputational damages (and thus recoverable money damages) are minimal.[95] There are three major flaws in this theory. First, a visitor may read the original post but never return to read the correction, thereby continuing to believe the damaging libel. Second, other blogs may repost the original post but fail to post the subsequent correction, leaving all their readers believing the damaging libel. And third, archival sites — like The Wayback Machine[96] and Google — cache and archive Web pages so one could easily come across the original post on a cached page without ever having seen the correction.

Yet another misconception is a blogger is not "entitled to the same free speech protection others are."[97] Bloggers are entitled to free speech; but they are not entitled to abuse it, or libel others in a capricious or malicious manner. When David Milum fired the lawyer representing him in a drunk driving case, he requested his $3,000 retainer back. The lawyer refused and Milum responded by accusing him in his blog of bribing judges on behalf of drug dealers. The attorney sued and since Milum could not prove the libelous statement, he earned the dubious distinction of becoming the first known blogger to lose a libel suit in a jury trial;[98] the Georgia Court of Appeals upheld the $50,000 verdict.[99]

A statement is not libelous because it says something bad about a person; it is libelous because it says something untrue that harms his reputation. Some defamation suits may be filed to silence critics, as in the case of SLAPP actions or gripe sites (both discussed in Chapter 19). Courts must factor in the motivation for the suit and the public interest served by preserving a forum for consumers to vent, with the truthfulness of the statement and the degree of reputational damage, if any. At least one federal court has held the **CDA** § 230 protects bloggers from liability for third-party comments on their blogs.[100] The court ruled even if the blogger exercised some editorial control over the posts, he is still protected. But this does not mean the blogger is not responsible for his own comments; nor does the **CDA** relieve third-parties themselves of responsibility for their comments.

A site owner thought it could rely on the **CDA** to shield him from defamation liability, but failure to respond to a complaint led to an $11 million judgment against it.[101] The plaintiff sued the gossip site after it posted her photograph, first name and last initial, jobs as a Kentucky teacher who also worked as a Cincinnati Bengals cheerleader, and the accusation her ex-boyfriend had cheated on her with more than 50 women, contracted Chlamydia and gonorrhea, and likely passed the diseases on to her. In addition to the **CDA**, the site owner relied on a disclaimer stating: "Postings may contain erroneous or inaccurate information. All images are credited to their original location. The owner of this site does not ensure the accuracy of any content presented on TheDirty.com." Apparently confident the disclaimer and the **CDA** provided immunity from prosecution for defamatory comments appearing on its site, the site owner failed to answer the charges or appear in court. Like the _Bock_ case above, the result was a default judgment. When one party fails to perform a court ordered action, such as appearing in court preventing the legal issue from being presented before the court, the judge may grant as default judgment, ruling in favor of the compliant party (the one who showed up, usually the plaintiff). Here, the defendant lost the case by default because it failed to respond to the suit. Note, this was not a judgment on the merits of the case, but rather a stark reminder mere reliance on the **CDA** or disclaimers without responding to the suit will still result in liability by default judgment.

## First Amendment Protection

Bloggers are entitled to the same First Amendment protection from censorship or punishment by the government (with exceptions for the military and public schools), no matter how contemptible or stupid the content of one's blog may be. A Wisconsin high school teacher was arrested after he posted an anonymous reply to a political blog in response to comments teachers were overworked and underpaid. Praising Eric Harris and Dylan Klebold, the students who killed 12 classmates and a teacher before committing suicide in the April 1999 Columbine High School massacre, he wrote: "They knew how to deal with the overpaid teacher union thugs. One shot at a time!" [102] He allegedly added teacher salaries made him sick because teachers are lazy and work only five hours a day. He was arrested, held in custody for an hour, and then released on $350 bail. While a blogger cannot be arrested for the blog's content—which is protected by the First Amendment—he can be arrested for inciting imminent lawless action. After reviewing the facts (the teacher had been the teachers' union president and claimed his comment was a "sarcastic attempt to discredit critics of education spending"), [103] the district attorney concluded the comment was not an incitement to lawless action and was protected by the First Amendment. [104] The blogger-teacher still faced disciplinary action from his school board for his inappropriate comments. [105]

## Vlogs

The newest form of blog is the *vlog*, short for video log. With easy availability of Webcams and rising popularity of "post your own video" sites like YouTube and Daily Motion, many bloggers have become vloggers. Vlogs range from one sitting before a Webcam discussing whatever is on her mind that day to attempts at stylish productions. Viewers can then leave text comments below the video. Many vloggers produce regular shows and develop a following. Some have tens of thousands of subscribers to their videos, turning bedroom broadcasters into Internet celebrities. A few vloggers have gone on to sign recording contracts or TV deals. This presents an interesting issue: Would a celebrity vlogger be considered a "public figure" in a defamation suit?

To prove defamation, a published false communication injuring one's reputation must be shown. But, if the defamed individual is a public figure, the statement must also have been made with "*actual malice*"—knowledge of falsity or reckless disregard of the truth. This standard, first enunciated by the U.S. Supreme Court in *New York Times Co. v. Sullivan* to apply to *public officials*, [106] has been extended to *public figures*: [107]

> 'Public figures' are those persons who, though not public officials, are 'involved in issues in which the public has a justified and important interest.'
> Such figures are, of course, numerous and include artists, athletes, business people, dilettantes, anyone who is famous or infamous because of who he is or what he has done.

The U.S. Supreme Court, in *Gertz v. Robert Welch, Inc.*, has also defined categories of public figures. *All-purpose public figures* are private individuals who occupy "positions of such persuasive power and influence that they are deemed public figure for all purposes * * * They invite attention and comment." [108] Celebrities like Lindsay Lohan and Donald Trump are examples. *Limited-purpose public figures* "thrust themselves to the forefront of particular public controversies in order to influence the resolution of the issues involved." [109] One can also become a limited public figure by engaging in actions that generate publicity within a narrow area of interest. For limited-purpose public figures, the actual malice standard extends only as far as the defamatory statements relate to the subjects about which they are considered public figures. In *Gertz*, the court noted public figures "invite attention and comment" and "usually enjoy significantly greater access to the channels of effective communication and hence have a more realistic opportunity to counteract false statements than private individuals normally enjoy."[110] That would seem to describe a YouTube "celebrity" who posts videos to invite attention and comment (YouTube allows both text comments posted below the video and "response videos" by others) and has access to channels of effective communication by posting his or her own response video or text comments.[111]

## Blogola

Reminiscent of the Payola scandals of the 1950s, the FTC announced it would begin policing blogs for bloggers touting products or services without revealing they have been compensated for doing so. One woman was paid $800 a month by advertisers to review products on her "mommy" blog offering her readers no clue she was paid to praise the products other than a common "support my sponsor" logo.[112] Section 5 of the **FTC Act** already bans deceptive and unfair business practices. The FTC believes consumers need to know if the blogger has an economic motive for what she blogs. Some bloggers routinely accept perks such as free computers, European vacations, luxury cruises, and cash to recommend or praise the gift provider's product or service without disclosing the compensation to readers. The new FTC guidelines might also cover affiliate marketing, where bloggers and other sites receive commissions when visitors click a link that leads to a purchase at an affiliated retailer, like Amazon affiliates.

# Defamation Versus Anonymous Free Speech

There is an inherent tension between First Amendment anonymous speech rights and the public policy interest in providing individuals with legal recourse to address defamation. An individual's personal reputation reflects on her standing within her community while one's business reputation is the lifeblood of his livelihood. Accordingly, people expect to have protection from, or redress for, damage to their reputation from defamation. At the same time, people want the freedom to speak their mind, but often have valid reasons for not wishing to disclose their identity.

## Rationales Favoring Anonymity

There are many rationales favoring anonymity. It enables speakers to express unpopular ideas and sentiments without fear of retribution. For example, many local governments maintain anonymous hotlines for citizens to report abuses by officials. Police have also established anonymous hotlines for those with knowledge of criminal activities to report it without fear of retaliation from the perpetrators. Whistleblowers will often only come forward to report organizational improprieties anonymously, out of fear of employer retaliation.

People may seek anonymity to avoid embarrassment or ostracism. Online support communities have formed for individuals who need emotional support or access to information regarding a shared situation, such as a medical condition or a sexual preference. For example, gay and lesbian teens may seek emotional support from peers but not wish to identify their sexual preference publicly. People also participate in online support communities to obtain medical information for embarrassing conditions (*e.g.*, impotence) or "loathsome diseases" (*e.g.*, leprosy or sexually transmitted diseases).

Public discourse is an essential component of democracy, and anonymity may fuel the free exchange of ideas from which society benefits. Individuals might desire to cloak their identities to protest political policies or regimes without fear of governmental retaliation. Maintaining their online anonymity might be a matter of life or death for dissidents and other citizens in totalitarian or theocratic societies. Hamza Kashgari, a Saudi Arabian blogger and columnist for the Al-Bilad newspaper, tweeted what was perceived as an insult about the Prophet Mohammed, which is considered blasphemy, a crime punishable by death in that country. In February 2012, he was deported from Malaysia to Saudi Arabia, where he was taken into custody. [113] It is not just the Saudi government, but the culture itself that inspires a climate of lethal consequences for online speech, creating a compelling argument for the value of anonymous speech. In 2008, a woman from Riyadh was killed by her father for chatting with a man on Facebook. She was beaten and shot when he discovered her in the middle of an online chat with the man. [114] This was not an aberrant act by the father; it occurred in the same culture whose judicial system sentenced a 19-year-old girl to 200 lashes and six months in prison after she was the victim of a gang rape, because she had been sitting alone in a car with an unrelated man when both were kidnapped and raped by seven Sunni men. [115]

Another rationale favoring anonymity is it places the focus on the message, not the messenger. This was the rationale behind the use of pseudonyms by the authors of the *Federalist Papers*, yet, as noted below, it has the effect of lessening credibility.

A final rationale for anonymity is to publicize a perceived inflicted wrong without being subjected to a lawsuit. This occurs in the case of cybergripers, who create gripe sites to complain about companies they believe has wronged them. Well-funded corporations and organizations often initiate Strategic Lawsuits Against Public Participation (SLAPPs), not for compensatory monetary damages but to intimidate and suppress speech. Anonymous speech deprives the plaintiff of a target to sue, however it is then likely to file a John Doe lawsuit seeking to unmask the anonymous speaker by subpoenaing the ISP to obtain the poster's IP address.

## Arguments Against Anonymity

There are compelling arguments against anonymity, primarily that it creates a lack of accountability for one's comments or actions and lessens the speaker's credibility. Defamation can be directed at a person, (as in the Liskula Cohen case, discussed below), or a business (as arises in the case of cybergripers). In the context of business defamation, companies can sue for the tort of **trade libel**, where there has been publication of a false statement of fact that is an intentional disparagement of the quality of the plaintiff's services or products. In trade libel cases, the defamation lies against the product or service, not the reputation of the company. Also, trade libel plaintiffs sue for special damages (compensation for monetary loss) and/or injunctive relief.

Anonymity can serve as a shield for cyberstalkers (as in the *Carafano* case, discussed above, where the plaintiff was left with no recourse, as the poster was an unknown individual in Berlin, Germany) and online harassers. Harassment may be targeted against a specific individual or take the form of general hate speech aimed at specific groups. An argument could be made against pseudonymity as well, given its use in cyberbullying (see the Megan Meier case, discussed in Chapter 21).

Anonymity can also create a lack of accountability for criminals engaging in fraudulent scams. These may take the form of fraudulent e-commerce scams or "pump and dump" schemes promoted by violators of securities laws in an effort to inflate stock prices through false online postings.

Anonymity also protects individuals who invade another person's privacy by disclosure of personal or confidential information, such as home phone numbers and addresses, street maps, fax numbers, which could lead to stalking or physical harm (*e.g.*, the Amy Boyer case discussed in Chapter 6 or the Nuremberg abortion files Website case, discussed in Chapter 18), [116] SSNs, and financial or medical records.

Lessened credibility is another downside of anonymity, especially for the speaker, or for those reporting on his comments or seeking to use them as substantive support on a given issue. Attributed statements, even if written pseudonymously, are generally viewed as more credible than anonymous ones. "'The threat is very serious and concerns me greatly,' an anonymous source said" carries less weight than were the same statement to be attributed to Dr. Thomas Frieden, an infectious disease specialist and director of the U.S. Centers for Disease Control and Prevention.

## The Tradition of Anonymous Speech

The U.S. Supreme Court has stated: [117]
> The decision in favor of anonymity may be motivated by fear of economic or official retaliation, by concern about social ostracism, or merely by a desire to preserve as much of one's privacy as possible. Whatever the motivation may be, at least in the field of literary endeavor, the interest in having anonymous works enter the marketplace of ideas unquestionably outweighs any public interest in requiring disclosure as a condition of entry. Accordingly, an author's decision to remain anonymous, like other decisions concerning omissions or additions to the content of a publication, is an aspect of the freedom of speech protected by the First Amendment

The previous chapter discussed how some justices, notably Hugo Black and William Douglas, argued for the absolutism of the First Amendment, believing defamation laws inherently unconstitutional as an impermissible suppression of free speech. Even Alexander Hamilton, one of the Founding Fathers, believed the federal government would lack the authority to suppress any speech. He argued (ironically, under a pseudonym) in *Federalist No. 84,* a Bill of Rights (which includes the First Amendment) was not a necessary component of the proposed Constitution: "Why for instance, should it be said, that the liberty of the press shall not be restrained, when no power is given by which restrictions may be imposed?"

The tradition of anonymous speech dates back to the Founding Fathers. Thomas Paine published the revolutionary pamphlet *Common Sense,* advocating the American colonies' independence from England, anonymously, to avoid charges of treason. Alexander Hamilton, James Madison, and John Jay published the *Federalist Papers* pseudonymously to encourage ratification of the Constitution. They wrote under a fictitious name so detractors would be forced to argue the merits of the content of their speech, rather than attack them ad hominem (*i.e.*, focus on the message, not the messenger).

Yet there remains a consensus or conviction wrongs should be righted, and a means should exist for redress. The pen may often inflict a deeper wound than the sword. More speech alone is not always the solution. Smaller voices may be drowned out in the Marketplace of Ideas by more influential or well-financed ones. The U.S. Supreme Court has held the First Amendment protects the right to anonymous speech, reasoning anonymity helps speech stay free.[118] It ruled activists have a constitutional right to pass out political literature anonymously in 1995,[119] stating "[a]nonymous pamphlets, leaflets, brochures and even books have played an important role in the progress of mankind,"[120] and held door-to-door solicitors or canvassers had a First Amendment right of anonymous speech that was violated by an ordinance requiring registration of their names with the mayor's office and the display of a government-issued name badge permit.[121]

## Unmasking the Speaker

A conflict arises when an anonymous online poster makes a defamatory comment on a blog or Web site. The right to free speech does not include a right to defame, but how does one sue a faceless entity? In the Classmates.com case, Carpenter was fortunate to be able to subpoena the poster's identity, but not all courts may be willing to issue such subpoenas. In a case where a corporation sued multiple "John Doe" defendants for alleged defamatory posts on a bulletin board,[122] a New Jersey Superior Court devised a five-prong test for where a defamation plaintiff seeks to discover the identities of anonymous online posters. In denying their discovery, the court announced the _Dendrite_ test, consisting of five prongs:

- Adequate Notice
- Time to Respond
- Stating Claims with Specificity
- Substantial Showing of Proof
- Balancing Test

Under the _Dendrite_ test, a plaintiff must (1) show it has tried to notify the anonymous poster he is the subject of a discovery procedure; (2) give reasonable time for response; (3) identify the poster's exact statements to the court; and (4) make a prima facie showing for each element of the defamation cause of action.[123] Only after the first four prongs have been met can the trial court apply the fifth prong by "balanc[ing] the defendant's First Amendment right of anonymous free speech against the strength of the prima facie case presented and the necessity for disclosure of the anonymous defendant's identity to allow the plaintiff to proceed."[124]

A Delaware court took a different approach toward protecting anonymous speech in crafting the _Cahill_ test, holding a plaintiff must: (1) make reasonable efforts to notify the defendant and (2) submit sufficient evidence to establish a genuine issue of material fact for each essential claim element within the plaintiff's control.[125] In _Cahill_, an elected official filed a "John Doe" suit to reveal a blogger's identity. The poster had referred to the politician's "character flaws", "mental deterioration", and "failed leadership."[126] The ISP notified "Doe" of the disclosure request, leading him to seek an emergency protective order preventing disclosure.[127] The trial court denied the order, and "Doe" appealed. The Delaware Supreme Court reversed, acknowledging the importance of the right to speak anonymously, particularly on political issues, while noting the First Amendment does not convey a right to defame. It recognized the need to balance these competing interests, but thought the _Dendrite_ test went too far:[128]

> [T]he _Dendrite_ standard goes further than is necessary to protect the anonymous speaker and, by doing so, unfairly limits access to the civil justice

system as a means to redress the harm to reputation caused by defamatory speech. Specifically, under _Dendrite_, the plaintiff is put to the nearly impossible task of demonstrating as a matter of law that a publication is defamatory before he serves his complaint or even knows the identity of the defendant(s). Indeed, under _Dendrite_, the plaintiff is not even able to place the alleged defamation in context by describing the relationship between the plaintiff and the speaker because the speaker's identity is protected until the prima facie case against him has been established.

The court's specious rationale implies one must know the context to determine if a statement is defamatory. While context is necessary to show _libel per quod_, it is not necessary in cases of **libel per se**. If one writes you are "a deadbeat, a thief, and a drunken wife-beater" that is libel per se (absent a showing of truth, an affirmative defense) and far from "an impossible task" to demonstrate the comments' defamatory nature (in terms of surviving a motion for summary judgment). In **libel per quod**, a harmless statement may become defamatory when placed in context of other facts. Most defamation claims are _per se_ and public figures have a higher standard of proof. [129] Nonetheless, the court reached the correct decision, realizing "there is reason to believe that many defamation plaintiffs bring suit merely to unmask the identities of anonymous critics" holding the plaintiff must present evidence creating a genuine issue of material fact for each element of the defamation claim before a court orders a speaker's identity disclosed. [130] Applying that standard, the court had no difficulty finding the phrases "character flaws", "mental deterioration", and "failed leadership" mere opinion and not defamatory.

Anonymous free speech is immensely important to a free society, especially in political matters. But the right is not absolute and must be balanced with individuals' interest in protecting themselves from defamatory anonymous comments. A Pennsylvania trial court, choosing not to follow either the New Jersey or Delaware rationales, compelled disclosure of anonymous posters who had referred to a Philadelphia law firm as "thieves" who committed "fraud" and had "lied to a judge." [131] It ruled the statements "_defamation per se_" as they amounted to accusations of criminal conduct. [132] It stated it chose not to fashion a balancing test as New Jersey and Delaware had done because it believed the state's existing civil procedure rules prohibiting discovery sought "in bad faith" or that would "cause unreasonable annoyance, embarrassment, oppression, burden or expense to the deponent or any person or party" would afford sufficient protection to both interests. [133] Under that standard, it concluded the statements were defamation per se and not entitled to First Amendment protection. But when a "Skanks in NYC" blog posted photos of fashion model Liskula Cohen, captioned with the phrases "psychotic", "ho", and "skank", she sued to learn the anonymous blogger's identity. The New York Supreme Court (one of the state's trial courts) ruled Google, owner of Blogger.com, had to reveal the bloggers' IP address and e-mail. [134] The court found the use of the words "skank", "skanky", "ho", and "whoring" appearing in captions near photos of the model in provocative poses might be defamatory because they "carry a negative implication of sexual promiscuity." [135]

Other courts have crafted their own tests. [136] An Illinois Appellate Court ordered a small town newspaper Web site to disclosure the identities of anonymous posters in a defamation suit, deeming the _Doe_ and _Cahill_ tests irrelevant. [137] In granting discovery, the court found neither test added any procedural protections not already assured by the state's discovery rules. It ruled: [138]

> Once the petitioner has made out a prima facie case for defamation, the potential defendant has no first amendment right to balance against the

petitioner's right to seek redress for damage to his reputation, as it is well settled that there is no first amendment right to defame.

However, the Court of Appeals of Maryland (the state's supreme court) held a newspaper Web site that allowed readers to post anonymous comments did not have to reveal the posters' identities in a defamation case where the plaintiff could not establish a valid cause of action against any of them. [139] The court, reversing the district court and quashing the subpoena, adopted the standard from _Dendrite_ (the fourth prong of the _Dendrite_ test).

## Barriers to Identifying an Anonymous Poster

There are at least five barriers to identifying an anonymous poster:

- **Lack of Cooperation**. The site owner or ISP might not be willing to release the poster's identity voluntarily.
- **Cost**. The expense of obtaining a court order and hiring an attorney might be prohibitive for many potential plaintiffs.
- **Verification**. The poster might not have provided accurate registration information to the site, so even if the plaintiff received a court order to access the site owner's data, it might be a false name and e-mail.
- **Delay**. Every Internet user is assigned an identifiable IP address by their ISP, which is attached to all data sent from the user's computer. While ISPs log these assigned IP addresses, they routinely purge their logs, so the poster's IP address may have been deleted by the time a subpoena is served.
- **Technology**. The poster might have hidden his or her identity by accessing the Internet through a _hotspot_ (a business establishment offering Wi-Fi Internet access) or _proxy server_ (which substitutes its own IP address for the user's). [140]

A hotspot transmits its own IP address, but not the user's, across the Internet. However, the user connects to the hotspot via a laptop network card that bears an identifying MAC address. Although the MAC address is not sent with the message, it is stored on the hotspot's router. Again, time is the enemy for potential plaintiffs, as router storage space is limited and if the router is heavily trafficked, the MAC address will be overwritten before a subpoena can be served and complied with. A poster might also buy a network card and register it with fictitious information and then, turning off his laptop's Wi-Fi switch, post anonymously with the card. The poster might also use MAC spoofing to substitute another MAC address for the real one.

## WikiLeaks

WikiLeaks is an international organization that publishes online submissions of private, secret, and classified information from anonymous sources. Effectively, it serves as a clearinghouse for contributors who wish to see their information disclosed while retaining their anonymity. A robust public debate has ensued over whether WikiLeaks serves a beneficial public purpose or is a source of malicious harm. WikiLeaks became the subject of an ongoing criminal investigation by the U.S. Department of Justice in February 2010, after leaking diplomatic cables sent to the U.S. State Department by 274 American consulates, embassies, and diplomatic missions, in what has become known as the world's largest release of classified material.

## Chapter 14 Notes

[1] *Bryson v. News Am. Publ'ns, Inc.*, 672 N.E.2d 1207 (Ill. 1996).

[2] *Smith v. Stewart*, 660 S.E.2d 822 (Ga. App. 2008).

[3] The intent element may not necessarily be the intent to defame. *See* Prosser, Law of Torts (4th ed., 1977, West Publishing, p. 771): "As in the case of deceit, the intention underlying a defamatory publication may involve a number of elements. The publisher may intend one or more of the following:

1. By words or conduct, to make a particular statement.
2. To communicate it to a person other than the plaintiff.
3. That it shall be understood to refer to the plaintiff.
4. It to convey a defamatory meaning.
5. That the meaning shall be false * * *
6. To cause damage to the plaintiff's reputation."

[4] *New York Times Co. v. Sullivan*, 376 U.S. 254 (1964). (Included in the Cases Section on the Issues in Internet Law site, www.IssuesinInternetLaw.com).

[5] Prosser, fn. 3 *supra*, p. 143.

[6] *New York Times Co. v. Sullivan*, 376 U.S. 254.

[7] *Noonan v. Staples, Inc.*, 556 F.3d 20 (1st Cir. 2009), panel reh'g *Noonan v. Staples, Inc.*, 539 F.3d 1 (1st Cir. 2008) granting motion for summary judgment.

[8] Cristin Schmitz, "Told with Ill Will, Even Truth is Grounds for Libel Suit: E-mail Humiliating Employee Leads to Defamation Suit," InsideCounsel, May 1, 2009.

[9] *Ibid.*

[10] *Ibid.*

[11] Mass. Gen. Laws ch. 231, § 92.

[12] *Sullivan*, 376 U.S. 254, *supra*.

[13] *Milkovich v. Lorain Journal Co.*, 497 U.S. 1 (1990).

[14] *Ibid.*

[15] *Hustler Magazine, Inc. v. Falwell*, 485 U.S. 46 (1988); *see also*, *Hamilton v. Prewitt* 860 N.E.2d 1234 at 1247 (Ind. Ct. App. 2007) ("Parody cannot constitute a false statement of fact and cannot support a defamation claim.").

[16] *Greenbelt Coop. Publ'g Ass'n, Inc. v. Bresler*, 398 U. S. 6 (1970); *Letter Carriers v. Austin*, 418 U. S. 264, 284-286 (1974).

[17] *Theophanous v. H & W Times*, 124 A.L.R. 1 (Austl. 1994).

[18] *Cubby v. CompuServe, Inc.*, 776 F. Supp. 135 (S.D.N.Y. 1991).

[19] *Stratton Oakmont, Inc. v. Prodigy Servs., Co.*, 1995 WL 323710 (N.Y. Sup. Ct. 1995). (Included in the Cases Section on the Issues in Internet Law site, www.IssuesinInternetLaw.com).

[20] The Communications Decency Act (CDA), 47 U.S.C. § 230.

[21] *Ibid.*, 47 U.S.C. § 230(c)(1).

[22] *Ibid.*, 47 U.S.C. § 230(c)(2).

[23] *Ibid.*, 47 U.S.C. § 230(f)(3).

[24] The Electronic Communications Privacy Act (ECPA), 18 U.S.C. § 2510, *et seq.*

[25] Thus, Tiffany's was able to sue eBay on an infringement claim based on auction posts by eBay users. *See Tiffany (NJ), Inc. v. eBay, Inc.*, 576 F. Supp. 2d 463 (S.D.N.Y. 2008), discussed in Chapter 4, *supra.*

[26] The Digital Millennium Copyright Act, 17 U.S.C. § 512. *See* Chapter 3, *supra.*

[27] *Perfect 10, Inc. v. CCBill, LLC*, 488 F.3d 1102 (9th Cir. 2007), reversing the district court's holding the claim for violation of the right of publicity was not barred by CDA § 230 immunity. The interesting aspect of this case is the court treated a right of publicity claim as an intellectual property claim and not as a privacy claim. *See also* Anne Broache, "Adult Site's Legal Battle Could Aid Web Hosting Services," CNET News.com, March 30, 2007.

[28] In *Universal Comm'n Sys., Inc. v. Lycos, Inc.*, 478 F.3d 413, 418 (1st Cir. 2007) the First Circuit noted, in dicta, the exclusion was not limited to federal intellectual property claims and a federal district court in New Hampshire, in *Doe v. FriendFinder Network, Inc.*, 540 F. Supp. 288 (D. N.H. 2008), held a state intellectual property claim should survive a motion to dismiss under § 230. Doe sued adult matchmaking

site FriendFinder when someone posted a fake sexually explicit profile on the site Doe alleged could be "reasonably identified" as portraying her. Doe claimed the fake profile violated her privacy and intellectual property rights under New Hampshire law. The court held her intrusion, public disclosure of private facts, and false light invasion of privacy claims were barred by § 230 but her fourth invasion of privacy claim — misappropriation — was actually the right of publicity and as such an intellectual property right. The right of publicity prevents unauthorized commercial use of someone's identity, including name, image, or likeness. There is debate over whether the right of publicity is a privacy right or an intellectual property right. It is a creation of state law and exists in 28 states, with varying characteristics in each.

[29] In the United Kingdom, the counterpart to the CDA § 230 is the U.K. Defamation Act of 1996, which has been held to immunize an ISP for third-party posts unless it knew about the posting but chose not to remove it from its server. *See* *Godfrey v. Demon Internet, Ltd.*, QBD, [1999] 4 All ER 342, [2000] 3 WLR 1020; [2001] QB 201 (Demon could not rely on the "innocent dissemination" defense because the ISP had been informed three times of the offending post and refused to delete it from the newsgroup.).

[30] *Zeran v. Am. Online, Inc.*, 129 F.3d 327 (4th Cir. 1997), cert. denied 524 U.S. 937 (1998).

[31] *Barrett v. Clark*, 2001 WL 881259, 2001 Extra LEXIS 46 (CA Super. Ct. 1996), rev'd *Barrett v. Rosenthal*, 114 Cal. App.4th 1379 (2003), rev'd *Barrett v. Rosenthal*, 146 P.3d 510 (Cal. 2006). The 1996 case is included in the Cases Section on the Issues in Internet Law site (www.IssuesinInternetLaw.com).

[32] *Ibid.*

[33] *Ibid.*

[34] *Ibid.*

[35] *Barrett v. Rosenthal*, 146 P.3d 510 (Cal. 2006).

[36] Kim Ficera, "Don't Quote Me: Online Anonymity Fosters Prejudice," AfterEllen.com, October 5, 2006, *available at* www.afterellen.com/column/2006/10/quote-online2.html (accessed Mar. 23, 2012).

[37] *Hollis v. Joseph*, Case No. GD 06-12677 (Allegheny Ct. Com. Pl., Pa. 2007).

[38] The Allegheny County (PA) Common Pleas court dismissed the case on jurisdictional grounds (see Chapter 1), even though the plaintiff was a Pennsylvania resident and Pennsylvanians posted messages on the Florida site. *See* Joe Mandak, "Judge Tosses Date-Dissing Web Site Suit," Associated Press wire service report, April 11, 2007.

[39] Ellen Nakashima, "Harsh Words Die Hard on the Web: Law Students Feel Lasting Effects of Anonymous Attacks," The Washington Post, p. A01, March 7, 2007.

[40] Comments such as "did jew (sic) bitches give head to get protein in concentration camps?" were representative of the vile nature of the message board. PrawfsBlawg, April 12, 2007 *available at* http://prawfsblawg.blogs.com/prawfsblawg/2007/04/theres_a_bit_mo.html (accessed Mar. 23, 2012).

[41] *Ibid.*

[42] *Ibid.* The comment has been analogized to the offensive platitude rape victims "invite" rape by the clothing they wear. Also, uploading photographs to a social network or photo archiving site does not imply one is inviting attention; often these sites are set to privacy settings that intend the photos only be seen by selected classes of viewers (*e.g.*, "friends only" settings). Reposting these photos in a different setting and context cannot be seen as an extension of the original posting; in fact, reposting without permission of the copyright holder is an infringement of her rights, and depending on the context, possibly an invasion of privacy (false light and/or appropriation).

[43] *Ibid.*

[44] Boston law firm Edwards Angell Palmer & Dodge rescinded its job offer to Anthony Ciolli, the "Chief Education Director" of AutoAdmit. *See* Amir Efrati, "Law Firm Rescinds Offer to Ex-AutoAdmit Executive," The Wall Street Journal law blog, May 3, 2007, *available at* http://blogs.wsj.com/law/2007/05/03/law-firm-rescinds-offer-to-ex-autoadmit-director (accessed Mar. 23, 2012); Ciolli subsequently countersued two women who had named (but later dropped) him as a co-defendant in a suit against AutoAdmit; *see* Maryclaire Dale, "Penn Law Grad Countersues over Web Posts about Women Law Students," Associated Press wire service report, March 6, 2008.

[45] "College Web Site Posts Sex Gossip, Hate, Rumor," Associated Press wire service report, February 18, 2008.

[46] *Ibid.*

[47] Eamon Mcniff and Ann Varney, "College Gossip Crackdown: Chelsea Gorman Speaks out," ABC News, May 14, 2008.

[48] "JuicyCampus, Home to Nasty School Gossip, Dries up," Associated Press wire service report, February 5, 2009.

[49] *Ibid.*

[50] *CCBill, LLC*, 488 F.3d 1102.

[51] John Borland, "Suit against Craigslist Claims Discriminatory Ads," CNET News.com, February 8, 2006.

[52] *Ramey v. Darkside Prods., Inc.*, 2004 U.S. Dist. LEXIS 10107, Case No. 00-1415, (D. D.C. 2004).

[53] *See* fn. 28, *supra.*

[54] The Fair Housing Act, 42 U.S.C. § 3601, *et seq.*, specifically 42 U.S.C. § 3604(a).

[55] *United States v. Spyder Web Enters., LLC*, Civil Action No. 03-1509 DMC (D.N.J. 2004).

[56] *Chicago Lawyers' Comm. for Civil Rights under the Law, Inc. v. Craigslist, Inc.*, 461 F. Supp. 2d 681 (N.D. Ill. 2006), aff'd 519 F.3d 666 (7th Cir. 2008).

[57] Rebecca Carr, "Web Sites Carry Discriminatory Ads, Civil Liberties Groups Say," Cox News Service, July 16, 2006; *see also* John Borland, "Suit against Craigslist Claims Discriminatory Ads," CNET News.com, February 8, 2006.

[58] *Craigslist, Inc.*, 461 F. Supp. 2d 681.

[59] *Ibid.*

[60] *Fair Hous. Council of San Fernando Valley v. Roommates.com, LLC*, 489 F.3d 921 (9th Cir. 2007) aff'd in part, rev'd in part, vacated in part, and remanded, *en banc* 521 F.3d 1157 (9th Cir. 2008).

[61] 42 U.S.C. § 3603(b)(2), known as the "Mrs. Murphy" exception to the FHA, permits discrimination in situations where the owner of a residence lives on the premises and rents to no more than three other people or families; but 42 U.S.C. § 3604(c) oddly bans all advertising about discriminatory preferences, including those the FHA allows in practice, like the "Mrs. Murphy" exception.

[62] *Fair Hous. Council of San Fernando Valley v. Roommates.com, LLC*, 521 F.3d 1157 (9th Cir. 2008) *at* 3.

[63] *Ibid.*

[64] *Fair Hous. Council* at 1162, where an online roommate matching service was liable for content created on its site by third-parties after providing prompts effectively requiring users to input information in violation of state and federal fair housing rules. But it was immune for illegal information it did not specifically solicit, *e.g.,* posted by third-parties in its "additional comments" section.

[65] *See Doe v. City of New York*, 583 F. Supp. 2d 444, 449 (S.D.N.Y. 2008).

[66] *See Ramey* fn. 52, *supra.*

[67] *See Barnes v. Yahoo!, Inc.*, 565 F.3d 560 (9th Cir. 2009), amended 570 F. 3d 1096 (9th Cir. 2009). *See also Scott P. v. Craigslist, Inc.*, CGC-10-496687 (Cal. Super. Ct. filed Feb. 2010), where a man criminally harassed by a series of fake Craigslist posts and allegedly promised on three occasions by Craigslist representatives it "would take care of it" sued Craigslist under the legal theory of *promissory estoppel* for failing to do so.

[68] *See MCW, Inc. v. Badbusinessbureau.com, LLC*, 2004 WL 833595 (N.D. Tex. 2004). The court also found the defendant lost immunity by soliciting a consumer to create disparaging material.

[69] *See Batzel v. Smith*, 333 F.3d 1018 (9th Cir. 2003).

[70] *Global Royalties, Ltd. v. Xcentric Ventures, LLC*, 544 F. Supp. 2d 929 (D. Ariz. 2008).

[71] *Global Royalties* at 932.

[72] *Gentry v. eBay, Inc.*, 99 Cal. App. 4th 816 (2002).

[73] *Goddard v. Google, Inc.*, 640 F. Supp. 2d 1193 (N.D. Cal. 2009).

[74] *Ibid.*

[75] *FriendFinder*, fn. 28, *supra.*

[76] *CCBill*, fn. 27, *supra.*

[77] *Carafano v. Metrosplash.com, Inc.*, 339 F.3d 1119 (9th Cir. 2003).

[78] *Ibid.*

[79] *Ibid.*

[80] "Lawyer's Joke Earns Reprimand from Court," The Oregonian, August 03, 2004.

[81] *In re Jim Carpenter*, Case No. OSB 02-32; SC S50321 (Ore. 2003) (Oregon State Bar complaint against Jim Carpenter), *available at* www.publications.ojd.state.or.us/S50321.htm (accessed Mar. 23, 2012). *See also* Jim Carpenter Public Reprimand OSB #00436, Oregon State Bar Bulletin, October 2004, *available at* www.osbar.org/publications/bulletin/04oct/discipline.html (accessed Mar. 23, 2012).

[82] *Was available at* www.blogACTIVE.com (accessed Sept. 25, 2007) but no longer available. *See also* Christian Grantham, "Virginia Republican Abruptly Retires over 'Allegations'," Outlet Radio Network,

August 30, 2004, *was available at* www.outletradio.com/grantham/archives/000525.php (accessed Jul. 1, 2009) but no longer available; *see also* Michael D. Shear and Chris L. Jenkins, "Va. Legislator Ends Bid for 3rd Term: Schrock Cites Unspecified Allegations Questioning His Ability to Serve," The Washington Post, p. A02, August 31, 2004.

[83] Declan McCullagh, "Professor's Web Posting at Center of Libel Suit," CNET News.com, January 25, 2005.

[84] A **summary judgment** is a ruling by the court there is no material issue of fact to be tried, and therefore the cause of action should be dismissed.

[85] *Ben-Tech Indus. Automation v. Mayer*, Case No. 247471, 2005 Mich. App. LEXIS 32 (Mich. App. Jan. 11, 2005) (Unpublished).

[86] McCullagh, fn. 83, *supra.*

[87] Laura Parker, "Courts are Asked to Crack down on Bloggers, Web Sites," USA Today, October 2, 2006.

[88] In *Wagner v. Miskin*, 660 N.W.2d 593 (N.D. 2003), reh'g denied (N.D. 2003), cert. denied, 540 U.S. 1154 (2004), a University of North Dakota student's site alleged a professor harassed her with sexually provocative phone calls; the professor sued and won $2 million for libel, $500,000 for slander, and $500,000 for tortious interference with his business relationships. *See also Draker v. Schreiber*, Case No. 06-08-17998-cv (D.C. Medina Cnty., Tex. 2006), aff'd 271 S.W.3d 318 (Tex. App. 2008), upholding the lower court's summary judgment in favor of the students on a claim of intentional infliction of emotional distress and in favor of their parents on claims of negligence and gross negligence; discussed *infra* in Chapter 12.

[89] Laura Parker, "Jury Awards $11.3M over Defamatory Internet Posts," USA Today, October 11, 2006.

[90] *Scheff v. Bock*, Case No. CACE03022837 (Broward Cnty., Fla. Cir. Ct., default verdict, Sept. 19, 2006).

[91] Parker, fn. 89, *supra.*

[92] Anna Badkhen, "Web Can Ruin Reputation with Stroke of a Key," San Francisco Chronicle, May 6, 2007.

[93] *Bock v. Scheff*, Case No. 4D07-3283 (Fla. 4th DCA 2009).

[94] This case is disturbing in several respects. First, is the issue of whether there was proper notice of trial. Normally, notice sent by U.S. Mail is sufficient for proper service; however in a situation where court papers sent to a federally-declared disaster area where entire homes (and presumably mailboxes) are several feet under water are returned as undeliverable by the Post Office, and the defendant admits she was not aware of the trial date, one might question the sufficiency of the notice. Second, while default judgments are common, it seems to fly in the face of notions of due process and equity to proceed with a trial against a defendant who is precluded from personally attending due to lack of proper notice and precluded from being represented by counsel due to lack of funds. Third, while the phrases "crook", "con artist", and "fraud" are undeniably pejorative and damaging to one's reputation, $11.3 million seems excessive, unless the plaintiff had an extremely lucrative business and these three words were proven to cost her that amount (or at least the $6.3 million in compensatory damages) from her bottom line.

[95] Parker, fn. 89, *supra.*

[96] *Available at* www.archive.org/index.php (accessed Mar. 23, 2012).

[97] Parker, fn. 89, *supra.*

[98] *Banks v. Milum*, Case No.A06A2394 (Ga. Super. Ct. 2006), aff'd 642 S.E.2d 892 (Ga. App. 2007).

[99] Greg Land, "Ga. Appeals Court Upholds Libel Verdict against Blogger," Fulton County Daily Report, March 9, 2007.

[100] *DiMeo v. Max*, 433 F. Supp. 2d 523 (E.D. Pa. dismissed May 26, 2006), dismissal aff'd 248 Fed. Appx. 280 (3d Cir. 2007).

[101] "Arizona Website Hit with $11 Million Judgment," Associated Press wire service report, August 26, 2010.

[102] Ryan J. Foley, "Wis. Teacher Arrested for Blog Comment," Associated Press wire service report, December 4, 2007.

[103] *Ibid.* Police seized two computers and two rifles from the teacher's home in a search prior to his arrest; his comment plus the rifles may have led police to make the arrest.

[104] Dan Benson, "Blog Won't Draw Charges; Teacher's Comment was Protected Speech, DA Says," The Milwaukee Journal, December 7, 2007.

[105] This situation raises several issues: Should the teacher have been arrested? Were the police correct to arrest the blogger based on complaints other people were "disturbed" by what he had written? Should the school board punish an employee for something written anonymously outside of work?

[106] *New York Times Co. v. Sullivan*, 376 U.S. 254 (1964).

[107] *Cepeda v. Cowles Magazines & Broad., Inc.*, 392 F.2d 417, 419 (9th Cir. 1968), cert. denied 393 U.S. 840 (1968).

[108] *Gertz v. Robert Welch, Inc.*, 418 U.S. 323, 345 (1974).

[109] *Ibid.*

[110] *Ibid.*

[111] However, when a socialite held press conferences about her divorce she was still deemed to be a private figure and not a limited-purpose public figure. *See Time, Inc. v. Firestone*, 424 U.S. 448 (U.S. 1976).

[112] Deborah Yao, "FTC Plans to Monitor Blogs for Claims, Payments," Associated Press wire service report, June 22, 2009.

[113] "Deported Blogger Could be Executed," The New Age (South Africa), February 12, 2012. His three consecutive tweets on Twitter, preceding anniversary of the Prophet Muhammad's birth, reportedly read:

> On your birthday, I will say that I have loved the rebel in you, that you've always been a source of inspiration to me, and that I do not like the halos of divinity around you. I shall not pray for you.
>
> On your birthday, I find you wherever I turn. I will say that I have loved aspects of you, hated others, and could not understand many more.
>
> On your birthday, I shall not bow to you. I shall not kiss your hand. Rather, I shall shake it as equals do, and smile at you as you smile at me. I shall speak to you as a friend, no more.

[114] Damien McElroy, "Saudi Woman Killed for Chatting on Facebook," The (U.K.) Telegraph, March 31, 2008.

[115] "200 Lashes for Saudi Gang Rape Victim," The (U.K.) Telegraph, November 17, 2007.

[116] While not all personal information falls under the privacy tort of public disclosure of private facts and may be available elsewhere online or through publicly available offline sources like the phone book, as evident from the Boyer and Nuremberg cases, such information can be misused to track down and harm or kill individuals.

[117] *MacIntyre v. Ohio Elections Comm'n*, 514 U.S. 334 (1995), invalidating an election law prohibiting anonymous campaign literature.

[118] *Ibid.*

[119] *Ibid.*

[120] *Talley v. California*, 362 U.S. 60, 64 (1960), invalidating an ordinance requiring identification of handbills; *see also Buckley v. Am. Constitutional Law Found.*, 525 U.S. 182, at 199-200 (1999), invalidating a state statute requiring individuals circulating petitions dealing with issue referenda to wear identification badges.

[121] *Watchtower Bible & Tract Soc'y of New York v. Village of Stratton*, 536 U.S. 150, 166-67 (2002).

[122] *Dendrite Int'l, Inc. v. Doe*, 775 A.2d 756 (N.J. Super. Ct. App. Div. 2001).

[123] What means of attempted notification are satisfactory under *Dendrite* remains unclear. In *Gallucci v. New Jersey On-Line, LLC*, Dkt. No. L-001107-07 (N.J. Super. Ct., Bergen Cnty. 2007), the plaintiff claimed he was not notified of the subpoena and only learned his identity had been disclosed when the target of his attack outted him on the forum. Although the case presented the court with the opportunity to clarify notice provisions under *Dendrite*, it was voluntarily dismissed.

[124] *Dendrite*, 342 N.J. Super. 134.

[125] *Doe v. Cahill*, 884 A.2d 451 (Del. 2005).

[126] "Delaware Supreme Court Protects Anonymous Blogger," Electronic Frontier Foundation site, *available at www.eff.org/press/archives/2005/10/06* (accessed Mar. 23, 2012).

[127] As required by the federal Cable Communications Policy Act of 1984, 47 U.S.C. § 551(c)(2).

[128] *Cahill*, 884 A.2d 451.

[129] *Gertz v. Robert Welch, Inc.*, 418 U.S. 323 (1974).

[130] *Cahill*, 884 A.2d 451.

[131] *Klehr Harrison Harvey Branzburg & Ellers v. JPA Dev., Inc.*, 2006 WL. 37020, 2006 Phila. Ct. Com. Pl. LEXIS 1 (Pa. Com. Pl. 2006), reversed without opinion at *Klehr v. JPA Dev.*, 898 A.2d 1141 (Pa. 2006).

[132] Shannon P. Duffy, "Law Firm's Defamation Claim Found to Trump Critics' Internet Anonymity," The Legal Intelligencer, January 23, 2006.

[133] Pa. R. Evid. 4011.

[134] _Cohen v. Google, Inc._, 887 N.Y.S.2d 424 (N.Y. Cty. 2009).

[135] _Ibid._ Cohen filed, but then dropped, her defamation suit against Rosemary Port, the outted blogger. _See_ "Model Cohen Drops Defamation Suit Against Blogger," The Gaea Times, August 23, 2009.

[136] The Southern District of New York, in _Sony Entm't, Inc. v. Does_, 326 F. Supp. 2d 556, 564-65 (S.D.N.Y. 2004), required "(1) a concrete showing of a prima facie claim of actionable harm * * * (2) specificity of the discovery request * * * (3) absence of alternative means to obtain the subpoenaed information * * * (4) a central need for the subpoenaed information to advance the claim * * * and (5) the party's expectation of privacy." The Northern District of California, in _Columbia Ins. Co. v. Seescandy.com_, 185 F.R.D. 573 (N.D. Cal. 1999), required the plaintiff to (1) identify the missing party with sufficient specificity to determine if the defendant could be sued in federal court; (2) make a good faith effort to communicate with the anonymous defendant and provide notice of the suit, assuring an opportunity to defend his or her anonymity; and (3) demonstrate viable claims. The Western District of Washington adopted a balancing test in _Doe v. 2theMart.com, Inc._, 140 F. Supp. 2d 1088 (W.D. Wash. 2001), asking "[W]hether: (1) the subpoena * * * was issued in good faith and not for any improper purpose, (2) the information sought relates to a core claim or defense, (3) the identifying information is directly and materially relevant to that claim or defense, and (4) [adequate] information * * * is unavailable from any other source." An Arizona appellate court held in _Mobilisa, Inc. v. Doe_, 170 P.3d 712 (Ariz. Ct. App. 2007) "to compel discovery of an anonymous [I]nternet speaker's identity, the requesting party must show: (1) the speaker has been given adequate notice and a reasonable opportunity to respond to the discovery request, (2) the requesting party's cause of action could survive a motion for summary judgment on elements not dependent on the speaker's identity, and (3) a balance of the parties' competing interests favors disclosure."

[137] _Maxon v. Ottawa Publ'g Co._, Case No. 08-MR-125 (Ill. App. Ct. filed Jun. 1, 2010).

[138] _Ibid._

[139] _Indep. Newspapers, Inc. v. Brodie_, 966 A. 2d 432 (Md. 2008).

[140] If the poster routes the message through multiple proxy servers, it is called _onion routing_.

# CHAPTER

# 15

## STUDENT SPEECH

This chapter is devoted to the First Amendment rights of student speech, on and off school grounds.

*"I think free speech on campus has to be important because the currency of universities is ideas."*
— *Neil Gaiman*

ONE OF THE ROLES of the state is to act as educator of its citizen's youth. To this end, every state has established a taxpayer-supported public school system. In its role as educator, the state and its agents—teachers, principals, and school boards—are constrained by, and subject to, the First Amendment. Since the First Amendment is a prohibition against government ("Congress shall make no law..."), private schools are unencumbered by such constitutional constraints. This chapter examines the free speech and free press rights of public school students in light of the four decisions the U.S. Supreme Court has issued in the past half century regarding student expression and the tangled array of their lower court progeny.

The U.S. Supreme Court has ruled students have free speech rights under the First Amendment and any regulation of such speech by public school administrators must be to prevent *"substantial disruption"* in the classroom.[1] However, those speech rights have been curtailed by subsequent decisions: schools may prohibit "indecent speech" (*e.g.*, a high school student's sexual innuendo-laced speech at a student assembly),[2] or speech at school events (even off school premises) promoting illegal drug use.[3]

State-supported public colleges have generally been held to have less control than elementary and high schools over their students' speech rights, partially because most college students are adults and partially because college and university campuses are "peculiarly marketplace[s] of ideas."[4] When speech issues do arise, they tend to revolve around whether the university administration has abridged the free speech rights of students in certain student organizations by refusing to fund those organizations. By officially recognizing specific groups, the university determines which ones will be allowed to share in the kitty of student activity fees it doles out and use campus offices for their meetings. Meeting facilities the college makes available such groups have been held to be "limited public forums".

## Forum Analysis

The level of judicial scrutiny applied to a restriction on speech depends on the nature of the forum in which it occurs. There are three types of public forums:

- **Open or Traditional.** This might be a public square or street corner. The government can impose *time, place, and manner restrictions* but not restrict content, unless it can show a *compelling governmental interest*.
- **Limited or Designated.** This might be a school meeting room or a government building. The government can limit access to types of speakers and use of the facilities to certain subjects, but may not restrict expression absent a *compelling interest*.
- **Closed or Nonpublic.** This might be a prison or military base. Governmental restrictions on access will be upheld if *reasonable* and not based on a desire to suppress any particular view.

The Supreme Court, in *Hazelwood School District v. Kuhlmeier*, held a high school newspaper was a nonpublic forum if produced as part of a journalism class, and therefore "part of the educational curriculum and a regular classroom activity."[5] That controversial decision allows schools to censor, for legitimate educational reasons, content of nonforum, school-sponsored newspapers. The Second Circuit has gone a step further in *R.O. v. Ithaca City School District*, distinguishing between a "limited" public forum and a "designated" public forum, holding the former can be censored consistent with the Supreme Court ruling.[6] Officials at New York's Ithaca High School prevented student editors from running an editorial cartoon about sex education in the school-sponsored newspaper, *The Tattler*, deeming it "inappropriate." The students then published an independent newspaper edition called "The March Issue," and printed the cartoon in it but school officials refused to allow them to distribute it on school grounds. They did allow distribution of two subsequent independently produced newspapers that did not contain the cartoon. There are two issues involved: Under what circumstances can a school censor school-sponsored speech? Can a school ban distribution of a newspaper produced by students independently, off school grounds? Even though *The Tattler*'s submissions were not restricted to current students and the paper was distributed at off-campus locations, the Second Circuit panel ruled *The Tattler* was a "limited public forum," and the school could nonetheless censor it. Turning to the second issue, the panel ruled the independent newspaper could be barred from school grounds based on the Supreme Court's *Kuhlmeier* decision "permitting suppression of vulgar, lewd, obscene, and plainly offensive speech in a public school".[7] The panel said "drawings of stick figures in sexual positions clearly qualify as 'lewd' — that is, 'inciting to sensual desire or imagination.'"[8]

Seven states — Arkansas, California, Colorado, Iowa, Kansas, Massachusetts and Oregon — responded to Kuhlmeier by enacting statutes to protect student journalists' free speech rights.[9] While each is drafted differently, they apply to public elementary, middle and high school students but not explicitly to colleges (with the exception of Oregon's statute, and California, which has separate statutes directed at colleges). Typically, they prohibit obscenity, defamation, invasion of privacy (Arkansas), incitement, encouragement of unlawful acts or violation of school rules, and a Tinkeresque "material and substantial disruption of the orderly operation of the school".[10] Some provide statutory protection for school administrators and teachers from lawsuits arising from student publications.[11] The California statute prohibits prior restraint "unless the content to be published is unprotected by the terms of the section".[12] Note *prior restraint* is the suppression of publication by the state, and should be distinguished from *prior review*, which is the requirement content be submitted for review and the state's (*i.e.*, school's) approval to be published. The Colorado statute provides school-sponsored publications substantially written by students and distributed throughout the school are expressly declared public forums, thus increasing First Amendment protection for those publications. [13] The Kansas statute says material cannot be censored merely because it is controversial. [14] The Massachusetts statute provides the right to freedom of expression in public schools "shall not be abridged" and defines freedom of expression to include "the rights and responsibilities of students… to write, publish, and disseminate their views." [15] The Oregon statute grants free expression rights to student journalists on "school-sponsored media" and is the only one to apply specifically to colleges, as well. [16]

Two states have code provisions relating to free expression of public school students. Pennsylvania's Administrative Code allows prior review by school officials but states: "School officials may not censor or restrict material simply because it is critical of the school or its administration." [17] The Code also makes a vague statement to the effect that "Students have the responsibility to be aware of the feelings and opinions of others and to give others a fair opportunity to express their views." [18] Washington's Administrative Code merely states: "All students possess the constitutional right to freedom of speech and press." [19]

Iowa's **Student Free Expression Law** read: [20]

> 1. Except as limited by this section, students of the public schools have the right to exercise freedom of speech, including the right of expression in official school publications.
>
> 2. Students shall not express, publish, or distribute any of the following:
>
>> a. Materials which are obscene.
>>
>> b. Materials which are libelous or slanderous under chapter 659.
>>
>> c. Materials which encourage students to do any of the following:
>>
>>> (1) Commit unlawful acts.
>>>
>>> (2) Violate lawful school regulations.
>>>
>>> (3) Cause the material and substantial disruption of the orderly operation of the school.
>
> 3. There shall be no prior restraint of material prepared for official school publications except when the material violates this section.

Ben Lange was a journalism teacher at Waukon High School in Iowa and served as faculty advisor for the student newspaper. He was reprimanded on two occasions by the principal for permitting students to publish "inappropriate articles" in two separate editions of the school newspaper. Lange sued the principal and the school district in state court seeking a declaratory judgment to establish the published articles did not violate Iowa's **Student Free Expression Law**. The district court granted summary judgment to the principal and the school district, concluding the articles encouraged students to "potentially commit unlawful acts, violate school regulations, or cause material and substantial disruption to the orderly operation of the school." It also held the statute codified the student speech standard enunciated by the U.S. Supreme Court in *Kuhlmeier*. On appeal, the court reversed summary judgment, rejecting the trial court's conclusion the state legislature intended to codify *Kuhlmeier*, holding instead, the legislature had enacted the statute for "the purpose of giving students more robust free-expression rights than those articulated by the Supreme Court" in *Kuhlmeier*. [21] The court found the articles did not violate any of the prohibitions in the **Student Free Expression Law** — they were not obscene, libelous, and did not encourage students to commit unlawful acts or disrupt school operations — and were, instead, speech protected by the statute: "Because school administrators cannot point to any specific content in the publications that encouraged students to engage in activities barred by the statute, we reverse." [22]

A Seventh Circuit decision in 2005 extended the Supreme Court's _Kuhlmeier_ holding, limiting First Amendment protections for high school students, to public college student expression. [23] In response, Illinois passed the **College Campus Press Act**, banning prior review of school-sponsored media at the state's colleges. [24] For school administrators, the right to censor is a double-edged sword. With editorial control comes increased liability for libelous statements in the student newspaper that they could have removed but did not. [25]

Assuming public schools can punish students for off-campus speech, how would that apply to student journalists who blog or write for independent student papers unaffiliated with a school, as opposed to school-sponsored publications? The tension between schools and student free speech is not new. In 1971, a dispute between the University of Florida and its school paper's editor and staff led to the _UF Alligator_ and its staff leaving the campus and changing the paper's name to _The Independent Florida Alligator._ The student editor had published the addresses of known abortion clinics at a time when abortion was illegal in Florida and the publication of abortion information violated state law. [26] More than 35 years later, Quinnipiac University and its student journalists found themselves in a similar rift. The student editor of the _Quinnipiac Chronicle_, the school-sponsored paper, editorialized against a university policy that prohibited it from publishing news online before it was published in the weekly print edition. The school agreed the paper would eventually become independent, but insisted on appointing the editors for the next year. Upset, the staff quit and formed its own independent, online newspaper, the _Quad News._ The school responded by allegedly threatening to shut down its Society of Professional Journalists chapter because of its support for the _Quad News_, and by barring the _Quad News'_ access to administrators and varsity coaches, staff, and athletes. [27] If one accepts the premise schools can punish students for off-campus speech, could the _Quad News_ student journalist be punished for the content of her blog? Or would she be protected by the First Amendment, like other reporters?

## Spare the Rod

> Love is a boy,
> by poets styl'd,
> Then spare the rod,
> and spoil the child.
> — Samuel Butler (1662)

The U.S. Supreme Court has yet to delineate a school's scope of authority to regulate expression that does not occur on school grounds or at a school-sponsored event. However, lower courts have applied the "on-campus" standard — whether the expression constituted true threats or caused a material and substantial disruption — to expression off-campus that causes a material and substantial disruption on-campus. [28] Whether this extension of the standard to off-campus activity (such as creating a Web site from home) will ultimately be approved by the U.S. Supreme Court remains unseen.[29] While schools have a legitimate concern in responding to speech representing a true threat of imminent harm, especially in light of the spate of school shootings beginning with Columbine High School, they must not punish speech that is merely offensive or unwelcome. School officials must consider what lessons they may be unintentionally teaching about free speech and free expression as they attempt to inhibit, ban, or punish the same.

In one of the first cases to address the issue, a court asked: "Has a school-master the right to punish his pupil for acts of misbehavior committed after the school has been dismissed, and the pupil has returned home?"[30] Eleven-year-old Peter Lander was walking his family's cow past his teacher's house in Vermont, an hour and a half after school had ended. As Peter and his classmates passed his teacher Jack Seaver's house, he called him "old Jack Seaver" and used "saucy and disrespectful language" toward him.[31] The next morning when school began, the teacher reprimanded Peter for his comments and then punished him — whipping him with a small rawhide strap, or as the court put it, "did, in his school, a little beat and bruise the plaintiff."[32] Peter sued for assault and battery. The jury returned a verdict for the teacher, and on appeal, the Vermont Supreme Court upheld the right of teachers to punish students for acts committed off school grounds. The jury's verdict was reversed on other grounds.[33]

The court reasoned:[34]

> It is conceded that [the teacher's] right to punish extends to school hours * * * the offense was committed an hour and a half after the school was dismissed, and after the boy had returned home. * * * When the child has returned home, or to his parents' control, then the parental authority is resumed and the control of the teacher ceases, and then, for all ordinary acts of misbehavior, the parent alone has the power to punish. It is claimed, however, that in this case "the boy, while in the presence of other pupils of the same school, used toward the master and in his hearing contemptuous language, with a design to insult him, and which had a direct and immediate tendency to bring the authority of the master over his pupils into contempt and lessen his hold upon them and his control over the school."

The court held:[35]

> [W]here the offense has a direct and immediate tendency to injure the school and bring the master's authority into contempt, as in this case, when done in the presence of other scholars and of the master, and with a design to insult him, we think he has the right to punish the scholar for such acts if he comes again to school.

But the court in 1859 also admonished, in language similar to the modern phraseology "*causing a material and substantial disruption on campus*"[36] that "the misbehavior must not have merely a remote and indirect tendency to injure the school."[37]

## The Material and Substantial Disruption Standard

Free speech rights of students, as Peter Lander discovered, were given little thought for most of the nation's history, in an era when the platitude "Children should be seen and not heard" was in vogue. It was not until 1943 that the Supreme Court conceded students were entitled to some First Amendment rights. In the midst of World War II, the West Virginia State Board of Education adopted a resolution requiring all students to give a stiff-arm salute the flag and recite the Pledge of Allegiance each day. Several students and their parents who were Jehovah's Witnesses challenged the policy, arguing their religion precluded them from saluting the flag. The Supreme Court ruled the kind of salutes mandated by the Board of Education was a form of utterance and therefore a means of communicating ideas. It concluded the rule violated their First Amendment right of free speech. [38]

While significant on confirming some degree of First Amendment protection for public school students, it would be a quarter century before the Court would revisit the issue. In 1969, as the Vietnam War raged in Southeast Asia and anti-war protests and unrest spread across American college campuses and among students of draftable age, students from universities to junior high schools found their long quieted voices and demanded to be heard. Shortly before Christmas, 1965, in Des Moines, 15-year-old John Tinker, his 13-year-old sister Mary Beth, and their 16-year-old friend Christopher Eckhardt, planned to wear black armbands to their schools (the local high school for the boys, and the junior high for Mary Beth) in protest of the Vietnam War. The school principals banned the wearing of armbands at school, under threat of suspension. Deciding to go forward with their protest, in an act of civil disobedience, the teenagers wore the armbands to school and were suspended until after January 1, 1966. Their suit against the school district reached the U.S. Supreme Court, which resulting in a 7-to-2 ruling in favor of the students. _Tinker_ became the landmark case by which future student free speech cases would be judged. The Court declared: [39]

> It can hardly be argued that either students or teachers shed their constitutional rights to freedom of speech or expression at the schoolhouse gate... School officials do not possess absolute authority over their students. Students in school as well as out of school are 'persons' under our Constitution. They are possessed of fundamental rights which the State must respect... In the absence of specific showing of constitutionally valid reasons to regulate their speech, students are entitled to freedom of expression of their views.

Ironically, while the majority recognized the communicative and expressive value of the students' symbolic speech, it was the First Amendment absolutist Hugo Black who wrote in his dissent he believed the First Amendment did not protect disruptive symbolic speech: [40]

> While I have always believed that under the First and Fourteenth Amendments neither the State nor the Federal Government has any authority to regulate or censor the content of speech, I have never believed that any person has a right to give speeches or engage in demonstrations where he pleases and when he pleases... I repeat that if the time has come when pupils of state-supported schools, kindergartens, grammar schools, or high schools, can defy and flout orders of school officials to keep their minds on their own schoolwork, it is the beginning of a new revolutionary era of permissiveness in this country fostered by the judiciary.

Perhaps in response to Justice Black's concern, Justice Abe Fortas, writing the majority opinion, made it clear First Amendment protection for student speech would encompass symbolic speech but not disruptive speech: [41]

> The school officials banned and sought to punish petitioners for a silent, passive expression of opinion, unaccompanied by any disorder or disturbance

on the part of petitioners. There is here no evidence whatever of petitioners' interference, actual or nascent, with the schools' work or of collision with the rights of other students to be secure and to be let alone. Accordingly, this case does not concern speech or action that intrudes upon the work of the schools or the rights of other students.

Justice Fortas noted mere "fear of disturbance" was insufficient to justify inhibiting student speech, which subsequent decisions have distinguished from "foreseeability of a material and substantial disruption, discussed later in this chapter:[42]

> The District Court concluded that the action of the school authorities was reasonable because it was based upon their fear of a disturbance from the wearing of the armbands. But, in our system, *undifferentiated fear or apprehension* of disturbance is not enough to overcome the right to freedom of expression.[43] [*Emphasis added*].

Justice Fortas enunciated a standard governing a school's right to suppress or punish free speech that has subsequently been applied at both primary and secondary educational levels as well as at public colleges and universities. He explained school administrators may not suppress student speech on a whim, based on convenience or personal preference, introducing the Material and Substantial Disruption standard, which has become known as the _Tinker_ test:[44]

> In order for the State in the person of school officials to justify prohibition of a particular expression of opinion, it must be able to show that its action was caused by something more than a mere desire to avoid the discomfort and unpleasantness that always accompany an unpopular viewpoint. Certainly where there is no finding and no showing that engaging in the forbidden conduct would *"materially and substantially interfere with the requirements of appropriate discipline in the operation of the school,"* the prohibition cannot be sustained. [*Emphasis added*].

Adhering to this distinction, a Missouri state court ruled in favor of a student where, after discovering a student's site criticizing school administrators, a principal suspended the student for 10 days, triggering the school's absenteeism policy which automatically lowered his grades as a result. In enjoining both the suspension and further restriction by the school of the student reposting the site from his home computer, the court — relying on the principal's testimony he had suspended the student because he was upset by the page's content, not because it had caused any substantial disruption at school—stated "Disliking or being upset by the content of a student's speech is not an acceptable justification for limiting student speech under _Tinker_."[45]

Next, Justice Fortas stated a student's speech, including expressive conduct, outside the classroom might still have a materially disruptive effect or substantially invade the rights of others within the classroom to the degree that it would not be constitutionally protected and hence subject to suppression or punishment:[46]

> [c]onduct by the student, *in class or out of it,* which for any reason — whether it stems from time, place, or type of behavior — materially disrupts classwork or involves substantial disorder or invasion of the rights of others is, of course, not immunized by the constitutional guarantee of freedom of speech. A student's rights, therefore, *do not embrace merely the classroom hours.* When he is in the

cafeteria, or on the playing field, or on the campus during the authorized hours, he may express his opinions, even on controversial subjects like the conflict in Vietnam, if he does so without "materially and substantially interfer[ing] with the requirements of appropriate discipline in the operation of the school" and without colliding with the rights of others. [*Emphasis added*].

Of course, *Tinker* was decided decades before the Internet. The idea of student speech in e-mails, blogs, Web sites, social network profiles, or online videos was inconceivable. In 1969, student speech meant speaking in class, handing out flyers or pinning them to bulletin boards, writing articles in the school newspaper (or possibly creating a nonschool-sponsored newspaper to be circulated on campus, or wearing expressive apparel (*e.g.*, armbands or T-shirts with messages written on them. The Internet presents the challenge of speech made by students away from school that nonetheless might reach in within the schoolhouse gates.

*Tinker* was a positive case for public school students, establishing their free speech rights, but subsequent Supreme Court decisions stated their rights were more limited than those of adults. [47] In 1986, in *Bethel School District v. Fraser*, [48] the court held lewd or indecent speech, even if not obscene, could be punished by school officials. At a school assembly of about 600 students, high school student Matthew Fraser gave a speech laced with sexual double entendres. [49] Fraser was suspended for three days and denied the opportunity to speak at graduation. He sued, claiming his free speech rights had been violated, and won both in the district court and on appeal to the Ninth Circuit. The U.S. Supreme Court overturned, in a 7-to-2 decision, allowing public school officials to prohibit vulgar and lewd speech on the rationale it was inconsistent with "the fundamental values of public school education": [50]

> The undoubted freedom to advocate unpopular and controversial views in schools and classrooms must be balanced against the society's countervailing interest in teaching students the boundaries of socially appropriate behavior.

Earlier in this chapter, we discussed *Kuhlmeier*, the third Supreme Court case, decided two years after *Fraser*, in which the Court held when an activity is school-sponsored, school officials may censor speech as long as the censorship is reasonably related to legitimate educational concerns. [51] School-sponsored activities could be school newspapers, concerts, and plays, so this decision grants school officials the final say over what articles appear in student newspapers, what songs are sung at school concerts, and what plays are presented at school drama performances. One way of looking at this decision is the school has an interest in regulating speech that bears the school's imprimatur, *i.e.*, published under the school's name and representing it.

The final Supreme Court student speech case in the quartet is *Morse v. Frederick*. [52] A student was suspended after displaying a banner reading "Bong Hits 4 Jesus" off school grounds but at a school-sanctioned and school-supervised event. The Court ruled against the student, notably not applying the Material and Substantial Disruption standard in its analysis of the case.

What do the four cases in which the Supreme Court has directly ruled on public school students' free speech rights tell us? The initial case, *Tinker*, might be read as establishing a broad protection for public school students that has been narrowed by the Court's subsequent three holdings. The first three cases involved speech taking place on campus while the fourth was characterized by the Court as a school-sanctioned and school-supervised event. [53]

Read together, public student have First Amendment free speech rights (*Tinker*) but school officials may suppress or punish speech if the speech causes or could foreseeably lead to a substantial or material disruption or an interference with rights of others (_Tinker_); or is lewd, vulgar, or indecent (_Fraser_); represents, or appears to represent, the school (_Kuhlmeier_); or advocates illegal drug use. (_Morse_) The Supreme Court has focused on the _effect_ of the speech (material and substantial disruption), its _content_ (lewd, vulgar, or indecent), and if it was _school-sponsored_ (as in an event or publication).

## Tinkering with Student Speech Rights

Online speech by students, often made from computers at home or on smart phones while they cruise the mall, has created a quandary for lower courts, that must determine if schools have any business punishing students for speech made off campus. As the post-Internet Supreme Court has not addressed that issue (Fortas' remark in _Tinker_ regarding "conduct by the student, in class or out of it" not having been directed at the Internet) the development of the law in this area has been relegated to the lower courts, resulting in no small degree of confusion among them. Some hold schools cannot regulate off campus speech, while others allow student speech to be disciplined if a sufficient nexus exists between the speech and the school. In 2012, the Supreme Court rejected the opportunity to rule on the issue and settle a split between two panels of the Third Circuit that had reached opposite decisions on essentially the same fact situation.

### A Bridge Too Far

Many lower courts have found public school officials to be overreaching when disciplining students for online activities outside of the school campus. In _Klein v. Smith_, a student saw a teacher in a restaurant parking lot and gave the teacher "the finger". Unlike the Peter Lander case more than a century earlier, the court held school officials lacked authority to punish a student for conduct not occurring on school grounds or during the school day. [54] A student was suspended for 10 days for creating a Web site criticizing his band teacher, but a federal court issued a temporary restraining order overturning the suspension, ruling it violated the student's free speech rights because school officials lacked authority to regulate speech made by students off campus. [55] A federal district court in Pennsylvania court found no evidence of actual disruption to school operations as a result of a student e-mailing a "Top 10" list to other students making fun of the athletic director's weight and sex life, ruling since the e-mail had been sent from an off-campus computer, the school's suspension of the student violated the student's free speech rights. [56] The same court held two years later schools must limit their authority to punish students to school grounds and school-sponsored events. [57] In _Flaherty v. Keystone Oaks School District_, a student posted a message critical of a teacher from his home computer on an online bulletin board devoted to volleyball at his high school. As punishment, the school had removed him from his school volleyball team, barred him from after-school activities, and revoked his school computer privileges. The district settled for $100,000. In _Latour v. Riverside Beaver School District_, the federal district court on Pennsylvania issued a preliminary injunction to prevent the expulsion of a student for posting four rap songs he had written and recorded on a Web site, because there was "not demonstrated that the songs constituted true threats or caused a material and substantial disruption." [58] The student received a $90,000 settlement.

Two 10th grade girls during a summer sleepover posed for some photographs with "phallic-shaped rainbow colored lollipops" simulating sex acts and posted them on Facebook, MySpace, and PhotoBucket, but did not identify them as Churubusco High School Students. When school officials found out, they suspended both girls from the school volleyball team. The school argued it should be allowed to regulate this speech, while the students claimed their First Amendment rights had been being violated. The Churubusco High School Student Handbook contained a "Code of Conduct" for extra-curricular activities that stated: "If you act in a manner in school or out of school that brings discredit or dishonor upon yourself or your school, you may be removed from extra-curricular activities for all or part of the year." After lamenting "one could reasonably question the wisdom of making a federal case out of a 6-game suspension from a high school volleyball schedule," the federal judge ruled, in _T.V. v. Smith-Green Community School Corp.,_ the school lacked authority to punish the girls for speech outside the school grounds: "The photographs were taken inside the privacy of their own homes and were published to the Internet from outside of school. Defendants contend that 'it is undisputed that the photographs did in fact make it into the school.' While this may be true, it's beside the point. Neither M.K. nor T.V. brought the material into the school environment. Others did." [59] The judge ruled the facts of the case failed to rise to the level of a substantial disruption as required by _Tinker_: [60]

> At most, this case involved two complaints from parents and some petty sniping among a group of 15 and 16 year olds. This can't be what the Supreme Court had in mind when it enunciated the "substantial disruption" standard in _Tinker_. To find otherwise would be to read the word "substantial" out of "substantial disruption."

The judge also reminded freedom of speech should be content-neutral: [61]

> And while the crass foolishness that is the subject of the protected speech in this case makes one long for important substantive expressions like the black armbands of _Tinker_, such a distinction between the worthwhile and the unworthy is exactly what the First Amendment does not permit.

An eighth-grader at Maple Place School in Oceanport, New Jersey created an "I Hate Maple Place" Web site from his home after school. The site was online for four days. His comments about the school and its teachers included: [62]

> 1) The worst teacher is Mrs. [ * * ] because she has a short temper.
> 2) The Principal, Dr. [ * * ] is not your friend and is a dictator.
> 3) It's fun to disrupt class especially in Mrs. [ * * ] room!
> 4) Mrs. [ * * ] is the coolest teacher because she is actually nice and has a brain…

The guestbook had a form for visitors to post comments. Although the boy requested posters refrain from posting threats or profanity, some nonetheless did. The 14-year-old student had no control over these messages; he could not edit them because of limitations imposed by his ISP and could not delete the comments without deleting the entire guestbook. The superintendent discovered the site and directed the principal to call the police. Having nothing better to do on a Saturday night in Oceanport, two police officers reviewed the site and printed out a copy. The boy was confronted with it; the principal and superintendent privately told him and his father it was "possibly a criminal matter." No criminal charges were filed. Ironically, despite the fact he made no offensive or threatening remarks and repeatedly warned others not to, he received far greater punishment than the students who wrote offensive remarks.

He was suspended from classes for five days and from the baseball team for a month, and barred from a class trip to Philadelphia and from taking Honors English and Honors Algebra placement tests during his suspension. Additionally, his school did not announce his award for a high SAT score when similar awards were announced.[63] The court held the **CDA** § 230 immunized the boy, as the site owner, from liability for the guestbook comments by others, and his own comments were entitled to First Amendment protection, as they could not reasonably cause a "specific and significant fear of disruption, [and] not just some remote apprehension of disturbance."[64] The school district settled, apologizing and paying $117,500 in damages and attorney's fees.

### Lobbing the Grenade

The potential disruptive effect of online student speech does not depend on the student's location at the moment he or she first created the speech. One could stand outside the schoolhouse gate, lob a grenade over it, and still yield a material and substantive disruption within the school, without the perpetrator ever setting foot on campus. If a student used a telephone from his home to call his school to report a fake bomb scare, there is no doubt there would be a material and substantial disruption. Classes would be canceled. The school building would be evacuated. Teachers and students would be panicked. No reasonable person would suggest, despite being physically off campus, the student could not be disciplined by school authorities for his actions. Many courts view off campus use of the Internet as the instrumentality the same way.

In _J.S. v. Bethlehem Area School District_, the Supreme Court of Pennsylvania court upheld the expulsion of an eighth-grader whose Web site featured a picture of his teacher's head morphing into that of Adolph Hitler, vile comments directed at the teacher, and a solicitation of $20 to cover the costs of a hit man to kill the teacher.[65] Despite the fact the student had created the Web site off campus, the court found a sufficient nexus between the site it and the school because it "materially disrupted the learning environment" since students were discussing it during school and at school-sponsored activities.

In _Wisniewski v. Board of Education_, a middle school student sent an instant message on America Online to a friend with an icon picturing a gun shooting bullets into a man's head and the words "Kill Mr. VanderMolen," the name of his English teacher. The court upheld Wisniewski's suspension, ruling his speech "crosses the boundary of protected speech and constitutes student conduct that poses a _reasonably foreseeable_ risk that the icon would come to the attention of school authorities and that it would materially and substantially disrupt the work and discipline of the school."[66] [_Emphasis added_]. Here, the court was focusing not merely on the fear of a material substantial disturbance but on its foreseeability. In the earlier _T.V. v. Smith-Green Community School Corp._ case, the plaintiff raised the issue of foreseeability but the court dismissed it:[67]

> But they offer little, either in evidence or argument, as to the nature of the feared disruption. [The Defendant merely asserts it] was familiar with the potential disruption that can result when photographs posted online are brought in to school. This thin record does not support a determination as a matter of law that the school officials made a reasonable forecast of substantial disruption. No reasonable jury could conclude that the photos of T.V. and M.K. posted on

the Internet caused a substantial disruption to school activities, or that there was a reasonably foreseeable chance of future substantial disruption.

There must be a specific reasonable basis to make the risk foreseeable; a general feeling or notion that the student speech might cause a material substantial disruption is not sufficient.

## A Tale of Two Cities

In the next two cases, school officials punished students for vulgar comments made off-campus on their respective social network profile pages. The comments were directed at school policies, using crude language to express disapproval of school administrators and their decisions and policies, yet the two state courts reached opposite conclusions as to whether the public school could punish each student's speech.

In _A.B. v. Indiana_, a middle school principal discovered a MySpace profile purporting to be his own, with a comment from a student, identified as "A.B." stating: [68]

> Hey you piece of greencastle shit.
> What the fuck do you think of me [now] that you can['t] control me? Huh? Ha ha ha guess what I'll wear my fucking piercings all day long and to school and you can['t] do shit about it! Ha ha fucking ha! Stupid bastard!
> Oh and kudos to whomever made this ([I'm] pretty sure I know who).

The comment referred to her displeasure over the school's policy on body piercings. A.B. did not create the fake profile; she merely posted a comment on it. Nonetheless, the state "filed a delinquency petition alleging A.B. committed acts that, if committed by an adult, would have constituted identity deception", and one count of identity theft, although it is not clear where there was any identity deception or theft committed by A.B. since she did not create the fake profile. [69] The state must have also realized this, as it dismissed the identity theft charge, but the juvenile court nonetheless adjudicated A.B. a "delinquent child" and placed her on probation for nine months.

The Juvenile Court wrote: [70]

> [A.B.'s comment] is obscene. As the well known U.S. Supreme Court decision "One knows Pornography when one sees it," this [c]ourt finds that such language is obscene in the context used by [A.B.]. [A.B.] was not exercising her constituted rights of free speech in such a tirade — but to use the most vulgar language she could. Moreover she was not expressing her opinion in her writing.

Obscenity is discussed in Chapter 17, which begins with Justice Potter Stewart's famous quote that he could not define obscenity but knew it when he saw it. However, it should be noted: (1) pornography, which is constitutionally protected, is distinct from obscenity, which is unprotected; and (2) Stewart's humorous remark was a quote within his opinion (_i.e._, dicta), not a holding or decision.

The Indiana Court of Appeals agreed with the appellant's argument: [71]

> A.B. asserts that her message, made in a public forum and criticizing Gobert, a state actor, in implementing a school policy proscribing decorative piercings is a legitimate communication envisioned within the bounds of protected political speech.
> A.B. openly criticizes Gobert's imposed school policy on decorative body piercings and forcefully indicates her displeasure with it. While we have little

regard for A.B.'s use of vulgar epithets, we conclude that her overall message constitutes political speech.

Students do have First Amendment free speech rights.[72] They may not be as articulate as one might wish, falling back on "vulgar language" to express themselves, but it is expression, protected when it concerns policies implemented by state school officials.

Contrast the result in *A.B. v. Indiana* with that of the next case, *Doninger v. Niehoff*. School officials disqualified 17-year-old high school junior Avery Doninger from running for student council for her senior year after she posted a comment in her LiveJournal blog.[73] Doninger and other students had worked on Jamfest—a council-sponsored battle of the bands. They feared school officials' refusal to allow use of the auditorium would mean another postponement of the event, diminishing attendance. They e-mailed students' parents, stating, in part: "[The school administration] says that the auditorium is the taxpayers', not the school's. We the students are asking you, the taxpayers, to please contact central office and ask that we be let to use our auditorium."[74] School officials charged the students with violating school policy by using a school computer for a school event. Doninger claimed the principal pulled her aside to say she was upset about the e-mail and that "as of now, Jamfest is canceled."[75] She went home and posted on her LiveJournal blog:[76]

> jamfest is cancelled due to douchebags in central office. here is an email that we sent out to a ton of people and asked them to forward to everyone in their address book to help get support for jamfest. basically, because we sent it out, Paula Schwartz is getting a TON of phone calls and emails and such. we have so much support and we really appriciate it. however, she got pissed off and decided to just cancel the whole thing all together. anddd so basically we aren't going to have it at all, but in the slightest chance we do it is going to be after the talent show on may 18th. anddd..here is the letter we sent out to parents.

In short, Doninger called school administrators "douchebags", challenged their job performance, and referred to one administrator as being "pissed off"—and when they learned of this, the "douchebags" removed her name from the class election ballot. Students showed up on election day wearing T-shirts that read "Team Avery" on the front and "Support L[ewis] M[ills] H[igh] Freedom of Speech" on the back (Avery wore a shirt that read "R.I.P. Democracy"). The principal stopped the students and told them they had to remove their T-shirts before they could enter the auditorium where the election was to be held.[77] In court, the principal admitted the shirts did not violate the dress code; she claimed her intent was not to stifle free speech but to keep out "electioneering materials [from] the election assembly [that] might unfairly prejudice students who lacked such advertising resources"—even though Doninger was no longer on the ballot and hence not a candidate.[78] Nonetheless, Doninger won with a plurality of write-in votes. The school then invalidated the results of the election.

The federal district court denied Doninger's request for a preliminary injunction, stating she could be punished for blogging because the blog addressed school issues and was likely to be read by other students, or as one critic put it, "In other words, Doninger lost the right to speak because of the likelihood that she'd be heard."[79] This is a particularly egregious comment for a court to make. "School issues" are the politics of the school, and as such, political speech about rules made by the state and how they are enforced goes to the essence of our democracy, which is why political speech is considered the highest form of protected speech, and any restrictions on it must be subjected to strict scrutiny. Nonetheless, the Second Circuit upheld the denial of the preliminary injunction, ruling:[80]

We have determined, however, that a student may be disciplined for expressive conduct, even conduct occurring off school grounds, when this conduct "would foreseeably create a risk of substantial disruption within the school environment," at least when it was similarly foreseeable that the off-campus expression might also reach campus.

The risk of "substantial disruption" in this case is, however, unclear.[81] The risk from decisions like this to society is much clearer. School officials alleged Doninger's use of the word "douchebag" did not comport with the values of "good citizenship" student government leaders should have. But their definition of good citizenship — do not speak out on matters of public concern, do not criticize authority, do not exercise free expression, do not vote for whom you wish ... and if you do, the election will be invalidated — is troubling to anyone familiar with the U.S. Constitution or history. Teaching is not always accomplished in the abstract; students will learn as much from their teachers' actions as they will from their words. Are these the lessons a school should be imparting to its students? Education of the populace is the foundation of democracy. Public schools should teach the value of freedom of expression, political discourse, and free elections in which the results are not ignored when they prove inconvenient. Freedom is not always polite. Teenagers often express thoughts and opinions in the language of their peers, which is not necessarily the language of polite society — but it is expression nonetheless and should be constitutionally protected. With *Doninger*, the Second Circuit extended a disturbing trend of cases diminishing student free speech rights, upholding school officials' right to punish students for out-of–school speech based on vulgarity without regard to whether the speech also contained substantive expression of political ideas (*e.g.*, school policies). If students are so inartful in their expression of ideas they must resort to vulgarity, then the school's purpose should be to teach them how to become expressive in a more polite, civil, or socially acceptable manner, not to suppress the content of their thoughts.

## Panel-demonium

Two Pennsylvania cases addressed, in opposite ways, the issue of whether a school can punish a student for vulgar speech, made off-campus. In both, students created an obscenity-filled MySpace profile purporting to belong to their principals, using vulgar language in a personal attack unrelated to any political issue or event (unlike the preceding cases).[82] In *J.S. v. Blue Mountain School District*, the district court wrote: "The speech does not make any type of political statement. It is merely an attack on the school's principal. It makes him out to be a pedophile and sex addict," ruling the school did not violate J.S.'s rights by punishing her speech "even though it arguably did not cause a substantial disruption of the school."[83] But in *Layshock v. Hermitage School District*, the district court ruled, because Layshock's off-campus expression did not disrupt school activities, the school had violated his First Amendment rights by punishing him.[84] Rejecting the plaintiffs' argument students may never be punished for off-campus speech, the *Blue Mountain* court focused on the fact the MySpace profile centered on the principal, its intended audience was the school's students, and the profile picture was taken from the school district's Web site. Both cases were appealed and two separate Third Circuit panels handed down ostensibly opposed rulings.

The *Layshock* panel unanimously upheld the lower court's finding for the student, holding the offensive profile protected free speech, basing its ruling on the fact the student created it off-campus and had not substantially disrupted the school with his behavior. [85] The _Blue Mountain_ panel, by a 2–to–1 vote, upheld the lower court's decision against the student, finding the offensive profile was not protected free speech, basing its ruling on the school's belief it would cause substantial disruption in the future, had it not been removed. [86] The seemingly contradictory decisions are reconcilable in one respect. Both panels relied on the _Tinker_ rationale, agreeing the school cannot punish or suppress student speech unless it "materially and substantially disrupt[s] the work and discipline of the school." They agreed on the principle of law; where they differed was in how they applied it to the facts of the two cases. In both cases, the panels found the profiles did not create a substantial material disruption in the school. But the _Blue Mountain_ panel focused on the question of whether it was reasonably foreseeable the profile _would_ cause a substantial disruption to the work and discipline of the school. While admitting it had caused only "minor inconvenience": [87]

> Were we examining the facts merely for evidence of a "substantial disruption of or material interference with school activities" that had already taken place, _see Tinker_, 393 U.S. at 514, we would have no trouble concluding, as the District Court did, that these incidents did not amount to a substantial disruption of the Middle School sufficient to discipline the students for their speech. The minor inconveniences associated with the profile, including [the principal]'s meetings related to it, students talking in class for a few minutes, and some school officials rearranging their schedules to assist [the principal], may have resulted in some disruption, but certainly did not rise to a substantial one. It is also difficult to separate the effects that the profile itself had on the school from the effects attributable to [the principal]'s investigation of the profile and subsequent punishment of J.S. and K.L.

The panel stressed: [88]

> [T]he "notion that a school may meet its burden of showing a substantial disruption through its well-founded belief that future disruption will occur," citing "_Doninger v. Niehoff_, 527 F.3d 41, 51 (2d Cir. 2008) (characterizing as "misguided" the notion "that _Tinker_ requires a showing of actual disruption to justify a restraint on student speech")".

But following the Second Circuit's questionable interpretation of _Tinker_ may lead the Third Circuit to an erroneous result. _Tinker_ dealt with an actual alleged substantial disruption on campus, not a potential one. _Tinker_'s holding speech cannot be suppressed unless school officials reasonably conclude it will "materially and substantially disrupt the work and discipline of the school" was a restriction on the authority of schools to punish student speech allowing for an exception only under extreme circumstances. It was not meant to restrict speech that caused minor inconvenience or no present material and substantial disruption. By broadening the scope of the school's power to punish speech for behavior that _might_ occur, the _Blue Mountain_ panel has extended _Tinker_ to an unwarranted degree. [89] Arguably, the "potential for disruption" standard is the antithesis of _Tinker_'s protection of student speech, as its vagueness creates a broad spectrum of scenarios that could subject student speech to suppression and its speakers to punishment. The Supreme Court, in 2012, declined to hear either case.

The principal in _Layshock_ subsequently sued Layshock and three other students in Pennsylvania state court for defamation. [90] Allowing a court of law to adjudicate the matter is arguably a better way to handle posting of a malicious, defamatory false Web profile than punishing or suppressing speech.[91] Students have a First Amendment right of free speech, but when speech crosses into defamation, then they must be responsible and accountable for what they have said. (An interesting question is whether they could argue the fake Web sites were constitutionally protected parodies. An important element of a defamation claim is whether the false statement is likely to be believed. But if the false material appears to have been posted by the parody's target, as in the case of a fake profile, then the reader may likely believe the statements.)

Anyone can create a MySpace profile and, as a result, many abound. As lampooned on the cover of this book, the Internet's anonymity allows people to pretend to be anyone they want. This has made sites like MySpace the technological equivalent of the schoolhouse bathroom stall: where students once scrawled derogatory comments about peers or teachers on bathroom walls, they now create a profile for the target of their ridicule. Similarly to the Classmates.com case in Chapter 14, many students have made fake profiles purporting to be the pages of fellow students, teachers, and principals. As discussed above, schools and courts are struggling to resolve how to deal with students' comments in blogs, on social networks, on personal sites, and on message boards. Malicious online comments directed against other students or teachers is a form of harassment called *cyberbullying* — schoolyard bullying taken from the school playground to the Internet. It includes defamatory statements, threats, ridicule, and harassment.

As they find themselves victimized, more educators and administrators are suing.[92] In Texas, two boys reportedly angered at their high school assistant principal, who had repeatedly disciplined them, made a fake MySpace profile with her photograph, lewd comments, obscene pictures, and images of sexual devices, written as if she had posted the information. It also falsely identified her as a lesbian.[93] MySpace immediately removed it after the assistant principal notified them she had not posted it. The school suspended the page's creator for three days and he was charged with misdemeanor retaliation and fraudulent use of identifying information.[94] What makes this different from the multitude of "fake teacher" profiles — besides the criminal prosecution — is the teacher herself sued the students and their parents, claiming defamation, libel, negligence, and negligent supervision.[95] The civil complaint raises a number of controversial issues:

- Do parents have a duty to supervise children's online activities?
- Can parents incur liability merely by "furnish[ing] the instrumentality" used by their children to create the MySpace page, namely, their personal computer?[96]
- Is it appropriate in this day and age for statements about one's sexuality to be deemed libel per se as a matter of state law?[97]
- Given that most parents of high school students are struggling to meet the costs of impending college tuition, is a lawsuit seeking monetary damages from such parents — possibly depriving the student from the means of attending college — a proper response by an educator to what is admittedly a mean-spirited and ill-advised juvenile prank?

There is no doubt what these boys did was wrong and caused embarrassment and distress. But teachers have been the butt of students' malicious scribblings and pranks since the first little red schoolhouse was built. Children do not necessarily appreciate the consequences of their actions — they may view this as a harmless prank or satire, failing to grasp the deep emotional harm or long-term injury to reputation their actions may cause. Do the potential consequences — a criminal conviction and a civil judgment that could devastate a family or preclude a college education — fit the act? As a society, we must devise appropriate legal responses for abuse of new technology which, while serving as deterrents, are not Draconian.

Additionally, a court may not always side with school administrators. A Florida court ruled suspension of a student for creating a Facebook page to criticize her teacher violated her First Amendment freedom of speech.[98] The high school senior had created a Facebook group entitled "Ms. Sarah Phelps is the worst teacher I've ever met" and wrote: "To those select students who have had the displeasure of having Ms. Sarah Phelps, or simply knowing her and her insane antics: Here is the place to express your feelings of hatred." The group, made after school from Evans' home computer, was removed after two days. The court wrote: "Evans' speech falls under the wide umbrella of protected speech. It was an opinion of a student about a teacher, that was published off-campus, did not cause any disruption on-campus, and was not lewd, vulgar, threatening, or advocating illegal or dangerous behavior."[99] This case strengthens the concept schools cannot punish students for online speech off-campus, absent a substantial disruption of school activities.

Public school administrators have resorted to suppression of speech (prior restraint) and sanctions (suspension from school and banning the student from participation in extra-curricular activities). Perhaps schools should adopt a more proactive, rather than reactive, approach to the way they handle online speech by students. Instead of restricting such expression or punishing students, schools might consider educating students about how to use digital media responsibly.

## Tinker's Overlooked Prong

All of the public school student free speech cases look for guidance to the Supreme Court decision in *Tinker*. Until now, they have uniformly focused on the first prong of *Tinker*—the Material Substantive Disruption standard. But *Tinker* also included a second prong—student conduct that "invades the rights of others" or "collides with the rights of others":[100]

> [C]onduct by the student, in class or out of it, which for any reason * * * materially disrupts classwork or involves substantial disorder *or invasion of the rights of others* is, of course, not immunized by the constitutional guarantee of freedom of speech. A student's rights, therefore, do not embrace merely the classroom hours. When he is in the cafeteria, or on the playing field, or on the campus during the authorized hours, he may express his opinions, even on controversial subjects * * * if he does so without "materially and substantially interfer[ing] with the requirements of appropriate discipline in the operation of the school" *and without colliding with the rights of others.* [*Emphasis added*].

Regardless of whether the student speech creates a material substantive disruption, courts may rule it unprotected speech if it invades or collides with the rights of others. At least one court has held *Tinker*'s second prong to apply to cyberbullying. Kara Kowalski created a group Web page on MySpace devoted to ridiculing a fellow student by claiming she was "a slut who had herpes". After creating the group, she invited about 100 of her MySpace "friends" to join it; about two dozen did so. Participants posted photos and comments ridiculing the victim and implying she had herpes. As the court described:[101]

> The webpage contained comments accusing Shay N. of having herpes and being a "slut," as well as photographs reinforcing those defamatory accusations by

depicting a sign across her pelvic area, which stated, "Warning: Enter at your own risk" and labeling her portrait as that of a "whore." ... The webpage called on classmates, in a pack, to target Shay N., knowing that it would be hurtful and damaging to her ability to sit with other students in class at Musselman High School and have a suitable learning experience.

School officials accused Kowalski of creating a "hate" Web site in violation of the school's policies against "harassment, bullying, and intimidation." She was suspended from school for five days and barred from the cheerleading squad. Kowalski sued, alleging the school district was not justified in punishing her speech because it did not occur during a "school-related activity," but instead was "private out-of-school speech." Relying on both prongs of _Tinker_, the Fourth Circuit held the school's sanctions were permissible because there was a sufficient nexus between Kowalski's online attack targeted against her classmate and the school environment, created a material substantial disruption, and interfered with the rights of another student: [102]

> Kowalski used the Internet to orchestrate a targeted attack on a classmate, and did so in a manner that was sufficiently connected to the school environment as to implicate the School District's recognized authority to discipline speech which "materially and substantially interfere[es] with the requirements of appropriate discipline in the operation of the school and collid[es] with the rights of others." * * *
>
> Although the Supreme Court has not dealt specifically with a factual circumstance where student speech targeted classmates for verbal abuse, in _Tinker_ it recognized the need for regulation of speech that interfered with the school's work and discipline, describing that interference as speech that "disrupts classwork," creates "substantial disorder," or "collid[es] with" or "inva[des]" "the rights of others." _Tinker_, 393 U.S. at 513. * * *
>
> Thus, the language of _Tinker_ supports the conclusion that public schools have a "compelling interest" in regulating speech that interferes with or disrupts the work and discipline of the school, including discipline for student harassment and bullying.

## Student Hate Web Sites

High schools and colleges routinely provide students with access to computers networked into the schools' server, as well as with e-mail accounts and Web page hosting on their servers. Suppose a student wishes to set up a hate site on the school server. Can the school prevent students from using its computers, servers, and network for the promotion of hate views? _Private_ schools are not agents of government and therefore can prohibit students from publishing offensive speech using university equipment or services. However, _public_ schools, as agents of the government, must follow the First Amendment's prohibition against speech restrictions based on content or view. As seen in _Kowalski_, a court may determine the second prong of the _Tinker_ Test permits school officials to regulate or punish cyberbullying or other harassment. Public schools may also simply choose to restrict student use of their server and computers to academic activities, which would likely prevent a student from creating a hate site or sending hate e-mail from his student e-mail account.

## Cyberbullying

Is cyberbullying a form of protected speech? While the Fourth Circuit in _Kowalski_ answered that question in the negative, a federal court in California held a school could not punish students for off-campus speech, even if the speech amounted to cyberbullying.[103] A student posted a four-minute and 36-second video to YouTube showing several students deriding the plaintiff as "spoiled," a "brat," and a "slut" and texted and IMed other students the link to view it. The eighth-grade victim complained to her school guidance counselor the next morning she was too upset and humiliated to go to class, distressed by the video and harassing text messages circulating around school. The girl who posted the video was suspended, and she sued the school, claiming the suspension violated her free speech rights. The court ruled, although reasonably foreseeable the video would be accessed on school grounds, it did not cause a substantial or material disruption sufficient to justify the poster's suspension. "The court cannot uphold school discipline of student speech simply because * * * teenagers are emotionally fragile," the court wrote. This case highlights the difficulty posed by the subjectivity of phrases like "material" and "substantial": what one court views as material another may deem trivial.

A California appeals court took a different approach to balancing free speech and cyberbullying, when a teenage boy created a Web site to promote his pursuit of an acting and singing career. His classmates posted derogatory remarks on his site, calling him a "faggot," and threatening him with bodily harm. The boy's father reported the incidents to the police, who advised him to withdraw his son from the private school. The police later decided the posts did not rise to the level of criminal prosecution and were protected speech. The father sued the students and the school board for defamation, intentional infliction of emotional distress, and hate crimes. In rejecting an anti-SLAPP motion and allowing the case to proceed, the court ruled the messages revealed a harmful intent and were not protected speech.[104]

Some threats are taken more seriously than others. A 14-year-old found herself pulled out of her biology class by two Secret Service agents who proceeded to interrogate her to the point of tears about her MySpace page.[105] The self-described "politically passionate" honor student had posted a picture of President George W. Bush on her MySpace page with the words "Kill Bush" written across it.[106] While it is a violation of federal law to threaten to harm or kill a U.S. president, one would hope the government could differentiate hyperbole or an inartful adolescent attempt at political expression from a legitimate threat to the chief executive.[107]

## Analysis

Lower courts have been confused by the paucity of Supreme Court opinions on the free speech rights of public school students. Of the four cases, one (_Morse_) was narrowly limited by its facts to apply to speech promoting illegal drug use. _Fraser_ would allow school officials to regulate speech if it were lewd or indecent, irrespective of whether it caused any disruption. This may be too broad a standard, as it does not distinguish between, for example, speech consisting of a string of profanities and speech containing political or ideological content laced with profanity. In fact, the _Fraser_ standard does not require profanity or obscenity, but merely "lewd" or "indecent" speech—a highly subjective standard that changes with each generation, as Justice Stevens, noted in his dissent.[108] *Kuhlmeier* allows schools to censor publications or productions produced under its imprimatur, but most of the student speech cases do not involve school newspapers or plays. The controlling case in most student speech cases is likely to be *Tinker*. A close reading of *Tinker* reveals the Court envisioned schools having the right to regulate speech that materially disrupted classwork, whether the speech occurs "in class or out of it":[109]

> [C]onduct by the student, *in class or out of it*, which for any reason—whether it stems from time, place, or type of behavior—materially disrupts classwork or involves substantial disorder or invasion of the rights of others is, of course, not immunized by the constitutional guarantee of freedom of speech. [*Emphasis added*].

In any event, the debate over regulation of off-campus speech is a false dichotomy. The relevant factor is not where the speech was made, but where the harm occurred. In the example of a student phoning in a bomb threat, a material, substantial disturbance occurs on campus, irrespective of the location of the speaker or the instrumentality used to convey the speech. Any other application of the standard would be unworkable and, as demonstrated by the split between the circuits and even between two panels of the same court, will led to confusing and conflicting decisions. For example, speech occurring enroute to school (*i.e.*, as a student is walking to school) might be held protected because it is technically made outside the campus, but the same offensive speech made on a school bus enroute to school might be deemed unprotected if the court viewed the bus as an extension of the campus.

## Chapter 15 Notes

[1] *Tinker v. Des Moines Indep. Cmty. Sch. Dist.*, 393 U.S. 503, 506 (1969), involving the right of students to wear black armbands to protest the Vietnam War, held schools can only punish student conduct that would "materially and substantially interfere with the requirements of appropriate discipline in the operation of the school" without violating the First Amendment.

[2] *Bethel Sch. Dist. v. Fraser*, 478 U.S. 675 (1986).

[3] *Morse v. Frederick*, 551 U.S. 393 (2007) where a student was suspended after displaying a banner reading "Bong Hits 4 Jesus" off campus but at a school-sanctioned and school-supervised event.

[4] *Healy v. James*, 408 U.S. 169, 180 (1972).

[5] *Hazelwood Sch. Dist. v. Kuhlmeier*, 484 U.S. 260 (1988).

[6] *R.O. v. Ithaca City Sch. Dist.*, Dkt. No. 09-1651-cv (2[d] Cir. May 2011).

[7] *Fraser*, 478 U.S. 675. *Cf. Burch v. Barker*, 861 F.2d 1149 (9th Cir. 1988), reaffirming the principle nonschool-sponsored student publications cannot be censored arbitrarily, but not precluding administrative sanctions if a specific publication contains offensive content. In *Burch*, a group of students produced and distributed an unofficial newspaper at a barbeque at a high school. The court overturned a school district policy requiring prior administrative review of all student-produced publications. It ruled a broad policy of prior restraint is unconstitutional, but school officials may punish students afterward for distributing offensive or disruptive materials.

[8] *R.O. v. Ithaca City Sch. Dist.*, Dkt. No. 09-1651-cv.

[9] Actually, California's statute predates *Kuhlmeier* by a decade and was the nation's first student expression law.

[10] The Arkansas Student Publications Act, Ark. Stat. Ann. §§ 6-18-1201-1204 (Apr. 10, 1995).

[11] The Colorado statute expressly forbids holding any district, employee, official, parent or guardian civilly or criminally liable for any "expression made by students in the exercise of freedom of speech or freedom of the press." CRS § 22-1-120(7). The Iowa statute provides "public school district and school employees or officials" cannot be held liable in any lawsuit or prosecution against student expression, "unless the school employees or officials have interfered with or altered the content of the student speech or expression, and then only to the extent of the interference or alteration of the speech or expression." IC § 280.22(6). The Kansas statute provides the board of education, the school district and their employees cannot be held responsible in any civil or criminal action for student expression under the statute. KSA § 72.1506(a).

[12] The California Student Free Expression Law, Calif. Educ. Code § 48907 (1977).

[13] The Colorado Student Free Expression Law, Colo. Rev. Stat. § 22-1-120 (1990).

[14] The Kansas Student Publication Act, Kan. Stat. Ann. §§ 72.1504 - 72.1506 (1992).

[15] The Massachusetts Student Free Expression Law, Mass. Gen. Laws Ann. ch. 71, § 82 (1988).

[16] The Oregon Student Free Expression Law, H.B. 3279, 74th Leg. Assem., Reg. Sess. (Or. 2007) (enacted).

[17] Pennsylvania Administrative Code: Student Rights and Responsibilities, 22 Pa. Code § 12.9 (Dec. 3, 2005).

[18] Pennsylvania Administrative Code: Student Rights and Responsibilities, 22 Pa. Code § 12.9(c)(2).

[19] Washington Administrative Code (WAC) 392-400-215, § 2.

[20] Iowa's Student Free Expression Law, Iowa Code §280.22.

[21] *Lange v. Diercks*, No. 11-0191 (Iowa App. Ct. Nov. 9, 2011).

[22] *Ibid.*

[23] *Hosty v. Carter*, 412 F.3d 731 (7th Cir. 2005) (*en banc*), cert. denied, 126 S. Ct. 1330 (2006).

[24] (Illinois) College Campus Press Act, 110 ILCS 13 (2007).

[25] "The choice of material to go into a newspaper and the decisions made as to the content of the paper constitute the exercise of editorial control and judgment, and with this editorial control comes increased liability." *Stratton Oakmont, Inc. v. Prodigy Servs., Co.*, 1995 WL 323710 (N.Y. Sup. Ct. 1995). (Included in the Cases Section on the Issues in Internet Law site, www.IssuesinInternetLaw.com).

[26] Bernie Machen, "Tribute to Alligator Publisher Ed Barber," University of Florida site, June 27, 2007, available at www.president.ufl.edu/speeches/2007/06/ed_barber062707.html (accessed Mar. 23, 2012).

[27] "The Quinnipiac Student Journalism Showdown," U.S. News & World Report, September 22, 2008.

[28] *See* Jason Cato, "Online Snooping Raises Free-speech Questions," Pittsburgh Tribune-Review, February 3, 2006. *See also Kowalski v. Berkeley Cnty. Schs.*, 652 F.3d 565 (4th Cir. 2011), cert. denied ___ U.S. ___ (2012), upholding discipline of a West Virginia high school student whose MySpace group contained crude insults about another student, because it was disruptive to the high school and interfered with the "rights of other students to be secure and to be let alone," even though the posting occurred off campus.

[29] The Supreme Court turned down the chance to address the issue in 2012 to resolve a split between two panels of the Third Circuit.

[30] *Lander v. Seaver*, 32 Vt. 114 (Vt. 1859). *Cf. Klein v. Smith*, 635 F. Supp. 1440 (D. Me. 1986) where a student saw a teacher in a restaurant parking lot and gave the teacher "the finger", the court held school officials lacked authority to punish a student for conduct not occurring on school grounds or during the school day.

[31] *Ibid.*

[32] *Ibid.*

[33] *Ibid.*

[34] *Ibid.*

[35] *Ibid.*

[36] *Tinker*, 393 U.S. 503.

[37] *Lander*, 32 Vt. 114.

[38] *West Virginia State Bd. of Educ. v. Barnette*, 319 U.S. 624 (1943).

[39] *Tinker*, 393 U.S. 503.

[40] *Tinker*, 393 U.S. at 517-18. (Black, J. dissenting).

[41] *Tinker*, 393 U.S. 503.

[42] *Ibid.*

[43] Thus, the Third Circuit in *Saxe v. State College Area Sch. Dist.*, 240 F.3d 200, *at* 211 (3ᵈ Cir. 2001) ruled *Tinker* requires a specific and significant fear of disruption, not just some remote apprehension of disturbance.

[44] *Tinker*, 393 U.S. 503.

[45] *Beussink v. Woodland R-IV Sch. Dist.*, 30 F. Supp. 2d 1175 (E.D. Mo. 1998).

[46] *Tinker*, 393 U.S. 503.

[47] *Fraser*, 478 U.S. 675. "It does not follow, however, that simply because the use of an offensive form of expression may not be prohibited to adults making what the speaker considers a political point, the same latitude must be permitted to children in a public school... constitutional rights of students in public school are not automatically coextensive with the rights of adults in other settings."

[48] *Ibid.*

[49] Fraser gave the following speech at a high school assembly in support of a candidate for student government office:

> I know a man who is firm — he's firm in his pants, he's firm in his shirt, his character is firm — but most...of all, his belief in you, the students of Bethel, is firm. Jeff Kuhlman is a man who takes his point and pounds it in. If necessary, he'll take an issue and nail it to the wall. He doesn't attack things in spurts — he drives hard, pushing and pushing until finally — he succeeds. Jeff is a man who will go to the very end — even the climax, for each and every one of you. So vote for Jeff for A. S. B. vice-president — he'll never come between you and the best our high school can be.

[50] *Ibid.* In his majority opinion, Chief Justice Warren Burger called the 17-year-old Fraser a "confused boy". In his concurring opinion, Justice Brennan wrote: "The Court, referring to these remarks as "obscene," "vulgar," "lewd," and "offensively lewd," concludes that school officials properly punished respondent for uttering the speech. Having read the full text of respondent's remarks, I find it difficult to believe that it is the same speech the Court describes." Justice Stevens, wrote in his dissent: "[Fraser] was an outstanding young man with a fine academic record. The fact that he was chosen by the student body to speak at the school's commencement exercises demonstrates that he was respected by his peers. This fact is relevant [because] it indicates that he was probably in a better position to determine whether an audience composed of 600 of his contemporaries would be offended by the use of a four-letter word — or a sexual metaphor — than is a group of judges who are at least two generations and 3,000 miles away from the scene of the crime."

[51] *Hazelwood Sch. Dist. v. Kuhlmeier*, 484 U.S. 260.

[52] *Morse v. Frederick*, 551 U.S. 393.

[53] *Ibid.* "Frederick cannot 'stand in the midst of his fellow students, during school hours, at a school-sanctioned activity and claim he is not at school."

[54] *Klein v. Smith*, 635 F. Supp. 1440

[55] *O'Brien v. Westlake City Sch. Bd. of Educ.*, Case No. 1:98CV 64 (E.D. Ohio 1998), granting a temporary restraining order to overrule a student's 10-day suspension for creating a Web site criticizing his band teacher. The federal court ruled the suspension violated the student's free speech rights and said school officials lack authority to regulate speech made by students off campus. School officials settled for $30,000, expunging the suspension from his record, and writing a letter of apology.

[56] *Killion v. Franklin Reg'l Sch. Dist.*, 136 F. Supp. 2d 446 (W.D. Pa. 2001), where the court found no evidence of disruption to school operations from a student e-mailing a "Top 10" list to other students making fun of the athletic director's weight and sex life, and holding since it was sent from an off-campus computer, the student's suspension violated the student's free speech rights. The school settled the case for $65,000.

[57] *Flaherty v. Keystone Oaks Sch. Dist.*, 247 F. Supp. 2d 698 (W.D. Pa. 2003), where a student who posted a message critical of a teacher from his home computer on an online bulletin board devoted to volleyball at his high school was removed from his school volleyball team, barred from after-school activities, and had his school computer privileges revoked. The court held schools must limit their authority to punish students to school grounds and school-sponsored events.

[58] *Latour v. Riverside Beaver Sch. Dist.*, 2005 WL 2106562 (W.D. Pa. 2005) granting a preliminary injunction against the expulsion of a student for posting four rap songs he had written and recorded on a Web site because there was "not demonstrated that the songs constituted true threats or caused a material and substantial disruption." The student received a $90,000 settlement.

[59] *See T.V. v. Smith-Green Cmty. Sch. Corp.*, Case No. 109-CV-290-PPS (N.D. Ind. Aug. 2011).

[60] *Ibid.*

[61] *Ibid.*

[62] *Dwyer v. Oceanport Sch. Dist.*, Case No. 03-6005, slip op. (D.N.J. 2005).

[63] "ACLU-NJ Announces Settlement In 8th Grade Webmaster Case," ACLU press release, November 6, 2005.

[64] The Third Circuit in *Saxe v. State College Area Sch. Dist.*, 240 F.3d 200, *at* 211 (3d Cir. 2001) held *Tinker* requires a specific and significant fear of disruption, not just some remote apprehension of disturbance."

[65] *J.S. v. Bethlehem Area Sch. Dist.*, 757 A.2d 412 (Pa. 2000).

[66] *Wisniewski v. Bd. of Educ.*, 494 F.3d 34, 40 (2d Cir. 2007), cert. denied, 552 U.S. 1296 (2008).

[67] *T.V. v. Smith-Green Cmty. Sch. Corp.*, Case No. 109-CV-290-PPS.

[68] *A.B. v. Indiana.*, 863 N.E.2d 1212 (Ind. Ct. App. 2007). As a minor, initials were substituted for the girl's name in court documents. On appeal, the state supreme court reversed but on different grounds. *A.B. v. Indiana*, 885 N.E.2d 1223 (2008).

[69] *A.B. v. Indiana*, 863 N.E.2d 1212.

[70] *Ibid.*, quoting the Juvenile Court opinion.

[71] *Ibid.*

[72] The Indiana Court of Appeals decided *A.B. v. Indiana*, fn. 69 *supra*, on the free speech clause in Art. 1, § 9, of the Indiana Constitution, and having determined the appellant's free speech rights had been violated, did not further analyze it under the U.S. Constitution's free speech clause.

[73] *Doninger v. Niehoff*, 514 F. Supp. 2d 199, 220 (D. Conn. 2007) denying requested preliminary injunction; aff'd 527 F.3d 41 (2d Cir. 2008). After Doninger graduated, the request for the injunction was moot, but she amended her complaint seeking damages. 594 F. Supp. 2d 211 (D. Conn. 2009). On appeal from a ruling on qualified immunity, the Second Circuit affirmed the district court's holding. 642 F.3d 334 (2d Cir. 2011), cert. denied, No. 11-113, 2011 WL 3204853 (U.S. Oct. 31, 2011).

[74] *Doninger v. Niehoff*, 514 F. Supp. 2d 199.

[75] *Ibid.*

[76] *Ibid.*

[77] *Ibid.*

[78] *Ibid.*

[79] Wendy Kaminer, "The Real Danger Online is Predatory Prosecutors," SpikedOnline, February 19, 2009, *available at* www.spiked-online.com/index.php?/behmnr/printable/6269 (accessed Mar. 23, 2012).

[80] *Doninger v. Niehoff*, 527 F.3d 41 (2d Cir. 2008).

[81] The court cited *Wisniewski v. Bd. of Educ.*, 494 F.3d 34, 40 (2d Cir. 2007), cert. denied, 552 U.S. 1296 (2008) for the proposition; however in that case a student, off-campus, created and IMed an icon "depict[ing] and call[ing] for the killing of his teacher" which would appear to pose a risk of "substantial disruption" of a degree not present in this case.

[82] In *J.S. ex rel. Snyder v. Blue Mountain Sch. Dist.*, 2007 WL 954245 (M.D. Pa. 2007), aff'd 593 F.3d 286 (2010), cert. denied ___ U.S. ___ (2012) the court described the fake profile: "[It] did not identify McGonigle by name, school, or location, though it did contain his official photograph from the School District's website. The profile was presented as a self-portrayal of a bisexual Alabama middle school principal named 'M-Hoe.' The profile contained crude content and vulgar language, ranging from nonsense and juvenile humor to profanity and shameful personal attacks aimed at the principal and his family." In *Layshock v. Hermitage Area Sch. Dist.*, 412 F. Supp. 2d 502 (W.D. Pa. 2007) four students posted three separate fake MySpace profiles of their principal, falsely portraying him as a pot smoking, beer guzzling, pornography lover. One student who was suspended for 10 days and sent to an alternative school sued the school district for violating his free speech rights.

[83] *Blue Mountain Sch. Dist.*, 2007 WL 954245 (M.D. Pa. 2007).

[84] *Layshock v. Hermitage Area Sch. Dist.*, 412 F. Supp. 2d 502 (W.D. Pa. 2007).

[85] *Layshock v. Hermitage Area Sch. Dist.*, 593 F.3d 249 (3d Cir. 2010), cert. denied ___ U.S. ___ (2012).

[86] *Blue Mountain Sch. Dist.*, 593 F.3d 286 (3d Cir. 2010).

[87] *Ibid.*

[88] *Ibid.*

[89] "Foreseeability" implies the likelihood of occurrence, whereas "might" implies the possibility of an event occurring. The sound of thunder would lead a reasonable man to conclude the possibility of rain was

foreseeable, leading him to retrieve his umbrella. It might rain. There might also be a meteor shower. Both events are possible, but few would consider a meteor shower foreseeable, absent some extrinsic fact making it likely to occur. Just because a material substantial disruption is possible (almost anything is possible) does not equate to foreseeability.

[90] *Trosch v. Layshock*, Case No. ___ (Pa. C.P., Mercer Cnty. filed Apr. 2007). In 2008, Trosch dropped his claims against three of the defendants, leaving only Layshock in the case.

[91] Although in some states it may be difficult for a public school employee to win a defamation suit, as many states consider school officials to be public officials, and therefore subject to the more stringent *Times* Malice standard.

[92] See *Felsher v. Univ. of Evansville*, 755 N.E.2d 589 (Ind. Sup. Ct. 2001), where the Indiana Supreme Court held a university could not sue for invasion of privacy but individual faculty members could, when a disgruntled fired employee created fake Web pages and e-mail accounts using faculty names to direct school officials to sites with defamatory statements about former colleagues.

[93] "Assistant Principal Sues Students over MySpace.com Page," Associated Press wire service report, September 25, 2006.

[94] Ken Rodriguez, "Lewd Web Posting about Principal Leads to Lawsuit, School Options," San Antonio Express-News, September 21, 2006; and Jenny LaCoste-Caputo, "Educator Sues Teens over Page on MySpace," San Antonio Express-News, September 21, 2006.

[95] *Draker v. Schreiber*, 271 S.W.3d 318 (Tex. App. 2008). The trial court granted summary judgment in favor of the students on a claim of intentional infliction of emotional distress and in favor of their parents on claims of negligence and gross negligence. The case was affirmed on appeal.

[96] Complaint, *Draker v. Schreiber*, Case No. 06-08-17998-cv (D. Medina Cnty., Tex. 2006).

[97] Interestingly, the complaint, *ibid.*, states "statements regarding Ms. Draker's sexuality are considered libel per se under Texas law."

[98] *Evans v. Bayer*, 684 F. Supp. 2d 1365 (S.D. Fla. 2010), denying the defendant's motion to dismiss. The case was settled with the school agreeing to remove any record of her suspension or the initial incident and pay her attorney fees and $1 in nominal damages.

[99] *Ibid.*

[100] *Tinker*, 393 U.S. 503.

[101] *Kowalski v. Berkeley Cnty. Schs.*, 652 F.3d 565 (4th Cir. 2011), cert. denied ___ U.S. ___ (Jan. 17, 2012).

[102] *Ibid.*

[103] *J.C. v. Beverly Hills Unified Sch. Dist.*, 711 F. Supp. 2d 1094 (C.D. Cal. 2010).

[104] *D.C. v. R.R.*, Case No. BC332406 (Cal. Sup. Ct. filed Mar. 15, 2010).

[105] "It's Big Brother's Space, Too," Associated Press wire service report, October 16, 2006.

[106] *Ibid.*

[107] 18 U.S.C. § 871(a), enacted in 1917, reads:

> Threats against President and successors to the Presidency:
> (a) Whoever knowingly and willfully deposits for conveyance in the mail or for a delivery from any post office or by any letter carrier any letter, paper, writing, print, missive, or document containing any threat to take the life of, to kidnap, or to inflict bodily harm upon the President of the United States, the President-elect, the Vice President or other officer next in the order of succession to the office of President of the United States, or the Vice President-elect, or knowingly and willfully otherwise makes any such threat against the President, President-elect, Vice President or other officer next in the order of succession to the office of President, or Vice President-elect, shall be fined under this title or imprisoned not more than five years, or both.

[108] "'Frankly, my dear, I don't give a damn.' When I was a high school student, the use of those words in a public forum shocked the Nation. Today Clark Gable's four-letter expletive is less offensive than it was then." *Fraser*, 478 U.S. 675 (Stevens, J. dissenting).

[109] *Tinker*, 393 U.S. 503.

# CHAPTER

# 16

## JOURNALISM IN THE DIGITAL AGE

This chapter discusses digital journalism, traditional journalism, professionalism, and citizen journalism. It also examines formats for digital journalism, including discussion boards, hyperlocal Web sites, blogs, podcasting, and wikis.

*"Don't quote me." — Anonymous*

THROUGHOUT HISTORY, THE RISE of one dominant power has usually meant the decline of another. The ascendancy of the Digital Age portends the extinction of newspapers and a redefinition of both the concept of journalism and who may be considered a journalist.

## The Rise of the Digital Age

From its inception, the newspaper business was a model of inefficiency. For the first 400 years after the invention of printing, all type was set by hand. Early presses required labor-intensive Linotype typesetting. Huge, costly printing presses are required to print newspapers — a modern web press is three stories high and can cost $40 million. Enormous quantities of ink and reams of newsprint drive up production costs. A large capital investment in a printing plant is required, including long-term leases. Distribution requires a fleet of delivery trucks and either vending racks, or in the old days, newsboys. The product shelf life was one day, so any product unsold 24 hours later was waste. Contrast this with the digital journalism model. Production requires no paper or ink, and the only necessary hardware is an inexpensive computer. Distribution is through computers or smart phones, which are ubiquitous in modern society. This means the individual consumer already possesses the means to receive the product. Delivery is electronic, requiring no deliverymen or delivery trucks. A business model laden with such Brobdingnagian production and distribution expenses cannot compete profitably with one unencumbered by them.

The newspaper business is organized around a model that was profitable when newspapers were the only medium from which to receive news, but as other media, such as radio, television, cable TV, and now the Internet have chipped away at that oligopoly, it find itself on the verge of extinction. The result has been an employment crisis for professional journalists. Between 2007 and 2010, U.S. daily newspapers shed 13,500 jobs. [1]

Another reason for the decline of newspapers is the societal demand for instant information. As a result of modern technology, consumers are no longer willing to wait for an evening edition or next morning delivery to learn of events occurring since publication of the morning newspaper. The launch of CNN in 1980 inaugurated the 24-hour news cycle. Deadlines no longer existed in an environment of constantly updated, streaming news reports. The newspaper, an iconic symbol of freedom of the press, could not compete with instantaneous electronic media.

## The Rise of "Citizen Journalism"

On Friday, November 22, 1963, at 12:30 p.m. CST, President John F. Kennedy was waving to a Dallas, Texas crowd as his motorcade drove through Dealey Plaza. Most of the media were waiting at the Dallas Trade Mart, Kennedy's destination, where he was scheduled to give a luncheon speech. A few reporters were in the caravan, several cars behind the president's limousine. When the fatal shots rang out from the Texas School Book Depository, there were no press photographers in position to capture the assassination on film. It was left to an ordinary citizen filming the procession to preserve one of history's most important moments. Abraham Zapruder happened to be in the crowd, filming the motorcade with his home-movie camera, a top-of-the-line 8mm Bell & Howell Zoomatic Director Series Model 414 PD. By being in the right place at the right time, with portable state-of-the-art recording equipment, in the absence of any professional media, Zapruder may have unintentionally become the first "citizen journalist." Today, nearly everyone carries a smart phone or digital camera capable of recording high quality photographic or video images. Combined with social networks like Twitter, where digitally filmed content can be uploaded and instantaneously disseminated, digital technology has transformed the notion of journalism, placing the power of reporting in the hands of the public. During the Arab Spring of 2011, when totalitarian governments tried to prevent news organizations from reporting their brutal crackdown on protesters, the story reached the world through amateur videos and concise tweets sent from smart phones. In the sections that follow, we will explore the pros and cons of citizen journalism.

The rise of digital journalism has brought new challenges for traditional media seeking its own Web presence. It must find an economically sustainable business model for Web-based delivery of news. Several newspapers, such as *The New York Times* and *The Wall Street Journal*, have concluded the free model is not viable and, in an effort to monetize content, are charging consumers for access. In this scenario, the newspaper displays a headline and *snippet*, with a link to the rest of the article, secured behind an online paywall. The model employed by *The Wall Street Journal* displays some content free and other content for paid subscribers only. In addition to economic sustainability, another challenge posed by digital journalism is adjusting to the interactivity of the Web. Traditional journalism, long used to being a one-way conduit of information, must now struggle with the interactivity of the Web and how to deal with an audience with a voice.

## Traditional Versus Digital Journalism

*"It's amazing that the amount of news that happens in the world every day always just exactly fits the newspaper."* — *Jerry Seinfeld*

Traditional journalism is based on a paradigm of scarcity of information and limited access, whereas digital journalism is distinguished by abundant information available to everyone. For generations, the press was the representative of the people, attending press conferences or covering news events and reporting back. Through digital journalism, the people are the press, sharing information with each other. The tremendous barriers to entry surrounding the professional media, such as the costs of labor, equipment, and initial capitalization, do not exist in digital journalism. With limited competition, local newspapers and TV news media were once sought out by news hungry consumers, but the massive competition for readers among online media means they must lure readers to their blogs or Web sites.

Digital journalism provides a different reader experience. Newspaper text is linear, as is television reporting in as much as it leads the viewer from one story to the next. But digital journalism consists of nonlinear multimedia pathways. It meshes text with audio and video through hyperlinks, and the nature of the hyperlinked Web means no two readers will navigate the same path through the site. News selection is driven by links in social media as opposed to the editorial selection process in traditional media. People link to news stories in e-mails, on their social networks, in their tweets, and in discussion threads. In the past, readers and viewers were exposed only to the news editors chose to present them. Today, digital readers are as likely to discover an article through a link on a friend's Twitter feed, bypassing the editorial selection process. The danger is people will substitute popular trending stories for the judgment of an experienced news editor trained to focus readers on what is important, no matter how popular the news item may be.

Whereas newspapers and magazines present material in greater depth, online media often use linking as a type of shorthand. Linking, in effect, has become digital footnoting. This can be problematic where either the reader ignores the link and the information it contains, or clicks on it and navigates away from the page, becoming so engrossed in the new article, or links from it to other pages, she fails to return to the initial article. Just as television viewers often watch TV with the remote control in hand, ready to channel surf at a moment's notice, so too do Web browsers read with one hand on their mouse, prepared to click onto the next site. Thus, consumers of digital journalism might speed through an online story, scanning it rather than giving it the thought and reflection they would to a print article.

Digital journalists may be more concerned with the speed of posting information than with the accuracy of what they post. In the slower print world, there is time for writers to reflect on, and revise, what they have written. Not so, in the digitized world, where the click of a mouse will send the writer's words to a global audience. Long used to writing for a silent, faceless audience, digital journalists must also adapt to consumers' demands for interactivity, through message boards, for example. No longer a one-way street, journalism now includes instant reader feedback on both the events reported and the reportage itself.

Professional journalists, employed by media organizations with a credo of impartial presentation of news, might have to share the digital realm with citizen journalists, whose blogs engender individual bias.

## Advantages of Digital Journalism

Digital journalism is easier and cheaper to produce and distribute. The amount of equipment needed to cover events has drastically decreased. Advances in technology have led to the development of significantly smaller, lighter, and less expensive audio, video, and still image photographic equipment. A generation ago, in addition to a pen and notepad, a typical reporter might need to lug a tape recorder, a clunky 35mm camera, a camera bag with multiple lenses, canisters of film, and photographic supplies, and perhaps a second camera bag with a videotape recording unit and a heavy video camera. Today, high quality digital images, audio, and video can be rendered from a smart phone small enough to fit inside a pocket or purse. This lowers cost and increases convenience and mobility for the digital journalist.

News grows stale, so it is important to get the story out as fast as possible. Gone are the days of intrepid reporters racing back to the office, handing off their film to be developed as they head to their typewriters. Digital journalists can write their stories in the field and send them electronically, along with digital photographs that need not be birthed in a darkroom, to their office in seconds. Conversely, a reporter back in the office needing a photograph of a noncelebrity to accompany a story does not need to send a photographer to the subject or request one from the family in the case of a kidnapping or murder victim. Instead, digital journalists often turn to the subject's social network profile for photographs and personal information. While quicker (some might suggest lazier), this approach raises an underlying copyright issue, because merely being in the public eye does not make a photograph in the public domain.

Most newspaper reporters write for local newspapers, which means their audience is limited to their locality.[2] Since the borderless nature of the Internet precludes geographic boundaries, the World Wide Web opens up a national and international readership that otherwise might not have existed. Anyone in any country can view a Web site or watch a video uploaded to YouTube. In fact, the notion of independent documentary filmmaking might be re-imagined as a series of shorter, linked videos uploaded to sites like YouTube, ensuring a larger and broader audience for low-budget reporting.

## Drawbacks of Digital Journalism

*"The public have an insatiable curiosity to know everything.*
*Except what is worth knowing. Journalism, conscious of this, and*
*having tradesman-like habits, supplies their demands." — Oscar Wilde*

One drawback of digital journalism is information overload. With millions of Web sites and indiscriminately filtered search results, individuals find themselves overwhelmed by too much information from too many unverified sources. Consumers are presented with quantity over quality, with no way to separate the wheat from the chaff. Valuable information may be returned in a search query but buried beneath an avalanche of irrelevant, incomplete, or inaccurate content. Information overload becomes a greater problem when decreasing attention spans of Internet users are factored in. An attention deficit has been observed in Web users, who show an inability to process large amounts of information as they become accustomed to reading tweets and blog posts rather than lengthy news articles. They have difficulty staying focused long enough to read multiple pages of information. For digital journalists, this means the Internet Generation's adoption of the 140-character tweet as a major means of communication leads to "soundbite journalism". The alternative, derided as "longform journalism", faces the challenge of how to hold the attention of an audience with one hand impatiently tapping on the computer mouse.

The rise of digital journalism has spawned news aggregators (sites that collect and categorize links from news sources). Reporting involves investigation, running down leads, interviewing sources of information, time, and travel. While the Internet may have significantly reduced the expense of producing and distributing the news, the cost of newsgathering remains. Just as wire services syndicate articles to many newspapers, syndication has come to the Web in the form of aggregation. Blogs generally rely on two sources of content: personal commentary and syndication for news. The majority of bloggers seldom conduct investigative reporting, lacking the funds and expertise, relying instead on content from aggregators. But if blogging and citizen journalism supplant traditional journalism, does that mean "cut and paste" journalism will replace in-depth reporting? Syndication leads to a homogenization of the news, with every blog reprinting the same story. Some have asked if this means we no longer need reporters. But perhaps it means the opposite, *i.e.*, we need more reporters, because only one perspective and one set of facts is being reprinted. Depth requires examination of different angles of a story, often accomplished by reading the perspectives of different reporters. Each reporter brings his or her unique perspective to a story and may choose to focus on a different aspect. That is the logic behind press conferences over interviews. Questions asked at a press conference represent the varied concerns, backgrounds, and interests of a cross section of journalists, whereas an interviewer brings only his own to the table.

Anyone can record events happening and send the video anywhere they wish, or put it on their site. Citizen journalists are individuals who are not professional journalists who regularly present news through their blogs or Web sites. The danger is these individuals have not been trained as professional journalists.

## Why Professionalism Matters

America began with a partisan press. Political bias, not objectivity, was the defining feature of newspapers. But it was not until fierce circulation wars, culminating in the rise of "yellow journalism", that the integrity of journalism itself was called into question. In 1898, Cuba revolted against Spanish rule, seeking autonomy. America sent the battleship U.S.S. Maine to Havana to ensure the safety of American citizens and interests in Cuba. The Maine sunk off the coast of Havana, Cuba after a massive explosion, killing 226 U.S. sailors. The explosion's cause was unknown, but that did not stop newspaper publishers William Randolph Hearst and Joseph Pulitzer from sensationalizing the incident in their respective papers, *The New York Journal* and *The New York World*. Their campaign of sensationalism and exaggeration, designed to increased newspaper sales, became known as *yellow journalism*. Hearst and Pulitzer accused Spain of sinking the Maine and soon America had declared war on Spain.

Many believed yellow journalism, replete with its unconfirmed facts and distortions, was to blame for the Spanish-America War. Over the next decade, there were calls for reform and professional journalism was born. Departing from the apprenticeship model, schools devoted to the teaching of journalism were established, the first being the University of Missouri in 1908. News would be determined not by publisher edicts, but by editors and reporters trained in standardized skills and ethics taught by journalism schools. The birth of professional journalism might be viewed in some ways as a form of self preservation. Many publishers, realizing some form of industry self-regulation was needed to curb excesses, funded the establishment of some schools. They might have thought establishment of professional standards would belay fears of the power of the press being concentrated in the hands of a few wealthy men. More important was the belief newspapers could gain the public's trust if reporters were viewed as trained professionals, accountable to the highest professional standards. Professionalism became inextricably tied to gaining and maintaining the public's trust. The hallmarks of professional journalism are fairness, objectivity, and accuracy.

The decline of journalistic professionalism began as conglomerates purchased newspaper and TV news outlets and sought to cut expenses and turn them from cash drains into profit centers. Foreign bureaus and Washington bureaus were closed to trim costs. News was transformed into entertainment. Print media began printing more "soft" news and feature stories, and genres like "literary journalism"—news stories relying on literary or narrative techniques similar to those found in novels or short stories—evolved. Splashy graphics and sets appeared on television news shows. Trivial topics and celebrity-related stories began to dominate the news. Coverage of the entertainment industry and its personalities displaced more substantive topics. Local TV stations moved news inside their entertainment divisions, insisting their news departments go from loss leaders to profit centers.[3] Critics claim professionalism has declined further in recent years: "On television, journalism is replaced by uninformed punditry and pointless prognostication, an inexpensive and entertaining way to maximize profit, but nothing remotely close to journalism."[4]

One concern is digital journalism may exacerbate the decline of, or perhaps replace, professional journalism. Several journalism critics have bemoaned the "snobbishness of education" but these critics miss the point: the skills taught to journalism students aspiring to professionalism—research, efficient writing, listening and observation, interpersonal communication, and critical thinking—are more important than any piece of technology. The computer, the Internet, and the smart phone may change many aspects of journalism, but the fundamental values of professionalism are what true journalism is about… be it digital journalism, traditional journalism, or whatever form of journalism the future may bring.

## Importance of Fact Checking

The advent of social networks has provided the temptation for journalists to become lazy and rely on the Internet as a substitute for doing their jobs. Similar to the situation in Chapter 2, where an advertising agency chose to pluck photographs off Flickr for its ad campaign rather than hire a photographer, journalists can rely too much on the ease of availability of information on the Web. But they must beware the maxim "If it's on the Internet, it must be true" and exercise independent fact checking. In Great Britain in 2008, six newspapers published a story about a wild 16ᵗʰ birthday party held by a girl at her family's £4.4 million villa in Spain. The girl described her birthday bash as "the party of the year" on the social network Bebo, detailing how 400 Facebook and Bebo "friends" attended, turning the seven bedroom home into "a war zone", with furniture and a television set thrown into the swimming pool while looters made off with £6,000 worth of jewelry and clothes.[5] The newspapers reprinted her account directly from her Bebo page and reprinted the photos she had posted. Not one newspaper bothered to fact check the story, relying completely on the accuracy and veracity of a 16-year-old girl's account on her social network page. "Teenage conversation has always involved a large amount of embellishment," the family's lawyer remarked with typical British understatement.[6] The girl's mother disputed everything stated in the news account, alleging the party was supervised by private security, there was no underage drinking or sex, no furniture in the pool, nothing stolen, and police were not called. She sued the newspapers for defamation and breach of privacy. The case also raises the issue of copyright in regard to the unauthorized use of photographs taken from the social network. Unlike American libel law, which places the burden of proof on the plaintiff to show the alleged libelous statement contained malice and caused damage, under British libel law the defendant must prove he did not commit libel. Additionally, British law does not require a plaintiff to show the defendant acted "with malice" as U.S. law does. Defenses to a charge of libel under British law include: (1) truth; (2) fair comment — so long as the opinion is based on true facts, is genuinely held, and not influenced by malice; (3) privilege (reporting of comments in Parliament, courts and other official arenas); and (4) qualified privilege protecting the widespread publication of false information about an individual — so long as it concerns a matter of public interest to the community and was published reasonably and without malice.[7] The plaintiff argued the newspapers could not rely on fair comment or qualified privilege defenses, since the information her daughter posted on Bebo was inaccurate and there was no legitimate public interest in publishing it. The lawsuit potentially could become a landmark British Internet defamation case. While social networks can be used by the press as leads to follow up on stories, their content should not be used as the story itself. The previous case poses many incredulous questions, not the least of which are how could so many newspapers print a story without verifying any facts, and how can the plaintiff claim a breach of privacy for the newspapers repeating information her own daughter posted online to the world? Another interesting question is would the case have a different outcome if the newspapers had clearly identified the source, e.g., "Jodie Hudson, age 16, reports on Bebo her birthday party turned into a…"?

The rest of the world press is as guilty as their counterparts on Fleet Street. When Oscar-winning French composer Maurice Jarre died, newspapers worldwide led his obituary with his quote, "When I die there will be a final waltz playing in my head." The only problem was, Jarre never spoke those words; they were the invention of Shane Fitzgerald, a 22-year-old Irish student. Fitzgerald posted the fake quotation on Wikipedia as a hoax to show the dangers of relying too heavily on the Internet for information. Newspapers from America, England, India, and other countries swallowed the bait, relying on a single Wikipedia entry without any further fact checking.[8]

These cases highlight the need for journalists to fact check their sources and not rely solely on the Web, and especially not on a wiki, which anyone can edit or change at a moment's notice. They also point out how the Web's viral nature can cause a false statement to be easily replicated across hundreds of Web sites instantaneously and given worldwide credibility.

## Dangers and Failings of Citizen Journalism

*"It was while making newspaper deliveries, trying to miss the bushes and hit the porch, that I first learned the importance of accuracy in journalism." — Charles Osgood*

The one-way nature of the news media was not solely a result of the limitations of production and distribution of traditional journalism. Even with the advent of digital journalism, there is still a need for a filter to weed out inaccurate, misleading, poorly researched reporting. Citizen journalists might be well-intentioned but their "reporting" may lack objectivity, context, and analysis. They might fail to consider the legal or ethical implications of their posts. Worse, their content might be inaccurate or biased, especially if they are not well-intentioned but instead promoting an agenda through misrepresentation. Through digital journalism, the means for informing the public are greater than ever, but so too are the means for misinforming it. The increase in misinformation becomes exponential, as individuals who are not qualified journalists are able to reach mass audiences with inaccurate or biased articles. The Internet Generation often places blind faith in the veracity of "facts" gleaned from the Internet, leading them to believe "If it's on the Internet, it must be true." Consumers of digital journalism must become Web literate and use critical thinking to evaluate the credibility of news sources.

What might have been a front page article in the newspaper may now simply be a tweet from anyone reporting the story. While social media may be unparalleled at spreading the news rapidly, they lack depth and perspective. There is only so much one can expect from a 140-character blurb. However, this limitation might be overcome by including a link to a full-length article, making the tweet analogous to newsboy's cry of "Wuxtry! Wuxtry! Read all about it!"

Unlike professional journalists engaging in digital journalism through their media organization's Web sites, citizen journalists produce their blogs and Web sites without the benefit of a professional editor to fix errors and peruse the content for legal liability. Their reportage may lack depth, perspective, expertise, or accountability. A participant in a journalism forum, responding to announcements by CNN and the *Huffington Post* suggesting a desire to substitute unpaid citizen journalists for more costly professional reporters, commented he would no sooner seek out the services of citizen journalist than he would those of a "citizen" surgeon or "citizen" mechanic. Ronald Steinman, executive editor of *The Digital Journalist*, writes:[9]

> No matter what the amateurs among us contend it does take training, guidance and experience to qualify as a working journalist. That does not happen overnight. Not everyone who tries succeeds. I prefer to call those who think they are citizen journalists "accidental journalists," especially those who are faux photojournalists because they happen to get a useful photo by being in the right place at the right time. Apologists for citizen journalists should think twice before anointing them the rescuers of mainstream media.

Who determines professional standards, the quality of reporting, and the accuracy of information in citizen journalism? Unlike professional journalists, citizen journalists are unschooled in journalism ethics. They may have a vague sense they should avoid plagiarism and defamation, but lack a detailed understanding of journalism ethics. Accuracy is an important ethical component of professional journalism, and that includes getting the story right, properly attributing quotes, fact-checking the story, and correcting post-publication errors. Another is objectivity, which is often confused with balance. It is acceptable to state there are multiple viewpoints to an issue, and even to present them within the article, but giving equal space or weight to each is not objectivity. An article on the Holocaust does not become objective by devoting an equal amount of space to a Holocaust denier. Another ethical concern is sensitivity when covering sensitive matters, such as interviewing a relative of a murder victim. Sticking a microphone in a grief-stricken woman's face and asking "How do you feel about your child being murdered?" is not only insensitive, it is a dumb question unlikely to elicit a response with any true news value. Certain practices, such as befriending people on Facebook to get information about them or image manipulation of photographs, are also unethical. Even professional news publications have had ethical lapses, especially in the area of image manipulation. In 1982, *National Geographic* used digital imaging manipulation to move a pyramid in a landscape photo so it would fit within its layout. The magazine referred to it as the "retroactive repositioning of the photographer." [10] *Time Magazine* altered a mug-shot of O.J. Simpson, to make him appear darker and unshaven, for its cover. The alterations stood out when competitor *Newsweek* used the same image, unaltered, on its cover. [11]

## News Formats

*"Freedom of the press is limited to those who own one." — A. J. Liebling*

Digital journalism offers new formats for journalists, including discussion boards, blogging, vlogging, live blogging, and hyperlocal journalism.

### Discussion Boards

In an effort to introduce interactivity with their online readers, many newspaper sites have set up message boards adjacent to news articles inviting reader comments discussing the article. While the **CDA** protects the newspaper from liability for third-party defamatory comments, interactivity carries other risks. One is the "Graffiti Factor" mentioned in Chapter 3. Several newspaper were forced to eliminate their discussion boards, citing lack of staff needed to monitor them 24 hours per day, after a deluge of profanity and racist comments from readers. [12] *The Washington Post* closed one blog to comments after a wave of posts that included personal attacks, profanity, and hate mail directed at its ombudsman. [13] Several months earlier, *The Los Angeles Times* had pulled the plug on its editorial page wiki, two days after inaugurating the forum, because visitors were posting pornographic material. [14]

Sometimes the Graffiti Factor can result from a well-intentioned source. *The Ventura County (California) Star* published a story about a man who killed four people before committing suicide in a store. *The Star* was uncertain of his identity, but a reader posted her guess on a comment section of the *Star*'s site. [15] While her guess turned out to be correct, the newspaper had not confirmed the man's identity and had refrained from publishing its own unconfirmed reports. As one commentator put it, "unbound by traditional journalism rules like making sure she was right, she posted the name." [16] The staff debated whether to remove the post, fearing the consequences if her guess was incorrect — an innocent person erroneously defamed as a murderer. Ultimately, it chose to leave it.

## Hyperlocal Web Sites

*Hyperlocal Web sites* focus on specialized topics — stories and issues of interest only to people within a small community. These geographically-based journalism Web sites are devoted to neighborhood-level news, covering topics like street repairs, Little League games, and restaurant health inspections. They tend to feature community events calendars, restaurant information, church listings, and daily police blotter information. Hyperlocal sites typically employ a small number of professionals, relying mainly on reader-provided content, such as blogs and videos, and local press releases. For that reason, they emphasize reader input and interaction more than mainstream news sites. Hyperlocal news sites might be considered an online blend of weekly community newspapers with citizen journalism.

Several media conglomerates have acquired hyperlocal sites. In 2009, MSNBC.com purchased the EveryBlock, and AOL bought two hyperlocal sites, Patch and Going. Critics argue hyperlocal journalism, with its shoestring budgets and meager revenue streams, is an economically unsustainable business model, but it might be the model has not fully evolved. EveryBlock transitioned from serving as an aggregated news feed of information about a locality to becoming a discussion forum for locals to opine about neighborhood news. The site redesign integrated social media, allowing users to create profiles and interact, in effect, creating a social network for a single neighborhood. While people have shown a desire to form social networks with their friends, it remains to be seen if they want the same kind of interaction with their neighbors.

## Blogs

Both professional journalists and citizen journalists may use a blog or a vlog (*e.g.*, blogging through YouTube videos) to tell a news story. Some bloggers offer news and commentary on social issues or industry-related topics, raising the question of whether a "news blogger" or "citizen journalist" is a journalist, and if so, entitled to the same statutory protections under state shield laws as professional journalists.[17]

*Shield laws* exist to protect a reporter from being forced to disclose his source of information to the government.[18] The issue of reporters protecting sources is not new. In 1848, *New York Herald* reporter John Nugent became the first American journalist jailed for refusing to identify a confidential source. He was held in contempt of Congress for refusing to reveal how he had gotten a secret draft of a treaty with Mexico.[19]

In modern times, American journalists have claimed a reporter's privilege, *i.e.*, a First Amendment right of a journalist to refuse to divulge sources of confidential information. The notion of a reporter's privilege is based on the legal concept of evidentiary privilege, which protects the confidentiality of communications based on certain relationships, such as husband–wife, attorney–client, accountant–client, doctor–patient, psychotherapist–patient, and priest–penitent. The law recognizes because of a special relationship between the parties, the interest in encouraging open communication between them overrides the state's interest in compelling testimony. In the case of reporters, protecting the anonymity of news sources encourage such sources to come forward with information. Thirty-six states and the District of Columbia have enacted shield laws codifying a reporter's privilege. Congress has considered a federal shield law but has failed to pass one. In 1972, in *Branzburg v. Hayes*, the

Supreme Court refused to recognize a First Amendment privilege for journalists to refuse to reveal their sources to a grand jury: "We are asked to create another by interpreting the First Amendment to grant newsmen a testimonial privilege that other citizens do not enjoy. This we decline to do." [20]

However, over time, courts have focused on Justice Powell's concurring opinion in *Branzburg*: [21]

> I add this brief statement to emphasize what seems to me to be the limited nature of the Court's holding. The Court does not hold that newsmen, subpoenaed to testify before a grand jury, are without constitutional rights with respect to the gathering of news or in safeguarding their sources. * * * As indicated in the concluding portion of the opinion, the Court states that no harassment of newsmen will be tolerated. If a newsman believes * * * his testimony implicates confidential source relationships without a legitimate need of law enforcement, he will have access to the court on a motion to quash and an appropriate protective order may be entered. * * * In short, the courts will be available to newsmen under circumstances where legitimate First Amendment interests require protection.

As a result, many federal and state courts have found exactly what the majority in *Branzburg* had rejected: a First Amendment privilege for reporters. Although these courts rely on Justice Powell's concurrence as their rationale for disregarding the *Branzburg* majority opinion, most reject his proposed balancing test in favor of a stricter test under which a reporter can be forced to testify only if the information sought is essential to the case and there is no other reasonable way to obtain it. Nonetheless, the Supreme Court has repeatedly affirmed its rejection of "the notion that under the First Amendment a reporter could not be required to appear or to testify as to information obtained in confidence without a special showing that the reporter's testimony was necessary." [22]

Courts have had to decided if the reporter's privilege is available to freelancers, authors, documentary filmmakers, and Web sites. But does it apply to bloggers? Can a news blogger who is not a professional journalist claim First Amendment protection? These issues arose when Apple Computer sued a news blogger [23] and two Web sites [24] to force them to reveal the identity of an Apple employee who had leaked advance product information. Apple claimed the revelations were trade secret violations. [25] The trial court allowed Apple to subpoena them to reveal their sources. [26] The appellate court reversed, holding the site constituted a "periodical publication" entitled to shield law's protection because it published regularly. [27] California's shield law is codified in its state constitution. [28] Most statutes do not address bloggers, but Hawaii's shield law likely would, as it protects: [29]

> [A]ny individual who can demonstrate by clear and convincing evidence that the individual has regularly and materially participated in the reporting or publishing of news or information of substantial public interest for the purpose of dissemination to the general public by means of tangible or electronic media [or the] position of the individual is materially similar or identical to that of a journalist or newscaster, taking into account the method of dissemination.

In the California case, Apple had contended in its complaint the First Amendment and the California shield law only applied to "legitimate members of the press." But what is a "legitimate member of the press"? Unlike many countries, such as Italy where one must first pass an examination and be licensed by the government to become a professional journalist, in the United States there is no litmus test to determine who is a journalist. A high school newspaper reporter may cover a news story for his readership just as *The Washington Post* reporter does for his constituency. A journalist may write on behalf of readers of a trade publication, a special interest magazine, or even a small town newspaper with only a few hundred readers. Should a writer for an online publication with hundreds of thousands of readers not be considered equally "legitimate"?

The First Amendment to the U.S. Constitution states: [30]

> Congress shall make no law respecting an establishment of religion, or prohibiting the free exercise thereof; or abridging the freedom of speech, or of the press; or the right of the people peaceably to assemble, and to petition the government for a redress of grievances.

Nowhere does it state freedom of the press applies only to organizations or "legitimate members of the press." No doubt the inspiration for "freedom of the press" came from Thomas Paine, who in 1776 used a printing press to print pamphlets like *Common Sense* that advocated the American Revolution. The First Amendment was drafted, not to protect an organized body called "the press", but to preserve the right of any individual to express and publish his views freely, as Paine did. The Internet allows every individual to have his own version of an electronic printing press that can reach practically anyone in the world who wishes to read it.

Since shield laws are drafted by each state's legislature, their applicability hinges on how each statute defines "journalist." Would the author of a controversial or exposé book be considered a "journalist" under a shield law? Ironically, in the Apple case, Santa Clara County Court Judge James Kleinberg stated: [31]

> Unlike the whistleblower who discloses a health, safety or welfare hazard affecting all, or the government employee who reveals mismanagement or worse by our public officials, [the sites] are doing nothing more than feeding the public's insatiable desire for information.

But is not "feeding the public's insatiable desire for information" the very job definition of what journalists and newspapers are supposed to do, and have been doing, for centuries?

New Jersey's shield law specifically applies to those affiliated with news media organizations, differentiating between bloggers and professional journalists. [32] A New Jersey trial court held a blogger's message board comments about a computer software firm were not protected by the state's shield law, [33] calling them "nothing more than the rants of a private person" that could not be given the same protections as information compiled though the news gathering process. [34] The court stated a need to distinguish between those engaged in the true dissemination of information and individuals expressing opinions. An appellate court upheld the decision, stating "new media should not be confused with news media." [35] Affirming the rulings of both the trial and appellate courts, the New Jersey Supreme Court held a blogger sued for defamation over comments on an Internet message board is not entitled to the same protections as a journalist. [36] "In essence, online message boards are little more than forums for discussion," the court explained. "The shield law requires a link to news media [as] the statute defines that term." While adding it also requires a purpose to gather or disseminate news, the court declined to restrict the shield law's protection to professional journalists. "It does not limit the privilege to professional journalists who follow certain norms." It rejected the appeals court interpretation the shield law mandated journalists identify themselves as reporters, carry certain credentials or follow professional standards like taking notes, fact-checking or disclosing conflicts of interest. Instead, it set out a three-part test to sustain a claim under the statute: (1) a connection to news media; (2) a purpose to gather or disseminate news; and (3) a showing the materials sought were obtained in the course of professional newsgathering activities. [37]

While the New Jersey court addressed a state statute, a North Carolina court ruled the First Amendment protects those who comment anonymously on stories on a newspaper's Web site. [38] In a ruling on a pre-trial motion, the court held an anonymous poster met the definition of a journalist and his identity was protected by both the First Amendment and that state's shield law. [39] It also rejected an argument the newspaper's comment section was more of a social network than a news gathering operation.

A federal district court ruled a blogger was not a journalist under the Oregon shield law. [40] Crystal Cox criticized Obsidian Finance Group and accused its co-founder of fraud on her blog, interlacing facts and opinions, and dubbing him a "thug, thief and a liar." [41] The plaintiff sued for defamation, demanding she reveal her source. She refused, relying on Oregon's shield law, which protects any person "employed by or engaged in any medium of communication to the public". [42] Despite the statute's definition of "medium of communication" as having "its ordinary meaning and includes, but is not limited to, any newspaper, magazine or other periodical, book, pamphlet, news service, wire service, news or feature syndicate, broadcast station or network, or cable television system," the court reasoned "although [the] defendant is a self-proclaimed 'investigative blogger' and defines herself as 'media,' the record fails to show that she is affiliated with any newspaper, magazine, periodical, book, pamphlet, news service, wire service, news or feature syndicate, broadcast station or network, or cable television system. Thus, she is not entitled to the protections of the law in the first instance." The plaintiff was awarded $2.5 million in damages. [43]

The issue of whether a blogger is considered a journalist in certain instances, such as whether a state shield law is applicable, may turn on the statute's language. States with shield laws can remove any ambiguity by addressing this within the statute.

In 2010, an Apple engineer left an iPhone prototype in a Silicon Valley bar. A customer found and sold it for $5,000 to Gizmodo, a technology Web site. [44] The site owners cracked open the prototype and posted images of it, despite Apple's demand to return it. A Gizmodo editor's home and car were searched pursuant to a search warrant and he was reported as under investigation for theft, receiving stolen property, and damaging property. No charges were filed, but the investigation sparked a debate over whether he was covered by California's shield law, which protects journalists from having to turn over unpublished notes and names of anonymous sources to police. The incident raised several issues. Did a technology Web site like Gizmodo fall within the shield law? Did the fact it paid its source ("checkbook journalism") remove any protection it might have had? Is a physical object, like the prototype, equivalent to unpublished notes? If it were, would the fact it was stolen property mandate it be returned to its rightful owner, despite the shield law? Was the prototype stolen property, or merely lost or abandoned property?

Rather than basing the reporter's privilege on a particular medium, some states define a journalist based on whether the individual is engaged in the function of journalism, *i.e.*, newsgathering and dissemination. Others look to whether the individual had the intent to disseminate the news to the public at the outset of the project. [45] The Free Flow of Information Act was a bill passed in the House of Representatives that would have created a federal shield law defining a journalist as one who "regularly gathers, photographs, records, writes, edits, reports, or publishes information concerning matters of public interest for dissemination to the public for a substantial portion of the person's livelihood or substantial financial gain."[46] Theoretically, ad-supported bloggers would have qualified, however the bill never reached a vote in the Senate.

Blogs have been criticized as unreliable and "opinion without expertise" because unlike professional journalists, bloggers do not submit their work for review by editors prior to publication. Some argue extending the journalist's privilege to anyone with a blog would make the exception the rule and the privilege would become meaningless. Yet, as professional news media organizations embrace the Web, they are launching sites for their own reporters to blog, as well as incorporating citizen journalism into their reporting. Both CNN and AOL's *Huffington Post* actively solicit content from bloggers and citizen journalists for their sites, further blurring the line between paid professional journalists and unpaid amateur citizen journalists. An example of this blurring occurred when a defamation plaintiff subpoenaed the identity of a poster to *The Billings Gazette's* blog. The *Gazette* argued it was privileged under the state's shield law, the **Media Confidentiality Act**, which protected "any information obtained or prepared" by a news agency from forced disclosure.[47] The plaintiff countered it was unprotected since it was not gathered as "news." In other words, are reader comments on newspaper blogs "news" or even "prepared by a news agency"? The court granted the *Gazette's* motion to quash the subpoena, ruling the state shield law that protected reporters from disclosing anonymous sources also protected the identity of anonymous posters on a newspaper's site. The court opined anonymous blog comments lack sufficient credibility to reach the legal requirements of defamation.[48]

## Live Blogging

Live blogging is real-time textual coverage of an ongoing event chronicled on a blog, continuously updated with time-stamped micro-updates. It might include audio and video in addition to text. Live blogging can be done from a laptop, netbook, tablet, or smart phone but requires Internet access from the event. It might also require permission from the event sponsors.

A *Louisville* (KY) *Courrier-Journal* reporter had his media credentials revoked and was evicted from a National Collegiate Athletic Association (NCAA) college baseball playoff game for violating NCAA rules against live blogging from the event.[49] In mid-game, college athletic staff told the reporter-blogger the school might lose its chance to host future NCAA games if it did not revoke his credentials. The newspaper admitted the college had sent an NCAA memo prior to the game stating no blogging was allowed during the game, as blogs were considered a "live representation of the game"; however it contended the blog was reporting facts, not broadcasting a game recreation. Live blogging has become common at sporting events, as Wi-Fi technology lets reporters access the Internet in the field. A similar case arose a decade earlier, when pagers, not Wi-Fi, were state-of-the-art. The National Basketball Association (NBA) challenged Motorola's text-message service designed to update subscribers with basketball scores. The Second Circuit held the NBA did not have a valid copyright claim over factual, statistical information about the game and Motorola's Sports Trax product was not a substitute for the product offered by the NBA (*i.e.*, the ability to be physically present at the game or watch it on TV).[50] By that logic, a blogger might also prevail.

Following the *Louisville Courrier-Journal* reporter's ouster, the NCAA announced new rules to allow credentialed reporters to live blog NCAA championship sporting events, but limiting the number of times reporters may live blog each event.[51] The rules also require bloggers to link their posts to the NCAA's Blog Central site and place an NCAA sports logo on their own sites.

Dallas Mavericks owner Mark Cuban tried to ban bloggers from his team's locker room, but after an NBA ruling bloggers from credentialed news organizations must be admitted, Cuban responded by opening the locker room doors to all bloggers, including newbies and students.[52] Sports executives view live blogging of games as a business issue rather than a free press issue. Major League Baseball Advanced Media—which runs the league's official Web site and 30 Major League Baseball club sites—brings in an estimated $400 million in annual revenue.[53] Sports executives fear live blogging could harm ad revenues from broadcasters who pay millions of dollars for rights to carry live games.

## RSS

*RSS* (*Really Simple Syndication*) is a distribution system that lets publishers share Web content, such as headlines and text, via XML feeds. The RSS feed (also known as a channel or stream) consists of a list of items, each containing a headline, description, and a link to a Web page for the full version of the article. When a site has an RSS feed, it is said to be "syndicated." Many Web sites and blogs use RSS to display headlines from other sites to provide additional content to readers. RSS is highly targeted because it delivers headlines only to those who have signed up for them, similar to an opt-in mailing list. Readers use a feed reader or RSS news aggregator to subscribe to and read feeds. Newer browsers include feed readers in their design. RSS data can also flow into other products and services, like smart phones, e-mail ticklers, and voice updates. RSS can also be used to automate e-mail newsletters.

As with other aspects of publishing content online, concerns of defamation, profanity, obscenity, and copyright and trademark infringement will have to be addressed in this emerging area. While the **CDA** will undoubtedly apply to RSS feeds, courts will have to determine if a Webmaster or blogger providing an RSS feed is a publisher or a distributor; after all, syndication is a form of distribution.

Many sites publish RSS aggregated news headlines in a bid to lure more readers and thus provide more eyeballs for advertisers. If a third-party creates an RSS news feed for the aggregated news headlines published on such a site, he would, in effect, be providing a means for the reader to access the information without viewing the ads. Recall the similar situation with framing and inline linking in Chapter 3, where content appeared "filtered" on a third-party site without the ads. Here, the headlines would be distributed via RSS feed, but none of the advertising would show with the feed. On the other hand, while the selection and order of the headlines may be proprietary to the site publishing them, the actual content, *i.e.*, the full articles, in most cases are not.

## Podcasting

Many news organizations, as well as individuals, deliver content in the form of podcasts. The concept of *podcasting* is similar to RSS feeds. A subscriber selects content from a collection of feeds, either individually or in the aggregate. The difference with podcasting is, instead of text feeds, they are mp3 audio files or video files, and rather than reading them on a monitor, the user listens to or views them on portable media players like the ubiquitous Apple iPod (hence the name "podcasting") or iPhone. Sites like ipodder.org list pod feeds available. Subscribers automatically receive audio file downloads, which they can play at their convenience. The downloaded podcast can be transferred to a portable media player. Podcasts may consist of music, lectures, or homemade talk shows. The growth of the popular new medium is spurred by the fact most podcasts are distributed free and without advertisements (though that may change, as the medium matures and podcasters need revenue to pay licensing fees or bandwidth expenses).

Unlike streaming (*i.e.*, continuous real-time) music offered by many radio sites, podcasts are individual audio files meant to be downloaded and listened to at a later date. Anyone can be a podcaster and anyone can download a podcast. All it takes to become a podcaster is the right software, a computer, a microphone, a Web site, and sufficient bandwidth. Podcasts can be downloaded by any type of computer. If the Internet brought publishing to the masses, then podcasting promises to bring broadcasting to them. Even schoolchildren can podcast and syndicate their own talk shows. Big media broadcasters, such as the BBC and NPR, are repackaging broadcasted segments into podcasts as marketing tools to promote their shows to a wider audience. TV networks offer entire shows for downloads as podcasts.

Since podcast content rests solely with the podcaster, it is important he not include copyrighted material without a license to do so. Apple iPods have a podcast menu button to take users to its online iTunes store, where they can subscribe to podcasts. [54] But this raises the possibility of offering a podcast containing infringing copyrighted material; unless Apple individually reviews each one, it cannot assure a podcaster/wannabee DJ has not submitted a podcast with a copyrighted song. Another area of potential liability is podcasts whose content may be legal in one country but illegal in another, *e.g.*, a broadcast protected under the First Amendment in the United States might run afoul of U.K. defamation laws.

Even radio stations should pause before packaging broadcasted syndicated material into podcasts, as many syndication agreements give only broadcast rights while reserving all other rights. Of course, a radio station can also specify podcast rights in its syndication agreements or later acquire a license to podcast such material. As podcasts increase in popularity and downloads, the Recording Industry Association of America will probably seek to enforce copyright laws against infringers, as it has with mp3 downloads through P2P file-sharing networks. [55]

Unlike broadcasters, podcasters are not subject to Federal Communications Commission (FCC) regulation, so both content and advertising are free from FCC censorship. Not only is Howard Stern free to say whatever comes to mind on his podcast without fear of FCC fines, but advertisers may hawk products the mainstream media might shy away from, as was the case with Durex, a condom manufacturer that became an early podcast advertiser. [56] Podcasts allow advertisers to narrowcast to a discrete target audience; indeed, the allure of podcasting is it provides an outlet for shows with formats so specialized they could never appear on commercial radio.

For its consumers, the attraction of podcasting can be summed up in four key points: access to highly specialized content; uncensored content; free distribution; and the option of time-shifting digital content. With podcasting, a consumer can choose exactly what he wants, free of FCC regulations, and listen to it at his convenience. For the podcaster, like blogging, it is a low-cost version of "personal publishing."

## Wikis

A *wiki* is server software that allows viewers to create and edit Web page content using any Web browser. Normally, a Web page is written by its creator and read by the viewer. A wiki Web page can be edited by anyone viewing it. Changes made by the viewer are visible to subsequent viewers. For example, *Wikipedia* is an online encyclopedia where entries are constantly updated, added to, or modified by viewers who become virtual contributors in what ultimately emerges as a community or consensus work. [57] The idea is multiple individuals are able to bring different aspects of knowledge to the project, resulting in a more complete and all-encompassing work — a collaborative aggregation of knowledge. Wikipedia's sponsors also sponsor the "Wiktionary" (dictionary and thesaurus), "Wikiquote" (collected quotations), "Wikispecies" (directory of species), "Wikinews" (free content news source), and "Wikibooks" (free textbooks and manuals). Wikis are not limited to reference works; they can be tailored to a focused audience or an affinity group, *e.g.*, a "Star Wars" wiki devoted to Wookies. The CIA has its own wiki called Intellipedia. [58]

Usually, modifications are not reviewed before they are published, so one major characteristic of wikis is the speed at which pages can be created or updated. This open philosophy might be a drawback, since defamatory comments, profanity, or hate speech could slip onto a page almost instantaneously. Another major characteristic is each page contains many hyperlinks. Pages often cite related pages, including those yet to be written. "Wikispam", where spammers (or their robots) add hyperlinks to irrelevant sites to boost the search engine page rankings of the linked site, is another potential problem. To combat this, most wikis have a "revision history" feature allowing an editor to view and restore a previous version of an article. Wikis may ban selected individuals from contributing by blocking their IP address. Wiki software provides for setting pages to "read only" mode, though this obviously defeats the purpose of a wiki. Like any democracy, the wiki's greatest feature — its openness — is also its greatest vulnerability.

A wiki is in some ways similar and yet in others completely different from a blog. Both offer ease of publication to anyone wishing to become a "Web publisher." A blog may allow viewers to reply to the blogger's comments, making it an interactive experience; however, the viewer cannot change the author's original text, which is not a limitation in a wiki. Many issues discussed earlier in this book relating to message boards and blogs, two areas where third-parties can add content to a Web site, may also become relevant to wikis as they develop. There have been reports of Wikipedia entries being changed to add defamatory content, delete embarrassing facts, "spruce up" one's own (or one's company's) entry, or add negative comments to a competitor's entry. [59]

During emergencies or natural disasters, wikis have proven important gathering sites, not just for news, but also to share resources, publish safety bulletins, locate missing persons, post vital information, and even serve as virtual support groups. When Hurricane Katrina struck Mississippi and Louisiana in September 2005, "Katrina wikis" provided updates from residents on the scene and let people post missing relatives' names or their own to show they had survived. One let users post status notes (*e.g.*, "flooded", "destroyed," "still standing") on an aerial photo map of houses in the hurricane-stricken area.

[1] "Decline in Newsroom Jobs Slows," American Society of Newspaper Editors, April 11, 2010, *available at* http://asne.org/annual_conference/conference_news/articleid/763/decline-in-newsroom-jobs-slows.aspx (accessed on Mar. 23, 2011).

[2] While some local news stories are syndicated to wider audiences, the majority are not viewed outside their local market.

[3] Martin Kaplan, "The Transformation of News Media from Journalism to Entertainment," November 3, 2010, *available at* www.virtualprofessors.com/the-transformation-of-news-media-from-journalism-to-entertainment-martin-kaplan (accessed Mar. 23, 2012).

[4] Robert McChesney and John Nichols, "The Rise of Professional Journalism," December 8, 2005, *available at* www.inthesetimes.com/article/2427 (accessed Mar. 23, 2012).

[5] Lester Haines, "Facebook Mob 'Trashed' £4.4m Spanish Villa," The Register, May 30, 2008.

[6] David Price, the family's solicitor. *See* Robert Verkaik, "Mother Sues over Tale of 'Drunken Party' Lifted from Bebo," The Independent, July 11, 2008.

[7] *Reynolds v. Times Newspapers, Ltd.* [2001] 2 AC 127 (House of Lords), on appeal from *Reynolds v. Times Newspapers, Ltd.* [1999] 3 All ER 961 (Court of Appeals) created a new form of qualified privilege protecting widespread publication of false information about an individual, if it concerns a matter of public interest to the community and was published reasonably and without malice. Reynolds sued the newspaper for defamation. He won, but was awarded no damages. Both sides appealed. The Court of Appeals ordered a retrial but denied the newspaper permission to use the qualified privilege defense. The newspaper appealed to the House of Lords. Lord Nicholls crafted what has become known as the *Reynolds* Defense. He devised 10 factors to consider in granting the defense of qualified privilege:

    1. The seriousness of the allegation.

    2. The nature of the information and extent to which the subject matter is of public concern.

    3. The source of the information.

    4. The steps taken to verify the information.

    5. The status of the information, *e.g.,* if it had already been the subject of an investigation.

    6. The urgency of the matter (as news is often a perishable commodity).

    7. Whether comment was sought from the plaintiff.

    8. Whether the article contained the gist of the plaintiff's side of the story.

    9. The article's tone.

    10. The circumstances of the publication, including the timing.

The *Reynolds* test balances free speech against the public's interest in not being misinformed by the media on important factual issues. *Reynolds* has been a limited defense in British libel proceedings, as subsequent judges have required defendants to satisfy all the criteria.

[8] Andras Gergely, "Irish Student's Jarre Wiki Hoax Dupes Journalists," Reuters wire service report, May 7, 2009.

[9] Ron Steinman, "Citizen Journalism: A Recipe for Disaster," The Digital Journalist, December 2009, *available at* http://digitaljournalist.org/issue0912/citizen-journalism-a-recipe-for-disaster.html (accessed Mar. 23, 2012).

[10] Ethics in the Age of Digital Photography," *available at* www.nppa.org/professional_development/self-training_resources/eadp_report/digital_manipulation.html (accessed Mar. 23, 2012).

[11] "Ethics in the Age of Digital Photography," *available at* www.nppa.org/professional_development/self-training_resources/eadp_report/ethics.html (accessed Mar. 23, 2012).

[12] "Paper Cuts off Web Site Forum," The Los Angeles Times, May 21, 2005. Many newspapers have a policy of banning comments during major news events. *The Roanoke* (VA) *Times* closed a message board set up to discuss the April 2007 Virginia Tech sniper massacre. Some papers, like *The Sacramento* (CA) *Bee*, ban anonymous comments and require readers to use real names in posts. *See* Janet Kornblum "Rudeness, Threats Make the Web a Cruel World," USA Today, July 30, 2007.

[13] Steve Outing, "When User Comments Become Community Journalism," E-Media Tidbits, June 2, 2005, *available at* www.poynter.org/column.asp?id=31&aid=83324 (accessed Mar. 23, 2012).

[14] Katharine Q. Seelye, "Paper Closes Reader Comments on Blog, Citing Vitriol," The New York Times, January 20, 2006.

[15] *Ibid.*

[16] Outing, fn. 13, *supra.*

[17] Random House Unabridged Dictionary defines a "journalist" as "a person who keeps a journal, diary, or other record of daily events", which would seem to qualify all bloggers as journalists. The question of who is a journalist has been debated in many contexts. The Third Circuit addressed the issue in deciding whether a district court erred by concluding Mark Madden, a witness in a civil case, was entitled to claim a journalist's privilege. *In re Madden*, 151 F. 3d 125 (3ᵈ Cir. 1998). Madden produced tape-recorded commentaries on wrestlers and wrestling events for a 900-number hotline. During a deposition, he refused to identify the sources of allegedly false and misleading statements, claiming the reporter's privilege. The court ruled he was not covered by the privilege because he was, by his own admission, "an entertainer, not a reporter." The Third Circuit established the *Madden* test to determine whether an individual is a journalist with standing to claim journalist's privilege. The individual must prove he (1) is engaged in investigative reporting, (2) is gathering news, and (3) possessed the intent at the inception of the news-gathering process to disseminate the news to the public.

[18] **"Shield laws"** protect journalists from being compelled to reveal their sources. Forty-nine states and the District of Columbia recognize a reporter's privilege, either through state shield laws or court decisions. Some journalists have been successfully sued by sources to whom they promised confidentiality but later revealed their identities. *See Cohen v. Cowles Media Co.*, 501 U.S. 663 (1991).

[19] "March 26, 1848: The Senate Arrests a Reporter," U.S. Senate Web site, *available at* www.senate.gov/ artandhistory/history/minute/The_Senate_Arrests_A_Reporter.htm (accessed Mar. 23, 2012).

[20] *Ibid.*

[21] *Branzburg v. Hayes*, 408 U.S. 665 (1972).

[22] *University of Pennsylvania v. EEOC*, 493 U.S. 182 (1990). *See also In re Grand Jury Subpoena, Judith Miller*, 397 F.3d 964, 976-980 (D.C. Cir. 2005).

[23] Nicholas M. Ciarelli's blog, *was available at* www.thinksecret.com (accessed September 25, 2007; as of August 5, 2008 the site was no longer accessible).

[24] PowerPage, *available at* www.powerpage.org (accessed Mar. 23, 2012), and Apple Insider, *available at* www.appleinsider.com, (accessed Mar. 23, 2012).

[25] The facts of the case are discussed in the Trade Secrets section of Chapter 5, *supra.*

[26] "Judge Says Web Sites Can Be Forced to Reveal Sources," Mercury News, March 04, 2005.

[27] *Apple Computer, Inc. v. Doe*, Case No. 1-04-cv-032178 (Cal. Super. Ct. 2005) granting discovery motion, rev'd *sub nom. O'Grady v. Super. Ct. of Santa Clara Cnty.*, 139 Cal. App. 4th 1423 (Cal. App. 6ᵗʰ Dist. 2006), holding when trade secrets law and freedom of speech conflict, First Amendment rights take precedence.

[28] The California Reporter's Shield Law, Art. I § 2(b) of the California Constitution.

[29] Hawaii's Shield Law, HRS Div. 4. Tit. 33. ch. 621.

[30] U.S. Supreme Court decisions have held the Fourteenth Amendment extended the prohibition against government abridgement of free speech or press to states as well as the federal government.

[31] Andrew Orlowski, "Bloggers Must Reveal Sources — Judge," The Register, March 12, 2005.

[32] New Jersey's Shield Law, N.J.S.A. 2A:84A-21.

[33] MaryAnn Spoto, "Judge Rules a Blogger Can Be Sued," New Jersey Star Ledger, July 3, 2009.

[34] *Ibid.*

[35] *Too Much Media, LLC v. Hale*, 413 N.J. Super. 135 (N.J. Super. Ct. App. Div. 2010).

[36] *Too Much Media, LLC v. Hale*, Case No. A-7-10 (N.J. Sup. Ct. Jun. 2011).

[37] *Ibid.*

[38] Kevin Ellis, "Judge Gives Online Commenters First Amendment Protection," The Gaston Gazette, July 28, 2010.

[39] North Carolina's Shield Law, N.C. Gen. Stat. § 8-53.11.

[40] *Obsidian Finance Group, LLC v. Cox*, Case No. CV-00057-hz (D. Ore. 2011)

[41] Cox's blog, *available at* www.bankruptcycorruption.com/2010/12/kevin-padrick-of-obsidian-finance-group.html (accessed on Mar. 23, 2012).

[42] Oregon Media Shield Law, ORS §44.510.

[43] Even if the defendant had qualified for shield law protection, under Oregon law it would not have protected the identity of the source of allegedly defamatory content in a civil trial.

[44] Paul Elias, "Jobs Made Phone Call Seeking Return of Lost iPhone," Associated Press wire service report, May 14, 2010.

[45] *von Bulow v. von Bulow*, 811 F.2d 136, 144 (2ᵈ Cir. 1987).

[46] H.R. 985: Free Flow of Information Act of 2009 was passed by the U.S. House of Representatives but S. 448 Free Flow of Information Act of 2009 died in the Senate. Sessions of Congress last two years, and at the end of each session any bills and resolutions that have not been passed are cleared from the books.

[47] Media Confidentiality Act § 26-1-901, *et al.*

[48] Greg Tuttle, "Judge: Law Protects Anonymous Newspaper Commenters," The Billings Gazette, September 3, 2008.

[49] Rick Bozich, "Courier-Journal Reporter Ejected from U of L Game," The Louisville Courier-Journal, June 11, 2007.

[50] *Nat'l Basketball Ass'n v. Motorola, Inc.*, 105 F.3d 841 (2ᵈ Cir. 1997).

[51] Heather Havenstein, "NCAA to Bloggers: Too Many Posts — and You're OUT!" Computerworld, December 20, 2007.

[52] Tim Arango, "Tension over Sports Blogging," The New York Times, April 21, 2008.

[53] *Ibid.*

[54] Charles Arthur, "Apple Pushes Podcasts through iTunes," The Register, June 28, 2005.

[55] In fact, ASCAP and BMI already offer a podcast license.

[56] "Durex Buys Condom Product Placements in Podcasts," AdAge.com, March 12, 2005.

[57] *Available at* http://en.wikipedia.org/wiki/Main_Page (accessed Mar. 23, 2012). Wikipedia describes itself as "the free-content encyclopedia that anyone can edit." *Ibid.*

[58] Cass R. Sunstein, "A Brave New Wikiworld," The Washington Post, p. A19, February 24, 2007.

[59] *Ibid.*

# CHAPTER

# 17

---

## OBSCENITY & PORNOGRAPHY:
## THE DARK SIDE OF THE WEB

> This chapter is the first of two chapters that examine restraints on free speech. In this chapter, obscenity, pornography and child pornography are discussed. The Children's Internet Protection Act of 2000 and the Child Protection and Obscenity Enforcement Act of 1988 are also covered.

*"But I know it when I see it" — Justice Potter Stewart*

I N *ROTH V. UNITED STATES*, in 1957, the U.S. Supreme Court ruled obscenity was not "within the area of constitutionally protected speech or press."[1] However, pornography is entitled to First Amendment protection unless it is obscene[2] or child pornography.[3] Thus, the question becomes: What is the definition of obscenity? This is a question courts have been unable to answer satisfactorily, although many attempts have been made. U.S. Supreme Court Justice Potter Stewart admitted he could not define obscenity, adding "but I know it when I see it."[4]

The current test for determining obscenity is the *Miller test*, first enunciated in 1973 in *Miller v. California*:[5]

> (a) Whether to the *average person*, applying *contemporary community standards*, the *dominant theme* of the material *taken as a whole* appeals to *prurient interest*; (b) Whether the work depicts or describes, in a patently offensive way, sexual conduct or excretory functions specifically defined by applicable state law, and (c) Whether the work, taken as a whole, *lacks serious literary, artistic, political or scientific value.*

Although still nebulous to apply, prior to the advent of the Internet, defendants could limit liability by avoiding geographic areas with restrictive standards. However, the borderless nature of the Internet makes applying community standards impossible. Since the Internet reaches every community, only the lowest common denominator (*i.e.*, the most restrictive) community standards would apply. However, the U.S. Supreme Court has more recently said "community standards" need not be defined by a precise geographic area.[6]

Community standards are usually thought of as subjective. Not everyone in the same community shares the same moral standards, and many pornography viewers may not want their neighbors to know of their interests and fetishes. So it can be hard to establish what a community's standards are when people may be reluctant to admit publicly their own standards; they often publicly condemn material they routinely view in private. Defense attorneys attempt to define community standards by showing which sexually explicit magazines and videos are available in the community, but this approach focuses on availability and not consumption. An attorney in a Florida obscenity case proposed a novel approach to establish community standards — contrasting the relative popularity of sexually-explicit search phrases local residents searched for in Google with ordinary phrases like "apple pie."[7] The search data, available through Google Trends, let users compare search trends in a specific area. The idea is if the defense attorney can show residents are searching in disproportionate volume for the same sexual matters displayed in the defendant's videos, then the videos do meet community standards.

## Federal Obscenity Statutes

### The Communications Decency Act (CDA) § 223

Earlier, we discussed § 230 of the **Communications Decency Act** (CDA). Another section of that act, § 223, made it illegal to transmit indecent material or display patently offensive material on the Internet.[8] In the 1997 case _Reno v. ACLU_, the U.S. Supreme Court unanimously ruled the **CDA** restrictions violated the First Amendment because the terms "indecent" and "patently offensive" were too broad.[9]

The U.S. Supreme Court turned down the chance to set online obscenity standards in 2006, when it rejected an appeal from a photographer who claimed the **CDA** violated her free speech rights to post pictures of sadomasochistic sexual behavior online.[10] A three-judge federal panel had held she failed to meet the evidentiary burden of proving the statute unconstitutional by not providing hard data on how many sites might have their free speech at risk from inconsistent applications of the _Miller_ test by local juries.[11] Barbara Nitke — whose site featured her bondage, sadomasochistic, and homoerotic photographs — along with the National Coalition for Sexual Freedom argued fear of prosecution created a _"chilling effect"_ on artists who might otherwise post such materials online, if legally protected speech in their own communities. In Nitke's case, what might not be considered "obscene" by her native New York City's community standards might be deemed so by a more conservative community, such as the Bible Belt or Salt Lake City. Nitke argued this chilling effect demonstrated the **CDA** was overbroad. (The **Overbreadth Doctrine** holds if a statute designed to prevent illegal speech has the effect of inhibiting protected speech, then that statute is deemed overbroad and therefore unconstitutional.)[12] By declining to hear the appeal, the U.S. Supreme Court let stand the earlier panel decision; as a result, federal prosecutors retain the option of selecting where to file obscenity charges. Obviously, under the _Miller_ test, their venue of choice would be the most conservative community. The problem is the Internet, unlike other methods of communication, is not targeted to a discrete audience, but available worldwide, without geographic boundaries. The borderless nature of the Internet effectively renders the _Miller_ test obsolete, a reality the U.S. Supreme Court has so far declined to address.[13]

## The Child Online Protection Act of 1998 (COPA)

After the U.S. Supreme Court struck down **CDA** § 223, Congress made yet another attempt to restrict online pornography. Hoping to resolve the First Amendment issues that had plagued the **CDA**, it enacted the **Child Online Protection Act** (COPA).[14] **COPA** criminalized publication of "any communication for *commercial* purposes that includes sexual material *harmful to minors, without restricting access* to such material by minors." "Harmful to minors" was defined in the Act as lacking "scientific, literary, artistic, or political value" and offensive to local "community standards." The maximum penalty was a $50,000 fine, six months in prison, and additional civil fees. The Act's "restricting access" requirement mandated adults use access codes or credit cards for age verification to view objectionable material.

However, **COPA** never took effect. The Third Circuit[15] upheld an injunction of **COPA** as unconstitutional.[16] The U.S. Supreme Court also let the injunction stand, though it cast doubt on the appellate court's reasoning, in *dicta*.[17] But in 2002, after rejecting the lower court's ruling use of "community standards" to define what is harmful to children was unconstitutional, the Supreme Court pointed out other constitutional issues the lower court failed to address.[18] The lower court, in turn, re-examined **COPA** and said, for the second time, it violated the First Amendment.[19] Then, in 2004, in *Ashcroft v. ACLU*, the Supreme Court sent the case back to the lower court for a new trial, citing rapid changes in technology that would make filtering software a more effective tool to block access than the more restrictive means proffered in **COPA**, such as age verification and credit card use.[20] (Indeed, how does one *really* verify online an individual's age or that an individual is the true owner of the credit card used?) In 2007, a federal district court again ruled **COPA** unconstitutional, noting the government's "own study shows that all but the worst performing filters are far more effective than **COPA** would be at protecting children from sexually explicit material on the Web."[21] In 2008, the Third Circuit agreed, ruling **COPA** unconstitutional because: (1) filtering technologies and other parental control tools offer a less restrictive way to protect children from inappropriate content online, and (2) the statute was overly broad and vague.[22]

**COPA** presented a constitutional conflict, pitting First Amendment free speech rights of adults against the power of Congress to control interstate commerce, derived from Article I, § 8 of the U.S. Constitution. Both the *Overbeadth Doctrine* and the *Vagueness Doctrine* applied. The statute was overbroad because it would deny adults access to "material harmful to children" (itself a vague phrase). Also, children could still access harmful material on foreign and noncommercial Web sites (since **COPA** only applied to commercial, U.S. sites) and via Internet protocols other than the World Wide Web, such as chat, message boards, instant messaging, and Usenet. The *Vagueness Doctrine* is derived from the Fifth and Fourteenth Amendments' due process clauses requiring criminal laws be drafted so individuals of "common intelligence" need not "necessarily guess as at its meaning and differ as to its application."[23]

## The Children's Internet Protection Act of 2000 (CIPA)

The **Children's Internet Protection Act of 2000** (CIPA) denies federal funds linked to Internet access to public libraries and schools refusing to filter their Internet-accessible computers.[24] It requires visual depictions (not text) of obscenity, child pornography, or "material harmful to minors" (defined as under age 17) be blocked. **CIPA** mandates libraries disable the filters on adult patrons' request. Initially not widely enforced, as its constitutionality was questioned (because of its limits on access to free speech), the U.S. Supreme Court upheld it in 2003, and now libraries nationwide have had to rethink their Internet safety policies.[25] Some have refused federal funds to be able to continue offering unfiltered Internet access.

**CIPA** does not force public libraries and schools to use filtering software, but threatens loss of federal funds if they do not. By 2007, 21 states had filtering laws applicable to public libraries and schools. Most required they adopt policies to keep minors from accessing sexually explicit, obscene, or "material harmful to minors," but some specifically required filtering software. A California appellate court ruled **CDA** § 230 protected a public library from attempts to use state law causes of action to force it to use filtering software.[26] The Phoenix, Arizona city council, in 2004, ended unrestricted Internet access for adults on public library computers,[27] attributing its policy change to a recent arrest of a child molester who admitted downloading child pornography at the Phoenix Public Library. The prior policy required filters remain on at all times in the libraries' children's areas and for patrons under 17, but allowed adults to disable them. Such filters block obscene images and Web pages by targeting keywords, phrases, or graphical images. Free speech advocates argue when libraries do not allow adults to turn off the filters, adult patrons are denied access to sites that deal with nonpornographic issues that might be mistakenly filtered, such as breast cancer, AIDS research, or sexual education.

## Obscene Words

Prior to _Miller_, several literature classics presently taught in colleges throughout America were banned as obscene, including James Joyce's _Ulysses_, and Voltaire's _Candide_. Since the _Miller_ test's introduction in 1973, obscenity prosecutions have been directed at images, not words. Drawings, photographs, movies, and videos have been subject to prosecution but songs and fictional stories have not. That changed in 2007, when federal prosecutors charged a woman with six counts of violating obscenity laws for writing fictional stories on her Web site.[28] Karen Fletcher, a 56-year-old home-bound agoraphobic on disability benefits, alleged she had left home at age 14 and lived on the streets of Michigan, where she had been physically and sexually abused. She claimed she wrote stories about the kidnapping, rape, and torture of children as a cathartic exercise, explaining she found refuge from the monster and demons that preyed on her in her nightmares by setting them loose on fictional characters. Her stories remained private until she discovered online bulletin boards where other writers posted stories. After gaining acceptance on one board, Fletcher created her own pay site, RedRoseStories.com, charging a $10 fee "to control access" to her stories (her site had 29 members, so presumably she had collected $290, which met the prosecution's definition of interstate commerce).[29] She created a chat room, which she likened to a support group, and let members contribute fictional stories. Fletcher did not allow images on her site.[30] The grand jury indicted her on obscenity charges, not child pornography, as there were no real children involved. For Fletcher to be convicted of obscenity, a jury would have to find her stories lacked serious literary, artistic, political, or scientific value. The danger of prosecuting a fictional work is the chilling effect such prosecution could have on other writers. Critics analogize prosecution of fictional works to prosecution of thought crimes.

Fletcher argued her work was no worse than Scooter Libby's fiction or the television show _South Park_, a cartoon about a group of young children. Libby's novel _The Apprentice_ details training a 10-year-old girl to become a frigid prostitute by placing the child in a cage to be repeatedly raped by a bear, as men pay to watch. Instead of being charged with obscenity, Libby went on to work in the White House as an aide to Vice President Dick Cheney. The three episodes of *South Park* described in Fletcher's brief include Eric Cartman, a little boy, joining the North American Man-Boy Love Association; Cartman playing a prank on a classmate by putting his penis in his classmate's mouth; and a five-year-old boy having sex with his teacher.[31] The *South Park* creators, rather than being charged with obscenity, won awards for "quality in arts and entertainment."[32]

Fletcher ultimately pleaded guilty to six counts of distributing obscenity rather than face trial; her attorney said Fletcher, who had been homebound and suffered from agoraphobia (fear of being in public), felt she could not endure a week-long public trial. The plea bargain called for her to be sentenced to a term of home detention rather than prison.[33] Since she voluntarily pleaded guilty, her plea bargain did not set any precedent in regard to text-only obscenity prosecutions.

## Child Pornography

In 1982, in <u>*New York v. Ferber*</u>, the U.S. Supreme Court ruled child pornography was not entitled to First Amendment protection.[34] Prior to this decision, child pornography had been treated as any other pornography, *i.e.*, requiring a showing of obscenity to be deemed unprotected speech. In <u>*Ferber*</u>, the U.S. Supreme Court created a new category of unprotected speech. The rationale for declaring child pornography de facto obscenity was *to protect children from physical abuse*.

In 2004, a federal court held unconstitutional a Pennsylvania statute designed to prevent viewing Web sites containing child pornography. The statute placed the burden on ISPs to police subscribers, rather than focusing on the violators posting the content, who are frequently hard to find, or overseas. The court found the law violated First Amendment free speech rights because it caused more than a million legitimate sites to be shut down while blocking only about 400 violators. The statute let prosecutors demand ISPs block access to offending sites or face potential criminal penalties. But blocking entire IP addresses also shut down many subaddresses with sites containing legitimate content. This was because Web site hosting companies, which are assigned blocks of addresses, often assign subaddresses to individual sites, since IP addresses are scarce. These subaddresses were difficult, if not impossible, for the ISPs to block individually, so closing down the IP address resulted in shutting down the sub addresses, as well.

Congress, in 1996, enacted the **Child Pornography Prevention Act** (CPPA).[35] The Act's stated goal was to protect children from sexual exploitation. However, it went further, prohibiting "virtual child pornography", *i.e.*, images completely computer-generated or morphed, and images of young-looking adult actors used to create the appearance of minors engaging in sexually explicit conduct. The Act carried criminal penalties of up to 15 years imprisonment *even where there was no real child involved*. Banning virtual child pornography runs counter to the rationale of protecting children, since no actual child is physically abused. In 2002, the U.S. Supreme Court, in <u>*Ashcroft v. Free Speech Coalition*</u>, ruled the **CPPA** violated the First Amendment.[36] In fact, the Court referred to previous decisions suggesting, where necessary for literary or artistic value to denote what would otherwise be child pornography, "a person over the statutory age who perhaps looked younger could be utilized", adding "simulation outside of the prohibition of the statute could provide another alternative."[37] So the **CPPA** had outlawed the very safe harbor advocated by the Court as a constitutional alternative.

The absurdity of the drive by some conservative legislators to outlaw virtual child pornography recalls an incident where a store owner faced child pornography charges for selling a comic book.[38] The comic book featured illustrations (no photographs) of elves — short, ancient, magical creatures with pointy ears and childlike appearance. Despite the fact no children (let alone real people) appeared in it, local authorities cited it as child pornography — a far cry from the stated purpose of child pornography laws, *i.e.*, protecting children from being sexually exploited in photographs and movies. Likewise, a Michigan singer-songwriter faced charges of manufacturing and distributing child pornography after posting a video to YouTube he had edited to make it appear school children were listening to him singing graphic lyrics.[39] A disclaimer said the children had not heard the song. If convicted, he faced up to 20 years in prison.

An Iowa comic book collector was sentenced in 2010 to six months in prison after pleading guilty to importing and possessing Japanese manga comic books depicting illustrations of child sex and bestiality.[40] Christopher Handley was charged under the **PROTECT Act**, the first individual convicted for possessing cartoon art, without any evidence he collected or viewed real photographs of child pornography. Had he not agreed to plead guilty to charges of possessing "obscene visual representations of the sexual abuse of children," Handley would have faced a maximum 15-year sentence. Customs agents had intercepted and opened a package from Japan addressed to him in 2006, discovering seven manga comic books.[41] The **PROTECT Act**, discussed below, criminalizes possession of cartoons, drawings, sculptures or paintings depicting minors engaging in sexually explicit conduct, and which lack "serious literary, artistic, political, or scientific value".

## The PROTECT Act

Undeterred by the **CPPA** being declared unconstitutional, Congress the following year enacted the **PROTECT Act of 2003**, also known as the Amber Alert Bill.[42] This Act established a national Amber Alert Program to locate missing children and authorized wiretaps for crimes using the Internet to lure children for sexual abuse and sex trafficking. Few congressmen would dare vote against a bill to "protect children" (the **PROTECT Act** passed 98-to-0 in the Senate and 400-to-25 in the House), but two items with significant First Amendment implications were tacked onto the bill. In response to *Ashcroft*, the 2002 U.S. Supreme Court decision that struck down key portions of the **CPPA**, the **PROTECT Act** amended child pornography laws to make virtual child pornography illegal. It banned "a computer image, computer-generated image, or digital image that is of, or is virtually indistinguishable from that of, an actual minor" thus criminalizing images that merely looked like children, even if computer-generated, or youthful-looking adult models.

Congress had enacted a near identical version of the **CPPA**, declared unconstitutional only a year earlier, and slipped it into a bill to locate and protect missing children, which no one was likely to vote against. The first edition of this book stated "Nevertheless, it stands to reason that this portion of the Act will most likely be held unconstitutional for the same reasons, if challenged."[43] Sure enough, an Eleventh Circuit panel unanimously struck down[44] that portion[45] of the **PROTECT Act** in 2006. The ruling affected only the Eleventh

Circuit—Florida, Georgia, and Alabama. But, on appeal, in _United States v. Williams_, the U.S. Supreme Court reversed, finding the statute not overly broad.[46] The **PROTECT Act** criminalizes production and possession of child pornography, as well as pandering material conveying the belief it contains minors engaged in sexually explicit conduct. The pandering provision includes anyone who "advertises, promotes, presents, distributes, or solicits" this material. Michael Williams was convicted under the Act for "pandering." The district court had held Congress could ban pandering of material as child pornography, even if not in fact child pornography. The Eleventh Circuit had reversed, striking down the **PROTECT Act** as unconstitutionally overbroad, but it was overruled by the U.S. Supreme Court on the rationale offers to engage in illegal transactions do not receive First Amendment protection.

The **PROTECT Act** has been used in other ways to fight child pornography. It amended a federal statute criminalizing behavior that "knowingly makes … or causes to be made … any notice … offering … to … distribute … or reproduce" child pornography across state lines."[47] That statute, which imposes a mandatory 15-year prison sentence without possibility of parole on anyone convicted of publishing "notice" offering to distribute child pornography across state lines, was originally designed to prosecute individuals who advertised child pornography in print ads or on computer bulletin board systems. But, in _United States v. Sewell_, a 43-year-old Missouri pharmacist was sentenced under the Act to the automatic 15-year prison term after downloading and sharing child pornography over the Kazaa file-sharing network.[48] The Eighth Circuit found, by placing files with descriptive names identifying them as child pornography in his Kazaa share folder, Sewell had met the statute's "notice" provision.

As discussed in Chapter 5, the **PROTECT Act** also criminalizes using misleading domain names with intent to deceive an adult into viewing obscenity online (punishable by a fine, or up to two years imprisonment, or both) or a minor into viewing material harmful to minors online (punishable by a fine, or up to four years imprisonment, or both). The terms "misleading", "obscenity", and "harmful to minors" are inherently vague, and therefore subject to a First Amendment challenge.

## Other Child Protection Statutes

The **Child Protection and Obscenity Enforcement Act of 1988** requires certain adult media, _e.g._, magazines and videos, maintain on-site records to verify all models or actors are of legal age.[49] Its purpose is to ensure minors are not engaged in production of pornography, and in 2005, it was extended to encompass Web sites. Webmasters who run adult-oriented sites must keep and provide extensive documentation about performers, including legal name, date of birth, and copies of documents with a photo ID. However, the rules do not extend to ISPs. The age regulations were inspired by congressional outrage at a hardcore video performance by then 15-year-old porn star Traci Lords.

The **Protect Our Children Act of 2008** requires "electronic communication or remote computing service providers" report incidences of child pornography, including the identity of anyone who appears to have violated a child exploitation or pornography law, his location, and images of any apparent child pornography.[50] It requires ISPs preserve child pornography images for evidentiary purposes. The Act also amends the federal criminal code to prohibit distribution of child pornography "that is an adapted or modified depiction of an identifiable minor", meaning Congress has again passed a law outlawing virtual child pornography. It remains to be seen if this provision will withstand a constitutional challenge.

The **Keeping the Internet Devoid of Sexual Predators Act of 2008** (KIDSPA) requires sex offenders provide the National Sex Offender Registry with all their Internet identifiers (*e.g.*, e-mail addresses). [51] It does not allow the identifiers to be made public, but requires the attorney general share the information with social networks so they can compare it with their users.

## What Is "Possession"?

What is the legal difference among pornography, obscenity, and child pornography? What constitutes "possession"? Should an individual or institution be liable for downloading pornography, obscenity, or child pornography if circumstances indicate they did not knowingly or intentionally do so?

Pornography is the depiction of sexual behavior intended to arouse sexual excitement, *i.e.*, appeal to prurient interests. But that quality alone will not render a work legally obscene. Pornography is legal but downloading it at one's workplace may lead to dismissal by employers fearing complaints from co-workers of sexual harassment due to the creation of a hostile work environment if the images or videos are visible by others, or for misusing company equipment. It could lead to criminal charges if allowed to be viewed by minors. A Connecticut substitute teacher was convicted of allowing her seventh-grade students to view pornography on a classroom computer, but was granted a new trial when the judge concluded it was possible spyware and adware programs might have been responsible for the pornographic pop-up ads viewed by students. The school computer did not have a firewall or anti-spyware software installed. The teacher had faced up to 40 years in prison after her conviction, until a state crime lab released findings casting doubt on evidence presented at the trial by the prosecution's computer expert. [52]

Obscenity goes beyond mere pornography, although as we have seen, no one can adequately describe it. According to the _Miller_ Test, it must appeal to prurient interests, which would mean videos of Nazis torturing concentration camp victims, the beheading of reporter Daniel Pearl, or a woman grinding her stiletto heel through the head of a kitten (all viewable online) are not considered legally obscene. Obscenity must depict sexual conduct or excretory functions in a patently offensive way as defined by state statute, the dominant theme taken as a whole must appeal to prurient interests as judged by one's neighbors (community standards) and the work, taken as a whole, must lack serious literary, artistic, political or scientific value. The problem is obscenity is a moving target, pegged to the social mores of the era. Novels like Henry Miller's *Tropic of Cancer*, D.H. Lawrence's *Lady Chatterley's Lover*, and James Joyce's *Ulysses*, [53] stage performances by comedian Lenny Bruce, and movies like *Carnal Knowledge* (written by Pulitzer Prize winner Jules Feiffer and starring Art Garfunkel, Jack Nicholson, Ann-Margret, Candice Bergen, and Rita Moreno) have all been declared obscene by the government. In the latter case, police raided a theater in Albany, Georgia, seized the film from the projector, and charged the theater manager with the crime of "distributing obscene material". The Supreme Court of Georgia upheld his conviction. Two years later, the U.S. Supreme Court overturned it. [54] Yesterday's obscenity may become tomorrow's classic. The term is not only vague and ill-defined, but open to subjective interpretation influenced by the mores of the times. As we have seen, what is considered obscene by societal standards in one generation may be viewed as harmless or even a serious artistic endeavor a generation later.

How many potential great works have been self-censored or perhaps abandoned by creators fearful of arrest for expressing themselves? The legality of popular culture (books, films, television, comic books, songs, video games, and Web sites) in America ebbs and flows with societal mores and cultural attitudes and may ultimately rest in the hands of the jury with no uniform national standard to apply, resulting in works being deemed obscene in one county but permissible in a neighboring county or state.

Radclyffe Hall wrote *The Well of Loneliness*, a novel about two lesbians who fall in love but are met with social ostracism for their perverse behavior. The book was judged obscene in Hall's native England and in America, where New York police seized 865 copies from the publisher's offices and charged him with selling an obscene publication. A New York magistrate refused to consider the book's literary qualities, stating it was "calculated to deprave and corrupt minds open to its immoral influences"[55] but on remand to the New York Court of Special Sessions the book was held not obscene.[56] The year was 1928 and Hall stated her reasons for writing *The Well of Loneliness* were social and political — to end public silence on the topic of homosexuality and encourage tolerance. Government efforts to ban obscenity have long been recognized as an attempt to legislate morality. One might ask if government attempts to ban books, films, and speech it labels "obscene" are a form of censorship, aimed at curtailing or suppressing speech. In fact, Justice Douglas wrote in his dissent in *Miller*:[57]

> That test would make it possible to ban any paper or any journal or magazine in some benighted place. The First Amendment was designed 'to invite dispute,' to induce 'a condition of unrest,' to 'create dissatisfaction with conditions as they are,' and even to stir 'people to anger.' The idea that the First Amendment permits punishment for ideas that are 'offensive' to the particular judge or jury sitting in judgment is astounding. No greater leveler of speech or literature has ever been designed. To give the power to the censor, as we do today, is to make a sharp and radical break with the traditions of a free society. The First Amendment was not fashioned as a vehicle for dispensing tranquilizers to the people. Its prime function was to keep debate open to 'offensive' as well as to 'staid' people. The tendency throughout history has been to subdue the individual and to exalt the power of government. The use of the standard 'offensive' gives authority to government that cuts the very vitals out of the First Amendment. As is intimated by the Court's opinion, the materials before us may be garbage. But so is much of what is said in political campaigns, in the daily press, on TV, or over the radio. By reason of the First Amendment — and solely because of it — speakers and publishers have not been threatened or subdued because their thoughts and ideas may be 'offensive' to some.

Under American law, it is illegal to purchase, sell, distribute, offer to sell, receive by mail,[58] or download obscene materials. One may, however, possess obscene materials in one's home.[59] But both distribution and possession of child pornography are illegal.[60] What constitutes "possession" in cyberspace? A Georgia man was sentenced to 20 years in prison for possession of child pornography, where the images were found on his computer in his Internet browser's cache.[61] A cache temporarily stores files automatically downloaded from visited Web sites. It is possible for one to click a link in a pop-up ad, e-mail, or search engine result and wind up on an unknown Web page. Suppose the man had arrived at the site unintentionally, or with no idea of its content and left immediately; the images would still reside in his browser's cache. The user has no control over the images being downloaded to the computer cache; should he be subject to criminal penalties of up to 20 years imprisonment? Should the existence of images in his cache amount to possession?

A Massachusetts man was fired when IT administrators found child pornography in his browser's cache. He hired a forensics expert to prove his work laptop was infected with malware surreptitiously visiting Web sites, leaving child pornography images in the cache. The virus had programmed his computer to visit up to 40 child pornography sites per minute! His computer was even accessed remotely, downloading child pornography while he was dining in a restaurant.[62] The evidence convinced the court to drop the case, but though exonerated, he did not get his job back.[63] A British hotel manager searching online for ways to play computer games without paying for them visited a pirated software site that redirected his browser to a child pornography site, leaving incriminating images in the cache. He was cleared by a computer forensic expert.[64] In another U.K. case, a virus reset a user's home page to a child pornography site, which his 7-year-old daughter stumbled on. He was jailed for more than a week, spent three months in a halfway house, and lost custody of his daughter.[65] We previously discussed the case of the teacher convicted of allowing her students to view pornography on a classroom computer that may have been installed by spyware without her knowledge.

At any moment, about 20 million computers plugged into the Web are infected with viruses enabling hackers to access them remotely.[66] Computer experts describe it as "painfully simple" for hackers to make a computer download files its owner may not want or be aware of. Pranksters may place illegal images on someone's hard drive, or an enemy may frame his victim by tapping viruses to make it seem he visits illegal sites. Individuals who collect or trade child pornography may exploit virus-infected computers to store and view their stash remotely, so as not to hold incriminating evidence on their own drives. The viruses force the victim's computer to browse child pornography sites, storing images along the way, or turn the computer into a warehouse for photographs and videos that can, surreptitiously, be viewed remotely whenever it is online.[67] The simplistic approach may be to conclude illegal material on a hard drive is evidence of illegal activity on the computer owner's part, but courts and prosecutors must become better educated about the technology of the Internet and how various aspects of that technology—including malware, Trojan horses, and browser caches—function.

Pornography, obscenity, and child pornography have been discovered in browser caches of unsuspecting Internet users, left by viruses or hackers. Just by clicking a link in a pop-up ad, e-mail, or search engine result, one may be sent to pornographic Web page, and even if the user leaves the page seconds later, images from the site will remain stored in the browser's cache. We have discussed wardriving scenarios where an individual's Wi-Fi connection is hijacked, and the wardriver, piggybacking on the network, downloads child pornography traceable back to the innocent individual's network. Globally, about 201 million households use Wi-Fi networks.[68] One study found 32 percent of adult Americans admitted trying to access someone else's Wi-Fi network.[69] Users with an open wireless router might not realize someone is piggybacking on the signal, which can reach 300–to–400 feet. Federal agents armed with assault weapons raided a Buffalo, New York man's home, accusing him of having downloaded thousands of child pornography images before concluding days later a neighbor had been piggybacking on his unsecured wireless connection.[70] A Sarasota, Florida man was mistakenly thought to be downloading child pornography until the FBI discovered someone on a boat docked in a marina outside his building was the real culprit, using a potato chip can as an antenna to boost his wireless signal.[71] A similar situation occurred in North Syracuse, New York, where a man's neighbor piggybacked on his Wi-Fi connection.[72] The legality of piggybacking is questionable: while state and federal laws prohibiting unauthorized access, there is no U.S. law mandating users secure their wireless connections and some might interpret an unsecured access point as implied permission to use it. By comparison, Germany's highest criminal court held Internet users have a duty to secure their wireless connections to prevent others from illegally downloading data and can be fined for failing to do so if someone piggybacks on their unsecured connection, but the user would not be held liable for illegal content downloaded by the third party.[73] A similar situation could be imagined in a public library or cybercafé, where an institution might be charged with displaying pornographic images left on the computer from a patron's use. Recall from Chapter 6, the U.K. pub owner fined after a patron illegally downloaded copyrighted material over the pub's open Wi-Fi hotspot. Suppose instead of copyrighted material, he had been viewing obscenity? Should such institutions be liable for the use their patrons make of the technology they provide? Must they apply filters to all their computers? If so, would that violate the First Amendment free speech rights of the patrons?

Technology may be ahead of the law here, especially with the advent of Web 2.0 and user-generated content, such as blogs and other Web pages that employ widgets that could contain malicious code to install spyware through a drive-by download. While there are ways to guard against (although not entirely prevent) such ambushes by porn, not every computer user is sophisticated enough to install firewalls, anti-spyware software, filters, or to secure a Wi-Fi network.

## Chapter 17 Notes

[1] *Roth v. United States*, 354 U.S. 476 (1957). (Included in the Cases Section on the Issues in Internet Law site, www.IssuesinInternetLaw.com).

[2] *Miller v. California*, 413 U.S. 15 (1973). (Included in the Cases Section on the Issues in Internet Law site, www.IssuesinInternetLaw.com).

[3] *New York v. Ferber*, 458 U.S. 747 (1982).

[4] *Jacobellis v. Ohio*, 378 U.S. 184 (1964).

[5] *Miller*, 413 U.S. 15.

[6] *Hamling v. United States*, 418 U.S. 87, 105 (1974). The Court noted a community was not any "precise geographic area." In *Ashcroft v. ACLU*, 535 U.S. 564, 577 (2002), the Court said, "Web publishers currently lack the ability to limit access to their sites on a geographic basis, so use of "community standards" to define obscenity "would effectively force all speakers on the Web to abide by the 'most puritan' community's standards."

[7] Matt Richtel, "What's Obscene? Google Could Have an Answer," The New York Times, June 24, 2008.

[8] The Communications Decency Act, 47 U.S.C. § 223, *et seq.*

[9] *Reno v. ACLU*, 521 U.S. 844 (1997).

[10] *Nitke v. Gonzales*, 413 F. Supp. 2d 262 (S.D.N.Y. 2005), aff'd 547 U.S. 1015 (2006).

[11] *Ibid.*

[12] *Broadrick v. Oklahoma*, 413 U.S. 601 (1973).

[13] Several justices did address it in *dicta* in *Ashcroft v. ACLU*, 535 U.S. 564, 587 (2002) (O'Connor, J., concurring) ("[A]doption of a national standard is necessary in my view for any reasonable regulation of Internet obscenity."); *Id.* at 589, (Breyer, J., concurring) ("I believe that Congress intended the statutory word 'community' to refer to the Nation's adult community taken as a whole, not to geographically separate local areas."). The 9th Circuit subsequently held "[A] national community standard must be applied in regulating obscene speech on the Internet, including obscenity disseminated via email." *United States v. Kilbride*, 584 F.3d 1240, 1254 (9th Cir. 2009) . However, a Florida court expressly rejected the 9th Circuit holding. *Cf. United States v. Little*, Crim. No. 8:07-cr-00170-SCB (M.D. Fla. 2010).

[14] The Child Online Protection Act (COPA), 47 U.S.C. § 231.

[15] *ACLU v. Reno*, 217 F. Supp. 3d 162 (3d Cir. 2000).

[16] *ACLU v. Reno*, 31 F. Supp. 2d 473 (E.D. Pa. 1999), aff'd 217 F.3d 162 (3d Cir. 2000), vacated and remanded *sub nom. Ashcroft v. ACLU*, 535 U.S. 564 (2002), aff'd on remand 322 F. Supp. 3d 240 (2003), aff'd and remanded, 542 U.S. 656 (2004).

[17] "**Dicta**" are portions of a judicial opinion that merely represent a judge's editorializing and do not directly address the case at hand.

[18] *Ashcroft v. ACLU*, 535 U.S. 564 (2002), vacating *ACLU v. Reno*, 217 F.3d 162 (3d Cir. 2000).

[19] *ACLU v. Ashcroft*, 322 F. Supp. 3d 240 (2003).

[20] *Ashcroft v. ACLU*, 542 U.S. 656 (2004) aff'g *ACLU v. Ashcroft*, 322 F.3d 240 (3d Cir. 2003).

[21] *ACLU v. Gonzales*, Final Order (98-5591, E.D. Pa. Mar. 22, 2007) [originally *ACLU v. Reno*, then *ACLU v. Ashcroft*].

[22] *ACLU v. Mukasey*, Case No. 07-2539 (3d Cir. 2008).

[23] *See Coates v. City of Cincinnati*, 402 U.S. 611 (1971).

[24] The Children's Internet Protection Act (CIPA), 47 U.S.C. § 254(h) and (l), (Pub. L. No. 106-554) denies e-rate funds (that provide technology discounts to public libraries and schools) and Library Services and Technology Act funds to public libraries and schools that refuse to put filter software on their Internet-accessible computers.

[25] *United States v. Am. Library Ass'n*, 539 U.S. 194 (2003), reversing the district court's holding in *Am. Library Ass'n v. United States*, 201 F. Supp. 2d 401 (E.D. Pa. 2002) that use of filtering software does not violate First Amendment rights of library patrons and CIPA is constitutional. (Included in the Cases Section on the Issues in Internet Law site, www.IssuesinInternetLaw.com).

[26] *Kathleen R. v. City of Livermore*, 87 Cal. App. 4th 684 (2001).

[27] Teri Metros, "Phoenix Public Library Filtering Policy Changed Due to City Council," Mountain Plains Library Association site, *was available at* www.mpla.us/documents/reports/state/az/20041021.html (accessed July 1, 2009) but no longer available.

[28] Indictment, *United States v. Fletcher*, No. 06-329 (W.D. Pa. Sept. 26, 2006).

[29] One of her 29 subscribers was likely a police informant. The fee requirement would effectively keep people from stumbling onto her stories; only those who sought access and were willing to pay were able to read them. Requiring a credit card also screened minors from accessing the site.

[30] Gina Passarella, "'Text-Only' Web Obscenity Case Attracts National Attention; Motions to Dismiss Said Obscenity Laws Should Not Be Applied to Text where No Pictures Were Involved," The Legal Intelligencer, February 5, 2008.

[31] Charlie Deitch, "Dirty Words: Could Successful Prosecution of Written Stories — Even "Vile" Ones — Set a Dangerous Precedent?" Pittsburgh City Paper, May 10, 2007.

[32] *Ibid.*

[33] Paula Reed Ward, "Afraid of Public Trial, Author to Plead Guilty in Online Obscenity Case," The Pittsburgh Post-Gazette, May 17, 2008.

[34] *Ferber*, 458 U.S. 747.

[35] The Child Pornography Prevention Act, 18 U.S.C. § 2252.

[36] *Ashcroft v. Free Speech Coal.*, 535 U.S. 234 (2002). (Included in the Cases Section on the Issues in Internet Law site, www.IssuesinInternetLaw.com).

[37] *Ibid.* The Court wrote:

> The second flaw in the Government's position is that *Ferber* did not hold that child pornography is by definition without value. On the contrary, the Court recognized some

works in this category might have significant value, *see id.*, *at* 761, but relied on virtual images — the very images prohibited by the CPPA — as an alternative and permissible means of expression: "[I]f it were necessary for literary or artistic value, a person over the statutory age who perhaps looked younger could be utilized. Simulation outside of the prohibition of the statute could provide another alternative." *Id.*, *at* 763. *Ferber*, then, not only referred to the distinction between actual and virtual child pornography, it relied on it as a reason supporting its holding. *Ferber* provides no support for a statute that eliminates the distinction and makes the alternative mode criminal as well.

[38] In September 1995, Oklahoma City police raided the Planet Comics comic book store and confiscated multiple comic books. The two store owners were charged with "displaying material harmful to minors"; "trafficking in obscene materials"; and one count of child pornography for a comic book titled "*The Devil's Angel.*" Despite the fact all the comics were sold to adults, not children, the store owners were charged with four felonies and four misdemeanors — the combined charges carried a maximum penalty of 43 years in prison. "*The Devil's Angel*" comic book contained illustrations of a demon, not a child. The child pornography charge was eventually dropped, but the store owners, in a plea bargain, pleaded guilty to two felony counts of trafficking in obscenity for selling the other comic books in exchange for a three-year deferred prison sentence and a $1,500 fine each. Their landlord evicted them and their business failed. *See* Susan Alston, "Censorship in Comics: Is This the United States?" Animation World Magazine, Issue 2.4, July 1997; *see also* "Planet Comics Opts for Deferred Sentence," Comic Book Legal Defense Fund Web site, *available at* www.awn.com/mag/issue2.7/2.7pages/2.7news_biz.html (accessed Mar. 23, 2012).

[39] Debra Cassens Weiss, "Singer Charged with Child Porn for Edited Video Showing Kids Listening to a Graphic Song," ABA Journal, March 8, 2011.

[40] David Kravets, "'Obscene' U.S. Manga Collector Jailed 6 Months," Wired.com, February 12, 2010.

[41] In Canada, where the legal definition of "child pornography" includes "visual representation" of children, a Canadian was convicted of importing child pornography — in this case, Japanese comic books (*i.e.*, "manga"). The comic books contained no real children, only pen and ink drawings. Canadian law imposes a minimum 90-day imprisonment for possession of child pornography. Canadian provincial Judge David Tilley was quoted: "I don't think this is the kind of filth that should be available to the public," unintentionally summing up the inherent problem with obscenity cases — society's fundamental freedoms are at risk when one individual can arbitrarily decide what material "should be available to the public" by applying his personal standards of what he considers acceptable and what he deems "filth." *See* Chris Purdy, "First Case of Child-porn Cartoons," Edmonton Journal, October 20, 2005.

[42] The PROTECT Act of 2003 (Pub. L. No. 108-21, 117 Stat. 650).

[43] Keith B. Darrell, *Issues in Internet Law*, p. 163, Amber Book Company (1st edition, 2005).

[44] *United State v. Williams*, 444 F.3d 1286 (11th Cir. 2006).

[45] Section 2252A(a)(3)(B) of the PROTECT Act of 2003 (Pub. L. No. 108-21, 117 Stat. 650).

[46] *United States v. Williams*, 553 U.S. 285 (2008).

[47] 18 U.S.C. § 2251(d)(1)(A).

[48] *United States v. Sewell*, 513 F.3d 820 (8th Cir. 2008).

[49] The Child Protection and Obscenity Enforcement Act, 18 U.S.C. § 2257.

[50] The Providing Resources, Officers, and Technology to Eradicate Cyber Threats to Our Children Act of 2008 (PROTECT Our Children Act of 2008) (Pub. L. No. 110–401).

[51] The Keeping the Internet Devoid of Sexual Predators Act (KIDSPA), (Pub. L. No. 110-400).

[52] Stephanie Reitz, "Teacher Gets New Trial on Pop-up Porn," Associated Press wire service report, June 7, 2007.

[53] *United States v. One Book Called "Ulysses,"* 5 F. Supp. 182 (S.D.N.Y. 1933), aff'd, 72 F.2d 705 (2d Cir. 1934), rejecting the *Hicklin* Test, *infra* fn. 55, and finding the book not obscene, suggesting a standard based on the effect on the average reader of the dominant theme of the work as a whole.

[54] *Jenkins v. Georgia*, 418 U.S. 153 (1974).

[55] Applying the standard of the English case *Regina v. Hicklin*, L.R. 3 Q.B. 360, 371 (1868).

[56] *People v. Friede*, 133 Misc. 611, 233 N.Y.S. 565 (N.Y.C. Magistrate's Ct. 1929), dismissed at trial by the Court of Special Sessions.

[57] *Miller v. California*, 413 U.S. 15, *supra*.

[58] *United States v. Reidel*, 402 U.S. 351 (1971).

[59] *Stanley v. Georgia*, 394 U.S. 557 (1969), holding the First Amendment prohibits criminalizing the private possession of obscene material.

[60] *Osborne v. Ohio*, 495 U.S. 103 (1990), holding the First Amendment allows states to outlaw possession of child pornography. *Cf. Stanley v. Georgia*, 394 U.S. 557, *supra.*

[61] Nathan Frick, "Lawyers in Walker County Child Porn Case Hope to Redefine Law," Walker County Messenger, June 14, 2005.

[62] Jordan Robertson, "Framed for Child Porn—by a PC Virus," Associated Press wire service report, November 8, 2009.

[63] Elinor Mills, "State Worker Cleared on Child Porn Charges That Were Due to Malware," CNET News. com, June 17, 2008.

[65] Robertson, fn. 62, *supra.*

[65] *Ibid.*

[66] Robertson, fn. 62, *supra.*

[67] *Ibid.*

[68] Carolyn Thompson, "Unsecured Home Routers Lead to Legal Troubles," Associated Press wire service report, April 24, 2011.

[69] *Ibid.*

[70] *Ibid.*

[71] *Ibid.*

[72] *Ibid.*

[73] *Ibid.*

# CHAPTER

# 18

---

## HATE SPEECH & REPRESSION:

## THE DARK SIDE OF THE WEB

> This chapter is the second of two chapters that examine restraints on free speech. In this chapter, hate speech, online harassment, prior restraint, and totalitarian restraints in other countries are discussed.

*"We hate some persons because we do not know them; and we will not know them because we hate them." — Charles Caleb Colton*

## Online Harassment

ONLINE HARASSMENT OCCURS WHEN one uses the Internet to cause *substantial emotional distress* to a victim. It can be through e-mail, chat, instant messages, newsgroup or message board posts, or words or images posted on Web sites or social networks. Harassment is distinct from, but may be in conjunction with, cyberstalking or hate groups. Rude people, unpopular ideas, spam, or simple disagreements — annoying as they may be — do not rise to the level of harassment.

In one form of harassment, *e-mail spoofing*, the harasser sends inflammatory e-mail using the victim's e-mail address. It results in masses of angry recipients replying to the victim, who never actually sent it. Spoofing wastes the victim's time receiving and/or responding to thousands of e-mails, damages his reputation, and can lead to suspension of his e-mail account. Finding the perpetrator is difficult, since he is using another's identity. One vindictive spoofer requested return receipts for each message; when the victim returned from a three-week vacation, he was greeted by 55,000 messages in his inbox. [1]

A woman allegedly harassed her ex-boyfriend by creating a fake Facebook profile in his name and posting, as him, he had herpes, frequented prostitutes and was "high" all the time. A New Jersey court ruled she could be prosecuted for identity theft under a state statute criminalizing impersonation of someone "for the purpose of obtaining a benefit for himself or another or to injure or defraud another." [2]

Perhaps the greatest degree of online harassment occurs among teens. Adults, so concerned with protecting children from adult "online predators", often forget sometimes children need protection from other kids. Psychologists note teens act impulsively and without empathy for peers; for the Internet Generation that means adolescent bullying has migrated from the schoolyard into cyberspace.[3] The new technologies associated with the Internet have intensified normal adolescent cruelty, creating a super bully — the "*cyberbully.*" Cyberbullying inflicts a deeper level of cruelty by enabling kids to harass peers from afar, without having to view the results of their actions.

Cyberbullies use Web sites, chat rooms, message boards, social networks, e-mail, instant messaging, and text messages via mobile phones to make anonymous threats and harass victims. Today, instant messaging is the lifeline to the Internet Generation teenager, as the telephone was to the previous generation's teens.[4] Teachers report students show up in class upset over incidents from the previous night, where they might have been harassed online by — or in the virtual presence of — peers.[5] Such online harassment usually goes unseen by adults and is often publicly humiliating, as e-mail and blogs allow gossip, put-downs, and embarrassing photographs to be widely distributed among their peers.

"Private" videos and photographs often are forwarded by the recipient to friends, who also pass them around. One boy made a video of himself singing for a girl he liked — the object of his affection posted it on the Web, much to his chagrin. A Quebec teen found a video he made practicing his "*Star Wars*" light saber moves and left on a school TV studio shelf had been discovered by classmates, digitally tweaked, and circulated to millions via the Web, quickly gaining him notoriety as "the Star Wars Kid."[6] He sued his classmates for $351,000 in damages for subjecting him to global ridicule by uploading digitalized versions of "May the Farce Be with You." The case was settled three years later. A girl made a "dirty dancing" video that ended with her words "If you show this to anyone else …" followed her hand slicing across her neck; undeterred, the boy to whom she sent it apparently decided to share it with a few million of his closest friends online. Another high school girl sent her nude photograph from her mobile phone to her boyfriend, who promptly e-mailed it to all his friends, who then circulated it online. Perhaps the most infamous incident was the Horace Mann School eighth-grader in the Bronx, New York who, in an attempt to win over a classmate, e-mailed him a video of her masturbating while declaring her love for him.[7] It soon made its way onto a popular file-sharing network and there were reports her classmates would go online at school to view the video.

Students often post insulting or derogatory comments about classmates on their Web pages and blogs. Some rank males as "stud or dud" and females as "hottest or ugliest." Others discuss rumored sexual promiscuity of particular girls, listing their names and mobile phone numbers. Online harassment among teens can include using another teen's screen name to send inflammatory or embarrassing messages to the victim's friends or crushes.

Unlike typical adolescent bullying, cyberbullying does not necessarily occur during school hours or on school property.[8] Running home and locking the door does not provide relief, as cyberbullying can continue 24 hours a day, invading the victim's home, computer, and mobile phone.[9] Unlike schoolyard bullies, the cyberbully has an infinite audience, a degree of protection through anonymity, and the ease of striking repeatedly through only a mouse click.[10]

A Vermont eighth-grader found herself the subject of a Web site created by two class-mates entitled "Kill Kylie Incorporated", "devoted to show people how gay Kylie [last name omitted] is" ending with "Kylie must die."[11] Another classmate, posing as Kylie, instant mes-saged her female field hockey teammates asking them out on dates and attempting to por-tray her as a lesbian.[12] The girl had to receive professional help and change schools twice, even being home-schooled for a semester.[13] Another Vermont teen, a 13-year-old cy-berbullied for two years, committed suicide. His classmates had spread rumors online he was gay and a girl from school befriended him online to lead him on so she could get him to reveal embarrassing personal details she would then forward to her friends.[14]

Thirteen-year-old Megan Meier knew she was too young to be on MySpace (which requires users be at least 14) but the lonely, overweight girl with self-esteem issues welcomed the opportunity to make new friends online. Diagnosed with depression, she had recently changed schools, and ended a friendship with a girl down the street. On MySpace, she met "Josh", who soon became her "online boyfriend." Messaging Josh each day after school was the bright spot in her life—until the day Josh dumped her. Josh shared Megan's messages with others, who posted bulletins calling her "fat" and a "slut." The final message from her beloved Josh read: "You are a bad person and everybody hates you. Have a shitty rest of your life. The world would be a better place without you." Megan replied: "You are the kind of boy a girl would kill herself over."[15] She ran from the computer straight to her bedroom. Twenty minutes later, her mother discovered Megan's body hanging in her closet.[16]

Six weeks after Megan's death, her parents were shocked to learn "Josh" never existed. Megan's online boyfriend, whose acceptance had meant so much to her and whose harsh rejection had shattered her fragile self-esteem, had actually been a creation of her former neighborhood friend; the ex-friend's mother, Lori Drew; and Drew's 18-year-old employee.[17] Despite public outrage, Missouri prosecutors did not pursue charges because they were unable to find a state statute on which to build a criminal case.[18] However, federal prosecutors in Los Angeles (where MySpace is located) charged Drew with violation of the **Computer Fraud and Abuse Act** (CFAA), a federal statute applied to hackers who illegally access online accounts to steal information.[19] The novel approach alleged by creating a fake MySpace account with a fictitious name, she had violated MySpace's Terms of Use and therefore had no authority to access its server, which in turn was a violation of the Act.[20]

While the goal of achieving justice in the Meier case is laudable, this innovative application of the statute to criminalize use of a pseudonym or fictitious name on a social network is troublesome, as there are often legitimate reasons why individuals might desire to keep their identities private (*e.g.*, whistleblowers making public posts, individuals wishing to avoid spam, or those simply desiring to remain anonymous online). The danger of applying the statute in this novel manner is such an interpretation could criminalize what is routine online behavior (use of pseudonym on social networks and in newsgroups). It would effectively give a business contract the force of a law, meaning violation of a site's Terms of Use agreement could carry criminal penalties in addition to potential civil liability. The result could be a chilling effect on free speech if people believe they cannot use an alias to speak freely. Nonetheless, in 2011, the U.S. Department of Justice argued it should be able to use the **CFAA**—a law against computer hacking—to prosecute violations of Web sites' Terms of Service policies or similar contractual agreements with an employer or provider."[21] Criminalizing violations of Web site Terms of Service or employment contracts could result in unintended—and unenforceable —consequences: using a false name on Facebook, lying about your age on Match.com, or using Google if a minor (*i.e.*, "not of legal age to form a binding contract")— all violations of those sites' Terms of Service—would automatically become crimes.

In the <u>Drew</u> case, the jury found the defendant not guilty of three of the four **CFAA** violations and the judge overturned its misdemeanor conviction on the fourth. In response to Megan Meier's suicide, Missouri passed a statute making cyberbullying a felony. A 40-year-old woman became the first individual charged under it, after allegedly posting a 17-year-old's photograph, e-mail address and mobile phone number on Craigslist's "Casual Encounters" page, stating the teen was seeking a sexual encounter. [22] Allegedly, the post was in retaliation after arguments among the woman, the teen, and the teen's mother on MySpace. The victim received lewd phone calls, e-mails, text messages and pornographic photos sent to her mobile phone. The felony harassment statute provides for up to four years in state prison, or up to a year in the county jail, and a $5,000 fine. The statute makes cyberbullying a felony if the victim is 17 or younger and the suspect 21 or older. [23]

Even where states have online harassment statutes, the actions must meet the statutory definition. For example, under the New York statute, "harassment" requires "the intent to harass, annoy, threaten or alarm" the victim. [24] An 18-year-old boy was charged under the New York statute — which carries a penalty of up to one-year imprisonment, and/or a $1,000 fine — after repeatedly sending electronic love notes to one of his MySpace "friends", a 14-year-old girl. She was not so enamored, and her father complained to the state attorney. The court held: [25]

> The question in this case is whether an 18-year-old defendant who, perhaps inartfully, expresses his love for the 14-year-old complainant — in person and through the social networking Web site MySpace — can be charged with aggravated harassment when his love goes unrequited. We hold that unrequited teenage love is not a crime, and is not elevated to a crime by the disapproval, and even annoyance, of the object of the erstwhile lover's affections, or by that of her father.

The judge pointed out the girl could have deleted the defendant as a "MySpace friend" to prevent receipt of further love notes and "conduct that is merely 'annoying' to a particular listener does not constitute harassment under the [statute]." In an entertaining opinion that references William Shakespeare and Dion and the Belmonts, Judge Michael Gerstein showed both uncommon 'common sense' and literary skill: [26]

> The complaint does not allege that the messages allegedly sent by the defendant were intended to threaten, incite alarm, or harass. * * * There is no evidence in the complaint that defendant intended anything other than to declare his love for the complainant.
> The words "we need to be together," "I will never stop talking to you," and "I love you" are not threats, but appear to be merely the symptoms of unrequited love — the same hopeless affection that, among countless others, Dante felt for Beatrice, Don Quixote for Dulcinea, Cyrano for Roxane, Quasimodo for Esmeralda, Young Werner for Lotte, Jay Gatsby for Daisy Buchanan, and that Charlie Brown felt for the Little Red Haired Girl. While these romances do not usually end well for the pursuing party, the People have cited neither statute nor case law that might punish the communication of unrequited love, even if such is undesired. * * *
> Teenagers are especially vulnerable to the "madness most discreet" that makes sad hours seem long. Mere pages before he met Juliet, Romeo pined for Rosaline; Adrian Mole longed for Pandora Braithwaite in volume after volume of his "secret diaries"; and Dion implored of the skies up above, "Why must I be a teenager in love?" — vowing, just a few verses later, that "If you should say

goodbye, I'd still go on loving you." When teenagers fall in love, as song lyrics and studies show, they are more likely to exhibit almost manic behaviors, take risks, act compulsively, and sometimes pursue, with reckless abandon, the objects of their affection. While the actions of a love-struck teenager may well be foolish, reckless, or otherwise acts which might not be expected from a mature adult, they are not, without more, elevated to crimes.

The allegations in the complaint merely establish that defendant declared his feelings for the complainant. Conversely, the complaint is devoid of allegations that the defendant knew his declarations would be coldly received. The alleged messages * * * that form the basis of the charge of aggravated harassment were transmitted through MySpace, a social networking Web site that allows each user to choose which friends will be part of his or her network. When another MySpace user receives an invitation to be friends, he or she must choose whether or not to communicate with the requesting user. * * * At any time, a MySpace user may remove friends from his or her network, or may block unwanted communications. Thus, while it is reasonable to assume that, at some point, complainant added the defendant under his nom de plume "looking4therightoneinmylife" to her list of friends, the complaint contains no allegations that complainant attempted to quell defendant's love by blocking defendant's messages or by asking him to cease writing her. We therefore find that the complaint fails to show that the defendant intended to alarm, threaten or annoy the complainant. Both counts of Penal Law § 240.30 are accordingly dismissed.

Sometimes, online harassment may be unintentional. A college student snapped pictures at a San Diego rock concert and posted them on his online photo gallery.[27] One photo of an unknown girl awkwardly "moshing" in mid-step motivated gallery visitors to contribute retouched photographs of the mosher, now dubbed "Moshzilla", morphed into various poses and scenarios (such as where she confronts Godzilla in hand-to-hand combat across the Tokyo skyline). The photographs were reposted to multiple message boards and seen by millions. While the original poster stated he had no malicious intent when posting it, the teenage girl dubbed "Moshzilla" said, "Some of the pictures that were Photoshopped were amazing, some were pretty malicious and cruel. So even though some of those pictures I laughed at hysterically with my boyfriend, you can't help but realize that you are being humiliated across the country. In a nutshell, I feel shitty."[28]

Cyberbullying is not limited to the United States. Ten percent of Japanese high school students have been harassed online.[29] In 2007, an 18-year-old leapt to his death at his high school in Kobe, western Japan, after classmates who had repeatedly e-mailed him demands for money posted a nude photograph of him on an unofficial school site.[30] A British teen who posted a death threat on Facebook became the first individual jailed for cyberbullying on a social network.[31] The 18-year-old threatened to kill a girl her age, a classmate whom she had bullied for four years. She was sentenced to three months in a young offenders institution and banned from contacting the victim in person, online, or in any other manner, for five years.

In July 2009, Megan Gillan, a 15-year-old from Macclesfield, Cheshire in the U.K., killed herself after being cyberbullied on the social network Bebo. Gillan's suicide led Vincent

Nichols, the Archbishop of Westminster, head of the U.K. Roman Catholic Church, to criticize the importance of social networks in the lives of today's Internet Generation, saying they encourage teenagers to place too much emphasis on the number of friends they have, rather than on the quality of their relationships:[32]

> Among young people, often a key factor in their committing suicide is the trauma of transient relationships. They throw themselves into a friendship or network of friendships, then it collapses and they're desolate.

Archbishop Nichols made a more general assessment of how the Internet has changed society:[33]

> Excessive use or an almost exclusive use of text and e-mails means that as a society we're losing some of the ability to build interpersonal communication that's necessary for living together and building a community. We're losing social skills, the human interaction skills, how to read a person's mood, to read their body language, how to be patient until the moment is right to make or press a point.

Teens who spend excessive time on Facebook tend to be more narcissistic, leading to antisocial personality disorder, paranoia, anxiety and alcohol use, according to one study.[34] Internet usage appears to affect their attention span, as well. Many are distracted from studying by electronic media, focusing on their lessons for only a few minutes before breaking to text friends or check their Facebook page. The study also reported the average teen texts 2,000 messages per month and attributes texting's popularity among teenagers to the concept of connection over quality. That might explain the phenomenon of social network users amassing large numbers of online "friends" with whom they share little or no closeness, valuing, as Archbishop Nichols notes, quantity over quality in online relationships.

## Happy Slapping

An outgrowth of online harassment is the trend of "*happy slapping*", where perpetrators use mobile phones to record physical assaults and upload the recorded videos to other phones and Web sites. The happy slapping craze began in London, England but has spread thanks to the Internet.[35] The craze has been linked to the popularity among teens of TV shows like MTV's "*Jackass*" where people are filmed doing dangerous or outrageous stunts. With a mobile phone camera and an Internet connection, anyone can become a mini-movie producer with worldwide distribution. Many videos show up on message boards, P2P networks, and YouTube. Of course, if the perpetrators are caught, the photographs or videos often become the best evidence against them. Nonetheless, happy slappers have been undeterred. Instances of happy slapping range from walking up to a classmate and unexpectedly slapping his or her face to violent assault. Three 14-year-olds filmed their rape of an 11-year-old girl and within minutes sent the video to hundreds of the girl's classmates at school.[36] Two other happy slapping teens shot a 17-year-old girl in the leg with a pellet gun to create their video.[37] A 16-year-old girl was brutally punched and knocked unconscious by teen happy slappers and shortly thereafter a fellow student showed the video to the girl's 13-year-old brother.[38] And two teens were arrested after a happy slapping incident where they filmed themselves setting fire to a man sleeping in a bus station.[39]

A French law against happy slapping makes it illegal for anyone except professional journalists to film and broadcast violent events in France.[40] French happy slapping incidents include a student using his mobile phone to film a classmate attacking a teacher, and photos of a young girl gang-raped in Nice being e-mailed around her school. [41]

Happy slapping has found its way into the United States, as teens seek their 15 megabytes of fame by beating up other teens and posting the videos on YouTube. In Lakeland, Florida, six girls and two boys — ranging in age from 14-to-18 — lured a 16-year-old girl to the home of one of the attackers and assaulted her as she curled into a fetal position. The 30-minute attack included a brief period when the girl was pummeled into unconsciousness. The attackers took turns filming the assault, intending to post the video on YouTube to humiliate and embarrass the girl, allegedly in retaliation for comments she had made on MySpace. [42]

## Hate Speech on the Internet

*"The mind of a bigot is like the pupil of the eye. The more light you shine on it, the more it will contract." — Justice Oliver Wendell Holmes, Jr.*

*Hate speech* denigrates, or attempts to inflame public opinion against, certain groups. The First Amendment guarantee of free speech protects hate speech in the United States. Hate groups target victims based on skin color, race, religion, ethnic origin, age, gender, or sexual orientation. They circulate elaborate conspiracy theories to blame the targeted groups for an array of social, economic, or political ills. Frequently, hate groups use the Bible to justify their positions, as in the case of Rev. Fred Phelps of the Westboro Baptist Church of Topeka, Kansas, who created his godhatesfags.com site. [43]

Hate groups have found a home on the Web — from 2000 to 2007, they increased from about 2,700 to 7,000. [44] Many hate sites are small, even one-man, operations. Hate group activities were once limited by geographical boundaries, but the Internet enables the smallest fringe group to spread hate and freely recruit members. The Internet is an *inexpensive* and *effective* means for hate groups to communicate their message, as well as a powerful recruitment tool. They depend on recruitment for survival and their primary audience is often impressionable teens. Many hate sites are designed to attract and indoctrinate children by using racist and anti-Semitic music and games. One of the most popular forms of racist music is "white power" rock 'n' roll, a mix of loud and violent music with hostile lyrics calling for the murder of blacks or a racial holy war. More than 50,000 white power rock 'n' roll CDs are sold annually. [45] One hate site sells a computer game called "Ethnic Cleansing" where players dress as Klansmen or skinheads in their quest to kill "subhumans" (*i.e.*, blacks and Latinos) and their "evil masters", the Jews. [46] The game's Web site promotes it as: [47]

> [T]he most politically incorrect video game ever made. Run through the ghetto blasting away various blacks and spics in an attempt to gain entrance to the subway system, where the Jews have hidden to avoid the carnage. Then, if YOU'RE lucky … you can blow away Jews as they scream 'Oy Vey!' on your way to their command center.

Hate groups find the Internet a fertile hunting ground for disaffected teens, who spend large portions of each day in the "virtual world." Some disguise themselves as legitimate information sources, but contain racist propaganda or "revisionist history." Others bring in revenue to fund hate groups through merchandise sales and donations. Most ISPs regulate, but do not ban, hate speech. Yahoo! prohibits "hate clubs" in its Terms of Service. Private businesses like Yahoo! may limit speech because the First Amendment only applies to the government. AOL has clear guidelines regulating acceptable behavior on its servers, whereas Earthlink states it "supports the free flow of information and ideas over the Internet" and does not actively monitor the content of sites it hosts. [48]

Hate speech remains protected in the United States under the First Amendment, except when it crosses into threats and intimidation. Threats involving racial epithets or motivated by racial animus are unprotected if directed at specific individuals, but blanket statements of hatred toward an ethnic, racial, or religious group are protected.

Speech inciting *imminent violence* is not protected. [49] In 1999, a coalition of anti-abortion groups was fined more than $100 million for providing information on a site called the "Nuremberg Files" that threatened the lives of doctors and clinic workers performing abortions. The site posted photographs of abortion providers, their home addresses, license plate numbers, and the names of their spouses and children. On three occasions after a doctor listed on the site was murdered, a line was drawn through his name. Although the site did not directly call for attacks on the physicians, the jury found the information it provided amounted to a real threat of bodily harm. [50]

## Remedies to Hate Speech

The anonymity provided by the Internet makes it difficult to track and prosecute individuals and hate groups who use it to threaten victims. But there are remedies to online hate speech. As seen in the Nuremberg files case above, lawsuits with huge monetary judgments are a powerful remedy that can financially cripple an organized hate group. The *"Marketplace of Ideas"* view proposes the best antidote to hate speech is more speech, *i.e.*, rebuttal. [51] *Filters* — software that can be installed with a Web browser to block access to sites containing inappropriate or offensive material — are often proposed as another remedy. The Anti-Defamation League created "HateFilter", which blocks access to sites advocating hatred, bigotry, or violence towards Jews or other groups based on their religion, race, ethnicity, or sexual orientation.

## Hate Speech in Foreign Jurisdictions

America and the rest of the world are diametrically opposed on the issue of hate speech on the Internet. While hate speech is *constitutionally protected* in the United States, most countries prohibit and even criminalize it. U.S. law prohibits interfering with the *content* of electronic communications. Europe, in contrast, is moving toward establishing international standards to define and regulate hate speech. But America has repeatedly stated its constitutional objection to any international legal means to outlaw hate speech and has indicated it will not join Europe in such a venture.

Publishing material likely to incite racial hatred is illegal in the United Kingdom under the Public Order Act of 1986, but there is nothing that can be done under U.K. law if the offending company's servers are located in another country, such as America. [52] In Germany, promoting Nazi ideology is illegal, while in many European countries it is illegal to deny the reality of the Holocaust. Britain, Canada, Denmark, France, and Germany have all charged individuals with crimes involving online hate speech.

Under U.S. law, an individual will not be extradited for engaging in a constitutionally protected activity, even if that activity violates a criminal law elsewhere. Since hate speech is protected in the United States, it has become a safe haven for hate groups seeking to escape Europe's strict hate speech laws. By hosting their hate sites from a U.S.–based server, European hate groups can avail themselves of the United State's broader protections, while their sites still remain accessible anywhere in the world, even in countries where the subject matter may be illegal.

Again, we see the problem of enforcing conflicting laws on a medium that transcends geographical boundaries. In 2001, there were reports Germany was contemplating denial of service attacks against U.S. servers hosting neo-Nazi sites.[53] While that would preclude German citizens from viewing the objectionable material, it would also prevent anyone, anywhere from seeing it, including U.S. citizens who have a constitutional right to view it. It would also shut down all other, non-hate sites hosted on the server. Had such a plan been implemented, it would not only mean a foreign government had launched an attack against physical assets (the servers) in the United States, but would have been able to shut down U.S. sites based solely on content.

A French court, in 2000, held Yahoo! violated French anti-hate laws by allowing online auctions of a thousand Nazi-related items.[54] While Yahoo! removed the items from its French subsidiary yahoo.fr, it did not remove them from its parent site yahoo.com, also accessible within France (and worldwide, though hosted in California). The lawsuit was brought by two anti-hate groups in Paris.[55] Yahoo! faced a daily $13,000 fine unless it blocked access within France to all Nazi objects listed on Yahoo.com (by 2006, the fine had reached $15 million). Rather than appeal the ruling in France, Yahoo! filed a complaint in the U.S. District Court for the Northern District of California, seeking a declaratory judgment the French court's orders were unenforceable under U.S. laws and a ruling the French judgment could not be collected in the United States. The district court ruled Web sites operated by Yahoo! were not subject to French laws, as the French court order posed a direct threat to Yahoo!'s First Amendment rights.[56] It stated:[57]

> What is at issue here is whether it is consistent with the Constitution and laws of the United States for another nation to regulate speech by a United States resident within the United States on the basis that such speech can be accessed by Internet users in that nation * * * [A]lthough France has the sovereign right to regulate what speech is permissible in France, this court may not enforce a foreign order that violates the protections of the United States Constitution.

However, the Ninth Circuit reversed, ruling U.S. courts did not have blanket power to block foreign countries from enforcing their laws against U.S. sites, adding obeying other nations' laws is the price of doing international business.[58] It ruled U.S. courts lack jurisdiction to override a foreign court's orders without that foreign government first bringing the dispute into the U.S. legal system. But, the court added, should the French government turn to the U.S. courts to enforce its order, then Yahoo! would be free to raise its First Amendment defense: "If Yahoo! violates the speech laws of another nation, it must wait for the foreign litigants to come to the United States to enforce the judgment before its First Amendment claim may be heard by a U.S. court."[59] Of course, a French judgment could still be enforced against whatever assets, if any, Yahoo! might have in France. This decision could expose U.S.–based sites to other nations' more restrictive laws. In 2006, a 6–to–5 majority of the Ninth Circuit dismissed the case, leaving unresolved the primary issue of whether U.S.–based sites are liable for damages in foreign courts for displaying content unlawful overseas but constitutionally protected in the United States. [60]

These cases illustrate the *fundamental conflict of values* between America, which views the alternative as ceding to foreign governments the authority to censor online speech contrary to the constitutional free speech guarantees granted in the First Amendment to the U.S. Constitution, and the other nations of the world, which feel the United States' position essentially forces American speech values on them.

## Repression of Online Speech

*"Since when have we Americans been expected to bow submissively to authority and speak with awe and reverence to those who represent us? " — Justice William O. Douglas*

In the 16th century, the English government controlled the printing presses through a system of patent grants, monopolies, and licensing. Licensing was a form of censorship or prior restraint. A ***prior restraint*** is a law requiring an individual to obtain government permission before speaking or conveying information. The practice of licensing continued into the American colonies, but ended in the 1720s. Prior restraint by the government in America was ultimately prohibited by the First Amendment (adopted in 1791). In *Near v. Minnesota*, the U.S. Supreme Court stated "the chief purpose" of the First Amendment was to prevent prior restraints and post-publication punishment was the preferred remedy for defamation. [61] In *Near*, a state statute allowed suppression of newspapers or periodicals as a public nuisance. While finding the statute unconstitutional, the court did note some limitations to the doctrine against prior restraint: [62]

> [T]he protection even as to previous restraint is not absolutely unlimited. But the limitation has been recognized only in exceptional cases. 'When a nation is at war many things that might be said in time of peace are such a hindrance to its effort that their utterance will not be endured so long as men fight and that no Court could regard them as protected by any constitutional right.' * * * No one would question but that a government might prevent actual obstruction to its recruiting service or the publication of the sailing dates of transports or the number and location of troops.

The concept of "permissible prior restraint in matters of national security", first hinted at in *Near*, reared its head 40 years later in what has become known as "The Pentagon Papers Case." [63] The Nixon White House turned to the U.S. Supreme Court to prevent *The New York Times* and *The Washington Post* from publishing a stolen, classified document titled "The History of U.S. Decision-Making on Viet Nam Policy" on grounds publication would endanger "national security." While each justice offered his own view on prior restraint, the court held the government had failed to meet the "heavy burden" required to sustain a prior restraint.

Perhaps the most straight-forward case of prior restraint versus national security was *United States v. Progressive, Inc.*, where the federal government sued to enjoin *The Progressive*, a left-wing magazine, from publishing its cover story titled "The H-Bomb Secret: How We Got It and Why We're Telling It." [64] The government argued a "how-to" manual for anyone wanting to build a hydrogen bomb was a "clear and present danger" and should be prevented from publication.[65] However, the issue was rendered moot when the article was published outside the United States.[66]

In 2008, WikiLeaks.org—a site that allowed whistleblowers to post government and corporate documents anonymously—posted internal documents accusing a Swiss bank's Cayman Islands branch of money laundering and tax evasion. The bank alleged a disgruntled fired executive had stolen the documents and illegally posted them. The hundreds of document pages included bank account numbers and Social Security numbers. The bank sued WikiLeaks and its California-based hosting company, alleging the site had posted stolen and confidential financial data. A federal judge issued a preliminary injunction shutting down the U.S. site. WikiLeaks argued shutting down the entire site—as opposed to a narrowly crafted order to remove the bank documents—was an unconstitutional prior restraint. Lawyers for several news organizations analogized the injunction to shutting down a newspaper because of controversy over one article.[67] The injunction only affected the main U.S. site; mirrored sites hosted in other countries remained accessible. But the breadth of the injunction was astounding. The judge had ordered the hosting company:[68]

1. Remove all traces of WikiLeaks from its servers

2. Prevent the domain name from resolving to WikiLeaks.org or "any other Web site or server other than a blank park page," *i.e.*, not point the domain to another DNS server

3. Lock the domain name to prevent its transfer to a different domain registrar to preclude changes to the site—effectively preventing transfer of the domain ownership, thereby restricting sale of the property

After heavy criticism for having issued the prior restraint, the judge dissolved the injunction against the hosting company, admitting: "It is clear that in all but the most exceptional circumstances, an injunction restricting speech pending final resolution of the constitutional concerns is impermissible."[69] The bank voluntarily dismissed its case, reserving the right to file or pursue it in an alternate jurisdiction.[70]

RateMyCop.com's owner obtained the names and badge numbers of police officers across the country and asked visitors to rate their experiences with individual officers. (No other personal information about the officers was listed, nor were any undercover officers named). A San Francisco TV news program reported police officers wanted the site shut down, claiming disclosure of their names and badge numbers—which are public information—somehow put them at risk. The hosting company shut down the site, claiming it had exceeded its three terabyte bandwidth limit, but the site owner disputed that, alleging he was censored after police complained.[71] The California Police Chiefs Association announced it would seek legislation to shut down the site, although such legislation would be a prior restraint and the **CDA § 230** protects the site from liability for third-party posts.[72]

An early Internet case illustrates the difficulty of balancing the First Amendment protection from prior restraint against an individual's right to privacy (see Chapter 12).[73] William Sheehan sued several credit reporting agencies for violating the **Fair Debt Collections Practices Act**[74] and the **Fair Credit Reporting Act**[75] and also created a gripe site (see Chapter 19). His site contained disparaging comments about one agency and contact information for its employees and attorneys. The information included home phone numbers and addresses, street maps, fax numbers, and SSNs. Sheehan claimed he obtained the information from public sources. The agency sought and received a temporary restraining order against the site. The credit agency agents and employees had legitimate concerns about disclosure of their private information. As made clear by the Amy Boyer case (see Chapter 12), threats of *cyberstalking* and *identity theft* posed by disclosure of such private information are sufficiently foreseeable.[76] But did they rise to the level of outweighing the constitutional protection against prior restraint? Whose right should prevail in such a conflict — Sheehan's right of free speech without prior restraint or the agency employees' right to privacy? Recall from Chapter 12, one of the four invasion of privacy torts is **public disclosure of private facts**. The employees might have a valid civil claim against Sheehan; however, a defense to that tort is the facts are not "private" and Sheehan claimed he obtained the information from public sources. Should a jury determine that to be the case, then Sheehan would have an adequate defense to an invasion of privacy claim.

Courts will issue a prior restraint on speech if it contains incitement to imminent unlawful action.[77] In the Sheehan case, the court initially denied the agency's motion to issue a *temporary restraining order* (TRO) against the allegedly defamatory speech, but later granted it against the disclosure of the private information, fearing it could be an incitement to imminent unlawful action (*i.e.*, the foreseeability of cyberstalking). After a TRO is granted, a hearing date is set for the court to decide whether to vacate (*i.e.*, eliminate) the TRO or issue a preliminary injunction based on it. Note, however, until the hearing, the TRO effectively was a prior restraint. Obtaining a *preliminary injunction* requires a showing of both a strong chance of success on the merits and the possibility of irreparable harm. Here, the court concluded since the information had been "available on plaintiff's Web site since early 1997, and there is no evidence that anyone has ever been harassed, approached, or contacted by a person who viewed the site" the posting could not be deemed an incitement to imminent unlawful action and it dissolved the TRO.[78] The court summed up:[79]

> Restraining orders and injunctions 'are classic examples of prior restraints'
> and as such are presumed to be unconstitutional * * * The First Amendment
> does not tolerate even temporary suppression of speech that might ultimately
> be found to be protected * * * In the absence of incitement to imminent
> unlawful action, the motion for a preliminary injunction must be denied.

A husband in a Vermont divorce case posted a "thinly-disguised, fictionalized account" of his marriage on his blog, along with excerpts from his wife's diary he had found after she moved out of the house.[80] The court ordered him to remove "any and all Internet postings" about his wife and their marriage pending a hearing. He claimed the judge's order was a prior restraint. The judge agreed and vacated his previous order, holding it had violated the husband's First Amendment rights.[81] As in most prior restraint cases, the constitutionally appropriate course is not to enjoin speech but to allow it and then hold the speaker legally accountable through damages, not an injunction. For example, the wife might have chosen to file a defamation claim (assuming the account was untrue) or an invasion of privacy (public disclosure of private facts) or copyright infringement claim (for publishing the diary).

Lyglenson Lemorin was one of seven men charged with conspiracy to commit terrorist acts with Al Queda and the only one acquitted. Because he was to be a witness in the retrial of the other defendants, a federal judge issued a gag order prohibiting both him and his attorney from speaking publicly about the case. The judge extended the order to include the attorney's "agents", which a criminal defense lawyer and law blogger — who represented the attorney in his fight against the gag order — interpreted as meaning he was now subject to the gag order, as well. As a result, he was unable to speak or blog about his client, effectively making the gag order a prior restraint.[82]

*"Fear of serious injury cannot alone justify suppression of free speech and assembly. Men feared witches and burned women. It is the function of speech to free men from the bondage of irrational fear. " — Justice Louis Brandeis*

On August 11, 2011, seeking to thwart a planned protest over a shooting of a man by transit police, San Francisco Bay Area Rapid Transit (BART) officials cut underground cell phone service for a several hours at multiple stations. Commuters stuck underground had no notice their phone service would be blocked. BART's intent was to prevent communication among those attempting to coordinate the protest, but its effect was to prevent all passengers in the affected areas from speaking to the outside world — no phone calls to friends, family, or the office. Commuters were unable to make emergency calls, or conduct business or personal affairs. Critics asked if a government agency in the business of providing transportation (BART) should engage in censorship. BART claimed its actions were legal because it owned the property and infrastructure. [83] But the government owns many properties, yet ownership does not convey the right to abridge the First Amendment. In this instance, a government agency effectively imposed a prior restraint on speech. The First Amendment guarantees both freedom of speech and freedom of assembly. Denying protestors the ability to discuss and plan a protest strikes at the heart of the First Amendment. Absent a threat of "imminent lawless action "government cannot prohibit speech. [84] Here, there was nothing to indicate the protest would not be peaceful.

A similar issue arose in England at about the same time, as the British government wrestled with how to deal with the London Riots (several nights of rioting in London's Tottenham neighborhood following protests over police shooting and killing a local man in August 2011). Police claimed criminals were using Twitter and smart phone instant messages to coordinate looting sprees during the rioting and the government considered limiting use of social networks and mobile phone carriers. Critics compared the government's consideration of that prospect to Egyptian president Hosni Mubarak's decision to shut down Internet access in Egypt to quell the protests that led to his resignation. Twitter played a key role in Mubarak's downfall: the number of tweets from Egypt increased from 2,300 to 230,000 in the week before Mubarak pulled the plug on the Internet. [85]

The First Amendment also protects *commercial speech* from government repression. A California law requiring online advertising companies be licensed real estate brokers to list or advertise homes for sale online was challenged on First Amendment grounds. The law was written broadly to include anyone acting as an agent or advertising or listing homes for a fee, but it specifically exempted newspapers. [86] In *ForSaleByOwner.com v. Zinneman*, the federal district court sided with a Web site, holding by requiring sites to obtain a license but specifically exempting newspapers publishing the same information, the statute was "wholly arbitrary" and violated the First Amendment guarantees of free speech and freedom of the press. [87] The court stated: "[T]here appears to be no justification whatsoever for any distinction between [either medium, *i.e.*, newspapers and Web sites]."

Canadian courts can issue gag orders on the press attending public trials. [88] The rationale for this ban on publication of trial details is to ensure a fair trial for the defendant since, unlike the United States, Canada does not sequester jurors. The gag order is meant to protect jurors from learning information the court does not want them to see or hear. But this has led to the odd situation where a reporter covering a trial is prohibited from revealing information from a government proceeding open to the public. With the advent of blogs, Canadian judges are now contending with nonjournalist bloggers who attend public trials and then blog the details while their press counterparts must remain silent or face judicial sanctions. In a one case, an American blogged[89] detailed reports of Canada's Adscam hearings, provided by a confidential source at the hearings.[90] The blogger reported a tenfold increase in news-hungry Canadian visitors to his blog. Ironically, when interviewing the blogger, the Canadian press was barred by the gag order from publishing the blog's URL. The chilling effect on speech was evident by one Canadian blogger's stated fear of linking to the U.S. blogger's site, after suggestions Canadian Web publishers linking to the American blog might be charged with contempt of court.

In another case of a democratic government repressing speech, ironically South Korea tried to ban access to a North Korean university site.[91] South Korea feared the Korean-language site ournation-school.com would spread Communist ideology among its Internet-obssessed youth. One South Korean official stated, "We need to block access to resources of one-sided information or knowledge which ordinary people can obtain easily," a comment more expected from a Communist regime like North Korea than a democracy.[92] Certainly, it is hardly an acceptance of the "marketplace of ideas" theory. In 2007, South Korea passed a law requiring citizens disclose their name and ID number before they opine online.[93]

Indeed, if the approach to online speech by democratic Western nations contrasts so sharply with that of the United States, how does the approach of totalitarian or authoritarian regimes compare?

## Web Speech Under Totalitarianism

*"Censorship reflects a society's lack of confidence in itself. It is the landmark of an authoritarian regime." — Justice Potter Stewart, Ginsberg v. United States*

The borderless nature of the Internet makes it difficult for governments to control the flow of information, yet totalitarian regimes, and even democratic governments, devote huge resources to controlling what information reaches people around the world. More than 20 countries use blocking and filtering systems for Internet content.[94] Internet filtering technology has grown more sophisticated, allowing governments to block particular words or phrases, without users ever knowing their online searches have been censored.

Communist China has struggled to control its citizens' Internet use, using both filtering software and human censors. Since many Chinese rely on cybercafés for Internet access, the government forces them to keep records of users and the pages they visit, and has installed cameras and monitoring software in cafés and bars to prevent customers from viewing "forbidden sites." The software automatically messages a "remote supervisory center" if it detects a banned sites — those deemed pornographic, or "superstitious" (such as those discussing the outlawed Falun Gong spiritual group), or that criticize the government or Communist Party. Dozens have been imprisoned for posting or downloading materials from banned sites. All computer users in cybercafés or bars must enter their ID card numbers (or passport number, if foreigners) to access the Internet.[95] China has also installed filters on public Internet terminals that block certain keyword searches and entire sites. The Chinese government employs more than 40,000 censors at dozens of regional centers.[96] It has a special task force of undercover online "commentators" whose job is to defend government positions when criticized on message boards, in an attempt to sway public opinion on controversial issues. [97] It also pays hundreds of thousands of students to flood the Web with government messages and drown out dissidents. [98]

Bloggers have become a major concern to the Chinese government. The Internet Society of China, an arm of Ministry of Information Industry, proposed bloggers be required to use their real names when they register blogs, though they would still be allowed to write under a pseudonym. [99] The result, of course, would be the bloggers would be anonymous to everyone except the government. The plan was abandoned as technologically impractical to administer and instead the government promoted a voluntary registration system by having bloggers sign a "self-discipline pledge." [100] Second only to the United States in the number of Internet users, China has 137 million citizens online, of whom 30 million are registered bloggers, while 100 million are regular blog readers. [101]

Despite employing thousands of its own censors, the Chinese government relies on private ISPs, including companies like Yahoo! China, Microsoft, and MySpace, to censor blogs. [102] It requires ISPs to police online content and weed out criticism of the government, calling on them to sign a "self-discipline pact" to stop the spread of "information that could harm national security." The pact describes the "basic principles of self-discipline for Internet" use as "patriotism, observance of law, fairness, and trustworthiness." ISPs must promise not to spread information "threatening national security, social stability, or containing superstitious or erotic content" and ensure they do not link to sites with "inappropriate material." The pact also requires Internet cafés to direct Web users to "healthy online information" and urges respect for intellectual property rights. [103] All these efforts are part of Communist China's struggle to gain and maintain control over Internet use by its online citizens.

Even American Web sites have felt Communist China's repressive grip. Google was allowed to launch a search engine in China only after agreeing to omit results from government-banned sites, including the Voice of America site. [104] Although omitted if the search requests were made through computers connecting to the Internet in China, the same queries submitted through a U.S. connection were able to retrieve the blocked Web site links. Google, in 2010, said it would stop censoring its search results in China.

Like China, Vietnam sees the Internet as a threat to the government, recognizing its capability as a powerful tool for recruitment and spreading dissent. Few Vietnamese can afford Internet connections, let alone their own computers, so Internet cafés have become a popular refuge for the country's online users, estimated at 20 percent of the nation's 83 million citizens. [105] Under Vietnamese law, Internet cafés are must inform on customers and cafés that do not comply are closed down. This has created a climate of fear and chilled free speech. The Vietnamese government claims it filters the Internet to protect citizens from socially objectionable topics like pornography, but according to one study, only material related to politics, religion, and human rights was being filtered. [106]

Arab nations have limited Web speech, too. Syria sentenced a man who downloaded material from a banned émigré site and e-mailed it to others to two-and-a-half years in prison for the crime of "publishing false news that saps the morale of the nation." Four other Syrians faced similar charges. Amnesty International called the verdict a "political decision that quells the right of expression in Syria." [107] Another Syrian was imprisoned for posting photographs of a Kurdish demonstration in Damascus. [108] Since then, dozens of bloggers and journalists have been imprisoned.[109] Syrian state-run media is closely controlled and the government bans sites deemed offensive or anti-Syrian.

In Bahrain, every Web site is required to register with the government, providing the names, addresses, and telephone numbers of its operators, and post a government-issued ID number on the site.[110] While not a prior restraint on what the site owner may wish to publish, it does have a chilling effect on speech by serving as a constant reminder Big Brother is watching over their shoulder.

In Morocco, where the press code for journalists makes it a crime to show disrespect to the king, a blogger was arrested, tried without a defense lawyer and with no opportunity to speak in his own defense, fined, and sentenced to two years in prison. He had written on a news site Morocco had been destroyed by the practice of giving charity or gifts such as taxi licenses to a lucky few, which encouraged people to become beggars. Those comments were interpreted as showing disrespect for the monarchy.[111]

An Iranian court sentenced an influential Iranian-Canadian blogger and government critic to 19½ years in prison for "conspiring with hostile governments, spreading propaganda against the Islamic system, spreading propaganda in favor of counter-revolutionary groups, blasphemy, and creating and managing obscene Web sites."[112]

Yet, no matter how often totalitarian regimes attempt to censor the Internet or punish online dissent, a significant number of their citizens continue to seek free expression.

## Chapter 18 Notes

[1] Noah Shachtman, "Return to Sender — 55,000 Times," Wired News, August 23, 2002, *available at* www.wired.com/news/culture/0,1284,54708,00.html (accessed Mar. 23, 2012).

[2] David Porter, "Case of Fake Facebook Profile Can Proceed, Judge Rules," Law.com, November 3, 2011.

[3] Amy Harmon, "Internet Gives Teenage Bullies Weapons to Wound from Afar," The New York Times, August 26, 2004.

[4] Amanda Lenhart, Mary Madden, and Paul Hitlin, "Teens and Technology Youth are Leading the Transition to a Fully Wired and Mobile Nation," Pew Internet & American Life Project, July 27, 2005. Pew observed "instant messaging has become the digital communication backbone of teens' daily lives" and "roughly 32% of all teens — use IM every single day."

[5] *Ibid.*

[6] Tu Thanh Ha, "'Star Wars Kid' Cuts a Deal with His Tormentors," (Quebec) Globe and Mail, July 4, 2006.

[7] The resulting scandal from the video — which included the girl simulating fellatio on a Swiffer mop — became known as "Swiffergate." *See* Gabriel Sherman, "After a Facebook Scandal, Horace Mann is Forced to Ask What Values It Should Teach," New York Magazine, March 30, 2008.

[8] Andrew Childers, "Bullying Moves to the Internet," Hometownannapolis.com, September 5, 2006.

[9] "1 of 3 Teens are Victims of Cyber Bullying," Spero News, August 17, 2006.

[10] Anne Marie Chaker, "Schools Act to Short-Circuit Spread of 'Cyberbullying,'" The Wall Street Journal, p. D1, January 24, 2007.

[11] Suzanne Struglinski, "Schoolyard Bullying Has Gone High-Tech," Deseret News (Salt Lake City, UT), August 21, 2006.

[12] *See* Anne Broache, "Anticrime Group Calls for Laws to Curb 'Cyber Bullying,'" CNET News.com, August 21, 2006, and Nicholas Zifcak, "Bullying Rampant in Cyberspace," Epoch Times, August 21, 2006.

[13] Struglinski, fn. 11, *supra*.

[14] John Flowers, "Cyber Bullying Hits Community," Addison County Independent, October 19, 2006.

[15] Renay San Miguel, "MySpace Suicide Case Exposes Legal Gap," TechNewsWorld, November 20, 2008.

[16] Steve Pokin, "'MySpace' Hoax Ends with Suicide of Dardenne Prairie Teen," Suburban Journals of Greater St. Louis, November 11, 2007.

[17] *Ibid.*

[18] *United States v. Drew*, Crim. No. CR 08-0582-GW (C.D. Cal. Aug. 28, 2009); *see also* Scott Glover and P.J. Huffstutter, "L.A. Grand Jury Issues Subpoenas in Web Suicide Case," The Los Angeles Times, January 9, 2008.

[19] The Computer Fraud and Abuse Act (CFAA), 18 U.S.C. § 1030. A federal grand jury convicted Lori Drew in November 2008 on three counts of accessing protected computers without authorization to obtain information to inflict emotional distress. Each count carried a penalty of up to five years in prison. Ashley Grills, the then 18-year-old employee, admitted on ABC-TV's *"Good Morning America"* show she had sent the final message to Megan posing as Josh, telling Megan the world would be better off without her. Federal prosecutors granted Grills immunity in exchange for her testimony against Drew. *See* Jonann Brady, "Exclusive: Teen Talks about Her Role in Web Hoax That Led to Suicide," ABCNews.com, April 1, 2008. In July 2009, a federal district court, ruling the application of the Computer Fraud and Abuse Act against Drew was selective and the statute was unconstitutionally vague, granted a defense motion to throw out the conviction. *See* Gina Keating, "MySpace Suicide Conviction Tentatively Dismissed," Reuters, July 2, 2009.

[20] Most states have anti-hacking statutes based on the federal Computer Fraud and Abuse Act. State prosecutors similarly made innovative use of the Ohio statute to convict a defendant, who used his work computer to upload nude photos of himself to an adult site and view other photos on porn sites, of felony hacking under the statute. The jury found he had exceeded his authorization to use the work computer by accessing the porn sites. The appellate court agreed his conduct was "beyond the scope of the express or implied consent", but critics argue the statute was misused to criminalize a violation of an internal policy that should have been handled by the human resources department. *See* *State v. Wolf*, Case No. 08 CA 16 (Ohio 5th App. Dist. 2009).

[21] Declan McCullagh, "DOJ: Lying on Match.com Needs to Be a Crime," CNET News.com, November 14, 2011.

[22] Betsey Taylor, "Mo. Woman Charged with Cyberbullying on Craigslist," Associated Press wire service report, August 18, 2009.

[23] *Ibid.*

[24] NY CLS Penal § 240.30.

[25] *People v. Rodriguez*, Case No. 2007KN085405, 2008 NY Slip Op. 28123 (N.Y. City Crim. Ct. Kings Cnty. 2008).

[26] *Ibid.*

[27] Leslie Katz, "When 'Digital Bullying' Goes Too Far," CNET News.com, June 22, 2005.

[28] *Available at* www.moshzilla.com (accessed Mar. 23, 2012).

[29] According to a Hyogo Prefectural Board of Education survey. *See* Yoko Kubota, "Cyber Bullying Common in Japan School Web Sites: Study," Reuters wire service report, April 16, 2008.

[30] *Ibid.*

[31] Individuals have previously been jailed for harassment and stalking on social networks but she is believed to be the first jailed for cyberbullying. *See* Luke Salkeld, "Facebook Bully Jailed: Death Threat Girl, 18, is First Person Put Behind Bars for Vicious Internet Campaign," (U.K.) Daily Mail, August 21, 2009.

[32] Jonathan Wynne-Jones, "Facebook and MySpace Can Lead Children to Commit Suicide, Warns Archbishop Nichols," Daily Telegraph (U.K.), August 1, 2009.

[33] *Ibid.*

[34] According to a study by psychologist Larry Rosen on how Facebook affects children. *See* Daniela Hernandez, "Too Much Facebook Time May Be Unhealthy for Kids," The Los Angeles Times, August 6, 2011.

[35] Katz, fn. 27, *supra*.

[36] Tosin Sulaiman, "Girl's Rape 'Filmed by Teenagers on Mobile,'" The London Times, June 18, 2005.

[37] *Ibid.*

[38] *Ibid.*

[39] *Ibid.*

[40] "New French Law Aimed at 'Happy Slapping,'" Associated Press wire service report, March 07, 2007.

[41] *Ibid.*

[42] "Suspects in Video Beating Could Get Life in Prison," CNN.com, April 11, 2008.

[43] "Fred Phelps and the Westboro Baptist Church," Anti-Defamation League site, *available at* www.adl.org/special_reports/wbc/default.asp (accessed Mar. 23, 2012).

[44] "Hate Web Sites Continue to Flourish," The Register, May 10, 2004, and Andy Levy-Ajzenkopf, "Online Hate Sites Grow Again, Wiesenthal Report Says," JUF News, August 24, 2007.

[45] Ros Davidson, "Web of Hate," Salon, October 16, 1998.

[46] "Racist Groups Using Computer Gaming to Promote Violence against Blacks, Latinos, and Jews," Anti-Defamation League, *available at* www.adl.org/videogames/default.asp (accessed Mar. 23, 2012).

[47] *Available at* www.resistance.com/ethniccleansing/catalog.htm (accessed Mar. 23, 2012).

[48] Christopher Wolff, "Racists, Bigots and the Law on the Internet," *available at* www.adl.org/internet/internet_law4.asp (accessed Mar. 23, 2012).

[49] *Brandenburg v. Ohio*, 395 U.S. 444 (1969). (Included in the Cases Section on the Issues in Internet Law site, www.IssuesinInternetLaw.com).

[50] *Planned Parenthood of the Columbia/Willamette, Inc. v. Am. Coal. of Life Activists*, 41 F. Supp. 2d 1130 (D. Or. 1999), aff'd *Planned Parenthood v. Am. Coal. of Life Activists*, reh'g *en banc*, 290 F.3d 1058 (9th Cir. 2002).

[51] *Abrams v. United States*, 250 U.S. 616 (1919).

[52] The Public Order Act 1986 (c 64), Parts 3 and 3A.

[53] Joris Evers, "Germany Plots Cyberattacks on Neo-Nazi Sites," IDG, April 10, 2001, *available at* http://edition.cnn.com/2001/TECH/internet/04/10/nazi.spam.idg/index.html (accessed Mar. 23, 2012).

[54] *La Ligue Contre le Racisme et L'Antisemitisme (LICRA) and L'Union des Etudiants Juifs de France (UEJF) v. Yahoo! Inc. and Yahoo! France*, Case No. 00/05308, (Tribunal de Grande Instance de Paris 2000).

[55] France's Union of Jewish Students and the International Anti-Racism and Anti-Semitism League.

[56] *Yahoo! Inc. v La Ligue Contre Le Racisme et L'antisemitisme*, 169 F. Supp. 2d 1181 (N.D. Cal. 2001).

[57] *Ibid.*

[58] *Yahoo! Inc. v. La Ligue Contre Le Racisme et L'Antisemitisme*, 04 C.D.O.S. 7742 (2004).

[59] *Ibid.*

[60] David Kravets, "Court Dismisses Yahoo Free Speech Suit," Associated Press wire service report, January 12, 2006.

[61] *Near v. Minnesota*, 283 U.S. 697 (1931), overturning an injunction obtained by Minnesota state officials preventing Jay Near from publishing a scandal sheet that routinely attacked state officials, under a state statute providing anyone who published "(a) an obscene, lewd and lascivious newspaper, magazine, or other periodical, or (b) a malicious, scandalous, and defamatory newspaper, magazine, or other periodical, is guilty of a nuisance, and all persons guilty of such nuisance may be enjoined."

[62] *Ibid.*

[63] *New York Times Co. v. United States*, 403 U.S. 713 (1971).

[64] *United States v. Progressive, Inc.*, 467 F. Supp. 990 (W.D. Wis. 1979) granting the government a temporary injunction against *The Progressive*. (Included in the Cases Section on the Issues in Internet Law site, www.IssuesinInternetLaw.com).

[65] A hydrogen bomb, which is fusion-based, can be many hundreds of times more powerful than a fission-based atomic bomb.

[66] *The Progressive* proceeded to publish the article.

[67] "Judge is Asked to Rescind Shutdown of Web Site," The Los Angeles Times, February 27, 2008.

[68] "Whistle-blower Site Taken Offline," BBC News, February 18, 2008.

[69] Declan McCullagh, "Judge: WikiLeaks Gets its Domain Name Back," CNET News.com, February 29, 2008.

[70] Declan McCullagh, "Swiss Bank in WikiLeaks Case Abruptly Abandons Lawsuit," CNET News.com, March 5, 2008.

[71] Elinor Mills, "Go Daddy Shuts down Police-Rating Web Site," CNET News.com, March 12, 2008.

[72] "Cop: New Web Site Has Police Furious," CBS13.com. March 9, 2008.

[73] *Sheehan v. King Cnty. Experian,* Case No. C97-1360WD (W.D. Wash., order denying preliminary injunction, issued Jul. 17, 1998).

[74] 15 U.S.C. § 1692, *et seq.*

[75] 15 U.S.C. § 1681, *et seq.*

[76] *Remsburg v. Docusearch, Inc.,* 816 A.2d 1001 (N.H. 2003). (Included in the Cases Section on the Issues in Internet Law site, www.IssuesinInternetLaw.com).

[77] *Brandenburg,* 395 U.S. 444.

[78] *Sheehan,* Case No. C97-1360WD.

[79] *Ibid.*

[80] *Garrido v. Krasnansky,* Case No. F 466-12-06 (Vt. Fam. Ct. 2008).

[81] *Ibid.*

[82] "Blogging Lawyer Silenced as Judge Expands Gag Order in Liberty City 7 Case," The (South Florida) Sun Sentinel, January 14, 2008.

[83] Terry Collins, "SF Cell Shutdown: Safety Issue, or Hint of Orwell?" Associated Press wire service report, August 13, 2011.

[84] In *Brandenburg,* 395 U.S. *at* 447, the Supreme Court ruled speech can be prohibited if (1) "directed at inciting or producing imminent lawless action" and (2) "likely to incite or produce such action."

[85] According to a University of Washington study. *See* Josh Smith, "Government Power in Cyberspace is Big and Growing," NationalJournal.com, September 23, 2011.

[86] The California statute broadly defined "real estate broker" to include any person who, for a fee, "sells or offers to sell, buys or offers to buy, solicits prospective sellers or purchasers of, solicits or obtains listings of, or negotiates the purchase, sale or exchange of real property."

[87] *ForSaleByOwner.com v. Zinneman,* 347 F. Supp. 2d 868 (E.D. Cal. 2004). Paula Reddish Zinneman was the commissioner of the California Department of Real Estate.

[88] *Dagenais v. Canadian Broad. Corp.,* [1994] 3 S.C.R. 835, holding publication bans did not violate Canada's Charter of Rights and Freedom.

[89] Declan McCullagh, "U.S. Blogger Thwarts Canadian Gag Order," CNET News.com, April 5, 2005.

[90] The Adscam hearings concerned allegations of corruption and illegal campaign contributions in Canada's Liberal party.

[91] "Seoul May Ban North Korea College Web Site," Reuters wire service report, November 12, 2004.

[92] *Ibid.*

[93] Dan Simmons, "Cyber Bullying Rises in S. Korea," BBC Click Online, November 3, 2006, *available at* http://news.bbc.co.uk/2/hi/programmes/click_online/6112754.stm (accessed Mar. 23, 2012).

[94] John Markoff, "Iranians and Others Outwit Net Censors," The New York Times, April 30, 2009.

[95] Associated Press wire service report, April 22, 2004.

[96] Markoff, fn. 94, *supra.*

[97] "China Goes Undercover to Sway Opinion on Internet," Reuters wire service report, May 19, 2005.

[98] Markoff, fn. 94, *supra.*

[99] "China Moves toward 'Real Name System' for Blogs," Reuters wire service report, October 23, 2006.

[100] Jason Leow, "Why China Relaxed Blogger Crackdown: Registration Plan was Dropped in Face of Tech-Industry Protests," The Wall Street Journal, May 17, 2007.

[101] "Chinese Blog Providers 'Encouraged' to Register Users with Their Real Names," Associated Press wire service report, August 22, 2007.

[102] Markoff, fn. 94, *supra.*

[103] "China Encourages ISPs to Sign 'Self-Discipline Pact,'" The Washington Post, June 21, 2004.

[104] Associated Press wire service report, September 25, 2004.

[105] John Boudreau, "Vietnam Tightens Grip on Internet; Cafés Closed for Not Reporting Dissenters," (San Jose, CA) Mercury News, October 24, 2006.

[106] *Ibid.*

[107] BBC News, June 21, 2004.

[108] Agence France Presse, "Syrian Gets 2 Years in Jail for Dissident E-Mail," The Daily Star (Lebanon), June 21, 2004.

[109] "Reporters without Borders: Detention of Journalists and Bloggers Continuously in Syria Despite the Presence of Arab Observers," LevantNews.com, January 2, 2012, *available at* www.levantnews.com/index.php?option=com_content&view=article&id=10654:2012-01-16-16-21-17&catid=77:civil-society-human-rights&Itemid=78 (accessed Mar. 23, 2012).

[110] "Bahrain Site Registration Sparks Protests," Associated Press wire service report, April 28, 2005.

[111] Tom Pfeiffer, "Moroccan Blogger Jailed for Disparaging King," Reuters wire service report, September 9, 2008.

[112] Robert Mackey, "Long Jail Term for Iran's 'Blogfather'," The New York Times, September 28, 2010.

# CHAPTER

# 19

---

## BUSINESS AND THE INTERNET

This chapter examines business on the Internet: e-discovery, SLAPPs, tortious interference with business relationships, corporate securities, cybergripers, interstate commerce, taxation, privacy policies, data retention, and employee blogging.

*"We are rapidly entering the age of no privacy, where everyone is open to surveillance at all times; where there are no secrets from government."*
*— William O. Douglas, dissenting, Osborn v. United States*

THE INTERNET HAS BECOME the lifeblood of most businesses but it brings many concerns for corporations, small businesses, employers, and employees. Companies face the threat of lawsuits, which can be costly and result in negative publicity, regardless of the outcome. Some might be suits against the company and some might be actions brought by the company, such as SLAPPs or tortious interference with business relations lawsuits. Companies might have to deal with cybergripers or securities-related issues. In any litigation, they face the prospect of e-discovery and must be prepared for it. Doing business on the Internet means doing business across state lines, which raises interstate commerce issues, especially in the area of taxation. Businesses typically establish privacy policies and must inform their customers about them and how they store, safeguard, and use customers' personally identifiable information, and how long they retain such information. Employers might use the Web to investigate job candidates and current employees, and they might fire employees based on employee posts to blogs or social networks.

## Litigation Concerns

### E-Discovery

Businesses, especially corporations because of their perceived deep pockets, are often targeted for lawsuits. Plaintiffs seek evidence to support their claims, typically turning to the discovery process to secure it. Computers have become the electronic filing cabinets of businesses, meaning most evidence will be electronic in nature. Electronic documents might not only contain incriminating evidence on their face but also hidden within the document itself. This metadata — data about data — while usually not visible on the printed page, can be extracted from the document. Some documents have hidden notes or saved changes, *i.e.* earlier versions of text that was re-edited or rewritten, that might show what was on the author's mind when the document was prepared. E-mails stored on office computers or servers might reveal incriminating details, such as the e-mails sent by Merrill Lynch stock analyst Henry Blodget denigrating as garbage stocks he was publicly touting to investors.[1] Metadata may include the identity of a document's author and the time and date it was written, and in the case of e-mail, to whom it was sent (*e.g.*, the header may reveal blind carbon copied [bcc] recipients in addition to the named recipient and listed carbon copied [cc] recipients).

Once a corporation becomes aware of a potential lawsuit (*i.e.*, the moment litigation is reasonably anticipated), it should initiate its **litigation hold** procedures on the relevant electronic data. The purpose of the litigation hold is to notify all relevant individuals within the firm what data must be kept and for how long, and to avoid **spoilation** (tampering with or destruction) of evidence. Two things it should not do are destroy the evidence or wait to receive a subpoena before initiating the hold. Spoilation is a crime that can result in fines and imprisonment. In some cases, spoilation may create a negative evidentiary inference that allows the finder of fact (*i.e.*, the judge in a bench trial, or otherwise the jury) to infer the defendant destroyed the evidence because it was incriminating. Simply put, one may assume the defendant destroyed the evidence because it would have proven her guilt. Under the revised Federal Rules of Civil Procedure, FRCP 37(f) provides a **safe harbor** for the good faith loss of data, or its destruction in the ordinary course of business. A New York federal court has held failure to issue a written legal hold constitutes negligence per se: "If a party fails to issue a written litigation hold, the court finds that it is grossly negligent, in which case relevance and prejudice are presumed. Point. Game. Match."[2] Other district courts have held there must be actual prejudice resulting from the loss of Electronically Stored Information (ESI).[3] One defendant who intentionally destroyed electronic evidence was held in civil contempt and imprisoned for up to two years unless and until he paid the plaintiff's attorney fees and costs related to the spoilation.[4]

FRCP 26(a) expanded the definition of e-discoverable material from "documents" or "data compilations" to include all ESI. This means e-mail, MS Word documents, voice mail, instant messages, databases, and backups are discoverable and may be subpoenaed. There is an exception in the case where data, such as backups, might prove too costly to produce. FRCP 26(b)(2) provides the responding party can show the discovery request would cause an undue burden because the ESI is not reasonably accessible (*e.g.*, deleted files, backup tapes, data stored on systems no longer in use). The requesting party must then show good cause for the request. The responding party nonetheless has an obligation to identify the existence of such ESI it has not searched for or produced because of the costs and burdens of accessing it. If the other party insists on seeing this data, the party holding it has the burden of proving to the court the information is not reasonably accessible. In *Zubulake v. UBS Warburg, LLC*, the district court concluded the issue of accessibility depends on the media on which data are stored and created a seven-pronged balancing test to determine when the cost of production of ESI should shift from the responding party to the requesting party.[5]

Sometimes, a responding party may inadvertently send the requesting party ESI that contains metadata with privileged information. FRCP 26(b)(5) allows for retrieval of such information under its "clawback" provision. Under a *clawback agreement*, the parties agree documents will be produced without any intent to waive privilege or protections, but if a privileged document is inadvertently produced, the responding party must advise the requesting party, who must return, sequester, or destroy the information promptly, and is barred from disclosing it until resolution of the lawsuit. Often, the court will have to determine whether to waive or forfeit a claim of privilege for electronic data inadvertently sent.

The ESI must be provided in a form in which ordinarily maintained or readily usable; however, FRCP 34(b) allows the requesting party ESI to specify the form to be used in production. This is important because it might include electronic data in its original format (*e.g.*, the actual spreadsheet file and not a PDF reproduction) with its metadata (*e.g.*, file creator, creation date, and document changes; and in e-mails, routing details such as sender, receivers, and subject line) intact. While more difficult to review, "native" files may be more advantageous for the requesting party, but for the responding party they pose the risk of exposing potentially damaging metadata or track changes.

## Corporate Securities

The Internet has changed the way information about securities is disseminated and how they are traded. However, businesses interested in using the Internet to trade securities or communicate with existing or potential investors may be unaware of the legal issues involved. Both criminal enforcement actions and civil lawsuits can arise from violation of securities laws.

**The Securities Act of 1933** requires any securities offered for sale to the public be registered with the U.S. Securities and Exchange Commission (SEC) unless the Act provides an exemption.[6] It requires full disclosure so investors may understand the nature of the risk they face should they decide to invest in the offered securities. The Act governs the initial issuance of securities and prohibits fraud, deceit, and misrepresentation. It also establishes a *"Quiet Period"* extending from the time a company files a registration statement with the SEC until the SEC staff declares the statement "effective." During the Quiet Period, federal securities laws limit what information a company and related parties can release to the public, including electronic road shows and information on or hyperlinked to an issuer's Web site.[7] Comments during the Quiet Period, either verbal or online by company officials, or information subsequently posted on the company's Web site, could jeopardize the offering. For example, an Initial Public Offering (IPO) was cancelled after an intra-office e-mail a CEO had sent during the Quiet Period, to the company's employees about its prospects was leaked to the media and published.[8]

**The Securities and Exchange Act of 1934** governs the purchase and sale of securities, securities brokerage firms, and the securities exchanges.[9] Under the authority of § 10(b) of the 1934 Act, the SEC has promulgated *Rule 10b-5* prohibiting any act or omission resulting in fraud or deceit in connection with the purchase or sale of any security.[10] Both criminal and civil liability can result from attempts to manipulate stock prices by wrongful posts in online forums (*e.g.*, rumors), e-mailing fake press releases or information, or creating phony Web sites. In a *"Pump and Dump" scheme*, an individual enters a message board or chat room, talks up stocks she owns and then surreptitiously sells them into the artificial demand she has created. The SEC has estimated 100 million stock spam e-mails are sent each week, spiking share prices and trading volume the spammers then sell into.[11] Stock spam has proven more efficient than boiler rooms and cold calls, as one study showed it can boost a stock price by 6 percent.[12]

The key liability provisions under federal securities laws are: Rule 10b-5 of the **Securities and Exchange Act of 1934**, which imposes liability for materially false or misleading statements made with intent to deceive investors or with reckless disregard of the truth, in connection with the purchase or sale of securities;[13] Section 12(a)(2) of the **Securities Act of 1933**, which prohibits offering or selling a security by use of an untrue or misleading statement of material fact;[14] and Section 11 of the 1933 Act, which provides liability for making an untrue or misleading statement of material fact in a registration statement.[15] State securities administrators and divisions enforce state securities laws, which consist of common law fraud statutes; specific securities fraud laws; and statutes dealing with registration to offer securities for sale within the state, known as "blue sky" laws. Using the Internet to promote an IPO and distribute literature about it raises compliance issues with various blue sky laws in the states where the securities are to be offered or sold. Many have amended their blue sky laws to allow use of an electronic prospectus but others have not.

The SEC has stated a public company may not include offering materials for a *private placement* on its Web site if the investors have not already been located without a general solicitation.[16] Under *Regulation A*, a company may conduct an IPO for less than $5 million on the Internet, instead of through an underwriter.[17] Companies would still be liable under the Section 12(a)(2) of the **Securities Act of 1933** for any materially false or misleading oral or written statement in connection with a solicitation to sell stock.

Public companies communicate with customers, shareholders, and prospective investors through their Web sites and through social media like blogs, Facebook, and Twitter. A company may be liable for fraudulent statements in third-party information it hyperlinks to from its Web site, or in social media posts, if it participated in its preparation or explicitly or implicitly approved or endorsed the statement. Where several reports about the company are available and it links only to a single favorable one, the company may face liability for fraudulent misrepresentation. Statements made on a publicly traded company's blog by company officials or employees are subject to the anti-fraud provisions of the federal securities laws. A company may not condition use of its Web site or blog on a user's waiver of the federal securities laws. However, while responsible for its own statements, a company bears no liability for the statements of third parties posted to its blog, and need not respond to or correct such statements.

The SEC promulgated *Regulation FD* (Fair Disclosure) to prohibit an issuer or associated persons from selectively disclosing material nonpublic information.[18] Under Regulation FD, if companies choose to disclose nonpublic information, they must disclose it publicly, not selectively. They must consider whether the posting of information on a company Web site or through social media constitutes a "public" disclosure under Regulation FD, *e.g.*, would the release of information on Twitter be considered a public release, or a release to a selective audience (*i.e.*, the company's Twitter followers)?

The Obama administration announced in September 2011 it was working with the SEC to establish a "crowdfunding" exemption for companies raising less than $1 million (with individual investments limited to $10,000, or 10 percent of the investor's annual income), as well as raising the cap on Regulation A offerings from $5 million to $50 million.[19] *Crowdfunding* is raising small amounts of money from a large number of investors, usually via the Internet.

The Financial Industry Regulatory Authority (FINRA), a self-regulating organization that does not make or enforce laws, also regulates stockbrokers and brokerage firms. It oversees approximately 5,100 brokerage firms with about 173,000 branch offices, and more than 676,000 registered securities representatives (*i.e.*, brokers). FINRA is the successor organization to the National Association of Securities Dealers (NASD). It regulates trading in stocks, corporate bonds, securities futures, and options. FINRA licenses brokers and establishes rules for their behavior. Under FINRA rules, stockbrokers must submit all "advertisements and sales literature" for review and approval by a registered principal of the broker-dealer, in writing. It considers Web sites, banner ads, bulletin boards, and static (*i.e.*, non-interactive) content on social networks and blogs to be *advertisements*, but a password-protected Web site is not considered an advertisement. E-mail or instant messages sent to 25 or more prospective retail customers are considered "*sales literature*", but if sent to a single customer it would be classified as "*correspondence*". Content posted in a real-time interactive electronic forum (*e.g.*, chat rooms, social networks, and blog comments) is considered a "*public appearance*" which does not require prior principal approval but must be supervised by the broker-dealer. [20] Social networks are usually composed of static and interactive content. *Static content*, considered an advertisement, is typically accessible to all visitors and visible until removed. *Interactive content*, such as real-time chat room discussions, is considered a public appearance. FINRA considers blogs to be static advertisements, but if the blog allows interactivity, *i.e.*, where a third-party comments in response to the initial blog post and the blogger responds, then the blogger's responses are deemed public appearances. FINRA cautions registered representatives not to link to third-party sites that contain misleading, incorrect, or outdated information.

## Cybergripers

Before the Internet, a consumer wronged by a large business had few alternatives. He could sue, but legal fees might exceed the claim's value; or he could try to bring public opinion to bear against the business, by contacting local print or television news reporters. The Web has leveled the playing field, allowing aggrieved consumers with limited resources to criticize firms with huge financial resources. The Web is the world's largest soapbox, a cyberspace version of Hyde Park, empowering a housewife or Joe Sixpack to tell millions about a bad experience he or she had with a company's product or services. However, a cybergriper must avoid violating defamation, trademark, or copyright laws while airing her gripe, lest she open herself up to a retaliatory suit from the company. Many firms, seeking to silence critics and stem negative publicity, countersue for defamation, trademark infringement, or tortious interference with business relationships. Although courts tend to side with cybergripers, upholding their free speech rights (where the gripe site is noncommercial), the expense of defending such suits often has the same chilling effect as a SLAPP (discussed below). One might argue they are identical to SLAPPs, as there is a public interest component in the cybergriper's speech.

Likewise, companies must weigh the public relations repercussions of attempts to quash cybergripers: unwanted negative publicity from a lawsuit may exceed the reach of the cybergriper's small site, blog, or message board post. Consider the case of Toys "R" Us, which took umbrage at "Roadkill "R" Us", a humor site listing prices paid for various roadkill (*e.g.*, "field mouse 10¢, armadillo $1.25, lawyer TOP $$$ — CALL!!!"). [21] A cease and desist letter from Toys "R" Us claiming trademark infringement led to the creation of a second site[22] detailing the ongoing legal battle and the addition of giraffes[23] at $88.25/linear neck inch on the Roadkill site.

A tenant who used Twitter to complain about mold in her Chicago apartment was sued for defamation by her landlord. The tenant tweeted, "Who said sleeping in a moldy apartment was bad for you? Horizon realty thinks it's okay."[24] Horizon Group Management sought damages of $50,000, alleging the tweet defamed it. A company owner admitted he never discussed the tweet with the tenant nor asked her to delete it before suing. Horizon claimed the tweet was "published throughout the world" and "severely damaged its good name" though the woman had only 20 Twitter followers and her Twitter account was subsequently closed. However, the blogosphere was vocal about the case, proving again companies risk a negative publicity backlash by attempting to stifle speech, as far more than her 20 followers learned of her complaint once Horizon sued.

Cybergripers often register a domain name that incorporates the business' name with an offensive prefix or suffix. Such sites have become known as "sucks sites" because many use "sucks" as a suffix. One site — WebGripeSites.com — lists gripe sites, such as: BMWlemon.com, FordReallySucks.com, MySuzukiLemon.com, FordLemon.com, BoycottDelta.org, AmexSux.com, PayPalSucks.com, EarthlinkSucks.net, VerizonEatsPoop.com, AllstateInsuranceSucks.com, and even GWBush.com (a parody site that "reportedly prompted the Bush campaign to buy preemptively many domain names such as BushSucks.net and BushSucks.org").[25] Corporations defensively register domain names potential cybergripers might register. Preemptive registrations include: CapitalOneIsEvil.com, IHateSprint.com, and SatanLovestheWashingtonPostcom (the last transferred to *The Washington Post* as a result of a trademark infringement suit).[26]

Where the name of the site's URL is identical to the business' name, it would appear to violate the firm's trademark. But courts have favored cybergripers over trademark holders, absent a showing of a profit motive by the cybergriper in creating the site.[27] A federal court in Minnesota denied a plaintiff injunctive relief under the **Anti-cybersquatting Consumer Protection Act** (ACPA), stating consumers were unlikely to be confused as to the gripe site's source or believe it was created by or affiliated with the plaintiff, though it bore the plaintiff's name.[28] The injunction was also denied under the **Lanham Act** (see Chapter 4), which requires a showing the defendant used the plaintiff's trademark in commerce, as the court determined the gripe site to be a noncommercial use. The Sixth Circuit held, absent a bad faith intent to profit from the use of another's trademark in a domain name, a use solely to criticize the trademark owner cannot be enjoined under the **ACPA**.[29] A disgruntled Bosley Medical Institute customer launched bosleymedical.com to hair, er, air his gripes about the hair restoration firm.[30] Bosley sued, claiming use of its business name in the domain name was trademark infringement. The Ninth Circuit disagreed on the grounds the site was not created to confuse current or potential customers, nor motivated by profit. The ruling further solidified the notion consumers can use a trade name as part of the domain name for a company they wish to criticize.[31]

Many "sucks sites" cases have been decided on whether Web visitors would realize "sucks" is a pejorative term and not confuse it with the company's site (consumer confusion being the test for finding trademark infringement, as discussed in Chapter 4). Most American cases have held consumers do not confuse "suck sites" with official trademarked sites.

However, in non-American jurisdictions where the slang meaning of the term "sucks" may not be familiar to the general public, trademark infringement claims have been upheld. The World Intellectual Property Organization (WIPO) sided with Air France in its arbitration claim for cybersquatting against a Florida corporation that had registered the domain AirFranceSucks.com, citing possible confusion by international customers. [32]

Typically, in a retaliatory lawsuit, a company charges trademark infringement and the defendant raises First Amendment free speech rights as a defense. A Georgia couple faced a retaliatory suit [33] from a siding company after creating a gripe site. [34] Unhappy with the sprayed-on siding applied to their house, they launched the site to complain and provide a forum for other dissatisfied customers. Visitor posts to the site's message board said the product, "Spray on Siding", cracked, bubbled, and buckled. The manufacturer, North Carolina-based Alvis Coatings Inc., sued, claiming the site infringed on its trademarks, intentionally misled and confused consumers, and defamed its product. Alvis alleged the gripe site's name, spraysiding.com, was "confusingly similar" to its own site, sprayonsiding.com, as well as its trademark "Spray on Siding." It also claimed tortious interference with business relationships, implying publication of negative comments would deter potential customers from doing business with them. [35] The defendants rejected settlement offers that would have barred them from talking about the product and required them to sell their site's domain to the company, choosing to fight, they said, so other potential customers could be better informed about the product. [36] The lawsuit sought $75,000 in actual damages plus punitive damages and attorney fees, leading the couple to remark they could lose their home. [37] Given the worldwide reach of the Internet and the negligible cost of a Web site, the gripe site perhaps served as their only viable means of communicating with other dissatisfied customers.

In a similar case, a New Jersey builder sued both gripe site RipOffReport.com and Google over an anonymous post characterizing his home construction as a "shoddy nightmare" and claiming he had "ripped off" a woman and "99 percent of the people" in her development. The builder alleged three banks rejected him after seeing the posts on a Google search. [38] RipOffReport.com refused to remove the comments but said it provided an opportunity for rebuttals to be posted. The builder countered since the poster had been subsequently "satisfied by a payment of a claim", the gripe site should remove the post, but it refused, stating its policy to keep all complaints on the site to maintain a "working history on the company or individual in question." [39] As with most gripe sites where the allegedly defamatory comments are posted by third-parties and not by the site owner, the gripe site would be protected by the CDA, although to avoid his own liability, the poster would need to substantiate the truth of any otherwise defamatory claims. Courts usually side with cybergripers over trademark owners in these cases. It is hard for companies to overcome the First Amendment argument, and resulting publicity from a lawsuit could backfire, bringing unwanted negative publicity and a potential public relations nightmare.

Other countries have confronted the issue of gripe sites. In France, students were able to log on to note2be.com and grade their teachers in six categories—interest, clarity, fairness, availability, respectfulness, and motivation. French teachers' unions and the education ministry sued, claiming the comments and gripes were a breach of privacy and an "incitement to public disorder." The French court agreed, holding the site could no longer identify teachers by name. [40] Such sites are common in America.

## Strategic Lawsuits Against Public Participation

A *Strategic Lawsuit Against Public Participation* (SLAPP) is a lawsuit lacking substantial merit by private interests to stop citizens exercising their political rights or to punish them for having done so. SLAPPs are typically marked by flimsy allegations and disproportionately large damage claims. Most are dismissed because of specious merits, and those that are tried often end favorably for the defendants. But the goal of companies and organizations filing SLAPPs is not to collect damages, but to harass, intimidate, and distract their opponents — in effect, to "slap down" the defendant. Since a lawsuit can last years, even if the defendant wins, he will have tens of thousands of dollars in costs and legal fees. The defendant, usually a private individual with limited means sued by a wealthy corporation or organization, must also endure emotional stress and lost work time resulting from the lawsuit.

A trend among corporations has been to sue anonymous message board posters (see the discussion of anonymous speech in Chapter 14). Not all such suits are SLAPPs — some have merit. But many are attempts to silence anonymous corporate critics and intimidate others who, on learning of a fellow poster being sued, cease their own critical posts. This *"chilling effect"* of a SLAPP — silencing others on the message board — is its goal, *i.e.,* to halt public discussion of an issue the plaintiff prefers remain undiscussed.

The elements of a SLAPP are:
- The defendants' speech forms the claim's basis
- No true legal merit exists for the claim (although the suit may typically *allege* defamation, breach of contract, and/or trade secret violations)
- The SLAPP is usually filed as a "John Doe" lawsuit, where the pseudonym "John Doe" represents the unknown defendant's name, since most message posters use screen names in lieu of their real names
- The plaintiff tries to discover (*i.e.,* subpoena) the poster's identity from his ISP
- There is a resulting chilling effect on others' speech

California is at the forefront in SLAPPs and ensuring some measure of protection for anonymous speech. Once an anti-SLAPP motion (the "special motion to strike") is filed there, all discovery is stayed (*i.e.,* frozen), so the plaintiff's attempts to discover the poster's identity must wait for the court to determine if the company's lawsuit has a "probability of success." If the motion is granted, then the SLAPP is dismissed and the defendant may recover attorney's fees and costs; otherwise the litigation (and discovery) proceeds. [41] As of 2010, 27 states had anti-SLAPP laws. [42]

## Tortious Interference with Business Relationships

To sue for *tortious interference with a business relationship*, a plaintiff must show all of the following:
1. Existence of a contract or business relationship
2. Defendant's knowledge of that relationship
3. Intentional interference with the contract or business relationship
4. That defendant's actions caused harm to the plaintiff (*i.e.,* causation)
5. Financial damage to the plaintiff

Where a contract exists, tortious interference with a business relationship may occur if the defendant interferes with a party's performance of the contract or induces the contracting party to breach the it. [43] Where there is no contract, tortious interference may still exist where the defendant has prevented the plaintiff from establishing or maintaining business relationships.

When an individual receiving spam complained to the ISP, who terminated the spammer's account, the spammer sued him for tortious interference with his business contract with his ISP. [44] A defendant used frames to put content from a newspaper's site within its own framed site, allowing users to bypass the newspaper's site and its paid ads. [45] The newspaper sued for tortious interference with its business relationship with its advertisers, claiming the framing made performance of its advertising contracts more burdensome. The parties settled and the frames were removed. A disgruntled former employee griped about the company to thousands of its employees at their workplace e-mail addresses. [46] Although he allowed recipients to opt-out from future mailings and apparently honored such requests, the company claimed the e-mails' content disrupted its workplace and was tortious interference with its business relationship with its employees. The court ruled the defendant had a First Amendment right to e-mail (*i.e.,* the plaintiff had only objected to the e-mails' *content,* not that it was an e-mail attack against its servers). These examples are presented not necessarily to illustrate successful claims, but to familiarize the reader with the concept and breadth of the tortious interference with business relationships cause of action.

## Interstate Commerce and the Internet

Borders act as constraints. Just as the borders of this page constrain the words from running off the page, so too do geographic borders restrain *interstate commerce* within the geographic confines of states. States determine their own laws regarding commerce, including what items may be shipped into or from the state and what taxes or tariffs may be applied to incoming goods. [47] States often maintain protectionist policies that aid local producers of goods while disadvantaging outside producers. The borderless nature of the Internet will raise many questions about the constraints states may place on commerce. Many regulate or prohibit items not regulated or prohibited in other states. Drugs, cigarettes, alcohol, and lottery tickets are examples. The legal age may vary by state. A 14-year-old in a state where gambling is legal for those over 14 may wish to buy a lottery ticket online from a state where the legal age is 18. A New York woman may seek to order a bottle of wine online from a California winery, which may be prohibited by New York state law. An Illinois man may view material on a Dutch server considered obscene in his state. Many states want to collect sales tax on items sold to their citizens online by out-of-state sellers (the rationale being the state is losing tax revenue it would have received had the buyer made the purchase within the state, giving out-of-state e-commerce firms a competitive advantage).

As people experience the freedom of the Internet that comes from its borderless nature, states will have a hard time enforcing, let alone justifying, constraints on interstate commerce. In 2005, the U.S. Supreme Court overturned a 70-year-old ruling letting states ban out-of-state wineries from shipping wine to consumers within the state. [48] The court held such protectionist laws, on the books in 23 states and barring online sales by out-of-state wineries to in-state residents, violated the Commerce Clause of the U.S. Constitution. As a result, states must now choose between allowing direct shipment to individual consumers residing within their territory by all wineries (within and without the state) or prohibiting direct shipment by local and out-of-state wineries. It remains to be seen what effect, if any, this holding will have on other Internet–interstate commerce conflicts. However, in late 2008, Amazon. com announced plans to sell American-produced wine from all regions of the country in approximately 26 states. Previously, only 7 percent of the $2.8 billion retail wine sales came from e-commerce, partly due to the shipping expense and confusing states rules on wine shipments. [49]

Like alcohol, there is a strong demand for cigarettes to be shipped interstate, especially as states increase their "sin taxes" on alcohol and cigarettes. A 2002 study showed 400 million packs of cigarettes were sold annually online. [50] In an attempt to prevent minors from purchasing cigarettes from out-of-state retailers, the Maine Legislature enacted the **Tobacco Delivery Law**, which imposed requirements on air and motor carriers transporting tobacco products into the state. Maine argued this was a valid use of its *police power* to protect the health and welfare of its citizens. Under the Maine statute, delivery companies must: check packages against a state-provided list of known unlicensed tobacco retailers; deliver only to the addressee; and verify a recipient is over the age of 27. The Maine law allowed only Maine-licensed retailers to ship tobacco to state residents. [51] Delivery companies argued to allow Maine — and the 40 other states that prohibit or severely restrict direct delivery of tobacco products purchased online — to enforce its own requirements would result in a burdensome patchwork of varying state regulations. The U.S. Supreme Court agreed, affirming two lower courts and holding unanimously the **Federal Aviation Administration Authorization Act of 1994** (FAAAA) preempted states from enacting laws "related to" the prices, routes, or services of air and motor carriers. [52]

The U.S. Supreme Court also dealt New York City's attempt to collect tax from online cigarette sellers a setback in 2010, when it ruled 5–to–3 the city cannot use the **RICO Act** against discount cigarette retailers in tax evasion cases involving Internet sales. [53] The city alleged more than 400 sites sold cigarettes, falsely advertised as "tax free". In 2003, it sued four online cigarettes retailers, alleging violation of the federal **Jenkins Act**, which requires businesses to report out-of-state tobacco sales to state tax authorities. [54] It had wanted to use the **RICO Act** in this case because it provides for *treble damages*. [55] However, despite the city's claim it would have used customer information from the online retailers to pursue unpaid taxes from their New York cigarette purchasers, the court ruled there was not a close enough connection between the retailers' alleged failure to supply that information and the city's inability to collect the taxes. The $4.25 New York City cigarette tax is the nation's highest (split $2.75 to the state and $1.50 to the city). Previously, the New York Court of Appeals, the state's highest court, had held the city lacked legal standing to sue online cigarette retailers for lost taxes under state business laws. [56]

Does Internet use automatically entail interstate commerce? When data travels across the Internet, is it traveling through interstate commerce? One might say, "of course." However, one circuit court has held the interstate nature of the Internet does not necessarily mean connecting to the World Wide Web invariably equals data moving in interstate commerce. [57] The Tenth Circuit overturned a conviction for receipt and possession of images involving sexual exploitation of minors because the federal statute required showing the images had traveled across state lines. The court reasoned while most Internet use involves movement of data between states, that cannot be assumed — it must be proved, at least in so far as to meet the statutory burden of proof. As the court stated: [58]

> Ultimately, the decision to uphold or overturn Mr. Schaefer's convictions turns
> on whether an Internet transmission, standing alone, satisfies the interstate
> commerce requirement of the statute. Mr. Schaefer asserts that [the statute]'s

> jurisdictional provisions requires movement across state lines, and it is not enough to assume that an Internet communication necessarily traveled across state lines in interstate commerce. We agree.
>
> [The statute] require[s] a movement between states. The government did not present evidence of such movement; instead, the government only showed that Mr. Schaefer used the Internet. We recognize in many, if not most, situations the use of the Internet will involve the movement of communications or materials between states. But this fact does not suspend the need for evidence of this interstate movement.

The First,[59] Third,[60] and Fifth[61] Circuits have taken a contrary position in similar cases, ruling connection to a Web site or server invariably involves data moving in interstate commerce.

## Sales Tax

*Sales tax* is another area where the Internet and interstate commerce are at odds. While states salivate at the prospect of taxing Internet transactions, the U.S. Supreme Court has held businesses can avoid paying sales tax to states where they have no physical presence.[62] In light of this ruling, most Internet business do not pay sales taxes in states other than where they are incorporated or have their principal place of business. However, the borderless nature of the Internet calls into question the concept of "physical presence." Ironically, a bookstore named "Borders" was found by California's First District Court of Appeal to owe that state sales tax on merchandise sold on its Web site.[63] Borders argued it was not required to collect California sales taxes because its online division did not own or lease property in California and all its online orders were received and processed outside the state. Based in Michigan, Borders did own a 414,000 square-foot distribution center and 129 "Borders" and "Waldenbooks" stores in California. The court reasoned the company's site (and therefore its online division) was too intertwined with its physical stores in the state, due to cross-promotion and the ability of customers to return merchandise purchased online to retail stores.

New York has further stretched the definition of physical presence. As part of its state budget, it passed a law requiring out-of-state online firms with $10,000 or more in New York sales to collect state sales tax on goods shipped to New York addresses, even if the firm lacked a brick-and-mortar presence, so long as it had at least one individual physically present in the state working as an online agent.[64] The concept of an "online agent" apparently included "*affiliates*" — sites linking to an online retailer and earning referral fees for customers sent to that retailer — should the affiliate site owner be a New York resident.[65] Under the law, even if only one affiliate were in the state, the online retailer must collect sales tax on all sales there. Amazon.com and Utah-based Overstock.com (which have no physical presence in New York and sell exclusively online) each sued New York, seeking the law declared unconstitutional.[66] The court dismissed both suits, finding Amazon had a nexus in the state, the law was "carefully crafted", and it did not target Amazon unfairly.[67] However, in a 5–to–0 ruling, a New York appeals court reinstated the lawsuits.[68] Amazon has ended affiliate programs in Arkansas, Colorado, Connecticut, Illinois, North Carolina, and Rhode Island over the state tax collection issue.[69] In late 2011, Amazon ended its fight to overturn California's law requiring out-of-state online retailers to collect sales taxes, in exchange for a year's moratorium on collecting it. The law required e-commerce sites collect state taxes in if they had offices, workers or other connections in California. Amazon's affiliate program had been deemed sufficient nexus to subject it to the law. Amazon had refused to collect the taxes and spent more than $5 million toward a ballot referendum challenging the law.

There remains the looming prospect Congress might settle the issue of whether, and under what circumstances, states may tax online sales. An act of Congress would supersede a state law regarding interstate commerce. Of course, that would require consensus from both houses of Congress to pass such a bill — a rarity in the current political climate — and, like all bills, would require the president's signature to become law. Even then, it would likely be challenged in court by states eager for new revenue sources in an economic downturn should Congress favor local retailers, or by online merchants should Congress favor the state governments.

In another Internet sales tax case, the city of Chicago sued eBay and its subsidiary StubHub for failing to comply with a local ordinance requiring sites collect city amusement taxes on cultural and sporting event tickets sold online. The federal district court in Illinois held StubHub had no collection duty but did need to place a prompt on its site advising ticket buyers of their obligation to pay the amusement tax. [70]

North Carolina's tax collectors sought detailed records, including names and addresses of customers and information about purchases, from Amazon.com. [71] The online retailer sued the state, claiming its demand violated Amazon's customers' privacy and First Amendment rights. North Carolina's Department of Revenue wanted information on nearly 50 million purchases made by state residents between 2003 and 2010. Amazon did provide anonymized information about which items were shipped to which zip codes, but the state demanded it reveal names and addresses linked to each order — personally identifiable information it could use to collect taxes from residents. As it involved the purchases of books and films, the case presented major First Amendment concerns. In 2002, the Colorado Supreme Court had held the First Amendment protects "an individual's fundamental right to purchase books anonymously, free from governmental interference," after police subpoenaed information from a bookstore about which books a customer had purchased. [72] Customers' privacy is also protected under federal law: the **Video Privacy Protection Act** prohibits retailers from disclosing the title, description, or subject matter of any video purchased by a specific customer. [73] In the North Carolina case, a federal court ruled the First Amendment protected Amazon's customers from having their selection of books, music, and movies disclosed to the government, but preserved the state's right to pursue tax collection from Amazon or its customers. [74]

Even if the courts ultimately rule in favor of online retailers, the Internet may not remain a tax-free zone. Seventeen states are members of the Streamlined Sales Tax Agreement, a coalition to implement laws to collect sales tax on Internet purchases, should Congress enact a federal law authorizing states to do so. [75]

## Privacy Concerns

### Privacy Policy

Businesses collect personal information from their online customers, both out of necessity and for marketing purposes. Marketers value personal identifiable information, such as name, address, birth date, occupation, income, age, gender, and hobbies to reach targeted audiences. When customers volunteer their information, they want to retain some control over what is done with it. They want to know what the business plans to do with it and assurance it will be stored safely, inaccessible to hackers or others who should not have access to it. To achieve this, companies place privacy policies on their Web sites, explaining how they collect information and what they do with it. In most circumstances, it is not a legal requirement to have a privacy policy, but most firms do because they make sites appear trustworthy. Privacy policies should be simple and straight-forward so they can be easily understood by site visitors, not filled with indecipherable legalese. Companies should review their policies periodically and update them as necessary. They should also ensure employees are familiar with the firm's privacy policy, so they can respond to questions regarding it and so they do not violate it.

## Data Breach

Personal information is valuable and, like anything of value, it is likely to be targeted by thieves. Unfortunately, most businesses are ill-equipped to provide adequate security against data breaches by hackers. Businesses lack a consensus on what qualifies as "reasonable security" for protecting against data breaches. Such breaches might occur from an intrusion by a third-party who infiltrates the computer network and steals the data, accidental disclosure by the company, insider breach, portable device breach, stationary device breach, hard copy loss, and payment card fraud at the point of purchase. Employees might keep customer information not just on company workstations and servers, but on portable (and easily lost or stolen) devices, such as smart phones, laptops, and tablets. Data may also be at risk from *cloud computing*, where it resides on third-party servers, with security beyond the control of the user, and possible access by employees of the third-party.

The consequences of a data breach are serious. Hackers could use stolen credit card information to purchase goods, or use other personally identifiable information for identity theft, financial scams, blackmail, or public humiliation. Even unintentional disclosure of personal information on the Web could be used to the detriment of the individuals involved by an employer to deny an applicant a job, or fire an employee; or an insurance company to deny coverage or payment of a claim, or raise premiums.

Many companies are reluctant to report breaches for fear of losing customer or investor confidence and opening themselves to lawsuits. A company whose data has been breached might expect to be sued by the affected individuals for negligence (for failing in its duties to have adequate procedures in place to prevent unauthorized access), breach of express and implied warranty (of a reasonable expectation of privacy for stored customer data), invasion of privacy, or possibly breach of an implied fiduciary duty (in cases where a company is entrusted with sensitive financial or medical data). In response, companies are placing waiver clauses in click-wrap agreements stating the customer agrees not to sue in the event of a data breach and purchasing "cyber insurance" to protect against customer claims for data loss and identity theft. An alternative is encryption, which not only makes it more difficult to access stolen data, but also may benefit the corporation because many state privacy laws do not require companies to report data breaches if the data were encrypted.

## Employer Concerns

### Job Applicants

Employers often search the Web to learn about job candidates. They routinely conduct Google searches on applicants, peruse their social network profiles, and read their blogs. The Internet has become a job applicant's online résumé and employers have learned individuals may be more honest on their Facebook profile than on their paper résumé. They look for mention (or photos) of alcohol and drug use, and provocative or inappropriate photographs; discriminatory remarks related to race, gender, or religion; an unprofessional screen name; and poor communication skills evident from the profile. They also scan social media for evidence of good communications skills, a professional image, and positive community involvement. Comments and photos posted on social networks by an applicant's friends are also factored into the evaluation process. Often the company's hiring personnel will have developed an image and opinion of the applicant before having met or interviewed her. A potential employer might reject an applicant solely based on the comments of others without the applicant having the opportunity to respond.

In 2012, privacy concerns were raised when reports surfaced of employers — such as Sears and the Maryland Department of Corrections — demanding job applicants give them their Facebook login information.[76] Facebook issued a statement that "sharing or soliciting" a Facebook password was a violation of its Terms of Use agreement, adding such action could create liability for the employers if they used certain uncovered information in their hiring decisions, such as age discrimination.[77]

### Employee Bloggers

If an employee posts information (*e.g.*, regarding products, sales, management, employees, or rumors) about his employer in a public forum, and had previously signed a confidentiality agreement, then he may have breached his fiduciary duty to the company and be in breach of contract. Sometimes, an employee will post anonymously on a message board to disclose corporate wrongdoing within his company (*i.e.*, a "whistleblower"), or merely to criticize his employer. Absent a confidentiality agreement, if the anonymous poster is later revealed as an employee, can the company fire him? Or does he have a First Amendment free speech right to criticize his employer?

Social network Friendster fired an employee for comments in her personal blog.[78] Joyce Park, a Web developer, made three posts about the new programming she had developed for the Friendster site that made it run much faster. The information in her blog was publicly available. Friendster did not have a stated policy on blog comments and did not warn Park or ask her to remove her comments before firing her. She had written:[79]

> As most of you probably know, I've spent the last six months working at Friendster. I have not managed to release any code in that entire time. Finally on Friday we launched a platform rearchitecture based on loose-coupling, Web standards, and a move from JSP (via Tomcat) to PHP. The Web site doesn't look much different, but hopefully we can now stop being a byword for unacceptably poky site performance. I also want to call out our first new user-facing feature in a long time, Friends in Common (upper left corner of your friends' profiles). Try it out and let me know what you think.

Presumably, someone in Friendster's management did not like the reference to "being a byword for unacceptably poky (sic) site performance." Imagine how they must have felt reading the 4,630 comments (culled from a September 2004 Google search) resulting from the negative backlash to Park's firing. Outraged commentators and fellow bloggers urged readers to cancel their Friendster memberships in protest, proving again companies need to realize the Internet is not a vacuum and beware the backlash to their actions.

Park was not the first to lose her job for blog comments. Microsoft fired contractor Michael Hanscom in 2003 after he posted photos of Apple G5 computers being unloaded at the software company to his blog under the title "Even Microsoft wants G5s." [80] (Despite the caption's implication, Microsoft had good reason to order Apple computers, as it is a major software producer for Apple). A Delta Airlines flight attendant was fired after posting suggestive pin-up photos of herself in her Delta uniform on her blog; she shot back by retitling her blog "Diary of a Fired Flight Attendant." [81] A Google employee was fired after only 11 days on the job, after blogging his impressions and criticisms of his new employer. [82] Reporter Rachel Mosteller blogged how much she hated her job: "I really hate my place of employment. Seriously." [83] While not naming her workplace — the *Durham* (N.C.) *Herald-Sun* — her employer sought to relieve her obvious suffering by giving her a pink slip the next day. [84] After an employee ranted about her boss on Facebook, he promptly reminded her she had added him as a 'friend', before firing her. [85] There have been so many "fired for blogging" cases there is now a name for it — getting "dooced." The phrase was coined by Web designer Heather B. Armstrong in 2002, after she was fired for comments about co-workers in her blog on her site Dooce.com. [86]

Beyond the private sector, government employees and contractors risk dismissal for blogging too. A CIA contractor was fired after she blogged her opinion American interrogation methods violated the Geneva Conventions. [87]

Union contracts (and some nonunion employment contracts) requiring "just cause" for firing may afford a blogger some protection, although a blogger would still be subject to termination for "just cause" if the blog violated the employer's work rules. Nonunion workers are at greater risk of losing their jobs over blogging if they criticize the company or disclose confidential information. An *"at-will"* employee — one who works for a private employer without a union contract — can be fired for any reason not specifically prohibited by law. Employers in "at-will" states can fire employees even if they wrote the blog on their own time on their own computer outside the office.

Employee blogs raise the issue of balancing freedom of speech with an employer's right to protect the company's public image. Some bloggers add disclaimers stating they do not represent the company for whom they work. Ideally, companies should establish written blogging policies. Often, it is a matter of common sense. As one blog reader put it, "Make your boss look bad, find another job. It's a no-brainer."

There has been at least one case of an employee fired for posting factual information to a wiki. NBC Washington bureau chief Tim Russert suffered a heart attack on the set of the *"Meet the Press"* news program he hosted; within 45 minutes he was taken to a hospital where he was pronounced dead. NBC waited slightly more than an hour to announce his death on the air, to allow the network time to notify his family. However, almost 40 minutes before NBC's on-air announcement, an Internet Broadcasting Services employee updated Russert's Wikipedia entry to include his time of death and change the entry's verbs to past tense. The employee was reportedly fired. [88]

In the early days of the Internet, a spate of employee firings based on Internet posts raised a due process issue. Employees were being fired for comments or photographs posted online without having been first told the company would object to such posts or consider them grounds for dismissal. Previous editions of this book discussed these cases in detail and concluded employers should draft guidelines for acceptable Internet use and ensure employees were aware of such guidelines before arbitrarily firing them. Now, most firms have social media policies in place, but the new issue in Internet law is how far their social media policies can go. The National Labor Relations Board (NLRB) has reported a surge in worker grievances stemming from uncertainty over what employees can or cannot post online.

The crux of the matter is the conflict between the NLRB's duty to protect both union and nonunion workers when they engage in "protected concerted activity" by joining to discuss working conditions and the legitimate concern of businesses not to be disparaged in a public forum where such comments might be seen by potential or current customers or investors. The **National Labor Relations Act** (NLRA) grants employees a federally protected right to form unions and prohibits employers from punishing them (whether or not they belong to a union) for discussing working conditions or unionization.[89] Are employees' criticisms of their employers on a social network a "protected concerted activity" within the meaning of the **NLRA** and would employers be breaking the law by punishing them for such statements?

The NLRB accused an employer of illegally firing an employee after she criticized her supervisor on Facebook but the matter was settled before it could be heard by an administrative law judge, meaning the case lacks precedential value.[90] It was the first time the NLRB had delineated legal limits on employers' Internet and social media policies, asserting the employer's policy was so overly broad it violated § 7 of the **NLRA**. The employer agreed to revise its rules and not discipline or discharge employees for discussing work issues away from the workplace; it also stipulated it would not deny employee requests for union representation or threaten discipline for such requests. The issue of employers punishing employees for comments posted on social networks about work matters from home computers is similar to the issue of students punished by schools for off-campus online speech, discussed in Chapter 15. Here, however, a federal statute specifically protects employee discussions with co-workers about working conditions, and terms and conditions of their employment, where there is "concerted activity". In this case, the employee had posted negative comments about her supervisor and responded to supportive responses from co-workers.

To be protected, there must be group activity; griping is not protected. If the employee had posted a message and no co-workers had responded, the comments might not be deemed a protected concerted activity. Disparaging comments or attacks against employers unrelated to work might also be unprotected. An employee of Hispanics United of Buffalo criticized other employees' job performance on Facebook.[91] The post generated responses from co-workers who defended their job performance and criticized working conditions, including work load and staffing issues. The employer fired the five employees who participated in the exchange, claiming they were in violation of its social media policy banning cyber harassment of co-workers. An administrative law judge ruled the employees' Facebook discussion protected concerted activity within the meaning of § 7 of the **NLRA** because it involved a conversation among employees about terms and conditions of employment.[92]

Expanding on that premise, an administrative law judge found a fired car salesman's criticism on Facebook of food served at a dealership event protected expression of concerns about the terms and conditions of his employment, since it could impact employees' sales compensation.[93] The judge reasoned the "lone act of a single employee is concerted if it 'stems from' or 'logically grew' out of prior concerted activity." But when the employee also posted a photo of a customer's 13-year-old driving a luxury SUV from the dealership into a pond, captioned as "This is your car: This is your car on drugs," the judge ruled it had no connection to any of the terms and conditions of the salesman's employment and was thus unprotected, justifying his termination.

As mentioned above, griping is not protected either. A Wal-Mart employee's Facebook complaint of management "tyranny" that included a derogatory reference to a female assistant manager was deemed "an individual gripe" instead of a protected effort to discuss work conditions with co-workers.[94] Even though two employees commented, one inquiring what had occurred and the other offering encouragement, the NLRB determined the employee had been lawfully fired and despite the co-workers' comments, there was no "protected concerted activity," characterizing his comments as an "individual gripe" and not an attempt to induce action by other employees. The key is whether the employee is looking to co-workers to engage in group action. In one case, the NLRB declined to hear the grievance of an Indiana emergency transportation and fire protection employee fired for posting a complaint on her U.S. senator's Facebook page stating her employer's cheap service compromised its quality of care.[95] The NLRB refused to equate making a public official (or the public) aware of employer related safety issues with a discussion of complaints with other workers.

A New Jersey high school teacher allegedly posted on her Facebook page homosexuality was "a perverted spirit that has existed from the beginning of creation" and "breeds like cancer."[96] The posts also allegedly objected to a school display celebrating Lesbian, Gay, Bisexual and Transgender History Month. The school district launched an investigation to determine if the teacher was performing her job in accordance with school policies and anti-bias laws. Gay rights groups argued the teacher had a responsibility to be a role model for students. But is that true? Do comments made outside of the classroom, not directed to, or in the presence of, students, have any bearing on job performance? Does a teacher, by virtue of her job, surrender her First Amendment free speech rights? Suppose her comments had been made in line at a supermarket, or in a political leaflet instead of on the Internet? Where is the line between an employee's right of free speech or, as discussed below, her expectation of privacy on her social network page outside of work, and the right of an employer to fire an employee for comments posted online? In the case of a school setting, the U.S. Supreme Court has said, "[I]t can hardly be argued that either students or teachers shed their constitutional rights of freedom of speech or expression at the schoolhouse gate."[97] Where should society — and ultimately, the law — draw the line?

## Privacy and Work — Lifestyle Privacy

Most people have an expectation their private life is separate from their work life and should not affect it. There are, of course, obvious situations when an extrinsic circumstance in one's private life may adversely affect one's career. For example, if a priest is caught soliciting sex from young boys; if a Disney starlet unintentionally circulates nude photos of herself on the Web; if a Miss Teen USA's racy photos appear on the Web — in these instances, the individuals have engaged in behavior that reflects poorly on the organization that employed them. The employee knew when he or she was hired the organization (*i.e.*, the Catholic church, Disney, or the Miss Teen USA Pageant) was built around a reputation of morality and wholesomeness, and as high profile employees, they would be seen as representing those organizations, even in their private lives. A truck driver might spend a night drinking with friends at a strip club and not expect to have to defend his actions the next day at work, whereas a congressman caught at the same club might have to hold a press conferences the next day in an attempt to keep his job.

Foolish employee behavior after hours was once merely the subject of next day banter around the office water cooler, but today, with smart phone cameras, high resolution pocket cameras, and the Internet, poor judgment can be immortalized in living color on every workstation by the next morning. With the advent of digital technology and the Internet, has privacy become an outdated notion? Closed circuit cameras film us as we walk down streets and enter businesses; Google Earth posts photographs of our homes and cars online; and people all around us carry smart phone and pocket digital cameras. Is any expectation of privacy even reasonable? Have we waived our right to privacy? As we discussed in an earlier chapter, the generation that has come of age with the Internet has also developed a lessened expectation of privacy. Thanks to Web sites, social networks, and YouTube, Andy Warhol's promise of 15 minutes of fame for everyone has become a reality. Anyone can post a homemade video on YouTube and be viewed by thousands of people. The Internet Generation thinks nothing of posting their lives' most intimate details in blogs, or on sites like Facebook, MySpace, or LiveJournal, or vlogging about their lives, loves, and the job or boss they hate. Many have been fired for blog comments posted after work, as in the case of a reporter fired after blogging how much she hated her job (turns out newspaper editors read blogs, too)![98] Should a job applicant really be shocked to learn he has been "Googled" by a prospective employer and his Facebook page and tweets taken into equal consideration with his application and résumé?

Let us set out some fundamental propositions:
- Employees are entitled to a reasonable expectation of privacy in off-work hours ("lifestyle privacy")
- Employees with high profile public personas should have a diminished expectation of privacy
- Employees or representatives of organizations that promote certain codes of behavior should not engage in behavior antithetical to those codes, even outside of work

How would these propositions be applied to real life situations? Suppose John Smith, a fictitious spokesman appearing in advertisements for the anti-lung cancer organization GASP (Group Against Smoke Pollution), is filmed smoking in public at various night clubs. While he may be entitled to a reasonable expectation of privacy outside of work, that expectation must be tempered by his job-related high profile persona. More importantly, by publicly smoking while serving as the spokesman for an anti-smoking organization, he has triggered our third proposition. His behavior might have been less egregious had both the second and third propositions been met, *e.g.*, if he had been a little-known employee and not a high profile spokesman.

In the next example, we will attempt to apply these propositions to an actual case and see how a court ruled. Stacy Snyder, a Millersville University senior in Pennsylvania, worked as a teaching assistant at nearby Conestoga Valley High School to fulfill her practicum requirement toward earning her teaching degree. Like many college students, the 25-year-old had a MySpace page. Snyder posted a photo of herself at a Halloween costume party (presumably after work and not on the high school campus) on her MySpace page. The head shot of Snyder in a pirate hat drinking from a yellow plastic cup bearing the words "Mr. Goodbar chocolate" did not show the cup's contents. The photo was captioned "Drunken Pirate." [99] Elsewhere on the profile, Snyder had written: [100]

> I figure a couple of students will actually send me a message when I am no longer their official teacher. They keep asking me why I won't apply there. Do you think it would hurt me to tell them the real reason (or who the problem was)?

The comment referred to students asking why she would not consider working at Conestoga Valley High School after her practicum had ended and she had obtained her teaching certificate. The "problem" alluded to in her comment was her strained relationship with her supervising teacher at the school, although that would not be apparent to most readers. The supervisor, allegedly unhappy with Snyder's job performance, discovered the profile page and showed it to the school's superintendent, who suspended Snyder from the student teacher program. [101] Barred from the high school campus days before the end of her semester-long practicum and her college graduation, Snyder was summoned by university officials and told the photo was "unprofessional", promoted underage drinking, and might be offensive to her students had any accessed her page and seen it (it is unknown if Snyder had set her profile page privacy settings to "public" or only those friends designated by her). [102] The university refused to award her an education degree, instead granting her an English degree. [103] Its refusal to confirm she had satisfactorily completed her student teaching requirements kept her from obtaining state certification; subsequently, she sought employment as a nanny. [104] Snyder sued the university for $75,000 in damages and injunctive relief requiring it to grant her a teaching degree, alleging violations of her free speech and due process rights.

As there is yet no body of established case law in this area, perhaps courts might consider adopting our three propositions and applying them on a case-by-case basis. Turning to the example above, most college students have MySpace or Facebook pages with photographs ranging from innocent to raunchy. For better or worse, college life has become synonymous with fraternities, sororities, partying, drinking, and football games, in addition to its primary purpose of education, and these activities will no doubt be reflected in the content one finds on such student profiles. While the photo was captioned "Drunken Pirate", there was no indication Snyder was drunk, nor that there was alcohol in the cup. Such captions are often tongue-in-cheek and this could have been a play on the "Yo-ho-ho and a bottle of rum" drunken pirate stereotype. As it was a costume party, there is no more reason to believe Snyder was actually drunk than to believe she was actually a pirate. Even if she had been drinking or inebriated, under our first proposition, employees would be entitled to a reasonable expectation of privacy in off work hours. Unless Snyder brought the photo or her MySpace page to the attention of her students, it would be unreasonable to think she would not be allowed to act as any other college student in her personal life. Snyder did not have a high profile public persona. Her job as a student teacher did not make her famous, nor did it make her a role model outside of the classroom, any more than posting the innocuous photo was "promoting underage drinking."

Did the organization (the university) promote certain codes of behavior? According to the pleadings, the school did have a code of conduct, but there was nothing cited in it prohibiting Snyder from maintaining a MySpace page or posting photographs from a costume party. [105] However, all student teachers were told at the start of the practicum to keep personal Web pages free of references to students and teachers at their assigned schools. Obviously, any employment agreements or relevant labor laws would also be a factor in such a case-by-case analysis. The importance of the pre-existence of codes of conduct or behavior, stated employee rules, employment contractual terms, or existing labor laws is they provide notice to the employee of what behavior outside of the office environment is considered acceptable or grounds for termination.

The _Snyder_ case was complicated by the issue of whether a student teacher should be subject to the legal standards applicable to student conduct or those applicable to teacher conduct. Legally, students have greater First Amendment speech rights than public employees, whose speech is constitutionally protected only if related to matters of public concern. [106] The court ruled against Snyder, finding "she was more a teacher than a student." [107] The court's classification of Snyder as an employee of the high school rather than as a university student effectively meant she had fewer rights than would be afforded the average student.

Reflecting on the _Snyder_ case four years later, Jeffrey Rosen wrote: [108]

> As social networking sites expanded, it was no longer quite so easy to have segmented identities: now that so many people use a single platform to post constant status updates and photos about their private and public activities, the idea of a home self, a work self, a family self and a high-school-friends self has become increasingly untenable.

The technology of the Internet, through social media — blogs, vlogs, and social networks — is eroding the barrier between our public and private lives. Both society and the law will have to recognize this overlap and craft rules that balance the reputational interests of employers with the reasonable expectations of privacy of employees. The Internet is forever and youthful indiscretions are etched upon it in indelible ink. Rosen noted the permanence of information posted on social media and mused, in a society where everything is recorded, "Now the worst thing you've done is often the first thing everyone knows about you." [109]

**Chapter 19 Notes**

[1] Thor Valdmanis, "Spitzer: Merrill Analyst Pitched Stock He Called 'Junk'," USA Today, April 14, 2002.

[2] _Pension Comm. of the Univ. of Montreal Pension Plan v. Banc of Am. Sec., LLC_, 2010 U.S. Dist. LEXIS 1839 (S.D.N.Y. 2010).

[3] _Davis v. Grant Park Nursing Home, LP_, 639 F. Supp. 2d 60 (D.D.C. 2009).

[4] _Victor Stanley, Inc. v. Creative Pipe, Inc._, ("_Victor Stanley II_"), 2010 U.S. Dist. LEXIS 93644 (D. Md. Sept. 9, 2010).

[5] _Zubulake v. UBS Warburg, LLC_, 217 F.R.D. 309 (S.D.N.Y. 2003).

[6] The Securities Act of 1933, text at U.S. Securities and Exchange Commission site, _available at_ www.sec.gov/about/laws/sa33.pdf (accessed Mar. 23, 2012).

[7] _See_ SEC Release No. 33-8591 — Securities Offering Reform.

[8] Deborah Lohse and Joan Indiana Rigdon, "Wired Kills IPO Amid Mishap With E-Mail," The Wall Street Journal, October 25, 1996, pp. C1, C17.

[9] The Securities Exchange Act of 1934, text at U.S. Securities and Exchange Commission site, _available at_ www.sec.gov/about/laws/sea34.pdf (accessed Mar. 23, 2012).

[10] 17 C.F.R. § 240.10b-5.

[11] Karey Wutkowski, "SEC Cracks down on Spam-driven Stocks," Reuters wire service report, March 8, 2007.

[12] Kit R. Roane, "Taking Penny Stocks out of the Boiler Room," U.S. News & World Report, June 4, 2007, pp. 55-56.

[13] Promulgated under § 10(b) of the Securities and Exchange Act of 1934, 15 U.S.C. § 78(j).

[14] The Securities Act of 1933, 15 U.S.C. § 77(l).

[15] The Securities Act of 1933, 15 U.S.C. § 77(k).

[16] *See* "Use of Electronic Media for Delivery Purposes," Exchange Act Release No. 33-7233, 60 S.E.C. Docket 1091, 1995 WL 588462, at *11 (S.E.C. Oct. 6, 1995).

[17] Regulation A [17 CFR § 230.251—230.263].

[18] Regulation FD [17 CFR § 243.100, *et seq.*].

[19] *See* Aneesh Chopra and Tom Kalil, "The President's American Jobs Act: Fueling Innovation and Entrepreneurship," White House Press Release, September 8, 2011, *available at* www.whitehouse.gov/blog/2011/09/08/president-s-american-jobs-act-fueling-innovation-and-entrepreneurship (accessed Mar. 23, 2012). *See also* Alex Goldmark, "Be Your Own Bank: New Laws Could Unleash Crowdfunding For Startups," Good Business, October 3, 2011, *available at* www.good.is/post/crowdfunding-why-the-sec-bans-it-obama-wants-it-and-banks-fear-it (accessed Mar. 23, 2012).

[20] NASD Rule 2210. Communications with the Public.

[21] "Roadkill "R" Us" Web site, *available at* www.rru.com (accessed Mar. 23, 2012).

[22] "Roadkill "R" Us" gripe site, *available at* www.rru.com/tru (accessed Mar. 23, 2012).

[23] Geoffrey the Giraffe is the Toys "R" Us mascot.

[24] "Defamation Lawsuit for US Tweeter," BBC News, July 29, 2009.

[25] *Available at* www.webgripesites.com/gripesites.shtml (accessed Mar. 23, 2012).

[26] Catherine Rampell, "Firms Fight Back in Site Name Game; Web Domains, or Variations thereof, Can Define a Company or Product," The Washington Post, p. D01, December 1, 2007.

[27] In *Taubman Co. v. Webfeats*, Case No. 01-72987 (E.D. Mich. 2001) (granting preliminary injunction), rev'd 319 F.3d 770 (6th Cir. 2003), the Sixth Circuit held use of plaintiff's trademarks with the word "sucks" in the domain names of noncommercial gripe sites did not violate the Lanham Act because there was no likelihood of consumer confusion and the First Amendment protects such speech.

[28] *Northland Ins. Cos. v. Blaylock*, 115 F. Supp. 2d 1108 (D. Minn. 2000).

[29] *Lucas Nursery & Landscaping, Inc. v. Grosse*, Civ. A. No. 01-73291 (E.D. Mich. 2002), aff'd 359 F.3d 806 (6th Cir. 2004).

[30] *Bosley Med. Inst., Inc. v. Kremer*, Case No. 01-1752, 2004 WL 964163 (S.D. Cal. 2004), aff'd in part and rev'd in part, 403 F.3d 672 (9th Cir. 2005).

[31] *Ibid*. However, the appellate court reinstated part of the lawsuit in which Bosley alleged Kremer violated the Anti-cybersquatting Consumer Protection Act by offering to sell the site to Bosley.

[32] *Société Air France v. Virtual Dates, Inc.*, Case No. D2005-0168 (2005), WIPO Arbitration and Mediation Center, *available at* http://arbiter.wipo.int/domains/decisions/html/2005/d2005-0168.html (accessed Mar. 23, 2012).

[33] *Alvis Coatings, Inc. v. Townsend*, Civil Action No. 3:04-cv-482-K (W.D.N.C. 2004).

[34] Associated Press wire service report, November 6, 2004.

[35] *Alvis Coatings*, Civil Action No. 3:04-cv-482-K.

[36] *Ibid*.

[37] *Ibid*.

[38] *RSA Enters., Inc. v. Rip-Off Report.com*, Case No. 2:2007-cv-01882 (D.N.J. 2007), dismissed by stipulation, Aug. 7, 2007.

[39] Jim Lockwood, "Builder Sues Web Site and Google over Posting," (New Jersey) Star-Ledger, April 27, 2007.

[40] "French Court Tells Web Site Not to Mark Teachers," Reuters wire service report, March 3, 2008.

[41] *Batzel v. Smith*, 333 F.3d 1018 (9th Cir. 2003), included in the Cases Section on the Issues in Internet Law site (www.IssuesinInternetLaw.com), is an interesting case discussing many of these topics — publisher analogy, *Stratton*, the CDA § 230, forums for potential defamation, and SLAPPs.

[42] Dan Frosch, "Venting Online, Consumers Can Find Themselves in Court," The New York Times, p. A1, June 1, 2010.

[43] *See* *Haelan Labs., Inc. v. Topps Chewing Gum, Inc.*, 202 F.2d 866 (2d Cir. 1953), cert. denied, 346 U.S. 816 (1953), where a chewing gum company induced baseball players to breach an exclusivity contract with a competitor to use their photographs on baseball trading cards.

[44] Bruce W. McCullough, "Internet Jurisdiction," Findlaw.com, *available at* http://library.findlaw.com/2000/Sep/1/127712.html (accessed Mar. 23, 2012).

[45] *Wash. Post Co. v. TotalNews, Inc.*, 97 Civ. 1190 (S.D.N.Y. filed Feb. 2, 1997, settled Jun. 5, 1997). (Included in the Cases Section on the Issues in Internet Law site, www.IssuesinInternetLaw.com).

[46] *Intel Corp. v. Hamidi*, 71 P.3d 296 (Cal. 2003). (Included in the Cases Section on the Issues in Internet Law site, www.IssuesinInternetLaw.com).

[47] "States" are referred to here both in the sense of nations as well as the individual states comprising the United States of America, the difference being international commerce is often subject to international treaties and agreements, while interstate commerce within the United States is subject to federal regulation by the Commerce Clause of the U.S. Constitution.

[48] *Granholm v. Heald*, 544 U.S. 460 (2005) consolidating *Granholm v. Heald*, 03-1116; *Mich. Beer & Wine Wholesalers Ass'n v. Heald*, 03-1120; and *Swedenburg v. Kelly*, 03-1274.

[49] Alexandria Sage, "Amazon to Sell U.S. Wine Online: Vintners," Reuters wire service report, September 11, 2008.

[50] Pete Yost, "Justices Skeptical of Maine Tobacco Law," Associated Press wire service report, November 28, 2007.

[51] Declan McCullagh, "Supreme Court Strikes down Law Targeting Online Cigarette Sales," CNET News.com, February 20, 2008.

[52] *Rowe v. N.H. Motor Transp. Ass'n*, 552 U.S. 364 (2008).

[53] *Hemi Grp., LLC v. City of New York*, 559 U.S. __ (2010). Newly-appointed Justice Sonia Sotomayor did not participate in the case because she had been a member of the Second Circuit panel that issued an earlier ruling in the case.

[54] Under the Jenkins Act, 15 U.S.C. § 376, an out-of-state retailer must report cigarette sales to state tax authorities, who can then collect the state use tax from the buyers, who remain liable for the tax regardless of where the purchase was made.

[55] The Racketeer Influenced and Corrupt Organizations Act ("RICO") is a fraud statute that allows treble (triple) damages to be awarded. New York City alleged Hemi's failure to file reports about who was buying cigarettes online was fraud and constituted a "predicate act" under RICO that caused the city to lose tens of millions of dollars in cigarette taxes.

[56] *City of New York v. Cyco.net, Inc.*, Dkt. No. 06-1665-cv(L) (N.Y. Ct. App. 2008). New York City sued 35 online cigarette sellers under civil RICO based on failure to file Jenkins Act reports. A federal district court dismissed the RICO claim, *City of New York v. Cyco.net, Inc.*, 383 F. Supp. 2d 526 (S.D.N.Y. 2005), but the Second Circuit reversed on appeal, *City of New York v. Smoke-Spirits.com, Inc.*, 541 F.3d 425 (2ᵈ Cir. 2008).

[57] *United States v. Schaefer*, 501 F.3d 1197 (10ᵗʰ Cir. 2007).

[58] *Ibid.*

[59] *United States v. Carroll*, 105 F.3d 740 (1ˢᵗ Cir. 1997), cert. denied, 520 U.S. 1258 (1997).

[60] *United States v. MacEwan*, 445 F.3d 237 (3ᵈ Cir. 2006), cert. denied, 549 U.S. 882 (2006).

[61] *United States v. Runyan*, 290 F.3d 223 (5ᵗʰ Cir. 2002), cert. denied, 537 U.S. 888 (2002).

[62] *Quill v. North Dakota*, 504 U.S. 298 (1992), holding states only have taxing jurisdiction over out-of-state sellers who have a sufficient physical nexus (contact or presence) within the state, finding in the specific case sending mail-order catalogs into a state did not constitute such a nexus.

[63] "Appeals Court: Borders Must Pay Online Sales Tax," Associated Press wire service report, June 14, 2005.

[64] The state estimated the tax would bring in $50 million in its first fiscal year and $73 million in 2009-2010.

[65] Affiliate programs allow a Web site owner or blogger to place a link on his site, or design an entire site as a storefront with multiple links, so when a customer clicks on the product link he is brought to the online retailer's site to complete the purchase, whereupon the retailer bills the customer, ships the product, and sends a commission to the referring site owner.

[66] *Amazon.com v. N.Y. State Dept. of Taxation & Fin.*, 877 N.Y.S.2d 842 (N.Y. Sup. Ct. 2009); *Overstock.com, Inc. v. N.Y. State Dept. of Taxation & Fin.*, No. 107581-08 (N.Y. Sup. Ct. 2008).

[67] "Judge Tosses Amazon Challenge to NYS Tax," Publishers Weekly, January 13, 2009.

[68] Declan McCullagh, "N.Y. Appeals Court Revives Amazon's Sales Tax Suit," CNET News.com, November 4, 2010.

[69] Lance Whitney, "Amazon Cuts Affiliate Ties in More States over Taxes," CNET News.com, June 13, 2011.

[70] *City of Chicago v. StubHub, Inc.*, 622 F. Supp. 2d 699 (N.D. Ill. 2009).

[71] Declan McCullagh, "Amazon Fights Demand for Customer Records," CNET News.com, April 19, 2010.

[72] *Tattered Cover, Inc. v. City of Thornton*, 44 P.3d 1044 (Colo. Sup. Ct. 2002).

[73] The Video Privacy Protection Act (18 U.S.C. 2710) makes it illegal to disclose what videotapes an individual has rented, unless given informed, written consent at the time the disclosure is sought.

[74] *Amazon.com, LLC v. Lay*, Case No. C10-664 MJP (W.D. Wash. 2010).

[75] "Arkansas Joins States to Push for Internet Tax," Associated Press wire service report, July 30, 2007.

[76] Stefanie Olsen, "Friendster Fires Developer for Blog," CNET News.com, August 31, 2004.

[77] Sam Favate, "Can Job Applicants Be Asked For Facebook Passwords?" The Wall Street Journal Law Blog, March 21, 2012.

[78] Facebook statement, *available at* https://www.facebook.com/notes/facebook-and-privacy/protecting-your-passwords-and-your-privacy/326598317390057 (accessed March 23, 2012).

[79] Joyce Park's blog entry, *available at* http://troutgirl.wordpress.com/2004/06 (accessed Mar. 23, 2012).

[80] David Becker, "Microsoft Photo Prompts Blogger's Regret," CNET News.com, November 3, 2003. Hanscom's version of the incident is on his blog *available at* www.michaelhanscom.com/eclecticism/2003/10/of_blogging_and.html (accessed Mar. 23, 2012).

[81] Time Magazine, December 19, 2004.

[82] Evan Hansen, "Google Blogger: 'I Was Terminated,'" CNET News.com, February 11, 2005.

[83] Amy Joyce, "Free Expression Can be Costly when Bloggers Bad-Mouth Jobs," The Washington Post, p. A01, February 11, 2005.

[84] *Ibid.*

[85] Julie Moult, "Woman 'Sacked' on Facebook for Complaining about Her Boss after Forgetting She Had Added Him as a Friend," (U.K.) Daily Mail, August 14, 2009, *available at* www.dailymail.co.uk/news/article-1206491/Woman-sacked-Facebook-boss-insult-forgetting-added-friend.html#ixzz1jERi8Ixe (accessed Mar. 23, 2012) and the actual post is *available at* http://i.huffpost.com/gadgets/slideshows/8636/slide_8636_117689_large.jpg?1326343899388 (accessed Mar. 23, 2012).

[86] Joyce, fn. 83, *supra.*

[87] David E. Kaplan, "Hey, Let's Play Ball," U.S. News & World Report, October 29, 2006.

[88] Noam Cohen, "Delaying News in the Era of the Internet," The New York Times, June 23, 2008.

[89] The National Labor Relations Act, 29 U.S.C. § 157.

[90] *Am. Med. Response of Conn.*, NLRB No. 34-CA-12576 (Oct. 27, 2010).

[91] *Hispanics United of Buffalo, Inc. v. Ortiz*, Case No. 3-CA-27872 (Sept. 2, 2011).

[92] "Administrative Law Judge Finds New York Nonprofit Unlawfully Discharged Employees Following Facebook Posts," NLRB Press Release, September 6, 2011.

[93] *Karl Knaux Motors, Inc. d/b/a Knauz BMW & Robert Becker*, Case No. 13-CA-46452 (Sept. 28, 2011).

[94] NLRB Advice Memorandum, Wal-Mart, Case No. 17-CA-25030 (Jul. 19, 2011).

[95] NLRB Advice Memorandum, Rural Metro, Case No. 25-CA-31802 (Jun. 29, 2011).

[96] "Teacher Criticized for Facebook Remarks on Gays," Associated Press wire service report, October 13, 2011.

[97] *Tinker v. Des Moines Indep. Cmty. Sch. Dist.*, 393 U.S. 503, 506 (1969).

[98] Joyce, fn. 83, *supra.*

[99] "College Sued over 'Drunken Pirate' Sanctions: Woman Claims Teaching Degree Denied Because of Single MySpace Photo," TheSmokingGun.com, April 26, 2007 *available at* www.thesmokinggun.com/archive/years/2007/0426072pirate1.html (accessed Mar. 23, 2012); *see also* Anita Ramasastry, "Can Universities Take Adverse Actions against Students Based on Their MySpace Profiles? It Depends in Part on Whether the University Followed Its Own Code of Conduct," FindLaw.com, May 4, 2007. The "Drunken Pirate" photograph can be viewed at http://i.cdn.turner.com/trutv/thesmokinggun.com/graphics/art3/0426072pirate1.jpg (accessed Mar. 23, 2012).

[100] *Snyder v. Millersville Univ.*, No. 07-1660 (E.D. Pa. 2008).

[101] *Ibid.*

[102] Complaint, *Snyder v. Millersville Univ.*, Case No. 2:2007-cv-01660 (E.D. Pa. filed Apr. 25, 2007) *was available at* http://casedocs.justia.com/pennsylvania/paedce/2:2007cv01660/228127/1/0.pdf (accessed July 23, 2010) but no longer available.

[103] *Snyder v. Millersville Univ.*, fn. 100, *supra.*

[104] Complaint, *Snyder v. Millersville Univ.*, fn. 102, *supra.*

[105] *Ibid.*

[106] Government employees have a First Amendment right to speak on issues of public concern and cannot be fired for doing so. *See Pickering v. Bd. of Educ.*, 391 U.S. 563 (1968), where a teacher was fired after writing a letter to a local newspaper critical of the board of education and the district superintendent. However, the First Amendment does not protect statements made by public employees pursuant to their official duties.

*See Garcetti v. Ceballos*, 547 U.S. 410 (2006), where a district attorney claimed he had been passed up for a promotion for criticizing a warrant's legitimacy, the Court ruled 5–to–4 the First Amendment did not protect his speech because his statements were made pursuant to his position as a public employee, and not as a private citizen.

[107] *Snyder v. Millersville Univ.*, fn. 100, *supra*.

[108] Jeffrey Rosen, "The Web Means the End of Forgetting," The New York Times, July 21, 2010.

[109] *Ibid.*

# CHAPTER

# 20

## WEB CONTRACTS

> This chapter explores basic principles of contract law, online contracts, legal capacity to contract, online signatures, sales contracts, Web site user agreements, and Web site development contracts.

*"A verbal contract isn't worth the paper it's printed on."* — Sam Goldwyn

I N THIS CHAPTER WE will discuss common contracts one might find on the Web, who has or lacks the legal capacity to be bound by a contract, and what constitutes a "signature" online. Two common forms of contracts encountered online are Web site user agreements and sales contracts to make an online purchase, which often take the form of click-wrap or browse-wrap agreements.

## Basic Principles of Contract Law

In the United States, contract law follows the **Objective Theory of Contracts**, which means an offer exists if a reasonable man would have believed the offeror's objective manifestations of intent (*i.e.*, his outward behavior by words and actions) constituted an offer. The offeror's subjective intent (*e.g.*, he was joking and did not intend to enter into a contract) is irrelevant. Courts do not look at whether an offer is fair or reasonable — only whether a reasonable man could have found it to exist. The elements necessary to form a contract are: (1) an *offer*, (2) *acceptance*, and (3) *consideration* (*i.e.*, an act or a promise to do or give up something of value). The contract must be for a lawful purpose and not violate public policy. Its terms must be certain and definite, and the parties must negotiate the contract in good faith.

If an offer is terminated before acceptance, then no contract has been formed. Offers may be terminated by: express expiration date; implied (*i.e.*, reasonable) expiration date; death or mental incapacity before acceptance;[1] offeror's revocation; offeree's rejection; destruction of the contract's subject matter; or supervening illegality (*i.e.*, enactment of a statute making the contract illegal). A counteroffer is a rejection and terminates the offer.

Once a contract is formed, a later counter-offer, if accepted, may be deemed a *modification* of the agreement. A district court in Florida held an instant message conversation between an employee of CX Digital, an online advertising lead provider, and the vice president of marketing at Smoking Everywhere, an online cigarette seller, constituted a modification of the companies' agreement, which contained a "no-oral modification clause."[2] The relevant chat session was:[3]

> pedramcx (2:49:45 PM): A few of our big guys are really excited about the new page and they're ready to run it
>
> pedramcx (2:50:08 PM): We can do 2000 orders/day by Friday if I have your blessing
>
> pedramcx (2:52:13 PM): those 2000 leads are going to be generated by our best affiliate and he's legit
>
> nicktouris is available (3:42:42 PM): I am away from my computer right now.
>
> pedramcx (4:07:57 PM): And I want the AOR when we make your offer #1 on the network
>
> nicktouris (4:43:09 PM): NO LIMIT
>
> pedramcx (4:43:21 PM): awesome!

The court found CX's suggestion of a 2000 sale per day limit was an offer of a new contract term. Smoking Everywhere's response of "NO LIMIT", the court held, was a counter-offer suggesting a new term, differing from the original offer and CX's response "awesome!" was an acceptance of this counter-offer.

A *bilateral contract* is one where the offeror gives a promise and the offeree accepts by giving a requested return promise (*i.e.*, promissory acceptance). A *unilateral contract* is a one where the offeror gives a promise and the offeree accepts by making the actual performance (*i.e.*, performance acceptance); it becomes irrevocable once performance has begun; but, it must be actual performance, not just preparations for performance.

A contract may be *implied-in-fact* where certain acts by the offeree act as acceptance, *i.e.*, the parties use conduct instead of words to form the contract. For example, a passenger who enters a taxi and arrives at his destination will have made an implied promise to pay the fare, even if no words were spoken. This is as an exception to the general rule silence does not act as acceptance of an offer.[4]

There must be consideration for the contract. *Consideration* is a bargained for exchange; a mutuality of promises. But some promises do not constitute valid consideration. An *illusory promise* — where the promissor has not obligated himself to perform, *i.e.*, one party receives only what the other was already obligated to provide — is a type of promise that is not good consideration. A second type would be a donative promise (*i.e.*, a gift) because the consideration is not mutual on the recipient's part. However, if the recipient were to bargain for the gift — by giving up a legal right or claim — such forbearance would be valid consideration, creating a mutuality of promises.[5] A third type would be a moral pressure promise — moral obligation is not sufficient consideration to support an express promise, absent a pre-existing duty.[6] Adequacy of consideration is irrelevant as long as not nominal; promises supported only by nominal (*i.e.*, token) consideration are unenforceable. There is one circumstance when consideration is unnecessary for a valid contract: promises that foreseeably induce detrimental reliance are enforceable without consideration — this is known as the doctrine of **promissory estoppel**.

An Oregon woman's ex-boyfriend created several fake Yahoo! profiles of her and posted her nude photos onto them. Then, he logged onto Yahoo! chat and pretended to be her, directing men to the fake profiles and soliciting them for sex. Several showed up at her office. She repeatedly asked Yahoo! to remove the profiles, but it delayed for months, until a local news program prepared to broadcast a report on the incident. Yahoo!'s director of communications called the woman and promised she would "personally walk the statements over to the division responsible for stopping unauthorized profiles and they would take care of it."[7] The woman relied on this promise and took no further action. The profiles remained online for two more months, until she sued Yahoo! for breach of contract. The court dismissed the case, but on appeal, the Ninth Circuit reinstated the breach of contract claim. It held because she had relied on a promise by a Yahoo! employee the photos and profiles would be taken down, she could state a breach of contract claim under the theory of promissory estoppel. The court said:[8]

> Contract liability here would come not from Yahoo!'s publishing conduct,
> but from Yahoo!'s manifest intention to be legally obligated to do something,
> which happens to be removal of material from publication.

Craigslist was also held liable under the legal theory of promissory estoppel for failing to keep its representatives' promises to remove a series of harassing fake posts and "take care of it", thereby denying Craigslist **CDA** § 230 immunity. [9]

If a contract is not well-drafted, *ambiguity* may arise. Then, the court will first look to the contract's definitions clause to see if the ambiguous term has been defined by the parties. If not defined, the court may apply the *Plain Meaning Rule*, a rule of interpretation where courts give words their ordinary or natural meaning. It may also look to trade or industry usage to see how the phrase is defined, if both parties are merchants in a common industry. The general common law rule is ambiguities in a contract are construed against the drafter of the contract.

Except as required by the Statute of Frauds, discussed below, oral contracts are valid, but it is difficult to prove their terms. Therefore, most people follow the adage, "Get it in writing." The parties' verbal agreement *is* the contract; the writing is merely the memorialization of that agreement. The written contract will usually contain an "*integration*" or "*merger*" clause stating the parties' entire agreement is contained within the document. This is because the common law *Parol Evidence Rule* bars extrinsic evidence of any prior agreements between the parties to contradict or supplement the integrated writing; however, extrinsic evidence is admissible to attack formation of the contract, by showing fraud, illegality, duress, mistake, or lack of consideration. Conversely, the contract may also incorporate by reference another document into the agreement. But one Florida case has held a written contract stating it "was subject to" an online User Agreement posted on the party's Web site was an insufficient expression of intent to incorporate the User Agreement into the contract. [10]

Contracts may contain conditions, which can be either express or implied. A *condition precedent* is where a stated event must occur before performance is due. A *condition subsequent* is where performance has already begun and the stated event cuts off that performance. Conditions may be implied-in-fact—meaning the court will assume the parties intended such conditions, even if not expressed in the contract; or implied-in-law—meaning the court will imply certain conditions as a matter of public policy.

## Affirmative Defenses

A party sued for breach of contract may raise three types of defenses: (1) there was no contract formed; (2) a contract was formed, but is unenforceable; or (3) a contract was formed, but the duty of performance has been discharged.

To attack a contract's existence or formation, the defendant must show either: (1) *indefiniteness* (*i.e.*, essential material terms were missing from the contract preventing the party from understanding his obligations)[11] or (2) *mistake.* The mistake may be a mutual mistake as to a material fact, in which case no contract has actually been formed and the parties are entitled to rescission (cancellation of the contract); or it may be a unilateral mistake on the part of one party, in which case most courts would not allow rescission.[12] If there is ambiguity or misunderstanding, *i.e.*, where the parties have two entirely different, but equally reasonable, interpretations of an ambiguous material term, then the court will find no contract was formed because there was no "*meeting of the minds.*"

A contract may have been formed but there are circumstances where courts will not enforce it due to *public policy.* Seven such affirmative defenses are:

- **Duress.** Where a party has been compelled by threat to enter into the contract. The threat can be of physical, emotional (*e.g.*, blackmail), or economic harm. For example, a dentist, apparently wary of consumer gripe sites, insisted a patient sign a privacy agreement before he would treat a painful infected cavity. The contract prohibited the patient from publishing comments about the dentist's work and assigned copyright to any commentary he might make to the dentist.[13] The patient paid the dentist, but he allegedly refused to send copies of his records for insurance reimbursement. This led the patient to post negative reviews on Yelp.com and DoctorBase.com. The dentist responded by billing the patient $100 for each day the reviews were online and threatened to sue for breach of contract. The patient claimed the privacy agreement was misleading, a breach of medical ethics and invalid under state law.[14] While parties may contract to almost anything not illegal (with some exceptions, noted below), there are reasons why a court might not uphold such an agreement.[15] In this case, the defense of duress springs to mind. When a patient is suffering extreme pain in his dentist's office, he is unlikely to risk being unable to find another dentist available to see him without waiting days for an appointment and may have no choice but to sign the contract.[16]

- **Undue Influence**. Where one party abuses a fiduciary relationship of trust and confidence to persuade the other to enter into the contract.

- **Fraud.** Where one party uses deceit to compel the other to enter into the contract. Fraud may take the form of misrepresentation (a false statement of fact with intent to deceive), concealment (where one party takes active steps to cover up information he is legally obligated to reveal or not withhold), or nondisclosure (where one party passively does not disclose information he has a duty to disclose).

- **Capacity.** Where one party lacks legal capacity, the contract is *voidable* at option of the incapacitated party. Mentally disabled individuals and minors (children under the state-defined age of majority, *i.e.*, 18 in most states)[17] lack legal capacity to contract. A contract with a minor is unenforceable by the other party and *voidable at the minor's option.* As long as the minor does not cancel the contract, it is *binding on the other party.* Though a minor may cancel a contract, he cannot be unjustly enriched by the ability to cancel it. So, if a minor makes a purchase and cancels the contract, he must return anything received under the contract. But, in at least one case, minors were held to the terms of an online contract. The minors entered into a click-wrap agreement with the defendant, a plagiarism checking site, but later sought to void the contract based on their minority. The court rejected their argument, as minors, they were not bound by the site's Terms of Use agreement. It ruled, having accepted the benefits of the agreement, the minors could not avoid their contractual obligations. [18]

- **Illegality.** Where either the consideration or purpose is illegal, a contract will be deemed void and unenforceable. Contracts contrary to public policy are also void and unenforceable, even if they do not violate a statute.

- **Unconscionability.** Where a contract is so one-sided as to be extremely unfair, the court may remove the provision or invalidate the entire contract. Such contracts may be an *adhesion contract* (where one party uses his disproportionate bargaining position to write the contract to his advantage — usually a standardized form offered on a take-it-or-leave-it basis); an *exculpatory clause* (a provision releasing a party from liability caused by his own wrongdoing or negligence); or *disclaimers and warranties* seeking to limit damages from defective products to replacement of the product.

- **The Statute of Frauds.** Where the *Statute of Frauds* requires a contract be in writing, an oral contract (or written contract that fails to meet its requirements) will be unenforceable. The Statute of Frauds requires a written agreement for suretyships; transfers of an interest in land; [19] contracts that cannot possibly be performed within one year; contracts in consideration of marriage; and the sale of goods in excess of $500. Even where there is a writing, it must meet the Statute's requirements: it must be signed by "the party to be charged" (*i.e.*, obligated party) and show evidence of the essential contract terms (*e.g.*, parties, subject matter, price, quantity, and terms). Noncompliance may be excused if there is material partial performance or a party's detrimental reliance on the other party caused the failure to put the agreement in writing.

Parties to a contract either perform or breach their duties, but in certain instances the duty of performance may be discharged. Such circumstances may arise due to:

- **Agreement of the Parties.** The parties may agree to substitute different parties (*i.e.*, novation) or different performance (*i.e.*, accord and satisfaction), or cancel the contract if no performance has yet occurred (*i.e.*, rescission).

- **Operation of Law.** A bankruptcy court-granted discharge, the statute of limitations, or a supervening illegality will discharge a party's duty of performance.

- **Impossibility of Performance.** An unforeseeable event — such as destruction of the contract's subject matter [20] or failure of an exclusive source of supply — that makes performance impossible will discharge a party's duty of performance.

- **Frustration of Purpose.** A change in circumstances or an intervening event may result in the contract no longer being able to be carried out for the essential purpose for which it was entered into. [21]

## Remedies

When a contract is breached, the nonbreaching party will turn to the court to remedy that breach. Courts may grant either equitable or legal remedies. *Equitable remedies* may take the form of rescission of the contract, restoring the parties to their original positions prior to contract's formation; reformation of the contract (*i.e.*, where the court rewrites an inaccurate written contract to conform with what was proven to be the accurate oral agreement); a declaratory judgment to determine the rights and responsibilities of the parties; an injunction, such as a covenant not to compete; or specific performance to compel a party to execute a contract according to its precise terms. *Legal remedies* usually take the form of money damages and fall into three categories: expectation damages, reliance damages, and restitution. Expectation damages give the plaintiff what he expected to receive financially from the contract. Reliance damages are granted in place of expectation damages and reimburse the plaintiff for out-of-pocket costs caused by his reliance on the defendant. Reliance damages are available even when there is no contract but the plaintiff has incurred expenses (*e.g.*, in preliminary negotiations) foreseeable and due to his detrimental reliance on the defendant. Restitution, also granted in place of expectation damages, is the recovery of the value to the defendant of the plaintiff's performance to prevent unjust enrichment of the plaintiff.

Often, when a contract is formed, parties may contemplate a specific dollar amount as damages for breach. Such remedies agreed on in advance are called **liquidated damages**. Courts will enforce a liquidated damages clause only if it is not a penalty, *i.e.*, if it attempts to estimate actual damages rather than penalize a breaching party by awarding more than actually suffered.

### Assignment and Delegation

*Assignment* is the transfer by a party of some or all rights under the contract. After an assignment, the assignor no longer has any claim to those rights he has assigned. *Delegation* is the transfer by a party of duties under the contract. After a delegation of duties, the delegating party remains secondarily liable for the performance of those duties. All contracts are assignable, unless the assignment:

- Materially alters the duty (*e.g.*, personal services contracts where there is a relationship of trust and confidence between the parties)
- Materially varies the risk (*e.g.*, contracts for insurance or extension of credit because the proposed party may be a greater coverage or credit risk)
- Impairs the chance to obtain return performance; *e.g.*, where the expected benefit of the contract was the ability to claim one worked with a prestigious individual or firm and the assignment is to a lesser or unprestigious individual or firm

All contracts can be delegated, unless a party has a substantial interest in having the other perform because of that party's particular skills (*e.g.*, doctor, artist) or because it is a personal services contract (*e.g.*, employment or independent contractors with special skills). As discussed, the delegant remains liable for obligations under the contract after delegation; the only way out of liability is a novation, where the parties make a new contract. Assignments are fully revocable; however, most state statutes make written assignments irrevocable. No consideration is required for an assignment, but if given, the assignment becomes irrevocable. Parties may put a nonassignment clause in the contract. If a party breaches it, he will be liable for damages, but the assignment to a third-party will be upheld, unless the nonassignment clause conditions the entire contract on nonassignability.

## Electronic Signatures

For centuries, a contract signing involved two people passing a pen to sign their names on a sheet of paper. Advances in technology have eliminated the necessity of both pen and paper, but the law has been slow to catch up with technology. As late as 1996, a court refused to accept the validity of a faxed signature on a legal document. In *Georgia Dept. of Transportation v. Norris*, Norris sought to sue the state department of transportation, after his wife was killed in an accident on what he claimed was a poorly maintained highway intersection.[22] Before he could sue, he was required to file a notice of claim in writing with the transportation department. He faxed it within the specified time and followed up with a mailed notice that arrived a day after the deadline. The court held he did not satisfy the notice requirement because, though the faxed notice was received in time, *"the transmission of beeps and chirps along a telephone line is not a writing."* The Georgia Supreme Court reversed, on grounds unrelated to whether a fax is a writing. The case, derisively known as the "beeps and chirps" case, highlights the difficulty courts have applying new technologies to traditional legal transactions.

### The Uniform Electronic Transactions Act (UETA)

The **Uniform Electronic Transactions Act** (UETA) is a model statute for states to adopt. A state's version may contain significant state-specific variations. To date, 46 states and the District of Columbia have adopted it. The Act provides "a record or signature may not be denied legal effect or enforceability solely because it is in electronic form." The **UETA** does not apply to wills.

### The E-SIGN Act

Congress enacted the **Electronic Signatures in Global and National Commerce Act** (the E-SIGN Act) in 2000.[23] It provides legal validity to contracts entered into electronically. The **E-SIGN Act** does not replace the **UETA**; it specifically states in any state that has adopted the **UETA**, the **E-SIGN Act** is preempted. It applies to e-mails, PDF documents, and encrypted digital signatures, but not to wills, family law (*e.g.*, adoption, divorce) documents, court documents, cancellation of utilities or health insurance, public recalls, or notices of default, repossession, foreclosure, or eviction. Under the Act, if another law requires written information to consumers, then they must affirmatively consent to receiving the electronic version. The **E-SIGN Act** does not apply to intrastate transactions that do not affect interstate or foreign commerce. The actual electronic "signature" can be either a scanned version of the signer's signature, the signer's name typed into the signature space, the clicking of an "I Accept" button, or a signature sent through encryption.

### E-mails as a Signed Writing

A New York appellate court ruled a series of e-mails between the parties proposing and accepting an employment contract modification were "signed writings" within the meaning of the Statute of Frauds. Under the *Doctrine of Integration*, a series of documents can be combined if they are "reasonably related." The court said the e-mails were within the Statute of Frauds because both parties' names appeared at the end of their respective e-mails, signifying their intent to authenticate the writing's contents.[24]

## Terms of Use Agreements

Almost all Web sites post some form of "Terms of Use" or "Terms of Service".[25] Since their primary purpose is to shield site owners from suits for copyright infringement, defamation, invasion of privacy, or other causes of action, their agreements contain many exculpatory clauses, disclaimers, and waivers of liability. A secondary purpose is to protect intellectual property rights — site owners do not want visitors infringing on their copyrighted material. A third purpose is to disclose how visitors' personally identifiable information is collected and retained: what collection methods are used; whether it is personally identifiable information or aggregate data; how long it is retained; how it is safeguarded; and with whom it is shared.[26] For e-commerce sites, one purpose is to provide terms of sale for products, accepted payment forms, how the product is shipped and which carriers are used, which countries the seller will ship to, what happens in event of damaged or missing shipments, how disputes are resolved, and similar transactional issues. Where a site holds itself out as a club, group, or organization, the agreement's purpose will include: if a social network, terms for acceptable behavior by members toward each other and what they may not post to their, or other members', pages; if an e-commerce site where users pay to use its services in exchange for membership benefits: the fee structure, terms and length of membership, rules of conduct, and benefits to be received. Such benefits may be the right to rent or purchase specific products, such as video rentals, or an online "Book of the Month" club; or the right to use a service provided exclusively for paid members, such as a dating or auction listing site, where the membership fee entitles members to interact and transact with other members.

Most online contracts take the form of click-wrap or browse-wrap agreements, where the terms are essentially offered on a "take-it-or-leave-it" basis, and assent is expressed by some action or inaction other than a handwritten signature. This raises issues as to the validity of these contracts; how assent may be legally expressed; how online agreements may be modified, what notice must be provided, and how notice should be provided; and what constitutes acceptance. As unilateral contracts, they raise concerns relating to adhesion contracts: unconscionable clauses; illusory promises; and unfair, one-sided provisions inserted by a party with superior bargaining power. Many Terms of Use agreements are buried deep within the Web site, where the visitor may never see them, or may not stumble on them until he has already used the site. Many are extremely long, difficult to comprehend, especially if written in legalese or using common phrases ascribed a different meaning (*e.g.*, "terms of art" — phrases given a special meaning in a particular context), or displayed in small scroll-down windows that require readers to maneuver a scroll bar while reading a document that may be more than 100 pages long within a small box on their screen.[27]

## Privacy Policies

Unlike the European Union, under current law, the United States does not require Web firms to explain their data collection or retention policies, unless they choose to have a privacy policy.[28] Companies can and do use personal information collected without consent (except in the case of children under age 13, where **COPPA** requires parental consent to collect personal information from children).[29] The greatest restriction on a firm's data collection is not the law, but its own privacy policy. Web visitors want assurance a site will not promise to use their collected personal information for a stated purpose but later market it to other companies. Some sites are legally required to post privacy policies, such as those collecting information from California residents (California requires any commercial site or online service operator collecting personally identifiable information from California residents to provide notice of its privacy policies); children under 13 (under **COPPA** requirements); or

European Union visitors (in compliance with the EU Data Protection Directive). [30] A privacy policy should disclose its policy regarding, and use of, behavioral marketing, including deep packet inspection. Privacy policies are discussed in-depth in Chapter 10, which covers why firms choose to have a one; how they are bound by it; what it should contain; and how it discloses the firm's behavioral marketing procedures.

## Membership Agreements

Certain Web sites market exclusive access to products or services based on payment of a membership fee. The service may involve facilitating access to other members for the purpose of conducting mutual social or business transactions, such as a dating site like Match.com, a video rental site like NetFlix or Blockbuster Online, or an auction listing site like eBay, where members pay to list items for auction or sale. In these situations, there is an obvious mutual exchange of consideration, *i.e.*, one party is giving money and the other is providing a service.

## Shrink-wrap Agreements

Agreements printed on back of, or inside, a commercial computer software box are *shrink-wrap agreements*. By breaking the package's cellophane shrink-wrap, a buyer agrees to be bound by the agreement's terms. Shrink-wrap agreements are controversial, especially if inside the box and not visible until after the purchase has been made and the box opened, as the purchaser is agreeing to terms he is unable to read, and the only way he can read them is to break the seal, automatically consenting to them. The Seventh Circuit has held a shrink-wrap agreement valid where there was a notice on the box with terms inside and a right to return it if the terms are unacceptable to the purchaser. [31]

## Click-wrap Agreements

Web users are increasingly encountering *click-wrap agreements*, where they must click a link or button indicating acceptance of the terms to proceed. Most click-wrap agreements are legally binding, even if the terms were not read, so long as terms were available to be read. A federal district court in Pennsylvania ruled a click-wrap agreement enforceable though the plaintiff claimed he had never read the terms, because a "reasonably prudent Internet user" would have been on notice of the terms, which were of reasonable length and clearly presented in readable text despite being in a window that required scrolling, and the user was required to click an "I agree" button to assent. [32] An Illinois court found a click-wrap agreement valid even when its terms were not prominently displayed, as long as the party had an opportunity to review them by clicking on an adjacent link. [33] However, a federal district court in California held PayPal's arbitration clause in its User Agreement unconscionable because it was not visible to customers prior to signing up for Paypal's services, even though accessible through a link on the same page as the "I Agree" button. [34]

But the trend is to find users bound to the terms, even if they accessed the site without authorization, using someone else's account, or if another party accessed the site using their account. A federal district court held an AOL customer's stepson who used his account without seeing or agreeing to AOL's Terms of Service was nonetheless bound by them as a sublicensee of the customer. [35] Other courts have also held an unauthorized user of a Web site consents to its Terms of Use agreement, even when the user is "borrowing" another person's account or subscription. When a travel Web site was sued for misrepresentation by a user, the site invoked the forum selection clause in its Terms of Use. The plaintiff claimed he never read it because a prior user in his office might have accessed the site and clicked past it. The court ruled he was still bound by the forum selection clause in the site's Terms of Use agreement. [36] Where two unauthorized users of an online real estate database accessed it using someone else's user name and password, the court ruled they were nonetheless bound by the Terms of Use forum selection clause. [37]

One federal district court has gone as far as to hold a party's repeated and automated use of a Web site could allow imputing knowledge of, and binding her to, the site's Terms of Use agreement. [38] However, in _Scarcella v. America Online, Inc._, a New York City court invalidated a choice of forum clause in AOL's click-wrap agreement. [39] The plaintiff argued the 91-page agreement was deceptive because it featured two "O.K., I agree" buttons midway through which, when clicked, allowed customers to "sign" the agreement before reaching its end. The court appeared to accept the argument, adding AOL might be seen as discouraging customers from reading the agreement by referring to it as "detailed" and "lengthy." But it did not go so far as to rule it a "deceptive practice". Instead, it ruled there was a strong public policy interest in providing access to a low cost, informal, local small claims forum rather than forcing the plaintiff to bear the expense of traveling to AOL's choice of forum in Virginia.

## Browse-wrap Agreements

Unlike a click-wrap agreement, a **browse-wrap agreement** is a contract a user may view online but need not do anything to indicate his acceptance. Most Terms of Use agreements (absent click-through boxes) fall into this category. [40] Although hard to see how this would be considered a valid contract, since one party to be bound has not consented by any affirmative act, some courts, notably the Second Circuit, have upheld browse-wrap agreements as legally binding. [41] The majority take the opposing view. [42] The logic of a browse-wrap agreement is similar to your neighbor saying, "If you walk past my house, you agree to pay me $200." If you then walk past his house, would he be entitled to collect $200 from you? Does the act of walking past his house indicate an affirmative assent to a contract or the complete opposite, an act of defiance? A fundamental concept of contract law is there must be a clear "meeting of the minds" between the parties. In _Ticketmaster Corp. v. Tickets.com, Inc._, a California district court remarked "It cannot be said that merely putting the terms and conditions [on the bottom of the Web page] necessarily creates a contract with anyone using the Web site." [43]

## ISP Contracts

Internet Service Providers (ISPs) serve as gatekeepers to the Internet. Every Internet customer's access is conditioned on agreement to their "Acceptable Use Policies" or "Terms of Service", though most consumers do not bother to read them. ISP contracts often contain broad rights for ISPs and limited recourse for customers. Some rights ISPs have granted themselves in their contracts include the right to: read customer e-mails; [44] look at sites customers visit; block customers from visiting sites; [45] cancel customers' accounts for excessive bandwidth use;[46] and block traffic—thereby interfering with customers' ability to download files.[47] Most ISPs reserve the right to change their contracts at any time without notice, other than an update on their site.

Some ISP contractual rights are extremely broad—at one point, AT&T's contract reserved the right to block any activity causing the company "to be viewed unfavorably by others."[48] Presumably, most of these provisions are seldom enforced and exist to allow ISPs to deal with spammers, hackers, and malware uploaders. However, they do apply to anyone who contracts with the ISP. They are able to use these adhesion contracts because broadband consumers' choices are limited to the phone or cable companies.

## Notification of Changes

Companies must notify customers of changes they make to their contracts. Under contract law principles, a unilateral change to a contract is not binding but results in the revised contract becoming an offer. The other party must then be notified so she can accept or reject this offer; on assent to the new terms, it becomes a binding agreement.

Is posting contract changes on a company's site adequate notice? One case illustrates the issue of what constitutes proper notice. The plaintiff had contracted for phone service through a division of AOL subsequently acquired by Talk America, Inc. After the acquisition, Talk America made several important changes to the contract (a price increase, an arbitration clause, a class-action suit waiver, and choice-of-law provision pointing to New York law). It posted these changes on its site, but did not send any notification directly to individual customers. After using the service for four years, the plaintiff became aware of the changes and sued Talk America. The trial court ruled, pursuant to the revised contract, the case had to go to arbitration, but the Ninth Circuit reversed, holding companies cannot change their contracts without first notifying customers and posting revisions online was not sufficient notification.[49] The court stated: "Parties to a contract have no obligation to check the terms on a periodic basis to learn whether they have been changed by the other side."[50]

## Unilateral Contracts

A 2009 federal district court decision may have enormous implications for online contracts. A Dallas, Texas resident sued Blockbuster, as lead plaintiff in a class action over the video firm sharing members' film rental or purchase history with Facebook, in violation of the **Video Privacy Protection Act**.[51] Forty-four affiliate sites participated in Facebook's Beacon marketing program, including Blockbuster.com. Affiliates placed a JavaScript code supplied by Facebook on their sites, which notified Facebook whenever an affiliate's customer bought or rented an item (*e.g.*, books, movies, movie tickets, jewelry, games).[52] This personally identifiable information was automatically posted as a news feed to all the Facebook users' friends on the social network.[53] Beacon was set up as an "opt-out" program, where Facebook members had to take affirmative steps not to be included.

Seeking to dismiss the class action, Blockbuster moved to compel arbitration, consistent with the arbitration clause in its online Terms of Use. As a registered Blockbuster.com site user, the plaintiff had to assent to its Terms of Use agreement by clicking a check box. An agreement clause gave Blockbuster the right to modify its terms "at any time, and at its sole discretion." Like most, if not all, click-wrap agreements, it sought to bind users who cannot negotiate terms (*e.g.*, an adhesion contract) and may contain disadvantageous and unfair, if not unconscionable, terms. While courts have generally upheld click-wrap contracts, they typically invalidated them in four instances:

- Unconscionable terms
- Lack of any evidence of assent (as with browse-wrap agreements, or lack of "click through" check boxes)[54]
- Terms not posted in a conspicuous manner[55]
- Lack of notice of changed terms[56]

Here, the court said it need not address the issue of unconscionability alleged by the plaintiff, because the fact the clause was unilaterally modifiable by Blockbuster made it illusory and hence unenforceable. Recall under contract law, both parties must promise something of value (*i.e.*, "consideration"). Where one's promise does not actually bind that party (*e.g.*, a promise depending solely on the promisor's whim), it is an *illusory promise*, and cannot serve as sufficient consideration. By retaining the right to unilaterally modify or remove the arbitration clause, Blockbuster had promised nothing of value:[57]

> There is nothing in the Terms and Conditions that prevents Blockbuster from unilaterally changing any part of the contract other than providing that such changes will not take effect until posted on the website.

While the decision applied only to Blockbuster's arbitration clause, its logic would extend to the entire contract. Under this reasoning, any online contract stating one party can unilaterally change its terms merely by placing notice of such changes on its Web site is an illusory contract.[58] The ruling's implications are profound, since most Terms of Use agreements contains a clause granting the service provider a similar unilateral right of modification.[59]

## Web Site Development Agreements

A *Web site development agreement* is a contract between a Web designer[60] and her client regarding terms and conditions of the job. Many do not realize they do not own the intellectual property rights to a site created by a designer they hire. Recall from Chapter 2, the *creator* of a copyrightable work is deemed by law the copyright holder, absent a *work-made-for-hire* agreement or *assignment* of rights, so the designer becomes the copyright owner unless the contract states otherwise. A contract may define "developer content" and "company content" and assign rights to each. It may grant the client a license to use a copyrighted work, while the designer retains the copyright. If rights are not assigned to the company in the contract, it may end up with a limited license to use the site, preventing it from changing it without the developer's permission.

No matter how detailed the contract, a project is likely to evolve in unforeseen ways. The Web site development agreement should be drafted to cover foreseeable contingencies. Typical clauses found in the contract are:

- **Definitions clause** — sets out the clear meaning and intent of phrases used in the contract. This not only avoids confusion over what may appear to be clear, common terminology, but also enables parties to refer to the stated definitions as a sort of shorthand throughout the document.

- **Authorized Contact clause** — identifies the individual with the authority to approve work and authorize changes. This prevents a situation where different members of the company or organization give the Web designer conflicting instructions.
- **Liquidated Damages clause** — provides compensation to the designer in the event the client breaches the contract.
- **Limitation of Liability clause** — limits the designer's liability to refunding client fees paid if the designer fails to perform as promised.
- **Warranties and Indemnification clause** — where a designer assures the client the text and graphic elements used in constructing the site do not infringe on copyrights and the client warrants he owns the rights to any materials provided to the designer for inclusion in the site.
- **Copyright to Web Pages clause** — advises the client the designer, by law, is the copyright holder of the site she creates and provides for assignment of various rights between the designer and client. It may also spell out a copyright notice on the site in the client's name applies only to the client content and not the site design or designer content.
- **Web Site Credits and Links clause** — gives the client an opportunity to grant the designer permission to advertise the fact she created the site.
- **Disclaimer of Warranties clause** — provides the designer does not warrant against error-free site operation or infringement on third-party copyrights and limits the designer's liability to the fees paid by the client.
- **Client Representations and Warranties clause** — assures the designer the client has authority to contract on behalf of his company or organization; will obtain necessary rights or licenses for content provided; and will indemnify the designer for claims arising from use of such content.
- **Payment of Fees clause** — a description of the initial deposit and a schedule for payments to be made at specified dates or "milestones." Some designers may charge an hourly rate because of difficulty in determining how long a project may take to complete. It may call for a combination of fixed fees and a capped hourly rate.
- **Payment of Designer's Costs clause** — allows for reimbursement to the designer for out-of-pocket expenses, such as travel, phone calls, postage or overnight shipping, courier services, and monies advanced to subcontractors.
- **Timely Payment of Fees clause** — establishes penalties for late payments.
- **Initial Payment and Refund Policy clause** — allows the client a predetermined number of days to cancel the contract, provided the client pays for work done prior to cancellation.
- **Venue clause** — establishes where disputes will be litigated or arbitrated.
- **Sole Agreement clause** — states the entire agreement between the parties is embodied in the document and there are no other written or oral agreements.
- **Severability clause** — provides if any portion of the contract is deemed illegal or unenforceable, that portion will be stripped from it and the rest will be considered valid and enforceable.
- **Termination of Agreement Other Than by Performance clause** — provides if the client terminates the contract prior to successful completion, he will stop using and return any designer content and forfeit all rights and licenses under the contract. It may also accelerate the balance payable to become due immediately.
- **Authorization clause** — gives the designer permission to access the client's server to upload files and make changes to the site.

- **Subcontractor clause** — allows the designer to assign work on the project to subcontractors. The designer may need to bring in help to complete the project on time, or assist in areas requiring expertise outside the designer's skill set.
- **Conditional Upon Client Performance clause** — provides if the client's actions, or inactions (*e.g.*, failing to provide necessary content in a timely fashion) prevent, delay, or otherwise hinder the designer's efforts to complete the site within a certain time frame and for a certain price, then the designer reserves the right to adjust the quoted time frame or price accordingly.
- **Changes in Project Scope clause** — sets up a process where the client can request major changes (since the client's needs may change from the contract formation date) and the designer can evaluate the scope of the changes and advise the client if he is able to make them and, if so, any additional cost. The client can then accept or reject the designer's proposal.
- **Completion Date clause** — establishes a project completion date, with allowances for delays and provisions for "rush" jobs.

Obviously all contract terms are subject to negotiation between the parties. These examples are illustrative of issues that need to be addressed in a Web site development agreement; the specifics may vary from contract to contract.

## Chapter 20 Notes

[1] Certain events, such as death of a party or destruction of the contract's subject matter, after acceptance, may discharge performance.

[2] *CX Digital Media, Inc. v. Smoking Everywhere, Inc.*, No. 09-62020-Civ (S.D. Fla. Mar. 23, 2011).

[3] *Ibid.*

[4] Silence may also constitute acceptance where: an offeror has given an offeree reasonable belief it is; where a party silently receives the benefit of services and 1) had a reasonable opportunity to reject services and 2) knew or should have known the other party expected compensation; where the offeree solicits the offer and drafts the terms; where property sent on approval is kept (but this does not apply to unsolicited goods from strangers); and where there is a prior course of dealing between the parties.

[5] *See Hamer v. Sidway*, 27 N.E. 256 (1891) holding irrelevant an uncle's intent to give a gift to his nephew, since he had conditioned it on the nephew's promise to give up drinking and smoking — forbearance of a legal right is adequate consideration for a legal contract when no direct benefit is conferred because the condition was bargained for, *i.e.*, the uncle gave an offer and the nephew performed.

[6] *Mills v. Wyman*, 3 Pick. 207 (Mass. 1825).

[7] *Barnes v. Yahoo!, Inc.*, 565 F.3d 560 (9th Cir. 2009), amended 570 F. 3d 1096 (9th Cir. 2009).

[8] *Ibid.*

[9] *Scott P. v. Craigslist, Inc.*, Case No. CGC-10-496687 (Cal. Super. Ct. Jun. 2, 2010).

[10] *Affinity Internet, Inc., v. Consol. Credit Counseling Servs., Inc.*, 920 So. 2d 1286 (Fla. 4th DCA 2006).

[11] If the missing information is not material (*i.e.*, essential to the contract), then the court may fill in the missing terms by implication.

[12] The mutual mistake must be a material mistake, made at the time of contract formation, and a mistake of fact, not judgment. The classic case used to illustrate the concept of mutual mistake is *Sherwood v. Walker*, 66 Mich. 568 (1887) where the parties contracted for the sale of a barren cow (with a lesser value as meat) and later discovered the cow was pregnant (thus more valuable as a breeder). The mistake was as to fact (the cow was not barren) not as to judgment (how good a breeder the cow was).

[13] The copyright issue would likely fall under the "Fair Use" exemption from copyright protection under the Copyright Act, 17 U.S.C. § 107.

[14] *Lee v. Makhnevich*, Case No. 1:11-cv-08665 (S.D.N.Y. filed Nov. 29, 2011).

[15] The contract was reportedly supplied by Medical Justice, an organization that offers legal advice and services to doctors. According to news reports, it yanked the form from its site and advised clients not to use it because of the lawsuit. *See* Jonathan Allen, "Patient Sues Dentist Who Charged Him for Bad Reviews," Reuters wire service report, December 1, 2011.

[16] More disturbing is the notion a doctor would insist patients sign a privacy contract demanding they surrender their right to speak freely about the quality of service received. One has to wonder why any doctor would include such a contract clause, unless he or she had been subjected to previous patient complaints. Such a clause runs counter to public policy, for the public has an interest in being informed of a doctor offering services to the general public whose practice has generated numerous public complaints. Silencing voices of patients who endured poor quality of care, negligence, or malpractice runs against public policy notions, as well as the concept of the Internet as a venue for the free exchange of information.

[17] The age of majority in the United States is 18 in all states except Alabama (19), Louisiana (17), Mississippi (21), and Nebraska (19). In American Samoa and Puerto Rico, the age of majority is 14.

[18] *A.V. v. IParadigms, LLC*, 544 F. Supp. 2d 473 (E.D. Va. 2008), (rev'd in part on other grounds in *A.V. v. iParadigms, LLC*, 562 F.3d 630 (4th Cir. 2009)).

[19] Leases for less than a year and contracts incidental to land (*e.g.,* a contract to construct a building on the land) do not fall within the Statute of Frauds.

[20] *Taylor v. Caldwell*, 122 Eng. Rep. 309 (1863). Where performance depends on the continued existence of a person or thing, there is an implied condition impossibility of performance by the destruction of that person or thing excuses performance.

[21] *Krell v. Henry*, 2 King's Bench 740 (1903).

[22] *Ga. Dept. of Transp. v. Norris*, 474 S.E.2d 216 (1996), rev'd on other grounds, 486 S.E.2d 826 (1997).

[23] The Electronic Signatures In Global And National Commerce Act ("E-SIGN Act") 15 U.S.C. § 7001-31 (2000).

[24] *Stevens v. Publicis, S.A.*, 854 N.Y.S.2d 690 (N.Y. App. Div. 1st Dept. 2008).

[25] The phrases "Terms of Use" and "Terms of Service" are used interchangeably.

[26] This is oftened detailed in a separate privacy policy, incorporated by reference into the Terms of Use agreement. *See* Chapter 8, *supra*.

[27] As in the case of the 91-page scroll-down agreement in *Scarcella v. Am. Online, Inc.*, 4 Misc. 3d 1024A (N.Y. Civ. Ct. 2004), aff'd 11 Misc. 3d 19 (N.Y.App. Term 2005).

[28] See the discussion on privacy policies in Chapter 10.

[29] The Children's Online Privacy Protection Act (COPPA), 15 U.S.C. § 6501, *et seq*.

[30] *See*, respectively, The California Online Privacy Protection Act, California Business and Professions Code § 22575-22579.; COPPA, fn. 29, *supra*; The EU's Data Protection Directive, Directive 95/46/EC, which requires users be informed their data may be collected and used for direct marketing, and provision for a right to object (*i.e.*, an "opt-out" provision).

[31] *ProCD, Inc. v. Zeidenberg*, 86 F.3D 1447 (7th Cir. 1996).

[32] *Feldman v. Google, Inc.*, 513 F. Supp. 2d 229 (E.D. Pa. 2007).

[33] *DeJohn v. The .TV Corp.*, 245 F. Supp. 2d 913 (N.D. Ill. 2003).

[34] *Comb v. PayPal, Inc.*, 218 F. Supp. 2d 1165 (N.D. Cal. 2002).

[35] *Motise v. Am. Online, Inc.*, 346 F. Supp.2d 563 (S.D.N.Y. 2004).

[36] *Burcham v. Expedia, Inc.* , 2009 WL 586513 (E.D.Mo. Mar. 6, 2009).

[37] *Costar Realty Info., Inc. v. Field*, 612 F. Supp. 2d 660 (2009).

[38] *Cairo, Inc. v. CrossMedia Servs., Inc.*, 2005 WL 756610 (N.D. Cal. Apr. 1, 2005).

[39] *Scarcella v. Am. Online, Inc.*, 4 Misc. 3d 1024A (N.Y. Civ. Ct. 2004), aff'd 11 Misc. 3d 19 (N.Y. App. Term 2005).

[40] In *Dyer v. Nw. Airlines Corp.*, 334 F. Supp. 2d 1196 (D. N.D. 2004), the court held a Web site privacy policy did not create a contract between the company and a site user.

[41] *Register.com, Inc. v. Verio, Inc.*, 126 F. Supp. 2d 238 (S.D.N.Y. 2000), aff'd 356 F.3d 393 (2d Cir. 2004) holding Register.com's Terms of Use created a binding contract between Verio and Register.com, despite the

fact the user could not read the Terms of Use until after performing a search on the WhoIs database, and was neither asked nor required to assent by clicking on an "I Agree" button.

[42] *Specht v. Netscape Commc'ns Corp.*, 150 F. Supp. 2d 585 (S.D.N.Y. 2001), aff'd 306 F.3d 17 (2ᵈ Cir. 2002) holding a browse-wrap agreement unenforceable where terms were located below the download button on the screen and no assent through an "I accept" button was required.

[43] *Ticketmaster Corp. v. Tickets.com, Inc.*, 54 U.S.P.Q.2D (BNA) 1344 (C.D. Cal. 2000).

[44] While the Electronic Communications Privacy Act protects e-mail from government and ISP surveillance absent a court order, its provisions can be waived by agreement between the ISP and the customer.

[45] Typically, such a clause would reserve the right to block traffic the ISP — in its sole discretion — deems "inappropriate." Comcast Corp. was the subject of a Federal Communications Commission investigation after charges the ISP was interfering with customers' downloads of large files. Comcast argued it had reserved the right to "manage traffic" under its Acceptable Use Policy. *See* the discussion in the Net Neutrality section of Chapter 21.

[46] Usually ISPs do not reveal how they define "excessive" bandwidth, making it difficult for users to know when they are using too much. Nonetheless, ISP contracts often reserve the right to terminate a customer's service for using excessive bandwidth.

[47] Peter Svensson, "Fine Print on ISP Contract Leave Few Rights for Subscribers," Associated Press wire service report, April 5, 2008.

[48] *Ibid.*

[49] *Douglas v. U.S. Dist. Ct. ex rel Talk Am., Inc.*, 495 F.3d 1062, 1065 (9ᵗʰ Cir. 2007).

[50] *Ibid.*

[51] *Harris v. Blockbuster, Inc.*, 622 F. Supp. 2d 396 (N.D. Tex. 2009) (Memorandum Denying Motion to Compel Arbitration). The Video Privacy Protection Act (18 U.S.C. 2710), which prohibits a videotape service provider from disclosing a customer's personally identifiable information unless given informed, written consent at the time the disclosure is sought. The Act provides for liquidated damages of $2,500 for each violation.

[52] *See* the discussion about Beacon in Chapter 9, *supra.*

[53] In a similar class action, a California Facebook user sued Facebook after a Beacon news feed revealed to his wife and other Facebook friends he had purchased a diamond ring from Overstock.com as a surprise for her. *See Lane v. Facebook, Inc.*, Case No. 08-3845 RS (N.D. Cal. Mar. 17, 2010).

[54] *Specht*, 150 F. Supp. 2d 585.

[55] *Ibid.*

[56] *Douglas*, 495 F.3d 1062, holding modified terms are unenforceable to the extent no notice was provided.

[57] *Harris*, 622 F. Supp. 2d 396.

[58] The court based its rationale on a Fifth Circuit decision, *Morrison v. Amway Corp.*, 517 F.3d 248 (5ᵗʰ Cir. 2008), holding Amway's contract with distributors illusory because it reserved the right to unilaterally modify all aspects merely by publishing notice of the changes.

[59] The court indicated a limitation on the ability to unilaterally modify or terminate the agreement might make it not illusory: "The Blockbuster contract only states that modifications 'will be effective immediately upon posting,' and the natural reading of that clause does not limit application of the modifications to earlier disputes;" however, it later backed away from this, adding as the *Morrison* court had "decided the issue on the basis that the ability to change the rules at any time made the contract merely illusory. The Court agrees with that analysis and finds that the *Morrison* rule applies even when no retroactive modification has been attempted." An example of a limitation suggested in *Morrison* was contract wording that would make the modification inapplicable to "disputes arising, or arising out of events occurring, before such publication" of the notice of changes to the agreement.

[60] In this chapter, the terms "Web designer" and "Web developer" are used synonymously. In practice, a Web developer specializes in applying programming-based applications (such as CGI, Perl, Java, PHP, and database integration) to Web sites, whereas a Web designer focuses on nonprogramming aspects (such as HTML, CSS, graphic design, site design, and usability). Many Web developers are also Web designers, and many Web design firms employ Web developers, so the terms are used interchangeably throughout this chapter.

# CHAPTER

# **21**

---

## ISSUES ON THE HORIZON

This chapter looks at Digital Estate Planning, Web Site Accessibility for the Disabled; Net Neutrality; Metadata; e-Books; and the Role of the Internet in Society.

*"It is a mistake to try to look too far ahead. The chain of destiny can only be grasped one link at a time." — Sir Winston Churchill*

A S WE CONTEMPLATE NEW laws to address issues raised by our present technology can we, any better than our forefathers, imagine the appearance of the technological landscape of the future those laws will have to address? Baby Boomer kids fantasized about one day being able to capture ephemeral television broadcasts of their favorite shows onto a permanent recording and ultimately having a library, not of traditional books, but of TV shows; or being able to catalog their growing comic book collections on a computer like the mammoth machines then used by NASA. Of course, they already knew one day everyone would have wireless communication, perhaps Dick Tracy's wristwatch TV or "*Star Trek*" 'communicators.' Such fantasies became realities through VCRs and videotapes, home computers and databases, and mobile phones — prosaic items to the Internet Generation that Baby Boomers could only dream of. Even these technological innovations have been supplanted by newer advances, such as DVDs, laptops, and smart phones. But the most imaginative Baby Boomer child could not have envisioned an invention that would allow anyone in the world to communicate instantaneously with anyone else, friend or random stranger, or for that matter, simultaneously with the entire world at once.

The Internet is here to stay. Technology, like an evil djinn, once freed from the bottle cannot be recorked. Advances in the technology of the Internet will lead to new legal issues, some as yet unimaginable, but some equally foreseeable. This chapter will spotlight some of those areas.

## Digital Estate Planning

*Digital estate planning* — the disposition of digital assets after death — is one of the evolving issues in Internet law on the horizon. Recall from Chapter Nine the case of the parents of a marine killed in Iraq who had difficulty obtaining his e-mail from Yahoo! State legislatures and attorneys have only begun addressing these concerns. Five states — Connecticut, Idaho, Indiana, Oklahoma, and Rhode Island — have drafted statutes governing digital asset management after death. Connecticut's [1] and Rhode Island's [2] laws are limited to e-mail. Indiana's statute grants access to "electronically stored documents of the deceased." [3] Oklahoma's [4] and Idaho's [5] laws covers a broad range of digital assets including e-mail, blogs, and social networks. The Oklahoma and Idaho statutes give an executor, "when authorized," the power "to take control of, conduct, or terminate" the online accounts of the deceased, including social networks, blogs and e-mail.

A Nebraska bill proposes granting an executor or personal representative access to and control over the decedent's digital accounts. [6] In January 2012, the Uniform Law Commission, formed a committee to study the digital assets issue. [7] The Commission is a national group of lawyers appointed by state governments to draft model laws states may adopt.

Digital assets can be categorized as: (1) an online account accessible only by a user name and password; (2) files stored on individual's computer, server, smart phone, or portable storage media; or (3) files stored "off site" at commercial online storage sites (e.g., Carbonite, DropBox, and iCloud). At issue are digital assets such as e-mail accounts, social networks, online storage accounts, personal or business Web sites and blogs, payment services (e.g., PayPal, Amazon Payments), virtual property accounts (e.g., Second Life), photo storage accounts (e.g., Flickr), auction sites (e.g., eBay, eBid); and online merchant accounts (e.g., Amazon).

At present, access to online assets are governed by Terms of Use agreements. Most grant companies the right to delete an online account within a set period after the account holder's demise. AOL deactivates a deceased's screen name after 90 days; PayPal's terms state an account will be closed if there is no activity for three years; Twitter's terms state a decedent's account may be "deactivated"; and Facebook's policy is to place the account in a memorialized state, freezing its content but allowing friends to comment on the page, although a decedent's heirs can request it be terminated after presenting a death certificate to the company. Personal representatives need the ability to preserve digital assets and, in some cases, access information they contain. For example, an e-mail account may hold information about contractual obligations the personal representative needs to be aware of. Some online accounts, however, may consist of music, videos, and e-books purchased by the decedent in which he received only a non-transferable license (i.e., a license expires on death). In planning for death, individuals should list all online accounts and assets with URLs, user names, and passwords to enable the personal representative to identify and access them. The list should be updated regularly, as passwords and other details change, and state the preferred disposition of the digital assets, i.e., which accounts should be closed, turned into memorial sites, or transferred to designated heirs.

Commercial alternatives, like Entrustet, Legacy Locker, and My Webwill exist to store one's digital assets and passwords, but there is the risk an individual might outlive any commercial enterprise. There is even a Facebook application called "If I Die" that allows users to leave a farewell message, to be played to survivors after they have died or posted to the deceased's Facebook page, taking 'having the last word' to the extreme.

## Internet Accessibility for the Disabled

While legally mandated for government sites, the extent to which private sites may be required, if at all, to be accessible to the disabled is unclear. The **Workforce Investment**

Act[8] includes the **Rehabilitation Act Amendments of 1998**,[9] one section of which—*Section 508*—requires disabled individuals seeking information or services from a federal agency have access to, and use of, information and data comparable to that provided to nondisabled individuals. This means federal, state, and local government sites must be accessible to disabled individuals. But what about nongovernment sites? Under the **Americans With Disabilities Act of 1990** (ADA), places of public accommodation, such as stores, restaurants, and hotels, must take reasonable steps to be accessible to those with physical limitations.[10] Is the Internet a "place of public accommodation"? The law was written before the World Wide Web became a ubiquitous presence in society, and might or might not apply to online services and sites. The **ADA** applies to common carriers like buses; would it apply to cyber common carriers, *i.e.*, ISPs like AOL?

The National Federation of the Blind (NFB) sued AOL, alleging its Internet service was inaccessible to the blind in violation of the **ADA**.[11] The suit was dropped after AOL agreed to make its software compatible with screen-access software. Screen-reading software reads content out loud (there are talking Web browsers that read Web site text and "alt" tags that describe graphics) or translates it into Braille text.[12] Since the case was dropped, no court decision was rendered on this issue.

Is the **ADA** applicable to a private business' Web site? The first federal court to address the issue said no. In *Access Now, Inc. v. Southwest Airlines*, a Florida district court ruled the **ADA** applies only to physical spaces, such as restaurants and movie theaters, and not to the Internet.[13] The Act defines a "public accommodation" as a facility, operated by a private entity, whose operations affect commerce and fall within at least one of 12 specified categories, including hotels, restaurants, shopping centers, universities, and bowling alleys. The court reasoned, because Congress so meticulously specified what kinds of physical spaces are covered by the **ADA**, it clearly did not intend for it to apply to the Internet. The Sixth[14] and Ninth[15] Circuits have sided with the Florida district court, holding a public place of accommodation must be a physical location. However, the First Circuit, while not specifically addressing the Internet, has held the **ADA** is not limited to purely physical structures.[16]

New York Attorney General Elliott Spitzer, arguing the **ADA** requires private Web sites be accessible to blind and visually impaired, launched an "investigation" into the accessibility of two major travel services' sites. Despite the unsettled status of that proposition, both Priceline.com and Ramada.com agreed to changes to enable users with screen reader software and other disability aiding technology to navigate and listen to text throughout their sites. While software and other devices, such as a vibrating mouse that lets the blind "feel" boxes and images on the computer screen, have existed for years, sites need special coding for the equipment to work. Ramada and Priceline, which faced no charges and made no admissions of guilt, agreed to pay New York $40,000 and $37,500 respectively to cover the investigation's cost.[17]

While accessibility is an admirable goal, and clearly good business sense, it is unclear if legally required by the **ADA** on private sites. That determination can only come from either an amendment to the statute or court rulings, the latter subject to appellate review before a final determination is made. If accessibility were to be required on private commercial sites, then not only large corporations, but every small business as well would have to redesign its Web site to comply, resulting in significant expense. If mandated for all Web sites, including noncommercial sites, then every individual with a nonconforming site would risk violating the **ADA**. This does not mean sites cannot or should not follow Web accessibility design standards.[18] But to force the **ADA** onto private sites would have a devastating effect on millions of Web sites, both commercial and noncommercial.[19]

Nonetheless, a 2006 case could have a profound impact on this issue. A class action filed by the NFB, with a visually-impaired[20] college student as lead plaintiff, alleged the Target department store chain's site was inaccessible to the blind because it did not use the ALT attribute in its HTML and parts of its shopping cart required use of a mouse instead of a keyboard.[21] The suit claimed Target violated the **ADA**, the California **Disabled Persons Act** (guaranteeing full and equal access for the disabled to all public places) and the state's **Unruh Civil Rights Act**. Target moved to dismiss, arguing the state laws were inapplicable because Web sites are not "physical" places of public accommodation. The federal district court rejected the motion and distinguished this case from *Access Now*:[22]

> In *Access Now*, the court held that plaintiff failed to state a claim under **ADA** because plaintiff alleged that the inaccessibility of southwest.com prevented access to Southwest's 'virtual' ticket counters. 'Virtual' ticket counters are not actual, physical places and therefore not places of public accommodation. Since there was no physical place of public accommodation alleged in *Access Now*, the court did not reach the precise issue presently in dispute: whether there is a nexus between a challenged service and an actual, physical place of public accommodation.

The court appeared to require a nexus between the site and a physical "bricks 'n mortar" location. In other words, the **ADA** requires a physical place of public accommodation; a site by itself is not a physical place and therefore does not fall under the **ADA**; however, if the site is merely a tool of an existing physical place of public accommodation, *i.e.*, using the Internet as a means to enhance services it offers at a physical location, then by extension it would fall under the **ADA**. (Here, Target customers could use the Web site to refill prescriptions and order photo prints for pick-up at a store). The court reasoned since the site was a gateway to a place of public accommodation and blind individuals were unable to use its services, Target may have violated the **ADA**. The court's logic seems strained. It parsed the statute's language in a manner likely unforeseen by its drafters, stating:[23]

> [The] statute applies to the services of a place *of* public accommodation, not services *in* a place of public accommodation. To limit the **ADA** to discrimination in the provision of services occurring on the premises of a public accommodation would contradict the plain language of the statute.

Rather than change its site to comply with California law, "Target could choose to make a [separate] California-specific Web site," the court wrote, oblivious to the onerous burden of requiring a business to have multiple versions of the same Web site to comply with a multitude of often conflicting state requirements.[24] The court added: "even if Target chooses to change its entire Web site in order to comply with California law, this does not mean that California is regulating out-of-state conduct"—although arguably that would be precisely the effect. Target, in this author's opinion, correctly argued the Internet requires uniform, national regulations. While other jurisdictions may choose not to follow this court's path, and its interpretation of the reach of the statute may eventually be repudiated by the U.S. Supreme Court, at present, the case is noteworthy because the court's order is believed to be the first ruling the **ADA** may apply to nongovernment sites.

Having denied Target's motion to dismiss, in 2007 the case was converted into a class action, with the court certifying two classes — one under the **ADA** requiring a physical nexus and one under the state statute not requiring a physical nexus:[25]

> The nationwide class consists of all legally blind individuals in the United States who have attempted to access Target.com and as a result have been denied access to the enjoyment of goods and services offered in Target stores. The California subclass includes all legally blind individuals in California who have attempted to access Target.com, for plaintiffs' claims arising under the California [statutes].

The parties settled in 2008, with Target agreeing to pay $6 million and work with the NFB to implement accessibility guidelines.[26] The following year, the NFB and the American Council of the Blind sued Arizona State University for allegedly violating the **ADA** by using Amazon's Kindle e-book reader to distribute electronic textbooks to students, complaining although the device had text-to-speech technology to read books out loud to blind students, its menus did not offer a way for them to buy books, choose books to read, or activate the text-to-speech feature. The case was settled in early 2010.[27] Although Amazon was not a party in the suit, it announced plans to add two new features to make Kindle more accessible to the visually impaired: read out loud menus and an extra large font for readers with impaired vision.

Internet accessibility for the disabled remains a major issue on the horizon. While clear government sites must be accessible, the extent to which accessibility may be required, if at all, for private sites is uncertain. In the Ninth Circuit, it would seem a physical business with a tangential Web site may be subject to the **ADA**, but, even there, no indication exists the **ADA** would apply to an online business with no physical retail environment.[28]

## Freedom of Online Association

eHarmony is an online dating service founded by Dr. Neil Clark Warren, a clinical psychologist and evangelical Christian with strong early ties to the religious conservative group Focus on the Family.[29] While heavily promoted by Christian evangelical leaders,[30] nowhere did eHarmony identify itself as a Christian Web site or require users follow its fundamental Christian values; nor did it mention Warren's fundamentalist Christian values, instead focusing on his expertise as a clinical psychologist who had devised a lengthy questionnaire to ensure compatibility between daters.[31] The questionnaire asked about religion and sexual preference, and advised complete honesty in answering the questions to ensure compatibility; it also warned eHarmony rejects a certain number of applicants but did not state why.

Eric McKinley, a New Jersey homosexual, after being rejected for membership by the site, complained against eHarmony and Warren to New Jersey's Division on Civil Rights.[32] He alleged the site's drop-down menus only had choices for a man seeking a woman, or a woman seeking a man. The Division issued a Finding of Probable Cause and eHarmony moved for reconsideration of the finding, which was held in abeyance as the parties settled.[33] Under the settlement terms, eHarmony was required to offer a same-sex matching services on its current site, or on a new site; give the first 10,000 same-sex registrants a free six-month subscription; and pay $50,000 to the state for administrative costs and $5,000 to

McKinley. eHarmony chose to create a new site for gays called Compatiblepartners.net. The settlement stated the Division made no findings or adjudication on the claim's merits. [34]

Shortly thereafter, Linda Carlson, a lesbian California resident, filed a class action suit against eHarmony and Warren, alleging eHarmony was denying equal treatment on the basis of sexual orientation, and creating a second site instead of modifying the original one constituted an unacceptable "separate but equal" policy. [35] Potential class members included any gay, lesbian, or bisexual who had tried to join the site since May 2004 but was denied. The issue was whether a private company's site can be required to offer its services to homosexuals. There are several factors to examine in analyzing this issue:

### Is There an Applicable Federal Law?

The Fourteenth Amendment's Equal Protection clause prohibits a state from denying any person within its jurisdiction equal protection of its laws. [36] It specifically applies to government, not private business. It mandates equal application of the laws, not of business practices. The equal protection clause only comes into play when a state grants a particular class of individuals the right to engage in an activity it denies others the right to engage in. Carlson argued [37] setting up separate Web sites for heterosexuals and homosexuals — a solution endorsed by the New Jersey case — was synonymous with the "separate but equal" doctrine established in _Plessy v. Ferguson_ [38] and held unconstitutional in _Brown v. Board of Education_. [39] The doctrine referred to the practice of state governments establishing separate schools and facilities for whites and blacks during America's period of segregation, with _Plessy_ holding such separate facilities were legal so long as they were "equal" in their accommodations. However, this is a false analogy, as there is no state actor in the eHarmony case: the dating site is run by a private business, not by the state; therefore the Fourteenth Amendment equal protection clause does not apply. [40]

### What Then, is the Underlying Statutory Basis for the Lawsuits?

The McKinley claim was filed under the New Jersey **Law Against Discrimination** (LAD), enacted to bar discrimination in housing, employment, or places of public accommodation. [41] Is a nongoverment Web site a "place of public accommodation"? This question was posed earlier in the accessibility for the blind case, and while it remains unanswered, note in that case there was a federal statute — the **Americans with Disabilities Act** — that specifically applied to places of public accommodation (and did not address sexual orientation); in this case, there is no applicable federal statute. Based on existing law, there is no reason to believe a Web site, let alone a nongovernment site, would be "a place of public accommodation". The New Jersey attorney general's Web site, which defines "public accommodation" under the **LAD**, lists examples of physical structures "such as a restaurant, hotel, doctor's office, camp, or theater," [42] but admits there are exceptions: "Places of public accommodation which, by their nature, are reasonably restricted to individuals of one gender (such as dressing rooms or gymnasiums) may deny access to the accommodation to members of the other gender." [43]

Carlson's class action was filed under California's **Unruh Civil Rights Act**, claiming denial of equal treatment on the basis of sexual orientation. [44] As eHarmony has established a separate site for homosexuals, it has provided equal accommodation; even if merged, the sites would still have to separate genders and sexual orientations in its search functions or else the search functionality — the utility of the entire matching site — would be rendered useless.

### Is eHarmony a Public Accommodation or a Private Organization or Club?

A public accommodation is a private business catering to the general public, whereas a private organization restricts membership. eHarmony's site stated it did not accept all who applied, though it did not explain its rejection criteria. It is established a private organization has a right to reject prospective members based on sexual orientation (Two of the three leading cases were from California involving the **Unruh Civil Rights Act**, while the third was from New Jersey and dealt with its public accommodations law). [45] In the California case, the court unanimously held the Boy Scouts was not a "business establishment" under the **Unruh Civil Rights Act**'s equal rights to public accommodations requirement, upholding a private organization's right to reject prospective members based on sexual orientation. [46] The U.S. Supreme Court reversed the New Jersey Supreme Court's ruling the state's public accommodations law required the Boy Scouts to re-admit an expelled gay scout leader, holding the statute violated the Boy Scouts' First Amendment right of expressive association. [47]

eHarmony members pay to associate with other members, characteristic of a club or private organization, many of which are run for profit. Private social organizations, like golf and country clubs, that perform no significant public function, have a First Amendment right of association and generally cannot be forced to accept members. The issue may come down to whether eHarmony is a private, members-only organization. It would have a stronger argument had it marketed itself as an evangelical Christian dating service, but its marketing was directed at a mass market. If a court were to rule against eHarmony, it should be based on the way it marketed itself to the public.

### Should a State Law Be Applied to the Internet?

This is an example of why it is a bad idea to apply local standards to the Internet; a patchwork of conflicting local laws and social or political influences should not be imposed on a borderless medium like the Internet. eHarmony went to the expense and effort of setting up a new Web site to meet the demands of one state jurisdiction, only to risk being told by another it must abandon that new site and change its business model. There are 50 states; what will the next one require? Questions like these should be preempted by federal law, and then only when that law is based on analysis of the policies and laws of foreign jurisdictions as well, since the Internet (and firms that do business on it) are not limited to any single jurisdiction.

### The Social and Business Impact

Had the class action prevailed, what would have been the effect? If eHarmony had to open its dating service to homosexuals, would JDate—the largest online Jewish dating site—have to accept Christians and Muslims? Would BlackSingles.com have to allow white daters? Would Gay.com have to accept straight daters? Such a ruling could extend beyond Web sites; would a heterosexual strip club be required to add male strippers?

### The Free Market Theory

A homosexual should, and does, have the right to enter any public business, like a heterosexual strip club, and use its services, *e.g.*, drink at the bar, watch the strippers. But it would be silly to suggest the strip club be legally required to hire male strippers to cater to his tastes. Most likely, there will be a nearby gay strip club, because in the free market system, if there is sufficient demand for a product or service, someone will provide it. There are many gay dating sites online. McKinley and Carlson had dozens from which to chose, yet they chose eHarmony. If they did so because eHarmony's marketing led them to believe it was open to all members of the public, then perhaps they should prevail. But if they did so merely to attack an organization they knew to be an evangelical Christian (presumably anti-gay) dating service, then perhaps they should fail.

The irony is "Compatible Partners," eHarmony's new site for gays mandated by the New Jersey settlement, might prove extremely profitable for the company. Another potential irony, had Carlson won, is the effect of such a decision would force gay dating sites to open their doors to straight members. The case was settled in 2010, establishing a $2 million settlement fund and providing, among other things, eHarmony would add a "gay and lesbian dating" category to its main site linking to the Compatible Partners site, and bisexual users would be able to access both sites for one subscription fee.

## Net Neutrality

One of the hottest Internet topics is *net neutrality*, the concept ISPs should treat all Internet traffic equally. The exponential increase in Internet usage, combined with sharing of large files (*e.g.,* movies) and legal broadband downloads, has strained broadband ISPs, especially cable companies. They have become victims of their own success — having promoted broadband as a means for subscribers to download large files like movies, they now find their pipelines clogged and need to change the way they convey Internet data. One alternative is to prioritize data by changing the Information Highway into a multilane highway with an express lane (*e.g.,* for e-mail and Web browsing) and another lane for slower traffic (*e.g.,* downloads). Subscribers might be charged more for faster service or for downloads that exceed a certain limit.

In 2008, the FCC investigated complaints Comcast Corp., America's largest cable ISP, was interfering with subscribers' file-sharing. FCC policy prohibits ISPs from blocking specific applications, but exempts "reasonable traffic management." The investigation centered on whether Comcast's techniques met the FCC's definition of "reasonable traffic management." Comcast admitted inserting "reset packets" into the data stream to break off communications between two computers, effectively flipping the "off" switch in the middle of subscribers' file-sharing sessions.[48] The subscriber's computer would read the return addresses on the packets as coming from the file-sharing computer when in reality they were coming from Comcast. The packet effectively told the subscriber's computer "so long, got to go", making it appear the file-sharing computer had ended the session. Comcast also set undisclosed monthly download limits, cutting off subscribers who exceeded them[49] The FCC ruled Comcast violated federal net neutrality rules by blocking Internet traffic for certain subscribers and ordered it to stop cutting off transfers of large data files among customers who use BitTorrent file-sharing software.[50] The 3–to–2 decision was the first time a broadband provider had been found to have violated net neutrality rules. On appeal, a unanimous three-judge panel of the U.S. Court of Appeals for the District of Columbia held the FCC lacks authority to enforce net neutrality. Siding with Comcast, it ruled the FCC had no statutory basis to require broadband providers treat all Internet traffic traveling over their networks equally. The ruling left the FCC with several options: appeal; seek express authority to regulate broadband from

Congress; or reclassify broadband services as Title II "Communications Services" instead of Title I "Information Services". Broadband had been under Title I until 2002, when the Bush Administration changed it in a deregulation move. By reclassifying broadband lines to be governed by the same rules as traditional phone networks, which the FCC has statutory legal authority over, the FCC would then be able to enforce net neutrality rules on ISPs.

In December 2010, the FCC by a 3–to–2 vote, adopted net neutrality rules granting it the power to ensure consumer access to large content files while allowing ISPs to manage networks to prevent congestion. FCC rules generally cannot be challenged until published in the Federal Register. The net neutrality rules were not published in the Federal Register until September 2011 and scheduled to go into effect in November 2011. Upon publication of the rules, at least one lawsuit had been filed against them.

One possible traffic management method—filtering out copyrighted material—was suggested by AT&T. While the **DMCA** provides a safe harbor for ISPs whose subscribers share copyrighted material, neither liability nor altruism, but instead practicality, may be behind this consideration. Filtering copyrighted files would eliminate a great deal of traffic from AT&T's network—studies show as much as 37 percent of net traffic emanates from P2P file-sharing (including illegal music and video file-sharing).[51] But such action would raise a privacy issue, as filtering would, by definition, require the ISP to look at the *content* its subscribers transmit. Would customers feel comfortable with the camel poking its nose under the tent?

## e-Books

Before warming up the modem to download e-books, readers might pause to ponder the ephemeral nature of digital bits and bytes, as contrasted with the durability of the progeny of dead trees, or as previous generations called them, books. E-book are not physical objects but merely electronic files. One does not "own" an e-book, but rather purchases a license to read its content on a specific device. With Orwellian irony, Amazon.com deleted George Orwell's novels "*1984*" and "*Animal Farm*" from all of its customers' Kindle e-book readers overnight in July 2009. Kindle owners were shocked, unaware Big Brother could reach into their devices and remotely erase content already purchased and downloaded to their e-book readers. Amazon gave customers no advance notice of the erasures. It later explained it deleted the e-books because they had been added to its catalog by someone who did not have the rights to the books. Amazon purchased the necessary rights to distribute them and they were once again available. But the damage had been done. Customers lost some degree of confidence in the integrity of Kindle and other e-book readers, realizing their e-libraries could vanish like a wisp of smoke without warning. One high school student sued Amazon, claiming his class notes on his Kindle vanished when his copy of "*1984*" got zapped. Amazon agreed to settle the lawsuit, and customers whose copies were erased were offered free books or $30.[52]

## Geolocation Filtering: Erecting Borders to the Internet

Three methods of filtering Internet content are distinguishable by where the filtering takes place. The first, OSP filtering, is done at the online service provider level. The OSP might be a Web site providing a service (*e.g.*, a search engine; a bulletin board system, or chat room) that it filters, or an ISP providing Internet access filtered at the request of a country's government (as discussed in Chapter 18). The second method is the employment of a hardware filter on the physical computer terminal, as in employer filtering software (discussed in Chapter 12) or filters applied to library computers (discussed in Chapter 17) and computer terminals at Chinese and Vietnamese cyber cafés (discussed in Chapter 18). The third method is geolocation filtering, which takes place at the target Web site. States have turned to geofiltering to counter the borderless nature of the Internet.

With *geolocation filtering*, a Web site can restrict access to, or modify, content it delivers based on geographical regions accessing the site. The geolocation technology identifies the visitor's IP address and cross-references it with a database of international IP addresses to determine the visitor's country of origin. Some comprehensive geolocation databases can match IP addresses with specific regions and cities.

There are several purposes for restricting access to content:

• **Political.** An individual in China conducting a search through Google China News portal will not receive the same results as one searching from outside China because Google filters the query results from China-based IP addresses. As discussed in Chapter 18, the Chinese government exercises tight control over the flow of information and wishes to keep certain political topics from the public discourse.

• **Legal.** As discussed in Chapter 18, the European Union takes the opposite approach from the United States by criminalizing hate speech. To comply with German and French laws forbidding hate sites or the sale of Nazi paraphernalia, Google excludes Nazi and hate sites from search results originating in those countries.[53] The mirrored Web site of the New York Times geofiltered out articles on a terrorism case in Britain for Web users in the UK. Those users were able to see headlines, but not the stories, instead being redirected to a message advising them: "This article is unavailable. On advice of legal counsel, this article is unavailable to readers of nytimes.com in Britain. This arises from the requirement in British law that prohibits publication of prejudicial information about the defendants prior to trial." American readers saw the headline "Details Emerge in British Terror Case" and an article about a bomb plot involving British airports.[54]

• **Cultural.** Some governments mandate geolocation filters on gambling and pornography sites.

• **Copyright licenses.** A Web site might be contractually bound with content providers to restrict access to video programs the provider has licensed only for certain countries or regions. The BBC sites, for example, use geofiltering to limit access to certain TV programming clips to U.K. residents. In the United States, Hulu and Netflix use geolocation filtering for the same reasons.

• **Security.** Some governments use geofiltering to thwart cyber terrorism and hackers. Certain businesses rely on geofiltering to restrict traffic from countries with high risk of credit card fraud.

Geofiltering, combined with keyword filtering, might prevent content deemed objectionable by a country from appearing on the Web within its borders. From such a government's standpoint, an effective prior restraint would be more efficacious than having to provide notice and wait for content to be removed after it has been posted and viewed. For example, India requires sites remove within 36 hours of notification any political satire and "blasphemous" content that might offend religious groups. Google and Facebook faced trial in 2012 in an Indian court on charges they failed to censor objectionable content from their sites. [55]

Governments may be tempted to view geofiltering as a "quick fix" for larger social and political woes. Following the 2011 London Riots, Prime Minister David Cameron told parliament he was considering restrictions on social media and the Internet: [56]

> Free flow of information can be used for good. But it can also be used for ill. And when people are using social media for violence we need to stop them. So we are working with the police, the intelligence services and industry to look at whether it would be right to stop people communicating via these Web sites and services.

In this respect, Internet filtering, including geofiltering, represents a significant threat to democracy.

Since geolocation filtering is based on IP addresses, Web users can employ proxy servers and anonymous communications systems to hide their location from geolocation technologies. In addition to Web proxies and anonymizers, other tools to evade geofiltering include dial-up to a foreign ISP and commercial services that allow one to acquire IP address from a foreign location.

Preventing individuals from obtaining something often increases their desire for it. As more people seek to evade geolocation filters and succeed, will they be exposing themselves to legal liability? Contractual liability may arise where a Web site has a clause in its Terms of Use agreement that users agree not to use geolocation evasion tools to access restricted content. In America, the **Computer Fraud and Abuse Act** (CFAA), which criminalizes knowingly accessing a computer without, or in excess of, authorization, might be invoked. Geolocation evasion tools might also violate the **DMCA**, which criminalizes circumventing an access control, whether or not there is actual infringement of copyright. Even were one to use geolocation evasion tools to disguise an IP address for purposes other than viewing or downloading copyrighted materials, the **DMCA,** as written, would appear to impute liability.

Geolocation technology presents a more fundamental issue for society. Is there a privacy right to obscure one's location? Must we show our identification papers as we travel across the Internet? Conversely, should the act of obscuring one's location be viewed as misrepresentation and punishable?

## The Blame Game

The Internet may be a nascent technology, but the social and legal problems it poses are not necessarily new. One of the great challenges society and lawmakers face is to resist the tendency to blame the Internet for society's perceived ills. After having turned their computers into babysitters, parents cannot abdicate their supervisory responsibilities and blame the Internet for content to which their children are exposed. Nor can government officials blame it for their own failings. Instead of calling for new laws to regulate the Internet, they need to regulate themselves better. For example, recall the situation discussed in Chapter 3 in which a government official who complained about the risk posed by P2P file-sharing networks — a risk that only existed because he (1) placed classified files on his home computer, (2) allowed his child access to a computer containing sensitive or classified files, and (3) allowed his daughter to install a P2P file-sharing program on that home computer, exposing the government documents to the network. [57] His cry for new regulation and new laws rings hollow — the solution to any perceived threat to national security is not to prohibit a technology that enables communication among its users (which would probably violate First Amendment free speech rights) but rather to regulate and control those in the government who handle sensitive or classified files. Likewise, when another government official complained "sensitive" military-issue equipment was being resold on eBay and Craigslist, rather than blaming the Internet and attempting to regulate online sales of such items, the focus should be on how the equipment was getting into the wrong hands in the first place and why there are no laws regulating the sale of such items through *any* means. [58]

## The New Nation-states

Throughout this book, we have discussed the borderless nature of the Internet, which transcends geographic boundaries. But perhaps the boundaries are being redrawn and the nation-states of the 22nd century will not be America, France, and China, but rather Google, Yahoo! and eBay — for the Internet giants have created fiefdoms that transcend nationality and function under their own rules. Certain companies have emerged as "first among equals" in discrete categories online. While there are other auction sites, eBay is the one most associate with online auctions, and hence provides the largest congregation of buyers and sellers. There are many search engines, but only one constantly has to protect its trademark from being used as a verb synonymous with Web searching, as in "Did you Google it?" Sites like Amazon, YouTube, eBay, Google, and Yahoo! are ubiquitous in their reach — Iranians and Israelis meet on eBay to sell items, Greeks and Turks upload their videos to YouTube, and the very book you hold in your hands is sold on dozens of foreign-language versions of Amazon's site. Citizens of different nations, while physically present in those countries, have joined to become citizens of online communities. But each online community, like the YouTube community for example, establishes and enforces its own rules for membership and participation within that community. From ISPs to social networks, private companies — not governments — through their Terms of Use and internal policies dictate their own rules for worldwide users.

As a result, the rules are not always clearly stated, if at all; enforcement is inconsistent and may vary based on the specific service representative interpreting her company's policies or invoking her own personal biases — leading to arbitrary and capricious outcomes. There is no guarantee of due process or equal protection, and no one to whom to appeal decisions made by the private company. Uploaded user content can be removed without notice and accounts terminated without a hearing. "Justice" becomes a commodity dispensed at the discretion of the private firm. Disputes are adjudicated behind closed doors by nameless individuals, who function as judge, jury, and executioner. They can delete user content they find "objectionable" or "controversial" regardless of its legality. One consequence of private businesses controlling public forums in cyberspace is the First Amendment limitations on government infringements on free expression do not apply to them. [59] An ISP or Web site's Terms of Use agreement grants it sole discretion to refuse or remove any content, without due process safeguards of notice, hearing, and a right of appeal. Should these private companies be vested with so much unchecked power? Should they even make such rules? If so, should they be required to provide a mechanism for consistent enforcement? Should there be government regulation of these private enterprises, similar to American regulation of the broadcast airwaves?

Or would such regulation be too restrictive and stifle growth? Should any government be entrusted with such authority? And if so, which? These are merely some of the issues on the horizon society shall have to confront.

**Chapter 21 Notes**

[1] Connecticut Public Act No. 05-136: An Act Concerning Access to Decedents' Electronic Mail Accounts.

[2] Rhode Island HB5647: Access to Decedents' Electronic Mail Accounts Act.

[3] Indiana Code 29-1-13 (SB 0212, 2007): Electronic Documents as Estate Property.

[4] Oklahoma HB2800: Control of Certain Social Networking, Microblogging or E-Mail Accounts of the Deceased.

[5] Idaho SB1044: Control of Certain Social Networking, Microblogging or E-Mail Accounts of the Deceased.

[6] A **decedent** is the deceased person; an **executor** or **personal representative** is the individual named in the will to administer the decedent's estate and distribution of assets.

[7] Steve Eider, "Deaths Pose Test for Facebook," The Wall Street Journal, February 11, 2012.

[8] The Workforce Investment Act of 1998 (Pub. L. No. 105-220).

[9] The Rehabilitation Act Amendments of 1993 (Pub. L. No. 103-73).

[10] The Americans With Disabilities Act of 1990 (Pub. L. No. 101-336), 42 U.S.C. § 12101, *et seq.*

[11] Sheri Qualters, "Discrimination Case Opens Door to Internet ADA Claims," The National Law Journal, September 28, 2006.

[12] For example, Simply Web 2000 talking browser, *was available at* www.econointl.com/sw (accessed July 23, 2010) but no longer available.

[13] *Access Now, Inc. v. Sw. Airlines*, 227 F. Supp. 2d 1312 (S.D. Fla. 2002) appeal denied, 385 F.3d 1324 (11th Cir. 2004).

[14] *Parker v. Metro. Life Ins. Co.*, 121 F.3d 1006 (6th Cir. 1997).

[15] *Weyer v. Twentieth Century Fox Film Corp.*, 198 F.3d 1104 (9th Cir. 2000).

[16] *Carparts Distribution Ctr., Inc. v. Auto. Wholesaler's Ass'n*, 37 F.3d 12, 22-23 (1st Cir. 1994).

[17] "Priceline, Ramada Agree to Make Web Sites More Accessible," ConsumerAffairs.com, August 20, 2004, available at www.consumeraffairs.com/news04/ada_webs.html (accessed Mar. 23, 2012).

[18] The University of Wisconsin has an excellent resource page on Web accessibility *available at* http://library.uwsp.edu/aschmetz/accessible/pub_resources.htm (accessed Mar. 23, 2012).

[19] Statutes prohibiting private companies from discriminating against disabled individuals (and theoretically that prohibition would extend to their Web sites) tend to define discrimination as the act of treating disabled customers in a worse manner than nondisabled customers and do not require provision of special or better treatment. The notable exception is the Americans with Disabilities Act, which applies to issues of employment and accessibility to public accommodations, although the ADA exempts smaller private companies.

[20] *Nat'l Fed'n of the Blind v. Target Corp.*, 452 F. Supp. 2d 946 (N.D. Cal. 2006). The lead plaintiff was "legally blind," a term that does not necessarily mean total blindness; 90 percent of legally blind individuals have some remaining vision. *See* Bonnie Azab Powell, "Transfer Student Bruce Sexton Has Target-ed Independence for Blind People as a Major Goal," UC Berkeley News, March 20, 2006. The plaintiff's "vision is just enough to see general shapes and to distinguish between light and dark." *Ibid.*

[21] HTML or Hyper Text Markup Language, is the computer language Web browsers use to format Web pages. The alt attribute allows text to be associated with a graphic on the pages so when the page is loading or the graphics are turned off in the browser settings, the images will be replaced with text describing them. Such text can then be read out loud by a "talking" browser using screen-reading software.

[22] *Nat'l Fed'n of the Blind*, 452 F. Supp. 2d 946.

[23] *Ibid.*

[24] "Target Lawsuit Tests Limits of U.S. Web Accessibility Law," OUT-LAW.com, September 12, 2006, *available at* www.out-law.com/page-7285 (accessed Mar. 23, 2012).

[25] *Nat'l Fed'n of the Blind*, 452 F. Supp. 2d 946.

[26] "Target Settles Case over Site's Access to Sightless," Associated Press wire service report, August 27, 2008.

[27] Minara El-Rahman, "Kindle Lawsuit Settled by ASU and Blind Groups," FindLaw.com, January 12, 2010, *available at* http://blogs.findlaw.com/injured/2010/01/kindle-lawsuit-settled-by-asu-and-blind-groups.html (accessed on Feb. 3, 2012).

[28] "Blind Web Users Fight, Sue for More Accessible Sites," Fox News.com, October 24, 2006.

[29] "eHarmony Sued in California for Excluding Gays," Reuters wire service report, May 31, 2007.

[30] David Colker, "eHarmony to Offer Same-sex Matches after New Jersey Settlement," The Los Angeles Times, November 19, 2008.

[31] eHarmony site, *available at* www.eharmony.com/about/eharmony (accessed Mar. 23, 2012).

[32] Colker, fn. 30, *supra.*

[33] *McKinley v. eHarmony, Inc.*, DCR Dkt. No. PQ27IB-02846 Administrative Action Settlement Agreement, Consent Order and General Release (2008).

[34] *Ibid.*

[35] *Carlson v. eHarmony, Inc.*, Case No. BC371958 (Los Angeles Sup. Ct. filed Nov. 19, 2008). *See also* Jon Hood, "eHarmony Faces New Lawsuits for 'Separate But Equal' Policy; Dating Site Accused of Segregating Same-sex Dating Partners," ConsumerAffairs.com, April 3, 2009.

[36] The Fourteenth Amendment, U.S. Const. states, in relevant part: "No state shall make or enforce any law which shall abridge the privileges or immunities of citizens of the United States; nor shall any state deprive any person of life, liberty, or property, without due process of law; nor deny to any person within its jurisdiction the equal protection of the laws."

[37] Hood, fn. 35, *supra.*

[38] *Plessy v. Ferguson*, 163 U.S. 537 (1896).

[39] *Brown v. Bd. of Educ. of Topeka*, 347 U.S. 483 (1954).

[40] Even if it were applicable, the Fourteenth Amendment's equal protection clause does not apply to sexual orientation, as that is not considered a protected class.

[41] N.J. Stat. § 10:5-1. The New Jersey attorney general's Web site explains the purpose and scope of the Act as follows: "The New Jersey Law Against Discrimination (LAD) makes it unlawful to subject people to differential treatment based on race, creed, color, national origin, nationality, ancestry, age, sex (including pregnancy), familial status, marital status, domestic partnership status, affectional or sexual orientation, atypical hereditary cellular or blood trait, genetic information, liability for military service, and mental or physical disability, perceived disability, and AIDS and HIV status. The LAD prohibits unlawful discrimination in employment, housing, places of public accommodation, credit and business contracts. Not all of the foregoing prohibited bases for discrimination are protected in all of these areas of activity. For example, familial status is only protected with respect to housing. The Division has promulgated regulations that explain that a place of public accommodation must make reasonable modifications to its policies, practices or procedures to ensure that people with disabilities have access to public places. The regulations also explain that under the LAD, these reasonable accommodations may include actions such as providing auxiliary aides and making physical changes to ensure paths of travel." New Jersey attorney general's Web site, available at www.state.nj.us/lps/dcr/law.html (accessed Mar. 23, 2012).

[42] "Public Accommodation: The New Jersey Law Against Discrimination (LAD) prohibits an owner, manager, or employee of any place that offers goods, services and facilities to the general public, such as a restaurant, hotel, doctor's office, camp, or theater, from directly or indirectly denying or withholding any accommodation, service, benefit, or privilege to an individual because of that individual's race, creed, color, national origin, nationality, ancestry, marital status, domestic partnership status, sex, affectional or sexual orientation, or disability. Further, individuals accompanied by a guide or service dog are entitled to full and equal access to all places of public accommodation." *Ibid.*

[43] *Ibid.*

[44] The Unruh Civil Rights Act, Cal. Civ. Code, § 51(b) All persons within the jurisdiction of this state are free and equal, and no matter what their sex, race, color, religion, ancestry, national origin, disability,

medical condition, marital status, or sexual orientation are entitled to the full and equal accommodations, advantages, facilities, privileges, or services in all business establishments of every kind whatsoever.

[45] *Curran v. Mount Diablo Council of Boy Scouts of Am.*, 952 P.2d 218 (Cal. 1998); *Randall v. Orange Cnty. Council*, 952 P.2d 261 (Cal. 1998), holding groups like the Boy Scouts were not "business establishments" subject to the Unruh Civil Rights Act provisions—the court found the Boy Scouts to be a "charitable organization" with interests unrelated its members' economic benefit, and no commercial interest in the activities provided to its members; *see also* *Boy Scouts of Am. v. Dale*, 530 U.S. 640 (2000).

[46] *Curran*, 952 P.2d 218.

[47] *Dale*, 530 U.S. 640.

[48] Peter Svensson, "Comcast Defends Internet Practices," Associated Press wire service report, December 12, 2008.

[49] Peter Svensson, "Demand for Video Reshaping Internet," Associated Press wire service report, February 11, 2008.

[50] John Dunbar, "FCC Rules against Comcast: Firm Ordered to End Delays on File-Sharing Traffic," Associated Press wire service report, August 2, 2008.

[51] Svensson, "Demand for Video Reshaping Internet," fn. 49, *supra*.

[52] "Amazon Agrees to Kindle Suit Settlement," Associated Press wire service report, October 2, 2009. *See also*, Caroline McCarthy, "Teen Sues Amazon: The Kindle Ate My Homework," CNET News.com, July 31, 2009.

[53] *See* *La Ligue Contre le Racisme et L'Antisemitisme (LICRA) and L'Union des Etudiants Juifs de France (UEJF) v. Yahoo! Inc. and Yahoo! France*, Case No. 00/05308, (Tribunal de Grande Instance de Paris, 2000).

[54] Julia Day, "UK Readers Blocked from NY Times Terror Article," The (U.K.) Guardian, August 29, 2006.

[55] Amol Sharma, "Facebook, Google to Stand Trial in India," The Wall Street Journal, March 13, 2012.

[56] Josh Halliday, "David Cameron Considers Banning Suspected Rioters from Social Media," The (U.K.) Guardian, August 11, 2011.

[57] Anne Broache, "Congress: P2P Networks Harm National Security," CNET News.com, July 24, 2007.

[58] Anne Broache, "Politicians Fret over Military Gear Resold on eBay, Craigslist," CNET News.com, April 10, 2008.

[59] In March 2012, a controversy ensued when PayPal warned several online publishers and booksellers it would "limit" their PayPal accounts or turn off their payment processing unless they removed e-books "containing themes of rape, incest, bestiality and underage subjects" from their Web sites. While the First Amendment applies only to government and does not prohibit a private business from restricting free speech, PayPal's market dominance as an online payment processor would cause any content-based restrictions it puts in place to have a chilling effect on speech. *See* Alistair Barr, "Paypal Sparks Furor over Limits on "Obscene" e-books," Reuters wire service report, March 7, 2012.

# APPENDIX

## Glossary

## Acronyms & Abbreviations

## Case Index

## Statute & Treaty Index

## Topic Index

## A Word About Style

## Author Biography

## Also Available From This Author

## Colophon

# GLOSSARY

**Abandonment of Trademark** occurs when a registered trademark falls into disuse or when a trademark holder fails to protest unauthorized use of the trademark (if the trademarked term becomes genericized, *i,e.,* part of the common usage).

**Actual Damages** are compensation for losses suffered by the plaintiff due to harm caused by the defendant.

**Actual Malice** at common law is "hatred or ill-will". Under "*Times* Malice", actual malice is "knowledge of falsity or reckless disregard of the truth". *See Times Malice.*

**Adware** is software in which ads are displayed while the program is running.

**Affiliates** are Web sites linking to an online retailer and earning referral fees for sending customers to that retailer.

**AllWhoIs** is a mega search engine site that searches WHO IS databases at multiple domain name registries.

**Amicus Curiae** is Latin for "friend of the court" and refers to a brief filed with the court by one who is not a party to the case.

**Anti-cybersquatting Consumer Protection Act (ACPA)** is a domain name dispute law giving trademark owners legal remedies against defendants who obtain domain names identical or confusingly similar to their trademark, with a "bad faith intent to profit from the mark."

**Appropriation** is use of an individual's name, likeness, or identity for trade or advertising (*i.e.,* commercial) purposes without consent. *See **right to privacy** and **right of publicity.***

**At-will Employee** is one who works for a private employer, has no union contract, and can be fired for any reason not specifically prohibited by law.

**Avatar** is an icon or animation representeng an online game player in a virtual world.

**Bandwidth Theft** is direct linking of images, scripts, sound files, movies, or zipped files to a Web site from another site's server without that site owner's knowledge or consent, resulting in costly charges for bandwidth usage to the victim's site. Also referred to as **hot-linking** or **direct linking**.

**Behavioral Marketing** targets consumers based on their behavior on Web sites by using clickstream data to track them and develop a profile of products that interest them, and then deliver related targeted advertising to them.

**Bench Trial** is a trial before a judge without a jury, where the judge sits as both trier of fact and of law.

**Betamax Standard** states if the technology is capable of commercially significant non-infringing uses, then it does not violate the copyright law.

**Bills** are proposed laws that only become law when passed by a legislature (state legislature or Congress) and signed into law by a chief executive (governor or president).

**Bloggers** are individuals who write and maintain blogs.

**Blogosphere** refers to the universe of interconnected blogs, as most blogs have multiple links to others, creating in effect, a network of blogs. The phrase may also refer to the collective community of bloggers.

**Blogs** (short for Web logs) are online diaries or commentaries by individuals.

**Blurring** is where consumers see a trademark used by someone other than the trademark holder to identify a noncompeting good, thereby diluting the unique and distinctive significance of the mark.

**Bot** is a Web robot that crawls the Web to index sites for search engines; some spam computers without an owner's knowledge or consent.

**Browse-wrap Agreement** is a contract a user may view online but need not do anything to indicate acceptance.

**Browser Caches** temporarily store files automatically downloaded from visited sites.

**Buckley Amendment** (the Family Educational Rights and Privacy Act of 1974) permits the federal government to cut funding to public schools violating student records privacy. It applies to state colleges, universities, and technical schools receiving federal funds.

**Buzz Marketing** is a marketing campaign creating a "buzz" about a product among the target market.

**CAN-SPAM Act of 2003** (Controlling Assault of Non-Solicited Pornography and Marketing Act) requires accurate headers in e-mail messages and procedures for recipients to opt-out of future e-mails, and forbids e-mail address harvesting.

**Canadian Privacy Act of 1983** protects personal information collected by the Canadian government.

**Carnivore** was a controversial Internet surveillance system developed by the FBI to monitor electronic transmissions of criminal suspects.

**Cashers** are individuals who encode stolen credit card numbers onto plastic cards and use them to withdraw money from ATMs.

**Casino-style Gambling Sites** offer the user a wide variety of games (*e.g.,* blackjack, poker, roulette, and slot machines) with colorful graphics and background music.

**Cause of Action** is the legal "grounds" for a lawsuit.

**Certiorari** is the writ issued by the U.S. Supreme Court to a lower court to review a judgment for legal error (reversible error) and review where no appeal is available as a matter of right.

**Chat Room** is a Web page using chat software that can display typed messages in real time.

**Child Online Protection Act (COPA)** makes it a crime to publish "any communication for commercial purposes that includes sexual material harmful to minors, without restricting access to such material by minors." COPA never took effect after the U.S. Supreme Court upheld a lower court's injunction.

**Children's Internet Protection Act of 2000 (CIPA)** denies federal funds for Internet access to public libraries and schools refusing to filters their Internet computers.

**Children's Online Privacy Protection Act (COPPA)** controls how Web sites collect and/or maintain personal information about children. It defines a "child" as under age 13 and applies to "sites directed at children" or where the "site knows it is collecting information from children."

**"Chilling Effect"** refers to the consequence of others being intimidated into silence after observing an action that inhibits or punishes someone's speech.

**Civil Law** is the body of law concerning the adjudication of disputes between individuals or organizations in noncriminal or nonmilitary matters.

**Clickstream** is a sequential log of page events collected by a server; a virtual trail left by a Web user as he navigates the Web site.

**Clickstream Data** are the information culled from the clickstream, such as what page or site the user visited, how long he stayed, the order he viewed the pages, newsgroups he participated in, keywords typed into search engines, and addresses of incoming and outgoing e-mail.

**Click-wrap Agreement** is an agreement displayed on a Web site to user, who must click a link or button indicating acceptance of the terms to proceed further.

**Cloud Computing** allows software to be hosted on a remote server rather than on one's own computer, with the result that data files are stored on the remote server.

**Common Law** is noncodified law derived from court decisions and precedence.

**Compensatory Damages** provide a plaintiff with the amount of money needed to replace what was lost.

**Computer Trespass** occurs when an individual gains unauthorized access to a computer system or exceeds authorized access.

**Consent Decree** is a court sanctioned agreement by a defendant to abide by the law, without admitting guilt.

**Constructive Notice** is a legal fiction creating a presumption a party has or should have had notice (based on a public display, filing, or advertisement), even if the party did not have actual notice.

**Content Aggregator** is a Web site that syndicates or links to, but does not host, third-party content, some of which may be infringing content.

**Contextual Marketing** targets consumers based on the content of pages they visit.

**Contributory Infringer** is one who knows or has reason to know of an infringement and induces, causes, or materially contributes to another's infringing conduct.

**Cookie** is a text file containing data stored on a user's computer to keep information allowing Web sites the user has visited to authenticate the user's identity, speed up transactions, monitor the user's behavior, and personalize presentations.

**Cookie Poisoning** is modification of a cookie by an attacker to gain unauthorized information about the user for purposes such as identity theft.

**"COPPA Gap"** is the unprotected age 13–to–17 gap between the preteen years (under 13) protected by COPPA and adulthood (over 18).

**Copyright Term Extension Act (CTEA)** is an amendment to the U.S. Copyright Act sponsored by Sonny Bono extending copyright protection.

**Copyright Act of 1976** is the federal statute governing U.S. copyright law.

**Corporate Cyberstalking** involves an organization stalking an individual online.

**Counter Notification** is a response to a DMCA takedown notice, sent to the OSP, claiming it has improperly removed noninfringing content.

**Coursepacks** are photocopied compilations of reading materials from assorted books and articles assigned to students by college professors.

**Creative Commons** is a licensing paradigm that emphasizes use over ownership.

**Creative Commons Licenses** offer a portion of rights subject to certain conditions: attribution, noncommercial use, nonderivative use, and "share alike" (permission to distribute derivative works only under a license identical to the license that governs the creator's work).

**Criminal Law** deals with crimes and their punishments.

**Crowdfunding** is raising small amounts of money from a large number of investors, usually via the Internet.

**Cyberbully** is one who uses electronic communication devices such as mobile phones and the Internet, to harass another.

**Cybergriper** is a dissatisfied consumer who airs gripes against a company in the form of a Web site devoted to publicizing complaints with the company.

**Cyberpoachers** grab domain names when a name previously registered by a company becomes available for any reason.

**Cybersquatter** is one who deliberately, and in bad faith, registers domain names in violation of the trademark owners' rights.

**Cyberstalking** is a crime where an attacker uses electronic communication (*e.g.*, e-mail, instant messaging, message board or chat room posts) to harass the victim.

**Data Breach** occurs when hackers steal stored data from a computer.

**De Facto** is in reality or in fact.

**De Jure** is lawful or in law

**De Minimis Copying** is the concept the amount of a work copied is too insignificant to be considered an infringement.

**Declaratory Judgment** is a conclusive and legally binding declaration by the court, in a civil case, advising the parties as to their rights and responsibilities, without awarding damages or ordering them to do anything.

**Deep-linking** refers to a hyperlink bypassing a Web site's home page and taking a user directly to an internal page.

**Deep Packet Inspection** is a controversial technique allowing ISPs to monitor everything a customer does online.

**Defamation** is a published false communication injuring one's reputation.

**Defamation by Implication** is a tort theory that provides literally true statements are defamatory if they create a false and negative impression of the plaintiff.

**Default Judgment** is granted when one party fails to perform a court ordered action, such as appearing in court preventing the legal issue from being presented before the court, and the judge rules in favor of the compliant party (the one who showed up, usually the plaintiff).

**Defendant** is the party sued in a civil case or prosecuted in a criminal case.

**Design Patents** protect the appearance of an object.

**Dicta** are comments in a judicial opinion not considered part of the holding, unrelated directly to the issue, and lacking binding or precedential effect.

**Digital Estate Planning** is the planning of disposition of one's digital assets after death.

**Digital Millennium Copyright Act (DMCA)** is a 1998 amendment to the U.S. Copyright Act of 1976 providing for criminal prosecution with up to 10 years imprisonment for circumventing technical measures that protect copyrighted works.

**Direct Infringer** is one who commits an infringing act, by making and sharing copies of a copyrighted work, or otherwise directly infringing on the copyright, trademark, or patent rights of another.

**Discovery** is the process during litigation where, prior to the start of a civil trial, both plaintiff and defendant can use civil procedural tools such as interrogatories, depositions, requests for production, and subpoenas to compel the production of evidence, in preparation for trial.

**Distinguish** is a phrase courts use to rationalize reaching a different result on the same fact pattern without directly overruling precedent.

**Diversity Jurisdiction** occurs in civil cases between citizens from different states where the amount at stake is more than $75,000, thus requiring the case be tried in federal rather than state court.

**Domain Name Registry** is a database showing which domain name maps to which IP address.

**Drive-by Download** is a program automatically and invisibly downloaded to a user's computer, often without the user's knowledge or consent.

**E-mail Opt-in Rule** mandates a recipient must have agreed in advance (*e.g.*, by signing up) to receive e-mail.

**E-mail Spoofing** is forgery of an e-mail header so the message appears to have originated from someone or somewhere other than the true source.

**Electronic Mailing List** is a list of e-mail addresses of individuals who have signed up to receive e-mails from all others on the list; such lists are managed through software programs like Majordomo and Listserv.

**Electronic Signatures in Global and National Commerce Act (the E-SIGN Act)** provides legal validity to certain contracts entered into electronically.

**En Banc Hearing** is a rehearing of a case by all the judges of an appellate court to reconsider a decision of the court's panel, where the case concerns a matter of exceptional public importance or conflicts with an earlier decision.

**Enjoin** is to command or instruct to do or not commit an act.

**Estoppel** is an evidentiary rule precluding a party from alleging or denying the truth of a fact already settled, due to that party's voluntary conduct. *See Promissory Estoppel.*

**European Union Directive on Data Protection** requires European Union member nations to implement national legislation to protect individuals' privacy. It prohibits transfer of personal data to non-European Union countries not meeting its "adequacy" standard for privacy protection.

**Fact Situation** is a description of facts specific to the case at hand.

**Fair Comment** is a statement of opinion, as opposed to fact, and as such is not actionable as (and thus serves as a defense to a claim of) defamation.

**"Fair Use" Doctrine** is an affirmative defense to a copyright infringement claim allowing limited use of a copyrighted work for criticism, comment, news reporting, research, scholarship, or teaching.

**False Light in the Public Eye** is a privacy tort involving a false or misleading statement that is highly offensive (but not necessarily defamatory) and creates a false impression about the plaintiff in the public eye. *See right to privacy.*

**Family Educational Rights and Privacy Act (FERPA) of 1974** requires all government agencies (federal, state, and local) requesting Social Security numbers provide a statement on the request form explaining if the disclosure is mandatory or optional, how it will be used, and under what statutory authority it is requested.

**Federalism** is a system of government where power is divided between a centralized government and a number of regional governments by a written constitution.

**Filters** are software programs that can block access to certain Web sites containing inappropriate or offensive material, by scanning for certain words and phrases.

**First Sale Doctrine** holds a buyer of a copyrighted work can sell or give away that work without the permission of the copyright owner.

**Framing** is the process allowing a user to view contents of a second Web site while it is framed by information from the first site.

**Gramm-Leach-Bliley Act of 1999** limits when financial institutions may disclose personal information; it also applies to companies, whether or not they are financial institutions, receiving such information.

**Geofiltering** enables a Web site to restrict access to, or modify, the content it delivers based on geographical regions accessing the site.

**Habeas Corpus** (Latin for "you have the body") is a writ directed to one holding an individual in custody or detention commanding the detained individual be brought before a court to determine the legality of his detention. Its purpose is to ensure individuals are not unlawfully detained. The writ dates back to 13th century England and was adopted by the United States.

**Happy Slapping** is a violent attack perpetrated on a victim for the purpose of filming and uploading it to the Web.

**Hate Speech** is speech denigrating or attempting to inflame public opinion against certain groups of people.

**Holding** is the court's actual ruling, the answer to the question raised in the Issue; *see ruling*.

**Hot News Tort** is a legal doctrine granting news organizations a short-term monopoly on their reporting, whether or not copied verbatim.

**Hotlinking** is the process of displaying a graphic file on one Web site that originates at another. *See bandwidth theft and inline linking*.

**Hotspot** is a business establishment offering Wi-Fi Internet access.

**HTML** is Hyper Text Mark-up Language, the computer language used to create Web pages.

**Hyperlocal Web Sites** focus on specialized topics: stories and issues of interest only to people within a small community.

**Identity Theft** is a crime in which an imposter obtains key pieces of personal information to impersonate the victim to get credit, merchandise, or services in the victim's name or to provide the thief with false credentials.

**Identity Theft Penalty Enhancement Act** provides mandatory prison sentences for anyone possessing another's identity-related information with the intent to commit a crime.

**Illusory Promise** is a promise that does not actually bind the promissor and therefore provides insufficient consideration for a contract.

**In Personam Jurisdiction** is a form of jurisdiction in which the plaintiff proceeds against a "person" as opposed to a "thing."

**In Rem Jurisdiction** is a form of jurisdiction in which the plaintiff proceeds against a "thing" as opposed to a "person."

**Inducement** is the active encouragement of copyright infringement.

**Injunction** is a court order requiring a party to do or refrain from doing a specific act.

**Inline Linking**, or inlining, is the process of displaying a graphic file on one Web site that originates at another. *See bandwidth theft and hotlinking*.

**Instant Message (IM)** or Private Message (PM) is a chat room feature allowing exchange of private messages among parties.

**Intellectual Property** is copyrights, trademarks, patents, and trade secrets.

**Internet Corporation for Assigned Names and Numbers (ICANN)** is the organization responsible for overseeing the registration of domain names.

**Internet Protocol (IP) Address** is a numeric identifier assigned by the user's ISP.

**Internet Service Provider (ISP)** is a company providing Internet access.

**Intrusion** is the invasion of one's privacy by intruding on an individual's solitude or seclusion, either physically, or by electronic or mechanical means. The tort occurs at the information gathering stage and does not require publication, but must be offensive and objectionable to a reasonable man. *See right to privacy.*

**Issue** is the question of law raised by the fact situation.

**Judicial Review** is the concept enabling courts to invalidate legislation found to conflict with the Constitution.

**Jurisdiction** is the limit or territory within which a court has the power, right, or authority to interpret and apply the law.

**Jurisprudence** is the philosophy or science of law.

**Keyword Advertising** is advertising generated by relevant keywords to appear in search engine results.

**Keystroke Logger** is malware that records keystrokes typed on a keyboard and writes the information (such as the victim's login user ID and passwords for online bank accounts) to a text log file, then sent back through the Internet to the phisher.

**Lanham Act** governs trademark law in the United States.

**Libel Per Quod** is a statement harmless by itself that becomes defamatory when placed in the context of extrinsic facts.

**Libel Per Se** is a statement defamatory on its face.

**Linking Disclaimer** is a notice on a Web site stating by linking to another site it does not endorse that site or its contents.

**Liquidated Damages** are damages for breach of contract, stipulated in advance by the parties in the contract.

**Litigation Hold** is a procedure, on notification of an anticipated lawsuit, to alert a firm's relevant employees what data must be kept and for how long.

**Long-Arm Statute** is a state law giving the state court jurisdiction over an out-of-state defendant whose actions caused damage in that state or to one of its residents.

**Madrid Protocol** provides for a process of international registration, not an international trademark — *i.e.,* applicants get a bundle of national rights, not a single international right.

**"Making Available" Theory** holds merely making an unauthorized copy of a copyrighted work available to the public, without evidence of distribution, constitutes copyright infringement under the Copyright Act.

**Mail Bomb** is a massive amount of e-mail sent to a specific person or computer network with the intent to disrupt service to all mail server customers.

**Malware** (short for "malicious software") is any software or file developed for the purpose of doing harm.

**"Marketplace of Ideas"** is a metaphor first enunciated by U.S. Supreme Court Justice Oliver Wendell Holmes that ideas compete for acceptance against each other — with the underlying faith the truth will prevail.

**Message Board** or **Forum** is a Web page where messages are posted and maintained in static form indefinitely, often permanently archived.

**Meta Tags** are relevant keywords used by search engines to index pages, allowing Web browsers to find tagged pages in searches.

**Metadata** is data about data; it may include the file creator and creation date, and document changes; and in e-mails, routing details such as the sender, recipients, and subject line.

**Milbloggers** are military bloggers.

*Miller* **Test** defines "obscene" as "Whether to the average person, applying contemporary community standards, the dominant theme of the material taken as a whole appeals to prurient interest."

**Minimum Contacts** with a forum state — if a defendant regularly solicits business in the state, derives substantial revenue from goods or services sold in the state, or engages in some other persistent course of conduct there — will enable the forum state to exercise personal jurisdiction.

**MMO** is a massively multiplayer online game with a capacity for thousands of simultaneous players engaging in a virtual world.

**Mousetrapping** occurs when a visitor cannot leave a Web site without clicking on a succession of pop-up windows.

**Murkogram** is spam with a disclaimer the message cannot be considered spam because it is in compliance with Bill S.1618 Title III, the Inbox Privacy Act.

**National Security Letters (NSLs)** are letters from the FBI typically requesting information from ISPs and other communication providers about subscribers, including home addresses, phone calls made, e-mail subject lines, and logs of Web sites visited.

**Net Neutrality** is the concept all Internet traffic should be treated equally by ISPs.

**New York Times "actual malice" standard** requires a defamation plaintiff prove "knowledge of falsity or reckless disregard of the truth" on the defendant's part in making the alleged defamatory remark.

**No Electronic Theft Act** prohibits unauthorized distribution of copyrighted material with a value greater than $2,500 over a computer network.

**Nominal Damages** are trivial amounts awarded where the plaintiff's legal right has been proven to have been violated but he has suffered minimal or no harm or loss.

**Nominative Fair Use** is permissible use of a trademarked term to describe a product or service not readily identified without using the trademark.

**Objective Theory of Contracts** states an offer exists if a reasonable man would have believed the offeror's objective manifestations of intent (*i.e.*, his outward behavior as demonstrated by his words and actions) constituted an offer — the offeror's subjective intent is irrelevant.

**Office Action** is a nonfinal rejection of a patent application by the USPTO because of the existence of "identical or similar marks" or if it finds the mark is "generic or descriptive."

**Onion Routing** is a technique of routing a message through multiple proxy servers.

**Online Harassment** occurs when a harasser uses the Internet to cause substantial emotional distress to the victim.

**Overbreadth Doctrine** holds if a statute designed to prevent illegal speech has the effect of inhibiting protected speech, then that statute is deemed overbroad and thus unconstitutional.

**Pagejacking** occurs where the offender steals a Web site's contents by copying some of its pages, putting them on a site appearing to be the real Web site, and then inviting people to the fake site through deceptive means.

**Paris Convention of 1883** provides if an inventor subsequently files patent applications for the same invention in other member countries within one year after filing the first one, the later applications receive a fictional filing date equal to the filing date of the first application.

**Parody** is literary or artistic work imitating the characteristic style of an author or work for comic effect or ridicule. A legal parody involves the conveyance of two simultaneous but contradictory messages — it must target the work but be apparent it is not the original.

**Patent** is a government-issued grant conferring on an inventor a right to exclude others from making, using, offering for sale, or selling the invention for a period of 20 years, measured from the filing date.

**Patent Agent** is a nonattorney who can prepare a patent application but not practice law (*e.g.,* litigate patent matters or write contracts related to patents).

**Patent Attorney** is a specialized attorney with knowledge and experience in patent law, having passed a special exam, and registered to practice before the USPTO.

**Patent Cooperation Treaty of 1970** makes it possible to seek patent protection for an invention simultaneously in each of a large number of countries by filing an "international" patent application.

**Peer-2-Peer (P2P) Networking** enables direct communication or sharing of information among individual users' computers.

**Pen Register** is a device recording outgoing phone numbers dialed from a phone.

**Permission-Based Marketing** occurs when a recipient has asked to receive bulk e-mail.

**Persistent Cookies** remain on a user's hard drive for an extended period rather than expiring when the browser is closed.

**Personal Attack Web Sites** are sites that actively solicit online posts containing personal attacks and offensive content that can be archived indefinitely and easily accessed through search engine queries.

**Personal Information Protection and Electronic Documents Act of 2000 (PIPEDA)** is a Canadian statute applying to the collection, storage, and use of personal information by nongovernmental organizations.

**Personal Jurisdiction** asks: Does the court have authority over the parties?

**Personalized Phishing** is where a victim receives e-mail containing personalized accurate account information the scammers have already obtained from other sources of misappropriated consumer data as part of a ruse to obtain even more sensitive information to sell to other scammers.

**Persuasive Precedents** are nonbinding precedents in other jurisdictions courts may look to for analysis and rationales of the issues before the court, which it may then adopt or discard.

**Pharming** is a malicious Web redirect exploiting the Domain Name System (DNS) used to translate a Web site's address into a numerical code for Internet routing.

**Phishing** (pronounced "fishing") is a scam in which unsuspecting users receive official-looking e-mails attempting to trick them into disclosing online passwords, user names, and personal information.

**Piggybacking** is use of a wireless Internet connection without permission.

**Plaintiff** is the party bringing a lawsuit in a civil proceeding.

**Plant Patents** protect the appearance and color of plants.

**Pod Burping** refers to the use of a portable media device to inject viruses or malicious code into a corporate network.

**Pod Slurping** is use of iPods or high-capacity mp3 players as portable drives to steal information from corporate PCs and networks.

**Podcasting** is a method of publishing audio and video files online to be downloaded and played offline on portable media players.

**Police Power** is a state's inherent authority to restrict private rights for the benefit of public health, safety, morals, and welfare.

**Precedence** is the principle prior decisions be followed by courts; *see stare decisis.*

**Pretexting** is using a false scenario to procure information (*e.g.,* pretending to work for the victim's bank and phoning for information). *See Social Engineering.*

**Prior Art** consists of prior published documents and activities related to a patent claim serving as evidence of state of the art, *i.e.,* everything publicly known before the invention, as shown in earlier patents and other published material.

**Prior Restraint** is a government prohibition of speech in advance of publication.

**Privacy Policy** is a statement on a Web site explaining how the site collects personal information and what it does with it.

**Privilege** is a legal concept protecting statements made in court by witnesses, attorneys, or judges; or on the floor of a legislative body.

**Procedural Law** governs the machinery of the courts, specifically the process and procedure of enforcing substantive rights.

**Promissory Estoppel** is a contract law doctrine that provides a party can enforce a promise even if the essential elements of a contract are not present, if he has detrimentally relied on that promise through action or forbearance.

**Pro Se** is a Latin term for a nonlaywer acting as his own attorney in court proceedings.

**Proxy Server** substitutes its own IP address for the user's.

**Public Disclosure of Private Facts** is a privacy tort involving publication of private and embarrassing facts unrelated to matters of public concern. *See right to privacy.*

**Public Domain** refers to created materials that either by law do not get copyright protection, or whose legal protection has lapsed.

**"Pump and Dump" Scheme** is a scam where an individual enters an investment message board or chat room and talks up stocks he already owns and then surreptitiously sell them into the artificial demand he has created.

**Punitive Damages** may be awarded in addition to actual damages to punish the defendant and serve as an example to prospective defendants not to commit the same act.

**Ransomware** is a type of malware that encrypts a user's hard drive or selected files (*e.g.,* music, photos, or documents) and then demands payment to decrypt it.

**Rationale** is the thought process used by a court in arriving at its *decision* or *holding.*

**Reciprocal Links** are mutually agreed on hyperlinks between two Web sites.

**Referrers** references the last URL the user has visited.

**Remand** is what a court does when it sends a case back to a lower court with instructions on how to proceed.

**Reporters** are books containing published court decisions, printed periodically and stocked by law libraries.

**Respondeat Superior** is the doctrine holding a principal is liable for his agent's acts.

**Right of Attribution** entitles an artist to be properly credited for work; or conversely, to demand her name be removed from any work distorted, mutilated, or modified; or to demand her name be removed from any work she did not create.

**Right of Integrity** precludes others from distorting, mutilating, or modifying an artist's work; it also prevents destruction of works of "recognized stature."

**Right of Publicity** is an individual's right to control and profit from commercial use of his name, likeness, and persona.

**Right to Privacy** is the right to control dissemination of information about one's self; *see appropriation, false light, intrusion,* and *public disclosure of private facts.*

**RSS (Really Simple Syndication)** is a distribution system letting publishers share Web content, such as headlines and text, via XML feeds.

**Ruling** is a court's actual Decision, the answer to the question raised in the Issue. *See holding.*

**Safe Harbor Provision** in regulations allows an individual or business to comply with specified standards which then provide shelter from liability under the statute.

**Session ID Cookies** expire when the browser is closed.

**Sexting** is sending sexually explicit photographs via mobile phone text messaging.

**Shield laws** protect journalists from being compelled to reveal their sources.

**Shrink-wrap Agreements** are agreements printed on back of, or included inside, a commercial software box. By breaking the package's shrink-wrap, a purchaser agrees to be bound by the agreement's terms.

**Shop Right** is common law right granting a nonexclusive and nontransferable license to an employer allowing use of an invention created during the course of employment by its employee.

**Snippet** is descriptive text about a link.

**Sock Puppet** is a false online identity to deceive others or promote a product or company.

**Social Engineering** is use of a variety of methods to trick or manipulate individuals into committing acts or revealing information.

**Social Graph** is an aggregate of an individual's online presence compiled to form a consumer profile.

**Social Media Marketing** is a process used by lenders and other firms to compile a social graph.

**Spam** is unsolicited bulk e-mail.

**Spear-phishing** is a targeted phishing variation occurring when a phisher poses as a high level executive in a targeted corporation and demands confidential information from an employee.

**Specific Performance** is a judicial order compelling a party to perform a specific act, usually pursuant to a contract.

**Spim** is spam sent as an Instant Message (IM).

**Spoilation** is the bad faith tampering with, or destruction of, evidence.

**Sports Gambling Sites** are gambling Web sites taking wagers on the outcome of sporting events.

**Spyware** is any software accessing and using a user's Internet connection in the background without the user's knowledge or explicit permission.

**Stare Decisis** is Latin for "let the decision stand", embodying the principle courts are to follow prior decisions. *See precedence.*

**Statute of Frauds** makes certain oral contracts unenforceable, usually those involving the sale or transfer of land or where performance cannot be completed within one year.

**Statutory Damages** are set amounts stipulated by a specific statute.

**Statutory Law** is law codified in statutes passed by a legislative body and signed into law by a chief executive.

**Stored Communication Messages** are e-mails stored on an ISP's server.

**Strategic Lawsuit Against Public Participation (SLAPP)** is a lawsuit without substantial merit brought by private interests to stop citizens from exercising their political rights or to punish them for having done so.

**Sua Sponte** is when a judge has acted of his own accord, without prompting from either party in a case.

**Subject Matter Jurisdiction** asks: Does the court have authority to hear the case?

**Substantive Law**, as contrasted with procedural law, creates, defines, and regulates rights.

**Summary Judgment** is a ruling by the court there is no material issue of fact to be tried, and therefore the cause of action should be dismissed.

**Sunshine Laws** allow public inquiry into government affairs, such as laws requiring meetings of governing bodies be open to the public (*i.e.*, "open meeting laws").

**Survey** is a social engineering technique where, using an innocent survey with innocuous questions, an identity thief can discover clues to passwords and user names. *See Social Engineering.*

**Takedown Notice** is notification under the DMCA by a copyright holder advising an OSP a third-party has uploaded copyrighted content to the OSP's Web site.

**Tarnishment** is where a third-party's use of a mark tarnishes, degrades, or brings ridicule to the mark's distinctive quality.

**Telecommunications Theft** is the crime of stealing Internet access or bandwidth.

**Terms of Use** is a policy statement on a Web site stating the rules for individuals who wish to use the site.

**Third-party Cookies** are set by a Web site other than the one the user is currently visiting.

*Times* **Malice** is the revised definition of "actual malice" announced by the U.S. Supreme Court in 1964 in *New York Times Co. v. Sullivan*, requiring "knowledge of falsity or reckless disregard of the truth". Often referred to as actual malice, but differing completely in meaning from the common law definition of that term. *See **Actual Malice**.*

**Trade Libel** occurs where there has been publication of a false statement of fact that is an intentional disparagement of the quality of the plaintiff's services or products.

**Transformative Use** is a the result of a secondary work that has added value to an original copyrighted work.

**Trap and Trace Device** captures phone numbers of incoming calls made to the target phone.

**Treble Damages** are a court award of three times the actual damages incurred. They are intended to penalize the guilty party and discourage others from similar behavior.

**Trier of Fact**, which may be the judge in a bench trial or the jury in a jury trial, decides the truthfulness of evidence presented in court.

**Trier of Law**, always the judge, applies the relevant law to the facts of a specific case.

**Trojan Horse** is a program in which malicious or harmful code is hidden inside an apparently harmless program or data to later gain control and cause damage. The phrase comes from Homer's *Iliad*; during the Trojan War, the Greeks presented the citizens of Troy with a large wooden horse in which they had secretly hidden their warriors. At night, the warriors emerged and overran and conquered Troy.

**Truth in Domain Names Act** is part of the PROTECT Act criminalizing use of a "misleading domain name" with the intent to deceive a person into viewing obscenity or to deceive a minor into viewing "material that is harmful to minors."

**Typosquatter** is a person who registers one or more domain names based on the most common typographical errors a user might make when entering a company's registered trademark name.

**Uniform Domain Name Dispute Resolution Policy (UDRP)** is a quick, cost-effective alternative to a lawsuit where there is a dispute over a registered domain name.

**Uniform Electronic Transactions Act (UETA)** is a model statute for states to adopt to give legal effect to electronic signatures.

**Unpublished Opinions** are court decisions not submitted to the reporters but filed at the clerk's office or accessible only on online databases.

**URL (Uniform Resource Locator)**, is the global address of documents and other resources on the World Wide Web.

**USPTO** is the U.S. Patent and Trademark Office.

**Utility Patent** is the most common type of patent and applies to inventions that have a use and protects functionality.

**Vagueness Doctrine** is derived from the due process clauses of the Fifth and Fourteenth Amendments that require criminal laws be drafted so individuals of "common intelligence" need not guess as at its meaning and differ as to its application.

**Venue** is the proper location for trial of a lawsuit.

**Verdict** is the judgment rendered by a jury.

**Vicarious Infringement** is liability for infringing acts of another; it occurs when a party has the right and ability to control an infringer's activity and receives a direct financial benefit from the infringement.

**Video Privacy Protection Act of 1988** criminalizes disclosing what videotapes an individual has rented.

**Vlog** is a video blog, *i.e.*, a vlogger sits in front of a Webcam and films a blog, which is then uploaded to a video site such as YouTube.com.

**Wardriving** is driving with a Wi-Fi enabled laptop computer, mapping houses and businesses with wireless access points.

**Web Bugs** (also called *Web Beacons* or *Clear GIFs*) are small, transparent image files placed on Web sites or in e-mail to identify a user's IP address; retrieve cookie information; find out when a page or an e-mail message was viewed; or determine if an e-mail message has been read.

**Web Site Development Agreement** is a contract between a Web site designer or developer and his client regarding terms and conditions pursuant to the job.

**Whaling** is when spear-phishers go after "big fish" like top executives.

**WHOIS** is a domain name database maintained by domain name registrars.

**Widgets** are self-contained pieces of code that can be placed within the HTML of any Web page without requiring any programming skills, to provide various functionalities.

**Wiki** is a collaborative Web site whose content can be edited by anyone who has access to it.

**Wikipedia** is an online encyclopedia where all the entries are constantly updated, added to, or modified by viewers who become virtual contributors in what ultimately emerges as a community or consensus work, each bringing different aspects of knowledge to the project.

**Wire Wager Act** is a 1961 law prohibiting use of "wire communication facilities for transmission in interstate or foreign commerce of bets or wagers or information assisting in placing of bets or wagers on any sporting event or contest."

**Work-made-for-hire** is a creative work where the employer, and not the employee, is considered the author.

**Working Requirement** is a requirement by many countries a patented product be manufactured in that country within a specified time frame (often three years).

**Worm** is a self-replicating virus that does not alter files but resides in the computer's active memory and duplicates itself.

# ACRONYMS & ABBREVIATIONS

**ACPA**  Anti-cybersquatting Consumer Protection Act

**ADA**  Americans with Disabilities Act

**AOL**  America On Line

**CAN-SPAM**  Controlling Assault of Non-Solicited Pornography and Marketing

**CDA**  Communications Decency Act

**C.f.**  Latin for *compare*, "compare and contrast with the immediately preceding statement"

**CFAA**  Computer Fraud and Abuse Act

**CIA**  Central Intelligence Agency

**CIPA**  Children's Internet Protection Act

**COPA**  Child Online Protection Act

**COPPA**  Children's Online Privacy Protection Act

**CPPA**  Child Pornography Prevention Act

**CTEA**  Copyright Term Extension Act

**DCA**  District Court of Appeals

**DMCA**  Digital Millennium Copyright Act

**DNS**  Domain Name System

**DOD**  Department of Defense

**DOJ**  Department of Justice

**DOT**  Department of Transportation

**DPI**  Deep Packet Inspection

**E-SIGN**  Electronic Signatures In Global And National Commerce

**ECPA**  Electronic Communications Privacy Act

**E.g.**  Latin for *exempli gratia*, "for the sake of example"

**ESI**  Electronically Stored Information

**Et Seq.**  Latin for *et sequentia*, "and the following"

**EU**  European Union

**EULA**  End User License Agreement

**FBI**  Federal Bureau of Investigation

**FCC**  Federal Communications Commission

**FERPA**  Family Educational Rights and Privacy Act

**FHA**  Fair Housing Act

**FINRA**  Financial Industry Regulatory Authority

**FISA**  Foreign Intelligence Surveillance Act

**FISC**  Foreign Intelligence Surveillance Court

**FOI**  Freedom of Information

**FRAP**  Federal Rules of Appellate Procedure

**FRCP**  Federal Rules of Civil Procedure

**FRCRP**  Federal Rules of Criminal Procedure

**FTC**  Federal Trade Commission

**GIF**  Graphics Interchange Format

**HIPAA**  Health Insurance Portability and Accountability Act

**HTML**  Hyper Text Markup Language

**HUD**  Department of Housing and Urban Development

**ICANN**  Internet Corporation for Assigned Names and Numbers

**ICP** Internet Content Provider

**ICS** Internet Content Service

**I.e.**  Latin for *id est*, "that is"

**IM**  Instant Message

**INDUCE Act**  Inducing of Copyright Infringement Act

**IP**  Internet Protocol

**IPO**  Initial Public Offering

**IRS**  Internal Revenue Service

**ISP**  Internet Service Provider

**MMO** Massively Multiplayer Online

**NAF** National Arbitration Forum

**NASA** National Aeronautics and Space Administration

**NASD** National Association of Securities Dealers

**NLRA** National Labor Relations Act

**NLRB** National Labor Relations Board

**NSL** National Security Letter

**OCILLA** Online Copyright Infringement Liability Limitation Act

**OHIM** Office for Harmonization in the Internal Market

**OSP** Online Service Provider

**P2P** Peer-to-Peer

**PIPEDA** Personal Information Protection and Electronic Documents Act

**PM** Private Message

**PROTECT** Prosecutorial Remedies and Other Tools to end the Exploitation of Children Today

**RIAA** Recording Industry Association of America

**RICO** Racketeer Influenced and Corrupt Organizations Act

**RSS** Really Simple Syndication

**SEC** Securities and Exchange Commission

**SEO** Search Engine Optimization

**SLAPP** Strategic Lawsuit Against Public Participation

**SSN** Social Security Number

**Sub Nom.** Latin for *sub nomine*, "under the name"

**TESS** Trademark Electronic Search System

**TRO** Temporary Restraining Order

**UCMJ** Uniform Code of Military Justice

**UDRP** Uniform Domain Name Dispute Resolution Policy

**UETA** Uniform Electronic Transactions Act

**U.K.** United Kingdom

**URRA**   Uruguay Round Agreements Act

**URL**   Uniform Resource Locator

**USA PATRIOT**   Uniting and Strengthening America by Providing Appropriate Tools Required to Intercept and Obstruct Terrorism

**U.S. CAFC**   United States Court of Appeals for the Federal Circuit

**USPTO**   United States Patent and Trademark Office

**UTSA**   Uniform Trade Secrets Act

**VARA**   Visual Artists Rights Act

**WIPO**   World Intellectual Property Organization

**WTO**   World Trade Organization

**XML**   EXtensible Markup Language

# Case Index

# Statute & Treaty Index

## U.S. STATE STATUTES

### * denotes a model code

## FOREIGN STATUTES

## CONVENTIONS & TREATIES

# Topic Index

# A Word About Style

Style is more than panache — it is also how a publisher maintains consistency for its readers. It would be rather jarring if the same words looked differently throughout a magazine or book, so publishers set a specific style and follow it from the first page up until the last. ***Issues in Internet Law: Society, Technology, and the Law*** is styled after the *AP Stylebook,* the *Chicago Manual of Style*, and the *Bluebook*. Where these authorities conflict, or worse, are silent, the author and publisher employ a mix of personal preference, common sense, and Magic 8-Ball to arrive at the proper style answers.

Is it e-mail or email? Website or Web site? Should Web be capitalized? Guestbook or guest book? News group or newsgroup? Meta data or metadata? Keyword or key word? Whistleblower or whistle-blower or even whistle blower? Fifth or 5th? F.T.C. or FTC? Cyberstalker or cyber stalker? These are all questions of style. Now for the answers.

This book follows the AP style of writing out numbers one through nine and using numerals for 10 and above. Amendments to the U.S. Constitution are spelled out and as are the Federal Circuits in the body text (but not in citations). Percentages are expressed as numerals with the word "percent" (*e.g.,* "9 percent" not "nine percent" or "9%"). The word "court" is lower-cased unless part of a name or when referencing the U.S. Supreme Court (as in "the Court held"). Quotes and citations (such as article titles) are reprinted verbatim without changing or adapting them to this book's style. Case names are italicized and underlined. Hyperlinks are underlined in the end notes citations but not in the body text. We have (reluctantly) come around to the growing consensus that it is "Web site" and not "website." We have also reluctantly joined the trend of removing periods from most acronyms (*e.g.,* "S.E.C." has become "SEC" and "E.U." has become "EU", but "U.S." and "U.K." remain unchanged). Another trend we are following is the compounding of many words formerly hyphenated and the elimination of hyphens from most prefixes (*e.g.,* "non-commercial" has become noncommercial"). Contractions are not used in the text and are only found within quoted material.

Some of the changes in style in recent editions include:
- Shortening "Web site" to "site", and
- Shortening "social networking sites" to "social networks"

This book follows *Bluebook* conventions for case citations and most legal references, except where doing so would prove confusing to readers with no legal background. Citations follow *Bluebook* abbreviations in the end notes but are not abbreviated in the cases index.

Since this book references many recent news articles published online, and as some Web sites change the URL for articles after they move them to their archives, we are limiting use of URLs in the endnotes for online sources. Rather than list a URL that is likely to become outdated, the endnote will include enough information to locate the article through a search engine query.

Phrases coined by the author, in this and previous editions, include: "borderless nature of the Internet", "COPPA Gap", "Creepy Factor," "Graffiti Factor", "Internet Generation", and "pod burping".

# Author Biography

Having been a journalist, Web designer, and attorney, Dr. Keith B. Darrell brings a unique perspective to the subject of Internet Law, as the courts and Congress struggle to adapt the 18th century First Amendment to the 21st century technology of the Internet.

By age 24, Dr. Darrell had earned his A.A. from Broward Community College, his B.S. in Journalism from the University of Florida, his M.B.A. from Emory University, and his J.D. from the Emory University School of Law. Dr. Darrell is a member of the State Bar of Georgia and the Florida Bar.

Other legal publications by Dr. Darrell include *"Redefining a 'Security': Is the Sale of a Business Through a Stock Transfer Subject to the Federal Securities Laws?"* 12 **Securities Regulation Law Journal** 22 (Warren, Gorham & Lamont), Spring 1984, and *"The Sale of Business Doctrine Revisited,"* 3 **JD/MBA Journal** 21, Winter 1987. Dr. Darrell's other books include **The Web Designer's Client Handbook**; **Putting Your Business on the Internet**; the short story collections **Randoms** and **Shards**; and the Halos & Horns fantasy series: **Paved With Good Intentions** (Book One), **And A Child Shall Lead Them** (Book Two) and **To Hell In A Handbasket** (Book Three). He has also written numerous fiction short stories and nonfiction articles.

Throughout his lifetime, Dr. Darrell has held many positions as a reporter, advertising representative, entrepreneur, retail business owner, insurance agent, stockbroker, real estate agent, Web designer, attorney, and author. His interests include his pets, photography, genealogy, art, literature, theater, old comic books, travel, and learning about different cultures and languages.

# ALSO AVAILABLE FROM THIS AUTHOR

## ALL NEW 2012-2013 EDITION!

Hardcover • ISBN: 978-1-935971-09-2
Softcover • ISBN: 978-1-935971-08-5
488 pages, 7 x 10

## AVAILABLE IN HARDCOVER AND SOFTCOVER!

Order from www.AmberBookCompany.com

**Amber Book Company LLC**

# Colophon

This book is printed on 50lb., white, acid-free paper and meets all ANSI standards for archival quality paper. The body text is set in 11pt. Minion Pro (9.5 pt. for end notes) and the subheads are set in Myriad Pro Bold.

CPSIA information can be obtained at www.ICGtesting.com
Printed in the USA
LVOW011225061212

310270LV00003B/17/P